SELF AND WORLD

Under the General Editorship of ROBERT J. FOGELIN, *Yale University*

SELF AND WORLD
Readings in Philosophy

edited by
JAMES A. OGILVY
Yale University

Harcourt New York
Brace Chicago
Jovanovich, San Francisco
Inc. Atlanta

ISBN: 0-15-579629-1

Library of Congress Catalog Card Number: 73-75318

Printed in the United States of America

Preface

The recent trend toward "relevance" in education has provoked a lively interest in the issues of philosophy, but the appeal of contemporary issues can be a seduction toward incoherence. In this book, by focusing on the reader himself and his relation to others and to the universe rather than on the ephemeral present, I have tried to bring philosophical coherence to the reader's quest for self-knowledge. This quest is eminently philosophical, for its faithful pursuit inevitably leads through all the major questions posed by philosophers past and present. The juxtaposition of both contemporary and classical readings in a pattern of concentric circles of self-awareness invites the reader to locate himself in relation to issues which are both timely and timeless.

The coherence of the book as a whole avoids the cynical relativism often bred by anthologies presenting an assortment of loosely related essays. The differing needs of many instructors, however, demand a collection that can be used in different ways. Consequently this book is divided into seven sections, each with its own introduction orienting that section to the whole. If these introductions serve as joints articulating the separate parts of the organism, the "transitions" are the circulatory system within each part and within the whole. Between introductions and transitions, groups of essays in each subsection function together and in opposition rather like extensor and flexor muscles. Following nature's guide in providing stronger bones for heavier loads, headnotes, introductions, and transitions to the more difficult texts offer more detailed analyses, so that all sections and readings may be clearly accessible to the student. The internal structure of the various parts achieves the coherence of the whole but invites flexible use of the book.

One hallmark of newer generations of students is their skepticism regarding postures of neutrality, whether the political neutrality of the university or the philosophical neutrality of a writer. I have happily abandoned the usual stance of editorial neutrality. The selections cover a range of views on each topic, though, so the reader will hardly experience indoctrination. In fact, respect for thought, reflected in honesty about one's own beliefs and one's reasons for holding them, is the surest guard against indoctrination. A well-informed doubt is discernibly different from a confused or dishonest neutrality.

Free of the claim to an impossible neutrality, this collection follows a course of self-development in which a position on one topic often dictates a move to another. For example, the discovery that the self is not a self-contained, particular entity dictates a critique of social theories that imagine society as an assemblage of isolated Robinson Crusoes. Because each self is a focus of relations with the world and with other selves, a philosophical examination of the self leads to a study of interpersonal relations and group psychology—topics well represented in the following selections. Contemporary writing on these topics, particularly that of R. D. Laing, is popular reading among students today. Laing is significant in this anthology, but not because he is "relevant" in the sense of being popular; his relevance follows from the importance of his concerns, an importance that is philosophically demonstrated. The same is true of topics like women's liberation. As the headnote to Germaine Greer's essay argues, the issues she raises are central to many essays throughout the volume. Similarly, the importance of ecology is shown by Bookchin, Snyder, Fromm, and others. Rather than allow narrowly topical and highly current essays to substitute relevance for philosophy, however, this book draws connections between the current and the traditional so that the reader may see both the relevance of traditional philosophy and the deeper significance of contemporary issues.

Like the discussions of women's liberation and ecology, the philosophical developments of some traditional topics cut across attempts to deal with several issues. The question "How do I know?" for example, is not dealt with under a single section labeled epistemology. Instead we see it first in relation to consciousness and the self, then as a problem of interpersonal perception, later in relation to education and art, and finally as a question of religious belief. While some readers may want to complete the material on the theory of knowledge before returning to other essays, others may want to pursue a shorter path that leads directly from Section One to the closely related essays in Section Four. This shorter course bypasses, incidentally, some of the book's more difficult essays in Sections Two and Three. Yet another alternative reading might take the essays on education first, rather than those of Section One. Though many signposts for alternative readings leave the reader considerable freedom in traveling about without losing his way, the arguments and metaphors of several essays and their introductions play important roles in the introductions to other essays. If the reader wishes to take full advantage of these editorial commentaries, he should find the introductions to Descartes, Ryle, James, Mead, and Laing particularly helpful for understanding how many of the other equally important essays relate to one another.

I would like to thank Ellen Black, Robin Evans, Cathy Gross, Nancy Kaplan, Heather Ogilvy, Richard Probst, Judy Solomon, and Susan Tuttle for their help in preparing the manuscript for press; Joan Levinson for her perceptive and intelligent editing; John McDermott and Patrick Hill for their very helpful comments on earlier stages of the book; and finally Robert J. Fogelin and William Pullin for both the initial suggestion to undertake the project and their constant encouragement toward its completion.

James A. Ogilvy

Contents

3   Consciousness and Knowledge

4   From Family to Society

5   Politics

6 Tradition and Upheaval: Esthetics and Education

7 The Community of Man and Cosmos

SELF AND WORLD

1 The Individual and Society

Introduction:
Self-Knowledge
in the
Contemporary
Situation

If philosophy is the love of wisdom (**philo-** in Greek means "love" and **sophia,** "wisdom"), and if wisdom is complete self-knowledge or self-consciousness, then presumably the best way to begin philosophizing would be an immediate turn to the self. But can the turn to the self be accomplished immediately? Or has it already been accomplished unknowingly? Are we already disengaged from our immediate situations? Is disengagement the same as a turn to the self, or could there be a disengagement that is unwilled and unconscious, a disengagement that separates the individual from his surroundings without provoking a consciousness of the self? The first of the following selections argues that many of us today are victims of precisely this kind of disengagement without self-knowledge.

In mediating the turn to the self by reflecting on how the contemporary situation provokes and determines that turn, we are following the guide of the German philosopher G. W. F. Hegel, who was born in 1770 and died in 1831. In his quest for self-knowledge Hegel was one of the first to acknowledge the importance of viewing one's contemporary situation as a culmination of all that precedes; which influences any attempt at contemporary self-consciousness. Rather than attempt an immediate turn to his own personal psyche, he analyzed the psyche, or spirit, of the age—the combined social and natural product of man's successive stages of growth. Hegel insisted that no one could go beyond his own historical period; he could only sum it up through the process of self-consciousness. He viewed history as being something like a single subject showing stages of growth through experimentation and self-reflection. An active man like Napoleon is a medium for history's experimentation; a reflective man like Hegel is a medium for history's self-reflection. Together they render history a dynamic and self-conscious whole.

We do not have to believe in some disembodied, widely dispersed "mind" in order to grasp some truth in Hegel's theory of history and its relation to the self. We have only to imagine what it would be like to have an up-to-date answer for questions such as, What is it to be a Christian? What is it to be a woman? What is it to be an American? What is it to be black? What is it to be a college student? What is it to be poor? Hegel took history seriously because he saw that to be self-conscious we would have to answer these questions, and the answers must constantly be changing. To know oneself requires that one know one's times; and the times are changing.

Naturally the answers to many questions remain the same, and philosophy helps us see samenesses in differences. However, if you are a woman you want to know what it is to be not just a human being in general but also a woman in particular. Just as we sometimes find it helpful to specify real differences and criticize false differences among human beings at one particular time, so we may need to specify real differences and criticize false differences between being a human at one time in history and being a human at another time in history. So even if Hegel succeeded in synthesizing all significant social, religious, and artistic phenomena up to 1807, the year he published his **Phenomenology of Mind,** still we have a right to remain skeptical, first, as to whether Hegel's self-consciously timebound synthesis remains adequate today, and second, whether a comparable but more contemporary synthesis is even possible today. The first source of skepticism partly explains why none of Hegel's work is included among the following readings; in addition, his prose is all but impenetrable. But further, were he alive today, Hegel himself would insist on the need for a contemporary attempt at historical self-consciousness.

The following four essays represent precisely such an attempt. But do they, or can they, succeed? Is a Hegelian description of an ordered whole possible today, or has what is known as history simply run amok? Is it possible that history, like an individual with a split personality, has become fractured into multiple systems of rationality in irresolvable conflict with each other? The next four essays contain frequent references to schizophrenia, a form of madness connoting a radical split or schism, as if one's reality had been rent in twain. I sincerely hope that references to social schizophrenia are either mistaken, or that we can somehow enjoin society, like the doctor, to heal itself. Each of us is a part of society and therefore as liable to illness as the whole. Can we assume right off that we do not reflect the ills of the society that nurtured us? Is it not possible that our actions, however well intended, are parts of the sickness? The radical quest for self-consciousness, the quest for that knowledge that makes it possible for me to say "I know what I am doing," demands the most far-reaching doubt about the sources of one's own consciousness. Sooner or later one must take one's stand, but for the most part, better later. We have suffered too many foolhardy ventures to fail to see the merits of reflection; so let us reflect on the sources of our consciousness.

PHILIP SLATER

(1927-   )

Philip Slater's first interest was the psychology of motivation: Why do we do what we do? Do we need a theory to answer such a question? Aren't our motives apparent? Certainly many of our motives are perfectly conscious, but cross-cultural studies in social psychology seem to show that some of our most important motives are not. In one of Slater's earlier books, **The Glory of Hera** (1968), he compares the psychology of the individual, the family, and the society of ancient Athens with what he sees in contemporary society. He finds evidence of matriarchal dominance in the Greek family, and his analysis of the mother-son relationship connects the aggressive character of the goddesses to the drivenness of the heroes in Greek mythology. His aim is hardly to uncover a conscious conspiracy on the part of Greek mothers. Rather he intends to show how patterns of family life, social customs, and religious practices all reinforce each other in producing deep-seated patterns of motivation that differ somewhat from culture to culture, patterns that those within the culture are usually unaware of.

In another book, **Microcosm** (1966), Slater turns his attention to small-group dynamics. What happens when eight or ten people, for example students in a seminar, are left to their own devices without active direction from their "leader"? At first none of the students can believe that the teacher really isn't going to teach. Then for a while there may be power conflicts over who will fill the vacuum. But sooner or later, almost invariably, the group joins together to reenact some version of the ancient "the king must die" myth. They resent the presence of the "leader" who does not lead, feel guilty about their resentment, become frustrated with their guilt, and the pot comes to a boil. The remarkable uniformity in Slater's observations of many groups shows that the same socially induced deep structures of motivational functioning must be operating in many of them, despite their members' lack of awareness of those structures.

Finally, in **The Pursuit of Loneliness** (1970), Slater turns to American society at large. Using insights derived from his other inquiries, he examines our frustrated needs and the built-in reasons for their frustration. He argues that our longstanding, culturally characteristic penchant for encouraging pioneer strength, self-sufficiency, and rugged individualism has tended to create a people systematically programmed to frustrate one another's needs for community, engagement, and dependence. The power of Slater's analysis lies in the possibility that things could be otherwise were we aware of the deepest motivations that drive us into our frustrations. Conscious awareness would permit an informed deliberation and choice. But who can choose when he does not know?

The loss of choice is a feature revealed by one of Slater's analytic tools: "identifying the shadow." Though he does not use this label, which was coined by the psychologist Carl Jung some forty years ago, the thought is the same: try to think of the kind of person who annoys you most. Describe his or her characteristics and personality type. You will then have identified your shadow, the part of you that you try hardest to deny and repress. Jung says that whenever you deny having that shadow, then it has you. You are no longer choosing; your actions are largely the result of the unknown battle between self and shadow. As you will see, Slater uses this dynamic of the shadow as a tool for understanding the often irrational actions of society as a whole.

THE PLIGHT OF LONELINESS

. . . I would like to suggest three human desires that are deeply and uniquely frustrated by American culture:

1. The desire for *community*—the wish to live in trust and fraternal cooperation with one's fellows in a total and visible collective entity.

2. The desire for *engagement*—the wish to come directly to grips with social and interpersonal problems and to confront on equal terms an environment which is not composed of ego-extensions.

3. The desire for *dependence*—the wish to share responsibility for the control of one's impulses and the direction of one's life.

When I say that these three desires are frustrated by American culture, this need not conjure up romantic images of the individual struggling against society. In every case it is fair to say that we participate eagerly in producing the frustration we endure—it is not something merely done to us. For these desires are in each case subordinate to their opposites in that vague entity called the American Character. The thesis of this chapter is that Americans have voluntarily created and voluntarily maintain a society which increasingly frustrates and aggravates these secondary yearnings, to

THE PLIGHT OF LONELINESS   From Philip Slater, *The Pursuit of Loneliness,* Chapter One: "I Only Work Here." Published by Beacon Press. Copyright © 1970 by Philip E. Slater. Reprinted by permission of Beacon Press.

the point where they threaten to become primary. Groups that in any way personify this threat are therefore feared in an exaggerated way, and will be until Americans as a group are able to recognize and accept those needs within themselves.

Community and Competition

We are so accustomed to living in a society that stresses individualism that we need to be reminded that "collectivism" in a broad sense has always been the more usual lot of mankind, as well as of most other species. Most people in most societies have been born into and died in stable communities in which the subordination of the individual to the welfare of the group was taken for granted, while the aggrandizement of the individual at the expense of his fellows was simply a crime.

This is not to say that competition is an American invention—all societies involve some sort of admixture of cooperative and competitive institutions. But our society lies near or on the competitive extreme, and although it contains cooperative institutions I think it is fair to say that Americans suffer from their relative weakness and peripherality. Studies of business executives have revealed, for example, a deep hunger for an atmosphere of trust and fraternity with their colleagues (with whom they must, in the short run, engage in what Riesman calls "antagonistic cooperation"). The competitive life is a lonely one, and its satisfactions are very short-lived indeed, for each race leads only to a new one.

In the past, as so many have pointed out, there were in our society many oases in which one could take refuge from the frenzied invidiousness of our economic system—institutions such as the extended family and the stable local neighborhood in which one could take pleasure from something other than winning a symbolic victory over one of his fellows. But these have disappeared one by one, leaving the individual more and more in a situation in which he must try to satisfy his affiliative and invidious needs in the same place. This has made the balance a more brittle one—the appeal of cooperative living more seductive, and the need to suppress our longing for it more acute.

In recent decades the principal vehicle for the tolerated expression of this longing has been the mass media. Popular songs and film comedies have continually engaged in a sentimental rejection of the dominant mores, maintaining that the best things in life are free, that love is more important than success, that keeping up with the Joneses is absurd, that personal integrity should take precedence over winning, and so on. But these protestations must be understood for what they are: a safety valve for the dissatisfactions that the modal American experiences when he behaves as he thinks he should. The same man who chuckles and sentimentalizes over a happy-go-lucky hero in a film would view his real-life counterpart as frivolous and irresponsible, and suburbanites who philosophize over their back fence with complete sincerity about their "dog-eat-dog-world," and what-is-it-all-for, and you-can't-take-it-with-you, and success-doesn't-make-you-happy-it-just-gives-you-ulcers-and-a-heart-condition—would be enraged should their children pay serious attention to such a viewpoint. Indeed, the degree of rage is, up to a point, a function of the degree of sincerity: if the individual did not feel these things he would not have to fight them so vigorously. The peculiarly exaggerated hostility that hippies tend to arouse suggests that the life they strive for is highly seductive to middle-aged Americans.

The intensity of this reaction can in part be attributed to a kind of circularity that characterizes American individualism. When a value is as strongly held as is individualism in America the illnesses it produces tend to be treated by increasing the dosage, in the same way an alcoholic treats a hangover or a drug addict his withdrawal symptoms. Technological change, mobility, and the individualistic ethos combine to rupture the bonds that tie each individual to a family, a community, a kinship network, a geographical location—bonds that give him a comfortable sense of himself. As this sense of himself erodes, he seeks ways of affirming it. But his efforts at self-enhancement automatically accelerate the very erosion he seeks to halt.

It is easy to produce examples of the many ways in which Americans attempt to minimize, circumvent, or deny the interdependence upon which all human societies are based. We seek a private house, a private means of transportation, a private garden, a private laundry, self-service stores, and do-it-yourself skills of every kind. An enormous technology seems to have set itself the task of making it unnecessary for one human being ever to ask anything of another in the course of going about his daily business. Even within the family Americans are unique in their feeling that each member should have a separate room, and even a separate telephone, television, and car, when economically possible. We seek more and more privacy, and feel more and more alienated and lonely when we get it. What accidental contacts we do have, furthermore, seem more intrusive, not only because they are unsought but because they are unconnected with any familiar pattern of interdependence.

Most important, our encounters with others tend increasingly to be competitive as a result of the search for privacy. We less and less often meet our fellow man to share and exchange, and more and more often encounter him as an impediment or a nuisance: making the highway crowded when we are rushing somewhere, cluttering and littering the beach or park or wood, pushing in front of us at the supermarket, taking the last parking place, polluting our air and water, building a highway through our house, blocking our view, and so on. Because we have cut off so much communication with each other we keep bumping into each other, and thus a higher and higher percentage of our interpersonal contacts are abrasive.

We seem unable to foresee that the gratification of a wish might turn out to be something of a monkey's paw if the wish were shared by many others. We cheer the new road that initially shaves ten minutes off the drive to our country retreat but ultimately transforms it into a crowded resort and increases both the traffic and the time. We are continually surprised to find, when we want something, that thousands or millions of others want it, too —that other human beings get hot in summer and cold in winter. The worst traffic jams occur when a mass of vacationing tourists departs for home early to "beat the traffic." We are too enamored of the individualistic fantasy that everyone is, or should be, different—that each person could somehow build his entire life around some single, unique eccentricity without boring himself and everyone else to death. Each of us of course has his quirks, which provide a surface variety that is briefly entertaining, but aside from this human beings have little basis for their persistent claim that they are not all members of the same species.

Since our contacts with others are increasingly competitive, unanticipated, and abrasive, we seek still more apartness and accelerate the trend. The desire to be somehow special inaugurates an even more competitive quest for progressively more rare and expensive symbols—a quest that is ultimately futile since it is individualism itself that produces uniformity.

This is poorly understood by Americans, who tend to confuse uniformity with "conformity," in the sense of compliance with or submission to group demands. Many societies exert far more pressure on the individual to mold himself to fit a particularized segment of a total group pattern, but there is variation among these circumscribed roles. Our society gives far more leeway to the individual to pursue his own ends, but, since *it* defines what is worthy and desirable, everyone tends, independently but monotonously, to pursue the same things in the same way. The first pattern combines cooperation, conformity, and variety; the second, competition, individualism, and uniformity.

These relationships are exemplified by two familiar processes in contemporary America: the flight to the suburb and the do-it-yourself movement. Both attempt to deny human interdependence and pursue unrealistic fantasies of self-sufficiency. The first tries to overlook our dependence upon the city for the maintenance of the level of culture we demand. "Civilized" means, literally, "citified," and the state of the city is an accurate index of the condition of the culture as a whole. We behave toward our cities like an irascible farmer who never feeds his cow and then kicks her when she fails to give enough milk. But the flight to the suburb is in any case self-defeating, its goals subverted by the mass quality of the exodus. The suburban dweller seeks peace, privacy, nature, community, and a child-rearing environment which is healthy and culturally optimal. Instead he finds neither the beauty and serenity of the countryside, the stimulation of the city, nor the stability and sense of community of the small town, and his children are exposed to a cultural deprivation equaling that of any slum child with a television set. Living in a narrow age-graded and class-segregated society, it is little wonder that suburban families have contributed so little to the national talent pool in proportion to their numbers, wealth, and other social advantages.[1] And this transplantation, which has caused the transplants to

_____

[1] Using cities, small towns, and rural areas for comparison. The small Midwestern town achieves its legendary dullness by a process akin to evaporation—all the

atrophy, has blighted the countryside and impoverished the city. A final irony of the suburban dream is that, for many Americans, reaching the pinnacle of one's social ambitions (owning a house in the suburbs) requires one to perform all kinds of menial tasks (carrying garbage cans, mowing lawns, shoveling snow, and so on) that were performed for him when he occupied a less exalted status.

Some of this manual labor, however, is voluntary—an attempt to deny the elaborate division of labor required in a complex society. Many Americans seem quite willing to pay this price for their reluctance to engage in interpersonal encounters with servants and artisans—a price which is rather high unless the householder particularly relishes the work (some find in it a tangible relief from the intangibles they manipulate in their own jobs) or is especially good at it, or cannot command a higher rate of pay in the job market than the servant or artisan.

The do-it-yourself movement has accompanied, paradoxically, increasing specialization in the occupational sphere. As one's job narrows, perhaps, one seeks the challenge of new skill-acquisition in the home. But specialization also means that one's interpersonal encounters with artisans in the home proliferate and become more impersonal. It is not a matter of a familiar encounter with the local smith or grocer—a few well-known individuals performing a relatively large number of functions, and with whom one's casual interpersonal contacts may be a source of satisfaction, and are in any case a testimony to the stability and meaningful interrelatedness of human affairs. One finds instead a multiplicity of narrow specialists—each perhaps a stranger (the same type of repair may be performed by a different person each time). Every relationship, such as it is, must start from scratch, and it is small wonder that the household turns away from such an unrewarding prospect in apathy and despair.

Americans thus find themselves in a vicious circle, in which their extrafamilial relationships are increasingly arduous, competitive, trivial, and irksome, in part as a result of efforts to avoid or minimize potentially irksome or competitive relationships. As the few vestiges of stable and familiar community life erode, the desire for a simple, cooperative life style grows in intensity. The most seductive appeal of radical ideologies for Americans consists in the fact that all in one way or another attack the competitive foundations of our society. Each touches a responsive doubt, and the stimuli arousing this doubt must be carefully unearthed and rooted out, just as the Puritan must unearth and root out the sexual stimuli that excite him.[2]

---

warm and energetic particles depart for coastal cities, leaving their place of origin colder and flatter than they found it. But the restless spirit in a small town knows he lives in the sticks and has a limited range of experience, while his suburban counterpart can sustain an illusion of cosmopolitanism in an environment which is far more constricted (*a small town is a microcosm, a suburb merely a layer*).

[2] Both efforts are ambivalent, since the "seek and destroy" process is in part a quest for the stimulus itself. The Puritanical censor both wants the sexual stimulus and

Now it may be objected that American society is far less competitive than it once was, and the appeal of radical ideologies should hence be diminished. A generation of critics has argued that the entrepreneurial individualist of the past has been replaced by a bureaucratic, security-minded, Organization Man. Much of this historical drama was written through the simple device of comparing yesterday's owner-president with today's assistant sales manager; certainly these nostalgia-merchants never visited a nineteenth-century company town. Another distortion is introduced by the fact that it was only the most ruthlessly competitive robber barons who survived to tell us how it was. Little is written about the neighborhood store that extended credit to the poor, or the small town industry that refused to lay off local workers in hard times—they all went under together. And as for the organization men—they left us no sagas.

Despite these biases real changes have undoubtedly occurred, but even if we grant that the business world as such was more competitive, the total environment contained more cooperative, stable, and personal elements. The individual worked in a smaller firm with lower turnover in which his relationships were more enduring and less impersonal, and in which the ideology of Adam Smith was tempered by the fact that the participants were neighbors and might have been childhood playmates. Even if the business world was as "dog-eat-dog" as we imagine it (which seems highly unlikely), one encountered it as a deviant episode in what was otherwise a more comfortable and familiar environment than the organization man can find today in or out of his office. The organization man complex is simply an attempt to restore the personal, particularistic, paternalistic environment of the family business and the company town; and the other-directed "group-think" of the suburban community is a desperate attempt to bring some old-fashioned small-town collectivism into the transient and impersonal life-style of the suburb. The social critics of the 1950's were so preoccupied with assailing these rather synthetic substitutes for traditional forms of human interdependence that they lost sight of the underlying pathogenic forces that produced them. Medical symptoms usually result from attempts made by the body to counteract disease, and attacking such symptoms often aggravates and prolongs the illness. This appears to be the case with the feeble and self-defeating efforts of twentieth-century Americans to find themselves a viable social context.

---

wants to destroy it, and his job enables him to gratify both of these "contradictory" desires. There is a similar prurience in the efforts of groups such as the House UnAmerican Activities Committee to "uncover subversion." Just as the censor gets to experience far more pornography than the average man, so the Congressional red-baiter gets to hear as much Communist ideology as he wants, which is apparently quite a lot.

Engagement and Uninvolvement

Many of the phenomena we have discussed can also be linked to a compulsive American tendency to avoid confrontation of chronic social problems. This avoiding tendency often comes as a surprise to foreigners, who tend to think of Americans as pragmatic and down-to-earth. But while trying to solve long-range social problems with short-run "hardware" solutions produces a lot of hardware—a down-to-earth result, surely—it can hardly be considered practical when it aggravates the problems, as it almost always does. American pragmatism is deeply irrational in this respect, and in our hearts we have always known it. One of the favorite themes of American cartoonists is the man who paints himself into a corner, saws off the limb he is sitting on, or runs out of space on the sign he is printing. The scientist of science-fiction and horror films, whose experimentation leads to disastrously unforeseen consequences, is a more anxious representation of this same awareness that the most future-oriented nation in the world shows a deep incapacity to plan ahead. We are, as a people, perturbed by our inability to anticipate the consequences of our acts, but we still wait optimistically for some magic telegram, informing us that the tangled skein of misery and self-deception into which we have woven ourselves has vanished in the night. Each month popular magazines regale their readers with such telegrams: announcing that our transportation crisis will be solved by a bigger plane or a wider road, mental illness with a pill, poverty with a law, slums with a bulldozer, urban conflict with a gas, racism with a goodwill gesture. Perhaps the most grotesque of all these telegrams was an article in *Life* showing a group of suburbanites participating in a "Clean-Up Day" in an urban slum. Foreigners are surprised when Americans exhibit this kind of naïveté and/or cynicism about social problems, but their surprise is inappropriate. Whatever realism we may display in technical areas, our approach to social issues inevitably falls back on cinematic tradition, in which social problems are resolved by gesture. Deeply embedded in the somnolent social consciousness of the broom-wielding suburbanites is a series of climactic movie scenes in which a long column of once surly natives, marching in solemn silence and as one man, framed by the setting sun, turn in their weapons to the white chief who has done them a good turn, or menace the white adventurer's enemy (who turns pale at the sight), or rebuild the missionary's church, destroyed by fire.

When a social problem persists (as they tend to do) longer than a few days, those who call attention to its continued presence are viewed as "going too far" and "causing the pendulum to swing the other way." We can make war on poverty but shrink from the extensive readjustments required to stop breeding it. Once a law is passed, a commission set up, a study made, a report written, the problem is expected to have been "wiped out" or "mopped up." Bombs abroad are matched by "crash programs" at home—the terminological similarity reveals a psychological one. Our approach to transportation problems has had the effect, as many people have observed, of making it easier and easier to travel to more and more places that have become less and less worth driving to. Asking us to consider the manifold consequences of chopping down a forest, draining a swamp, spraying a field with poison, making it easier to drive into an already crowded city, or selling deadly weapons to everyone who wants them arouses in us the same impatience as a chess problem would in a hyperactive six-year-old.

The avoiding tendency lies at the very root of American character. This nation was settled and continuously repopulated by people who were not personally successful in confronting the social conditions obtaining in their mother country, but fled these conditions in the hope of a better life. This series of choices (reproduced in the westward movement) provided a complex selection process—populating America disproportionately with a certain kind of person.

In the past we have always, explicitly or implicitly, stressed the positive side of this selection, implying that America thereby found itself blessed with an unusual number of energetic, mobile, ambitious, daring, and optimistic persons. Now there is no reason to deny that a number of traits must have helped to differentiate those who chose to come from those who chose to stay, nor that these differences must have generated social institutions and habits of mind that tended to preserve and reproduce these characteristics. But very little attention has been paid to the more negative aspects of the selection. If we gained the energetic and daring we also gained the lion's share of the rootless, the unscrupulous, those who value money over relationships, and those who put self-aggrandizement ahead of love and loyalty. And most of all, we gained a critically undue proportion of persons who, when faced with a difficult situation, tended to chuck the whole thing and flee to a new environment. Escaping, evading, and avoiding are responses which lie at the base of much that is peculiarly American—the suburb, the automobile, the self-service store, and so on.

These responses also contribute to the appalling discrepancy between our material resources and our treatment of those who cannot adequately care for themselves. This is not an argument against institutionalization: American society is not geared to handle these problems in any other way, and this is in fact the point I wish to make. One cannot successfully alter one facet of a social system if everything else is left the same, for the patterns are interdependent and reinforce one another. In a cooperative, stable society the aged, infirm, or psychotic person can be absorbed by the local community, which knows and understands him. He presents a difficulty which is familiar and which can be confronted daily and directly. This condition cannot be reproduced in our society today—the burden must be carried by a small, isolated, mobile family unit that is not really equipped for it.

But understanding the forces that require us to incarcerate those who cannot function independently in our society does not give us license to ignore the significance of doing so. The institutions we provide for those who cannot care for themselves are human garbage heaps—they result from and reinforce our tendency to avoid confronting social and interpersonal problems. They make life "easier" for the rest of society, just as does the automobile. And just as we find ourselves having to devise ridiculous exercises to counteract the harmful effect of our dependence upon the automobile, so the "ease" of our nonconfronting social technology makes us bored, flabby, and interpersonally insensitive, and our lives empty and mechanical.

Our ideas about institutionalizing the aged, psychotic, retarded, and infirm are based on a pattern of thought that we might call the Toilet Assumption—the notion that unwanted matter, unwanted difficulties, unwanted complexities and obstacles will disappear if they are removed from our immediate field of vision. We do not connect the trash we throw from the car window with the trash in our streets, and we assume that replacing old buildings with new expensive ones will alleviate poverty in the slums. We throw the aged and psychotic into institutional holes where they cannot be seen. Our approach to social problems is to decrease their visibility: out of sight, out of mind. This is the real foundation of racial segregation, especially its most extreme case, the Indian "reservation." The result of our social efforts has been to remove the underlying problems of our society farther and farther from daily experience and daily consciousness, and hence to decrease, in the mass of the population, the knowledge, skill, resources, and motivation necessary to deal with them.

When these discarded problems rise to the surface again—a riot, a protest, an exposé in the mass media—we react as if a sewer had backed up. We are shocked, disgusted, and angered, and immediately call for the emergency plumber (the special commission, the crash program) to ensure that the problem is once again removed from consciousness.

The Toilet Assumption is not merely a facetious metaphor. Prior to the widespread use of the flush toilet all of humanity was daily confronted with the immediate reality of human waste and its disposal. They knew where it was and how it got there. Nothing miraculously vanished. Excrement was conspicuously present in the outhouse or chamber pot, and the slops that went out the window went visibly and noticeably into the street. The most aristocratic Victorian ladies strolling in fashionable city parks thought nothing of retiring to the bushes to relieve themselves. Similarly, garbage did not disappear down a disposal unit—it remained nearby.

As with physical waste, so with social problems. The biblical adage, "the poor are always with us," had a more literal meaning before World War I. The poor were visible and all around. Psychosis was not a strange phenomenon in a textbook but a familiar neighbor or village character. The aged were in every house. Everyone had seen animals slaughtered and knew what they were eating when they ate them; illness and death were a part of everyone's immediate experience.

In contemporary life the book of experience is filled with blank and mysterious pages. Occupational specialization and plumbing have exerted a kind of censorship over our understanding of the world we live in and how it operates. And when we come into immediate contact with anything that does not seem to fit into the ordinary pattern of our somewhat bowdlerized existence our spontaneous reaction is to try somehow to flush it away, bomb it away, throw it down the jail.

But in some small degree we also feel bored and uneasy with the orderly chrome and porcelain vacuum of our lives, from which so much of life has been removed. Evasion creates self-distaste as well as comfort, and radical confrontations are exciting as well as disruptive. The answering chord that they produce within us terrifies us, and although we cannot entirely contain our fascination, it is relatively easy to project our self-disgust onto the perpetrators of the confrontations.

This ambivalence is reflected in the mass media. The hunger for confrontation and experience attracts a lot of attention to social problems, but these are usually dealt with in such a way as to reinforce the avoidance process. The TV documentary presents a tidy package with opposing views and an implication of progress. Reports in popular magazines attempt to provide a substitute for actual experience. Important book and film reviews, for example, give just the blend of titillation and condescension to make the reader imagine that he is already "in" and need not undergo the experience itself—that he has not only participated in the novel adventure but already outgrown it. Thus the ultimate effect of the media is to reinforce the avoiding response by providing an effigy of confrontation and experience. There is always the danger with such insulating mechanisms, however, that they at times get over-loaded, like tonsils, and become carriers of precisely the agents against which they are directed. This is an increasingly frequent event in our society today.

A corollary of this latent desire for social confrontation is the desire for an incorruptible man—a man who cannot be bribed, who does not have his price. Once again this desire is a recessive trait, relegated largely to the realm of folk drama and movie script, but it exists nonetheless, as a silent rebellion against the oppressive democratic harmony of a universal monetary criterion.

In the hard reality of everyday life, however, the incorruptible man is at best an inconvenience, an obstacle to the smooth functioning of a vast institutional machinery. Management leaders, for example, tend to prefer corrupt union leaders—"people you can do business with"—to those who might introduce questions and attitudes lying outside the rules of a monetary game. The man who cannot be bought tends to be mistrusted as a fanatic, and the fact that incorruptible men are so often called Communists may be understood in the same light. As in the case of the mass media, however, this mechanism has become overloaded, so that having been jailed and/or called a Communist or traitor is now regarded by young adults as a medal attesting to one's social concern.

Also closely related to the latent desire for confrontation is an inarticulate wish to move in an environment consisting of something other than our own creations. Human beings evolved as organisms geared to mastery of the natural environment. Within the past few thousand years we have learned to perform this function so well that the natural environment poses very little threat to civilized peoples. Our dangers are self-made ones— subtle, insidious, and meaningless. We die from our own machines, our own poisons, our own weapons, our own despair. Furthermore, we are separated from primitive conditions by too few millennia to have evolved any comfortable adaptation to a completely man-made environment. We still long for and enjoy struggling against the elements, even though such activity can only occasionally be considered meaningful or functional.[3] We cross the ocean in artificially primitive boats, climb mountains we could fly over, kill animals we do not eat. Natural disasters, such as floods, hurricanes, blizzards, and so on, generate a cheerfulness which would seem inappropriate if we did not all share it. It is as if some balance between man and nature had been restored, and with it man's "true function." Like the cat that prefers to play with a ball around the obstacle of a chair leg, so man seems to derive some perverse joy from having a snowstorm force him to use the most primitive mode of transportation. It is particularly amusing to observe people following the course of an approaching hurricane and affecting a proper and prudent desire that it veer off somewhere, in the face of an ill-concealed craving that it do nothing of the kind. There is a satisfaction that comes from relating to nature on equal terms, with respect and even deference to forms of life different from ourselves—as the Indian respects the deer he kills for food and the tree that shields him from the sun.

We interact largely with extensions of our own egos. We stumble over the consequences of our past acts. We are drowning in our own excreta (another consequence of the Toilet Assumption). We rarely come into contact with a force which is clearly and cleanly Not-Us. Every struggle is a struggle with ourselves, because there is a little piece of ourselves in everything we encounter—houses, clothes, cars, cities, machines, even our foods. There is an uneasy, anesthetized feeling about this kind of life—like being trapped forever inside an air-conditioned car with power steering and power brakes and only a telephone to talk to. Our world is only a mirror, and our efforts mere shadowboxing—yet shadowboxing in which we frequently manage to hurt ourselves.

Even that part of the world which is not man-made impinges upon us through a symbolic network we have created. We encounter primarily our

---

[3] The cholesterol problem provides an illustration: one theory proposes that the release of cholesterol into the bloodstream was functional for hunting large animals with primitive weapons. Since the animal was rarely killed but only wounded, he had to be followed until he dropped, and this was a matter of walking or running for several days without food or rest. A similar response would be activated today in fields such as advertising, in which a sustained extra effort over a period of time (to obtain a large contract, for example) is periodically required. But these peak efforts do not involve any physical release—the cholesterol is not utilized.

own fantasies: we have a concept and image of a mountain, a lake, or a forest almost before we ever see one. Travel posters tell us what it means to be in a strange land, the events of life become news items before they actually happen—all experience receives preliminary structure and interpretation. Public relations, television drama, and life become indistinguishable.

The story of Pygmalion is thus the story of modern man, in love with his own product. But like all discreet fairy tales, that of Pygmalion stops with the consummation of his love. It does not tell us of his ineffable boredom at having nothing to love but an excrescence of himself. But we know that men who live surrounded by that which and those whom they have molded to their desires—from the Caliph of Baghdad to Federico Fellini—suffer from a fearsome ennui. The minute they assume material form our fantasies cease to be interesting and become mere excreta.

Dependence and Independence

Independence training in American society begins almost at birth—babies are held and carried less than in most societies and spend more time in complete isolation—and continues, despite occasional parental ambivalence, throughout childhood and adolescence. When a child is admonished to be a "big boy" or "big girl" this usually means doing something alone or without help (the rest of the time it involves strangling feelings, but this norm seems to be on the wane). Signs of independence are usually rewarded, and a child who in too obvious a manner calls attention to the fact that human intelligence is based almost entirely on the process of imitation is ridiculed by calling him a copycat or a monkey (after the paradoxical habit humans have of projecting their most uniquely human attributes onto animals).

There have been many complaints in recent years that independence training is less rigorous than it once was, but again, as in the case of competitiveness, this is hard to assess. To be on one's own in a simple, stable, and familiar environment requires a good deal less internal "independence" than to be on one's own in a complex, shifting, and strange one. Certainly a child could run about more freely a century ago without coming to harm, and his errors and misdeeds had far more trivial consequences than today; but this decline in the child's freedom of movement says nothing about the degree to which the child is asked to forego the pleasures of depending upon his parents for nurturance and support. If the objective need is greater, it may offset a small increase in parental tolerance for dependent behavior, and cause the child to experience the independence training as more severe rather than less.

In any case, American independence training is severe relative to most of the rest of the world, and we might assume this to have emotional consequences. This is not to say that such training is not consonant with the demands of adult society: the two are quite in accord. Sociologists and anthropologists are often content to stop at this point and say that as long as this accord exists there is no problem worth discussing. But the frustration of any need has its effects (one of them being to increase the society's vulnerability to social change) and these should be understood.

An example might help clarify this issue. Ezra and Suzanne Vogel observe that Japanese parents encourage dependency as actively as American parents push independence, and that healthy children and adults in Japan rely heavily on others for emotional support and decisions about their lives. A degree of dependence on the mother which in America would be considered "abnormal" prepares the Japanese for a society in which far more dependency is expected and accepted than in ours. The Japanese firm is highly paternalistic and takes a great deal of responsibility for making the individual employee secure and comfortable. The Vogels observe, however, that just as the American mother tends to complain at the success of her efforts and feel that her children are *too* independent, so the Japanese mother tends to feel that her children are too *dependent,* despite the fact that she has trained them this way.[4]

What I am trying to point out is that regardless of the congruence between socialization practices and adult norms, any extreme pattern of training will produce stresses for the individuals involved. And just as the mothers experience discomfort with the effects of these patterns, so do the children, although barred by cultural values from recognizing and naming the nature of their distress, which in our society takes the form of a desire to relinquish responsibility for control and decision-making in one's daily life. Deeply felt democratic values usually stand in the way of realizing this goal through authoritarian submission, although our attitudes toward democracy are not without ambivalence, as has been suggested elsewhere;[5] but the temptation to abdicate self-direction in more subtle ways is powerful indeed. Perhaps the major problem for Americans is that of choice: Americans are forced into making more choices per day, with fewer "givens," more ambiguous criteria, less environmental stability, and less social structural support, than any people in history.

Many of the mechanisms through which dependency is counteracted in our society have already been discussed in the preceding sections, but a word should be said about the complex problem of internalized controls. In stable societies, as many authors have pointed out, the control of human impulses is usually a collective responsibility. The individual is viewed as not having within himself the controls required to guarantee that his im-

---

[4] Ezra F. Vogel and Suzanne H. Vogel, "Permissive Dependency in Japan," in H. Kent Geiger (ed.), *Comparative Perspectives on Marriage and the Family* (Boston: Little, Brown, 1968), pp. 68–77.

[5] See Erich Fromm, *Escape from Freedom* (New York: Rinehart, 1941); W. G. Bennis and P. E. Slater, *The Temporary Society* (New York: Harper and Row, 1968), Chapter 1. Bennis and I attempt to show that the "efficiency" Americans attribute to autocratic systems applies only to situations involving simple, routine tasks. Such systems function poorly under conditions of change and complexity. They have an awkward tendency to run a "tight ship" which nevertheless sinks.

pulses will not break out in ways disapproved by the community. But this matters very little, since the group is always near at hand to stop him or shame him or punish him should he forget himself.

In more fluid, changing societies we are more apt to find controls that are internalized—that do not depend to so great an extent on control and enforcement by external agents. This has long been characteristic of American society—de Tocqueville observed in 1830 that American women were much more independent than European women, freer from chaperonage, and able to appear in what a European would consider "compromising" situations without any sign of sexual involvement.

Chaperonage is in fact the simplest way to illustrate the difference between external and internalized controls. In chaperon cultures—such as traditional Middle-Eastern and Latin societies—it simply did not occur to anyone that a man and woman could be alone together and not have sexual intercourse. In America, which represents the opposite extreme, there is almost no situation in which a man and a woman could find themselves in which sexual intercourse could not at least be considered problematic (Hollywood comedies have exploited this phenomenon—well past the point of exhaustion and nausea—over the past 35 years). Americans are virtuosi of internalized control of sexual expression (the current relaxation of sexual norms in no way changes this), and this has caused difficulties whenever the two systems have come into contact. An unchaperoned girl in a bikini or mini-skirt means one thing in America, another in Baghdad. It is a mistake to consider a chaperon society more prudish—the compliment is likely to be returned when the difference is understood. Even Americans consider some situations inherently sexual: if a girl from some mythical culture came to an American's house, stripped, and climbed into bed with him, he would assume she was making a sexual overture and would be rather indignant if he found that she was merely expressing casual friendship according to her native customs. He would also be puzzled if *he* were called prudish, and we need not speculate as to what he would call *her*.

But how are internalized controls created? We know that they are closely tied to what are usually called "love-oriented" techniques of discipline in childhood. These techniques avoid physical punishment and deprivation of privileges and stress reasoning and the withdrawal of parental affection. The basic difference between "love-oriented" and "fear-oriented" techniques (such as physical punishment) is that in the latter case the child simply learns to avoid punishment while in the former he tends to incorporate parental values as his own in order to avoid losing parental love and approval. When fear-oriented techniques prevail, the child is in the position of inhabitants of an occupied country, who obey to avoid getting hurt but disobey whenever they think they can get away with it. Like them, the child does not have any emotional commitment to his rulers—he does not fear losing their love.

Love-oriented techniques require by definition that love and discipline emanate from the same source. When this happens it is not merely a question of avoiding the punisher: the child wishes to anticipate the displeasure of the loved and loving parent, wants to be like the parent, and takes into himself as a part of himself the values and attitudes of the parent. He wants to please, not placate, and because he has taken the parent's attitudes as his own, pleasing the parent comes to mean making him feel good about himself. Thus while individuals raised with fear-oriented techniques tend to direct anger outward under stress, those raised with love-oriented techniques tend to direct it inward in the form of guilt—a distinction that has important physiological correlates.[6]

Under stable conditions external controls work perfectly well. Everyone knows his own place and his neighbor's, and deviations from expected behavior will be quickly met from all sides. When social conditions fluctuate, social norms change, and people move frequently from one social setting to another and are often among strangers, this will no longer do. An individual cannot take his whole community with him wherever he goes, and in any case the rules differ from place to place. The mobile individual must travel light, and internalized controls are portable and transistorized, as it were.

Anger directed inward is also made for mobile conditions. In a stable community two youths who start to get into a fight will be held back by their friends—they depend upon this restraint and can abandon themselves to their passion, knowing that it will not produce harmful consequences. But where one moves among strangers it becomes increasingly important to have other mechanisms for handling aggression. In situations of high mobility and flux the individual must have a built-in readiness to feel himself responsible when things go wrong.

Most modern societies are a confused mixture of both systems, a fact that enables conservative spokesmen to attribute rising crime rates to permissive child-rearing techniques. The overwhelming majority of ordinary crimes, however, are committed by individuals who have *not* been reared with love-oriented techniques, but, insofar as the parent or parents have been able to rear them at all, by the haphazard use of fear-oriented discipline. Love-oriented child-rearing techniques are a luxury that slum parents, for example, can seldom afford.

Furthermore, it is rather misleading to refer to the heavily guilt-inducing socialization techniques of middle-class parents as "permissive." Misbehavior in a lower class child is more often greeted with a cuff, possibly accompanied by some non-informative response such as "stop that!" But it may not be at all clear to the child which of the many motions he is now performing "that" is; and, indeed, "that" may be punished only when the parent is feeling irritable. A child would have to have achieved an enormously high intelligence level (which, of course, it has not, for this very reason) to be able to form a moral concept out of a hundred irritable stop-

---

[6] S. H. King and A. F. Henry, "Aggression and Cardiovascular Reactions Related to Parental Control over Behavior," *Journal of Abnormal and Social Psychology,* LIII, 1955, pp. 206–210.

thats. What he usually forms is merely a crude sense of when the "old man" or the "old lady" is to be avoided. The self-conscious, highly verbal, middle-class parent is at the opposite extreme. He or she feels that discipline should relate to the child's act, not the parent's own emotional state, and is very careful to emphasize verbally the principle involved in the misbehavior ("it's bad to hit people" or "we have to share with guests"). Concept-formation is made very easy for the middle-class child, and he tends to think of moral questions in terms of principles.

As he grows older this tendency is reinforced by his encounter with different groups with different norms. In a mobile society, one cannot simply accept the absolute validity of any rule because one experiences competing moral codes. As a result the middle-class child tends to evolve a system of meta-rules, that is, rules for assessing the relative validity of these codes. The meta-rules tend to be based upon the earliest and most general principles expressed by the parents; such as prohibitions on violence against others, egalitarianism, mutuality, and so on. This ability to treat rules in a highly secular fashion while maintaining a strong moral position is baffling to those whose control mechanisms are more primitive, but it presupposes a powerful and articulate conscience. Such an individual can expose himself to physical harm and to violence-arousing situations without losing control and while maintaining a moral position. This may seem inconceivable to an uneducated working-class policeman whose own impulses are barely held in line by a jerry-built structure of poorly articulated and mutually contradictory moral absolutes. Hence he tends to misinterpret radical middle-class behavior as a hypocritical mask for mere delinquency.

The point of this long digression, however, is that internalization is a mixed blessing. It may enable one to get his head smashed in a good cause, but the capacity to give oneself up completely to an emotion is almost altogether lost in the process. Where internalization is high there is often a feeling that the controls themselves are out of control—that emotion cannot be expressed when the individual would like to express it. Life is muted, experience filtered, emotion anesthetized, affective discharge incomplete. Efforts to shake free from this hypertrophied control system include not only drugs, and sensation-retrieval techniques such as those developed at the Esalen Institute in California, but also confused attempts to reestablish external systems of direction and control—the vogue currently enjoyed by astrology is an expression of this. The simplest technique, of course, would be the establishment of a more authoritarian social structure, which would relieve the individual of the great burden of examining and moderating his own responses. He could become as a child, lighthearted, spontaneous, and passionate, secure in the knowledge that others would prevent his impulses from causing harm.

Realization of this goal is prevented by democratic values and the social conditions that foster them (complexity, fluidity, change). But the desire plays a significant part in conventional reactions to radical minorities, who are all felt to be seeking the abandonment of self-restraints of one kind or another and at the same time demanding *more* responsible behavior from the establishment. This is both infuriating and contagious to white middle-class adults, who would like very much to do the same, and their call for "law and order" (that is, more *external* control) is an expression of that desire as well as an attempt to smother it. This conflict over dependency and internalization also helps explain why official American anticommunism always lays so much stress on the authoritarian (rather than the socialistic) aspects of Communist states.

Individualism Reassessed

The three variables we have been discussing—community, engagement, dependency—can all trace their suppression in American society to our commitment to individualism. The belief that everyone should pursue autonomously his own destiny has forced us to maintain an emotional detachment (for which no amount of superficial gregariousness can compensate) from our social and physical environment, and aroused a vague guilt about our competitiveness and indifference to others; for, after all, our earliest training in childhood does not stress competitiveness, but cooperation, sharing, and thoughtfulness—it is only later that we learn to reverse these priorities. Radical challenges to our society, then, always tap a confused responsive chord within us that is far more disturbing than anything going on outside. They threaten to reconnect us with each other, with nature, and with ourselves, a possibility that is thrilling but terrifying—as if we had grown a shell-like epidermis and someone was threatening to rip it off.

Individualism finds its roots in the attempt to deny the reality and importance of human interdependence. One of the major goals of technology in America is to "free" us from the necessity of relating to, submitting to, depending upon, or controlling other people.[7] Unfortunately, the more we have succeeded in doing this the more we have felt disconnected, bored, lonely, unprotected, unnecessary, and unsafe.

Individualism has many expressions: free enterprise, self-service, academic freedom, suburbia, permissive gun-laws, civil liberties, do-it-yourself, oil-depletion allowances. Everyone values some of these expressions and condemns others, but the principle is widely shared. Criticisms of our society since World War II have almost all embraced this value and expressed fears for its demise—the organization man, the other-directed man, conformity, "group-think," and so on. In general these critics have failed to

[7] The peculiar germ-phobia that pervades American life (and supports several industries) owes much to this insulation machinery. So far have we carried the fantasy of individual autonomy that we imagine each person to have his own unique species of germs, which must therefore not be mixed and confused with someone else's. We are even disturbed at the presence of the germs themselves: despite the fact that many millions of them inhabit every healthy human body from the cradle to the grave we regard them as trespassers. We feel that nature has no business claiming a connection with us, and perhaps one day we will prove ourselves correct.

see the role of the value they embrace so fervently in generating the phenomena they so detest.

The most sophisticated apologist for individualism is David Riesman, who recognizes at least that uniformity and community are not the same thing, and does not shrink from the insoluble dilemmas that these issues create. Perhaps the definitive and revealing statement of what individualism is all about is his: "I am insisting that no ideology, however noble, can justify the sacrifice of an individual to the needs of the group."[8]

Whenever I hear such sentiments I recall Jay Haley's discussion of the kind of communication that characterizes the families of schizophrenics. He points out that people who communicate with one another necessarily govern each other's behavior—set rules for each other. But an individual may attempt to avoid this human fate—to become independent, uninvolved: ". . . he may choose the schizophrenic way and indicate that nothing he does is done in relationship to other people." The family of the schizophrenic establishes a system of rules like all families, but also has "a prohibition on any acknowledgement that a family member is setting rules. Each refuses to concede that he is circumscribing the behavior of others, and each refuses to concede that any other family member is governing him." The attempt, of course, fails. "The more a person tries to avoid being governed or governing others, the more helpless he becomes and so governs others by forcing them to take care of him."[9] In our society as a whole this caretaking role is assigned to technology, like so much else.

Riesman overlooks the fact that the individual is sacrificed either way. If he is never sacrificed to the group the group will collapse and the individual with it. Part of the individual is, after all, committed to the group. Part of him wants what "the group" wants, part does not. No matter what is done some aspect of the individual—id, ego, or whatever—will be sacrificed.

An individual, like a group, is a motley collection of ambivalent feelings, contradictory needs and values, and antithetical ideas. He is not, and cannot be, a monolithic totality, and the modern effort to bring this myth to life is not only delusional and ridiculous, but also acutely destructive, both to the individual and to his society.

Recognition of this internal complexity would go a long way toward resolving the dilemma Riesman implicitly poses. For the reason a group needs the kind of creative deviant Riesman values is the same reason it needs to sacrifice him: the failure of the group members to recognize the complexity and diversity and ambivalence within themselves. Since they have oversimplified and rejected parts of themselves, they not only lack

[8] David Riesman, *Individualism Reconsidered* (Garden City, New York: Doubleday Anchor, 1954), p. 27. This is a principle for which nature has shown a fine disregard—evolution proceeds on a diametrically opposite principle.

[9] Jay Haley, "The Family of the Schizophrenic: A Model System," in G. Handel (ed.), *The Psychosocial Interior of the Family* (Chicago: Aldine, 1967), pp. 271–272.

certain resources but also are unable to tolerate their naked exposure by others. The deviant is a compensatory mechanism to mitigate this condition. He comes along and tries to provide what is "lacking" in the group (that is, what is present but denied, suppressed). His role is like that of the mutant —most are sacrificed but a few survive to save the group from itself in times of change. Individualism is a kind of desperate plea to save all mutants, on the grounds that we do not know what we are or what we need. As such it is horribly expensive—a little like setting a million chimps to banging on a typewriter on the grounds that eventually one will produce a masterpiece.

But if we abandon the monolithic pretense and recognize that any group sentiment, and its opposite, represents a part of everyone but only a part, then the prophet is unnecessary since he exists in all of us. And should he appear it will be unnecessary to sacrifice him since we have already admitted that what he is saying is true. And in the meantime we would be able to exercise our humanity, governing each other and being governed, instead of encasing ourselves in the leaden armor of our technological schizophrenia.

TOM WOLFE

(1931-　　)

Tom Wolfe is a contemporary popular journalist with a passion for what is new and different. He wants to see and describe the countless mini-hierarchies now replacing traditional society and its institutions. He takes the dispersion of traditional society to its logical extreme: from a single pyramid topped by a single set of social elite, through a multiplicity of pyramids among which one may choose, finally to the single individual, his own lord and master in a technological paradise. The modern hero, the finest example of this final extreme, is Hugh Hefner, whom Wolfe portrays with less irony than one might first expect. Opposed to Slater's dour portrait of the plight of the individual, Wolfe's picture of the individualistic society leads him to exclaim that we are in the midst of a happiness explosion. He suggests that, instead of bemoaning the demise of utopian communities, we contemplate the politics of pleasure and the pharmacology of overjoy.

The contrast between Slater and Wolfe is stark. We may be inclined to resolve their contradictory views in the noncontroversial thought that the contemporary social situation is neither as bad as Slater sees it nor as good as Wolfe sees it. But that won't do, for within the different pictures they paint of the way things **are,** you will find clear suggestions of the way things **ought** to be, and their suggestions about the way things ought to be differ as widely as their estimates about the way they are. Slater thinks we ought to have more community. Wolfe thinks we ought to forget our utopian tales of community and concentrate on our real and new-found capacities to function as independent entities. Slater and Wolfe are finally divided by their philosophies of what it is to be a human being. Does one find one's most complete fulfillment in oneself alone or in community with others? This is a central question running throughout many of the following essays. I show my hand as an undisguised champion of community, but there must be a place for the likes of Tom Wolfe within the community. I resist dourness too. Joy sounds good, but what about "overjoy"? And do we need individualism to get it?

LONELINESS AFFIRMED

It was a strange time for me. Many rogue volts of euphoria. I went from one side of this country to the other and then from one side of England to the other. The people I met—the things they did—I was entranced. I met Carol Doda. She blew up her breasts with emulsified silicone, the main ingredient in Silly Putty, and became the greatest resource of the San Francisco tourist industry. I met a group of surfers, the Pump House Gang. They attended the Watts riot as if it were the Rose Bowl game in Pasadena. They came to watch "the drunk niggers" and were reprimanded by the same for their rowdiness. In London I met a competitive 17-year-old named Nicki who got one-up on her schoolgirl chums by taking a Kurdish clubfoot lover. I met a £9-a-week office boy named Larry Lynch. He spent his lunch hour every day with hundreds of other child laborers in the crazed pitchblack innards of a noonday nightclub called Tiles. All of them *in ecstasis* from the frug, the rock 'n' roll, and God knows what else, for an hour—then back to work. In Chicago I met Hugh Hefner. He revolved on his bed, offering scenic notes as his head floated by—

Now, about Hefner. I was heading for California from New York and I happened to stop off in Chicago. I was walking down North Michigan Avenue when I ran into a man from the Playboy organization, Lee Gottlieb. Something he said made me assume that Hefner was out of town.

"Out of town?" said Gottlieb. "Hef never leaves his house."

"Never?"

Never, said Gottlieb. At least not for months at a time, and even then only long enough to get in a limousine and go to the airport and fly to New York for a TV show or to some place or other for the opening of a new Playboy Club. This fascinated me, the idea that Hefner, the Main Playboy himself, was now a recluse. The next afternoon I went to the Playboy offices on East Ohio Street to see about getting in to see him. In the office they kept track of Hefner's physical posture in his Mansion, which was over on North State Parkway, as if by play-by-play Telex. He was flat out in bed asleep, they told me, and wouldn't be awake until around midnight. That night I was killing time in a dive in downtown Chicago when a courier materialized and told me Hefner was now on his feet and could see me.

Hefner's Playboy Mansion had a TV eye at the front portals and huge black guards or major-domos inside. *Nubian slaves,* I kept saying to myself. One of the blacks led me up a grand staircase covered in red wall-to-wall, to a massive carved-wood doorway bearing the inscription, *Si Non Oscillas, Noli Tintinnare,* "If you don't swing, don't ring." Inside were Hefner's private chambers. Hefner came charging out of a pair of glass doors within. He was wound up and ready to go. "Look at this!" he said. "Isn't this fantastic!" It was an issue of *Ramparts* magazine that had just come. It had a glossy foldout, like the one in *Playboy.* Only this one had a picture of Hefner. In the picture he was wearing a suit and smoking a pipe. "Isn't this fantastic!" Hefner kept saying. Right now he was wearing silk pajamas, a bathrobe, and a pair of slippers with what looked like embroidered wolf heads on them. This was not, however, because he had just gotten up. It was his standard wear for the day, this day, every day, the uniform of the contemporary recluse.

There were several people in attendance at the midnight hour. The *dame d'honneur* of the palace, who was named Michele; Gottlieb; a couple of other Playboy personnel; the blacks: they were all dressed, however. Hefner showed me through his chambers. The place was kept completely draped and shuttered. The only light, day or night, was electric. It would be impossible to keep track of the days in there. And presently Hefner jumped onto . . . the center of his world, the bed in his bedroom. Aimed at the bed was a TV camera he was very proud of. Later on *Playboy* ran a cartoon showing a nude man and woman in a huge bed with a TV set facing them, and the man is saying, "And now, darling, how about an instant replay." Hefner hit a dial and the bed started revolving . . .

All I could think of at that moment was Jay Gatsby in the Fitzgerald novel. Both were scramblers who came up from out of nowhere to make their fortunes and build their palaces and ended up in regal isolation. But there was a major difference between Hefner and Gatsby. Hefner no longer dreamed, if he ever did, of making the big social leap to East Egg. It was at least plausible for Gatsby to hope to make it into Society. But Hefner? He has made a fortune, created an empire, and the Playboy Beacon shines out over the city and the Great Lakes. But socially Hefner is still a man who runs a tit magazine and a string of clubs that recall the parlor floor—not the upper floors but the parlor floor—of a red-flock whorehouse. There is no Society in Chicago for Hugh Hefner.

So he has gone them one better. He has started his own league. He has created his own world, in his own palace. He has created his own status-phere. The outside world comes to him, including the talented and the cele-brated. Jules Feiffer stays awhile in his scarlet guest suite. Norman Mailer skinnydips in his Playboy swimming pool. He has his courtiers, his girls, and his Nubian slaves. Not even God's own diurnal light rhythm intrudes upon the order that Hefner has founded inside.

What a marvelous idea! After all, the community has never been one great happy family for all men. In fact, I would say the opposite has been true. Community status systems have been games with few winners and many who feel like losers. What an intriguing thought—for a man to take his new riches and free time and his machines and *split* from *communitas* and start his own league. He will still have status competition—but he in-vents the rules.

Why has no one ever done it before? Well, of course, people have. Robin Hood did it. Spades, homosexuals, artists, and street gangs have done it. All sorts of outlaws, and outcasts, by necessity or choice. The intriguing thing today, I was to find, is that so many Americans and Englishmen of middle and lower incomes are now doing the same thing. Not out of "rebel-lion" or "alienation"—they just want to be happy winners for a change.

What is a California electronics worker making $18,000 a year sup-posed to do with his new riches? Set about getting his son into Culver Mili-tary and himself and the wife into the Doral Beach Country Club? Socially, he is a glorified mechanic. Why not, à la Hefner, put it all into turning his home into a palace of technological glories—and extend that abroad in the land with a Buick Estate Wagon and a Pontiac GTO—and upon the seas with an Evinrude cruiser and even into the air with a Cessna 172? Why not surround the palace with my favorite piece of landscaping of the happy worker suburbs of the American West, the Home Moat. It is about three feet wide and a foot and a half deep. Instructions for placing rocks, flowers, and shrubs are available. The Home Moat is a psychological safeguard against the intrusion of the outside world. The Home Moat guards against the fear that *It* is going to creep up in the night and press its nose against your picture window.

Southern California, I found, is a veritable paradise of statuspheres. For example, the move to age segregation. There are old people's housing de-velopments, private developments, in which no one under 50 may buy a home. There are apartment developments for single persons 20 to 30 only. The Sunset Strip in Los Angeles has become the exclusive hangout of the 16 to 25 set. In 1966 they came close to street warfare to keep it that way, against the police who moved in to "clean up."

And . . . the Pump House Gang. Here was a group of boys and girls who had banded together in a way that superficially resembled a street gang's. They had very little of the street gang's motivation, however. They came from middle-class and upper-middle-class homes in perhaps the most high-class beach community in California, La Jolla. They had very little sense of resentment toward their parents or "society" and weren't rebels. Their only "alienation" was the usual hassle of the adolescent, the feeling that he is being prodded into adulthood on somebody else's terms. So they did the latest thing. They split off—*to the beach! into the garages!*—and started their own league, based on the esoterica of surfing. They didn't resent the older people around them; they came to pity the old bastards because they couldn't partake of this esoteric statusphere.

The day I met the Pump House Gang, a group of them had just been thrown out of "Tom Coman's garage," as it was known. The next summer they moved up from the garage life to a group of apartments near the beach, a complex they named "La Colonia Tijuana." By this time some were shifting from the surfing life to the advance guard of something else— the psychedelic *head* world of California. That is another story. But even the *hippies,* as the heads came to be known, did not develop *sui generis.* Their so-called "dropping out" was nothing more than a still further elaboration of the kind of worlds that the surfers and the car kids I met—"The Hair Boys"—had been creating the decade before.

The Pump House Gang lived as though age segregation were a permanent state, as if it were inconceivable that any of them would ever grow old, i.e., 25. I foresaw the day when the California coastline would be littered with the bodies of aged and abandoned *Surferkinder,* like so many beached whales.

In fact, however, many of these kids seem to be able to bring the mental atmosphere of the surfer life forward with them into adulthood—even into the adult world where you have to make a living. I remember going to the motorcycle races at Gardena, California, which is just south of Watts, with a surfer who is now about 30 and has developed a large water-sport equipment business. This was a month after the Watts riots. We were sitting in the stands at Gardena. The motorcycles were roaring around the half-mile track below and flashing under the lights. Just beyond the track from where we sat were Watts and Compton.

"Tom," he said to me, "you should have been here last month."

"Why?"

"The riots," he said. "You should have been here. We were all sitting here right where we are now and the bikes were going around down below here. And over here"—over to the left you could look over the edge of the stands and see the highway—"the National Guard units were pulling and jumping off the trucks and getting into formation and everything with the bayonets and all. It was terrific. And then, there"—and his gaze and his voice got a far-off quality, going beyond the track and toward Watts—"and there, there in the distance, was Los Angeles . . . *burning!*"

A few minutes later ten motorcycles came into the first turn, right in front of where we were sitting. Five went down in a pile-up. Bodies shot through the air every which way. I saw one, a rider in black and white racing leathers, get hit in midair by one motorcycle and run over by the one behind it. This was a kid named Clemmie Jackson. He was dead. Everybody could see that. His neck was broken like a stick. Two other riders were seriously injured. The p.a. announcer didn't mention those who were lying there, however. He only mentioned those who got up. "There's No. 353, Rog Rogarogarog, he's up and his bike looks O.K. . . ." As soon as the bodies were removed, the race resumed. Luckily they hadn't had to take both the ambulances. They have two ambulances at the track, and if both have to leave, the races have to stop until one returns. They were able to get the three worst bodies into one ambulance. The ambulance, a big white Cadillac, left very quietly. It didn't even flash a light. About three minutes later you could hear the siren start up, way down the highway. Off in the distance, as they say. It was a freaking ghastly sound, under the circumstances. Within seconds, however, the race was on again, with five bikes instead of ten, and all was forgotten. As usual, there were only a couple of paragraphs in the papers about the death.

I don't think that is a very morbid incident, taken in context. The half-mile racers are the wildest and most suicidal crowd in the motorcycle life, but all the motorcycle crowds get a lot of their juice out of the luxury of risking their necks. The motorcycle life has been perfect as a statusphere. It is dangerous and therefore daring. It is as esoteric as surfing. It can liberate you physically from the *communitas*.

When you mention the motorcycle life, people tend to think—again—of outlaws. Namely, the Hell's Angels. The Angels and other motorcycle outlaws, however, make up only a small part of the people who have started their own league with their bikes. I'll never forget the Harley-Davidson agency in Columbus, Ohio. A guy came in the back there dragging a big Harley. It was all bent and mashed, the spokes, the headers, the cylinder heads, the sprocket, the drive chain. Everybody said, You had a wreck! The guy said, Naw, it was my wife. Everybody said, Was she hurt bad! The guy said, Naw, she took a block of cement about this big and she— well, it seems she had smashed the hell out of it. He had first bought the Harley just for a little recreation away from the wife and kids. Then he had discovered hundreds of motorcyclists around Columbus—all drifting away from the wife and kids. Pretty soon he was meeting the boys every day after work at a place called Gully's and they would drink beer and ride up to Lake Erie before coming home, a mere 200-mile trip. By and by they had a whole new life for themselves—blissful liberation!—based on the motorcycle. Until his wife decided to sort that little situation out . . .

Columbus is the world capital of the motorcycle life. This statement, I find, comes as a surprise and an annoyance—the damnable Hell's Angels again—to a lot of people in Columbus, despite the fact that the American Motorcycle Association has its headquarters there. On the surface, Columbus could not be more conservative and traditional. A few big property-owning families seem to control everything. Well, they don't control the motorcycle life, which has proliferated in and around the town over the past ten years in full rich variety, from half-mile racing daredevils to Honda touring clubs. They also have a local version of the Hell's Angels, the Road Rogues. The vast majority of Columbus motorcyclists, however, are perfectly law-abiding citizens who happen to have found an infinitely richer existence than being a standard wage–mule for whoever does run Columbus.

The two great motorcyclists of Columbus are Dick Klamforth, a former half-mile racing champion and now owner of the Honda agency there, the biggest in the country, and Tom Reiser. Reiser is truly one of the greats. He built "Tom's Bomb." He achieved an ultimate. He flew through the air of the American Midwest, astride a 300-horsepower Chevrolet V-8 engine . . . riding bareback . . .

Now, this is not exactly what the great Utopian thinkers of the nineteenth century, the Saint-Simons, the Fouriers, and the Owens, had in mind when they envisioned a world of the future in which the ordinary working man would have the time and the money to extend his God-given potential to the fullest. The old Utopians believed in industrialism. In fact, it was Saint-Simon who coined the word. Yet the worker paradise industrialism would make possible was to take a somewhat more pastoral form. They saw it as a kind of Rousseauvian happy-primitive village with modern conveniences. In short, a community, with everyone, great and small, knit together forever after, grateful as spaniels. More recently, in the 1920's and 1930's, the vision was amended. It now put the happy workers into neat lead-white blocks of Bauhaus apartments and added Culture. Every night, in this vision, the family would gather around the hearth and listen to Dad read from John Strachey or Mayakovsky while WQXR droned in the background. The high point of the week would be Saturday afternoon, when Dad would put on his electric-blue suit—slightly gauche, you understand, but neat and clean and pressed, "touching," as it were—and the whole family would hold hands and walk up to the Culture Center to watch the Shock Workers of the Dance do a ballet called "Factory." Well, today, in the 1960's, the Culture Centers have sprouted up, sure enough. We have them in most of the metropolises of America. But where have all the happy workers gone? These temples to breeding and taste are usually constructed at great cost, in the name of "the people." But the people, the happy people, have left them to the cultivated, educated classes, the "diploma elite," who created them.

And even the cultivated classes—the term "upper classes" no longer works—are in a state of rather amusing confusion on the subject. When great fame—the certification of status—is available without great property, it is very bad news for the old idea of a class structure. In New York, for example, it is done for, but no one has bothered to announce its death. As a result, New York "Society" is now made up of a number of statuspheres—all busily raiding the old class order for trappings to make their fame look genuine. Business and other corporate statuspheres have been so busy cannibalizing the old aristocratic modes, I have had to write an entire new gull's handbook on the subject ("Tom Wolfe's New Book of Etiquette"). The great hotel corporations now advertise Luxury (equals "class") to the same crowd who used to go to those durable second-raters, the commercial or businessman's hotel. It is a pretty amusing invention, this second-class *class,* unless you happen to stay at The Automated Hotel without knowing the name of the game. Meanwhile, individual climbers are busy moving into separate little preserves that once made up the happy monolith of "the upper class"—such as charities and *Yes!* Culture—and I offer the golden example of Bob and Spike Scull for those who want to make it *Now,* without having to wait three generations, as old-fashioned sorts, such as the Kennedy family, had to do. Of course, with so many statuspheres now in operation, and so many short cuts available, there is a chronic chaos in Society. People are now reaching the top without quite knowing what on earth they have reached the top of. They don't know whether they have reached *The* Top or whether they have just had a wonderful fast ride up the service elevator. But as Bob Scull himself says: "Enjoy!"

What struck me throughout America and England was that so many people have found such novel ways of doing just that, *enjoying,* extending their egos way out on the best terms available, namely, their own. It is curious how many serious thinkers—and politicians—resist this rather obvious fact. Sheer ego extension—especially if attempted by all those rancid proles and suburban petty burghers—is a perplexing prospect. Even scary, one might say. Intellectuals and politicians currently exhibit a vast gummy nostalgia for the old restraints, the old limits, of the ancient ego-crusher: *Calamity.* Historically calamity has been the one serious concern of serious people. War, Pestilence—Apocalypse! I was impressed by the profound relief with which intellectuals and politicians discovered poverty in America in 1963, courtesy of Michael Harrington's book *The Other America.* And, as I say, it was *discovered.* Eureka! We have found it again! We thought we had lost it! That was the spirit of the enterprise. When the race riots erupted—and when the war in Vietnam grew into a good-sized hell—intellectuals welcomed all that with a ghastly embrace, too. War! Poverty! Insurrection! Alienation! O Four Horsemen, you have not deserted us entirely. The game can go on.

One night, in the very middle of the period when I was writing these stories, I put on *my* electric-blue suit—it is truly electric blue—and took part in a symposium at Princeton with Günter Grass, Allen Ginsberg, and Gregory Markopoulos, who is an "underground" filmmaker, before 1,200 students. The subject was "The Style of the Sixties." Paul Krassner was the moderator, and Krassner has a sense of humor, but the Horsemen charged on. Very soon the entire discussion was centered on police repression, Gestapo tactics, the knock on the door, the Triumph of the Knout. I couldn't believe what was happening, but there it was.

"What are you talking about?" I said. "We're in the middle of a . . . Happiness Explosion!" But I didn't know where to begin. I might as well have said let's talk about the Fisher King. Happiness, said Saint-Just a century ago, is a new concept in Europe. Apparently it was new here, unheard-of almost. Ah, *philosophes!*—if we want to be *serious,* let us discuss the real apocalyptic future and things truly scary: ego extension, the politics of pleasure, the self-realization racket, the pharmacology of Overjoy . . .

But why discuss it now. I, for one, will be content merely to watch the faces of our leaders, political and intellectual, the day they wake up and look over their shoulders and catch the first glimpse of their erstwhile followers—streaking—*happy workers!*—in precisely the opposite direction, through God's own American ozone—*apocalyptic riders!*—astride their own custom versions—*enjoy!*—of the 300-horsepower Chevrolet V-8 engines of this world . . . riding bareback . . .

ERICH FROMM

(1900-   )

Erich Fromm is a true man of our century. Educated in Germany, he was trained in psychoanalysis at a time when a number of scholars, including Herbert Marcuse, were intrigued by the possibility of a synthesis between the political thought of Marx and the new school of Freudian psychoanalysis. Both traditions seemed to offer powerful analyses of the fundamental workings of self and society.

When the Nazis came to power, Fromm came to the United States. His contributions to the American intellectual scene include many of his own books and one of the first translated editions of Marx's **1844 Manuscripts,** reprinted in part later in this volume. Fromm's broad background has equipped him to take the kind of historical view we are now pursuing.

In reading the following essay try to see how Fromm agrees and disagrees with Slater. While Fromm would undoubtedly disagree with most of the norms implicit and explicit in Wolfe's essay, would he agree wholeheartedly with Slater? In his defense of man against a dehumanizing technology, Fromm seems most concerned about technology's capacity for disrespecting the individual. He places a high premium on privacy and the rights of the individual.

Is it possible that Fromm shares a disease that renders him unable to cure society's sickness, assuming, that is, that Slater is right about the price of individualism? Or is Fromm's concern for the individual of a different sort than Slater's? Has Slater lost sight of the importance of the individual as a result of **his** conditioning in a technological society?

I ask these questions and include these essays because it is important to see that on such complex issues we cannot divide everyone into neatly opposed partisan camps. Even when two men agree on many important issues, subtle differences may lead to substantive differences on other important issues.

The Present Technological Society

Its Principles

The technetronic society may be the system of the future, but it is not yet here; it can develop from what is already here, and it probably will, unless a sufficient number of people see the danger and redirect our course. In order to do so, it is necessary to understand in greater detail the operation of the present technological system and the effect it has on man.

What are the guiding principles of this system as it is today?

It is programed by two principles that direct the efforts and thoughts of everyone working in it: The first principle is the maxim that something *ought* to be done because it is technically *possible* to do it. If it is possible to build nuclear weapons, they must be built even if they might destroy us all. If it is possible to travel to the moon or to the planets, it must be done, even if at the expense of many unfulfilled needs here on earth. This principle means the negation of all values which the humanist tradition has developed. This tradition said that something should be done because it is needed for man, for his growth, joy, and reason, because it is beautiful, good, or true. Once the principle is accepted that something ought to be done because it is technically possible to do it, all other values are dethroned and technological development becomes the foundation of ethics.[1]

THE PRESENT TECHNOLOGICAL SOCIETY   "The Present Technological Society" (pp. 32–46) in *The Revolution of Hope* by Erich Fromm. Copyright © 1968 by Erich Fromm. By permission of Harper & Row, Publishers, Inc.

[1] While revising this manuscript I read a paper by Hasan Ozbekhan, "The Triumph of Technology: 'Can' Implies 'Ought.' " This paper, adapted from an invited presentation at MIT and published in mimeographed form by System Development Corporation, Santa Monica, California, was sent to me by the courtesy of Mr.

The second principle is that of *maximal efficiency and output*. The requirement of maximal efficiency leads as a consequence to the requirement of minimal individuality. The social machine works more efficiently, so it is believed, if individuals are cut down to purely quantifiable units whose personalities can be expressed on punched cards. These units can be administered more easily by bureaucratic rules because they do not make trouble or create friction. In order to reach this result, men must be de-individualized and taught to find their identity in the corporation rather than in themselves.

The question of economic efficiency requires careful thought. The issue of being economically efficient, that is to say, using the smallest possible amount of resources to obtain maximal effect, should be placed in a historical and evolutionary context. The question is obviously more important in a society where real material scarcity is the prime fact of life, and its importance diminishes as the productive powers of a society advance.

A second line of investigation should be a full consideration of the fact that efficiency is only a known element in already existing activities. Since we do not know much about the efficiency or inefficiency of untried approaches, one must be careful in pleading for things as they are on the grounds of efficiency. Furthermore, one must be very careful to think through and specify the area and time period being examined. What may appear efficient by a narrow definition can be highly inefficient if the time and scope of the discussion are broadened. In economics there is increasing awareness of what are called "neighborhood effects"; that is, effects that go beyond the immediate activity and are often neglected in considering benefits and costs. One example would be evaluating the efficiency of a particular industrial project only in terms of the immediate effects on this enterprise—forgetting, for instance, that waste materials deposited in nearby streams and the air represent a costly and a serious inefficiency with regard to the community. We need to clearly develop standards of efficiency that take account of time and society's interest as a whole. Eventually, the human element needs to be taken into account as a basic factor in the system whose efficiency we try to examine.

Dehumanization in the name of efficiency is an all-too-common occurrence; e.g., giant telephone systems employing Brave New World techniques of recording operators' contacts with customers and asking customers to evaluate workers' performance and attitudes, etc.—all aimed at instilling "proper" employee attitude, standardizing service, and increas-

---

George Weinwurm. As the title indicates, Ozbekhan expresses the same concept as the one I present in the text. His is a brilliant presentation of the problem from the standpoint of an outstanding specialist in the field of management science, and I find it a very encouraging fact that the same idea appears in the work of authors in fields as different as his and mine. I quote a sentence that shows the identity of his concept and the one presented in the text: "Thus, feasibility, which is a strategic concept, becomes elevated into a normative concept, with the result that whatever technological reality indicates we *can* do is taken as implying that we *must* do it" (p. 7).

ing efficiency. From the narrow perspective of immediate company purposes, this may yield docile, manageable workers, and thus enhance company efficiency. In terms of the employees, as human beings, the effect is to engender feelings of inadequacy, anxiety, and frustration, which may lead to either indifference or hostility. In broader terms, even efficiency may not be served, since the company and society at large doubtless pay a heavy price for these practices.

Another general practice in organizing work is to constantly remove elements of creativity (involving an element of risk or uncertainty) and group work by dividing and subdividing tasks to the point where no judgment or interpersonal contact remains or is required. Workers and technicians are by no means insensitive to this process. Their frustration is often perceptive and articulate, and comments such as "We are human" and "The work is not fit for human beings" are not uncommon. Again, efficiency in a narrow sense can be demoralizing and costly in individual and social terms.

If we are only concerned with input-output figures, a system may give the impression of efficiency. If we take into account what the given methods do to the human beings in the system, we may discover that they are bored, anxious, depressed, tense, etc. The result would be a twofold one: (1) Their imagination would be hobbled by their psychic pathology, they would be uncreative, their thinking would be routinized and bureaucratic, and hence they would not come up with new ideas and solutions which would contribute to a more productive development of the system; altogether, their energy would be considerably lowered. (2) They would suffer from many physical ills, which are the result of stress and tension; this loss in health is also a loss for the system. Furthermore, if one examines what this tension and anxiety do to them in their relationship to their wives and children, and in their functioning as responsible citizens, it may turn out that for the system as a whole the seemingly efficient method is most inefficient, not only in human terms but also as measured by merely economic criteria.

To sum up: efficiency is desirable in any kind of purposeful activity. But it should be examined in terms of the larger systems, of which the system under study is only a part; it should take account of the human factor within the system. Eventually efficiency as such should not be a *dominant* norm in any kind of enterprise.

The other aspect of the same principle, that of *maximum output,* formulated very simply, maintains that the more we produce of whatever we produce, the better. The success of the economy of the country is measured by its rise of total production. So is the success of a company. Ford may lose several hundred million dollars by the failure of a costly new model, like the Edsel, but this is only a minor mishap as long as the production curve rises. The growth of the economy is visualized in terms of ever-increasing production, and there is no vision of a limit yet where production may be stabilized. The comparison between countries rests upon the same principle. The Soviet Union hopes to surpass the United States by accomplishing a more rapid rise in economic growth.

Not only industrial production is ruled by the principle of continuous and limitless acceleration. The educational system has the same criterion: the more college graduates, the better. The same in sports: every new record is looked upon as progress. Even the attitude toward the weather seems to be determined by the same principle. It is emphasized that this is "the hottest day in the decade," or the coldest, as the case may be, and I suppose some people are comforted for the inconvenience by the proud feeling that they are witnesses to the record temperature. One could go on endlessly giving examples of the concept that constant increase of quantity constitutes the goal of our life; in fact, that it is what is meant by "progress."

Few people raise the question of *quality,* or what all this increase in quantity is good for. This omission is evident in a society which is not centered around man any more, in which one aspect, that of quantity, has choked all others. It is easy to see that the predominance of this principle of "the more the better" leads to an imbalance in the whole system. If all efforts are bent on doing *more,* the quality of living loses all importance, and activities that once were means become ends.[2]

If the overriding economic principle is that we produce more and more, the consumer must be prepared to want—that is, to consume—more and more. Industry does not rely on the consumer's spontaneous desires for more and more commodities. By building in obsolescence it often forces him to buy new things when the old ones could last much longer. By changes in styling of products, dresses, durable goods, and even food, it forces him psychologically to buy more than he might need or want. But

---

[2] I find in C. West Churchman's *Challenge to Reason* (New York: McGraw-Hill, 1968) an excellent formulation of the problem:

"If we explore this idea of a larger and larger model of systems, we may be able to see in what sense completeness represents a challenge to reason. One model that seems to be a good candidate for completeness is called an *allocation* model; it views the world as a system of activities that use resources to 'output' usable products.

The process of reasoning in this model is very simple. One searches for a central quantitative measure of system performance, which has the characteristic: the more of this quantity the better. For example, the more profit a firm makes, the better. The more qualified students a university graduates, the better. The more food we produce, the better. It will turn out that the particular choice of the measure of system performance is not critical, so long as it is a measure of general concern.

We take this desirable measure of performance and relate it to the feasible activities of the system. The activities may be the operations of various manufacturing plants, of schools and universities, of farms, and so on. Each significant activity contributes to the desirable quantity in some recognizable way. The contribution, in fact, can often be expressed in a mathematical function that maps the amount of activity onto the amount of the desirable quantity. The more sales of a certain product, the higher the profit of a firm. The more courses we teach, the more graduates we have. The more fertilizer we use, the more food [pp. 156–57]."

industry, in its need for increased production, does not rely on the consumer's needs and wants but to a considerable extent on advertising, which is the most important offensive against the consumer's right to know what he wants. The spending of 16.5 billion dollars on direct advertising in 1966 (in newspapers, magazines, radio, TV) may sound like an irrational and wasteful use of human talents, of paper and print. But it is not irrational in a system that believes that increasing production and hence consumption is a vital feature of our economic system, without which it would collapse. If we add to the cost of advertising the considerable cost for restyling of durable goods, especially cars, and of packaging, which partly is another form of whetting the consumer's appetite, it is clear that industry is willing to pay a high price for the guarantee of the upward production and sales curve.

The anxiety of industry about what might happen to our economy if our style of life changed is expressed in this brief quote by a leading investment banker:

> Clothing would be purchased for its utility; food would be bought on the basis of economy and nutritional value; automobiles would be stripped to essentials and held by the same owners for the full 10 or 15 years of their useful lives; homes would be built and maintained for their characteristics of shelter, without regard to style or neighborhood. And what would happen to a market dependent upon new models, new styles, new ideas?[3]

Its Effect on Man

What is the effect of this type of organization on man? It reduces man to an appendage of the machine, ruled by its very rhythm and demands. It transforms him into *Homo consumens,* the total consumer, whose only aim is to *have* more and to *use* more. This society produces many useless things, and to the same degree many useless people. Man, as a cog in the production machine, becomes a thing, and ceases to be human. He spends his time doing things in which he is not interested, with people in whom he is not interested, producing things in which he is not interested; and when he is not producing, he is consuming. He is the eternal suckling with the open mouth, "taking in," without effort and without inner activeness, whatever the boredom-preventing (and boredom-producing) industry forces on him—cigarettes, liquor, movies, television, sports, lectures—limited only by what he can afford. But the boredom-preventing industry, that is to say, the gadget-selling industry, the automobile industry, the movie industry, the television industry, and so on, can only succeed in preventing the boredom from becoming conscious.

[3] Paul Mazur, *The Standards We Raise,* New York, 1953, p. 32.

In fact, they increase the boredom, as a salty drink taken to quench the thirst increases it. However unconscious, boredom remains boredom nevertheless.

The passiveness of man in industrial society today is one of his most characteristic and pathological features. He takes in, he wants to be fed, but he does not move, initiate, he does not digest his food, as it were. He does not reacquire in a productive fashion what he inherited, but he amasses it or consumes it. He suffers from a severe systemic deficiency, not too dissimilar to that which one finds in more extreme forms in depressed people.

Man's passiveness is only one symptom among a total syndrome, which one may call the "syndrome of alienation." Being passive, he does not relate himself to the world actively and is forced to submit to his idols and their demands. Hence, he feels powerless, lonely, and anxious. He has little sense of integrity or self-identity. Conformity seems to be the only way to avoid intolerable anxiety—and even conformity does not always alleviate his anxiety.

No American writer has perceived this dynamism more clearly than Thorstein Veblen. He wrote:

> In all the received formulations of economic theory, whether at the hands of the English economists or those of the continent, the human material with which the inquiry is concerned is conceived in hedonistic terms; that is to say, in terms of a passive and substantially inert and immutably given human nature. . . . The hedonistic conception of man is that of a lightning calculator of pleasures and pains, who oscillates like a homogeneous globule of desire of happiness under the impulse of stimuli that shift him about the area, but leave him intact. He has neither antecedent nor consequent. He is an isolated, definitive human datum, in stable equilibrium except for the buffets of the impinging forces that displace him in one direction or another. Self-imposed in elemental space, he spins symmetrically about his own spiritual axis until the parallelogram of forces bears down upon him, whereupon he follows the line of the resultant. When the force of the impact is spent, he comes to rest, a self contained globule of desire as before. Spiritually, the hedonistic man is not a prime mover. *He is not the seat of a process of living, except in the sense that he is subject to a series of permutations enforced upon him by circumstances external and alien to him.*[4]

Aside from the pathological traits that are rooted in passiveness, there are others which are important for the understanding of today's pathology of normalcy. I am referring to the growing split of cerebral-intellectual function from affective-emotional experience; the split between thought from feeling, mind from the heart, truth from passion.

[4] "Why Is Economics Not an Evolutionary Science?" in *The Place of Science in Modern City Civilization and Other Essays* (New York: B. W. Huebsch, 1919), p. 73. (Emphasis added.)

Logical thought is not rational if it is merely logical[5] and not guided by the concern for life, and by the inquiry into the total process of living in all its concrctcness and with all its contradictions. On the other hand, not only thinking but also emotions can be rational. *"Le coeur a ses raisons que la raison ne connaît point,"* as Pascal put it. (The heart has its reasons which reason knows nothing of.) Rationality in emotional life means that the emotions affirm and help the person's psychic structure to maintain a harmonious balance and at the same time to assist its growth. Thus, for instance, irrational love is love which enhances the person's dependency, hence anxiety and hostility. Rational love is a love which rclatcs a person intimately to another, at the same time preserving his independence and integrity.

Reason flows from the blending of rational thought and feeling. If the two functions are torn apart, thinking deteriorates into schizoid intellectual activity, and feeling deteriorates into neurotic life-damaging passions.

The split between thought and affect leads to a sickness, to a low-grade chronic schizophrenia, from which the new man of the technetronic age begins to suffer. In the social sciences it has become fashionable to think about human problems with no reference to the feelings related to these problems. It is assumed that scientific objectivity demands that thoughts and theories concerning man be emptied of all emotional concern with man.

An example of this emotion-free thinking is Herman Kahn's book on thermonuclear warfare. The question is discussed: how many millions of dead Americans are "acceptable" if we use as a criterion the ability to rebuild the economic machine after nuclear war in a reasonably short time so that it is as good as or better than before. Figures for GNP and population increase or decrease are the basic categories in this kind of thinking, while the question of the human results of nuclear war in terms of suffering, pain, brutalization, etc., is left aside.

Kahn's *The Year 2000* is another example of the writing which we may expect in the completely alienated megamachine society. Kahn's concern is that of the figures for production, population increase, and various scenarios for war or peace, as the case may be. He impresses many readers because they mistakc thc thousands of little data which he combines in ever-changing kaleidoscopic pictures for erudition or profundity. They do not notice the basic superficiality in his reasoning and the lack of the human dimension in his description of the future.

When I speak here of low-grade chronic schizophrenia, a brief explanation seems to be needed. Schizophrenia, like any other psychotic state, must be defined not only in psychiatric terms but also in social terms. Schizophrenic experience *beyond* a certain threshold would be considered a sickness in any society, since those suffering from it would be unable to func-

---

[5] Paranoid thinking is characterized by the fact that it can be completely logical, yet lack any guidance by concern or concrete inquiry into reality; in other words, logic does not exclude madness.

tion under any social circumstances (unless the schizophrenic is elevated into the status of a god, shaman, saint, priest, etc.). But there are low-grade chronic forms of psychoses which can be shared by millions of people and which—precisely because they do not go beyond a certain threshold—do not prevent these people from functioning socially. As long as they share their sickness with millions of others, they have the satisfactory feeling of not being alone; in other words, they avoid that sense of complete isolation which is so characteristic of full-fledged psychosis. On the contrary, they look at themselves as normal and at those who have not lost the link between heart and mind as being "crazy." In all low-grade forms of psychoses, the definition of sickness depends on the question as to whether the pathology is shared or not. Just as there is low-grade chronic schizophrenia, so there exist also low-grade chronic paranoia and depression. And there is plenty of evidence that among certain strata of the population, particularly on occasions where a war threatens, the paranoid elements increase but are not felt as pathological as long as they are common.[6]

The tendency to install technical progress as the highest value is linked up not only with our overemphasis on intellect but, most importantly, with a deep emotional attraction to the mechanical, to all that is not alive, to all that is man-made. This attraction to the non-alive, which is in its more extreme form an attraction to death and decay (necrophilia), leads even in its less drastic form to indifference toward life instead of "reverence for life." Those who are attracted to the non-alive are the people who prefer "law and order" to living structure, bureaucratic to spontaneous methods, gadgets to living beings, repetition to originality, neatness to exuberance, hoarding to spending. They want to control life because they are afraid of its uncontrollable spontaneity; they would rather kill it than to expose themselves to it and merge with the world around them. They often gamble with death because they are not rooted in life; their courage is the courage to die and the symbol of their ultimate courage is the Russian roulette.[7] The rate of our automobile accidents and the preparation for thermonuclear war are a testimony to this readiness to gamble with death. And who

[6] The difference between that which is considered to be sickness and that which is considered to be normal becomes apparent in the following example. If a man declared that in order to free our cities from air pollution, factories, automobiles, airplanes, etc., would have to be destroyed, nobody would doubt that he was insane. But if there is a consensus that in order to protect our life, our freedom, our culture, or that of other nations which we feel obliged to protect, thermonuclear war might be required as a last resort, such opinion appears to be perfectly sane. The difference is not at all in the kind of thinking employed but merely in that the first idea is not shared and hence appears abnormal while the second is shared by millions of people and by powerful governments and hence appears to be normal.

[7] Michael Maccoby has demonstrated the incidence of the life-loving versus the death-loving syndrome in various populations by the application of an "interpretative" questionnaire. Cf. his "Polling Emotional Attitudes in Relation to Political Choices" (to be published).

would not eventually prefer this exciting gamble to the boring unaliveness of the organization man?

One symptom of the attraction of the merely mechanical is the growing popularity, among some scientists and the public, of the idea that it will be possible to construct computers which are no' different from man in thinking, feeling, or any other aspect of functioning.[8] The main problem, it seems to me, is not whether such a computer-man can be constructed; it is rather why the idea is becoming so popular in a historical period when nothing seems to be more important than to transform the existing man into a more rational, harmonious, and peace-loving being. One cannot help being suspicious that often the attraction of the computer-man idea is the expression of a flight from life and from humane experience into the mechanical and purely cerebral.

The possibility that we can build robots who are like men belongs, if anywhere, to the future. But the present already shows us men who act like robots. When the majority of men are like robots, then indeed there will be no problem in building robots who are like men. The idea of the manlike computer is a good example of the alternative between the human and the inhuman use of machines. The computer can serve the enhancement of life in many respects. But the idea that it replaces man and life is the manifestation of the pathology of today.

The fascination with the merely mechanical is supplemented by an increasing popularity of conceptions that stress the animal nature of man and the instinctive roots of his emotions or actions. Freud's was such an instinctive psychology; but the importance of his concept of libido is secondary in comparison with his fundamental discovery of the unconscious process in waking life or in sleep. The most popular recent authors who stress instinctual animal heredity, like Konrad Lorenz (*On Aggression*) or Desmond Morris (*The Naked Ape*), have not offered any new or valuable insights into the specific human problem as Freud has done; they satisfy the wish of many to look at themselves as determined by instincts and thus to camouflage their true and bothersome human problems.[9] The dream of many people seems to be to combine the emotions of a primate with a computerlike brain. If this dream could be fulfilled, the problem of human freedom and of responsibility would seem to disappear. Man's feelings would be determined by his instincts, his reason by the computer; man would not have to give an answer to the questions his existence asks him.

[8] Dean E. Wooldridge, for instance, in *Mechanical Man* (New York: McGraw-Hill, 1968), writes that it will be possible to manufacture computers synthetically which are "completely undistinguishable from human beings produced in the usual manner" [!] (p. 172). Marvin L. Minsky, a great authority on computers, writes in his book *Computation* (Englewood Cliffs, N.J.: Prentice-Hall, 1967): "There is no reason to suppose machines have any limitations not shared by man" (p. vii).

[9] This criticism of Lorenz refers only to that part of his work in which he deals by analogy with the psychological problems of man, not with his work in the field of animal behavior and instinct theory.

Whether one likes the dream or not, its realization is impossible; the naked ape with the computer brain would cease to be human, or rather "he" would not *be*.[10]

Among the technological society's pathogenic effects upon man, two more must be mentioned: the disappearance of *privacy* and of *personal human contact*.

"Privacy" is a complex concept. It was and is a privilege of the middle and upper classes, since its very basis, private space, is costly. This privilege, however, can become a common good with other economic privileges. Aside from this economic factor, it was also based on a hoarding tendency in which *my* private life was *mine* and nobody else's, as was *my* house and any other property. It was also a concomitant of *cant,* of the discrepancy between moral appearances and reality. Yet when all these qualifications are made, privacy still seems to be an important condition for a person's productive development. First of all, because privacy is necessary to collect oneself and to free oneself from the constant "noise" of people's chatter and intrusion, which interferes with one's own mental processes. If all private data are transformed into public data, experiences will tend to become more shallow and more alike. People will be afraid to feel the "wrong thing"; they will become more accessible to psychological manipulation which, through psychological testing, tries to establish norms for "desirable," "normal," "healthy" attitudes. Considering that these tests are applied in order to help the companies and government agencies to find the people with the "best" attitudes, the use of psychological tests, which is by now an almost general condition for getting a good job, constitutes a severe infringement on the citizen's freedom. Unfortunately, a large number of psychologists devote whatever knowledge of man they have to his manipulation in the interests of what the big organization considers efficiency. Thus, psychologists become an important part of the industrial and governmental system while claiming that their activities serve the optimal development of man. This claim is based on the rationalization that what is best for the corporation is best for man. It is important that the managers understand that much of what they get from psychological testing is based

---

[10] In revising this manuscript I became aware that Lewis Mumford had expressed the same idea in 1954 in *In the Name of Sanity* (New York: Harcourt, Brace & Co.):

"Modern man, therefore, now approaches the last act of his tragedy, and I could not, even if I would, conceal its finality or its horror. We have lived to witness the joining, in intimate partnership, of the automaton and the id, the id rising from the lower depths of the unconscious, and the automaton, the machine-like thinker and the manlike machine, wholly detached from other life-maintaining functions and human reactions, descending from the heights of conscious thought. The first force has proved more brutal, when released from the whole personality, than the most savage of beasts; the other force, so impervious to human emotions, human anxieties, human purposes, so committed to answering only the limited range of questions for which its apparatus was originally loaded, that it lacks the saving intelligence to turn off its own compulsive mechanism, even though it is pushing science as well as civilization to its own doom [p. 198]."

on the very limited picture of man which, in fact, management requirements have transmitted to the psychologists, who in turn give it back to
management, allegedly as a result of an independent study of man. It
hardly needs to be said that the intrusion of privacy may lead to a control
of the individual which is more total and could be more devastating than
what totalitarian states have demonstrated thus far. Orwell's 1984 will
need much assistance from testing, conditioning, and smoothing-out psychologists in order to come true. It is of vital importance to distinguish
between a psychology that understands and aims at the well-being of man
and a psychology that studies man as an object, with the aim of making
him more useful for the technological society.

PETER MARIN
(1936-   )

In the late 1960's Peter Marin
was the director of Pacific High School, an experimental school in
California. During that period California was a spawning ground
for cultural influences that have since been felt across the nation.
Marin's sensitivity to what was happening around him at that time
and place gave him a uniquely contemporary grasp of a number of
issues that reappear later in this book. Even his style reflects a
contemporary esthetic that Brown and Leonard explore later. His
hope, "to articulate a way of seeing, of feeling, that will restore
to the young a sense of manhood and potency without at the
same time destroying the past," could serve as a motto for this
volume. Yet here, too, we find a radical concern for the individual
that may be in conflict with Slater's objections to individualism.
Certainly Marin emphasizes the importance of community differently from Fromm. Is Marin's concern perhaps for the socially situated self rather than for the "rugged individual" attacked by
Slater?

The Open Truth
and Fiery Vehemence
of Youth

It is midnight and I am sitting here with my notes, enough of them to make two books and a half and a volume of posthumous fragments, trying to make some smaller sense of them than the grand maniacal design I have in my mind. I don't know where to begin. Once, traveling in summer across the country with a friend from Hollywood and my young son in a battered green Porsche, I stopped for lunch somewhere in Kansas on a Sunday morning. As we walked into the restaurant, bearded, wearing dark glasses and strange hats, and followed by my long-haired boy, one Kansas matron bent toward another and whispered: "I bet those two men have kidnapped that little girl." I took a deep breath and started to speak, but I did not know where to begin or how to explain just how many ways she was mistaken. Now, trying to write clearly about education and adolescence, I feel the same way.

For that reason I have chosen an eccentric method of composition, one that may seem fragmentary, jumpy, and broken. This article will be more like a letter, and the letter itself is an accumulation of impressions and ideas, a sampling of thoughts at once disconnected but related. There is a method to it that may disappear in its mild madness, but I do not know at this juncture how else to proceed. Shuffling through my notes I feel like an archeologist with a mass of uncatalogued shards. There is a pattern to all this, a coherence of thought, but all I can do here is assemble the bits and pieces and lay them out for you and hope that you can sense how I get from one place to another.

An entire system is hiding behind this, just beginning to take form, and these notes are like a drawing, a preliminary sketch. I feel comfortable with that notion, more comfortable than with the idea of forcing them together, cutting and pasting, to make a more conventional essay. I can perceive in myself at this moment what I also see in the young: I am reluctant to deal in sequence with my ideas and experience, I am impatient with transition, the habitual ways of getting "from here to there." I think restlessly; my mind, like the minds of my students, works in flashes, in sudden perceptions and brief extended clusters of intuition and abstraction—and I have stuck stubbornly to that method of composition. There is still in me the ghost of an apocalyptic adolescent, and I am trying to move it a few steps toward the future.

THE OPEN TRUTH AND FIERY VEHEMENCE OF YOUTH From Peter Marin, "The Open Truth and Fiery Vehemence of Youth," First appeared in *The Center Magazine,* a publication of the Center for the Study of Democratic Institutions in Santa Barbara, California (January 1969). Copyright 1969 by Peter Marin. Reprinted by permission of International Famous Agency.

One theme, as you will see, runs through what I have written or thought: we must rethink our ideas of childhood and schooling. We must dismantle them and start again from scratch. Nothing clse will do. Our visions of adolescence and education confine us to habit, rule perception out. We make do at the moment with a set of ideas inherited from the nineteenth century, from an industrial, relatively puritanical, repressive, and "localized" culture; we try to gum them like labels to new kinds of experience. But that won't do. Everything has changed. The notions with which I began my job as a high-school director have been discarded one by one. They make no sense. What emerges through these children as the psyche of this culture is post-industrial, relatively unrepressed, less literate and local: a new combination of elements, almost a new strain. Adolescents are, each one of them, an arena in which the culture transforms itself or is torn between contrary impulses; they are the victims of a culture raging within itself like man and wife, a schizoid culture—and these children are the unfinished and grotesque products of that schism.

They are grotesque because we give them no help. They are forced to make among themselves adjustments to a tension that must be unbearable. They do the best they can, trying, in increasingly eccentric fashions, to make sense of things. But we adults seem to have withdrawn in defeat from that same struggle, to have given up. We are enamored, fascinated, and deluded by adolescence precisely because it is the last life left to us; only the young rebel with any real passion against media, machines, the press of circumstance itself. Their elders seem to have no options, no sense of alternative or growth. Adult existence is bled of life and we turn in that vacuum toward children with the mixed repulsion and desire of wanton Puritans toward life itself.

As for me, an adult, I think of myself as I write as an observer at a tribal war—an anthropologist, a combination of Gulliver and a correspondent sending home news by mule and boat. By the time you hear of it, things will have changed. And that isn't enough, not enough at all. Somebody must step past the children, must move into his own psyche or two steps past his own limits into the absolute landscape of fear and potential these children inhabit. That is where I am headed. So these ideas, in effect, are something like a last message tacked to a tree in a thicket or tucked under a stone. I mean: we cannot *follow* the children any longer, we have to step ahead of them. Somebody has to mark a trail.

Adolescence: a few preliminary fragments . . .

(FROM MY STUDENT, V): yr whole body moves in a trained way & you know that youve moved this way before & it contains all youve been taught its all rusty & slow something is pushing under that rusted mesh but STILL YOU CANNOT MOVE you are caught between 2 doors & the old one is much closer & you can grab it all the time but the other door it disappears that door you cant even scratch & kick (like the early settlers were stung by the new land) but this new land doesnt even touch you & you wonder if youre doing the right thing to get in

(FROM FRANZ KAFKA): He feels imprisoned on this earth, he feels constricted; the melancholy, the impotence, the sicknesses, the feverish fancies of the captive afflict him; no comfort can comfort him, since it is merely comfort, gentle headsplitting comfort glazing the brutal fact of imprisonment. But if he is asked what he wants he cannot reply. . . . He has no conception of freedom.

(FROM TAPES RECORDED IN PACIFIC PALISADES, 1966, SEVERAL BOYS AND GIRLS AGED 12–14):—Things are getting younger and younger. Girls twelve will do it now. One guy said I fuck a girl every Friday night. What sexual pleasure do you get out of this (he's very immature you know) and he would say, I don't know I'm just going to fuck.

or

—*How old are you?* —Twelve. —*Will you tell us your first experience with drugs, how you got into it?* —Well, the people I hung around with were big acidheads. So one day my friend asked me if I wanted to get stoned and I said yes. That was about five months ago and I've been getting on it ever since. Started taking LSD about one month ago. Took it eleven times in one month. I consider it a good thing. For getting high, smoking grass is better, or hashish—its about six times stronger than marijuana.

(FROM PAUL RADIN: *Primitive Man As Philosopher*): It is conceivably demanding too much of a man to whom the pleasures of life are largely bound up with the life of contemplation and to whom analysis and introspection are the self-understood prerequisites for a proper understanding of the world, that he appreciate . . . expressions which are largely non-intellectual—where life seems, predominatingly, a discharge of physical vitality, a simple and naive release of emotions or an enjoyment of sensations for their own sake. Yet . . . it is just such an absorption in a life of sensations that is the outward characteristic of primitive peoples.

Can you see where my thought leads? It is precisely at this point, adolescence, when the rush of energies, that sea-sex, gravitation, the thrust of the ego up through layers of childhood, makes itself felt, that the person is once more like an infant, is swept once more by energies that are tidal, unfamiliar, and unyielding. He is in a sense born again, a fresh identity beset inside and out by the rush of new experience. It is at this point, too—when we seem compelled by a persistent lunacy to isolate him—that what is growing within the adolescent demands expression, requires it, and must, in addition, be received by the world and given form—or it will wither or turn to rage. Adolescence is a second infancy. It is then that a man desires solitude and at the same time contact with the vivid world; must test within social reality the new power within himself; needs above all to discover himself for the first time as a bridge between inner and outer, a maker of value, a vehicle through which culture perceives and transforms itself. It is now, ideally, that he begins to understand the complex and delicate nature of the ego itself as a thin skin between living worlds, a synaptic jump, the self-conscious point at which nature and culture combine.

In this condition, with these needs, the adolescent is like a primitive man, an apocalyptic primitive; he exists for the moment in that stage of single vision in which myth is still the raw stuff of being, he knows at first hand through his own energies the possibilities of life—but he knows these in muddled, sporadic, contradictory ways. The rush of his pubescent and raw energy seems at odds with public behavior, the *order* of things, the tenor of life around him, especially in a culture just emerging—as is ours—from a tradition of evasion, repression, and fear.

The contradictions within the culture itself intensify his individual confusion. We are at the moment torn between future and past: in the midst of a process of transformation we barely understand. The development of adolescent energy and ego—difficult at any time—is complicated in our own by the increase in early sexuality, the complicated messages of the media, and the effects of strong and unfamiliar drugs. These three elements are, in themselves, the salient features of a culture that is growing more permissive, less repressive. They are profound, complex, and strong: heavy doses of experience demanding changes in attitude, changes in behavior. The direction and depth of feeling responds accordingly; the adolescent tries—even as a form of self-defense against the pressure of his own energies—to move more freely, to change his styles of life, to "grow." But it is then that he finds he is locked into culture, trapped in a web of ideas, law, and rituals that keep him a child, deprive him of a chance to test and assimilate his newer self. It is now that the culture turns suddenly repressive. His gestures are evaded or denied; at best he is "tolerated," but even then his gestures, lacking the social support of acknowledgment and reward, must seem to him lacking in authenticity—more like forms of neurosis or selfishness than the natural stages in growth.

He is thrust back upon himself. The insistent natural press within him toward becoming whole is met perpetually by unbudging resistance. Schools, rooted as they are in a Victorian century and seemingly suspicious of life itself, are his natural enemies. They don't help, as they might, to make that bridge between his private and the social worlds; they insist, instead, upon their separation. Indeed, family, community, and school all combine—especially in the suburbs—to isolate and "protect" him from the adventure, risk, and participation he needs; the same energies that relate him at this crucial point to nature result in a kind of exile from the social environment.

Thus the young, in that vivid confrontation with the thrust of nature unfolding in themselves, are denied adult assistance. I once wrote that education through its limits denied the gods, and that they would return in the young in one form or another to haunt us. That is happening now. You can sense it as the students gather, with their simplistic moral certainty, at the gates of the universities. It is almost as if the young were once more possessed by Bacchanalian gods, were once again inhabited by divinities whose honor we have neglected. Those marvelous and threatening energies! What disturbs me most about them is that we lack rituals for their use and balance, and the young—and perhaps we ourselves—now seem at their mercy. The young have moved, bag and baggage, into areas where adults cannot help them, and it is a scary landscape they face, it is crowded with strange forms and faces, and if they return from it raddled, without balance and pitched toward excess, who can pretend to be surprised—or blameless?

At times they seem almost shell-shocked, survivors of a holocaust in which the past has been destroyed and all the bridges to it bombed. I cannot describe with any certainty what occurs in their minds, but I do know that most adults must seem to the young like shrill critics speaking to them in an alien language about a Greek tragedy in which they may lose their lives. The words we use, our dress, our tones of voice, the styles of adult lives—all of these are so foreign to that dramatic crisis that as we approach them we seem to increase the distance we are trying to cross. Even our attention drives them further away, as if adolescents perceived that adults, coming closer, diminish in sense and size.

The inner events in an adolescent demand from what surrounds him life on a large scale, in a grand style. This is the impulse to apocalypse in the young, as if they were in exile from a nation that does not exist—and yet they can sense it, they know it is there—if only because their belief itself demands its presence. Their demand is absolute and unanswerable, but it exists and we seem unable at this point in time to suppress or evade it. For one reason or another, massive shifts in cultural balances, the lessening of repression for whatever reasons—economic, technological, evolutionary— those energies, like gods, have appeared among us again. But what can we make of them? The simple problem is that our institutions are geared to another century, another set of social necessities, and cannot change quickly enough to contain, receive, or direct them—and as we suppress or refuse them they turn to rage.

Primitive cultures dealt with this problem, I think, through their initiation rites, the rites of passage; they legitimized and accepted these energies and turned them toward collective aims; they were merged with the life of the tribe and in this way acknowledged, honored, and domesticated—but not destroyed. In most initiation rites the participant is led through the mythical or sacred world (or a symbolic version) and is then returned, transformed, to the secular one as a new person, with a new role. He is introduced through the rites to a dramatic reality coexistent with the visible or social one and at its root; he is put in direct touch with sources of energy, the divinities of the tribe. In many cultures the symbolic figures in the rites are unmasked at the end, as if to reveal to the initiate the interpenetration of the secular and sacred worlds. Occasionally the initiate is asked at some point to don the ritual mask himself—joining, as he does, one world with another and assuming the responsibility for their connection. This shift in status, in *relation,* is the heart of the rite; a liturgized merging of the individual with shared sources of power.

Do you see what I am driving at? The rites are in a sense a social contract, a binding up; one occurring specifically, profoundly, on a deep psychic level. The individual is redefined in the culture by his new relation to its mysteries, its gods, to one form or another of nature. His experience of that hidden and omnipotent mythical world is the basis for his relation to the culture and his fellows, each of whom has a similar bond—deep, personal, and unique, but somehow shared, invisibly but deeply. These ritualized relationships of each man to the shared gods bind the group together; they form the substance of culture: an invisible landscape that is real and felt, commonly held, a landscape which resides in each man and in which, in turn, each man resides.

I hope that makes sense. That is the structure of the kaleidoscopic turning of culture that Blake makes in "The Crystal Cabinet," and it makes sense too, in America, in relation to adolescents. What fascinates me is that our public schools, designed for adolescents—who seem, as apocalyptic men, to demand this kind of drama, release, and support—educate and "socialize" their students by depriving them of everything the rites bestow. They manipulate them through the repression of energies; they isolate them and close off most parts of the community; they categorically refuse to make use of the individual's private experience. The direction of all these tendencies is toward a cultural schizophrenia in which the student is forced to choose between his own relation to reality or the one demanded by the institution. The schools are organized to weaken the student so that he is forced, in the absence of his own energies, to accept the values and demands of the institution. To this end we deprive the student of mobility and experience; through law and custom we make the only legal place for him the school, and then, to make sure he remains dependent, manipulable, we empty the school of all vivid life.

We appear to have forgotten in our schools what every primitive tribe with its functional psychology knows: allegiance to the tribe can be forged only at the deepest levels of the psyche and in extreme circumstances demanding endurance, daring, and awe; that the participant must be given *direct* access to the sources of cultural continuity—by and in himself; and that only a place in a coherent community can be exchanged for a man's allegiance.

I believe that it is precisely this world that drugs replace; adolescents provide for themselves what we deny them: a confrontation with some kind of power within an unfamiliar landscape involving sensation and risk. It is there, I suppose, that they hope to find, by some hurried magic, a new way of seeing, a new relation to things, to discard one identity and assume another. They mean to find through their adventures the *ground* of reality, the resonance of life we deny them, as if they might come upon their golden city and return still inside it: at home. You can see the real veterans sometimes on the street in strange costumes they have stolen from dreams: American versions of the Tupi of Brazil, who traveled thousands of miles each year in search of the land where death and evil do not exist. Theirs is a world totally alien to the one we discuss in schools; it is dramatic, it enchants them; its existence forms a strange brotherhood among them and they cling to it—as though they alone had been to a fierce land and back. It is that which draws them together and makes of them a loose tribe. It is, after all, some sort of shared experience, some kind of foray into the risky dark; it is the best that they can do.

When you begin to think about adolescence in this way, what sense can you make of our schools? None of the proposed changes makes sense to me: revision of curriculum, teaching machines, smaller classes, encounter groups, redistributions of power—all of these are stopgap measures, desperate attempts to keep the young in schools that are hopelessly outdated. The changes suggested and debated don't go deeply enough; they don't question or change enough. For what needs changing are not the methods of the school system but its aims, and what is troubling the young and forcing upon their teachers an intolerable burden is the *idea* of childhood itself; the ways we think about adolescents, their place in the culture itself. More and more one comes to see that changes in the schools won't be enough; the crisis of the young cuts across the culture in all its areas and includes the family and the community. The young are displaced; there seems no other word for it. They are trapped in a prolonged childhood almost unique.

In few other cultures have persons of fifteen or eighteen been so uselessly isolated from participation in the community, or been deemed so unnecessary (in their elders' eyes), or so limited by law. Our ideas of responsibility, our parental feelings of anxiety, blame, and guilt, all of these follow from our curious vision of the young; in turn, they concretize it, legitimize it so that we are no longer even conscious of the ways we see childhood or the strain that our vision puts upon us. That is what needs changing: the definitions we make socially and legally of the role of the young. They are trapped in the ways we see them, and the school is simply one function, one aspect, of the whole problem. What makes real change so difficult in the schools is only in part their natural unwieldiness; it is more often the difficulty we have in escaping our preconceptions about things.

In general the school system we have inherited seems to me based upon three particular things:

1. What Paul Goodman calls the idea of "natural depravity": our puritanical vision of human nature in which children are perceived as sinners or "savages" and in which human impulse or desire is not to be trusted and must therefore be constrained or "trained."

2. The necessity during the mid-nineteenth century of "Americanizing" great masses of immigrant children from diverse backgrounds and creating, through the schools, a common experience and character.

3. The need in an industrialized state for energy and labor to run the machines: the state, needing workers, educates persons to be technically capable but relatively dependent and responsive to authority so that their energies will be available when needed.

These elements combine with others—the labor laws that make childhood a "legal" state, and a population explosion that makes it necessary now to keep adolescents off both the labor market and the idle street—to "freeze" into a school system that resists change even as the culture itself and its needs shift radically. But teachers can't usually see that, for they themselves have been educated in this system and are committed to ideas that they have never clearly understood. Time and again, speaking to them, one hears the same questions and anguish:

"But what will happen to the students if they don't go to school?" "How will they learn?" "What will they do without adults?"

What never comes clear, of course, is that such questions are, at bottom, statement. Even while asking them teachers reveal their unconscious and contaminating attitudes. They can no longer imagine what children will do "outside" schools. They regard them as young monsters who will, if released from adult authority or help, disrupt the order of things. What is more, adults no longer are capable of imagining learning or child-adult relationships outside the schools. But mass schooling is a recent innovation. Most learning—especially the process of socialization or acculturation—has gone on outside schools, more naturally, in the fabric of the culture. In most cultures the passage from childhood to maturity occurs because of social necessity, the need for responsible adults, and is marked by clear changes in role. Children in the past seem to have learned the ways of the community or tribe through constant contact and interchange with adults, and it was taken for granted that the young learned continually through their place close to the heart of the community.

We seem to have lost all sense of that. The school is expected to do what the community cannot do and that is impossible. In the end, we will have to change far more than the schools if we expect to create a new coherence between the experiences of the child and the needs of the community. We will have to rethink the meaning of childhood; we will begin to grant greater freedom *and* responsibility to the young; we will drop the compulsory-schooling age to fourteen, perhaps less; we will take for granted the "independence" of adolescents and provide them with the chance to live alone, away from parents and with peers; we will discover jobs they can or want to do in the community—anything from mail delivery to the teaching of smaller children and the counseling of other adolescents. At some point, perhaps, we will even find that the community itself—in return for a minimum of work or continued schooling—will provide a minimal income to young people that will allow them to assume the responsibility for their own lives at an earlier age, and learn the ways of the community outside the school; finally, having lowered the level of compulsory schooling, we will find it necessary to provide different *kinds* of schools, a wider choice, so that students will be willing voluntarily to continue the schooling that suits their needs and aims. [. . .]

I remember a talk I had with a college student.

"You know what I love to do," he said. "I love to go into the woods and run among the trees."

"Very nice," I said.

"But it worries me. We shouldn't do it."

"Why not?" I asked.

"Because we get excited. It isn't *orderly.*"

"Not orderly?"

"Not orderly."

"Do you run into the trees?" I asked.

"Of course not."

"Then it's orderly," I said.

In a small way this exchange indicates the kind of thinking we encourage in the schools: the mistaking of rigidity and stillness for order, of order as the absence of life. We try to create and preserve an order which depends upon the destruction of life both inside and out and which all life, when expressed, must necessarily threaten or weaken.

The natural process of learning seems to move naturally from experience through perception to abstraction in a fluid continuous process that cannot be clearly divided into stages. It is in that process that energy is somehow articulated in coherent and meaningful form as an act or thought or a made object. The end of learning is wisdom and wisdom to me, falling back as I do on a Jewish tradition, is, in its simplest sense, "intelligent activity" or, more completely, the suffusion of activity with knowledge, a wedding of the two. For the Hassidic Jews every gesture was potentially holy, a form of prayer, when it was made with a reverence for God. In the same way a gesture is always a form of wisdom—an act is wisdom—when it is suffused with knowledge, made with a reverence for the truth.

Does that sound rhetorical? I suppose it does. But I mean it. The end of education is intelligent activity, *wisdom,* and that demands a merging of opposites, a sense of process. Instead we produce the opposite: immobility, insecurity, an inability to act without institutional blessing or direction, or, at the opposite pole, a headlong rush toward motion without balance or thought. We cut into the natural movement of learning and try to force upon the students the end product, abstraction, while eliminating experience and ignoring their perception. The beginning of thought is in the experience through one's self of a particular environment—school, community, culture. When this is ignored, as it is in schools, the natural relation of self and knowledge is broken, the parts of the process become polar opposites, antitheses, and the young are forced to choose between them:

objectivity, order, and obedience as against subjectivity, chaos, and energy. It doesn't really matter which they choose; as long as the two sets seem irreconcilable their learning remains incomplete. Caught between the two, they suffer our intellectual schizophrenia until it occupies them, too. They wait. They sit. They listen. They learn to "behave" at the expense of themselves. Or else—and you can see it happening now—they turn against it with a vengeance and may shout, as they did at Columbia, "Kill all adults," for they have allied themselves with raw energy against reason and balance—our delicate, hard-won virtues—and we should not be surprised. We set up the choices ourselves, and it is simply that they have chosen what we hold to be the Devil's side. [. . .]

One thing alone of all I have read has made recent sense to me concerning adolescents. That is the implicit suggestion in Erik Erikson's *Young Man Luther* that every sensitive man experiences in himself the conflicts and contradictions of his age. The great man, he suggests, is the man who articulates and resolves these conflicts in a way that has meaning for his time; that is, he is himself, as was Luther, a victim of his time and its vehicle and, finally, a kind of resolution. But all men, not only the great, have in some measure the capacity to experience in themselves what is happening in the culture around them. I am talking here about what is really shared among the members of a particular culture is a condition, a kind of internal "landscape," the psychic shape that a particular time and place assumes within a man as the extent and limit of his perceptions, dreams, and pleasure and pain.

If there is such a shared condition it seems to me a crucial point, for it means that there is never any real distance between a man and his culture, no real isolation or alienation from society. It means that adolescents are not in their untutored state cut off from culture nor outside it. It means instead that each adolescent is an arena in which the contradictions and currents sweeping through the culture must somehow be resolved, must be resolved by the person himself, and that those individual resolutions are, ideally, the means by which the culture advances itself.

Do you see where this leads? I am straining here to get past the idea of the adolescent as an isolate and deviant creature who must be joined—as if glued and clamped—to the culture. For we ordinarily think of schools, though not quite consciously, as the "culture" itself, little models of society. We try to fit the student into the model, believing that if he will adjust to it he will in some way have been "civilized." That approach is connected to the needs of the early century, when the schools were the means by which the children of immigrant parents were acculturated and moved from the European values of their parents toward more prevalent American ones. But all of that has changed now. The children in our schools, all of them, are little fragments of *this* culture; they no longer need to be "socialized" in the same ways. The specific experiences of every adolescent —his fears, his family crises, his dreams and hallucinations, his habits, his sexuality—all these are points at which the general culture reveals itself in some way. There is no longer any real question of getting the adolescent to "adjust" to things.

The problem is a different one: What kind of setting will enable him to discover and accept what is already within him; to articulate it and perceive the extent to which it is shared with others; and, finally, to learn to change it within and outside himself? For that is what I mean when I call the adolescent a "maker of value." He is a trustee, a trustee of a world that already exists in some form within himself—and we must both learn, the adolescent and his teachers, to respect it.

In a sense, then, I am calling for a reversal of most educational thought. The individual is central; the individual, in the deepest sense, *is* the culture, not the institution. His culture resides in him, in experience and memory, and what is needed is an education that has at its base the sanctity of the individual's experience and leaves it intact.

What keeps running through my mind is a line I read twelve years ago in a friend's first published story: *The Idea in that idea is: there is no one over you.* I like that line: *There is no one over you.* Perhaps that signifies the gap between these children and their parents. For the children it is true, they sense it: there is no one over them; believable authority has disappeared; it has been replaced by experience. As Thomas Altizer says, God is dead; he is experienced now not as someone above or omnipotent or omniscient or "outside," but inwardly, as conscience or vision or even the unconscious or Tillich's "ground of being." This is all too familar to bother with here, but this particular generation is a collective dividing point. The parents of these children, the fathers, still believe in "someone" over them, insist upon it; in fact, demand it for and from their children. The children themselves cannot believe it; the idea means nothing to them. It is almost as if they are the first real Americans—suddenly free of Europe and somehow fatherless, confused, forced back on their own experience, their own sense of things, even though, at the same time, they are forced to defy their families and schools in order to keep it.

This is, then, a kind of Reformation. Arnold was wrong when he said that art would replace religion; education replaced it. Church became School, the principal vehicle for value, for "culture," and just as men once rebelled against the established Church as the mediator between God and man, students now rebel against the *public* school (and its version of things) as the intermediary between themselves and experience, between themselves and experience and the making of value. Students are expected to reach "reality" (whether of knowledge or society) through their teachers and school. No one, it is said, can participate in the culture effectively without having at one time passed through their hands, proven his allegiance to them, and been blessed. This is the authority exercised by priests or the Church. Just as men once moved to shorten the approach to God, they are moved now to do the same thing in relation to learning and to the community. For just as God was argued to appear within a man—

unique, private, and yet shared—so culture is, in some way, grounded in the individual; it inhabits him. The schools, like the Church, must be the expression of that habitation, not its exclusive medium. This is the same reformative shift that occurred in religion, a shift from the institutional (the external) to the individual (the internal), and it demands, when it occurs, an agony, an apocalyptic frenzy, a destruction of the past itself. I believe it is happening now. One sees and feels it everywhere: a violent fissure, a kind of quake.

I remember one moment in the streets of Oakland during the draft demonstrations. The students had sealed off the street with overturned cars and there were no police; the gutters were empty and the students moved into them from the sidewalks, first walking, then running, and finally almost dancing in the street. You could almost see the idea coalesce on their faces: The street is ours! It was as if a weight had been lifted from them, a fog; there was not at that moment any fury in them, any vengefulness or even politics; rather, a lightness, delight, an exhilaration at the sudden inexplicable sense of being free. George Orwell describes something similar in *Homage to Catalonia:* that brief period in Barcelona when the anarchists had apparently succeeded and men shared what power there was. I don't know how to describe it, except to say that one's inexplicable sense of invisible authority had vanished: the oppressive father, who is not really there, was gone.

That sudden feeling is familar to us all. We have all had it from time to time in our own lives, that sense of "being at home," that ease, that feeling of a Paradise which is neither behind us nor deferred but is around us, a natural household. It is the hint and beginning of Manhood: a promise, a clue. One's attention turns to the immediate landscape and to one's fellows: toward what is there, toward what can be felt as a part of oneself. I have seen the same thing as I watched Stokely Carmichael speaking to a black audience and telling them that they must stop begging the white man, like children, for their rights. They were, he said, neither children nor slaves, no, they were—and here they chanted, almost cried, in unison —a beautiful people: *yes our noses are broad and our lips are thick and our hair is kinky . . . but we are beautiful, we are beautiful, we are black and beautiful.* Watching, you could sense in that released joy an emergence, a surfacing of pride, a refusal to accept shame or the white man's dominance—and a turning to one another, to their own inherent value.

But there is a kind of pain in being white and watching that, for there is no one to say the same things to white children; no "fathers" or brothers to give them that sense of manhood or pride. The adolescents I have seen—white, middle-class—are a long way from those words *we are beautiful, we are beautiful.* I cannot imagine how they will reach them, deprived as they are of all individual strength. For the schools exist to deprive one of strength. That is why one's own worth must be proven again and again by the satisfaction of external requirements with no inherent

value or importance; it is why one must satisfy a set of inexplicable demands; it is why there is a continual separation of self and worth and the
intrusion of a kind of institutional guilt: failure not of God but of *the
system,* the nameless "others," the authority that one can never quite see;
and it explains the oppressive sense of some nameless transgression, almost
a shame at Being itself. [. . .]

The crisis of youth and education is symptomatic of some larger, deeper
fault in our cities and minds, and perhaps nothing can be done consciously
in those areas until the air itself is violently cleared one way or another.

So I have no easy conclusions, no startling synthesis with which to
close. I have only a change in mood, a softening, a kind of sadness. It may
be, given that, that the best thing is simply to close with an unfinished fragment in which I catch for myself the hint of an alternative:

> . . . I am trying to surround you, I see that, I am trying to make with
> these words a kind of city so natural, so familiar, that the other world,
> the one that appears to be, will look by comparison absurd and flat,
> limited, unnecessary. What I am after is liberation, not my own, which
> comes often enough these days in solitude or sex, but yours, and that is
> arrogant, isn't it, that is presumptuous, and yet that is the function of
> art: to set you free. It is that too which is the end of education: a libera-
> tion from childhood and what holds us there, a kind of midwifery, as
> if the nation itself were in labor and one wanted to save both the fu-
> ture and the past—for we are both, we are, we are the thin bridge sway-
> ing between them, and to tear one from the other means a tearing of
> ourselves, a partial death.
>
> And yet it may be that death is inevitable, useful. It may be. Perhaps,
> as in the myth, Aphrodite can rise only where Cronos' testicles have
> fallen into the sea. It may be that way with us. The death of the Father
> who is in us, the death of the old authority which is part of us, the death
> of the past which is also our death; it may all be necessary: a rending
> and purgation. And yet one still seeks another way, something less (or is
> it more) apocalyptic, a way in which the past becomes the future in our-
> selves, in which we become the bridges between: makers of culture.
>
> *Unless from us the future takes place, we are Death only,* said Law-
> rence, meaning what the Chassids do: that the world and time reside
> within, not outside, men; that there is no distance, no "alienation," only
> a perpetual wedding to the world. It is that—the presence in oneself of
> Time—that makes things interesting, is more gravid and interesting than
> guilt. I don't want to lose it, don't want to relinquish that sense in the
> body of another dimension, a distance, the depth of the body as it ex-
> tends backward into the past and forward, as it contains and extends and
> transforms.

What I am after is an alternative to separation and rage, some kind of
connection to things to replace the system of dependence and submission
—the loss of the self—that now holds sway, slanted toward violence. I am
trying to articulate a way of seeing, of feeling, that will restore to the

young a sense of manhood and potency without at the same time destroying the past. That same theme runs through whatever I write: the necessity for each man to experience himself as an extension and maker of culture, and to feel the whole force of the world within himself, not as an enemy—but as himself:

> . . . An act of learning is a meeting, and every meeting is simply the discovery in the world of a part of oneself that had previously been unacknowledged by the self. It is the recovery of the extent of one's being. It is the embrace of an eternal but elusive companion, the shadowy "other" in which one truly resides and which blazes, when embraced, like the sun.

2 The Self

Introduction:
The
Metaphysics
of
Self-Identity

Individualism is as much a theory about collectivities as about individuals: the individualist claims that the best society puts the fewest limits on the liberty of the individual. Conversely, anti-individualism is as much a theory about individuals as about society: the anti-individualist claims that individualism sets the self adrift from its natural social context and thereby inhibits the development of selfhood. Both individualism and its critics affirm the existence of individual self and social collectivities; they differ in their accounts of the nature of that self and its relation to society. Even the strongest opponent of individualism as a social theory may acknowledge a private part of the self, removed from historical flux and social determination. He may grant that even after the question "Who am I?" has been answered with public titles like "student" or "teacher," "male" or "female," "lover" or "spouse," even after all the public titles have been determined in countless questionnaires, a sense of incompleteness may remain. The public titles say **what** I am, but do they determine **who** I am? Is there an inner core that bears these titles? Is there a nonsocially defined "me" who determines the choice of one title rather than another? Is there a part of me that defines me uniquely and not merely as one among many bearing the same title?

Efforts to answer these questions take many forms. Where philosophers speak of the quest for self-knowledge and psychologists speak of identity crises, frustrated parents and teachers sometimes speak of the adolescent's attempt to find himself. Adolescence seems to provoke this difficult inner quest, since growth away from one's parents forces one to come to grips with life on one's own, but the quest for self-knowledge ought not be regarded as a "stage" that one passes through and leaves behind. Finding and maintaining one's self-identity can be a lifelong process. While it makes sense to expect that we can carry on the process without the pain and desperation often experienced in adolescence, it is a mistake to assume that once the pain has stopped the process is over. Rather than suffer the doubts and uncertainties of growth toward an indeterminate destination, many people fix a destination very early in life and then define themselves in terms of that destination: "I am a good mother"; "I am an engineer"; "I am a dropout." Many people imagine they can settle the account of self-identity once and for all and then live in the security of their certainty. But that premature decision is a subtle form of suicide. It amounts to opting out of life, for to live is to grow and change.

How, then, to live? How to find oneself and, once found, avoid petrifaction? The task can be performed well or poorly. Philosophy is largely about following the quest well rather than poorly. It is possible to make mistakes in the way we think about ourselves, not only in the public titles we ascribe to ourselves, but about the kind of thing a self is. We may be amused when someone treats his car as if it were an animate being by talking to it or kicking it when it fails to start. It is less amusing when people are treated like machines, yet this is precisely the kind of mistake a person makes when he prematurely fixes a destination and transforms himself into a machine for getting there. But if the self is not a machine, if it is not a mechanism with a clearly describable structure and function, then what is it?

Metaphysics is the branch of philosophy that deals with the question of kinds of being. The name was first assigned in a quite arbitrary way around 70 B.C. to one of Aristotle's books. He had written a **Physics** and then another book, scholars thought, **after** that, which they named the **Metaphysics; meta** in Greek means "after." But since then the name metaphysics has been used to describe any attempt to answer the questions Aristotle posed in his **Metaphysics.** Aristotle described his inquiry as the science of being, as such, meaning that he was not asking about particular beings and their properties, but about what it is in general "to be": what is it to be something rather than nothing? Although metaphysics does not describe particular beings, it does inquire into **ways** of being. Are there different ways of being—physical being on the one hand and nonspatiotemporal being on the other—or is there only one mode of being—the physical, material mode?

Metaphysics is necessary to the quest for self-knowledge because if you cannot locate the self with a scalpel, if the self is not like physical entities that have a simple location in space and time, then we want to know what other kind of being it can have, if any. If we are mistaken about the kind of being the self exhibits, then we can hardly help making mistakes when it comes to defining and determining the nature and identity of particular selves, including one's own self. Once again, it may be amusing when someone mistreats his car, but the subtle suicide involved in mistreating oneself is not. We can take the car to a mechanic, but can we take the self to a metaphysician? The quest for self-knowledge is necessarily a do-it-yourself enterprise, but the philosophical tradition contains priceless aids for exploring the metaphysics of self-identity.

The following six essays include representative samples from very different branches of the philosophical tradition, but the sampling is hardly random. Beginning with Descartes' argument for the self as "a thing which thinks," and Ryle's contemporary critique of the Cartesian metaphysics, we move to the problem of free will and determinism, a metaphysical problem in that it turns partially on the concept of causality as such rather than an examination of particular causes. Further, the denial of freedom is a denial of any autonomy for the self and hence a denial of an ongoing, self-identical, responsible agent. The two essays by Hume and Erikson then discuss the process character that distinguishes the being of this ongoing self from the being of inanimate entities.

RENÉ DESCARTES
(1596-1650)

Descartes' influence on modern philosophy would be hard to overestimate. His **Meditations** (1641) and his **Discourse on Method** (1637) mark the beginning of a major concern with the **methods** of philosophy. **How** can we know whatever we do know? How can we know when we are being deceived? How, for example, can we tell whether we are asleep or awake? The most frightening nightmares are often those in which one dreams that one has awakened only to find the horror continuing: you dream that you wake up, reach for the light, and feel a slimy hand.

If objects provide no indubitable marks of their reality, then perhaps we can find certainty in subjective states; perhaps the subjective quality of an experience provides more proof of its truthfulness than its objective contents. In his inauguration of what we now refer to as the "Subjective Turn," Descartes singled out as most important the subjective qualities of clarity and distinctness.

Whatever the limitation of his method, we owe Descartes a great debt for focusing on the importance of method. Whether or not philosophy can provide prepackaged answers to anyone asking a given question, at least we should expect philosophy to assist us in knowing how to go about asking and answering questions that do not merely increase confusion. Descartes presents us with a clear method: doubt everything you can until you get down to what is clear and distinct. But how much can you doubt? Descartes admits that his method imposes upon him a "laborious wakeful-ness." The labors of meditation are not always easy, but the fruits of those labors can be worth the effort.

Meditations I and II

Meditation I

Of the things which may be brought within the sphere of the doubtful.

It is now some years since I detected how many were the false beliefs that I had from my earliest youth admitted as true, and how doubtful was everything I had since constructed on this basis; and from that time I was convinced that I must once for all seriously undertake to rid myself of all the opinions which I had formerly accepted, and commence to build anew from the foundation, if I wanted to establish any firm and permanent structure in the sciences. But as this enterprise appeared to be a very great one, I waited until I had attained an age so mature that I could not hope that at any later date I should be better fitted to execute my design. This reason caused me to delay so long that I should feel that I was doing wrong were I to occupy in deliberation the time that yet remains to me for action. To-day, then, since very opportunely for the plan I have in view I have delivered my mind from every care [and am happily agitated by no passions] and since I have procured for myself an assured leisure in a peaceable retirement, I shall at last seriously and freely address myself to the general upheaval of all my former opinions.

Now for this object it is not necessary that I should show that all of these are false—I shall perhaps never arrive at this end. But inasmuch as reason already persuades me that I ought no less carefully to withhold my assent from matters which are not entirely certain and indubitable than from those which appear to me manifestly to be false, if I am able to find in each one some reason to doubt, this will suffice to justify my reject-ing the whole. And for that end it will not be requisite that I should examine each in particular, which would be an endless undertaking; for owing to the fact that the destruction of the foundations of necessity brings with it the downfall of the rest of the edifice, I shall only in the first place attack those principles upon which all my former opinions rested.

All that up to the present time I have accepted as most true and cer-

MEDITATIONS I AND II   From René Descartes, *Meditations on the First Philosophy in Which the Existence of God and the Distinction Between Mind and Body Are Demonstrated.*

tain I have learned either from the senses or through the senses; but it is sometimes proved to me that these senses are deceptive, and it is wiser not to trust entirely to any thing by which we have once been deceived.

But it may be that although the senses sometimes deceive us concerning things which are hardly perceptible, or very far away, there are yet many others to be met with as to which we cannot reasonably have any doubt, although we recognise them by their means. For example, there is the fact that I am here, seated by the fire, attired in a dressing gown, having this paper in my hands and other similar matters. And how could I deny that these hands and this body are mine, were it not perhaps that I compare myself to certain persons, devoid of sense, whose cerebella are so troubled and clouded by the violent vapours of black bile, that they constantly assure us that they think they are kings when they are really quite poor, or that they are clothed in purple when they are really without covering, or who imagine that they have an earthenware head or are nothing but pumpkins or are made of glass. But they are mad, and I should not be any the less insane were I to follow examples so extravagant.

At the same time I must remember that I am a man, and that consequently I am in the habit of sleeping, and in my dreams representing to myself the same things or sometimes even less probable things, than do those who are insane in their waking moments. How often has is happened to me that in the night I dreamt that I found myself in this particular place, that I was dressed and seated near the fire, whilst in reality I was lying undressed in bed! At this moment it does indeed seem to me that it is with eyes awake that I am looking at this paper; that this head which I move is not asleep, that it is deliberately and of set purpose that I extend my hand and perceive it; what happens in sleep does not appear so clear nor so distinct as does all this. But in thinking over this I remind myself that on many occasions I have in sleep been deceived by similar illusions, and in dwelling carefully on this reflection I see so manifestly that there are no certain indications by which we may clearly distinguish wakefulness from sleep that I am lost in astonishment. And my astonishment is such that it is almost capable of persuading me that I now dream.

Now let us assume that we are asleep and that all these particulars, e.g. that we open our eyes, shake our head, extend our hands, and so on, are but false delusions; and let us reflect that possibly neither our hands nor our whole body are such as they appear to us to be. At the same time we must at least confess that the things which are represented to us in sleep are like painted representations which can only have been formed as the counterparts of something real and true, and that in this way those general things at least, i.e. eyes, a head, hands, and a whole body, are not imaginary things, but things really existent. For, as a matter of fact, painters, even when they study with the greatest skill to represent sirens and satyrs by forms the most strange and extraordinary, cannot give them natures which are entirely new, but merely make a certain medley of the members of different animals; or if their imagination is extravagant enough to invent something so novel that nothing similar has ever before been seen, and that then their work represents a thing purely fictitious and absolutely false, it is certain all the same that the colours of which this is composed are necessarily real. And for the same reason, although these general things, to wit, [a body], eyes, a head, hands, and such like, may be imaginary, we are bound at the same time to confess that there are at least some other objects yet more simple and more universal, which are real and true; and of these just in the same way as with certain real colours, all these images of things which dwell in our thoughts, whether true and real or false and fantastic, are formed.

To such a class of things pertains corporeal nature in general, and its extension, the figure of extended things, their quantity or magnitude and number, as also the place in which they are, the time which measures their duration, and so on.

That is possibly why our reasoning is not unjust when we conclude from this that Physics, Astronomy, Medicine and all other sciences which have as their end the consideration of composite things, are very dubious and uncertain; but that Arithmetic, Geometry and other sciences of that kind which only treat of things that are very simple and very general, without taking great trouble to ascertain whether they are actually existent or not, contain some measure of certainty and an element of the indubitable. For whether I am awake or asleep, two and three together always form five, and the square can never have more than four sides, and it does not seem possible that truths so clear and apparent can be suspected of any falsity [or uncertainty].

Nevertheless I have long had fixed in my mind the belief that an all-powerful God existed by whom I have been created such as I am. But how do I know that He has not brought it to pass that there is no earth, no heaven, no extended body, no magnitude, no place, and that nevertheless [I possess the perceptions of all these things and that] they seem to me to exist just exactly as I now see them? And, besides, as I sometimes imagine that others deceive themselves in the things which they think they know best, how do I know that I am not deceived every time that I add two and three, or count the sides of a square, or judge of things yet simpler, if anything simpler can be imagined? But possibly God has not desired that I should be thus deceived, for He is said to be supremely good. If, however, it is contrary to His goodness to have made me such that I constantly deceive myself, it would also appear to be contrary to His goodness to permit me to be sometimes deceived, and nevertheless I cannot doubt that He does permit this.

There may indeed be those who would prefer to deny the existence of a God so powerful, rather than believe that all other things are uncertain. But let us not oppose them for the present, and grant that all that is here said of a God is a fable; nevertheless in whatever way they suppose that I have arrived at the state of being that I have reached—whether they attribute it to fate or to accident, or make out that it is by a continual succession of antecedents, or by some other method—since to err and deceive oneself is a defect, it is clear that the greater will be the probability of my being so imperfect as to deceive myself ever, as is the Author to whom they assign my origin the less powerful. To these reasons I have certainly nothing to reply, but at the end I feel constrained to confess that there is nothing in all that I formerly believed to be true, of which I cannot in some measure doubt, and that not merely through want of thought or through levity, but for reasons which are very powerful and maturely considered; so that henceforth I ought not the less carefully to refrain from giving credence to these opinions than to that which is manifestly false, if I desire to arrive at any certainty [in the sciences].

But it is not sufficient to have made these remarks, we must also be careful to keep them in mind. For these ancient and commonly held opinions still revert frequently to my mind, long and familiar custom having given them the right to occupy my mind against my inclination and rendered them almost masters of my belief; nor will I ever lose the habit of deferring to them or of placing my confidence in them, so long as I consider them as they really are, i.e. opinions in some measure doubtful, as I have just shown, and at the same time highly probable, so that there is much more reason to believe in than to deny them. That is why I consider that I shall not be acting amiss, if, taking of set purpose a contrary belief, I allow myself to be deceived, and for a certain time pretend that all these opinions are entirely false and imaginary, until at last, having thus balanced my former prejudices with my latter [so that they cannot divert my opinions more to one side than to the other], my judgment will no longer be dominated by bad usage or turned away from the right knowledge of the truth. For I am assured that there can be neither peril nor error in this course, and that I cannot at present yield too much to distrust, since I am not considering the question of action, but only of knowledge.

I shall then suppose, not that God who is supremely good and the fountain of truth, but some evil genius not less powerful than deceitful, has employed his whole energies in deceiving me; I shall consider that the heavens, the earth, colours, figures, sound and all other external things are nought but the illusions and dreams of which this genius has availed himself in order to lay traps for my credulity; I shall consider myself as having no hands, no eyes, no flesh, no blood, nor any senses, yet falsely believing myself to possess all these things; I shall remain obstinately attached to this idea, and if by this means it is not in my power to arrive at the knowledge of any truth, I may at least do what is in my power [i.e. suspend my judgment], and with firm purpose avoid giving credence to any false thing, or being imposed upon by this arch deceiver, however powerful and deceptive he may be. But this task is a laborious one, and insensibly a certain lassitude leads me into the course of my ordinary life. And just as a captive who in sleep enjoys an imaginary liberty, when he begins to suspect that his liberty is but a dream, fears to awaken, and conspires with these agreeable illusions that the deception may be prolonged, so insensibly of my own accord I fall back into my former opinions, and I dread awakening from this slumber, lest the laborious wakefulness which would follow the tranquility of this repose should have to be spent not in daylight, but in the excessive darkness of the difficulties which have just been discussed.

Meditation II

Of the Nature of the Human Mind; and that it is more easily known than the Body.

The Meditation of yesterday filled my mind with so many doubts that it is no longer in my power to forget them. And yet I do not see in what manner I can resolve them; and, just as if I had all of a sudden fallen into very deep water, I am so disconcerted that I can neither make certain of setting my feet on the bottom, nor can I swim and so support myself on the surface. I shall nevertheless make an effort and follow anew the same path as that on which I yesterday entered, i.e. I shall proceed by setting aside all that in which the least doubt could be supposed to exist, just as if I had discovered that it was absolutely false; and I shall ever follow in this road until I have met with something which is certain, or at least, if I can do nothing else, until I have learned for certain that there is nothing in the world that is certain. Archimedes, in order that he might draw the terrestrial globe out of its place, and transport it elsewhere, demanded only that one point should be fixed and immoveable; in the same way I shall have the right to conceive high hopes if I am happy enough to discover one thing only which is certain and indubitable.

I suppose, then, that all the things that I see are false; I persuade myself that nothing has ever existed of all that my fallacious memory represents to me. I consider that I possess no senses; I imagine that body, figure, extension, movement and place are but the fictions of my mind. What, then, can be esteemed as true? Perhaps nothing at all, unless that there is nothing in the world that is certain.

But how can I know there is not something different from those things that I have just considered, of which one cannot have the slightest doubt? Is there not some God, or some other being by whatever name we call it, who puts these reflections into my mind? That is not necessary, for is it not possible that I am capable of producing them myself? I myself, am I not at least something? But I have already denied that I had senses and body. Yet I hesitate, for what follows from that? Am I so dependent on body and senses that I cannot exist without these? But I was persuaded that there was nothing in all the world, that there was no heaven, no earth, that there were no minds, nor any bodies: was I not then likewise persuaded that I did not exist? Not at all; of a surety I myself did exist since I persuaded myself of something [or merely because I thought of something]. But there is some deceiver or other, very powerful and very cunning, who ever employs his ingenuity in deceiving me. Then without doubt I exist also if he deceives me, and let him deceive me as much as he will, he can never cause me to be nothing so long as I think that I am something. So that after having reflected well and carefully examined all things, we must come to the definite conclusion that this proposition: I am, I exist, is necessarily true each time that I pronounce it, or that I mentally conceive it.

But I do not yet know clearly enough what I am, I who am certain that I am; and hence I must be careful to see that I do not imprudently take some other object in place of myself, and thus that I do not go astray in respect of this knowledge that I hold to be the most certain and most evident of all that I have formerly learned. That is why I shall now consider anew what I believed myself to be before I embarked upon these last reflections; and of my former opinions I shall withdraw all that might even in a small degree be invalidated by the reasons which I have just brought forward, in order that there may be nothing at all left beyond what is absolutely certain and indubitable.

What then did I formerly believe myself to be? Undoubtedly I believed myself to be a man. But what is a man? Shall I say a reasonable animal? Certainly not; for then I should have to inquire what an animal is, and what is reasonable; and thus from a single question I should insensibly fall into an infinitude of others more difficult; and I should not wish to waste the little time and leisure remaining to me in trying to unravel subtleties like these. But I shall rather stop here to consider the thoughts which of themselves spring up in my mind, and which were not inspired by anything beyond my own nature alone when I applied myself to the consideration of my being. In the first place, then, I considered myself as having a face, hands, arms, and all that system of members composed of bones and flesh as seen in a corpse which I designated by the name of body. In addition to this I considered that I was nourished, that I walked, that I felt, and that I thought, and I referred all these actions to the soul: but I did not stop to consider what the soul was, or if I did stop, I imagined that it was something extremely rare and subtle like a wind, a flame, or an ether, which was spread throughout my grosser parts. As to body I had no manner of doubt about its nature, but thought I had a very clear knowledge of it; and if I had desired to explain it according to the notions that I had then formed of it, I should have described it thus: By the body I understand all that which can be defined by a certain figure: something which can be confined in a certain place, and which can fill a given space in such a way that every other body will be excluded from it; which can be perceived either by touch, or by sight, or by hearing, or by taste, or by smell: which can be moved in many ways not, in truth, by itself, but by something which is foreign to it, by which it is touched [and from which it receives impressions]: for to have the power of self-movement, as also of feeling or of thinking, I did not consider to appertain to the nature of body: on the contrary, I was rather astonished to find that faculties similar to them existed in some bodies.

But what am I, now that I suppose that there is a certain genius which is extremely powerful, and, if I may say so, malicious, who employs all his powers in deceiving me? Can I affirm that I possess the least of all those things which I have just said pertain to the nature of body? I pause to consider, I revolve all these things in my mind, and I find none of which I can say that it pertains to me. It would be tedious to stop to enumerate them. Let us pass to the attributes of soul and see if there is any one which is in me? What of nutrition or walking [the first mentioned]? But if it is so that I have no body it is also true that I can neither walk nor take nourishment. Another attribute is sensation. But one cannot feel without body, and besides I have thought I perceived many things during sleep that I recognised in my waking moments as not having been experienced at all. What of thinking? I find here that thought is an attribute that belongs to me; it alone cannot be separated from me. I am, I exist, that is certain. But how often? Just when I think; for it might possibly be the case if I ceased entirely to think, that I should likewise cease altogether to exist. I do not now admit anything which is not necessarily true: to speak accurately I am not more than a thing which thinks, that is to say a mind or a soul, or an understanding, or a reason, which are terms whose significance was formerly unknown to me. I am, however, a real thing and really exist; but what thing? I have answered: a thing which thinks.

And what more? I shall exercise my imagination [in order to see if I am not something more]. I am not a collection of members which we call the human body: I am not a subtle air distributed through these members, I am not a wind, a fire, a vapour, a breath, nor anything at all which I can imagine or conceive; because I have assumed that all these were nothing. Without changing that supposition I find that I only leave myself certain of the fact that I am somewhat. But perhaps it is true that these same things which I supposed were non-existent because they are unknown to me, are really not different from the self which I know. I am not sure about this, I shall not dispute about it now; I can only give judgment on things that are known to me. I know that I exist, and I inquire what I am, I whom I know to exist. But it is very certain that the knowledge of my existence taken in its precise significance does not depend on things whose existence is not yet known to me; consequently it does not depend on those which I can feign in imagination. And indeed the very term *feign* in imagination[1] proves to me my error, for I really do this if I image myself a something, since to imagine is nothing else than to contemplate the figure or image of a corporeal thing. But I already know for certain that I am, and that it may be that all these images, and, speaking generally, all things that relate to the nature of body are nothing but dreams [and chi-

---

[1] Or 'form an image' (effingo).

meras]. For this reason I see clearly that I have as little reason to say, 'I shall stimulate my imagination in order to know more distinctly what I am,' than if I were to say, 'I am now awake, and I perceive somewhat that is real and true: but because I do not yet perceive it distinctly enough, I shall go to sleep of express purpose, so that my dreams may represent the perception with greatest truth and evidence.' And, thus, I know for certain that nothing of all that I can understand by means of my imagination belongs to this knowledge which I have of myself, and that it is necessary to recall the mind from this mode of thought with the utmost diligence in order that it may be able to know its own nature with perfect distinctness.

But what then am I? A thing which thinks. What is a thing which thinks? It is a thing which doubts, understands, [conceives], affirms, denies, wills, refuses, which also imagines and feels.

Certainly it is no small matter if all these things pertain to my nature. But why should they not so pertain? Am I not that being who now doubts nearly everything, who nevertheless understands certain things, who affirms that one only is true, who denies all the others, who desires to know more, is averse from being deceived, who imagines many things, sometimes indeed despite his will, and who perceives many likewise, as by the intervention of the bodily organs? Is there nothing in all this which is as true as it is certain that I exist, even though I should always sleep and though he who has given me being employed all his ingenuity in deceiving me? Is there likewise any one of these attributes which can be distinguished from my thought, or which might be said to be separated from myself? For it is so evident of itself that it is I who doubts, who understands, and who desires, that there is no reason here to add anything to explain it. And I have certainly the power of imagining likewise; for although it may happen (as I formerly supposed) that none of the things which I imagine are true, nevertheless this power of imagining does not cease to be really in use, and it forms part of my thought. Finally, I am the same who feels, that is to say, who perceives certain things, as by the organs of sense, since in truth I see light, I hear noise, I feel heat. But it will be said that these phenomena are false and that I am dreaming. Let it be so; still it is at least quite certain that it seems to me that I see light, that I hear noise and that I feel heat. That cannot be false; properly speaking it is what is in me called feeling; and used in this precise sense that is no other thing than thinking.

From this time I begin to know what I am with a little more clearness and distinction than before; but nevertheless it still seems to me, and I cannot prevent myself from thinking, that corporeal things, whose images are framed by thought, which are tested by the senses, are much more distinctly known than that obscure part of me which does not come under the imagination. Although really it is very strange to say that I know and understand more distinctly these things whose existence seems to me dubious, which are unknown to me, and which do not belong to me, than others of the truth of which I am convinced, which are known to me and which pertain to my real nature, in a word, than myself. But I see clearly how the case stands: my mind loves to wander, and cannot yet suffer itself to be retained within the just limits of truth. Very good, let us once more give it the freest rein, so that, when afterwards we seize the proper occasion for pulling up, it may the more easily be regulated and controlled.

Let us begin by considering the commonest matters, those which we believe to be the most distinctly comprehended, to wit, the bodies which we touch and see; not indeed bodies in general, for these general ideas are usually a little more confused, but let us consider one body in particular. Let us take, for example, this piece of wax: it has been taken quite freshly from the hive, and it has not yet lost the sweetness of the honey which it contains; it still retains somewhat of the odour of the flowers from which it has been culled; its colour, its figures, its size are apparent; it is hard, cold, easily handled, and if you strike it with the finger, it will emit a sound. Finally all the things which are requisite to cause us distinctly to recognise a body, are met with in it. But notice that while I speak and approach the fire what remained of the taste is exhaled, the smell evaporates, the colour alters, the figure is destroyed, the size increases, it becomes liquid, it heats, scarcely can one handle it, and when one strikes it, no sound is emitted. Does the same wax remain after this change? We must confess that it remains; none would judge otherwise. What then did I know so distinctly in this piece of wax? It could certainly be nothing of all that the senses brought to my notice, since all these things which fall under taste, smell, sight, touch, and hearing, are found to be changed, and yet the same wax remains.

Perhaps it was what I now think, viz. that this wax was not that sweetness of honey, nor that agreeable scent of flowers, nor that particular whiteness, nor that figure, nor that sound, but simply a body which a little while before appeared to me as perceptible under these forms, and which is now perceptible under others. But what, precisely, is it that I imagine when I form such conceptions? Let us attentively consider this, and, abstracting from all that does not belong to the wax, let us see what remains. Certainly nothing remains excepting a certain extended thing which is flexible and movable. But what is the meaning of flexible and movable? Is it not that I imagine that this piece of wax being round is capable of becoming square and of passing from a square to a triangular figure? No, certainly it is not that, since I imagine it admits of an infinitude of similar changes, and I nevertheless do not know how to compass the infinitude by my imagination, and consequently this conception which I have of the wax is not brought about by the faculty of imagination. What now is this extension? Is it not also unknown? For it becomes greater when the wax is melted, greater when it is boiled, and greater still when the heat increases; and I should not conceive [clearly] according to truth what wax is, if I did not think that even this piece that we are considering is capable of receiving more variations in extension than I have ever imagined. We must then grant that I could not even understand through the imagination what this piece of wax is, and that it is my mind alone which perceives it. I say this piece of wax in particular, for as to wax in general it is yet clearer. But what is this piece of wax which cannot be understood excepting by the [understanding or] mind? It is certainly the same that I see, touch, imagine, and finally it is the same which I have always believed it to be from the beginning. But what must particularly be observed is that its perception is neither an act of vision, nor of touch, nor of imagination, and has never been such although it may have appeared formerly to be so, but only an intuition of the mind, which may be imperfect and confused as it was formerly, or clear and distinct as it is at present, according as my attention is more or less directed to the elements which are found in it, and of which it is composed.

Yet in the meantime I am greatly astonished when I consider [the great feebleness of mind] and its proneness to fall [insensibly] into error; for although without giving expression to my thoughts I consider all this in my own mind, words often impede me and I am almost deceived by the terms of ordinary language. For we say that we see the same wax, if it is present, and not that we simply judge that it is the same from its having the same colour and figure. From this I should conclude that I knew the wax by means of vision and not simply by the intuition of the mind; unless by chance I remember that, when looking from a window and saying I see men who pass in the street, I really do not see them, but infer that what I see is men, just as I say that I see wax. And yet what do I see from the window but hats and coats which may cover automatic machines? Yet I judge these to be men. And similarly solely by the faculty of judgment which rests in my mind, I comprehend that which I believed I saw with my eyes.

A man who makes it his aim to raise his knowledge above the common should be ashamed to derive the occasion for doubting from the forms of speech invented by the vulgar; I prefer to pass on and consider whether I had a more evident and perfect conception of what the wax was when I first perceived it, and when I believed I knew it by means of the external senses or at least by the common sense as it is called, that is to say by the imaginative faculty, or whether my present conception is clearer now that I have most carefully examined what it is, and in what way it can be known. It would certainly be absurd to doubt as to this. For what was there in this first perception which was distinct? What was there which might not as well have been perceived by any of the animals? But when I distinguish the wax from its external forms, and when, just as if I had taken from it its vestments, I consider it quite naked, it is certain that although some error may still be found in my judgment, I can nevertheless not perceive it thus without a human mind.

But finally what shall I say of this mind, that is, of myself, for up to this point I do not admit in myself anything but mind? What then, I who seem to perceive this piece of wax so distinctly, do I not know myself, not only with much more truth and certainty, but also with much more distinctness and clearness? For if I judge that the wax is or exists from the fact that I see it, it certainly follows much more clearly that I am or that I exist myself from the fact that I see it. For it may be that what I see is not really wax, it may also be that I do not possess eyes with which to see anything; but it cannot be that when I see, or (for I no longer take account of the distinction) when I think I see, that I myself who think am nought. So if I judge that the wax exists from the fact that I touch it, the same thing will follow, to wit, that I am; and if I judge that my imagination, or some other cause, whatever it is, persuades me that the wax exists, I shall still conclude the same. And what I have here remarked of wax may be applied to all other things which are external to me [and which are met with outside of me]. And further, if the [notion or] perception of wax has seemed to me clearer and more distinct, not only after the sight or the touch, but also after many other causes have rendered it quite manifest to me, with how much more [evidence] and distinctness must it be said that I now know myself, since all the reasons which contribute to the knowledge of wax, or any other body whatever, are yet better proofs of the nature of my mind! And there are so many other things in the mind itself which may contribute to the elucidation of its nature, that those which depend on body such as these just mentioned, hardly merit being taken into account.

But finally here I am, having insensibly reverted to the point I desired, for, since it is now manifest to me that even bodies are not properly speaking known by the senses or by the faculty of imagination, but by the understanding only, and since they are not known from the fact that they are seen or touched, but only because they are understood, I see clearly that there is nothing which is easier for me to know than my mind. But because it is difficult to rid oneself so promptly of an opinion to which one was accustomed for so long, it will be well that I should halt a little at this point, so that by the length of my meditation I may more deeply imprint on my memory this new knowledge.

Transition:
Mind,
Matter,
and Philosophic
Method

Was Descartes true to his method? His doubts are certainly radical, but are they radical enough? He showed the way into the introspective well of doubt, but did he plumb its depths? Just to show how difficult his method is to master, let me pose some of the questions raised by other philosophers.

First, is Descartes correct in his estimation of the point at which the drill of doubt meets the bedrock of certainty? For example, in his analysis of the identity of the piece of wax, is he correct in his description of what is left behind when all the changeable qualities are removed? Other philosophers have attempted the same thought experiment and come up with different answers. Aristotle (384–322 B.C.), in his **Metaphysics** (Book Zeta, Chapter 3), attempts the same metaphysical undressing and in his estimation the "length and breadth and depth" of a thing can be stripped away just as easily as its color and weight. In that passage Aristotle identifies matter as the ultimate substratum (bedrock) of identity, but he does not define matter in terms of extension as Descartes does. Similarly, Kant shows us a metaphysical striptease in his **Critique of Pure Reason** (B xxxv/A xxi): "if I take away from the representation of a body that which the understanding thinks in regard to it, substance, force, divisibility, etc., and likewise what belongs to sensation, impenetrability, hardness, colour, etc., something still remains over from this empirical intuition, namely, extension and figure." But Kant attributes this extension and figure not to the object in itself but to the cognitive faculties of the subject. For Kant, space and time are not objective realities but subjective forms of the way we see things. Thus the bedrock of identity is located even more subjectively than Descartes had imagined. On the basis of these passages from Aristotle and Kant we can see that the metaphysical striptease is not easy to perform. Even with a careful articulation of the method of doubt, what is certain to one man is not always certain to another.

This leads us to a second and even more radical objection to Descartes' method: what if we should doubt the method of doubt itself? Is subjective certainty a reliable criterion of truth? Perhaps the whole metaphor suggested by Descartes' method is a mistake; perhaps there is no bedrock. Or to use another metaphor, perhaps philosophic inquiry is more like peeling an onion than an orange. Descartes' method presupposes that beneath the rind of illusion one will find the fruit of truth. What if the truth is simply the totality of all the layers our doubt so briskly peels away? This is not to say there is no truth any more than the lack of a differentiated center denies the existence of an onion. The onion theory of reality, to coin a phrase, simply denies the notion that truth is to be found in a bedrock of reality that lies separate from and beneath appearances. According to the onion theory, reality is the totality of the appearances, not something separate from appearances. The distinction between reality and appearance still makes sense, however, because as long as one remains preoccupied with one layer one is necessarily cut off from the totality, and hence cut off from reality and truth. Descartes' method remains helpful in encouraging us to doubt the finality of any "truth" we apprehend. Whether or not we reach bedrock, the method of doubt spurs us on to regard each successive layer as another level of appearance. Thus the method of doubt leads to a totality in which each of the appearances is reclaimed as a part of the whole and not dismissed as a simple falsehood.

This method of totalizing is the method I embrace. Its major exponent in the western tradition is Hegel, whose writings, not surprisingly, rely so heavily on the relatedness of their various parts that no single part can be justly excerpted for an anthology. The reader will get a taste of the method of totalizing as he sees that method inform the organization of the rest of this anthology.

Gilbert Ryle limits the use of the metaphor of interior layers to the simple distinction of inside and outside. He accuses Descartes of having bifurcated man into a mental inside and physical outside. Without anticipating the details of Ryle's argument, I would like to call attention to the fact that Ryle's essay, too, can be read as a discourse on method. Just as Descartes' **Meditations** bear not only on the content of the mind-body problem but also on the method of the Subjective Turn, so Ryle's essay combines reflection on the mind-body problem with an application of the Linguistic Turn. That is, just as Descartes turned from a reflection on objects to a reflection on subjective experience, so Ryle turns from the method of introspection to an examination of the language we use in articulating our puzzlements. Ryle was not the first to make the Linguistic Turn. Perhaps its most famous initiators were Bertrand Russell (1872–1970), Ludwig Wittgenstein (1889–1951), and Rudolph Carnap (1891–   ). Through an examination of the language we use in talking about mind, matter, and existence, they showed how we are deceived by surface similarities among certain types of sentences. The sentence, 'She insists,' may look very like the sentence, 'She exists,' but a closer examination shows that the word 'exists' functions very differently from 'insists,' and if we insist on treating existence as a predicate that ascribes a particular property or activity to a subject, then our reliance on superficial linguistic similarities will end in confusion. The surface similarity of the two words muddies the distinction between **what** a thing is and **that** it is; the surface similarity between the sentences above leads us to think that 'exists,' since it is located in the predicate position, tells us something in particular about **what** the subject is or is doing, whereas in fact the word 'exists' only reasserts **that** there is a subject to which we may ascribe particular properties. The point may seem insignificant if regarded merely as an esoteric observation about our language, but when we realize that proofs for the existence of God as well as discussions of the existence of values turn on such points, then the results of linguistic analysis may seem more important. (For a full representation of this important movement in twentieth-century philosophy Richard Rorty's anthology, appropriately titled **The Linguistic Turn,** is excellent.)

The transition from Descartes to Ryle is a big transition. While Ryle places himself in a direct dialogue with Descartes, more than three hundred years passed between the publication of Descartes' **Meditations** and Ryle's **Concept of Mind.** During that time many philosophers not only followed Descartes' footsteps around the Subjective Turn but broke new paths in their own investigations of mind, matter, and philosophic method. Throughout the long transition from Descartes to Ryle the history of philosophy teaches the lesson that **what** we see depends on **how** we look: philosophic method influences the resultant metaphysics. Conversely, a commitment to a given metaphysics influences the method of inquiry most appropriate to expounding that metaphysics: if we are convinced that reality is nothing but matter and motion in space and time, then a Cartesian mathematical physics is the most appropriate method of inquiry. If, instead, we regard the logical space of discourse as the most significant reality for philosophical inquiry, then an examination of the logic of our language will be the most appropriate method of inquiry. And once we have taken the Linguistic Turn, its method not only replaces the method of the Subjective Turn; the metaphysics of Cartesianism comes under attack as well. Descartes' pictures of mind and matter fall under the charge that the Cartesian metaphysics follows from linguistic confusions.

GILBERT RYLE

(1900-   )

Gilbert Ryle is one of the most important of the contemporary British philosophers interested in examining our ordinary language, and as professor at Oxford and editor of the philosophical journal **Mind,** Ryle has influenced the course of philosophical debate in the English-speaking world for almost a generation. Since the publication of **The Concept of Mind** in 1949 and the posthumous publication of Wittgenstein's **Philosophical Investigations** in 1953, a whole tradition known as the "philosophy of mind" has centered around the issues raised in these two books. This tradition is characterized not only by its primary object, mind, but also by its method of inquiry, the examination of ordinary language. The same tradition is as often referred to as "ordinary language philosophy."

In the following essay, the first chapter of his **Concept of Mind,** Ryle shows how the Cartesian view of mind is the result of what Ryle calls a "category-mistake." Ryle finds it easiest to use examples to show the meaning of the term "category-mistake," but he generalizes from the examples to the claim that category-mistakes are generated by an "inability to use certain items in the English vocabulary." A close reading of Ryle's analysis of category-mistakes is well worth the effort, for the analytic tool of identifying category-mistakes proves helpful later in this book.

Descartes' Myth

The Official Doctrine

There is a doctrine about the nature and place of minds which is so prevalent among theorists and even among laymen that it deserves to be described as the official theory. Most philosophers, psychologists and religious teachers subscribe, with minor reservations, to its main articles and, although they admit certain theoretical difficulties in it, they tend to assume that these can be overcome without serious modifications being made to the architecture of the theory. It will be argued here that the central principles of the doctrine are unsound and conflict with the whole body of what we know about minds when we are not speculating about them.

The official doctrine, which hails chiefly from Descartes, is something like this. With the doubtful exceptions of idiots and infants in arms every human being has both a body and a mind. Some would prefer to say that every human being is both a body and a mind. His body and his mind are ordinarily harnessed together, but after the death of the body his mind may continue to exist and function.

Human bodies are in space and are subject to the mechanical laws which govern all other bodies in space. Bodily processes and states can be inspected by external observers. So a man's bodily life is as much a public affair as are the lives of animals and reptiles and even as the careers of trees, crystals and planets.

But minds are not in space, nor are their operations subject to mechanical laws. The workings of one mind are not witnessable by other observers; its career is private. Only I can take direct cognisance of the states and processes of my own mind. A person therefore lives through two collateral histories, one consisting of what happens in and to his body, the other consisting of what happens in and to his mind. The first is public, the second private. The events in the first history are events in the physical world, those in the second are events in the mental world.

It has been disputed whether a person does or can directly monitor all or only some of the episodes of his own private history; but, according to the official doctrine, of at least some of these episodes he has direct and

unchallengeable cognisance. In consciousness, self-consciousness and introspection he is directly and authentically apprised of the present states and
operations of his mind. He may have great or small uncertainties about
concurrent and adjacent episodes in the physical world, but he can have
none about at least part of what is momentarily occupying his mind.

It is customary to express this bifurcation of his two lives and of his
two worlds by saying that the things and events which belong to the physical world, including his own body, are external, while the workings of his
own mind are internal. This antithesis of outer and inner is of course
meant to be construed as a metaphor, since minds, not being in space,
could not be described as being spatially inside anything else, or as having
things going on spatially inside themselves. But relapses from this good
intention are common and theorists are found speculating how stimuli, the
physical sources of which are yards or miles outside a person's skin, can
generate mental responses inside his skull, or how decisions framed inside
his cranium can set going movements of his extremities.

Even when 'inner' and 'outer' are construed as metaphors, the problem
how a person's mind and body influence one another is notoriously
charged with theoretical difficulties. What the mind wills, the legs, arms
and the tongue execute; what affects the ear and the eye has something
to do with what the mind perceives; grimaces and smiles betray the mind's
moods and bodily castigations lead, it is hoped, to moral improvement.
But the actual transactions between the episodes of the private history and
those of the public history remain mysterious, since by definition they can
belong to neither series. They could not be reported among the happenings
described in a person's autobiography of his inner life, but nor could they
be reported among those described in some one else's biography of that
person's overt career. They can be inspected neither by introspection nor
by laboratory experiment. They are theoretical shuttlecocks which are forever being bandied from the physiologist back to the psychologist and
from the psychologist back to the physiologist.

Underlying this partly metaphorical representation of the bifurcation of
a person's two lives there is a seemingly more profound and philosophical
assumption. It is assumed that there are two different kinds of existence
or status. What exists or happens may have the status of physical existence,
or it may have the status of mental existence. Somewhat as the faces of
coins are either heads or tails, or somewhat as living creatures are either
male or female, so, it is supposed, some existing is physical existing, other
existing is mental existing. It is a necessary feature of what has physical
existence that it is in space and time, it is a necessary feature of what has
mental existence that it is in time but not in space. What has physical existence is composed of matter, or else is a function of matter; what has
mental existence consists of consciousness, or else is a function of consciousness.

There is thus a polar opposition between mind and matter, an opposition which is often brought out as follows. Material objects are situated in

a common field, known as 'space,' and what happens to one body in one part of space is mechanically connected with what happens to other bodies in other parts of space. But mental happenings occur in insulated fields, known as 'minds,' and there is, apart maybe from telepathy, no direct causal connection between what happens in one mind and what happens in another. Only through the medium of the public physical world can the mind of one person make a difference to the mind of another. The mind is its own place and in his inner life each of us lives the life of a ghostly Robinson Crusoe. People can see, hear and jolt one another's bodies, but they are irremediably blind and deaf to the workings of one another's minds and inoperative upon them.

What sort of knowledge can be secured of the workings of a mind? On the one side, according to the official theory, a person has direct knowledge of the best imaginable kind of the workings of his own mind. Mental states and processes are (or are normally) conscious states and processes, and the consciousness which irradiates them can engender no illusions and leaves the door open for no doubts. A person's present thinkings, feelings and willings, his perceivings, rememberings and imaginings are intrinsically 'phosphorescent'; their existence and their nature are inevitably betrayed to their owner. The inner life is a stream of consciousness of such a sort that it would be absurd to suggest that the mind whose life is that stream might be unaware of what is passing down it.

True, the evidence adduced recently by Freud seems to show that there exist channels tributary to this stream, which run hidden from their owner. People are actuated by impulses the existence of which they vigorously disavow; some of their thoughts differ from the thoughts which they acknowledge; and some of the actions which they think they will to perform they do not really will. They are thoroughly gulled by some of their own hypocrisies and they successfully ignore facts about their mental lives which on the official theory ought to be patent to them. Holders of the official theory tend, however, to maintain that anyhow in normal circumstances a person must be directly and authentically seized of the present state and workings of his own mind.

Besides being currently supplied with these alleged immediate data of consciousness, a person is also generally supposed to be able to exercise from time to time a special kind of perception, namely inner perception, or introspection. He can take a (non-optical) 'look' at what is passing in his mind. Not only can he view and scrutinize a flower through his sense of sight and listen to and discriminate the notes of a bell through his sense of hearing; he can also reflectively or introspectively watch, without any bodily organ of sense, the current episodes of his inner life. This self-observation is also commonly supposed to be immune from illusion, confusion or doubt. A mind's reports of its own affairs have a certainty superior to the best that is possessed by its reports of matters in the physical world. Sense-perceptions can, but consciousness and introspection cannot, be mistaken or confused.

On the other side, one person has no direct access of any sort to the events of the inner life of another. He cannot do better than make problematic inferences from the observed behaviour of the other person's body to the states of mind which, by analogy from his own conduct, he supposes to be signalised by that behaviour. Direct access to the workings of a mind is the privilege of that mind itself; in default of such privileged access, the workings of one mind are inevitably occult to everyone else. For the supposed arguments from bodily movements similar to their own to mental workings similar to their own would lack any possibility of observational corroboration. Not unnaturally, therefore, an adherent of the official theory finds it difficult to resist this consequence of his premises, that he has no good reason to believe that there do exist minds other than his own. Even if he prefers to believe that to other human bodies there are harnessed minds not unlike his own, he cannot claim to be able to discover their individual characteristics, or the particular things that they undergo and do. Absolute solitude is on this showing the ineluctable destiny of the soul. Only our bodies can meet.

As a necessary corollary of this general scheme there is implicitly prescribed a special way of construing our ordinary concepts of mental powers and operations. The verbs, nouns and adjectives, with which in ordinary life we describe the wits, characters and higher-grade performances of the people with whom we have do, are required to be construed as signifying special episodes in their secret histories, or else as signifying tendencies for such episodes to occur. When someone is described as knowing, believing or guessing something, as hoping, dreading, intending or shirking something, as designing this or being amused at that, these verbs are supposed to denote the occurrence of specific modifications in his (to us) occult stream of consciousness. Only his own privileged access to this stream in direct awareness and introspection could provide authentic testimony that these mental-conduct verbs were correctly or incorrectly applied. The onlooker, be he teacher, critic, biographer or friend, can never assure himself that his comments have any vestige of truth. Yet it was just because we do in fact all know how to make such comments, make them with general correctness and correct them when they turn out to be confused or mistaken, that philosophers found it necessary to construct their theories of the nature and place of minds. Finding mental-conduct concepts being regularly and effectively used, they properly sought to fix their logical geography. But the logical geography officially recommended would entail that there could be no regular or effective use of these mental-conduct concepts in our descriptions of, and prescriptions for, other people's minds.

The Absurdity of the Official Doctrine

Such in outline is the official theory. I shall often speak of it, with deliberate abusiveness, as 'the dogma of the Ghost in the Machine.' I hope to prove that it is entirely false, and false not in detail but in principle. It is not merely an assemblage of particular mistakes. It is one big mistake and a mistake of a special kind. It is, namely, a category-mistake. It represents the facts of mental life as if they belonged to one logical type or category (or range of types or categories), when they actually belong to another. The dogma is therefore a philosopher's myth. In attempting to explode the myth I shall probably be taken to be denying well-known facts about the mental life of human beings, and my plea that I aim at doing nothing more than rectify the logic of mental-conduct concepts will probably be disallowed as mere subterfuge.

I must first indicate what is meant by the phrase 'Category-mistake.' This I do in a series of illustrations.

A foreigner visiting Oxford or Cambridge for the first time is shown a number of colleges, libraries, playing fields, museums, scientific departments and administrative offices. He then asks 'But where is the University? I have seen where the members of the Colleges live, where the Registrar works, where the scientists experiment and the rest. But I have not yet seen the University in which reside and work the members of your University.' It has then to be explained to him that the University is not another collateral institution, some ulterior counterpart to the colleges, laboratories and offices which he has seen. The University is just the way in which all that he has already seen is organized. When they are seen and when their co-ordination is understood, the University has been seen. His mistake lay in his innocent assumption that it was correct to speak of Christ Church, the Bodleian Library, the Ashmolean Museum *and* the University, to speak, that is, as if 'the University' stood for an extra member of the class of which these other units are members. He was mistakenly allocating the University to the same category as that to which the other institutions belong.

The same mistake would be made by a child witnessing the march-past of a division, who, having had pointed out to him such and such battalions, batteries, squadrons, etc., asked when the division was going to appear. He would be supposing that a division was a counterpart to the units already seen, partly similar to them and partly unlike them. He would be shown his mistake by being told that in watching the battalions, batteries and squadrons marching past he had been watching the division marching past. The march-past was not a parade of battalions, batteries, squadrons *and* a division; it was a parade of the battalions, batteries and squadrons *of* a division.

One more illustration. A foreigner watching his first game of cricket learns what are the functions of the bowlers, the batsmen, the fielders, the umpires and the scorers. He then says 'But there is no one left on the field to contribute the famous element of team-spirit. I see who does the bowling, the batting, and the wicket-keeping; but I do not see whose role it is to exercise *esprit de corps*.' Once more, it would have to be explained that he was looking for the wrong type of thing. Team-spirit is not another cricketing-operation supplementary to all of the other special tasks. It is, roughly, the keenness with which each of the special tasks is performed, and performing a task keenly is not performing two tasks. Certainly exhibiting team-spirit is not the same thing as bowling or catching, but nor is it a third thing such that we can say that the bowler first bowls *and* then exhibits team-spirit or that a fielder is at a given moment *either* catching *or* displaying *esprit de corps*.

These illustrations of category-mistakes have a common feature which must be noticed. The mistakes were made by people who did not know how to wield the concepts *University, division* and *team-spirit*. Their puzzles arose from inability to use certain items in the English vocabulary.

The theoretically interesting category-mistakes are those made by people who are perfectly competent to apply concepts, at least in the situations with which they are familiar, but are still liable in their abstract thinking to allocate those concepts to logical types to which they do not belong. An instance of a mistake of this sort would be the following story. A student of politics has learned the main differences between the British, the French and the American Constitutions, and has learned also the differences and connections between the Cabinet, Parliament, the various Ministries, the Judicature and the Church of England. But he still becomes embarrassed when asked questions about the connections between the Church of England, the Home Office and the British Constitution. For while the Church and the Home Office are institutions, the British Constitution is not another institution in the same sense of that noun. So inter-institutional relations which can be asserted or denied to hold between the Church and the Home Office cannot be asserted or denied to hold between either of them and the British Constitution. 'The British Constitution' is not a term of the same logical type as 'the Home Office' and 'the Church of England.' In a partially similar way, John Doe may be a relative, a friend, an enemy or a stranger to Richard Roe; but he cannot be any of these things to the Average Taxpayer. He knows how to talk sense in certain sorts of discussions about the Average Taxpayer, but he is baffled to say why he could not come across him in the street as he can come across Richard Roe.

It is pertinent to our main subject to notice that, so long as the student of politics continues to think of the British Constitution as a counterpart to the other institutions, he will tend to describe it as a mysteriously occult institution; and so long as John Doe continues to think of the Average Taxpayer as a fellow-citizen, he will tend to think of him as an elusive insubstantial man, a ghost who is everywhere yet nowhere.

My destructive purpose is to show that a family of radical category-mistakes is the source of the double-life theory. The representation of a person as a ghost mysteriously ensconced in a machine derives from this argument. Because, as is true, a person's thinking, feeling and purposive doing cannot be described solely in the idioms of physics, chemistry and physiology, therefore they must be described in counterpart idioms. As the human body is a complex organised unit, so the human mind must be another complex organised unit, though one made of a different sort of stuff and with a different sort of structure. Or, again, as the human body, like any other parcel of matter, is a field of causes and effects, so the mind must be another field of causes and effects, though not (Heaven be praised) mechanical causes and effects.

The Origin of the Category-mistake

One of the chief intellectual origins of what I have yet to prove to be the Cartesian category-mistake seems to be this. When Galileo showed that his methods of scientific discovery were competent to provide a mechanical theory which should cover every occupant of space, Descartes found in himself two conflicting motives. As a man of scientific genius he could not but endorse the claims of mechanics, yet as a religious and moral man he could not accept, as Hobbes accepted, the discouraging rider to those claims, namely that human nature differs only in degree of complexity from clockwork. The mental could not be just a variety of the mechanical.

He and subsequent philosophers naturally but erroneously availed themselves of the following escape-route. Since mental-conduct words are not to be construed as signifying the occurrence of mechanical processes, they must be construed as signifying the occurrence of non-mechanical processes; since mechanical laws explain movements in space as the effects of other movements in space, other laws must explain some of the non-spatial workings of minds as the effects of other non-spatial workings of minds. The difference between the human behaviours which we describe as intelligent and those which we describe as unintelligent must be a difference in their causation; so, while some movements of human tongues and limbs are the effects of mechanical causes, others must be the effects of non-mechanical causes, i.e. some issue from movements of particles of matter, others from workings of the mind.

The differences between the physical and the mental were thus represented as differences inside the common framework of the categories of 'thing,' 'stuff,' 'attribute,' 'state,' 'process,' 'change,' 'cause' and 'effect.' Minds are things, but different sorts of things from bodies; mental processes are causes and effects, but different sorts of causes and effects from bodily movements. And so on. Somewhat as the foreigner expected the University to be an extra edifice, rather like a college but also considerably different, so the repudiators of mechanism represented minds as extra centers of causal processes, rather like machines but also considerably different from them. Their theory was a para-mechanical hypothesis.

That this assumption was at the heart of the doctrine is shown by the fact that there was from the beginning felt to be a major theoretical difficulty in explaining how minds can influence and be influenced by bodies. How can a mental process, such as willing, cause spatial movements like the movements of the tongue? How can a physical change in the optic nerve have among its effects a mind's perception of a flash of light? This notorious crux by itself shows the logical mould into which Descartes pressed his theory of the mind. It was the self-same mould into which he and Galileo set their mechanics. Still unwittingly adhering to the grammar of mechanics, he tried to avert disaster by describing minds in what was merely an obverse vocabulary. The working of minds had to be described by the mere negatives of the specific descriptions given to bodies; they are not in space, they are not motions, they are not modifications of matter, they are not accessible to public observation. Minds are not bits of clock-work, they are just bits of not-clockwork.

As thus represented, minds are not merely ghosts harnessed to machines, they are themselves just spectral machines. Though the human body is an engine, it is not quite an ordinary engine, since some of its workings are governed by another engine inside it—this interior governor-engine being one of a very special sort. It is invisible, inaudible and it has no size or weight. It cannot be taken to bits and the laws it obeys are not those known to ordinary engineers. Nothing is known of how it governs the bodily engine.

A second major crux points the same moral. Since, according to the doctrine, minds belong to the same category as bodies and since bodies are rigidly governed by mechanical laws, it seemed to many theorists to follow that minds must be similarly governed by rigid non-mechanical laws. The physical world is a deterministic system, so the mental world must be a deterministic system. Bodies cannot help the modifications that they un-dergo, so minds cannot help pursuing the careers fixed for them. *Responsi-bility, choice, merit* and *demerit* are therefore inapplicable concepts—unless the compromise solution is adopted of saying that the laws governing mental processes, unlike those governing physical processes, have the con-genial attribute of being only rather rigid. The problem of the Freedom of the Will was the problem how to reconcile the hypothesis that minds are to be described in terms drawn from the categories of mechanics with the knowledge that higher-grade human conduct is not of a piece with the be-haviour of machines.

It is an historical curiosity that it was not noticed that the entire argu-ment was broken-backed. Theorists correctly assumed that any sane man could already recognise the differences between, say, rational and non-rational utterances or between purposive and automatic behaviour. Else there would have been nothing requiring to be salved from mechanism. Yet the explanation given presupposed that one person could in principle never recognise the difference between the rational and the irrational utter-ances issuing from other human bodies, since he could never get access to the postulated immaterial causes of some of their utterances. Save for the doubtful exception of himself, he could never tell the difference between a man and a Robot. It would have to be conceded, for example, that, for all that we can tell, the inner lives of persons who are classed as idiots or lunatics are as rational as those of anyone else. Perhaps only their overt behaviour is disappointing; that is to say, perhaps 'idiots' are not really idiotic, or 'lunatics' lunatic. Perhaps, too, some of those who are classed as sane are really idiots. According to the theory, external observers could never know how the overt behaviour of others is correlated with their mental powers and processes and so they could never know or even plausibly conjecture whether their applications of mental-conduct concepts to these other people were correct or incorrect. It would then be hazardous or impossible for a man to claim sanity or logical consistency even for himself, since he would be debarred from comparing his own performances with those of others. In short, our characterisations of persons and their performances as intelligent, prudent and virtuous or as stupid, hypocritical and cowardly could never have been made, so the problem of providing a special causal hypothesis to serve as the basis of such diagnosis would never have arisen. The question, 'How do persons differ from machines?' arose just because everyone already knew how to apply mental-conduct concepts before the new causal hypothesis was introduced. This causal hypothesis could not therefore be the source of the criteria used in those applications. Nor, of course, has the causal hypothesis in any degree improved our handling of those criteria. We still distinguish good from bad arithmetic, politic from impolitic conduct and fertile from infertile imaginations in the ways in which Descartes himself distinguished them before and after he speculated how the applicability of these criteria was compatible with the principle of mechanical causation.

He had mistaken the logic of his problem. Instead of asking by what criteria intelligent behaviour is actually distinguished from non-intelligent behaviour, he asked 'Given that the principle of mechanical causation does not tell us the difference, what other causal principle will tell it us?' He realised that the problem was not one of mechanics and assumed that it must therefore be one of some counterpart to mechanics. Not unnaturally psychology is often cast for just this role.

When two terms belong to the same category, it is proper to construct conjunctive propositions embodying them. Thus a purchaser may say that he bought a left-hand glove and a right-hand glove, but not that he bought a left-hand glove, a right-hand glove and a pair of gloves. 'She came home in a flood of tears and a sedan-chair' is a well-known joke based on the absurdity of conjoining terms of different types. It would have been equally ridiculous to construct the disjunction 'She came home either in a flood of tears or else in a sedan-chair.' Now the dogma of the Ghost in the Machine does just this. It maintains that there exist both bodies and minds; that there occur physical processes and mental processes; that there are mechanical causes of corporeal movements and mental causes of corporeal movements. I shall argue that these and other analogous conjunctions are absurd; but, it must be noticed, the arguments will not show that either of the illegitimately conjoined propositions is absurd in itself. I am not, for example, denying that there occur mental processes. Doing long division is a mental process and so is making a joke. But I am saying that the phrase 'there occur mental processes' does not mean the same sort of thing as 'there occur physical processes,' and, therefore, that it makes no sense to conjoin or disjoin the two.

If my argument is successful, there will follow some interesting consequences. First, the hallowed contrast between Mind and Matter will be dissipated, but dissipated not by either of the equally hallowed absorptions of Mind by Matter or of Matter by Mind, but in quite a different way. For the seeming contrast of the two will be shown to be as illegitimate as would be the contrast of 'she came home in a flood of tears' and 'she came home in a sedan-chair.' The belief that there is a polar opposition between Mind and Matter is the belief that they are terms of the same logical type.

It will also follow that both Idealism and Materialism are answers to an improper question. The 'reduction' of the material world to mental states and processes, as well as the 'reduction' of mental states and processes to physical states and processes, presuppose the legitimacy of the disjunction 'Either there exist minds or there exist bodies (but not both).' It would be like saying, 'Either she bought a left-hand and a right-hand glove or she bought a pair of gloves (but not both).'

It is perfectly proper to say, in one logical tone of voice, that there exist minds and to say, in another logical tone of voice, that there exist bodies. But these expressions do not indicate two different species of existence, for 'existence' is not a generic word like 'coloured' or 'sexed.' They indicate two different senses of 'exist,' somewhat as 'rising' has different senses in 'the tide is rising,' 'hopes are rising,' and 'the average age of death is rising.' A man would be thought to be making a poor joke who said that three things are now rising, namely the tide, hopes and the average age of death. It would be just as good or bad a joke to say that there exist prime numbers and Wednesdays and public opinions and navies; or that there exist both minds and bodies. In the succeeding chapters I try to prove that the official theory does rest on a batch of category-mistakes by showing that logically absurd corollaries follow from it. The exhibition of these absurdities will have the constructive effect of bringing out part of the correct logic of mental-conduct concepts.

Historical Note

It would not be true to say that the official theory derives solely from Descartes' theories, or even from a more widespread anxiety about the implications of seventeenth century mechanics. Scholastic and Reformation theology had schooled the intellects of the scientists as well as of the laymen, philosophers and clerics of that age. Stoic-Augustinian theories of the will were embedded in the Calvinist doctrines of sin and grace; Platonic and Aristotelian theories of the intellect shaped the orthodox doctrines of the immortality of the soul. Descartes was reformulating already prevalent theological doctrines of the soul in the new syntax of Galileo. The theologian's privacy of conscience became the philosopher's privacy of consciousness, and what had been the bogy of Predestination reappeared as the bogy of Determinism.

It would also not be true to say that the two-worlds myth did no theoretical good. Myths often do a lot of theoretical good, while they are still new. One benefit bestowed by the para-mechanical myth was that it partly superannuated the then prevalent para-political myth. Minds and their Faculties had previously been described by analogies with political superiors and political subordinates. The idioms used were those of ruling, obeying, collaborating and rebelling. They survived and still survive in many ethical and some epistemological discussions. As, in physics, the new myth of occult Forces was a scientific improvement on the old myth of Final Causes, so, in anthropological and psychological theory, the new myth of hidden operations, impulses and agencies was an improvement on the old myth of dictations, deferences and disobediences.

Transition:
Free Will
and
Determinism

Ryle calmly affirmed, "The problem of the Freedom of the Will was the problem how to reconcile the hypothesis that minds are to be described in terms drawn from the categories of mechanics with the knowledge that higher-grade human conduct is not of a piece with the behaviour of machines." In his "Historical Note," he identified "Stoic-Augustinian theories of the will" as playing a supporting role in the "official doctrine" of the ghost in the machine. Let us now take a longer look at the problem of the Freedom of the Will, and let us see what Augustine has to say about it. Not everyone would agree with Ryle's description of the problem. Or if we do, and if we further agree with Ryle in rejecting "the hypothesis that minds are to be described in terms drawn from the categories of mechanics," and if we consequently **dissolve** the problem by eliminating the need to reconcile that rejected hypothesis with "the knowledge that higher-grade human conduct is not of a piece with the behaviour of machines," we may still want to know something about how higher-grade human conduct does in fact differ from that of machines. In short, there is not just one problem of the Freedom of the Will; there are many, and Ryle's dissolution of one of them, admirable as it may be, does not answer all our doubts about the Freedom of the Will. Even if Ryle is right in attacking the notion of an inner will that not only causes overt behavior but also suffers the effects of other causes, and even if he dissolves the problem of the freedom of the **Will,** has he dissolved the problem of freedom? True, the Will as it is described in the "official doctrine" may be a mythical entity, a mere name that refers to nothing behind voluntary acts, but we still do distinguish between voluntary acts and involuntary acts. Is the distinction legitimate? How is it made?

Clearly, there seem to be differences between going downstairs to get the mail, falling down the stairs, and being dragged down the stairs by the police. In the first case I intentionally do what I want to do. In the second my act is involuntary, an accident. The third case may be no accident, but my descent is still involuntary. And we can see the need for distinguishing among various kinds of involuntary behavior: accidents, behavior influenced by the active constraint of others, or the beating of one's heart, which seems to be another kind of involuntary behavior. Among voluntary actions we may want to distinguish between those actions we do consciously, like getting the mail, and those we do unconsciously, like balancing a bike while riding. The latter is hardly involuntary like a heartbeat; it is a learned behavior, and during the process of learning is most certainly conscious. But once learned it becomes quite unconscious, and thus a candidate for a different species of the voluntary.

Such proliferation of distinctions could, and indeed does, go on without limit. I am not arguing for any finality that qualifies any particular set or subset of distinctions among the voluntary and the involuntary. I merely wish to show the **kinds** of distinctions swept aside by the claims of the determinist.

The determinist may choose to make one of several different possible claims. If he claims that **no** distinctions can be made among voluntary and involuntary actions he is clearly wrong. We have just seen that some distinctions can be made. The question is, then, their legitimacy. If the ultimate court of appeals is ordinary linguistic usage, then the determinist is wrong unless he is making some particular claim about the **significance** of the distinctions. He may, for example, be saying something analogous to the claim that you can distinguish among fishes, horses, flies, snakes, and men, but in the end they're all animals. In other words, the determinist may admit that there are grounds for making certain distinctions, but he will claim that in the end all behavior is **caused**. There are no violations of the laws of causality. Your thought processes may be quite different when you go down to get the mail and when you are dragged down the stairs by the police, but **finally,** says the determinist, all your actions can be explained through an analysis of interlocking, never ending chains of cause and effect.

At this point the determinist has shifted the ground of the argument. He has moved from an analysis of the distinctions we find useful in our experience to an analysis of principles he claims to be operative beneath our experience. In short, he has shifted into metaphysics. Now I,

for one, am not an enemy of metaphysics, the quest for those fundamental principles we can use to make sense of what we find around us.
To disown metaphysics as many twentieth-century philosophers have
done is to discount the possibility that our ordinary way of looking at
things could be simply wrong. The metaphysician will not take ordinary
linguistic usage as the ultimate court of appeals. Like Aristotle, the
metaphysician will go to the trough of ordinary language to make sure
he is not simply engaging in idle fancy. But he will not discount the
possibility that unanimity of usage might still hide falsehood. After all,
there was a time when everyone thought the earth was flat. Was that
theory adequately verified by the currency of expressions like, "I would
go to the edge of the earth for you"?

No, the metaphysician may be right with some of his claims. But he
may be wrong, too. If he claims infallibility he may be mad, or the truth
he is espousing may be a disguised tautology—that is, a less obvious
case of such a statement as "All bachelors are unmarried." The truth
of a tautology is guaranteed by the fact that the predicate is contained
in the definition of the subject. Thus, if the determinist makes the statement, "All behavior is subject to causal laws," the statement may be
true but empty if he defines behavior as motion in space and time. Signing one's name is a motion in space and time, and as such it is subject
to causal laws. But what is the determinist to say about the differences
between writing one's name for the fun of it and signing a contract? If
behavior is defined not merely in terms of motion in space and time but
as action in the world of persons and legal statutes, then his claim that
all behavior is subject to causal laws becomes somewhat vapid. The law
of gravity is of much less interest than the law of torts where signing
a contract is concerned.

A further claim that the determinist might make is that all action is
in principle predictable. This is a curious claim for at least two reasons.
First, the phrase "in principle": what does it mean? If it means that the
determinist thinks he **will** be able to find a way around any obstacle to
prediction, then his claim is a mere hope and deserves no more attention than we accord other yet-to-be-realized hopes. But second, even if
someone could predict my future behavior, were that behavior anything
like my past behavior it would include all sorts of distinctions between
voluntary and involuntary acts. So the determinist might find his claim
of predictability entailing a prediction of freedom—not exactly what he
set out to prove.

If this second peculiarity of determinism as in principle predictability
sounds a bit too peculiar to be digested without further question, then
read the following piece by St. Augustine. Augustine knew nothing of
nineteenth-century physicalistic determinism, but freedom was an issue
for him as he struggled with the problem of predestination in God's
omniscience. As Ryle noted, "the bogy of Predestination reappeared as
the bogy of determinism." Such reappearances of philosophical prob-

lems is an important feature of the history of philosophy. The fact that the same problems keep coming up in different guises speaks for the need to identify a guise as a guise and at the same time appreciate the thinking of earlier philosophers who dealt with our problems in their earlier guises.

ST. AUGUSTINE

(354-430)

In the following passage from **On Free Will,** Augustine establishes an argument not too different from the one I have been tracing. Just as modern courts of law distinguish between the voluntary and the involuntary in order to attribute responsibility for punishable acts, so Augustine begins by discussing "culpable" acts—that is, acts that are blameworthy in the sight of God. The initial problem concerns God's omnipotence: isn't He responsible for the evil done? The modern lawyer might argue that society in its omnipotence is responsible for the action of the criminal. In both cases a fairly subtle argument is required to identify properly the agent of an action. Next, the argument moves to "predictability in principle" on the basis of God's omniscience. Here the modern correlate is the physical determinist. Consider whether it is significant that men have always been able to find some sense in which they seemed to be involuntarily determined, whether by God, physical causality, unconscious instincts, economic and social determinants, technology, or whatever. What if we are, in fact, determined in all these different ways? How does that reflect on the apparent bindingness of any one form of determinism?

On Free Will

(i, 1)   *Evodius*—It is sufficiently evident to me that free will is to be numbered among the good things, and, indeed, not among the least of our good things. We are, therefore, compelled to confess that it has been given us by God, and that he has rightly given it to us. But now, if you think a suitable time has come, I want to

ON FREE WILL   From *Augustine: Earlier Writings,* Vol. VI, Book III, The Library of Christian Classics. Edited by John H. S. Burleigh. Published in the U.S.A. by The Westminster Press, 1953. Used by permission.

learn from you whence arises the movement by which the will itself turns from the unchangeable good, which is the common property of all, to its own interests or to the interests of others or to things beneath it, and so turns to mutable goods.

Augustine—Why must you know this?

Ev.—Because if free will is so given that it has that movement by nature, it turns of necessity to mutable goods; and no blame attaches where nature and necessity prevail.

Aug.—Do you like or dislike that movement?

Ev.— I dislike it.

Aug.—So you find fault with it?

Ev.—I do.

Aug.—Then you find fault with a movement of the mind though it is faultless.

Ev.—No, I do not. But I do not know whether there is any fault in abandoning the unchangeable good and turning towards the mutable goods.

Aug.—Then you are finding fault with something which you do not know.

Ev.—Don't insist on a verbal point. I said that I did not know whether there was any fault, but I meant to be understood really as having no doubt about it. Certainly I said I do not know, but obviously I was being ironical in suggesting that there could be any doubt about so clear a matter.

Aug.—Just consider what is that truth you hold to be so certain that it has caused you so soon to forget what you said a moment ago. If that movement of the will exists by nature or necessity, it is in no way culpable. And yet you are so firmly convinced that it is culpable that you think fit to wax ironical about hesitation over a matter so certain. Why did you think it right to affirm, or at least to say with some hesitation, what you yourself show to be obviously false? You said: "If free will has been given in such fashion that it has that movement by nature, then it turns to mutable things of necessity and no fault can be found where nature and necessity rule." But you ought to have had no doubt that it was not given in that fashion, since you do not doubt that that movement is culpable.

Ev.—I said that the movement is culpable, and that therefore it displeases me, and that I cannot doubt that it is reprehensible. But I hold that a soul which is thereby drawn from the unchangeable good to mutable goods is not to be blamed if its nature is such that it is so moved by necessity.

(2) *Aug.*—To whom belongs the movement which you admit is blameworthy?

Ev.—I see that it is in the soul, but to whom it belongs I know not.

Aug.—You do not deny that the soul is moved by that motion?

Ev.—No.

Aug.—Do you then deny that the motion by which a stone is moved is the motion of the stone? I don't mean the motion that we give to it, or that is given to it by some other force, when it is thrown upwards, but that by which of its own accord it falls back to carth.

Ev.—I do not deny that the motion you refer to, by which it turns and falls downward, is the motion of the stone, but it is its natural motion. If the motion of the soul is like that, it too is natural, and it cannot rightly be blamed for a motion that is natural. Even if it moves to its own destruction, it is compelled by the necessity of its own nature. Moreover because we have no doubt that the soul's motion is culpable we must absolutely deny that it is natural, and therefore not like the motion of the stone, which is natural motion.

Aug.—Did we achieve anything in our two previous discussions?

Ev.—I am sure we did.

Aug.—No doubt you remember that in the first discussion we discovered that the mind can become the slave of lust only by its own will. No superior thing and no equal thing compels it to such dishonour, because that would be unjust. And no inferior thing has the power. It remains that that must be the mind's own motion when it turns its will away from enjoyment of the Creator to enjoyment of the creature. If that motion is accounted blameworthy—and you thought anyone who doubted that deserved to be treated ironically—it is not natural but voluntary. It is like the motion of the falling stone, in so far as it is a motion of the soul as the former is the motion of the stone. But it is dissimilar in this, that it is not in the power of a stone to arrest its downward motion, while if the soul is not willing it cannot be moved to abandon what is higher and to love what is lower. Thus the stone's motion is natural, the soul's voluntary. Hence anyone who says that a stone sins when it is carried downwards by its own weight is, I will not say more senseless than the stone but, completely mad. But we charge the soul with sin when we show that it has abandoned the higher things and prefers to enjoy lower things. What need is there, therefore, to seek the origin of the movement whereby the will turns from the unchangeable to the changeable good? We acknowledge that it is a movement of the soul, that it is voluntary and therefore culpable. And all useful learning in this matter has its object and value in teaching us to condemn and restrain that movement, and to convert our wills from falling into temporal delights to the enjoyment of the eternal good.

(3)   *Ev.*—I see, and in a sense grasp that what you say is true. There is nothing that I feel more certainly and more personally than that I have a will, and that it moves me to enjoy this or that. I know nothing I could call my own if the will by which I will "yea" or "nay" is not my own. If I use it to do evil, to whom is the evil to be attributed if not to myself? Since a good God has made me, and I can do nothing right except by willing, it is clearly evident that it was to this end that the will has been given to me by God who is good. Moreover, unless the movement of the will towards this or that object is voluntary and within our power, a man would not be praiseworthy when he turns to the higher objects nor blame-

worthy when he turns to lower objects, using his will like a hinge. There would be no use at all in warning him to pay no attention to temporal things and to will to obtain the eternal things, or to will to live aright and to be unwilling to live an evil life. But whoever thinks that man is not to be so warned ought to be cut off from membership in the human race.

(ii, 4)   That being so, I have a deep desire to know how it can be that God knows all things beforehand and that, nevertheless, we do not sin by necessity. Whoever says that anything can happen otherwise than as God has foreknown it, is attempting to destroy the divine foreknowledge with the most insensate impiety. If God foreknew that the first man would sin—and that anyone must concede who acknowledges with me that God has foreknowledge of all future events—I do not say that God did not make him, for he made him good, nor that the sin of the creature whom he made good could be prejudicial to God. On the contrary, God showed his goodness in making man, his justice in punishing his sin, and his mercy in delivering him. I do not say, therefore, that God did not make man. But this I say. Since God foreknew that man would sin, that which God foreknew must necessarily come to pass. How then is the will free when there is apparently this unavoidable necessity?

(5)   *Aug.*—You have knocked vigorously. May God in his mercy grant us his presence and open the door to those who knock. But I verily believe that the vast majority of men are troubled by that question for no other reason than that they do not ask it in a pious fashion. They are swifter to make excuses for their sins than to make confession of them. Some are glad to hold the opinion that there is no divine providence presiding over human affairs. They commit themselves, body and soul, to fortuitous circumstances, and deliver themselves to be carried about and tormented by lusts. They deny that there is any divine judgment, and deceive human judges when they are accused. They imagine that they are driven on by the favour of fortune. In sculpture or painting they are wont to represent Fortune as blind, either because they are better than the goddess by whom they think they are ruled, or because they confess that in their sentiments they are afflicted with that same blindness. In the case of such people it is not absurd to admit that they do everything by chance, seeing that they stumble in all that they do. But against this opinion, so full of foolish and senseless error, we have, I think, sufficiently spoken in our second disputation. Others do not venture to deny that the providence of God presides over human affairs, but they would rather indulge in the wicked error of believing that providence is weak or unjust or evil than confess their sins with suppliant piety. If all these would suffer themselves to be persuaded to believe that the goodness, justice and power of God are greater far, and far superior to any thought they can have of goodness, justice or might, if they would but take thought to themselves, they would know that they owe thanks to God, even if he had willed them to be somewhat lower in the scale of being than they actually are, and with all that is within them they would exclaim with the Psalmist: "I have spoken: Lord

have mercy upon me; heal my soul for I have sinned against thee" (Ps. 41:5). So by stages the divine mercy would bring them to wisdom. They would be neither inflated by what they discover, nor rebellious when they fail to find the truth; by learning they would become better prepared to see the truth, and by recognizing their ignorance they would become more patient in seeking it. I am quite sure that these are your views too. Now first answer a few questions I am going to put to you, and you will see how easily I can find a solution to your tremendous problem.

(iii, 6)   Your trouble is this. You wonder how it can be that these two propositions are not contradictory and incompatible, namely that God has foreknowledge of all future events, and that we sin voluntarily and not by necessity. For if, you say, God foreknows that a man will sin, he must necessarily sin. But if there is necessity there is no voluntary choice in sinning, but rather fixed and unavoidable necessity. You are afraid that by that reasoning the conclusion may be reached either that God's foreknowledge of all future events must be impiously denied, or, if that cannot be denied, that sin is committed not voluntarily but by necessity. Isn't that your difficulty?

Ev.—Exactly that.

Aug.—You think, therefore, that all things of which God has foreknowledge happen by necessity and not voluntarily.

Ev.—Yes. Absolutely.

Aug.—Try an experiment, and examine yourself a little, and tell me what kind of will you are going to have to-morrow. Will you want to sin or to do right?

Ev.—I do not know.

Aug.—Do you think God also does not know?

Ev.—I could in no wise think that.

Aug.—If God knows what you are going to will to-morrow, and foresees what all men are going to will in the future, not only those who are at present alive but all who will ever be, much more will he foresee what he is going to do with the just and the impious?

Ev.—Certainly if I say that God has foreknowledge of my deeds, I should say with even greater confidence that he has foreknowledge of his own acts, and foresees with complete certainty what he is going to do.

Aug.—Don't you see that you will have to be careful lest someone say to you that, if all things of which God has foreknowledge are done by necessity and not voluntarily, his own future acts will be done not voluntarily but by necessity?

Ev.—When I said that all future events of which God has foreknowledge happen by necessity, I was having regard only to things which happen in God himself. Indeed, in God nothing happens. Everything is eternal.

Aug.—God, then, is not active within his creation?

Ev.—He determined once for all how the order of the universe he created was to go on, and he never changes his mind.

Aug.—Does he never make anyone happy?

Ev.—Indeed he does.

Aug.—He does it precisely at the time when the man in question actually becomes happy.

Ev.—That is so.

Aug.—If, then, for example, you yourself are happy one year from now, you will be made happy at that time.

Ev.—Exactly.

Aug.—God knows to-day what he is going to do a year hence?

Ev.—He eternally had that foreknowledge, but I agree that he has it now, if indeed it is to happen so.

(7) *Aug.*—Now tell me, are you not God's creature? And will not your becoming happy take place within your experience?

Ev.—Certainly I am God's creature, and if I become happy it will be within my experience.

Aug.—If God, then, makes you happy, your happiness will come by necessity and not by the exercise of your will?

Ev.—God's will is my necessity.

Aug.—Will you then be happy against your will?

Ev.—If I had the power to be happy, I should be so at once. For I wish to be happy but am not, because not I but God makes me happy.

Aug.—The truth simply cries out against you. You could not imagine that "having in our power" means anything else than "being able to do what we will." Therefore there is nothing so much in our power as is the will itself. For as soon as we will [*volumus*] immediately will [*voluntas*] is there. We can say rightly that we do not grow old voluntarily but necessarily, or that we do not die voluntarily but from necessity, and so with other similar things. But who but a raving fool would say that it is not voluntarily that we will? Therefore though God knows how we are going to will in the future, it is not proved that we do not voluntarily will anything. When you said that you did not make yourself happy, you said it as if I had denied it. What I say is that when you become happy in the future it will take place not against your will but in accordance with your willing. Therefore, though God has foreknowledge of your happiness in the future, and though nothing can happen otherwise than as he has foreknown it (for that would mean that there is no foreknowledge) we are not thereby compelled to think that you will not be happy voluntarily. That would be absurd and far from true. God's foreknowledge, which is even to-day quite certain that you are to be happy at a future date, does not rob you of your will to happiness when you actually attain happiness. Similarly if ever in the future you have a culpable will, it will be none the less your will because God had foreknowledge of it.

(8) Observe, pray, how blind are those who say that if God has foreknowledge of what I am going to will, since nothing can happen otherwise than as he has foreknown it, therefore I must necessarily will what he has foreknown. If so, it must be admitted that I will, not voluntarily but from

necessity. Strange folly! Is there, then, no difference between things that happen according to God's foreknowledge where there is no intervention of man's will at all, and things that happen because of a will of which he has foreknowledge? I omit the equally monstrous assertion of the man I mentioned a moment ago, who says I must necessarily so will. By assuming necessity he strives to do away with will altogether. If I must necessarily will, why need I speak of willing at all? But if he puts it in another way, and says that, because he must necessarily so will, his will is not in his own power, he can be countered by the answer you gave me when I asked whether you could become happy against your will. You replied that you would be happy now if the matter were in your power, for you willed to be happy but could not achieve it. And I added that the truth cries out against you; for we cannot say we do not have the power unless we do not have what we will. If we do not have the will, we may think we will but in fact we do not. If we cannot will without willing, those who will have will, and all that is in our power we have by willing. Our will would not be will unless it were in our power. Because it is in our power, it is free. We have nothing that is free which is not in our power, and if we have something it cannot be nothing. Hence it is not necessary to deny that God has foreknowledge of all things, while at the same time our wills are our own. God has foreknowledge of our will, so that of which he has foreknowledge must come to pass. In other words, we shall exercise our wills in the future because he has foreknowledge that we shall do so; and there can be no will or voluntary action unless it be in our power. Hence God has also foreknowledge of our power to will. My power is not taken from me by God's foreknowledge. Indeed I shall be more certainly in possession of my power because he whose foreknowledge is never mistaken, foreknows that I shall have the power.

Ev.—Now I no longer deny that whatever God has foreknown must necessarily come to pass, nor that he has foreknowledge of our sins, but in such a way that our wills remain free and within our power.

(iv, 9)   *Aug.*—What further difficulty do you have? Perhaps you have forgotten what we established in our first disputation, and now wish to deny that we sin voluntarily and under no compulsion from anything superior, inferior or equal to us.

Ev.—I do not venture to deny that at all. But I must confess I do not yet see how God's foreknowledge of our sins and our freedom of will in sinning can be other than mutually contradictory. We must confess that God is just and knows all things beforehand. But I should like to know with what justice he punishes sins which must necessarily be committed; or how they are not necessarily committed when he knows that they will be committed; or how the Creator is to escape having imputed to him anything that happens necessarily in his creature.

(10)   *Aug.*—Why do you think our free will is opposed to God's foreknowledge? Is it because it is foreknowledge simply, or because it is God's foreknowledge?

Ev.—In the main because it is God's foreknowledge.

Aug.—If you knew in advance that such and such a man would sin, there would be no necessity for him to sin.

Ev.—Indeed there would, for I should have no real foreknowledge unless I knew for certain what was going to happen.

Aug.—So it is foreknowledge generally and not God's foreknowledge specially that causes the events foreknown to happen by necessity? There would be no such thing as foreknowledge unless there was certain foreknowledge.

Ev.—I agree. But why these questions?

Aug.—Unless I am mistaken, you would not directly compel the man to sin, though you knew beforehand that he was going to sin. Nor does your prescience in itself compel him to sin even though he was certainly going to sin, as we must assume if you have real prescience. So there is no contradiction here. Simply you know beforehand what another is going to do with his own will. Similarly God compels no man to sin, though he sees beforehand those who are going to sin by their own will.

(11)   Why then should he not justly punish sins which, though he had foreknowledge of them, he did not compel the sinner to commit? Just as you apply no compulsion to past events by having them in your memory, so God by his foreknowledge does not use compulsion in the case of future events. Just as you remember your past actions, though all that you remember were not actions of your own, so God has foreknowledge of all his own actions, but is not the agent of all that he foreknows. Of evil actions he is not the agent but the just punisher. From this you may understand with what justice God punishes sins, for he has no responsibility for the future actions of men though he knows them beforehand. If he ought not to award punishment to sinners because he knew beforehand that they would sin, he ought not to reward the righteous, because he knew equally that they would be righteous. Let us confess that it belongs to his foreknowledge to allow no future event to escape his knowledge, and that it belongs to his justice to see that no sin goes unpunished by his judgment. For sin is committed voluntarily and not by any compulsion from his foreknowledge.

JEAN-PAUL SARTRE

(1905-   )

Jean-Paul Sartre carries the argument for freedom even further than Augustine. Augustine said, "we charge the soul with sin when we show that it has abandoned the higher things and prefers to enjoy the lower things."

The soul's freedom extends to choosing between what Christian doctrine fixes as higher and lower. Sartre argues that the denominations of higher and lower are not fixed. Our freedom extends to the determination and creation of 'higher values.'

Sartre's radicalization of the argument for freedom extends so far that we begin to question whether Evodius was right when he said, "free will is to be numbered among the good things." Freedom becomes an almost impossible burden. Recall Marin's double-edged declaration that the adolescents he knew were perhaps the first generation who felt that 'there is no one over you' and that those young people were setting out on a frightening landscape.

Freedom is anguished, says Sartre, so difficult to bear that we are inclined to fall into what he calls "bad faith." We are inclined to view ourselves as things, as not free, because it is easier that way: we no longer bear the burden of responsibility for our acts and for determining the values by which we judge our acts. Note the difference between these two responsibilities. Augustine affirmed the first, but anguish follows from the combination of the first with the second. It is easier to accept only the first responsibility, and then acknowledge guilt before a table of values we are not responsible for. To accept the burden of responsibility for both the act **and** the criteria of judgment is to accept the role of a creator of values. And that is hard. To take on the role of the creator is to end all possibility of scapegoating. You cannot say, "Oh, it was the devil in me." Nor can you even take credit for doing the "right thing," where "right" is determined by some other. As Sartre says, you cannot **justify** your actions. All you can do is accept the fact that whatever happens, **you** did it, even if what you did was try to get out of a responsibility for your acts and values.

Here it is worth introducing another theme that reappears in later discussions. One easy way to misread Sartre is to interpret him as espousing a shallow form of subjective relativism. That is, one can jump to the simple conclusion, "Whatever I do is all right because there are no objective values, only subjective tastes. I like what I like and you like what you like and there's no point in discussing values because they're all relative." True, Sartre is denying the objective givenness of absolute values, but between the security of objective absolutes and the simplicity of subjective relativism there lies a position I like to call objective relativism: roughly put, one can deny objective values but one cannot deny certain objective facts, and the process of valuation is relative to both the subject **and** the objective facts. We are creators, but we are not creators in a void. To ignore the nature and being of the materials we have to work with is to foredoom the product of creation—namely, ourselves.

FREEDOM AND SELF-CREATION

Value derives its being from its exigency and not its exigency from its being. It does not deliver itself to a contemplative intuition which would apprehend it as *being* value and thereby would remove from it its right over my freedom. On the contrary, it can be revealed only to an active freedom which makes it exist as value by the sole fact of recognizing it as such. It follows that my freedom is the unique foundation of values and that *nothing,* absolutely nothing, justifies me in adopting this or that particular value, this or that particular scale of values. As a being by whom values exist, I am unjustifiable. My freedom is anguished at being the foundation of values while itself without foundation. It is anguished in addition because values, due to the fact that they are essentially revealed to a freedom, can not disclose themselves without being at the same time "put into question," for the possibility of overturning the scale of values appears complementarily as *my* possibility. It is anguish before values which is the recognition of the ideality of values.

Ordinarily, however, my attitude with respect to values is eminently reassuring. In fact I am engaged in a world of values. The anguished apperception of values as sustained in being by my freedom is a secondary and mediated phenomenon. The immediate is the world with its urgency; and in this world where I engage myself, my acts cause values to spring up like partridges. My indignation has given to me the negative value "baseness," my admiration has given the positive value "grandeur." Above all my obedience to a multitude of tabus, which is real, reveals these tabus to me as existing in fact. The bourgeois who call themselves "respectable citizens" do not become respectable as the result of contemplating moral values. Rather from the moment of their arising in the world they are thrown into a pattern of behavior the meaning of which is respectability. Thus respectability acquires a being; it is not put into question. Values are sown on my path as thousands of little real demands, like the signs which order us to keep off the grass.

Thus in what we shall call the world of the immediate, which delivers itself to our unreflective consciousness, we do not first appear to ourselves, to be thrown subsequently into enterprises. Our being is immediately "in situation"; that is, it arises in enterprises and knows itself first in so far as it is reflected in those enterprises. We discover ourselves then in a world peopled with demands, in the heart of projects "in the course of realization." I write. I am going to smoke. I have an appointment this evening with Pierre. I must not forget to reply to Simon. I do not have

FREEDOM AND SELF-CREATION   Used by permission of Philosophical Library, Inc. From *Being and Nothingness* by Jean-Paul Sartre, © Copyright 1956 by Philosophical Library, Inc., New York.

the right to conceal the truth any longer from Claude. All these trivial passive expectations of the real, all these commonplace, everyday values, derive their meaning from an original projection of myself which stands as my choice of myself in the world. But to be exact, this projection of myself toward an original possibility, which causes the existence of values, appeals, expectations, and in general a world, appear to me only beyond the world as the meaning and the abstract, logical signification of my enterprises. For the rest, there exist concretely alarm clocks, signboards, tax forms, policemen, so many guard rails against anguish. But as soon as the enterprise is held at a distance from me, as soon as I am referred to myself because I must await myself in the future, then I discover myself suddenly as the one who gives its meaning to the alarm clock, the one who by a signboard forbids himself to walk on a flower bed or on the lawn, the one from whom the boss's order borrows its urgency, the one who decides the interest of the book which he is writing, the one finally who makes the values exist in order to determine his action by their demands. I emerge alone and in anguish confronting the unique and original project which constitutes my being; all the barriers, all the guard rails collapse, nihilated by the consciousness of my freedom. I do not have nor can I have recourse to any value against the fact that it is I who sustain values in being. Nothing can ensure me against myself, cut off from the world and from my essence by this nothingness which I am. I have to realize the meaning of the world and of my essence; I make my decision concerning them—without justification and without excuse.

Anguish then is the reflective apprehension of freedom by itself. In this sense it is mediation, for although it is immediate consciousness of itself, it arises from the negation of the appeals of the world. It appears at the moment that I disengage myself from the world where I had been engaged —in order to apprehend myself as a consciousness which possesses a preontological comprehension of its essence and a pre-judicative sense of its possibilities. Anguish is opposed to the mind of the serious man who apprehends values in terms of the world and who resides in the reassuring, materialistic substantiation of values. In the serious mood I define myself in terms of the object by pushing aside *a priori* as impossible all enterprises in which I am not engaged at the moment; the meaning which my freedom has given to the world, I apprehend as coming from the world and constituting my obligations. In anguish I apprehend myself at once as totally free and as not being able to derive the meaning of the world except as coming from myself.

We should not however conclude that being brought on to the reflective plane and envisaging one's distant or immediate possibilities suffice to apprehend oneself in *pure* anguish. In each instance of reflection anguish is born as a structure of the reflective consciousness in so far as the latter considers consciousness as an object of reflection; but it still remains possible for me to maintain various types of conduct with respect to my own anguish—in particular, patterns of flight. Everything takes place, in fact, as if our essential and immediate behavior with respect to anguish is flight. Psychological determinism, before being a theoretical conception, is first an attitude of excuse, or if you prefer, the basis of all attitudes of excuse. It is reflective conduct with respect to anguish; it asserts that there are within us antagonistic forces whose type of existence is comparable to that of things. It attempts to fill the void which encircles us, to re-establish the links between past and present, between present and future. It provides us with a *nature* productive of our acts, and these very acts it makes transcendent; it assigns to them a foundation in something other than themselves by endowing them with an inertia and externality eminently reassuring because they constitute a permanent game of *excuses*. Psychological determinism denies that transcendence of human reality which makes it emerge in anguish beyond its own essence. At the same time by reducing us to *never being anything but what we are,* it reintroduces in us the absolute positivity of being-in-itself and thereby reinstates us at the heart of being.

But this determinism, a reflective defense against anguish, is not given as a reflective *intuition*. It avails nothing against the *evidence* of freedom; hence it is given as a faith to take refuge in, as the ideal end toward which we can flee to escape anguish. That is made evident on the philosophical plane by the fact that deterministic psychologists do not claim to found their thesis on the pure givens of introspection. They present it as a satisfying hypothesis, the value of which comes from the fact that it accounts for the facts—or as a necessary postulate for establishing all psychology. They admit the existence of an immediate consciousness of freedom, which their opponents hold up against them under the name of "proof by intuition of the inner sense." They merely focus the debate on the *value* of this inner revelation. Thus the intuition which causes us to apprehend ourselves as the original cause of our states and our acts has been discussed by nobody. It is within the reach of each of us to try to mediate anguish by rising above it and by *judging* it as an illusion due to the mistaken belief that we are the real causes of our acts. The problem which presents itself then is that of the degree of faith in this mediation. Is an anguish placed under judgment a disarmed anguish? Evidently not. However here a new phenomenon is born, a process of "distraction" in relation to anguish which, once again, supposes within it a nihilating power.

By itself determinism would not suffice to establish distraction since determinism is only a postulate or an hypothesis. This process of detachment is a more complete activity of flight which operates on the very level of reflection. It is first an attempt at distraction in relation to the possibles opposed to *my* possible. When I constitute myself as the comprehension of a possible as *my* possible, I must recognize its existence at the end of my project and apprehend it as myself, awaiting me down there in the future and separated from me by a nothingness. In this sense I apprehend myself as the original source of my possibility, and it is this which ordinarily we call the consciousness of freedom. It is this structure of consciousness and this alone that the proponents of free-will have in mind when they speak of the intuition of the inner sense. But it happens that I force myself at the same time to *be distracted* from the constitution of other possibilities which contradict *my* possibility. In truth I can not avoid positing their existence by the same movement which generates the chosen possibility as mine. I cannot help constituting them as *living* possibilities; that is, *as having the possibility of becoming my possibilities.* But I force myself to see them as endowed with a transcendent, purely logical being, in short, as things. If on the reflective plane I envisage the possibility of writing this book as *my* possibility, then between this possibility and my consciousness I cause a nothingness of being to arise which constitutes the writing of the book as a possibility and which I apprehend precisely in the permanent possibility that the possibility of not writing the book is *my* possibility. But I attempt to place myself on the other side of the possibility of not writing it as I might do with respect to an observable object, and I let myself be penetrated with what I wish to see there; I try to apprehend the possibility of not writing as needing to be mentioned merely as a reminder, as not concerning me. It must be an external possibility in relation to me, like movement in relation to the motionless billiard ball. If I could succeed in this, the possibilities hostile to *my* possibility would be constituted as logical entities and would lose their effectiveness. They would no longer be threatening since they would be "outsiders," since they would surround my possible as purely *conceivable* eventualities; that is, fundamentally, conceivable *by* another or as *possibles of another who might find himself in the same situation.* They would belong to the objective situation as a transcendent structure, or if you prefer (to utilize Heidegger's terminology)—*I* shall write this book but *someone* could also not write it. Thus I should hide from myself the fact that the possibles are *myself* and that they are immanent conditions of the possibility of my possible. They would preserve just enough being to preserve for my possible its character as gratuitous, as a free possibility for a free being, but they would be disarmed of their threatening character. They would not *interest* me; the chosen possible would appear—due to its selection—as my only concrete possible, and consequently the nothingness which separates me from it and which actually confers on it its possibility would collapse.

But flight before anguish is not only an effort at distraction before the future; it attempts also to disarm the past of its threat. What I attempt to flee here is my very transcendence in so far as it sustains and surpasses my essence. I assert that I *am* my essence in the mode of being of the in-itself. At the same time I always refuse to consider that essence as being historically constituted and as implying my action as a circle implies its properties. I apprehend it, or at least I try to apprehend it as the original beginning of my possible, and I do not admit at all that it has in itself a beginning. I assert then that an act is free when it exactly reflects my essence. However this freedom which would disturb me if it were freedom before myself, I attempt to bring back to the heart of my essence—i.e., of my self. It is a matter of envisaging the self as a little God which inhabits me and which possesses my freedom as a metaphysical virtue. It would be no longer my being which would be free *qua* [as] being but my Self which would be free in the heart of my consciousness. It is a fiction eminently reassuring since freedom has been driven down into the heart of an opaque being; to the extent that my essence is not translucency, that it is transcendent in immanence, freedom would become one of its properties. In short, it is a matter of apprehending my freedom in my self as the freedom of another. We see the principal themes of this fiction: My self becomes the origin of its acts as the other of his, by virtue of a personality already constituted. To be sure, he (the self) lives and transforms himself; we will admit even that each of his acts can contribute to transforming him. But these harmonious, continued transformations are conceived on a biological order. They resemble those which I can establish in my friend Pierre when I see him after a separation. Bergson expressly satisfied these demands for reassurance when he conceived his theory of the profound self which endures and organizes itself, which is constantly contemporary with the consciousness which I have of it and which can not be surpassed by consciousness, which is found at the origin of my acts not as a cataclysmic power but as a father begets his children, in such a way that the act without following from the essence as a strict consequence, without even being foreseeable, enters into a reassuring relation with it, a family resemblance. The act goes farther than the self but along the same road; it preserves, to be sure, a certain irreducibility, but we recognize ourselves in it, and we find ourselves in it as a father can recognize himself and find himself in the son who continues his work. Thus by a projection of freedom—which we apprehend in ourselves—into a psychic object which is the self, Bergson has contributed to disguise our anguish, but it is at the expense of consciousness itself. What he has established and described in this manner is not our freedom as it appears to itself; *it is the freedom of the Other.*

Such then is the totality of processes by which we try to hide anguish from ourselves; we apprehend our particular possible by avoiding considering all other possibles, which we make the possibles of an undifferentiated Other. The chosen possible we do not wish to see as sustained in being by a pure nihilating freedom, and so we attempt to apprehend it as engendered by an object already constituted, which is no other than our self, envisaged and described as if it were another person. We should like to preserve from the original intuition what it reveals to us as our independence and our responsibility but we tone down all the original nihilation in it; moreover we are always ready to take refuge in a belief in determinism if this freedom weighs upon us or if we need an excuse. Thus we flee from anguish by attempting to apprehend ourselves from without as an Other or as *a thing.* What we are accustomed to call a revelation of the inner sense or an original intuition of our freedom contains nothing original; it is an already constructed process, expressly designed to hide from ourselves anguish, the veritable "immediate given" of our freedom.

Do these various constructions succeed in stifling or hiding our anguish? It is certain that we can not overcome anguish, for we *are* anguish. As for veiling it, aside from the fact that the very nature of consciousness and its translucency forbid us to take the expression literally, we must note the particular type of behavior which it indicates. We can hide an external object because it exists independently of us. For the same reason we can turn our look or our attention away from it—that is, very simply, fix our eyes on some other object; henceforth each reality—mine and that of the object—resumes its own life, and the accidental relation which united consciousness to the thing disappears without thereby altering either existence. But if I *am* what I wish to veil, the question takes on quite another aspect. I can in fact wish "not to see" a certain aspect of my being only if I am acquainted with the aspect which I do not wish to see. This means that in my being I must indicate this aspect in order to be able to turn myself away from it; better yet, I must think of it constantly in order to take care not to think of it. In this connection it must be understood not only that I must of necessity perpetually carry within me what I wish to flee but also that I must aim at the object of my flight in order to flee it. This means that anguish, the intentional aim of anguish, and a flight from anguish toward reassuring myths must all be given in the unity of the same consciousness. In a word, I flee in order not to know, but I can not avoid knowing that I am fleeing; and the flight from anguish is only a mode of becoming conscious of anguish. Thus anguish, properly speaking, can be neither hidden nor avoided.

Yet to flee anguish and to be anguish can not be exactly the same thing. If I am my anguish in order to flee it, that presupposes that I can decenter myself in relation to what I am, that I can be anguish in the form of "not-being it," that I can dispose of a nihilating power at the heart of anguish itself. This nihilating power nihilates anguish in so far as I flee it and nihilates itself in so far as *I am anguish in order to flee it*. This attitude is what we call *bad faith*. There is then no question of expelling anguish from consciousness nor of constituting it in an unconscious psychic phenomenon; very simply I can make myself guilty of bad faith while apprehending the anguish which I am, and this bad faith, intended to fill up the nothingness which I *am* in my relation to myself, precisely implies the nothingness which it suppresses.[. . .]

. . . We should examine more closely the patterns of bad faith and attempt a description of them. This description will permit us perhaps to fix more exactly the conditions for the possibility of bad faith; that is, to reply to the question we raised at the outset: "What must be the being of man if he is to be capable of bad faith?"

Take the example of a woman who has consented to go out with a particular man for the first time. She knows very well the intentions which the man who is speaking to her cherishes regarding her. She knows also that it will be necessary sooner or later for her to make a decision. But she does not want to realize the urgency; she concerns herself only with what is respectful and discreet in the attitude of her companion. She does not apprehend this conduct as an attempt to achieve what we call "the first approach": that is, she does not want to see possibilities of temporal development which his conduct presents. She restricts this behavior to what is in the present; she does not wish to read in the phrases which he addresses to her anything other than their explicit meaning. If he says to her, "I find you so attractive!" she disarms this phrase of its sexual background; she attaches to the conversation and to the behavior of the speaker, the immediate meanings, which she imagines as objective qualities. The man who is speaking to her appears to her sincere and respectful as the table is round or square, as the wall coloring is blue or gray. The qualities thus attached to the person she is listening to are in this way fixed in a permanence like that of things, which is no other than the projection of the strict present of the qualities into the temporal flux. This is because she does not quite know what she wants. She is profoundly aware of the desire which she inspires, but the desire cruel and naked would humiliate and horrify her. Yet she would find no charm in a respect which would be only respect. In order to satisfy her, there must be a feeling which is addressed wholly to her *personality*—i.e., to her full freedom—and which would be a recognition of her freedom. But at the same time this feeling must be wholly desire; that is, it must address itself to her body as object. This time then she refuses to apprehend the desire for what it is; she does not even give it a name; she recognizes it only to the extent that it transcends itself toward admiration, esteem, respect and that it is wholly absorbed in the more refined forms which it produces, to the extent of no longer figuring anymore as a sort of warmth and density. But then suppose he takes her hand. This act of her companion risks changing the situation by calling for an immediate decision. To leave the hand there is to consent in herself to flirt, to engage herself. To withdraw it is to break the troubled and unstable harmony which gives the hour its charm. The aim is to postpone the moment of decision as long as possible. We know what happens next; the young woman leaves her hand there, but she *does not notice* that she is leaving it. She does not notice because it happens by chance that she is at this moment all intellect. She draws her companion up to the most lofty regions of sentimental speculation; she speaks of Life, of her life, she shows herself in her essential aspect—a personality, a consciousness. And during this time the divorce of the body from the soul is accomplished; the hand rests inert between the warm hands of her companion—neither consenting nor resisting—a thing.

We shall say that this woman is in bad faith. But we see immediately that she uses various procedures in order to maintain herself in this bad faith. She has disarmed the actions of her companion by reducing them to being only what they are.[. . .]

. . . We have seen also the use which our young lady made of our being-in-the-midst-of-the-world—*i.e.,* of our inert presence as a passive object among other objects—in order to relieve herself suddenly from the functions of her being-in-the-world—that is, from the being which causes there to be a world by projecting itself beyond the world toward its own possibilities. Let us note finally the confusing syntheses which play on the nihilating ambiguity of these temporal ekstases, affirming at once that I am what I have been (the man who deliberately *arrests himself* at one period in his life and refuses to take into consideration the later changes) and that I am not what I have been (the man who in the face of re-proaches or rancor dissociates himself from his past by insisting on his freedom and on his perpetual re-creation). In all these concepts, which have only a transitive role in the reasoning and which are eliminated from the conclusion, (like hypochondriacs in the calculations of physicians), we find again the same structure. We have to deal with human reality as a being which is what it is not and which is not what it is.

Transition:
The Self's Being
as a
Process
of Becoming

Descartes identifies man as a thinking thing, but Ryle cautions against locating the thinker as a ghost inside a machine. He gives us reasons to reject the hypothesis that "minds are to be described in terms drawn from the categories of mechanism." His argument introduces the problem of free will. In their efforts to articulate man's freedom, Augustine and Sartre show us a picture of man as a process in time. Sartre's description takes us beyond the categories of mechanism. A refrigerator is a refrigerator, but "we have to deal with human reality as a being which is what it is not and which is not what it is." Sartre's paradoxical plunge into nonmechanistic categories threatens to leave us in confusion. What kind of being is he talking about?

If there is any such thing as a self, its kind of being is not the kind of being we are used to dealing with when we talk about the being of physical entities in space and time. This is not to say that the self is a nonphysical, immaterial thing. The self, as I and others later argue, is eminently physical. The point is rather to imagine a way of being that is different from the way many physical things are.

Many things exist in such a way that their properties are never separated from each other. Even though the properties of Descartes' piece of wax may change when it is held near the heat, the color is always found where the shape is, and the smell and taste go together as well. Consequently, Descartes is led to suppose that there is something **in which** all these properties inhere, something that accounts for the substantiality, the unity, and togetherness of the various properties. Extension is his answer.

Ryle, however, points to the category-mistake involved in immediately assuming that everything is like the piece of wax in that it can be located in one extension. The university is nonetheless existent even though it cannot be located as its separate buildings can. Ryle's example of a category-mistake pertains to the existence of things in space. Just because a thing cannot be located in one continuous portion of space, it does not follow that it does not exist. Nor does it follow that it is nonspatial and mystical. Similarly, I argue that we make category-mistakes with respect to time. Just because something cannot be located in a specific stretch of time, it does not follow that it does not exist, nor does it follow that it is mystically nontemporal.

The problem with examples like the piece of wax, or chairs, or tables, is not that they are spatiotemporal, but rather that they present us with a paradigm of existence in which continuity and simplicity are the criteria for existence. If the space occupied by the properties of the wax becomes discontinuous, then we say there are two pieces of wax and not one. There are many other kinds of examples. The university shows the being of something discontinuous in space. A game is another example that can show discontinuity in time. If you break off playing a game of Monopoly and return to it the next day, you return to the same game. You have one game, not two. Or you could end one game and start another during a continuous stretch of time. Try to think of other examples.

In any case, the point is that the self may be a kind of process rather than a complete and underlying, continuous thing. The following two essays reflect on the nature of that process.

DAVID HUME

(1711-1776)

The name David Hume is insepa-
rable from the school known as British Empiricism. Following
John Locke (1632–1714) and Bishop Berkeley (1685–1753),
Hume developed a philosophy whose main points stand in almost
diametrical opposition to the philosophy of the Continental Rationalists Descartes, Leibniz (1646–1716), and Spinoza (1632–
1677). Where the rationalists founded knowledge on innate ideas
and the functions of understanding, the empiricists denied the existence of innate ideas and trusted rather to the evidence of the
senses. Where Leibniz saw perceptions as confused ideas, Hume
sees complex ideas as combinations of simple sensations. Where
the rationalists saw the world as a vast pattern of necessary connections, all similar in kind from the truths of mathematics down
to the tiniest details of historical fact, the empiricists distinguished
sharply between the logical necessity of truths of reason and the
empirical contingency of truths of fact. It was Hume above all who
attacked the rationalist idea that causal connections exhibit the
same necessity found in logic or mathematics.

In the following selection Hume attacks the concept of identity
as it was developed by Descartes, among others. Compare Hume's
analysis with Descartes' **Meditations** concerning the differences
between rationalists and empiricists. And most important, compare Hume's analysis with your own meditations. Try to follow his
directions for introspection just as you tried to follow Descartes'
method of doubt. Hume reports that he never finds his **self** on his
inner quest, but only bundles of perceptions connected by relations of resemblance, contiguity, or causation. Those perceptions,
he argues, are not connected by any underlying identity, and our
tendency to import some substratum of identity is a mistaken attempt to account for the felt continuity of our experience. Sometimes, of course, our experience does not feel terribly continuous.
Sometimes we experience an identity crisis, as the psychologist
Erik Erikson puts it. We come to doubt just who it is that we are.
How would you relate Hume's discussion of self-identity to the experience of an identity crisis?

ON SELF-IDENTITY

There are some philosophers, who imagine we are every moment intimately conscious of what we call our *self;* that we feel its existence and its continuance in existence; and are certain, beyond the evidence of a demonstration, both of its perfect identity and simplicity. The strongest sensation, the most violent passion, say they, instead of distracting us from this view, only fix it the more intensely, and make us consider their influence on *self* either by their pain or pleasure. To attempt a farther proof of this were to weaken its evidence; since no proof can be derived from any fact, of which we are so intimately conscious; nor is there any thing, of which we can be certain, if we doubt of this.

Unluckily all these positive assertions are contrary to that very experience, which is pleaded for them, nor have we any idea of *self,* after the manner it is here explained. For from what impression could this idea be derived? This question 'tis impossible to answer without a manifest contradiction and absurdity; and yet 'tis a question, which must necessarily be answered, if we would have the idea of self pass for clear and intelligible. It must be some one impression, that gives rise to every real idea. But self or person is not any one impression, but that to which our several impressions and ideas are supposed to have a reference. If any impression gives rise to the idea of self, that impression must continue invariably the same, through the whole course of our lives; since self is supposed to exist after that manner. But there is no impression constant and invariable. Pain and pleasure, grief and joy, passions and sensations succeed each other, and never all exist at the same time. It cannot therefore be from any of these impressions, or from any other, that the idea of self is derived; and consequently there is no such idea.

But farther, what must become of all our particular perceptions upon this hypothesis? All these are different, and distinguishable, and separable from each other, and may be separately considered, and may exist separately, and have no need of any thing to support their existence. After what manner therefore do they belong to self; and how are they connected with it? For my part, when I enter most intimately into what I call *myself,* I always stumble on some particular perception or other, of heat or cold, light or shade, love or hatred, pain or pleasure. I never can catch *myself* at any time without a perception, and never can observe any thing but the perception. When my perceptions are removed for any time, as by sound sleep; so long am I insensible of *myself,* and may truly be said not to exist. And were all my perceptions removed by death, and could I neither think, nor feel, nor see, nor love, nor hate after the dissolution of my body, I

ON SELF-IDENTITY   From David Hume, "Of Personal Identity," in *Of the Understanding,* Book I, Part IV, Section 6 of *The Treatise of Human Nature.*

should be entirely annihilated, nor do I conceive what is farther requisite to make me a perfect non-entity. If any one upon serious and unprejudiced reflection, thinks he has a different notion of *himself,* I must confess I can reason no longer with him. All I can allow him is, that he may be in the right as well as I, and that we are essentially different in this particular. He may, perhaps, perceive something simple and continued, which he calls *himself;* though I am certain there is no such principle in me.

But setting aside some metaphysicians of this kind, I may venture to affirm of the rest of mankind, that they are nothing but a bundle or collection of different perceptions, which succeed each other with an inconceivable rapidity, and are in a perpetual flux and movement. Our eyes cannot turn in their sockets without varying our perceptions. Our thought is still more variable than our sight; and all our other senses and faculties contribute to this change; nor is there any single power of the soul, which remains unalterably the same, perhaps for one moment. The mind is a kind of theatre, where several perceptions successively make their appearance; pass, re-pass, glide away, and mingle in an infinite variety of postures and situations. There is properly no *simplicity* in it at one time, nor *identity* in different; whatever natural propension we may have to imagine that simplicity and identity. The comparison of the theatre must not mislead us. They are the successive perceptions only, that constitute the mind; nor have we the most distant notion of the place, where these scenes are represented, or of the materials, of which it is composed.

What then gives us so great a propension to ascribe an identity to these successive perceptions, and to suppose ourselves possessed of an invariable and uninterrupted existence through the whole course of our lives? In order to answer this question, we must distinguish betwixt personal identity, as it regards our thought or imagination, and as it regards our passions or the concern we take in ourselves. The first is our present subject; and to explain it perfectly we must take the matter pretty deep, and account for that identity, which we attribute to plants and animals; there being a great analogy betwixt it, and the identity of a self or person.

We have a distinct idea of an object, that remains invariable and uninterrupted through a supposed variation of time; and this idea we call that of *identity* or *sameness.* We have also a distinct idea of several different objects existing in succession, and connected together by a close relation; and this to an accurate view affords as perfect a notion of *diversity,* as if there was no manner of relation among the objects. But though these two ideas of identity and a succession of related objects be in themselves perfectly distinct, and even contrary, yet 'tis certain, that in our common way of thinking they are generally confounded with each other. That action of the imagination, by which we consider the uninterrupted and invariable object, and that by which we reflect on the succession of related objects, are almost the same to the feeling, nor is there much more effort of thought required in the latter case than in the former. The relation facilitates the transition of the mind from one object to another, and renders its passage as smooth as if it contemplated one continued object. This resemblance is the cause of the confusion and mistake, and makes us substitute the notion of identity, instead of that of related objects. However at one instant we may consider the related succession as variable or interrupted, we are sure the next to ascribe to it a perfect identity, and regard it as invariable and uninterrupted. Our propensity to this mistake is so great from the resemblance above-mentioned, that we fall into it before we are aware; and though we incessantly correct ourselves by reflection, and return to a more accurate method of thinking, yet we cannot long sustain our philosophy, or take off this bias from the imagination. Our last resource is to yield to it, and boldly assert that these different related objects are in effect the same, however interrupted and variable. In order to justify to ourselves this absurdity, we often feign some new and unintelligible principle, that connects the objects together, and prevents their interruption or variation. Thus we feign the continued existence of the perceptions of our senses, to remove the interruption; and run into the notion of a *soul,* and *self,* and *substance,* to disguise the variation. But we may farther observe, that where we do not give rise to such a fiction, our propension to confound identity with relation is so great, that we are apt to imagine something unknown and mysterious, connecting the parts, beside their relation; and this I take to be the case with regard to the identity we ascribe to plants and vegetables. And even when this does not take place, we still feel a propensity to confound these ideas, though we are not able fully to satisfy ourselves in that particular, nor find any thing invariable and uninterrupted to justify our notion of identity.

Thus the controversy concerning identity is not merely a dispute of words. For when we attribute identity, in an improper sense, to variable or interrupted objects, our mistake is not confined to the expression, but is commonly attended with a fiction, either of something invariable and uninterrupted, or of something mysterious and inexplicable, or at least with a propensity to such fictions. What will suffice to prove this hypothesis to the satisfaction of every fair inquirer, is to shew from daily experience and observation, that the objects, which are variable or interrupted, and yet are supposed to continue the same, are such only as consist of a succession of parts, connected together by resemblance, contiguity, or causation. For as such a succession answers evidently to our notion of diversity, it can only be by mistake we ascribe to it an identity; and as the relation of parts, which leads us into this mistake, is really nothing but a quality, which produces an association of ideas, and an easy transition of the imagination from one to another, it can only be from the resemblance, which this act of the mind bears to that, by which we contemplate one continued object, that the error arises. Our chief business, then, must be to prove, that all objects, to which we ascribe identity, without observing their invariableness and uninterruptedness, are such as consist of a succession of related objects.

In order to this, suppose any mass of matter, of which the parts are contiguous and connected, to be placed before us; 'tis plain we must at-

tribute a perfect identity to this mass, provided all the parts continue unin-
terruptedly and invariably the same, whatever motion or change of place
we may observe either in the whole or in any of the parts. But supposing
some very *small* or *inconsiderable* part to be added to the mass, or subtracted from it; though this absolutely destroys the identity of the whole,
strictly speaking; yet as we seldom think so accurately, we scruple not to
pronounce a mass of matter the same, where we find so trivial an alteration. The passage of the thought from the object before the change to the
object after it, is so smooth and easy, that we scarce perceive the transition, and are apt to imagine, that 'tis nothing but a continued survey of
the same object.

There is a very remarkable circumstance that attends this experiment;
which is, that though the change of any considerable part in a mass of
matter destroys the identity of the whole, yet we must measure the greatness of the part, not absolutely, but by its *proportion* to the whole. The
addition or diminution of a mountain would not be sufficient to produce a
diversity in a planet; though the change of a very few inches would be able
to destroy the identity of some bodies. 'Twill be impossible to account for
this, but by reflecting that objects operate upon the mind, and break or
interrupt the continuity of its actions not according to their real greatness,
but according to their proportion to each other: and therefore, since this
interruption makes an object cease to appear the same, it must be the uninterrupted progress of the thought, which constitutes the imperfect identity.

This may be confirmed by another phænomenon. A change in any considerable part of a body destroys its identity; but 'tis remarkable, that
where the change is produced *gradually* and *insensibly* we are less apt to
ascribe to it the same effect. The reason can plainly be no other, than that
the mind, in following the successive changes of the body, feels an easy
passage from the surveying its condition in one moment to the viewing of
it in another, and at no particular time perceives any interruption in its
actions. From which continued perception, it ascribes a continued existence
and identity to the object.

But whatever precaution we may use in introducing the changes gradually, and making them proportionable to the whole, 'tis certain, that where
the changes are at last observed to become considerable, we make a scruple
of ascribing identity to such different objects. There is however another
artifice, by which we may induce the imagination to advance a step farther; and that is, by producing a reference of the parts to each other, and
a combination to some *common end* or purpose. A ship, of which a considerable part has been changed by frequent reparations, is still considered
as the same; nor does the difference of the materials hinder us from ascribing an identity to it. The common end, in which the parts conspire, is the
same under all their variations, and affords an easy transition of the imagination from one situation of the body to another.

But this is still more remarkable, when we add a *sympathy* of parts to
their *common end,* and suppose that they bear to each other the reciprocal

relation of cause and effect in all their actions and operations. This is the case with all animals and vegetables; where not only the several parts have a reference to some general purpose, but also a mutual dependance on, and connexion with each other. The effect of so strong a relation is, that though every one must allow, that in a very few years both vegetables and animals endure a *total* change, yet we still attribute identity to them, while their form, size, and substance are entirely altered. An oak, that grows from a small plant to a large tree, is still the same oak; though there be not one particle of matter, or figure of its parts the same. An infant becomes a man, and is sometimes fat, sometimes lean, without any change in his identity.

We may also consider the two following phænomena, which are remarkable in their kind. The first is, that though we commonly be able to distinguish pretty exactly betwixt numerical and specific identity, yet it sometimes happens, that we confound them, and in our thinking and reasoning employ the one for the other. Thus a man who hears a noise, that is frequently interrupted and renewed, says, it is still the same noise; though 'tis evident the sounds have only a specific identity or resemblance, and there is nothing numerically the same, but the cause, which produced them. In like manner it may be said without breach of the propriety of language, that such a church, which was formerly of brick, fell to ruin, and that the parish rebuilt the same church of free-stone, and according to modern architecture. Here neither the form nor materials are the same, nor is there any thing common to the two objects, but their relation to the inhabitants of the parish; and yet this alone is sufficient to make us denominate them the same. But we must observe, that in these cases the first object is in a manner annihilated before the second comes into existence; by which means, we are never presented in any one point of time with the idea of difference and multiplicity; and for that reason are less scrupulous in calling them the same.

Secondly, we may remark, that though in a succession of related objects, it be in a manner requisite, that the change of parts be not sudden nor entire, in order to preserve the identity, yet where the objects are in their nature changeable and inconstant, we admit of a more sudden transition, than would otherwise be consistent with that relation. Thus as the nature of a river consists in the motion and change of parts; though in less than four and twenty hours these be totally altered; this hinders not the river from continuing the same during several ages. What is natural and essential to any thing is, in a manner, expected; and what is expected makes less impression, and appears of less moment, than what is unusual and extraordinary. A considerable change of the former kind seems really less to the imagination, than the most trivial alteration of the latter; and by breaking less the continuity of the thought, has less influence in destroying the identity.

We now proceed to explain the nature of *personal identity,* which has become so great a question in philosophy, especially of late years in England, where all the abstruser sciences are studied with a peculiar ardour and application. And here 'tis evident, the same method of reasoning must be continued, which has so successfully explained the identity of plants, and animals, and ships, and houses, and of all the compounded and changeable productions either of art or nature. The identity which we ascribe to the mind of man, is only a fictitious one, and of a like kind with that which we ascribe to vegetables and animal bodies. It cannot therefore have a different origin, but must proceed from a like operation of the imagination upon like objects.

But lest this argument should not convince the reader; though in my opinion perfectly decisive; let him weigh the following reasoning, which is still closer and more immediate. 'Tis evident, that the identity, which we attribute to the human mind, however perfect we may imagine it to be, is not able to run the several different perceptions into one, and make them lose their characters of distinction and difference, which are essential to them. 'Tis still true, that every distinct perception, which enters into the composition of the mind, is a distinct existence, and is different, and distinguishable, and separable from every other perception, either contemporary or successive. But as, notwithstanding this distinction and separability, we suppose the whole train of perceptions to be united by identity, a question naturally arises concerning this relation of identity; whether it be something that really binds our several perceptions together, or only associates their ideas in the imagination. That is, in other words, whether in pronouncing concerning the identity of a person, we observe some real bond among his perceptions, or only feel one among the ideas we form of them. This question we might easily decide, if we would recollect what has been already proved at large, that the understanding never observes any real connexion among objects, and that even the union of cause and effect, when strictly examined, resolves itself into a customary association of ideas. For from thence it evidently follows, that identity is nothing really belonging to these different perceptions, and uniting them together; but is merely a quality, which we attribute to them, because of the union of their ideas in the imagination, when we reflect upon them. Now the only qualities, which can give ideas an union in the imagination, are these three relations above-mentioned. These are the uniting principles in the ideal world, and without them every distinct object is separable by the mind, and may be separately considered, and appears not to have any more connexion with any other object, than if disjoined by the greatest difference and remoteness. 'Tis therefore on some of these three relations of resemblance, contiguity, and causation, that identity depends; and as the very essence of these relations consists in their producing an easy transition of ideas; it follows, that our notions of personal identity proceed entirely from the smooth and uninterrupted progress of the thought along a train of connected ideas, according to the principles above-explained.

The only question, therefore, which remains is, by what relations this uninterrupted progress of our thought is produced, when we consider the successive existence of a mind or thinking person. And here 'tis evident we must confine ourselves to resemblance and causation, and must drop contiguity, which has little or no influence in the present case.

To begin with *resemblance;* suppose we could see clearly into the breast of another, and observe that succession of perceptions, which constitutes his mind or thinking principle, and suppose that he always preserves the memory of a considerable part of past perceptions; 'tis evident that nothing could more contribute to the bestowing a relation on this succession amidst all its variations. For what is the memory but a faculty, by which we raise up the images of past perceptions? And as an image necessarily resembles its object, must not the frequent placing of these resembling perceptions in the chain of thought, convey the imagination more easily from one link to another, and make the whole seem like the continuance of one object? In this particular, then, the memory not only discovers the identity, but also contributes to its production, by producing the relation of resemblance among the perceptions. The case is the same whether we consider ourselves or others.

As to *causation;* we may observe, that the true idea of the human mind, is to consider it as a system of different perceptions or different existences, which are linked together by the relation of cause and effect, and mutually produce, destroy, influence, and modify each other. Our impressions give rise to their correspondent ideas; and these ideas in their turn produce other impressions. One thought chases another, and draws after it a third, by which it is expelled in its turn. In this respect, I cannot compare the soul more properly to any thing than to a republic or commonwealth, in which the several members are united by the reciprocal ties of government and subordination, and give rise to other persons who propagate the same republic in the incessant changes of its parts. And as the same individual republic may not only change its members, but also its laws and constitutions; in like manner the same person may vary his character and disposition, as well as his impressions and ideas, without losing his identity. Whatever changes he endures, his several parts are still connected by the relation of causation. And this view our identity with regard to the passions serves to corroborate that with regard to the imagination, by the making our distant perceptions influence each other, and by giving us a present concern for our past or future pains or pleasures.

As memory alone acquaints us with the continuance and extent of this succession of perceptions, 'tis to be considered, upon that account chiefly, as the source of personal identity. Had we no memory, we never should have any notion of causation, nor consequently of that chain of causes and effects, which constitute our self or person. But having once acquired this notion of causation from the memory, we can extend the same chain of causes, and consequently the identity of our persons beyond our memory, and can comprehend times, and circumstances, and actions, which we have entirely forgot, but suppose in general to have existed. For how few of our past actions are there, of which we have any memory? Who can tell me, for instance, what were his thoughts and actions on the first of January, 1715, the eleventh of March, 1719, and the third of August, 1733? Or will he affirm, because he has entirely forgot the incidents of these days, that the present self is not the same person with the self of that time; and by that means overturn all the most established notions of personal identity? In this view therefore memory does not so much *produce* as *discover* personal identity, by shewing us the relation of cause and effect among our different perceptions. 'Twill be incumbent on those who affirm that memory produces entirely our personal identity, to give a reason why we can thus extend our identity beyond our memory.

The whole of this doctrine leads us to a conclusion, which is of great importance in the present affair, viz. that all the nice and subtile questions concerning personal identity can never possibly be decided, and are to be regarded rather as grammatical than as philosophical difficulties. Identity depends on the relations of ideas; and these relations produce identity, by means of that easy transition they occasion. But as the relations, and the easiness of the transition may diminish by insensible degrees, we have no just standard by which we can decide any dispute concerning the time, when they acquire or lose a title to the name of identity. All the disputes concerning the identity of connected objects are merely verbal, except so far as the relation of parts gives rise to some fiction or imaginary principle of union, as we have already observed.

What I have said concerning the first origin and uncertainty of our notion of identity, as applied to the human mind, may be extended with little or no variation to that of *simplicity*. An object, whose different co-existent parts are bound together by a close relation, operates upon the imagination after much the same manner as one perfectly simple and indivisible, and requires not a much greater stretch of thought in order to its conception. From this similarity of operation we attribute a simplicity to it, and feign a principle of union as the support of this simplicity, and the centre of all the different parts and qualities of the object.

ERIK ERIKSON

(1902-   )

Erik Erikson was trained in psychoanalysis at Vienna, close to the influence of Freud's genius. Since then he has practiced psychoanalysis, taught at Harvard, and written several books including **Childhood and Society** (1950), **Young Man Luther** (1958), and **Gandhi's Truth** (1969). Followed by younger men like Robert Jay Lifton and Kenneth Keniston, Erikson has pioneered the application of psychological insights to biography, history, and social change. In the following selection

from the Prologue to his **Identity, Youth and Crisis,** Erikson examines the history of the term 'identity-crisis,' a phrase he first
used some twenty-five years ago. His self-conscious application of
historical perspective to his own achievements, and their influence on others and, finally, on himself makes Erikson a model of
the phenomenon he is discussing: the changing patterns not only
of one's own identity, but of the very nature of the identity problem itself.

Certainly Erikson's formulation of the problem of self-identity is
different from Hume's, but the two are not necessarily opposed.
Rather, Erikson's formulation can be regarded as a set of directions for the concrete application of Hume's relatively abstract insights. Hume and Ryle argue that the identity of the self is not
established by some inner, substantial, unalterable core. Relations of contiguity, resemblance, and causation constitute one's
feelings of continuity. But what criteria are we to use for resemblance? As Hume noted in closing, simplicity is a relative concept
requiring choices in its application. Similarly, resemblance is a
relative concept requiring the application of specific criteria of
resemblance. For example, if you are presented with a green
square, a green circle, and a blue circle and then asked which two
resemble one another most, you would have to choose whether
you regarded sameness of shape or color as the more important
criterion of resemblance. This example is very simple. We can
clearly see the difference between the typologies of color and
shape, and we know how to use both. But now substitute the typologies of individual selfhood implicit in the two essays by Slater
and Wolfe. For Slater's engaged and dependent self in the community the important criteria for resemblance derive from the
values and norms of his social group. His very experience of self-
continuity depends to a large extent on those values. The individual can feel himself growing continuously from childhood to adulthood if his experiences resemble each other, cause each other,
and remain contiguous with each other according to a socially
defined pattern on which the individual is willing to depend. For
Wolfe's individual in his technological fortress, however, a different source of criteria for resemblance must be either found or
created.

By relating issues of individual identity to the historically changing patterns of social organization, Erikson brings together the issues of this and the preceding section. As Erikson makes perfectly
clear, the metaphysics of self-identity must be made concrete and
specific in terms of one's own historical time. Furthermore, his
argument points ahead to the rest of this volume: since it is true
that the quest for self-identity requires, as Erikson calls it, an ever
renewed "consolidation" of self and world, the wider circles of self-

awareness reflect back into the constitution of self-identity. As he says of the process of realizing self-identity, "the process described is always changing and developing: at its best it is a process of increasing differentiation, and it becomes ever more inclusive as the individual grows aware of a widening circle of others significant to him, from the maternal person to 'mankind'."

Identity, Youth and Crisis

To review the concept of identity means to sketch its history. In the twenty years since the term was first employed in the particular sense to be discussed in this book, its popular usage has become so varied and its conceptual context so expanded that the time may seem to have come for a better and final delimitation of what identity is and what it is not. And yet, by its very nature, what bears such a definitive name remains subject to changing historical connotations.

"Identity" and "identity crisis" have in popular and scientific usage become terms which alternately circumscribe something so large and so seemingly self-evident that to demand a definition would almost seem petty, while at other times they designate something made so narrow for purposes of measurement that the over-all meaning is lost, and it could just as well be called something else. If, to give examples of the wider use of the term, the papers run a headline "The Identity Crisis of Africa" or refer to the "identity crisis" of the Pittsburgh glass industry; if the outgoing president of the American Psychoanalytic Association titles his farewell address "The Identity Crisis of Psychoanalysis"; or if, finally, the Catholic students at Harvard announce that they will hold an "Identity Crisis" on Thursday night at eight o'clock sharp, then the dignity of the term seems to vary greatly. The quotation marks are as important as the term they bracket: everybody has heard of "identity crisis" and it arouses a mixture of curiosity, mirth, and discomfort which yet promises, by the very play on the word "crisis," not to turn out to be something quite as fatal as it sounds. In other words, a suggestive term has begun to lend itself to ritualized usage.

Social scientists, on the other hand, sometimes attempt to achieve greater specificity by making such terms as "identity crisis," "self-identity," or "sexual identity" fit whatever more measurable item they are investigating at a given time. For the sake of logical or experimental maneuverability (and in order to keep in good academic company) they try to treat these terms as matters of social roles, personal traits, or conscious self-images,

IDENTITY, YOUTH AND CRISIS   Reprinted from *Identity, Youth and Crisis* by Erik H. Erikson. By permission of W. W. Norton & Company, Inc. Copyright © 1968 by W. W. Norton & Company, Inc.

shunning the less manageable and more sinister—which often also means the more vital—implications of the concept. Such usages have, in fact, become so indiscriminate that the other day a German reviewer of the book in which I first used the term in the context of psychoanalytic ego theory called it the pet subject of the *amerikanische Populaerpsychologie.*

But one may note with satisfaction that the conceptualization of identity has led to a series of valid investigations which, if they do not make clearer what identity is, nevertheless have proved useful in social psychology. And it may be a good thing that the word "crisis" no longer connotes impending catastrophe, which at one time seemed to be an obstacle to the understanding of the term. It is now being accepted as designating a necessary turning point, a crucial moment, when development must move one way or another, marshaling resources of growth, recovery, and further differentiation. This proves applicable to many situations: a crisis in individual development or in the emergence of a new elite, in the therapy of an individual or in the tensions of rapid historical change.

The term "identity crisis" was first used, if I remember correctly, for a specific clinical purpose in the Mt. Zion Veterans' Rehabilitation Clinic during the Second World War, a national emergency which permitted psychiatric workers of different persuasions and denominations, among them Emanuel Windholz and Joseph Wheelwright, to work together harmoniously. Most of our patients, so we concluded at that time, had neither been "shellshocked" nor become malingerers, but had through the exigencies of war lost a sense of personal sameness and historical continuity. They were impaired in that central control over themselves for which, in the psychoanalytic scheme, only the "inner agency" of the ego could be held responsible. Therefore, I spoke of a loss of "ego identity."[1] Since then, we have recognized the same central disturbance in severely conflicted young people whose sense of confusion is due, rather, to a war within themselves, and in confused rebels and destructive delinquents who war on their society. In all these cases, then, the term "identity confusion" has a certain diagnostic significance which should influence the evaluation and treatment of such disturbances. Young patients can be violent or depressed, delinquent or withdrawn, but theirs is an acute and possibly passing crisis rather than a breakdown of the kind which tends to commit a patient to all the malignant implications of a fatalistic diagnosis. And as has always been the case in the history of psychoanalytic psychiatry, what was first recognized as the common dynamic pattern of a group of severe disturbances (such as the hysterias of the turn of the century) revealed itself later to be a pathological aggravation, an undue prolongation of, or a regression to, a normative crisis "belonging" to a particular stage of individual development. Thus, we have learned to ascribe a normative "identity crisis" to the age of adolescence and young adulthood.

---

[1] Erik H. Erikson, "A Combat Crisis in a Marine," *Childhood and Society,* Second Edition, New York: W. W. Norton, 1963, pp. 38–47.

Referring to the first use of the term "identity crisis," I said "if I remember correctly." Perhaps one should be able to remember such things. But the fact is that a term which later becomes so distinctive is often first used as something one takes, and thinks others take, for granted. This brings to mind one of the innumerable stories with which Norman Reider could be counted on to lighten those often weary war days. An old man, he recounted, used to vomit every morning, but he showed no inclination to consult a doctor about it. His family finally prevailed on him to go to Mt. Zion for a general checkup. When Dr. Reider approached him cautiously, "How are you?" he was told promptly, "I'm fine. Couldn't be better." And, indeed, on further examination the constituent parts of the old man seemed to be in as good shape as could be expected. Finally, Dr. Reider became a bit impatient. "But I hear you vomit every morning?" The old man looked mildly surprised and said, "Sure. Doesn't everybody?"

In telling this story, I am not implying that "identity crisis" is a symptom of mine that I simply assumed everybody else had also—although there is, of course, something to that too. But I did assume that I had given the most obvious name to something that everybody had had at one time and would, therefore, recognize in those who were having it acutely.

Judged by the clinical origin of these terms, then, it would seem reasonable enough to link the *pathological* and the *developmental aspects* of the matter and to see what might differentiate the identity crisis typical for a case history from that of a life history. This emphasis on individual lives, however, would make the other and wider uses of the terms "identity" and "identity crisis" appear all the more suspect as mere analogies not admissable in any court of definition. That Catholic students would try to pool their individual crises, enjoy them together, and get them over with in one evening makes at least humorous sense. But what possible connection could adolescence as such have with the state of an African nation or of a scientific body? *Is* this a mere analogistic usage such as is employed, with a mixture of boastfulness and apology, when a nation is said to be in its historical and economic "adolescence," or to have developed a "paranoid political style"? And if a nation cannot be said to be "adolescent," can a type of individual identity crisis be shared by a significant section of the young population? And further, to return to the faddish use of the term "identity confusion," would some of our youth act so openly confused and confusing if they did not *know* they were *supposed* to have an identity crisis?

The history of the last twenty years seems to indicate that there are clinical terms which are taken over not only by diagnosticians, but also by those who have been overdiagnosed, and, in this case, by a section of a whole age group who echo our very terms and flamboyantly display a conflict which we once regarded as silent, inner, and unconscious.

[. . .] Today when the term identity refers, more often than not, to something noisily demonstrative, to a more or less desperate "quest," or to an almost deliberately confused "search" let me present two formulations which assert strongly what identity feels like when you become aware of the fact that you do undoubtedly *have* one.

My two witnesses are bearded and patriarchal founding fathers of the psychologies on which our thinking on identity is based. As a *subjective sense* of an *invigorating sameness* and *continuity,* what I would call a sense of identity seems to me best described by William James in a letter to his wife:[2]

> A man's character is discernible in the mental or moral attitude in which, when it came upon him, he felt himself most deeply and intensely active and alive. At such moments there is a voice inside which speaks and says: *"This* is the real me!"

Such experience always includes

> . . . an element of active tension, of holding my own, as it were, and trusting outward things to perform their part so as to make it a full harmony, but without any *guaranty* that they will. Make it a guaranty . . . and the attitude immediately becomes to my consciousness stagnant and stingless. Take away the guaranty, and I feel (provided I am *ueberhaupt* [totally or generally] in vigorous condition) a sort of deep enthusiastic bliss, of bitter willingness to do and suffer anything . . . and which, although it is a mere mood or emotion to which I can give no form in words, authenticates itself to me as the deepest principle of all active and theoretic determination which I possess . . .

James uses the word "character," but I am taking the liberty of claiming that he describes a sense of identity, and that he does so in a way which can in principle be experienced by any man. To him it is both mental and moral in the sense of those "moral philosophy" days, and he experiences it as something that "comes upon you" as a recognition, almost as a surprise rather than as something strenuously "quested" after. It is an active tension (rather than a paralyzing question)—a tension which, furthermore, must create a challenge "without guaranty" rather than one dissipated in a clamor for certainty. But let us remember in passing that James was in his thirties when he wrote this, that in his youth he had faced and articulated an "identity crisis" of honest and desperate depth, and that he became *the* Psychologist-Philosopher of American Pragmatism only after having experimented with a variety of cultural, philosophic, and national identity elements: the use in the middle of his declaration of the untranslatable German word *"ueberhaupt"* is probably an echo of his conflictful student days in Europe.

One can study in James's life history a protracted identity crisis as well

---

[2] *The Letters of William James,* edited by Henry James (his son), Vol. I, Boston: The Atlantic Monthly Press, 1920, p. 199.

as the emergence of a "self-made" identity in the new and expansive American civilization. We will repeatedly come back to James, but for the sake of further definition, let us now turn to a statement which asserts a unity of *personal and cultural* identity rooted in an ancient people's fate. In an address to the Society of B'nai B'rith in Vienna in 1926,[3] Sigmund Freud said:

> What bound me to Jewry was (I am ashamed to admit) neither faith nor national pride, for I have always been an unbeliever and was brought up without any religion though not without a respect for what are called the "ethical" standards of human civilization. Whenever I felt an inclination to national enthusiasm I strove to suppress it as being harmful and wrong, alarmed by the warning examples of the peoples among whom we Jews live. But plenty of other things remained over to make the attraction of Jewry and Jews irresistible—many obscure emotional forces, which were the more powerful the less they could be expressed in words, as well as a clear consciousness of inner identity, the safe privacy of a common mental construction. And beyond this there was a perception that it was to my Jewish nature alone that I owed two characteristics that had become indispensable to me in the difficult course of my life. Because I was a Jew I found myself free from many prejudices which restricted others in the use of their intellect; and as a Jew I was prepared to join the Opposition, and to do without agreement with the "compact majority."

No translation ever does justice to the distinctive choice of words in Freud's German original. "Obscure emotional forces" are *"dunkle Gefuehlsmaechte";* the "safe privacy of a common mental construction" is *"die Heimlichkeit der inneren Konstruktion"*—not just "mental," then, and certainly not "private," but a deep communality known only to those who shared in it, and only expressible in words more mythical than conceptual.

These fundamental statements were taken not from theoretical works, but from special communications: a letter to his wife from a man who married late, an address to his "brothers" by an original observer long isolated in his profession. But in all their poetic spontaneity they are the products of trained minds and therefore exemplify the main dimensions of a positive sense of identity almost systematically. Trained minds of genius, of course, have a special identity and special identity problems often leading to a protracted crisis at the onset of their careers. Yet we must rely on them for formulating initially what we can then proceed to observe as universally human.

This is the only time Freud used the term identity in a more than casual way and, in fact, in a most central ethnic sense. And as we would expect of him, he inescapably points to some of those aspects of the matter which I called sinister and yet vital—the more vital, in fact, "the less they could be

[3] Sigmund Freud, "Address to the Society of B'nai B'rith" [1926], *Standard Edition,* 20:273, London: Hogarth Press, 1959.

expressed in words." For Freud's "consciousness of inner identity" includes a sense of bitter pride preserved by his dispersed and often despised people throughout a long history of persecution. It is anchored in a particular (here intellectual) gift which had victoriously emerged from the hostile limitation of opportunities. At the same time, Freud contrasts the *positive identity* of a fearless freedom of thinking with a *negative* trait in "the peoples among whom we Jews live," namely, "prejudices which restrict others in the use of their intellect." It dawns on us, then, that one person's or group's identity may be relative to another's, and that the pride of gaining a strong identity may signify an inner emancipation from a more dominant group identity, such as that of the "compact majority." An exquisite triumph is suggested in the claim that the same historical development which restricted the prejudiced majority in the free use of their intellect made the isolated minority sturdier in intellectual matters. To all this, we must come back when discussing race relations.

And Freud goes farther. He admits in passing that he had to suppress in himself an inclination toward "national enthusiasm" such as was common for "the peoples among whom we Jews live." Again, as in James's case, only a study of Freud's youthful enthusiasms could show how he came to leave behind other aspirations in favor of the ideology of applying the methods of natural science to the study of psychological "forces of dignity." It is in Freud's dreams, incidentally, that we have a superb record of his suppressed (or what James called "abandoned," or even "murdered") selves—for our "negative identity" haunts us at night.

The two statements and the lives behind them serve to establish a few dimensions of identity and, at the same time, help to explain why the problem is so all-pervasive and yet so hard to grasp: for we deal with a process "located" *in the core of the individual* and yet also *in the core of his communal culture,* a process which establishes, in fact, the identity of those two identities. If we should now pause and state a few minimum requirements for fathoming the complexity of identity we should have to begin by saying something like this (and let us take our time in saying it): in psychological terms, identity formation employs a process of simultaneous reflection and observation, a process taking place on all levels of mental functioning, by which the individual judges himself in the light of what he perceives to be the way in which others judge him in comparison to themselves and to a typology significant to them; while he judges their way of judging him in the light of how he perceives himself in comparison to them and to types that have become relevant to him. This process is, luckily, and necessarily, for the most part unconscious except where inner conditions and outer circumstances combine to aggravate a painful, or elated, "identity-consciousness."

Furthermore, the process described is always changing and developing: at its best it is a process of increasing differentiation, and it becomes ever more inclusive as the individual grows aware of a widening circle of others significant to him, from the maternal person to "mankind." The process "begins" somewhere in the first true "meeting" of mother and baby as two persons who can touch and recognize each other,[4] and it does not "end" until a man's power of mutual affirmation wanes. As pointed out, however, the process has its normative crisis in adolescence, and is in many ways determined by what went before and determines much that follows. And finally, in discussing identity, as we now see, we cannot separate personal growth and communal change, nor can we separate (as I tried to demonstrate in *Young Man Luther*) the identity crisis in individual life and contemporary crises in historical development because the two help to define each other and are truly relative to each other. In fact, the whole interplay between the psychological and the social, the developmental and the historical, for which identity formation is of prototypal significance, could be conceptualized only as a kind of *psychosocial relativity*. A weighty matter then: certainly mere "roles" played interchangeably, mere self-conscious "appearances," or mere strenuous "postures" cannot possibly be the real thing, although they may be dominant aspects of what today is called the "search for identity." [. . .]

It must be confessed that at least those of us who are occupied with making sense of case histories or of biographies (which so often superficially resemble case histories) and who are teaching either young psychiatrists or the humanistically privileged college youth, are often out of touch with the resources of identity available to that majority of youths whose ideology is a product of the machine age. That youth, on the whole, does not need us, and those who do assume the "patient role" created by us. Nor do we seem to think that our theories need to include them. And yet we must assume that masses of young people both here and abroad are close enough both by giftedness and by opportunity to the technological trends and the scientific methods of our time to feel at home in it as much as anybody ever felt at home in human life. I, for one, have never been able to accept the claim that in mercantile culture or in agricultural culture, or, indeed, in book culture, man was in principle less "alienated" than he is in technology. It is, I believe, our own retrospective romanticism which makes us think that peasants or merchants or hunters were less determined by their techniques. To put it in terms of what must be studied concertedly: in every technology and in every historical period there are types of individuals who ("properly" brought up) can combine the dominant techniques with their identity development, and *become* what they *do*. Independently of minor superiorities or inferiorities, they can settle on the *cultural consolidation* which secures them what joint verification and what transitory salvation lies in doing things together and in doing them right—a rightness proven by the bountiful response of "nature," whether in the form of the prey bagged, the food harvested, the goods produced, the money made, or the technological

---

[4] Joan M. Erikson, "Eye to Eye," *The Man Made Object*, Gyorgy Kepes (ed.), New York: Braziller, 1966.

problems solved. In such consolidation and accommodation a million daily tasks and transactions fall into practical patterns and spontaneous ritualizations which can be shared by leaders and led, men and women, adults and children, the privileged and the underprivileged, the specially gifted and those willing to do the chores. The point is that only such consolidation offers the coordinates for the range of a period's identity formations and their necessary relation to a sense of inspired activity, although for many or most it does so only by also creating compartments of pronounced narrowness, of enforced service, and of limited status. Each such consolidation, by dint of its very practicality (the fact that "it works" and maintains itself by mere usage and habituation), also works for entrenched privileges, enforced sacrifices, institutionalized inequalities, and built-in contradictions, which become obvious to the critics of any society. But how such consolidation leads to a sense of embeddedness and natural flux among the very artifacts of organization: how it helps to bring to ascendance some style of perfection and of self-glorification; and how it permits man at the same time to limit his horizon so as *not* to see what might destroy the newly won familiarity of the world and expose him to all manner of strangeness and, above all, to the fear of death or of killing—all of this we have hardly approached from the point of view of depth psychology. Here the discussion of the "ego" should take on new dimensions.

The history of cultures, civilizations, and technologies is the history of such consolidations, while it is only in periods of marked transition that the innovators appear: those too privileged in outlook to remain bound to the prevailing system; too honest or too conflicted not to see the simple truths of existence hidden behind the complexity of daily "necessities"; and too full of pity to overlook "the poor" who have been left out. As therapists and ideologists, we understand the uppermost and the lowest fringe better, because of our own therapeutic ideology. Thus we often take for granted the vast middle which, for reasons of its own, maintains us. Yet insofar as we aspire to contribute to "normal psychology" we must learn to understand cultural and technological consolidation, for it, ever again, inherits the earth.

And always with it comes a new definition of adulthood, without which any question of identity is self-indulgent luxury. The problem of adulthood is how to *take care* of those to whom one finds oneself committed as one emerges from the identity period, and to whom one now owes *their* identity.

Another question is what the "typical" adult of any era's consolidation is able and willing to renounce for himself and demand of others, for the sake of a style of cultural balance and, perhaps, perfection. Judging from the way Socrates, the philosopher, in his Apologia, exposed the fabric of Athenian consolidation, it was probably not only for himself that, at the very end, he pronounced death to be the only cure for the condition of living. Freud, the doctor, revealed for the mercantile and early industrial period what havoc the hypocritical morality was wreaking, not only in his era, but in all of human history. In doing so, he founded what Philipp Rieff has described as the *therapeutic orientation,* which goes far beyond the clinical cure of isolated symptoms. But we cannot know what technological conformity does *to* man unless we know what it does *for* him. The ubiquitous increase in mere number, of course, at first transforms many erstwhile problems of quality into matters of mere quantitative management.

If the majority of young people, therefore, can go along with their parents in a kind of fraternal identification, it is because they jointly leave it to technology and science to carry the burden of providing a self-perpetuating and self-accelerating way of life. This would make it plausible that the young are even expected to develop new values-as-you-go. But the fact is that the values associated with indefinite progress, just because it strains orientation as well as imagination, are often tied to unbelievably old-fashioned ideas. Thus technological expansion can be seen as the due reward of generations of hard-working Americans. No need is felt to limit expansionist ideals, as long as—together with technical discipline—old-fashioned decencies and existing political machineries survive, with all their hometown oratory. There is always hope (a hope which has become an important part of an implicit American ideology) that in regard to any possible built-in evil in the very nature of supermachines, appropriate brakes and corrections will be invented in the nick of time, without any undue investment of strenuously new principles. And while they "work," the super-machineries, organizations, and associations provide a sufficiently "great," or at any rate adjustable, identity for all those who feel actively engaged in and by them.

Thus, also, that major part of youth which sees no reason to oppose the war in Vietnam is animated by a combination of a world-war patriotism, anticommunism, obedience to the draft and to military discipline, and finally by that unshakable solidarity, the highest feeling among men, which comes from having renounced the same pleasures, facing the same dangers, and having to obey the same obnoxious orders. But there is a new element in all this which comes from the technological ideology and makes a soldier an expert whose armament is mechanized and whose fidelity is an almost impersonal technical compliance with a policy or strategy which puts a certain *target* into the range of one of the admirable weapons at hand. No doubt certain "character structures" fit such a world view better than others, and yet, on the whole, each generation is prepared to participate in a number of consolidated attitudes in one lifetime.

But until a new ethics catches up with progress, one senses the danger that the limits of technological expansion and national assertion may not be determined by known facts and ethical considerations or, in short, by a certainty of identity, but by a willful and playful testing of the range and the limit of the supermachinery which thus takes over much of man's conscience. This could become affluent slavery for all involved, and this seems to be what the new "humanist" youth is trying to stop by putting its own existence "on the line" and insisting on a modicum of a self-sustaining quality of living.

3 **Consciousness and Knowledge**

Introduction:
The Determinants
of Consciousness

To be a self is to be conscious of oneself. Without self-consciousness there is no self, for consciousness is the glue that binds experiences together into the unity of a self. But what is consciousness? How does consciousness establish the continuity of selfhood?

We begin by asking about consciousness as if it were equivalent to knowledge: How do we know? Plato's answer is innocent of Cartesian doubt. He believed that different kinds of objects elicit different kinds of knowledge. The object is the main determinant of consciousness. Kant's answer reflects the influence of Descartes' Subjective Turn; for Kant the subjective apparatus of cognition plays a major role in determining consciousness. Both Plato and Kant share the tendency to view consciousness as knowledge, as an intellectual function of cognition. In his essay, William James suggests several ways that the traditional view of consciousness has been overintellectualized. There are modes of consciousness quite different from rational thought and cognition, and a fuller investigation of the determinants of consciousness must go beyond the question of the subjective and objective sources of knowledge.

The essays by Nietzsche, Brown, and Epicurus develop the concept of the body as a determinant of consciousness. Though the body is hardly like the logical categories that Kant sees as subjectively determining our knowledge, Kant's analysis of subjective determinants of knowledge facilitates an understanding of the body's role as a subjective determinant of consciousness in general. Similarly, Plato's analysis of the objective determinants of knowledge anticipates the way our relationships with other people determine our consciousness. Mead, Polanyi, and Goffman develop a theory of interpersonal perception that includes not only subjective and objective determinants but also noncognitive, bodily determinants as well as the cognitive dimensions of conscious-ness explored by Plato and Kant. Where Kant and Plato stress the roles of self and other, respectively, in determining purely **cognitive** con-sciousness or knowledge, the essays on incarnate consciousness and interpersonal perception stress the roles of self and others, respec-tively, in determining the **noncognitive** aspects of consciousness as well. Finally, Laing's essay incorporates both psychological and philo-sophical insights in an examination of how this enriched, subjective-objective-bodily-socially determined consciousness influences the con-sciousness of self. The progressive enrichment of consciousness leaves Laing with more problems than he can solve in the still-too-narrow con-text of the self in its intimate relations with its closest companions, and the contradictions developed in Laing's essay drive us on to consider the wider circle of social and political involvement as a further source for the enrichment of self-consciousness.

PLATO

(428-347 B.C.)

Plato's philosophy, written dur-ing the fourth century B.C. in Athens, is the first of the major western philosophies. The twentieth-century philosopher Alfred North Whitehead has even gone so far as to suggest that the en-tire history of western philosophy can be regarded as a series of footnotes to Plato. Plato had some important predecessors. The pre-Socratic philosophers Thales, Anaximander, Anaxagoras, Hera-clitus, and Parmenides each had profound influences on early Greek thought. The Sophists were a group of teachers who trained young Athenians in rhetoric and who also claimed expertise in other matters. And there was, of course, Socrates, who wrote nothing but was Plato's teacher and model in the way he demon-strated to the Sophists and others that they did not in fact know what they thought they knew. Socrates was a great talker, a bril-liant man whose wit and will to get to the bottom of things, to play the gadfly stinging the soft underbelly of some "proper" Athe-nians, eventually earned him a condemnation to death in 399 B.C. A public court of more than five hundred Athenians voted him guilty on charges of corrupting the youth, not believing in the public gods, and introducing divinities of his own making. The details of the charges are obscure, but clearly Socrates was a severe embarrassment to the Athenian Establishment. Aristophanes' play **The Clouds** draws a picture of what many of his countrymen thought of Socrates: a strange old man who talked about silly things, and in such a way that his young listeners lost respect for their fathers and opposed them in matters sacred and profane. Plato wrote his dialogues, many of which are understood to be fairly close accounts of conversations between Socrates and his fellow Athenians, partly to clear his teacher by showing his conviction to be unjust, and partly to continue his teacher's quest. The two aims go well together, for in pursuing the first he was showing the Athenians that they did not know what they thought they knew, which is what Socrates used to do.

Plato's dialogues are written substitutes for the living person of Socrates. Keeping this fact in mind facilitates a just reading of the dialogues. Otherwise one is liable to dismiss the dialogues as many dismissed Socrates: he angered them by his apparent simplicities, by his continual questioning, by his irony, by not coming out with the truths they always suspected he was holding up his sleeve, by putting what he knew in the form of myths or parables that obviously couldn't represent the literal truth. Similarly, Plato's dialogues taunt the reader, not merely by representing Socrates at work, but by the way the dialogues themselves work even when Socrates is not present. Often they end without explicitly answering the question they set out to answer. Plato purposely hides certain lines of inquiry beneath the literal or surface level of the dialogue, and the reader has to go back and dig for a deeper level of interpretation to find what lies hidden. Interestingly enough, in the dialogue called the **Symposium** Plato has Alcibiades describe Socrates as like the Silenus figures: statuettes that reveal one thing on the surface but can be opened up to disclose an inner beauty. Such are Plato's dialogues. And consequently they are sometimes frustrating, but purposely so. The reader has to supply his own resources. Reading a Platonic dialogue is not at all like watching television, but then neither was talking to Socrates. The pedagogy of the Platonic dialogue (or the Socratic conversation) is one that demands participation.

Despite the fact that Plato is represented by more selections than any other philosopher in this anthology, I must still apologize for not presenting more of his writings, particularly in the following selection and the later one on art. These two selections are excerpted from one of his longest and best known dialogues, the **Republic.** Although neither selection can really be interpreted in its full significance apart from surrounding passages, both are such classic passages in the history of philosophy that they reward study even in truncated form. One has to begin reading Plato somewhere, and these excerpts provide at least a good beginning.

The following passage comes from the end of Book Six and the beginning of Book Seven of the **Republic** (Jowett translation) and offers a picture (but only a picture) of Plato's ideas about knowledge. Four different kinds of knowing correspond to four different kinds of objects of knowledge. Each kind of object is known by the corresponding capacity for knowledge. The objects themselves are ranked in an order from appearance to reality. Finally, the idea of the Good, symbolized by the sun, renders possible both knowledge and its objects. It is worth thinking a long time about why this principle of supreme value is located on neither side of the divided line, neither merely subjective nor wholly objective. It is also worth thinking about what is involved in the scene down in the cave. (Plato's description of watching the shadows on the wall bears an uncanny resemblance to watching television.) And what does he mean by "when any of them is liberated and compelled suddenly to stand up and turn his neck round and walk towards the light, he will suffer sharp pains"? What does he mean by each detail of the tale? And how, precisely, does the ascent out of the cave parallel the course of the divided line?

The Divided Line and the Myth of the Cave

. . . Let us not at present ask what is the actual nature of the good, for to reach what is now in my thoughts would be an effort too great for me. But of the child of the good who is likest him, I am ready to speak, if I could be sure that you wished to hear —otherwise, not.

By all means, he said, tell us about the child, and you shall remain in our debt for the account of the parent.

[507] I do indeed wish, I replied, that I could pay, and you receive, the account of the parent, and not, as now, of the offspring only; take, however, this latter by way of interest,[1] and at the same time have a care that I do not pay you in spurious coin, although I have no intention of deceiving you.

THE DIVIDED LINE AND THE MYTH OF THE CAVE From Plato, *The Dialogues of Plato*, Fourth Edition, Volume II, *The Republic*, from Books VI and VII, translated by B. Jowett. Copyright © 1953. Reprinted by permission of The Clarendon Press, Oxford.

The numbers in brackets refer to the pages of the Stephanus edition of the Greek text of Plato's works. Scholarly editions in all languages bear these numbers, making it easy to go from one edition or translation to another.

[1] A play upon τόκος, which means both 'offspring' and 'interest.'

Yes, we will take all the care that we can: proceed.

Yes, I said, but I must first come to an understanding with you, and remind you of what I have mentioned in the course of this discussion, and at many other times.

What?

The old story, that there are many beautiful things and many good. And again there is a true beauty, a true good; and all other things to which the term *many* has been applied, are now brought under a single idea, and, assuming this unity, we speak of it in every case as *that which really is*.

Very true.

The many, as we say, are seen but not known, and the Ideas are known but not seen.

Exactly.

And what is the organ with which we see the visible things?

The sight, he said.

And with the hearing, I said, we hear, and with the other senses perceive the other objects of sense?

True.

But have you remarked that sight is by far the most costly and complex piece of workmanship which the artificer of the senses ever contrived?

Not exactly, he said.

Then reflect: have the ear and voice need of any third or additional nature in order that the one may be able to hear and the other to be heard?

Nothing of the sort.

No, indeed, I replied; and the same is true of most, if not all, the other senses—you would not say that any of them requires such an addition?

Certainly not.

But you see that without the addition of some other nature there is no seeing or being seen?

How do you mean?

Sight being, as I conceive, in the eyes, and he who has eyes wanting to see; colour being also present in the objects, still unless there be a third nature specially adapted to the purpose, sight, as you know, will see nothing and the colours will be invisible.

Of what nature are you speaking?

Of that which you term light, I replied.

True, he said.

[508] Then the bond which links together the sense of sight and the power of being seen, is of an evidently nobler nature than other such bonds —unless sight is an ignoble thing?

Nay, he said, the reverse of ignoble.

And which, I said, of the gods in heaven would you say was the lord of this element? Whose is that light which makes the eye to see perfectly and the visible to appear?

I should answer, as all men would, and as you plainly expect—the sun.

May not the relation of sight to this deity be described as follows?

How?

Neither sight nor the organ in which it resides, which we call the eye, is the sun?

No.

Yet of all the organs of sense the eye is the most like the sun?

By far the most like.

And the power which the eye possesses is a sort of effluence which is dispensed from the sun?

Exactly.

Then the sun is not sight, but the author of sight who is recognized by sight?

True, he said.

And this, you must understand, is he whom I call the child of the good, whom the good begat in his own likeness, to be in the visible world, in relation to sight and the things of sight, what the good is in the intellectual world in relation to mind and the things of mind:

Will you be a little more explicit? he said.

Why, you know, I said, that the eyes, when a person directs them towards objects on which the light of day is no longer shining, but the moon and stars only, see dimly, and are nearly blind; they seem to have no clearness of vision in them?

Very true.

But when they are directed towards objects on which the sun shines, they see clearly and there is sight in them?

Certainly.

And the soul is like the eye: when resting upon that on which truth and being shine, the soul perceives and understands, and is radiant with intelligence; but when turned towards the twilight and to those things which come into being and perish, then she has opinion only, and goes blinking about, and is first of one opinion and then of another, and seems to have no intelligence?

Just so.

Now, that which imparts truth to the known and the power of knowing to the knower is, as I would have you say, the Idea of good, and this Idea, which is the cause of science and of truth, you are to conceive as being apprehended by knowledge, and yet, fair as both truth and knowledge are, you will be right to [509] esteem it as different from these and even fairer; and as in the previous instance light and sight may be truly said to be like the sun and yet not to be the sun, so in this other sphere science and truth may be deemed to be like the good, but it is wrong to think that they are the good; the good has a place of honour yet higher.

What a wonder of beauty that must be, he said, which is the author of science and truth, and yet surpasses them in beauty; for you surely cannot mean to say that pleasure is the good?

God forbid, I replied; but may I ask you to consider the image in another point of view?

In what point of view?

You would say, would you not, that the sun is not only the author of visibility in all visible things, but of generation and nourishment and growth, though he himself is not generation?

Certainly.

In like manner you must say that the good not only infuses the power of being known into all things known, but also bestows upon them their being and existence, and yet the good is not existence, but lies far beyond it in dignity and power.

Glaucon said, with a ludicrous earnestness: By the light of heaven, that is far beyond indeed!

Yes, I said, and the exaggeration may be set down to you; for you made me utter my fancies.

And pray continue to utter them; at any rate let us hear if there is anything more to be said about the similitude of the sun.

Yes, I said, there is a great deal more.

Then omit nothing, however slight.

I expect that I shall omit a great deal, I said, but shall not do so deliberately, as far as present circumstances permit.

I hope not, he said.

You have to imagine, then, that there are two ruling powers, and that one of them is set over the intellectual world, the other over the visible. I do not say heaven, lest you should fancy that I am playing upon the name. May I suppose that you have this distinction of the visible and intelligible fixed in your mind?

I have.

Now take a line which has been cut into two unequal parts, and divide each of them again in the same proportion, and suppose the two main divisions to answer, one to the visible and the other to the intelligible, and then compare the subdivisions in respect of their clearness and want of clearness, and you will find that the first section in the sphere of the [510] visible consists of images. And by images I mean, in the first place, shadows, and in the second place, reflections in water and in solid, smooth and polished bodies and the like: Do you understand?

Yes, I understand.

Imagine, now, the other section, of which this is only the resemblance, to include the animals which we see, and every thing that grows or is made.

Very good.

Would you not admit that both the sections of this division have different degrees of truth, and that the copy is to the original as the sphere of opinion is to the sphere of knowledge?

Most undoubtedly.

Next proceed to consider the manner in which the sphere of the intellectual is to be divided.

In what manner?

Thus:—There are two subdivisions, in the lower of which the soul, using as images those things which themselves were reflected in the former division, is forced to base its enquiry upon hypotheses, proceeding not towards a principle but towards a conclusion; in the higher of the two, the soul proceeds *from* hypotheses, and goes up to a principle which is above hypotheses, making no use of images as in the former case, but proceeding only in and through the Ideas themselves.

I do not quite understand your meaning, he said.

Then I will try again; you will understand me better when I have made some preliminary remarks. You are aware that students of geometry, arithmetic, and the kindred sciences assume the odd and the even and the figures and three kinds of angles and the like in their several branches of science; these are their hypotheses, which they and everybody are supposed to know, and therefore they do not deign to give any account of them either to themselves or others; but they begin with them, and go on until they arrive at last, and in a consistent manner, at the solution which they set out to find?

Yes, he said, I know.

And do you not know also that although they make use of the visible forms and reason about them, they are thinking not of these, but of the ideals which they resemble; not of the figures which they draw, but of the absolute square and the absolute diameter, and so on—the forms which they draw or make, and which themselves have shadows and reflections in water, are in turn converted by them into images; for they are really seeking to behold the things themselves, which can only be seen with the eye of the mind?

[511] That is true.

And this was what I meant by a subdivision of the intelligible, in the search after which the soul is compelled to use hypotheses; not ascending to a first principle, because she is unable to rise above the region of hypothesis, but employing now as images those objects from which the shadows below were derived, even these being deemed clear and distinct by comparison with the shadows.

I understand, he said, that you are speaking of the province of geometry and the sister arts.

And when I speak of the other division of the intelligible, you will understand me to speak of that other sort of knowledge which reason herself attains by the power of dialectic, using the hypotheses not as first principles, but literally as hypotheses—that is to say, as steps and points of departure into a world which is above hypotheses, in order that she may soar beyond them to the first principle of the whole; and clinging to this and then to that which depends on this, by successive steps she descends again without the aid of any sensible object, from Ideas, through Ideas, and in Ideas she ends.

I understand you, he replied; not perfectly, for you seem to me to be describing a task which is really tremendous; but, at any rate, I understand you to say that that part of intelligible Being, which the science of dialectic contemplates, is clearer than that which falls under the arts, as they are termed, which take hypotheses as their principles; and though the objects are of such a kind that they must be viewed by the understanding, and not by the senses, yet, because they start from hypotheses and do not ascend to a principle, those who contemplate them appear to you not to exercise the higher reason upon them, although when a first principle is added to them they are cognizable by the higher reason. And the habit which is concerned with geometry and the cognate sciences I suppose that you would term understanding and not reason, as being intermediate between opinion and reason.

You have quite conceived my meaning, I said; and now, corresponding to these four divisions, let there be four faculties in the soul—reason answering to the highest, understanding to the second, faith (or conviction) to the third, and perception of shadows to the last—and let there be a scale of them, and let us suppose that the several faculties have clearness in the same degree that their objects have truth.

I understand, he replied, and give my assent, and accept your arrangement. [. . .]

Book VII

[514] And now, I said, let me show in a figure how far our nature is enlightened or unenlightened:—Behold! human beings housed in an underground cave, which has a long entrance open towards the light and as wide as the interior of the cave; here they have been from their childhood, and have their legs and necks chained, so that they cannot move and can only see before them, being prevented by the chains from turning round their heads. Above and behind them a fire is blazing at a distance, and between the fire and the prisoners there is a raised way; and you will see, if you look, a low wall built along the way, like the screen which marionette players have in front of them, over which they show the puppets.

I see.

And do you see, I said, men passing along the wall carrying all sorts of vessels, and statues and figures of animals made of wood and stone and various materials, which appear over the wall? While carrying their burdens, some of them, as you would expect, are talking, others silent.

You have shown me a strange image, and they are strange prisoners.

Like ourselves, I replied; for in the first place do you think they have seen anything of themselves, and of one another, except the shadows which the fire throws on the opposite wall of the cave?

How could they do so, he asked, if throughout their lives they were never allowed to move their heads?

And of the objects which are being carried in like manner they would only see the shadows?

Yes, he said.

And if they were able to converse with one another, would they not suppose that the things they saw were the real things?[2]

Very true.

And suppose further that the prison had an echo which came from the other side, would they not be sure to fancy when one of the passers-by spoke that the voice which they heard came from the passing shadow?

No question, he replied.

To them, I said, the truth would be literally nothing but the shadows of the images.

That is certain.

And now look again, and see in what manner they would be released from their bonds, and cured of their error, whether the process would naturally be as follows. At first, when any of them is liberated and compelled suddenly to stand up and turn his neck round and walk and look towards the light, he will suffer sharp pains; the glare will distress him, and he will be unable to see the realities of which in his former state he had seen the shadows; and then conceive someone saying to him that what he saw before was an illusion, but that now, when he is approaching nearer to being and his eye is turned towards more real existence, he has a clearer vision,—what will be his reply? And you may further imagine that his instructor is pointing to the objects as they pass and requiring him to name them,—will he not be perplexed? Will he not fancy that the shadows which he formerly saw are truer than the objects which are now shown to him?

Far truer.

And if he is compelled to look straight at the light, will he not have a pain in his eyes which will make him turn away to take refuge in the objects of vision which he can see, and which he will conceive to be in reality clearer than the things which are now being shown to him?

True, he said.

And suppose once more, that he is reluctantly dragged up that steep and rugged ascent, and held fast until he is forced into the presence of the sun himself, is he not likely to be pained [516] and irritated? When he approaches the light his eyes will be dazzled, and he will not be able to see anything at all of what are now called realities.

Not all in a moment, he said.

He will require to grow accustomed to the sight of the upper world. And first he will see the shadows best, next the reflections of men and other objects in the water, and then the objects themselves; and, when he turned to the heavenly bodies and the heaven itself, he would find it easier

---

[2] [Text uncertain: perhaps 'that they would apply the name *real* to the things which they saw'.]

to gaze upon the light of the moon and the stars at night than to see the sun or the light of the sun by day?

Certainly.

Last of all he will be able to see the sun, not turning aside to the illusory reflections of him in the water, but gazing directly at him in his own proper place, and contemplating him as he is.

Certainly.

He will then proceed to argue that this is he who gives the seasons and the years, and is the guardian of all that is in the visible world, and in a certain way the cause of all things which he and his fellows have been accustomed to behold?

Clearly, he said, he would arrive at this conclusion after what he had seen.

And when he remembered his old habitation, and the wisdom of the cave and his fellow-prisoners, do you not suppose that he would felicitate himself on the change, and pity them?

Certainly, he would.

And if they were in the habit of conferring honours among themselves on those who were quickest to observe the passing shadows and to remark which of them went before and which followed after and which were together, and who were best able from these observations to divine the future, do you think that he would be eager for such honours and glories, or envy those who attained honour and sovereignty among those men? Would he not say with Homer, "Better to be a serf, labouring for a landless master," and to endure anything, rather than think as they do and live after their manner?

Yes, he said, I think that he would consent to suffer anything rather than live in this miserable manner.

Imagine once more, I said, such a one coming down suddenly out of the sunlight, and being replaced in his old seat; would he not be certain to have his eyes full of darkness?

To be sure, he said.

And if there were a contest, and he had to compete in measuring the shadows with the prisoners who had never [517] moved out of the cave, while his sight was still weak, and before his eyes had become steady (and the time which would be needed to acquire this new habit of sight might be very considerable), would he not make himself ridiculous? Men would say of him that he had returned from the place above with his eyes ruined; and that it was better not even to think of ascending; and if anyone tried to loose another and lead him up to the light, let them only catch the offender, and they would put him to death.

No question, he said.

This entire allegory, I said, you may now append, dear Glaucon, to the previous argument; the prison-house is the world of sight, the light of the fire is the power of the sun, and you will not misapprehend me if you interpret the journey upwards to be the ascent of the soul into the intellectual world according to my surmise, which, at your desire, I have expressed —whether rightly or wrongly God knows. But, whether true or false, my opinion is that in the world of knowledge the Idea of good appears last of all, and is seen only with an effort; although, when seen, it is inferred to be the universal author of all things beautiful and right, parent of light and of the lord of light in the visible world, and the immediate and supreme source of reason and truth in the intellectual; and that this is the power upon which he who would act rationally either in public or private life must have his eye fixed.

I agree, he said, as far as I am able to understand you.

Moreover, I said, you must agree once more, and not wonder that those who attain to this vision are unwilling to take any part in human affairs; for their souls are ever hastening into the upper world where they desire to dwell; which desire of theirs is very natural, if our allegory may be trusted.

Yes, very natural.

And is there anything surprising in one who passes from divine contemplations to the evil state of man, appearing grotesque and ridiculous; if, while his eyes are blinking and before he has become accustomed to the surrounding darkness, he is compelled to fight in courts of law, or in other places, about the images or the shadows of images of justice, and must strive against some rival about opinions of these things which are entertained by men who have never yet seen the true justice?

Anything but surprising, he replied.

[518] Anyone who has common sense will remember that the bewilderments of the eyes are of two kinds and arise from two causes, either from coming out of the light or from going into the light, and, judging that the soul may be affected in the same way, will not give way to foolish laughter when he sees anyone whose vision is perplexed and weak; he will first ask whether that soul of man has come out of the brighter life and is unable to see because unaccustomed to the dark, or having turned from darkness to the day is dazzled by excess of light. And he will count the one happy in his condition and state of being, and he will pity the other; or, if he have a mind to laugh at the soul which comes from below into the light, this laughter will not be quite so laughable as that which greets the soul which returns from above out of the light into the cave.

That, he said, is a very just distinction.

But then, if I am right, certain professors of education must be wrong when they say that they can put a knowledge into the soul which was not there before, like sight into blind eyes.

They undoubtedly say this, he replied.

Whereas our argument shows that the power and capacity of learning exists in the soul already; and that just as if it were not possible to turn the eye from darkness to light without the whole body, so too the instrument of knowledge can only by the movement of the whole soul be turned from the world of becoming to that of being, and learn by degrees to endure the sight of being, and of the brightest and best of being, or in other words, of the good.

Very true.

And must there not be some art which will show how the conversion can be effected in the easiest and quickest manner; an art which will not implant the faculty of sight, for that exists already, but will set it straight when it has been turned in the wrong direction, and is looking away from the truth?

Yes, he said, such an art may be presumed.

And whereas the other so-called virtues of the soul seem to be akin to bodily qualities, for even when they are not originally innate they can be implanted later by habit and exercise, the virtue of wisdom more than anything else contains a divine element which never loses its power, and by this conversion is rendered useful and profitable; or, by conversion of another [519] sort, hurtful and useless. Did you never observe the narrow intelligence flashing from the keen eye of a clever rogue—how eager he is, how clearly his paltry soul sees the way to his end; he is the reverse of blind, but his keen eye-sight is forced into the service of evil, and he is mischievous in proportion to his cleverness?

Very true, he said.

But what if such natures had been gradually stripped, beginning in childhood, of the leaden weights which sink them in the sea of Becoming, and which, fastened upon the soul through gluttonous indulgence in eating and other such pleasures, forcibly turn its vision downwards—if, I say, they had been released from these impediments and turned in the opposite direction, the very same faculty in them would have seen the truth as keenly as they see what their eyes are turned to now.

Very likely.

Yes, I said; and there is another thing which is likely, or rather a necessary inference from what has preceded, that neither the uneducated and uninformed of the truth, nor yet those who are suffered to prolong their education without end, will be able ministers of State; not the former, because they have no single aim of duty which is the rule of all their actions, private as well as public; nor the latter, because they will not act at all except upon compulsion, fancying that they are already dwelling apart in the islands of the blest.

Very true, he replied.

Then, I said, the business of us who are the founders of the State will be to compel the best minds to attain that knowledge which we have already shown to be the greatest of all, namely, the vision of the good; they must make the ascent which we have described; but when they have ascended and seen enough we must not allow them to do as they do now.

What do you mean?

They are permitted to remain in the upper world, refusing to descend again among the prisoners in the cave, and partake of their labours and honours, whether they are worth having or not.

But is not this unjust? he said; ought we to give them a worse life, when they might have a better?

You have again forgotten, my friend, I said, the intention of our law, which does not aim at making any one class in the State happy above the rest; it seeks rather to spread happiness over the whole State, and to hold the citizens together by persuasion and necessity, making each share with others any benefit [520] which he can confer upon the State; and the law aims at producing such citizens, not that they may be left to please themselves, but that they may serve in binding the State together.

True, he said, I had forgotten.

Observe, Glaucon, that we shall do no wrong to our philosophers but rather make a just demand, when we oblige them to have a care and providence of others; we shall explain to them that in other States, men of their class are not obliged to share in the toils of politics: and this is reasonable, for they grow up spontaneously, against the will of the governments in their several States; and things which grow up of themselves, and are indebted to no one for their nurture, cannot fairly be expected to pay dues for a culture which they have never received. But we have brought you into the world to be rulers of the hive, kings of yourselves and of the other citizens, and have educated you far better and more perfectly than they have been educated, and you are better able to share in the double duty. Wherefore each of you, when his turn comes, must go down to rejoin his companions, and acquire with them the habit of seeing things in the dark. As you acquire that habit, you will see ten thousand times better than the inhabitants of the cave, and you will know what the several images are and what they represent, because you have seen the beautiful and just and good in their truth. And thus our State, which is also yours, will be a reality and not a dream only, and will be administered in a spirit unlike that of other States, in which men fight with one another about shadows only and are distracted in the struggle for power, which in their eyes is a great good. Whereas the truth is that the State in which those who are to govern have least ambition to do so is always the best and most quietly governed, and the State in which they are most eager, the worst.

Transition:
Plato and Kant
on the
A Priori

A passage in Kant's major work, **The Critique of Pure Reason** (1781), contains the key to his thought, namely, his "Copernican revolution" in philosophy. Copernicus revolutionized the way we see the heavens, not by discovering any new heavenly bodies, but by suggesting a difference in our perspective as viewers of the heavens: rather than seeing the stars, planets, and sun as all rotating around the earth as the fixed center of the universe, Copernicus showed how the paths of the heavenly bodies could be more easily calculated and understood if we took the sun as the center and saw ourselves as rotating about that center with the rest of the planets. Kant's revolution also introduced not new things but a new way of looking at things; both revolutions involve discoveries about our roles and perspectives as viewers. Unlike Christopher Columbus, Kant does not show us a new land; he shows us a new way of understanding how we look at familiar terrain. Basically, he argues that the terrain is familiar only because human minds order experience in the same way, and the way we see things determines the structure of what we see. Kant argued that we are not merely passive recipients of an already structured, determinate world. On the contrary, each of us uses the same set of categories actively to synthesize our experience. The phenomenon of an objectively fixed and determinate world is a function of the intersubjectively shared categories that structure experience in the same way for every human mind.

Kant describes this set of intersubjectively shared categories as **a priori** concepts. The term **'a priori'** connotes a special sense of "prior to." When Kant speaks of **a priori** knowledge of objects he is contrasting it to knowledge gained through experience, or knowledge only possible **a posteriori** (that is, **after** experience). The distinction has less to do with a time sequence than with an ordering in terms of actuality, possibility, and necessity. **A priori** knowledge is necessary knowledge. It is certain even before experience, in the sense that no experienced datum could possibly undermine that certainty. For example, you may experience big squares, little squares, green squares, heavy squares, but all your experience of squares could not shake your **a priori** certainty that squares have four sides. If a big, green, heavy thing presents a plane surface that is three-sided, then it is not a square. All the data about squares reconfirm an **a priori** certainty that squares have four sides— so that we regard this truth not as a **fact,** not as something about the world that might be otherwise, but hold the proposition "squares have four sides" as a truth by definition. Like prejudices, **a priori** knowledge colors our perception of facts in such a way that our experiences cannot alter our certainty in that knowledge. But like definitional truths, **a priori** knowledge is innocent of vested interests and the falsifying effects of prejudice. Somewhere between definitional and prejudicial certainty, Kant is looking for what he calls synthetic **a priori** truths: truths whose necessity depends more on logic than the psychological stubbornness characterizing prejudice; but truths whose necessity is not purely logical, not purely definitional.

Though the truths Kant is after are more like factual truths than are definitional truths, the **role** of definitional truths shows us more about the meaning of **'a priori'.** Our definitional truths, our **rules** for the way we use certain words, play the role of necessary conditions for the possibility of speech. If I say 'square' and mean by 'square' a figure that may have three sides, and you understand 'square' to denote a figure that is necessarily four-sided, we will not understand one another. When you say "the table is square," if you are abiding by the same definitions or rules that I am, then I tacitly infer other truths that peripherally constitute the world of communication we build by using words according to **a priori** rules. For example, I know immediately and without being conscious of it that the table is unlike a thought in that the table has a spatiotemporal shape. I know this because 'square' is the name for a particular kind of shape, so that anything that is square must be the kind of thing that has a shape. This tacit inference follows from the definition of 'square.'

Kant's use of **a priori** extends from the truths of definition, which render speech possible by defining the meanings of words, to what I like to call "truths of determination," which render experience possible by determining the character of objects. Just as speech is not possible without a set of rules that language users follow in their use of words, so Kant's insight was to see that experience is not possible apart from a set of rules governing our perceptions of things; and, like the rules of language, we carry around with us our truths of determination as the baggage **we** bring **to** experience. Fundamentally, Kant is claiming that each of us is master of a complex system of ordering the inputs to our perceptual apparatus. Without that system of ordering, our awareness would not constitute the relatively coherent whole we know as experience, but would on the contrary be what William James called a "blooming, buzzing confusion"—an experiential analogue to the Tower of Babel, where speech became impossible because everyone used words according to different rules.

To return to the meaning of **a priori,** just as children can learn to speak properly before learning to formulate the rules of grammar explicitly, so the knowledge Kant claims as **a priori** may not become explicit until **after** a good deal has been experienced. Indeed, reading **The Critique of Pure Reason** is the experience required for us to become explicitly aware of our **a priori** knowledge. Nonetheless, it is part of Kant's argument that whether we were explicitly aware of this **a priori** or not, the possession of that knowledge was **necessary** for experience to be **possible,** just as following the basic rules of grammar and definition is necessary for speech to be possible, whether or not one can explicitly formulate those rules.

The phrase "necessary for experience to be possible" captures a large part of the meaning of **'a priori.'** The same phrase is also closely tied to the term 'transcendental.' "I entitle **transcendental** all knowledge which is occupied not so much with objects as with the mode of our knowledge of objects in so far as this mode of knowledge is to be possible **a priori,"** writes Kant in his "Introduction." Elsewhere he is careful to distinguish 'transcendental' from 'transcendent.' The latter refers to that which **goes beyond** experience in that it falls forever outside of experience, cutting off all links with experience. The transcendent is the unknown beyond. The transcendental, too, falls outside of experience in that, as Kant says, it "is occupied not so much with objects as with the mode of our knowledge of objects." But the transcendental is **this side** of experience rather than beyond experience. Transcendental knowledge is concerned with the **a priori** that renders experience possible by structuring input according to a set of fixed rules.

Just how these rules work, how the structuring happens psychologically, is not so much Kant's concern as is the argument that some such rules are in fact necessary for experience to be possible. Kant's agnosticism on the psychological mechanisms, his inclination to speak of "an art concealed in the depths of the human soul," or of "a blind but indispensable function of the soul . . . of which we are scarcely ever conscious," recalls aspects of Plato's epistemology. In dialogues like the **Phaedo** and the **Meno,** Plato speaks of learning as a kind of remembering. His analysis of knowledge shows a need for some kind of **a priori,** some sense in which knowledge must be already had before it can be learned. As the riddle of the **Meno** goes, how could you ever learn anything if you could not recognize what you were looking for when you found it; but if you already know it, why look? So Plato adopts a myth of remembering: consistent with the importance of self-knowledge, the myth says that all knowledge lies within the soul prior to experience, and all one needs is a way to get it out, a spur to the memory, a Socrates. And like Kant, Plato confesses that while the logic of the learning riddle is real enough, the character of the solution leaves a lot unexplained.

Whether we refer the **a priori** to a body of knowledge acquired by the soul in a previous life and remembered in this life, or to a set of rules operating in an unknown way, both Plato and Kant present us with the idea that knowing is not at all like simply taking something outside the head and putting it inside the head. The head and the body—the knower in all his capacities—do a lot of their own work in rendering experience knowable. Before tracing the similarity between Plato and Kant too far, however, it is important to see how their accounts of knowledge differ. Here the reader should pursue his own inquiry. A good question to begin with is whether Kant does not condemn us to the first two or three sections of the divided line. And if Plato thinks we can attain to the fourth level, to a knowledge of things themselves rather than their sensible imitations, how would he answer Kant's **Critique of Pure Reason?**

IMMANUEL KANT

(1724-1804)

Outwardly Kant did not live an exciting life. Supposedly he never traveled more than fifty miles from Königsburg, the Prussian city where he was born, and the townspeople would set their watches according to his highly regular afternoon walk. He began his academic career studying nature and cosmology, and in 1755 he published a treatise on the origins of the solar system. His nebular hypothesis, similar in many ways to that developed later by Pierre Simon de Laplace, anticipates contemporary theories. Kant's mature philosophical publications really begin with **The Critique of Pure Reason,** published first in 1781 when he was fifty-seven. Fortunately, Kant lived long enough and retained the intellectual energy to publish a second edition in 1787, followed by **The Critique of Practical Reason** in 1788, and **The Critique of Judgment** in 1789 and 1793. In addition to many smaller tracts, his three major critiques brought an end to the Enlightenment's glorification of "pure reason." Although Kant hardly intended all that followed in his wake, his philosophy ushered in the spiritual chaos of the nineteenth and twentieth centuries. Without faith in the unbounded power of pure reason, later thinkers have been encouraged to embrace romanticism, antirationalism, and countless forms of less-than-pure reason as guides for the conduct of human life. Kant, whose humble pietism restricted reason only from its improper extensions but not from its proper use, would doubtless be offended by the claim that his philosophy encouraged later extravagances. But at least we can say that without an understanding of Kant's influence it is difficult to understand what followed.

THE COPERNICAN REVOLUTION

[B vii] Whether the treatment of such knowledge as lies within the province of reason does or does not follow the secure path of a science, is easily to be determined from the outcome.

THE COPERNICAN REVOLUTION From Immanuel Kant, *Critique of Pure Reason,* translated by Norman Kemp Smith. Copyright © 1929 by St. Martin's Press. Reprinted by permission of St. Martin's Press and the permission of The Macmillan Company of Canada and Macmillan, London and Basingstoke.
  The letters and numbers in brackets refer to the page numbers of the Second Edition. This entire selection is from the Preface.

For if after elaborate preparations, frequently renewed, it is brought to a
stop immediately it nears its goal; if often it is compelled to retrace its
steps and strike into some new line of approach; or again, if the various
participants are unable to agree in any common plan of procedure, then
we may rest assured that it is very far from having entered upon the secure
path of a science, and is indeed a merely random groping. In these circumstances, we shall be rendering a service to reason should we succeed in
discovering the path upon which it can securely travel, even if, as a result
of so doing, much that is comprised in our original aims, adopted without
reflection, may have to be abandoned as fruitless.

[B viii] That logic has already, from the earliest times, proceeded upon
this sure path is evidenced by the fact that since Aristotle it has not required to retrace a single step, unless, indeed, we care to count as improvements the removal of certain needless subtleties or the clearer exposition
of its recognised teaching, features which concern the elegance rather than
the certainty of the science. It is remarkable also that to the present day
this logic has not been able to advance a single step, and is thus to all
appearance a closed and completed body of doctrine. If some of the mod-
erns have thought to enlarge it by introducing *psychological* chapters on
the different faculties of knowledge (imagination, wit, etc.), *metaphysical*
chapters on the origin of knowledge or on the different kinds of certainty
according to difference in the objects (idealism, scepticism, etc.), or *anthropological* chapters on prejudices, their causes and remedies, this could
only arise from their ignorance of the peculiar nature of logical science.
We do not enlarge but disfigure sciences, if we allow them to trespass upon
one [B ix] another's territory. The sphere of logic is quite precisely delim-
ited; its sole concern is to give an exhaustive exposition and a strict proof
of the formal rules of all thought, whether it be *a priori* or empirical, whatever be its origin or its object, and whatever hindrances, accidental or
natural, it may encounter in our minds.

That logic should have been thus successful is an advantage which it
owes entirely to its limitations, whereby it is justified in abstracting—indeed,
it is under obligation to do so—from all objects of knowledge and their
differences, leaving the understanding nothing to deal with save itself and
its form. But for reason to enter on the sure path of science is, of course,
much more difficult, since it has to deal not with itself alone but also with
objects. Logic, therefore, as a propaedeutic, forms, as it were, only the
vestibule of the sciences; and when we are concerned with specific modes
of knowledge, while logic is indeed presupposed in any critical estimate of
them, yet for the actual acquiring of them we have to look to the sciences
properly and objectively so called.

Now if reason is to be a factor in these sciences, something in them
must be known *a priori,* and this knowledge may be related to its object
in one or other of two ways, either as merely *determining* it and its concept (which must be supplied [B x] from elsewhere) or as also *making it
actual.* The former is *theoretical,* the latter *practical* knowledge of reason.

In both, that part in which reason determines its object completely *a priori,* namely, the *pure* part—however much or little this part may contain— must be first and separately dealt with, in case it be confounded with what comes from other sources. For it is bad management if we blindly pay out what comes in, and are not able, when the income falls into arrears, to distinguish which part of it can justify expenditure, and in which line we must make reductions.

Mathematics and physics, the two sciences in which reason yields theoretical knowledge, have to determine their objects *a priori,* the former doing so quite purely, the latter having to reckon, at least partially, with sources of knowledge other than reason.

In the earliest times to which the history of human reason extends, *mathematics,* among that wonderful people, the Greeks, had already entered upon the sure path of science. But it must not be supposed that it was as easy for mathematics as it was for logic—in which reason has to deal with itself alone—[B xi] to light upon, or rather to construct for itself, that royal road. On the contrary, I believe that it long remained, especially among the Egyptians, in the groping stage, and that the transformation must have been due to a *revolution* brought about by the happy thought of a single man, the experiment which he devised marking out the path upon which the science must enter, and by following which, secure progress throughout all time and in endless expansion is infallibly secured. The history of this intellectual revolution—far more important than the discovery of the passage round the celebrated Cape of Good Hope—and of its fortunate author, has not been preserved. But the fact that Diogenes Laertius, in handing down an account of these matters, names the reputed author of even the least important among the geometrical demonstrations, even of those which, for ordinary consciousness, stand in need of no such proof, does at least show that the memory of the revolution, brought about by the first glimpse of this new path, must have seemed to mathematicians of such outstanding importance as to cause it to survive the tide of oblivion. A new light flashed upon the mind of the first man (be he Thales or some other) who demonstrated the properties of the isosceles triangle. [B xii] The true method, so he found, was not to inspect what he discerned either in the figure, or in the bare concept of it, and from this, as it were, to read off its properties; but to bring out what was necessarily implied in the concepts that he had himself formed *a priori,* and had put into the figure in the construction by which he presented it to himself. If he is to know anything with *a priori* certainty he must not ascribe to the figure anything save what necessarily follows from what he has himself set into it in accordance with his concept.

Natural science was very much longer in entering upon the highway of science. It is, indeed, only about a century and a half since Bacon, by his ingenious proposals, partly initiated this discovery, partly inspired fresh vigour in those who were already on the way to it. In this case also the discovery can be explained as being the sudden outcome of an intellectual revolution. In my present remarks I am referring to natural science only in so far as it is founded on *empirical* principles.

When Galileo caused balls, the weights of which he had himself previously determined, to roll down an inclined plane; when Torricelli made the air carry a weight which he had calculated beforehand to be equal to that of a definite volume of water; or in more recent times, when Stahl changed metals [B xiii] into oxides, and oxides back into metal, by withdrawing something and then restoring it,[1] a light broke upon all students of nature. They learned that reason has insight only into that which it produces after a plan of its own and that it must not allow itself to be kept, as it were, in nature's leading-strings, but must itself show the way with principles of judgment based upon fixed laws, constraining nature to give answer to questions of reason's own determining. Accidental observations, made in obedience to no previously thought-out plan, can never be made to yield a necessary law, which alone reason is concerned to discover. Reason, holding in one hand its principles, according to which alone concordant appearances can be admitted as equivalent to laws, and in the other hand the experiment which it has devised in conformity with these principles, must approach nature in order to be taught by it. It must not, however, do so in the character of a pupil who listens to everything that the teacher chooses to say, but of an appointed judge who compels the witnesses to answer questions which he has himself formulated. Even physics, therefore, owes the beneficent revolution in its point of view [B xiv] entirely to the happy thought, that while reason must seek in nature, not fictitiously ascribe to it, whatever as not being knowable through reason's own resources has to be learnt, if learnt at all, only from nature, it must adopt as its guide, in so seeking, that which it has itself put into nature. It is thus that the study of nature has entered on the secure path of a science, after having for so many centuries been nothing but a process of merely random groping.

Metaphysics is a completely isolated speculative science of reason, which soars far above the teachings of experience, and in which reason is indeed meant to be its own pupil. Metaphysics rests on concepts alone—not, like mathematics, on their application to intuition. But though it is older than all other sciences, and would survive even if all the rest were swallowed up in the abyss of an all-destroying barbarism, it has not yet had the good fortune to enter upon the secure path of a science. For in it reason is perpetually being brought to a stand, even when the laws into which it is seeking to have, as it professes, an *a priori* insight are those that are confirmed by our most common experiences. Ever and again we have to retrace our steps, as not leading us in the direction in which we desire to go. So [B xv] far, too, are the students of metaphysics from exhibiting any kind of unanimity in their contentions, that metaphysics has rather to be regarded as a

---

[1] I am not, in my choice of examples, tracing the exact course of the history of the experimental method; we have indeed no very precise knowledge of its first beginnings.

battle-ground quite peculiarly suited for those who desire to exercise themselves in mock combats, and in which no participant has ever yet succeeded in gaining even so much as an inch of territory, not at least in such manner as to secure him in its permanent possession. This shows, beyond all questioning, that the procedure of metaphysics has hitherto been a merely random groping, and, what is worst of all, a groping among mere concepts.

What, then, is the reason why, in this field, the sure road to science has not hitherto been found? Is it, perhaps, impossible of discovery? Why, in that case, should nature have visited our reason with the restless endeavour whereby it is ever searching for such a path, as if this were one of its most important concerns? Nay, more, how little cause have we to place trust in our reason, if, in one of the most important domains of which we would fain have knowledge, it does not merely fail us, but lures us on by deceitful promises, and in the end betrays us! Or if it be only that we have thus far failed to find the true path, are there any indications to justify the hope that by renewed efforts we may have better fortune than has fallen to our predecessors?

The examples of mathematics and natural science, which [B xvi] by a single and sudden revolution have become what they now are, seem to me sufficiently remarkable to suggest our considering what may have been the essential features in the changed point of view by which they have so greatly benefited. Their success should incline us, at least by way of experiment, to imitate their procedure, so far as the analogy which, as species of rational knowledge, they bear to metaphysics may permit. Hitherto it has been assumed that all our knowledge must conform to objects. But all attempts to extend our knowledge of objects by establishing something in regard to them *a priori,* by means of concepts, have, on this assumption, ended in failure. We must therefore make trial whether we may not have more success in the tasks of metaphysics, if we suppose that objects must conform to our knowledge. This would agree better with what is desired, namely, that it should be possible to have knowledge of objects *a priori,* determining something in regard to them prior to their being given. We should then be proceeding precisely on the lines of Copernicus' primary hypothesis. Failing of satisfactory progress in explaining the movements of the heavenly bodies on the supposition that they all revolved round the spectator, he tried whether he might not have better success if he made the spectator [B xvii] to revolve and the stars to remain at rest. A similar experiment can be tried in metaphysics, as regards the *intuition* of objects. If intuition must conform to the constitution of the objects, I do not see how we could know anything of the latter *a priori;* but if the object (as object of the senses) must conform to the constitution of our faculty of intuition, I have no difficulty in conceiving such a possibility. Since I cannot rest in these intuitions if they are to become known, but must relate them as representations to something as their object, and determine this latter through them, either I must assume that the *concepts,* by means of which I obtain this determination, conform to the object, or else I assume that the objects, or what is the same thing, that the *experience* in which alone, as given objects, they can be known, conform to the concepts. In the former case, I am again in the same perplexity as to how I can know anything *a priori* in regard to the objects. In the latter case the outlook is more hopeful. For experience is itself a species of knowledge which involves understanding; and understanding has rules which I must presuppose as being in me prior to objects being given to me, and therefore as being *a priori*. They find expression in *a priori* [B xviii] concepts to which all objects of experience necessarily conform, and with which they must agree. As regards objects which are thought solely through reason, and indeed as necessary, but which can never—at least not in the manner in which reason thinks them —be given in experience, the attempts at thinking them (for they must admit of being thought) will furnish an excellent touchstone of what we are adopting as our new method of thought, namely, that we can know *a priori* of things only what we ourselves put into them.[2]

This experiment succeeds as well as could be desired, and promises to metaphysics, in its first part—the part that is occupied with those concepts *a priori* to which the corresponding objects, commensurate with them, can be given in experience—the secure path of science. [B xix] For the new point of view enables us to explain how there can be knowledge *a priori;* and, in addition, to furnish satisfactory proof of the laws which form the *a priori* basis of nature, regarded as the sum of the objects of experience— neither achievement being possible on the procedure hitherto followed. But this deduction of our power of knowing *a priori,* in the first part of metaphysics, has a consequence which is startling, and which has the appearance of being highly prejudicial to the whole purpose of metaphysics, as dealt with in the second part. For we are brought to the conclusion that we can never transcend the limits of possible experience, though that is precisely what this science [B xx] is concerned, above all else, to achieve. This situation yields, however, just the very experiment by which, indirectly, we are enabled to prove the truth of this first estimate of our *a priori* knowledge of reason, namely, that such knowledge has to do only with appearances, and must leave the thing in itself as indeed real *per se,* but as not known by us. For what necessarily forces us to transcend the limits of

---

[2] This method, modelled on that of the student of nature, consists in looking for the elements of pure reason in *what admits of confirmation or refutation by experiment.* Now the propositions of pure reason, especially if they venture out beyond all limits of possible experience, cannot be brought to the test through any experiment with their *objects,* as in natural science. In dealing with those *concepts* and *principles* which we adopt *a priori,* all that we can do is to contrive that they be used for viewing objects from two different points of view—on the one hand, in connection with experience, [B xix] as objects of the senses and of the understanding, and on the other hand, for the isolated reason that strives to transcend all limits of experience, as objects which are thought merely. If, when things are viewed from this twofold standpoint, we find that there is agreement with the principle of pure reason, but that when we regard them only from a single point of view reason is involved in unavoidable self-conflict, the experiment decides in favour of the correctness of this distinction.

experience and of all appearances is the *unconditioned,* which reason, by necessity and by right, demands in things in themselves, as required to complete the series of conditions. If, then, on the supposition that our empirical knowledge conforms to objects as things in themselves, we find that the unconditioned *cannot be thought without contradiction,* and that when, on the other hand, we suppose that our representation of things, as they are given to us, does not conform to these things as they are in themselves, but that these objects, as appearances, conform to our mode of representation, *the contradiction vanishes;* and if, therefore, we thus find that the unconditioned is not to be met with in things, so far as we know them, that is, so far as they are given to us, but only so far as we do not know them, that is, so far as they are things in themselves, we are justified in concluding that what we at first assumed for the purposes of experiment is [B xxi] now definitely confirmed.[3] But when all progress in the field of the supersensible has thus been denied to speculative reason, it is still open to us to enquire whether, in the practical knowledge of reason, data may not be found sufficient to determine reason's transcendent concept of the unconditioned, and so to enable us, in accordance with the wish of metaphysics, and by means of knowledge that is possible *a priori,* though only from a practical point of view, to pass beyond the limits of all possible experience. Speculative reason has thus at least made room for such an extension; and if it must [B xxii] at the same time leave it empty, yet none the less we are at liberty, indeed we are summoned, to take occupation of it, if we can, by practical data of reason.[4]

This attempt to alter the procedure which has hitherto prevailed in metaphysics, by completely revolutionising it in accordance with the example set by the geometers and physicists, forms indeed the main purpose of this critique of pure speculative reason. It is a treatise on the method, not a system of the science itself.

[3] This experiment of pure reason bears a great similarity to what in chemistry is sometimes entitled the experiment of *reduction,* or more usually the *synthetic* process. The *analysis of the metaphysician* separates pure *a priori* knowledge into two very heterogeneous elements, namely, the knowledge of things as appearances, and the knowledge of things in themselves; his *dialectic* combines these two again, in *harmony* with the necessary idea of the *unconditioned* demanded by reason, and finds that this harmony can never be obtained except through the above distinction, which must therefore be accepted.

[4] Similarly, the fundamental laws of the motions of the heavenly bodies gave established certainty to what Copernicus had at first assumed only as an hypothesis, and at the same time yielded proof of the invisible force (the Newtonian attraction) which holds the universe together. The latter would have remained for ever undiscovered if Copernicus had not dared, in a manner contradictory of the senses, but yet true, to seek the observed movements, not in the heavenly bodies, but in the spectator. The change in point of view, analogous to this hypothesis, which is expounded in the *Critique,* I put forward in this preface as an hypothesis only, in order to draw attention to the character of these first attempts at such a change, which are always hypothetical. But in the *Critique* itself it will be proved, apodeictically not hypothetically, from the nature of our representations of space and time and from the elementary concepts of the understanding.

Transition:
Kant's Legacy

Kant's transcendental method was put to limited use in **The Critique of Pure Reason** where the transcendental method found application mainly in exposing the cognitive conditions for the possibility of experience. Though Kant distinguished between sensation and understanding, his attention to the former was for the most part restricted to an exposition of space and time as the so-called 'forms of intuition.' That is to say, all our perceptions are spatial and temporal; spatiality and temporality are **our ways** of perceiving things, and not properties of the things themselves. This is a powerful idea, but the subsequent history of philosophy shows that Kant's application of transcendental methodology was incomplete. Edmund Husserl, among others, for example, concerned himself with an extension of Kant's categories of understanding. Just as the faculty of sensibility has its forms—space and time—so the Understanding (distinguished from sensibility as conception is distinguished from perception) contains **a priori** forms known as categories or concepts of understanding. Kant derived from Aristotle's analysis of Judgments a set of twelve categories. The table of categories includes unity, plurality, totality, reality, negation, limitation, substance, causality, reciprocity, possibility, existence, and necessity. To show how these categories function, take as an example the categories of causality and substance: in order to be included as part of a coherently structured experience, whatever input we receive must find a place according to some ordering principle. The causal principle generates the temporal sequence of before and after according to the order of cause and effect. The principle of substance generates the order of properties inhering in the enduring subjects of those properties. But the enduring subjects are not the predicateless substrata conceived by Aristotle as matter and by Descartes as extension. These metaphysical curiosities, never met with in ordinary experi-

the table of categories. Not only the twelve categories named by Kant, showed that the articulation of things (substances) in our experience is the result of **our** ordering of perceptual data into coherent blocks of properties. Substance is not a property of things in themselves but a result of the way we order experience. Similarly causality, as Hume showed, is not a property of things in themselves. I see a door close, I hear a loud noise; I say the slamming door caused the bang, but I do not **see** the causal link the way I see the door and hear the noise.

Thinkers like Husserl concerned themselves largely with expanding the table of categories. Not only the twelve categories named by Kant but a great many other features of our experience are a function of our own categorial organization. But it may be more interesting to expand the transcendental approach in general to noncognitive dimensions of experience. As we shall see later, the course of nineteenth- and twentieth-century philosophy can be read in part as an extension of Kant's transcendental method from examining our categories of understanding to examining all the baggage we bring to experience. Later thinkers discover all sorts of **a priori's**, from instinctual structures to economic and social determinations. We may haggle over whether later invocations of **a priori** status conform to Kant's definition of the **a priori,** but clearly the basic thrust of the transcendental method remains central to much of the philosophy that followed Kant: thinkers concerned themselves not so much with the objects of experience themselves as with our modes of dealing with those objects, and with how those modes are unconsciously brought to experience rather than read out of experience.

William James reflects on the metaphysics of the world seen by Kantian and post-Kantian philosophy. How do Kantian insights affect the arguments by Descartes, Ryle, and Hume for and against an inner self, a Cogito, or a "ghost in the machine"? Kant himself retained a very important place for the Cogito—the 'I think,' which he said must accompany all our awarenesses. If I bring a lot to experience, then there must be an **I** who does the bringing. James doubts the cogency of this inference.

WILLIAM JAMES

(1842-1910)

Though the following essay begins with reflections upon Kant's legacy, its implications extend far beyond Kant's philosophy. Recall that Descartes attempted a kind of metaphysical undressing in order to uncover the bedrock of identity in the piece of wax. Hume argued that he could find no such underlying source of identity, either in changing things or in himself. Yet Erikson and Hume both agree that certain relations of continuity and resemblance do constitute a "consolidation" sufficient for us to identify both others and ourselves as numerically singular and enduring.

James is in effect arguing that Kant and his followers are backtracking on Hume's theory of relational identity. In his effort to see what the subject brings to experience, Kant effects a kind of epistemological striptease: he tries to abstract all particular features from the experience of knowing in order to get down to the ultimate knower, the 'I think,' the **Cogito,** which according to Kant must be able to accompany every experience.

While James' answer to Kant is in some ways very similar to Hume's answer to Descartes—namely, in substituting a relational concept of identity for an underlying substratum of identity—it is important to see how James' essay goes beyond Hume's. Though Hume denied the existence of a substratum of identity in the self, the bundle of perceptions in relation to one another constituted a subjective experience different in kind and cut off from objective reality. Hume's theory of knowledge was ultimately skeptical because he could not bridge the subject-object gap. According to Hume we know only our ideas of things and not the things themselves. The ideas are in the subject while the things remain in a separate, objective realm.

James' great insight was to see a vestigial influence of the concept of substratum identity in this separation of subject and object. Even though Hume and thinkers like him denied the existence of a particular entity tying subjective experience together the way the island of Manhattan joins all its buildings, still they regarded subjective experience as irrevocably separate from objective entities, a separateness modeled after that of different, self-identical entities. Those thinkers had developed the concept of relational identity as a denial of substratum identity where the substratum could not be found, but they had not come to the corresponding concept of **relational difference.** They still thought in terms of difference of substrata as the ultimate criterion of difference.

James uses the metaphor of a single point lying at the intersection of two different lines. Taking one line as the continuity of a subjective experience and the other as the continuity of an objective history, he argues that the experience of, say, a room is both subjective and objective. The experience, like the point, is numerically one, not two, but it reflects a difference to the extent that it can be related to two different and equally continuous contexts: the history of the person and the history of the room. The subject-object split arises from regarding the single experience as numerically two, from regarding the relational difference as a difference of substratum—as if the two lines never do and never can really intersect. Consequently, we come to think of the single experience as split into two substantially different halves: the room as it exists in objective reality and a subjective representation of the room. Those halves are then transformed into wholes: a self-contained objective reality and a self-contained mental experience. But if James is right, this separating transformation is a bit of myth-making we carry on as a result of a confusion between relational difference and differences among substrata.

This confusion is fairly widespread, so it might be worth taking up another example in preparation for James' argument. Meat and potatoes and melon are examples of different substrata. If a given piece of food is a piece of meat you can be sure that it is not and cannot be a potato. But what about some of our other ways of distinguishing among foods? What about the terms 'dessert' and 'appetizer'? It is true that in a three-course meal the appetizer will usually be separated from the dessert by the main course, but the same kind of substratum—say melon—can be either appetizer or dessert. If melon plays the role of dessert, a role defined by a temporal relation to the main course, does it follow that melon can never be an appetizer? Further, while it makes sense to ask how many melons there are in the world, does it make sense to ask how much dessert there is in the world? Dessert is a role-concept, not a substratum-concept. Roles are defined by contextual relations in such a way that one and the same thing may play two or more roles. James is arguing not only that the unity of our mental experience is not given by a single substratum called consciousness, but also that subjectivity and objectivity are role-concepts. They no more denote two separate metaphysical substrata than do appetizer and dessert.

Does 'Consciousness' Exist?

'Thoughts' and 'things' are names for two sorts of object, which common sense will always find contrasted and will always practically oppose to each other. Philosophy, reflecting on the contrast, has varied in the past in her explanations of it, and may be expected to vary in the future. At first, 'spirit and matter,' 'soul and body,' stood for a pair of equipollent substances quite on a par in weight and interest. But one day Kant undermined the soul and brought in the transcendental ego, and ever since then the bipolar relation has been very much off its balance. The transcendental ego seems nowadays in rationalist quarters to stand for everything, in empiricist quarters for almost nothing. In the hands of such writers as Schuppe, Rehmke, Natorp, Münsterberg— at any rate in his earlier writings, Schubert-Soldern and others, the spiritual principle attenuates itself to a thoroughly ghostly condition, being only a name for the fact that the 'content' of experience *is known*. It loses personal form and activity—these passing over to the content—and becomes

DOES 'CONSCIOUSNESS' EXIST? From William James, *Essays in Radical Empiricism*. First appeared in the *Journal of Philosophy, Psychology and Scientific Methods*, Vol. 1, No. 18, September 1, 1904.

a bare *Bewusstheit* [consciousness] or *Bewusstsein überhaupt* [general awareness], of which in its own right absolutely nothing can be said.

I believe that 'consciousness,' when once it has evaporated to this estate of pure diaphaneity, is on the point of disappearing altogether. It is the name of a nonentity, and has no right to a place among first principles. Those who still cling to it are clinging to a mere echo, the faint rumor left behind by the disappearing 'soul' upon the air of philosophy. During the past year, I have read a number of articles whose authors seemed just on the point of abandoning the notion of consciousness,[1] and substituting for it that of an absolute experience not due to two factors. But they were not quite radical enough, not quite daring enough in their negations. For twenty years past I have mistrusted 'consciousness' as an entity; for seven or eight years past I have suggested its non-existence to my students, and tried to give them its pragmatic equivalent in realities of experience. It seems to me that the hour is ripe for it to be openly and universally discarded.

To deny plumply that 'consciousness' exists seems so absurd on the face of it—for undeniably 'thoughts' do exist—that I fear some readers will follow me no farther. Let me then immediately explain that I mean only to deny that the word stands for an entity, but to insist most emphatically that it does stand for a function. There is, I mean, no aboriginal stuff or quality of being, contrasted with that of which material objects are made, out of which our thoughts of them are made; but there is a function in experience which thoughts perform, and for the performance of which this quality of being is invoked. That function is *knowing*. 'Consciousness' is supposed necessary to explain the fact that things not only are, but get reported, are known. Whoever blots out the notion of consciousness from his list of first principles must still provide in some way for that function's being carried on.

1

My thesis is that if we start with the supposition that there is only one primal stuff or material in the world, a stuff of which everything is composed, and if we call that stuff 'pure experience,' then knowing can easily be explained as a particular sort of relation towards one another into which portions of pure experience may enter. The relation itself is a part of pure experience; one of its 'terms' becomes the subject or bearer of the knowledge, the knower,[2] the other becomes the object known. This will need much explanation before it can be understood. The best way to get it understood is to contrast it with the

---

[1] Articles by Baldwin, Ward, Bawden, King, Alexander and others. Dr. Perry is frankly over the border.

[2] In my *Psychology* I have tried to show that we need no knower other than the 'passing thought.' [*Principles of Psychology,* vol. 1, pp. 338 ff.]

alternative view; and for that we may take the recentest alternative, that in which the evaporation of the definite soul-substance has proceeded as far as it can go without being yet complete. If neo-Kantism has expelled earlier forms of dualism, we shall have expelled all forms if we are able to expel neo-Kantism in its turn.

For the thinkers I call neo-Kantian, the word consciousness to-day does no more than signalize the fact that experience is indefeasibly dualistic in structure. It means that not subject, not object, but object-plus-subject is the minimum that can actually be. The subject-object distinction meanwhile is entirely different from that between mind and matter, from that between body and soul. Souls were detachable, had separate destinies; things could happen to them. To consciousness as such nothing can happen, for, timeless itself, it is only a witness of happenings in time, in which it plays no part. It is, in a word, but the logical correlative of 'content' in an Experience of which the peculiarity is that *fact comes to light* in it, that *awareness of content* takes place. Consciousness as such is entirely impersonal—'self' and its activities belong to the content. To say that I am self-conscious, or conscious of putting forth volition, means only that certain contents, for which 'self' and 'effort of will' are the names, are not without witness as they occur.

Thus, for these belated drinkers at the Kantian spring, we should have to admit consciousness as an 'epistemological' necessity, even if we had no direct evidence of its being there.

But in addition to this, we are supposed by almost every one to have an immediate consciousness of consciousness itself. When the world of outer fact ceases to be materially present, and we merely recall it in memory, or fancy it, the consciousness is believed to stand out and to be felt as a kind of impalpable inner flowing, which, once known in this sort of experience, may equally be detected in presentations of the outer world. "The moment we try to fix our attention upon consciousness and to see *what,* distinctly, it is," says a recent writer, "it seems to vanish. It seems as if we had before us a mere emptiness. When we try to introspect the sensation of blue, all we can see is the blue; the other element is as if it were diaphanous. Yet it *can* be distinguished, if we look attentively enough, and know that there is something to look for."[3] "Consciousness" (Bewusstheit), says another philosopher, "is inexplicable and hardly describable, yet all conscious experiences have this in common that what we call their content has this peculiar reference to a centre for which 'self' is the name, in virtue of which reference alone the content is subjectively given, or appears. . . . While in this way consciousness, or reference to a self, is the only thing which distinguishes a conscious content from any sort of being that might be there with no one conscious of it, yet this only ground of the distinction defies all closer explanations. The existence of consciousness, although it is the fundamental fact of psychology, can

[3] G. E. Moore: *Mind,* vol. XII, N.S. [1903], p. 450.

indeed be laid down as certain, can be brought out by analysis, but can neither be defined nor deduced from anything but itself."[4]

'Can be brought out by analysis,' this author says. This supposes that the consciousness is one element, moment, factor—call it what you like —of an experience of essentially dualistic inner constitution, from which, if you abstract the content, the consciousness will remain revealed to its own eye. Experience, at this rate, would be much like a paint of which the world pictures were made. Paint has a dual constitution, involving, as it does, a menstruum[5] (oil, size or what not) and a mass of content in the form of pigment suspended therein. We can get the pure menstruum by letting the pigment settle, and the pure pigment by pouring off the size or oil. We operate here by physical subtraction; and the usual view is, that by mental subtraction we can separate the two factors of experience in an analogous way—not isolating them entirely, but distinguishing them enough to know that they are two.

2

Now my contention is exactly the reverse of this. *Experience, I believe, has no such inner duplicity; and the separation of it into consciousness and content comes, not by way of subtraction, but by way of addition*—the addition, to a given concrete piece of it, of other sets of experiences, in connection with which severally its use or function may be of two different kinds. The paint will also serve here as an illustration. In a pot in a paint-shop, along with other paints, it serves in its entirety as so much saleable matter. Spread on a canvas, with other paints around it, it represents, on the contrary, a feature in a picture and performs a spiritual function. Just so, I maintain, does a given undivided portion of experience, taken in one context of associates, play the part of a knower, of a state of mind, of 'consciousness'; while in a different context the same undivided bit of experience plays the part of a thing known, of an objective 'content.' In a word, in one group it figures as a thought, in another group as a thing. And, since it can figure in both groups simultaneously we have every right to speak of it as subjective and objective both at once. The dualism connoted by such double-barrelled terms as 'experience,' 'phenomenon,' 'datum,' 'Vorfindung' [anticipation] —terms which, in philosophy at any rate, tend more and more to replace the single-barrelled terms of 'thought' and 'thing'—that dualism, I say, is still preserved in this account, but reinterpreted, so that, instead of being

---

[4] Paul Natorp: *Einleitung in die Psychologie,* 1888, pp. 14, 112.

[5] "Figuratively speaking, consciousness may be said to be the one universal solvent, or menstruum, in which the different concrete kinds of psychic acts and facts are contained, whether in concealed or in obvious form." G. T. Ladd: *Psychology, Descriptive and Explanatory,* 1894, p. 30.

mysterious and elusive, it becomes verifiable and concrete. It is an affair of relations, it falls outside, not inside, the single experience considered, and can always be particularized and defined.

The entering wedge for this more concrete way of understanding the dualism was fashioned by Locke when he made the word 'idea' stand indifferently for thing and thought, and by Berkeley when he said that what common sense means by realities is exactly what the philosopher means by ideas. Neither Locke nor Berkeley thought his truth out into perfect clearness, but it seems to me that the conception I am defending does little more than consistently carry out the 'pragmatic' method which they were the first to use.

If the reader will take his own experiences, he will see what I mean. Let him begin with a perceptual experience, the 'presentation,' so called, of a physical object, his actual field of vision, the room he sits in, with the book he is reading as its centre; and let him for the present treat this complex object in the common-sense way as being 'really' what it seems to be, namely, a collection of physical things cut out from an environing world of other physical things with which these physical things have actual or potential relations. Now at the same time it is just *those self-same things* which his mind, as we say, perceives; and the whole philosophy of perception from Democritus's time downwards has been just one long wrangle over the paradox that what is evidently one reality should be in two places at once, both in outer space and in a person's mind. 'Representative' theories of perception avoid the logical paradox, but on the other hand they violate the reader's sense of life, which knows no intervening mental image but seems to see the room and the book immediately just as they physically exist.

The puzzle of how the one identical room can be in two places is at bottom just the puzzle of how one identical point can be on two lines. It can, if it be situated at their intersection; and similarly, if the 'pure experience' of the room were a place of intersection of two processes, which connected it with different groups of associates respectively, it could be counted twice over, as belonging to either group, and spoken of loosely as existing in two places, although it would remain all the time a numerically single thing.

Well, the experience is a member of diverse processes that can be followed away from it along entirely different lines. The one self-identical thing has so many relations to the rest of experience that you can take it in disparate systems of association, and treat it as belonging with opposite contexts. In one of these contexts it is your 'field of consciousness'; in another it is 'the room in which you sit,' and it enters both contexts in its wholeness, giving no pretext for being said to attach itself to consciousness by one of its parts or aspects, and to outer reality by another. What are the two processes, now, into which the room-experience simultaneously enters in this way?

One of them is the reader's personal biography, the other is the history of the house of which the room is part. The presentation, the experience, the *that* in short (for until we have decided *what* it is it must be a mere *that*) is the last term of a train of sensations, emotions, decisions, movements, classifications, expectations, etc., ending in the present, and the first term of a series of similar 'inner' operations extending into the future, on the reader's part. On the other hand, the very same *that* is the *terminus ad quem* [end toward which] of a lot of previous physical operations, carpentering, papering, furnishing, warming, etc., and the *terminus a quo* [origin from which] of a lot of future ones, in which it will be concerned when undergoing the destiny of a physical room. The physical and the mental operations form curiously incompatible groups. As a room, the experience has occupied that spot and had that environment for thirty years. As your field of consciousness it may never have existed until now. As a room, attention will go on to discover endless new details in it. As your mental state merely, few new ones will emerge under attention's eye. As a room, it will take an earthquake, or a gang of men, and in any case a certain amount of time, to destroy it. As your subjective state, the closing of your eyes, or any instantaneous play of your fancy will suffice. In the real world, fire will consume it. In your mind, you can let fire play over it without effect. As an outer object, you must pay so much a month to inhabit it. As an inner content, you may occupy it for any length of time rent-free. If, in short, you follow it in the mental direction, taking it along with events of personal biography solely, all sorts of things are true of it which are false, and false of it which are true if you treat it as a real thing experienced, follow it in the physical direction, and relate it to associates in the outer world.

3

So far, all seems plain sailing, but my thesis will probably grow less plausible to the reader when I pass from percepts to concepts, or from the case of things presented to that of things remote. I believe, nevertheless, that here also the same law holds good. If we take conceptual manifolds, or memories, or fancies, they also are in their first intention mere bits of pure experience, and, as such, are single *thats* which act in one context as objects, and in another context figure as mental states. By taking them in their first intention, I mean ignoring their relation to possible perceptual experiences with which they may be connected, which they may lead to and terminate in, and which then they may be supposed to 'represent.' Taking them in this way first, we confine the problem to a world merely 'thought-of' and not directly felt or seen. This world, just like the world of percepts, comes to us at first as a chaos of experiences, but lines of order soon get traced. We find that any bit of it which we may cut out as an example is connected with distinct groups of associates, just as our perceptual experiences are, that these associates link themselves with it by different relations,[6] and that one forms the inner history of a person, while the other acts as an impersonal 'objective' world, either spatial and temporal, or else merely logical or mathematical, or otherwise 'ideal.'

The first obstacle on the part of the reader to seeing that these non-perceptual experiences have objectivity as well as subjectivity will probably be due to the intrusion into his mind of *percepts,* that third group of associates with which the non-perceptual experiences have relations, and which, as a whole, they 'represent,' standing to them as thoughts to things. This important function of the non-perceptual experiences complicates the question and confuses it; for, so used are we to treat percepts as the sole genuine realities that, unless we keep them out of the discussion, we tend altogether to overlook the objectivity that lies in non-perceptual experiences by themselves. We treat them, 'knowing' percepts as they do, as through and through subjective, and say that they are wholly constituted of the stuff called consciousness, using this term now for a kind of entity, after the fashion which I am seeking to refute.[7]

Abstracting, then, from percepts altogether, what I maintain is, that any single non-perceptual experience tends to get counted twice over, just as a perceptual experience does, figuring in one context as an object or field of objects, in another as a state of mind: and all this without the least internal self-diremption on its own part into consciousness and content. It is all consciousness in one taking; and, in the other, all content.

I find this objectivity of non-perceptual experiences, this complete parallelism in point of reality between the presently felt and the remotely thought, so well set forth in a page of Münsterberg's *Grundzüge,* that I will quote it as it stands.

"I may only think of my objects," says Professor Münsterberg; "yet, in my living thought they stand before me exactly as perceived objects would do, no matter how different the two ways of apprehending them may be in their genesis. The book here lying on the table before me, and the book in the next room of which I think and which I mean to get, are both in the same sense given realities for me, realities which I acknowledge and of which I take account. If you agree that the perceptual object is not an idea within me, but that percept and thing, as indistinguishably one, are really experienced *there, outside,* you ought not to believe that the merely thought-of object is hid away inside of the thinking subject. The object of which I think, and of whose existence I take cognizance without letting it now work upon my senses, occupies its definite place in the outer world as much as does the object which I directly see."

[6] Here as elsewhere the relations are of course *experienced* relations, members of the same originally chaotic manifold of nonperceptual experience of which the related terms themselves are parts.

[7] Of the representative function of non-perceptual experience as a whole, I will say a word in a subsequent article: it leads too far into the general theory of knowledge for much to be said about it in a short paper like this.

"What is true of the here and the there, is also true of the now and the then. I know of the thing which is present and perceived, but I know also of the thing which yesterday was but is no more, and which I only remember. Both can determine my present conduct, both are parts of the reality of which I keep account. It is true that of much of the past I am uncertain, just as I am uncertain of much of what is present if it be but dimly perceived. But the interval of time does not in principle alter my relation to the object, does not transform it from an object known into a mental state. . . . The things in the room here which I survey, and those in my distant home of which I think, the things of this minute and those of my long-vanished boyhood, influence and decide me alike, with a reality which my experience of them directly feels. They both make up my real world, they make it directly, they do not have first to be introduced to me and mediated by ideas which now and here arise within me. . . . This not-me character of my recollections and expectations does not imply that the external objects of which I am aware in those experiences should necessarily be there also for others. The objects of dreamers and hallucinated persons are wholly without general validity. But even were they centaurs and golden mountains, they still would be 'off there,' in fairy land, and not 'inside' of ourselves."[8]

This certainly is the immediate, primary, naïf, or practical way of taking our thought-of world. Were there no perceptual world to serve as its 'reductive,' in Taine's sense, by being 'stronger' and more genuinely 'outer' (so that the whole merely thought-of world seems weak and inner in comparison), our world of thought would be the only world, and would enjoy complete reality in our belief. This actually happens in our dreams, and in our day-dreams so long as percepts do not interrupt them.

And yet, just as the seen room (to go back to our late example) is *also* a field of consciousness, so the conceived or recollected room is *also* a state of mind; and the doubling-up of the experience has in both cases similar grounds.

The room thought-of, namely, has many thought-of couplings with many thought-of things. Some of these couplings are inconstant, others are stable. In the reader's personal history the room occupies a single date —he saw it only once perhaps, a year ago. Of the house's history, on the other hand, it forms a permanent ingredient. Some couplings have the curious stubbornness, to borrow Royce's term, of fact; others show the fluidity of fancy—we let them come and go as we please. Grouped with the rest of its house, with the name of its town, of its owner, builder, value, decorative plan, the room maintains a definite foothold, to which, if we try to loosen it, it tends to return, and to reassert itself with force.[9] With these associates, in a word, it coheres, while to other houses, other

[8] Münsterberg: *Grundzüge der Psychologie,* vol. 1, p. 48.

[9] Cf. A. L. Hodder: *The Adversaries of the Sceptic,* pp. 94–99.

towns, other owners, etc., it shows no tendency to cohere at all. The two collections, first of its cohesive, and, second, of its loose associates, inevitably come to be contrasted. We call the first collection the system of external realities, in the midst of which the room, as 'real,' exists; the other we call the stream of our internal thinking, in which, as a 'mental image,' it for a moment floats.[10] The room thus again gets counted twice over. It plays two different rôles, being *Gedanke* and *Gedachtes,* the thought-of-an-object, and the object-thought-of, both in one; and all this without paradox or mystery, just as the same material thing may be both low and high, or small and great, or bad and good, because of its relations to opposite parts of an environing world.

As 'subjective' we say that the experience represents; as 'objective' it is represented. What represents and what is represented is here numerically the same; but we must remember that no dualism of being represented and representing resides in the experience *per se.* In its pure state, or when isolated, there is no self-splitting of it into consciousness and what the consciousness is 'of.' Its subjectivity and objectivity are functional attributes solely, realized only when the experience is 'taken,' *i.e.,* talked-of, twice, considered along with its two differing contexts respectively, by a new retrospective experience, of which that whole past complication now forms the fresh content.

The instant field of the present is at all times what I call the 'pure' experience. It is only virtually or potentially either object or subject as yet. For the time being, it is plain, unqualified actuality, or existence, a simple *that.* In this *naïf* immediacy it is of course *valid;* it is *there,* we *act* upon it; and the doubling of it in retrospection into a state of mind and a reality intended thereby, is just one of the acts. The 'state of mind,' first treated explicitly as such in retrospection, will stand corrected or confirmed, and the retrospective experience in its turn will get a similar treatment; but the immediate experience in its passing is always 'truth,'[11] practical truth, *something to act on,* at its own movement. If the world were then and there to go out like a candle, it would remain truth absolute and objective, for it would be 'the last word,' would have no critic, and no one would ever oppose the thought in it to the reality intended.[12]

---

[10] For simplicity's sake I confine my exposition to 'external' reality. But there is also the system of ideal reality in which the room plays its part. Relations of comparison, of classification, serial order, value, also are stubborn, assign a definite place to the room, unlike the incoherence of its places in the mere rhapsody of our successive thoughts.

[11] Note the ambiguity of this term, which is taken sometimes objectively and sometimes subjectively.

[12] In the *Psychological Review* for July [1904], Dr. R. B. Perry has published a view of Consciousness which comes nearer to mine than any other with which I am acquainted. At present, Dr. Perry thinks, every field of experience is so much 'fact.' It becomes 'opinion' or 'thought' only in retrospection, when a fresh experi-

I think I may now claim to have made my thesis clear. Consciousness connotes a kind of external relation, and does not denote a special stuff or way of being. *The peculiarity of our experiences, that they not only are, but are known, which their 'conscious' quality is invoked to explain, is better explained by their relations—these relations themselves being experiences—to one another.*

4

Were I now to go on to treat of the knowing of perceptual by conceptual experiences, it would again prove to be an affair of external relations. One experience would be the knower, the other the reality known; and I could perfectly well define, without the notion of 'consciousness,' what the knowing actually and practically amounts to—leading-towards, namely, and terminating-in percepts, through a series of transitional experiences which the world supplies. But I will not treat of this, space being insufficient.[13] I will rather consider a few objections that are sure to be urged against the entire theory as it stands.

5

First of all, this will be asked: "If experience has not 'conscious' existence, if it be not partly made of 'consciousness,' of what then is it made? Matter we know, and thought we know, and conscious content we know, but neutral and simple 'pure experience' is something we know not at all. Say *what* it consists of—for it must consist of something—or be willing to give it up!"

To this challenge the reply is easy. Although for fluency's sake I myself spoke early in this article of a stuff of pure experience, I have now to say that there is no *general* stuff of which experience at large is made. There are as many stuffs as there are 'natures' in the things experienced. If you ask what any one bit of pure experience is made of, the answer is always the same: "It is made of *that*, of just what appears, of space, of intensity, of flatness, brownness, heaviness, or what not." Shadworth Hodgson's analysis here leaves nothing to be desired. Experience is only a collective

---

ence, thinking the same object, alters and corrects it. But the corrective experience becomes itself in turn corrected, and thus experience as a whole is a process in which what is objective originally forever turns subjective, turns into our apprehension of the object. I strongly recommend Dr. Perry's admirable article to my readers.

[13] I have given a partial account of the matter in *Mind,* vol. x, p. 27, 1885 [reprinted in *The Meaning of Truth,* pp. 1–42], and in the *Psychological Review,* vol. II, p. 105, 1895 [partly reprinted in *The Meaning of Truth,* pp. 43–50]. See also C. A. Strong's article in the *Journal of Philosophy, Psychology and Scientific Methods,* vol. 1, p. 253, May 12, 1904. I hope myself very soon to recur to the matter.

name for all these sensible natures, and save for time and space (and, if you like, for 'being') there appears no universal element of which all things are made.

6

The next objection is more formidable, in fact it sounds quite crushing when one hears it first.

"If it be the self-same piece of pure experience, taken twice over, that serves now as thought and now as thing"—so the objection runs—"how comes it that its attributes should differ so fundamentally in the two takings. As thing, the experience is extended; as thought, it occupies no space or place. As thing, it is red, hard, heavy; but who ever heard of a red, hard or heavy thought? Yet even now you said that an experience is made of just what appears, and what appears is just such adjectives. How can the one experience in its thing-function be made of them, consist of them, carry them as its own attributes, while in its thought-function it disowns them and attributes them elsewhere. There is a self-contradiction here from which the radical dualism of thought and thing is the only truth that can save us. Only if the thought is one kind of being can the adjectives exist in it 'intentionally' (to use the scholastic term); only if the thing is another kind, can they exist in it constitutively and energetically. No simple subject can take the same adjectives and at one time be qualified by it, and at another time be merely 'of' it, as of something only meant or known."

The solution insisted on by this objector, like many other common-sense solutions, grows the less satisfactory the more one turns it in one's mind. To begin with, *are* thought and thing as heterogeneous as is commonly said?

No one denies that they have some categories in common. Their relations to time are identical. Both, moreover, may have parts (for psychologists in general treat thoughts as having them); and both may be complex or simple. Both are of kinds, can be compared, added and subtracted and arranged in serial orders. All sorts of adjectives qualify our thoughts which appear incompatible with consciousness, being as such a bare diaphaneity. For instance, they are natural and easy, or laborious. They are beautiful, happy, intense, interesting, wise, idiotic, focal, marginal, insipid, confused, vague, precise, rational, casual, general, particular, and many things besides. Moreover, the chapters on 'Perception' in the psychology-books are full of facts that make for the essential homogeneity of thought with thing. How, if 'subject' and 'object' were separated 'by the whole diameter of being,' and had no attributes in common, could it be so hard to tell, in a presented and recognized material object, what part comes in through the sense organs and what part comes 'out of one's own head'? Sensations and apperceptive ideas fuse here so intimately that you can no more tell where one begins and the other ends, than you can tell, in those cunning circular panoramas that have lately been exhibited, where the real foreground and the painted canvas join together.[14]

Descartes for the first time defined thought as the absolutely unextended, and later philosophers have accepted the description as correct. But what possible meaning has it to say that, when we think of a footrule or a square yard, extension is not attributable to our thought? Of every extended object the *adequate* mental picture must have all the extension of the object itself. The difference between objective and subjective extension is one of relation to a context solely. In the mind the various extents maintain no necessarily stubborn order relatively to each other, while in the physical world they bound each other stably, and, added together, make the great enveloping Unit which we believe in and call real Space. As 'outer,' they carry themselves adversely, so to speak, to one another, exclude one another and maintain their distances; while, as 'inner,' their order is loose, and they form a *durcheinander* [hodgepodge] in which unity is lost.[15] But to argue from this that inner experience is absolutely inextensive seems to me little short of absurd. The two worlds differ, not by the presence or absence of extension, but by the relations of the extensions which in both worlds exist.

Does not this case of extension now put us on the track of truth in the case of other qualities? It does; and I am surprised that the facts should not have been noticed long ago. Why, for example, do we call a fire hot, and water wet, and yet refuse to say that our mental state, when it is 'of' these objects, is either wet or hot? 'Intentionally,' at any rate, and when the mental state is a vivid image, hotness and wetness are in it just as much as they are in the physical experience. The reason is this, that, as the general chaos of all our experiences gets sifted, we find that there are some fires that will always burn sticks and always warm our bodies, and that there are some waters that will always put out fires; while there are other fires and waters that will not act at all. The general group of experiences that *act,* that do not only possess their natures intrinsically, but wear them adjectively and energetically, turning them against one another, comes inevitably to be contrasted with the group whose members, having identically the same natures, fail to manifest them in the 'energetic' way. I make for myself now an experience of blazing fire; I place it near my body; but it does not warm me in the least. I lay a stick upon it, and the stick either burns or remains green, as I please. I call up water, and pour it on the fire, and absolutely no difference ensues. I account for all

[14] Spencer's proof of his 'Transfigured Realism' (his doctrine that there is an absolutely non-mental reality) comes to mind as a splendid instance of the impossibility of establishing radical heterogeneity between thought and thing. All his painfully accumulated points of difference run gradually into their opposites, and are full of exceptions. [Cf. Spencer: *Principles of Psychology,* part VII, ch. XIX.]

[15] I speak here of the complete inner life in which the mind plays freely with its materials. Of course the mind's free play is restricted when it seeks to copy real things in real space.

such facts by calling this whole train of experiences unreal, a mental train. Mental fire is what won't burn real sticks; mental water is what won't necessarily (though of course it may) put out even a mental fire. Mental knives may be sharp, but they won't cut real wood. Mental triangles are pointed, but their points won't wound. With 'real' objects, on the contrary, consequences always accrue; and thus the real experiences get sifted from the mental ones, the things from our thoughts of them, fanciful or true, and precipitated together as the stable part of the whole experience-chaos, under the name of the physical world. Of this our perceptual experiences are the nucleus, they being the originally *strong* experiences. We add a lot of conceptual experiences to them, making these strong also in imagination, and building out the remoter parts of the physical world by their means; and around this core of reality the world of laxly connected fancies and mere rhapsodical objects floats like a bank of clouds. In the clouds, all sorts of rules are violated which in the core are kept. Extensions there can be indefinitely located; motion there obeys no Newton's laws.

7

There is a peculiar class of experiences to which, whether we take them as subjective or as objective, we *assign* their several natures as attributes, because in both contexts they affect their associates actively, though in neither quite as 'strongly' or as sharply as things affect one another by their physical energies. I refer here to *appreciations,* which form an ambiguous sphere of being, belonging with emotion on the one hand, and having objective 'value' on the other, yet seeming not quite inner nor quite outer, as if a diremption had begun but had not made itself complete.

Experiences of painful objects, for example, are usually also painful experiences; perceptions of loveliness, of ugliness, tend to pass muster as lovely or as ugly perceptions; intuitions of the morally lofty are lofty intuitions. Sometimes the adjective wanders as if uncertain where to fix itself. Shall we speak of seductive visions or of visions of seductive things? Of wicked desires or of desires for wickedness? Of healthy thoughts or of thoughts of healthy objects? Of good impulses, or of impulses towards the good? Of feelings of anger, or of angry feelings? Both in the mind and in the thing, these natures modify their context, exclude certain associates and determine others, have their mates and incompatibles. Yet not as stubbornly as in the case of physical qualities, for beauty and ugliness, love and hatred, pleasant and painful can, in certain complex experiences, coexist.

If one were to make an evolutionary construction of how a lot of originally chaotic pure experiences became gradually differentiated into an orderly inner and outer world, the whole theory would turn upon one's success in explaining how or why the quality of an experience, once active, could become less so, and, from being an energetic attribute in some cases, elsewhere lapse into the status of an inert or merely internal 'nature.' This would be the 'evolution' of the psychical from the bosom of the physical, in which the esthetic, moral and otherwise emotional experiences would represent a halfway stage.

8

But a last cry of *non possumus* [we cannot] will probably go up from many readers. "All very pretty as a piece of ingenuity," they will say, "but our consciousness itself intuitively contradicts you. We, for our part, *know* that we are conscious. We *feel* our thought, flowing as a life within us, in absolute contrast with the objects which it so unremittingly escorts. We can not be faithless to this immediate intuition. The dualism is a fundamental *datum:* Let no man join what God has put asunder."

My reply to this is my last word, and I greatly grieve that to many it will sound materialistic. I can not help that, however, for I, too, have my intuitions and I must obey them. Let the case be what it may in others, I am as confident as I am of anything that, in myself, the stream of thinking (which I recognize emphatically as a phenomenon) is only a careless name for what, when scrutinized, reveals itself to consist chiefly of the stream of my breathing. The 'I think' which Kant said must be able to accompany all my objects, is the 'I breathe' which actually does accompany them. There are other internal facts besides breathing (intracephalic muscular adjustments, etc., of which I have said a word in my larger Psychology), and these increase the assets of 'consciousness,' so far as the latter is subject to immediate perception; but breath, which was ever the original of 'spirit,' breath moving outwards, between the glottis and the nostrils, is, I am persuaded, the essence out of which philosophers have constructed the entity known to them as consciousness. *That entity is fictitious, while thoughts in the concrete are fully real. But thoughts in the concrete are made of the same stuff as things are.*

I wish I might believe myself to have made that plausible in this article. In another article I shall try to make the general notion of a world composed of pure experiences still more clear.

Transition: Incarnate Consciousness and Philosophy of the Body

Descartes is generally credited with (or blamed for) having drawn too deep a distinction between mind and body, or as he put it, between thinking substance and extended substance. Many contemporary Anglo-American philosophers have criticized the Cartesian split, but their movement, often referred to as "philosophy of mind," has curiously tended to perpetuate the split between mind and body. Ryle purged contemporary thought of the "ghost in the machine," but who has devoted attention to the machine on the ghost, that is, to the myth of the body as something separate and simply worn as a cloak by the person beneath? To the extent that philosophers of mind eliminate the Cartesian dualism, an adequate philosophy of body is implicit in their writings, but an explicit statement of a philosophy of body would prevent our slipping back into the same old dualism when talking about bodily phenomena.

European philosophy in the last century deals with philosophy of body more than our Anglo-American tradition. Particularly in the movement known as "phenomenology," many thinkers have written on the necessarily **incarnate** character of human consciousness. Though Friedrich Nietzsche predates the flourishing of the phenomenological movement, his writings influenced some of its major figures, particularly Martin Heidegger, Maurice Merleau-Ponty, and Jean-Paul Sartre. Though Husserl and later phenomenologists devote many pages to the precise meaning of the term 'phenomenology,' we can begin by saying that 'phenomenology' stands for a method of inquiry rather than a fixed set of truths, and that the key to the method lies in paying attention to the phenomena of experience themselves without interpreting them in terms of the theoretical presuppositions or dogmas we bring to experience. What Husserl described as the "phenomenological reduction" is for the most part an attempt to lay bare the presuppositions that **we** bring to experience, presuppositions that common sense imagines it finds in the object of experience. So, for example, Nietzsche uncovers how we presuppose a division between properties and the subject that lies behind them. What we thought we **found in** experience, namely things (subjects) with properties (predicates) Nietzsche tells us we put there through our own **interpretation** of the phenomena.

Nietzsche's point is fairly Kantian, but with an important difference: while Kant showed us how we constitute our experience using our cognitive apparatus with its various forms and categories, Nietzsche, along with several other nineteenth- and twentieth-century thinkers, tried to show how **noncognitive** aspects of the self assist in constituting experience. Later thinkers have adopted a version of Kant's Copernican revolution—that the experienced objects must conform to our means of cognition rather than that our knowledge must conform to things in themselves—but they have taken this transcendental perspective and expanded it to the range of the noncognitive.

Karl Marx, for example, held that economic factors played a major role in determining the kind of reality certain people are capable of seeing.

> The production of ideas, of conceptions, of consciousness is directly interwoven with the material activity and the material relationships of men; it is the language of actual life. Conceiving, thinking, and the intellectual relationships of men appear here as the direct result of their material behavior. The same applies to intellectual production as manifested in a people's language of politics, law, morality, religion, metaphysics, etc.[1]

Freud argued that instincts play the major role in determining how we experience life. Whether we are consciously aware of it or not, what we do and what we experience is largely determined by the play of instincts. For both Freud and Marx, the conscious reasons we offer for our actions are better understood as **rationalizations** for following the deeper determinants we bring to our experience.

Naturally, the reduction of reasoning to rationalization is a tough pill for most philosophers to swallow, and many simply turn away rather than take up the argumentative gambit. But some, like Nietzsche and Norman O. Brown, are ruthless in their will to face the possibility of false consciousness. (This term appears frequently in the Marxist tradition of ideological debates: one accuses another of false consciousness when one wishes to claim that the other is not only wrong, but incapable of seeing the truth because of the nature of the noncognitive determinants playing on his consciousness. The victim of false consciousness is like a deaf man in a concert hall; he cannot be expected to make good judgments. The term 'false consciousness' is obviously transferable to contexts in which the determinants of experience are other than economic.)

To return now to the philosophy of body, more and more of our contemporaries attribute a type of false consciousness directly to bodily determinants. How is this physiological influence possible? In order to break down the Cartesian distinction between thinking consciousness

[1] Karl Marx and Friedrich Engels, "The German Ideology," in *Writings of the Young Marx on Philosophy and Society*, ed. and trans. Easton and Guddat, Doubleday & Company, Garden City, New York, 1967, p. 414.

and body, it is sufficient to show that both exhibit a certain identity with a crucial third realm, that of mood, emotion, and feeling.

First let's examine the distinction between moods and feelings on the one hand and thoughts on the other. How clear is the distinction? Following the Cartesian split between mind and body, we tend to think of mathematics as the paradigm of thought, and then we imagine, with Descartes, that all thought, insofar as it is really **thinking,** is clear and distinct and utterly independent of emotional affect. But if you examine what happens, even in mathematics, isn't there almost always some emotional affect, like the "Whew!" when the long division problem comes out without a remainder, or the "Aha" when you see how to reach a geometrical proof? Now if we take the phenomenological stance of really looking at what happens, then we may come to wonder whether we describe the situation properly when we say that thought (one process) often **has** emotional affect (another process), as if thought and emotion were two separate things, like milk and cream, and the two could be separated out in the skim milk of logical inquiry. Another metaphor (though still only a metaphor) would be viewing thought as a river and emotion as the water: there is no river without water, but sometimes the river runs smoothly and sometimes it is turbulent. We talk about the river and the water in different ways: the river bends and drops, the water flows and gurgles. But the river **is** the water in some sense, so our different ways of talking about the river and the water don't confuse us into thinking there can be a river without water. There is, of course, a riverbed; but no one would take an empty riverbed for a river. Where thought runs smoothly, however, people have imagined that thought in its purest form was the empty riverbed of emotionless thought.

Now, to complete the "connection" between thinking and the body (I use quotes because the connection is only one of argumentative sequence; the argument's conclusion claims an identity: one thing with different aspects rather than different things connected together as if by a rope), let us argue the bodily character of emotions. Some may think that emotions are confused thoughts, just as the rationalist philosopher Leibniz thought perceptions were confused ideas. So, for example, anger might be conceived as a kind of intellectual contradiction: "I'm mad at her because she wants me to go home and I want to stay at the party." We often hear people asking others who are emotionally upset to "be reasonable!" as if a well-thought-out resolution to a contradiction would end the emotional upset. But this is often an absurd expectation, and the request to "be reasonable" can itself be an emotional outburst meaning "Do it **my** way!"

Surely emotions often do refer to situations that can be described and articulated in intellectual terms, but the very fact that we call certain experiences more emotional than intellectual stems from the fact that those experiences are felt in our bodies. Joy is not simply holding an opinion that something is nice; it is a state in which smiling or laughing or jumping up and down play an essential part. And grief calls for crying.

Just as the Cartesian view sees thought and emotion like milk and cream—similar but separable—so it sees the emotions and the body as two separate things often linked by causal relationships, as if **thinking** that something is nice **caused** a smile. In fact, as William James saw, the smile **is** at least a large part of the joy. James' insight is put succinctly in the following statement that makes the connection between emotions and the body:

> The more closely I scrutinize my states, the more persuaded I become that whatever moods, affections, and passions I have are in very truth constituted by, and made up of, those bodily changes which we ordinarily call their expression or consequence; and the more it seems to me that if I were to become corporeally anaesthetic, I should be excluded from the life of the affections, harsh and tender alike, and drag out an existence of merely cognitive or intellectual form.[2]

During the past decade more and more people have been discovering that they were corporeally anesthetized. I do not think that the movement in sensitivity training is a mere fad; it has philosophical significance. It is as if our culture is now discovering that the Cartesian mind-body split had actually made its way from the pages of a philosophical text into the very fabric of our lives, and that a mistake in thought had filtered down into mistaken life styles. Once the body comes alive again, once the life is changed, the mistake in the thought is easier to see, and the new realization cannot fail to have philosophic import in an influence on the character of thought pursued.

If precedents are needed (since the philosophical movement I am describing is so new as to be almost nonexistent), one need only look, as many are now looking, to the East. In marked contrast to the western tradition of philosophy, Indian and Chinese thinkers have always recognized the unity of mind and body. Yoga is not just a form of exercise to keep you fit so you'll live longer and look better. Westerners have often dismissed Yoga because the claims made for its suprabodily effects seemed mystical. But as the following selection shows, Nietzsche's arguments for the importance of the body are hardly mystical.

2 William James, *The Principles of Psychology*, 2 vols., New York, Dover, 1890.

FRIEDRICH NIETZSCHE

(1844-1900)

Friedrich Nietzsche's thought lends itself to expression in aphoristic form. Rather than develop long, detailed arguments leading from premises to conclusions through further premises to further conclusions, Nietzsche preferred to leap from peak to peak in long strides. The wonder is that he so often landed squarely on each peak. As the numbers and parenthesized dates show, the following aphorisms from his posthumously published work **The Will to Power** were neither written together nor were they intended to appear together. Nevertheless, the reader should be able to draw his own connections among Nietzsche's various reflections on a single topic.

Before relating the different aphorisms to one another it may help to unpack the condensed statement of each by connecting it to other discussions. For example, No. 492 addresses "the idea of the nature of our subject-unity," the main topic of Part 2. But more specifically, Nietzsche's choice of the model of a regent "at the head of a communality" is the subject of Ryle's remarks in his historical note at the end of his essay. Nos. 485, 547, and 549 carry further the reflections on the metaphysics of subject, substance, self, and identity most explicitly developed by Descartes and Hume. No. 676 shows an anticipation of the Freudian concept of the unconscious, a concept that comes up again, particularly in the essays by Laing and Reich. Finally Nietzsche's concern for the immediate quality of life in No. 1016 seems very close to our contemporary concerns as they were expressed by Slater, Fromm, and Marin.

As each aphorism is explored we see emerging a unified picture of the self: the self is radically physical, and any attempts to deny that physicality can be interpreted only as conscious or unconscious attempts to deny life.

THE SOUL IS SOMETHING
ABOUT THE BODY

[492 (*1885*)] The body and physiology the starting point: why?— We gain the correct idea of the nature of our subject-unity, namely as regents at the head of a communality (not as "souls" or "life forces"), also of the dependence of these regents upon the ruled and of an order of rank and division of labor as the conditions that make possible the whole and its parts. In the same way, how living unities continually arise and die and how the "subject" is not eternal; in the same way, that the struggle expresses itself in obeying and commanding, and that a fluctuating assessment of the limits of power is part of life. The relative ignorance in which the regent is kept concerning individual activities and even disturbances within the communality is among the conditions under which rule can be exercised. In short, we also gain a valuation of *not-knowing,* of seeing things on a broad scale, of simplification and falsification, of perspectivity. The most important thing, however, is: that we understand that the ruler and his subjects are of the same kind, all feeling, willing, thinking—and that, wherever we see or divine movement in a body, we learn to conclude that there is a subjective, invisible life appertaining to it. Movement is symbolism for the eye; it indicates that something has been felt, willed, thought.

The danger of the direct questioning of the subject *about* the subject and of all self-reflection of the spirit lies in this, that it could be useful and important for one's activity to interpret oneself *falsely.* That is why we question the body and reject the evidence of the sharpened senses: we try, if you like, to see whether the inferior parts themselves cannot enter into communication with us.

[485 (*Spring–Fall 1887*)] The concept of substance is a consequence of the concept of the subject: not the reverse! If we relinquish the soul, "the subject," the precondition for "substance" in general disappears. One acquires degrees of being, one loses that which *has* being.

Critique of "reality": where does the "more or less real," the gradation of being in which we believe, lead to?—

The degree to which we feel life and power (logic and coherence of experience) gives us our measure of "being," "reality," not-appearance.

The subject: this is the term for our belief in a unity underlying all the different impulses of the highest feeling of reality: we understand this belief

THE SOUL IS SOMETHING ABOUT THE BODY   From *The Will to Power,* by Friedrich Nietzsche. Translated by Walter Kaufmann and R. J. Hollingdale. Copyright © 1967 by Walter Kaufmann. Reprinted by permission of Random House, Inc. (The title I have chosen to head this assemblage of aphorisms is a line from *The Antichrist* by Nietzsche.)

as the *effect* of one cause—we believe so firmly in our belief that for its sake we imagine "truth," "reality," "substantiality" in general.— "The subject" is the fiction that many similar states in us are the effect of one substratum: but it is we who first created the "similarity" of these states; our adjusting them and making them similar is the fact, not their similarity (—which ought rather to be denied—).

[547 (*1885–1886*)] Psychological history of the concept "subject." The body, the thing, the "whole" construed by the eye, awaken the distinction between a deed and a doer; the doer, the cause of the deed, conceived ever more subtly, finally left behind the "subject."

[549 (*1885*)] "Subject," "object," "attribute"—these distinctions are fabricated and are now imposed as a schematism upon all the apparent facts. The fundamental false observation is that I believe it is *I* who do something, suffer something, "have" something, "have" a quality.

[659 (*1885*)] *The evidence of the body.*— Granted that the "soul" is an attractive and mysterious idea which philosophers have rightly abandoned only with reluctance—perhaps that which they have since learned to put in its place is even more attractive, even more mysterious. The human body, in which the most distant and most recent past of all organic development again becomes living and corporeal, through which and over and beyond which a tremendous inaudible stream seems to flow: the body is a more astonishing idea than the old "soul." In all ages, there has been more faith in the body, as our most personal possession, our most certain being, in short our ego, than in the spirit (or the "soul," or the subject, as school language now has it instead of soul). It has never occurred to anyone to regard his stomach as a strange or, say, a divine stomach: but to conceive his ideas as "inspired," his evaluations as "implanted by a God," his instincts as activity in a half-light—for this tendency and taste in men there are witnesses from all ages of mankind. Even now there is ample evidence among artists of a sort of wonderment and respectful suspension of judgment when they are faced with the question of the means by which they achieved their best work and from which world the creative idea came to them; when they ask this, they exhibit something like innocence and childlike shamefacedness; they hardly dare to say "it came from me, it was my hand that threw the dice."

Conversely, even those philosophers and religious teachers who had the most compelling ground in their logic and piety to consider their bodies a deception (and, indeed, as a deception overcome and done with) could not help acknowledging the foolish fact that the body has not gone away; of which the strangest witnesses are to be found partly in Paul, partly in the Vedanta philosophy. But what, after all, does *strength of belief* mean? It could still be a very foolish belief!— This should be reflected on:—

And after all, if belief in the body is only the result of an inference: supposing it were a false inference, as the idealists assert, is it not a question mark against the spirit itself that it should be the cause of such false inferences? Supposing multiplicity, space and time, and motion (and whatever else may be the presuppositions of a belief in what is bodily) were errors —what mistrust would this arouse against the spirit that had prompted such presuppositions? Let it suffice that, for the present, belief in the body is always a stronger belief than belief in the spirit; and whoever desires to undermine it, also undermines at the same time most thoroughly belief in the authority of the spirit!

[676 (*1883–1888*)] *On the Origin of Our Evaluations.*—We can analyze our body spatially, and then we gain precisely the same image of it as we have of the stellar system, and the distinction between the organic and inorganic is no longer noticeable. Formerly, one explained the motions of the stars as effects produced by entities conscious of a purpose. One no longer needs this explanation, and in regard to bodily motions and changes, too, one has long since abandoned the belief in an explanation by means of a consciousness that determines purposes. By far the greater number of motions have nothing whatever to do with consciousness; nor with sensation. Sensations and thoughts are something extremely insignificant and rare in relation to the countless number of events that occur every moment.

On the other hand, we perceive that a purposiveness rules over the smallest events that is beyond our understanding: planning, selectivity, coordination, reparation, etc. In short, we discover an activity that would have to be ascribed to a far higher and more comprehensive intellect than we know of. We learn to think less highly of all that is conscious; we unlearn responsibility for ourselves, since we as conscious, purposive creatures, are only the smallest part of us. Of the numerous influences operating at every moment, e.g., air, electricity, we sense almost nothing: there could well be forces that, although we never sense them, continually influence us. Pleasure and pain are very rare and scarce appearances compared with the countless stimuli that a cell or organ exercises upon another cell or organ.

We are in the phase of modesty of consciousness. Ultimately, we understand the conscious ego itself only as a tool in the service of a higher, comprehensive intellect; and then we are able to ask whether all conscious willing, all conscious purposes, all evaluations are not perhaps only means through which something essentially different from what appears in consciousness is to be achieved. We think: it is a question of our pleasure and displeasure——but pleasure and displeasure could be means through which we have to achieve something that lies outside our consciousness.—— It must be shown to what exent everything conscious remains on the surface; how an action and the image of an action differ, how little one knows of what precedes an action; how fantastic are our feelings of "freedom of will," "cause and effect"; how thoughts and images are, like words, only signs of thoughts; the inexplicability of every action; the superficiality of all praise and blame; how essential fiction and conceits are in which we dwell consciously; how all our words refer to fictions (our affects, too), and how the bond between man and man depends on the transmission and elaboration of these fictions; while fundamentally the real bond (through procreation) goes its unknown way. Does this belief in common fictions really *change* men? Or is the entire realm of ideas and evaluations itself only an expression of unknown changes? *Are* there really will, purposes, thoughts, values? Is the whole of conscious life perhaps only a reflected image? And even when evaluation seems to determine the nature of a man, fundamentally something quite different is happening! In short: supposing that purposiveness in the work of nature could be explained without the assumption of an ego that posits purposes: could *our* positing of purposes, our willing, etc., not perhaps be also only a language of signs for something altogether different, namely something that does not will and is unconscious? Only the faintest reflection of that natural expediency in the organic but not different from it?

Put briefly: perhaps the entire evolution of the spirit is a question of the body; it is the history of the development of a higher body that emerges into our sensibility. The organic is rising to yet higher levels. Our lust for knowledge of nature is a means through which the body desires to perfect itself. Or rather: hundreds of thousands of experiments are made to change the nourishment, the mode of living and of dwelling of the body; consciousness and evaluations in the body, all kinds of pleasure and displeasure, are signs of these changes and experiments. In the long run, it is not a question of man at all: he is to be overcome.

[314 (*Nov. 1887–March 1888*)] Our most sacred convictions, the unchanging elements in our supreme values, are judgments of our muscles.

[392 (*March–June 1888*)] Moral values as illusory values compared with physiological values.

[461 (*March–June 1888*)] *Why philosophers are slanderers.*— The treacherous and blind hostility of philosophers towards the senses—how much of mob and middle class there is in this hatred!

The common people always consider an abuse of which they feel the ill consequences as an objection to that which is abused: all insurrectionary movements aimed against principles, whether political or economic, argue thus, with the idea of representing an abuse as being necessary to, and inherent in, the principle.

It is a miserable story: man seeks a principle through which he can despise men—he invents a world so as to be able to slander and bespatter this world: in reality, he reaches every time for nothingness and construes nothingness as "God," as "truth," and in any case as judge and condemner of *this* state of being—

If one wants a proof of how profoundly and thoroughly the actually barbarous needs of man seek satisfaction, even when he is tamed and "civilized," one should take a look at the "leitmotifs" of the entire evolution of philosophy:—a sort of revenge on reality, a malicious destruction of the valuations by which men live, an unsatisfied soul that feels the tamed state as a torture and finds a voluptuous pleasure in a morbid unraveling of all the bonds that tie it to such a state.

The history of philosophy is a secret raging against the preconditions of life, against the value feelings of life, against partisanship in favor of life. Philosophers have never hesitated to affirm a world provided it contradicted this world and furnished them with a pretext for speaking ill of this world. It has been hitherto the grand school of slander; and it has imposed itself to such an extent that today our science, which proclaims itself the advocate of life, has accepted the basic slanderous position and treated this world as apparent, this chain of causes as merely phenomenal. What is it really that hates here?

I fear it is still the Circe of philosophers, morality, that has here bewitched them into having to be slanderers forever— They believed in moral "truths," they found there the supreme values—what else could they do but deny existence more firmly the more they got to know it?— For this existence is immoral— And this life depends upon immoral preconditions: and all morality *denies* life—.

Let us abolish the real world: and to be able to do this we first have to abolish the supreme value hitherto, morality— It suffices to demonstrate that even morality is immoral, in the sense in which immorality has always been condemned. If the tyranny of former values is broken in this way, if we have abolished the "real world," then a new order of values must follow of its own accord.

The apparent world and the world invented by a lie—this is the antithesis. The latter has hitherto been called the "real world," "truth," "God." This is what we have to abolish.

Logic of my conception:

1. Morality as supreme value (master over all phases of philosophy, even over the skeptics). Result: this world is good for nothing, it is not the "real world."

2. What here determines the supreme value? What is morality, really?— The instinct of decadence; it is the exhausted and disinherited who *take revenge* in this fashion. Historical proof: philosophers are always decadents —in the service of the *nihilistic* religions.

3. The instinct of decadence which appears as will to power. Proof: the absolute immorality of means throughout the entire history of morality.

General insight: the highest values hitherto are a special case of the will to power; morality itself is a special case of immorality.

[820 (*1885*)] In the main, I agree more with the artists than with any philosopher hitherto: they have not lost the scent of life, they have loved the things of "this world"—they have loved their senses. To strive for "desensualization": that seems to me a misunderstanding or an illness or a cure, where it is not merely hypocrisy or self-deception. I desire for myself and for all who live, *may* live, without being tormented by a puritanical conscience, an ever-greater spiritualization and multiplication of the senses; indeed, we should be grateful to the senses for their subtlety, plenitude, and power and offer them in return the best we have in the way of spirit. What are priestly and metaphysical calumnies against the senses to us! We no longer need these calumnies: it is a sign that one has turned out well when, like Goethe, one clings with ever-greater pleasure and warmth to the "things of this world":—for in this way he holds firmly to the great conception of man, that man becomes the transfigurer of existence when he learns to transfigure himself.

[226 (*March–June 1888*)] They despised the body: they left it out of the account: more, they treated it as an enemy. It was their delusion to believe that one could carry a "beautiful soul" about in a cadaverous abortion— To make this conceivable to others they needed to present the concept "beautiful soul" in a different way, to revalue the natural value, until at last a pale, sickly, idiotically fanatical creature was thought to be perfection, "angelic," transfiguration, higher man.

[1016 (*March–June 1888*)] *What does us honor.*— If anything does us honor, it is this: we have transferred seriousness: we regard as important the lowly things that have at all times been despised and left aside—on the other hand, we let "beautiful feelings" go cheap.

Is there a more dangerous aberration than contempt for the body? As if it did not condemn all spirituality to become sickly—to the *vapeurs* of "idealism"!

Whatever Christians and idealists have devised has neither rhyme nor reason: we are more radical. We have discovered the "smallest world" as that which is decisive everywhere.

The way our streets are paved, good air in our room, food—we grasp their value; we have taken all the necessities of existence seriously and despise all "beautiful-soulism" as a kind of "levity and frivolity."— What was formerly most despised has been brought to the front.

[1046 (*1884*)]
1. We want to hold fast to our senses and to our faith in them—and think their consequences through to the end! The nonsensuality of philosophy hitherto as the greatest nonsensicality of man.

2. The existing world, upon which all earthly living things have worked so that it appears as it does (durable and changing *slowly*), we want to go on building—and not criticize it away as false!

3. Our valuations are a part of this building; they emphasize and underline. Of what significance is it if entire religions say: "all is bad and false and evil"! This condemnation of the entire process can only be a judgment of the ill-constituted!

4. To be sure, the ill-constituted can be the greatest sufferers and the most subtle? The contented could be of little value?

5. One must understand the artistic basic phenomenon that is called "life"—the building spirit that builds under the most unfavorable conditions: in the slowest manner—— A demonstration of all its combinations must first be produced afresh: it preserves itself.

[1047 (*Nov. 1887–March 1888*)] Sexuality, the lust to rule, pleasure in appearance and deception, great and joyful gratitude for life and its typical states—these are of the essence of the pagan cults and have a good conscience on their side.— Unnaturalness (already in Greek antiquity) fights against the pagan, as morality, as dialectic.

NORMAN O. BROWN
(1913-   )

If Nietzsche's praise of the body was avowedly antimystical and this-worldly, Norman O. Brown's resurrection of the body would seem to be its contrary. Brown cites the importance of the traditional writings on the mystical body. But what **is** the mystical body?

Part of Brown's aim is to undercut any attempt at a single answer to that question. In fact, he attacks the spirit of literalism, that seriousness seeking a single, definitive picture of the world. "To make in ourselves a new consciousness, an erotic sense of reality, is to become conscious of symbolism. Symbolism is mind making connections (correspondences) rather than distinctions (separations)." Brown's erotic sense of reality is an attempt to join all systems of relational determination in one "body." His emphasis on the importance of the body is hardly a physicalism. Rather, the body is significant both in itself as a part of the totality **and** as a metaphor for union and communion among all the facets of reality.

Because Brown's own words forbid single, literal interpretation, it seems most appropriate to look for their communion with the rest of the essays in this anthology. Brown's style of bringing together the words of others is an inspiration for the nature and intent of an anthology. I encourage the reader to reflect again and again on Brown's ideas as he seeks a unified vision from the varied essays pulled together here. Brown's insights might serve as a kind of methodological preface to the whole book. Surely his reflections help to explain why, for example, Peter Marin finds it

necessary to write in fits and starts without a clear, linear organization; Marin is seeking the new consciousness that Brown describes. But note that Brown's reflections are no excuse for slop-
piness. The quest for wholeness includes the passionate and the
erotic, but in communion with care and discipline.

Brown's symbolic consciousness returns us once again to the
complex business of taking each experience many times over, as
James put it. Further, Brown explicitly relates this pluralism of
vision to the problem of freedom. Rather than finding freedom in
a denial of determinism, Brown finds freedom in "over-determination." Each event is the subject of many different relational determinations. The attempt to constrict the meaning of the event
to a single set of determinations is the mistake of literalism.
Polymorphous perversity in sexuality becomes the metaphor for a
polymorphous reality in union with itself. The joyous spontaneity
of sexuality symbolizes the height of freedom in that polymorphous
reality.

SYMBOLIC CONSCIOUSNESS
AND SEXUALITY

Unity

Is there a way out; an end to analysis; a cure; is there such a thing as health?

To heal is to make whole, as in wholesome; to make one again; to unify
or reunify: this is Eros in action. Eros is the instinct that makes for union,
or unification, and Thanatos, the death instinct, is the instinct that makes
for separation, or division.

Crazy Jane in William Butler Yeats—Crazy Jane who is both the student and the teacher—says,

> Nothing can be sole or whole
> That has not been rent.

We have been rent; there is no health in us. We must acknowledge the
rents, the tears, the splits, the divisions; and then we can pray, as Freud

prays at the end of *Civilization and Its Discontents,* "that the other of the two heavenly forces, eternal Eros, will put forth his strength so as to maintain himself alongside his equally immortal adversary."

Yeats, "Crazy Jane Talks with the Bishop."

There is only one political problem in our world today: the unification of mankind. The Internationale shall be the human race. That they may be one—*ut unum sint.* This is Christ's last prayer before the crucifixion, which was also the last prayer of the late Pope John; it must be set beside Freud's prayer in *Civilization and Its Discontents.* For indeed they will not be one until Freud and Pope John are found to speak in unison; or Freud and Marx and Pope John: the thing is to bring them together. John X, 16: Other sheep I have, which are not of this fold: them also must I bring, and they shall hear my voice; and there shall be one fold, and one shepherd.

John XVII, 21.

The unification of the human race: a mental fight, a struggle in and about men's minds. The rents, the tears, splits and divisions are mindmade; they are not based on the truth but on what the Buddhists call illusion, what Freud calls unconscious fantasies. The prevailing sense of reality, the prevailing forms of knowledge, are ruled by the instinct of aggression and division, are under the dominion of the death instinct. We are in Satan's kingdom; to build a Heaven in Hell's despite is to construct an erotic sense of reality.

To make in ourselves a new consciousness, an erotic sense of reality, is to become conscious of symbolism. Symbolism is mind making connections (correspondences) rather than distinctions (separations). Symbolism makes conscious interconnections and unions that were unconscious and repressed. Freud says, symbolism is on the track of a former identity, a lost unity: the lost continent, Atlantis, underneath the sea of life in which we live enisled; or perhaps even our union with the sea (Thalassa); oceanic consciousness, the unity of the whole cosmos as one living creature, as Plato said in the *Timaeus.*

Cf. Freud, "Interpretation of Dreams," 370.

Union and unification is of bodies, not souls. The erotic sense of reality unmasks the soul, the personality, the ego; because soul, personality and ego are what distinguish and separate us; they make us individuals, arrived at by dividing till you can divide no more—atoms. But psychic individuals, separate, unfissionable on the inside, impenetrable on the outside, are, like physical atoms, an illusion; in the twentieth century, in this age of fission, we can split the individual even as we can split the atom. Souls, personalities, and egos are masks, spectres, concealing our unity as body. For it is as one biological species that mankind is one—"the species-essence" that

Karl Marx looked for; so that to become conscious of ourselves as body is to become conscious of mankind as one.

Cf. K. Marx and F. Engels, *Kleine ökonomische Schriften,* 42–166.

It is the erotic sense of reality that discovers the inadequacy of fraternity, or brotherhood. It is not adequate as a form for the reunification of the human race: we must be either far more deeply unified, or not at all. The true form of unification—which can be found either in psychoanalysis or in Christianity, in Freud or Pope John, or Karl Marx—is: "we are all members of one body." The true form of the unification of the human race is not the brothers, Cain and Abel, but Adam the first man, and Christ the second man: for as in Adam all die, even so in Christ shall all be made alive.

I Corinthians XV, 22. Cf. Daniélou, *Origen,* 205: "When we expound the dogma of the Mystical Body we do not take the dogma itself from Karl Marx but we do bring out the factors in it that correspond to what Karl Marx taught."

Christ is the second Adam; these two are one; there is only one man. This is not a new idea, but part of the great tradition, to be made new and alive today. St. Thomas Aquinas says, "many men are derived from Adam, as members of one body"—*tanquam membra unius corporis;* and, "the human race is to be considered as one body, which is called the mystical body, whose head is Christ himself, both with regard to the souls and with regard to the bodies"—*et quantum ad animas et quantum ad corpora.* The mystical body is not, because mystical, therefore non-bodily. And St. Augustine: "the whole human race which was to become Adam's posterity through the first woman, was present in the first man." "We all existed in that one man, since, taken together, we were the one man who fell into sin." Even as in Hebrew *adham* is man and mankind in one; and the man Adam. "All mankind, whose life from Adam to the end of this world is as the life of one man."

St. Thomas Aquinas in Gierke, *Political Theories of the Middle Age,* 103, n.7. Augustine, *De Civitate Dei,* XIII, 3–14, *de vera religione,* 27, 50. Cf. Pedersen, *Israel,* I, 110. Ladner, *The Idea of Reform,* 264–265.

And the resurrection is the resurrection of the body; but not the separate body of the individual, but the body of mankind as one body. The fall of man is the fall into division of the human race, the dismemberment of the first man, Adam; and the resurrection or rebirth through the second man, Christ, is to reconstitute the lost unity. "His fall into Division & his Resurrection to Unity"; till we all come to one perfect man. St. Athanasius, commenting on Christ's last prayer, "that they may be all one, as Thou in Me, and I in Thee," says it means that "born as it were by Me, they may all be one body and one spirit, and may combine to form one perfect man . . . so that, made divine, they may be one in us." The unification of mankind into one is also the unification of humanity and divinity; St.

Gregory of Nyssa says, "Christ, by whom all mankind was united into divinity." Unification is deification.

Blake, *Night* I, 1. 21. Scheeben, *Mysteries*, 367n., 386n.
Cf. Augustine, *De Civitate Dei,* XXII, 17–18. Dante, *De Monarchia,* I, 8. Ephesians IV, 13; John XVII, 21.

If we are all members of one body, then in that one body there is neither male nor female; or rather there is both: it is an androgynous or hermaphroditic body, containing both sexes. In this way St. Augustine explains that other old story: the creation of Eve out of the rib of Adam. "God did not wish to create the woman who was to be mated with man in the same way that He created man, but, rather, out of him, in order that the whole human race might be derived entirely from one single man." The division of the one man into two sexes is part of the fall; sexes are sections.

Galatians III, 28. Augustine, *De Civitate Dei,* XII, 21.

Hence according to the Epistle to the Ephesians the true meaning of the mystery of sexual intercourse is that it is a symbolic representation, or adumbration, of that mystical body in which we are all members of one body.

> So ought men to love their wives as their own bodies. He that loveth his wife loveth himself.
> For no man ever yet hated his own flesh; but nourisheth and cherisheth it, even as the Lord the church.
> For we are members of his body, of his flesh, and of his bones.
> For this cause shall a man leave his father and mother, and shall be joined unto his wife, and they two shall be one flesh.
> This is a great mystery: but I speak concerning Christ and the church.

Ephesians V, 28–32.

The fantastic hypothesis of Freud in *Beyond the Pleasure Principle* and Ferenczi in *Thalassa* turns out to be right after all. The tendency of the sexual instinct is to restore an earlier state of things, an earlier state of unity, before life was sexually differentiated; ultimately going back to a state "before living substance was torn apart into separate particles." Freud illustrated his hypothesis with the myth in Plato's *Symposium,* deriving sexual differentiation from the bisection of a primal hermaphroditic body.

Freud, *Beyond the Pleasure Principle,* 79–80.

What else is to be found in psychoanalysis, by those determined to find, about the one body, the mystical body? The truth, the healing truth, the wholesome truth, the truth that will make us whole, is not in individual psychology, nor in the currently so fashionable ego psychology, but in what the later Freud called "mass-psychology." Freud said his last work, *Moses and Monotheism,* was an attempt "to translate the concepts of individual psychology into mass-psychology." "Mass-psychology" is not mob psychology, but the psychology of mankind as a whole, as one mass, or one body. Mass, then, in the same sense as Augustine's *massa perditionis; universa massa in vitiata radice damnata* [the condemned human race; the whole mass damned as if in a vitiated root]. The word "enmasse." [. . .]

Cf. Augustine, *De Civitate Dei,* XIV, 26. Whitman, "One's-Self I Sing."

Resurrection

II Corinthians III, 6: The letter killeth, but the spirit giveth life. Literal meanings as against spiritual or symbolical interpretations, a matter of Life against Death. The return to symbolism, the rediscovery that everything is symbolic—*alles Vergängliche nur ein Gleichniss*—a penis in every convex object and a vagina in every concave one—is psychoanalysis. A return or turning point, the beginning of a new age; the Third Kingdom, the age of the spirit prophesied by Joachim of Fiore; or the second coming, the resurrection of the body. It is raised a spiritual or symbolical body; the awakening to the symbolical life of the body.

The return to symbolism would be the end of the Protestant era, the end of Protestant literalism. Symbolism in its pre-Protestant form consisted of typological, figural, allegorical interpretations, of both scripture and liturgy. But the great Protestant Reformers were very explicit in their condemnation of the typological method: "The literal sense of Scripture alone is the whole essence of faith and of Christian theology." *Sola fide, sola litera:* faith is faith in the letter.

Luther in Miller, *Roger Williams,* 34–35.

Protestant literalism: the crux is the reduction of meaning to a single meaning—univocation. Luther's word is *Eindeutigkeit:* the "single, simple, solid and stable meaning" of scripture; *unum simplicem solidum et constantem sensum.* Compare Calvin on Galatians IV, 22–26: "But as the apostle declares that these things are allegorized, Origen, and many others along with him, have seized the occasion of torturing Scripture in every possible manner away from the true sense. Scripture they say is fertile, and thus produces a variety of meanings. I acknowledge that Scripture is a most rich and inexhaustible fountain of wisdom: but I deny that its fertility consists in the various meanings which any man at his pleasure may assign. Let us know that the true meaning of Scripture is the natural and obvious meaning, and let us embrace and abide by it resolutely."

Cf. Holl, "Luthers Bedeutung für den Fortschritt der Auslegungskunst," 551. Hahn, "Luthers Auslegungsgrundsätze," 210.

Augustine had said: "What more liberal and more fruitful provision could God have made in regard to Sacred Scriptures than that the same words might be understood in several senses, all of which are sanctioned by the concurring testimony of other passages equally divine?" The Medieval schema of a fourfold meaning in everything—the quadriga, the four-horsed chariot—however mechanical in practice, is at least a commandment not to rest in one simple solid and constant meaning. As in Blake also:

> Now I a fourfold vision see,
> And a fourfold vision is given to me;
> 'Tis fourfold in my supreme delight
> And threefold in soft Beulah's night
> And twofold Always. May God us keep
> From Single vision and Newton's sleep!

So also the psychoanalytic principle of over-determination: "Psychical acts and structures are invariably over-determined." The principle of over-determination declares that there cannot be just one "true" interpretation of a symptom or symbol: it forbids literal-mindedness.

Augustine, *De Doctrina Christiana,* III, 38. Blake, Letter to Butts, 22 November 1802. Freud, *Totem and Taboo,* 100.

Protestant literalism is modern scholarship. Parallel to the emphasis on the one true meaning of scripture there was an increase in Luther's interest in grammar and textual criticism; to establish the text, *die feste Schrift,* a mighty fortress; the authoritative text.

Cf. Hahn, "Luthers Auslegungsgrundsätze," 207.

Textual criticism is part of the search for the one true and literal meaning. The old spiritual or symbolical consciousness had not hunted that will-o'-the-wisp, the one true text; instead it found symbolical meaning in every textual variation. Even the slips of the scribe were significant, as even the slips of the tongue become significant again for Freud. The early Luther, who, as he himself acknowledged later, was enthusiastic for symbolical interpretations, brought variant readings into happy harmony by applying the principle of over-determination: *"Die Anwendung des vierfachen Schriftsinnes geht sogar so weit, dass abweichende Lesarten durch den verschiedenen Gebrauch der Sinne zur Übereinstimmung gebracht werden* [the application of fourfold meaning extends even to bringing variant readings into agreement through different uses of the meaning]."

Hahn, "Luthers Auslegungsgrundsätze," 200.

Modern humanistic, literary, and historical scholarship, *Geisteswissenschaft,* is the pursuit of the literal truth; and it was the commitment to a literal interpretation of the Bible that modernized scholarship. Modern humanistic scholarship is the Renaissance counterpart of Reformation literalism.

Dilthey, "Die Entstehung der Hermeneutik," 324.

The basic assumption of modern hermeneutics, the organic unity of the document, is a commitment to univocation; and was elaborated by Protestantism to set up the one true meaning of scripture. Thus for example the Lutheran explicator *par excellence,* Flacius: "It was no little obstacle to the clarity of Scripture and to the truth and purity of Christian doctrine, that practically all the writers and fathers in their interpretations and explications of the sacred writings treated them as if they were a miscellaneous collection of sentiments, and not as an artistic unity conforming to correct principles of composition. In sacred scripture, as in all works of literature, the true meaning depends on the context, on the purpose of the work as a whole, and on the organic relations which unite the parts as members are united in one body."

Flacius cited in Dilthey, "Das natürliche System der Geisteswissenschaften," 118.

The crux in the reduction of meaning to a single meaning—both in scriptural and in literary exegesis—the crux in univocation, is the reduction of meaning to conscious meaning: *intentio auctoris,* the author's intention. But the unconscious is the true psychic reality; and the unconscious is the Holy Spirit. The opposite of the letter is the spirit. "The *sensus plenior* is that additional, deeper meaning, intended by God but not clearly intended by the human author."

Brown, *The Sensus Plenior of Sacred Scripture,* 92.
Cf. Lubac, *Histoire et esprit,* 387, 408.

The spirit inspires (the god is Dionysus). The orthodox Protestant faith is Protestan fundamentalism; if meaning is restricted to the conscious intention of the author, then divine inspiration means that the holy spirit is literally the author; the holy scripture is literally inspired. The inspiration of scripture is reduced to the infallibility of scripture, literally understood.

Cf. Hahn, "Luthers Auslegungsgrundsätze," 166. Ebeling, "Die Anfänge von Luthers Hermeneutik," 223.

The identification of God's word with scripture, the written or printed word; somewhat to the neglect of the word made flesh. The book is a materialization of the spirit; instead of the living spirit, the worship of a new material idol, the book.

Freedom

Meaning is new, or not at all; a new creation, or not at all; poetry or not at all. The newness is the metaphor, or nonsense—saying one thing and meaning another. It is the legal fiction, which liberates from the letter of the law and from the tyranny of literal meaning.

Cf. Barfield, "Poetic Diction and Legal Fiction."

A vast pun, a free play, with unlimited substitutions. A symbol is never a symbol but always polysymbolic, overdetermined, polymorphous. Freedom is fertility; a proliferation of images, in excess. The seed must be sown wastefully, extravagantly. Too much, or not enough; overdetermination is determination made into chance; chance and determination reconciled. Too much meaning is meaning and absurdity reconciled.

Cf. Sèchehaye, *A New Psychotherapy in Schizophrenia,* 142. Storch, *Primitive Archaic Forms,* 15–16. Onians, *Origins of European Thought,* 474–476. Chenu, "Histoire et allégorie au douzieme siècle," 66.

Symbolism is polymorphous perversity, the translation of all of our senses into one another, the interplay between the senses, the metaphor, the free translation. The separation of the senses, their mutual isolation, is sensuality, is sexual organization, is bondage to the tyranny of one partial impulse, leading to the absolute and exclusive concentration of the life of the body in the representative person.

Cf. McLuhan, *Gutenberg Galaxy,* 5, 65–66, 138.

Knowledge is carnal knowledge, a copulation of subject and object, making these two one. *Cognitio nihil aliud est quam coitio quaedam cum suo cognobili*—"Sex becomes not only an object of thought but in some sense an imaginative method of comprehension." Polymorphously perverse sexuality, in and through every organ of perception:

> If in the morning sun I find it, there my eyes are fix'd
> In happy copulation.

Patrizzi cited in Cassirer, *Individual and Cosmos,* 134. Sewell, *The Orphic Voice,* 209 (on Novalis). Blake, *Vision of the Daughters of Albion,* 194.

Knowledge is carnal knowledge. A subterranean passage between mind and body underlies all analogy; no word is metaphysical without its first being physical; and the body that is the measure of all things is sexual. All metaphors are sexual; a penis in every convex object and a vagina in every concave one.

Cf. Sharpe, "Psycho-Physical Problems Revealed in Language: an Examination of Metaphor," 202. Ferenczi, "Stages in the Development of the Sense of Reality," 227.

Symbolism is polymorphous perversity. Orthodox psychoanalysis warns against the resexualization of thought and speech; orthodox psychoanalysis bows down before the reality-principle. The reality-principle is based on desexualization; in symbolic consciousness thought and speech become resexualized. As in schizophrenia. For example, the patient who refused to play his violin in public; psychoanalysis can find nothing wrong: "Behind

every form of play lies a process of discharge of masturbatory phantasies."
Nothing wrong, except the refusal to play: when our eyes are opened to
the symbolic meaning, our only refuge is loss of shame, polymorphous
perversity, pansexualism; penises everywhere. As in Tantric Yoga, in which
any sexual act may become a form of mystic meditation, and any mystic
state may be interpreted sexually.

Klein, *Psychoanalysis of Children*, 31.
Cf. Fenichel, *Psychoanalytical Theory of the Neuroses*, 296. Storch, *Primitive Archaic Forms*, 17. Eliade, *Le Yoga*, 235.

Speech resexualized.

> *Sei das Wort die Braut genannt*
> *Bräutigam der Geist.*

The tongue made potent again, out of his mouth goeth a sharp sword. The
spermatic word, the word as seed; the sower soweth the word. Annuncia-
tions, messages, messengers, angels, having intercourse with the daughters
of men, making pregnant through the ear; angels or birds, winged words or
doves of the spirit. The flying bird or angel is an erection or a winged
phallus; "a single word stands for the penis and the sentence for the thrust
of the penis in coitus." A supernatural pregnancy: "A being, be it man or
woman, who has the Holy Ghost within him is pregnant or full of semen
and in ejaculating words of prophecy the wizard either ejaculates semen or
gives birth to a child."

Goethe, "Buch Hafis," *West-Östlicher Divan*. Roheim, *Animism*, 383; cf. 159–160.
Klein, "Infant Analysis," 112.
Cf. Freud, "Interpretation of Dreams," 390. Leisegang, *Pneuma Hagion*, 21, 25,
33, 35, 40, 49–50. Jones, "The Madonna's Conception through the Ear."

Speech resexualized. Sexual potency, linguistic power, abolished at
Babel and restored at Pentecost. At Pentecost, tongues of fire, a flame in
the shape of a male member. Speaking with tongues is fiery speech, speech
as a sexual act, a firebird or phoenix.

Cf. Flügel, "The International Language Movement," 196. Freud, "Acquisition of
Power over Fire," 291–292.

Speech resexualized: overcoming the consequences of the fall. The
tongue was the first unruly member. Displacement is first from above
downwards; the penis is a symbolic tongue, and disturbances of ejaculation
a kind of genital stuttering. "In the beginning the serpent, getting possession of the ears of Eve, thence spread his poison through her whole body;
today Mary through her ears received the champion of everlasting bliss."

St. Ephrem in Jones, "The Madonna's Conception through the Ear," 292.
Cf. Ferenczi, *Thalassa*, 9. Blake, *Night* I, 17–18.

Thought and speech resexualized. Symbolic correspondence is a marriage. The things beneath are related to the things above as Man and Wife.

Bring them together in a new conjunction, a *parallelismus membrorum* [parallelism of members], a rhyme, a couplet or copulation. In puns, "two words get on top of each other and become sexual"; in metaphor, two become one. What God hath joined no philosophy can put asunder.

Bion, "Language and the Schizophrenic," 237.
Cf. Paracelsus in Raine, "Blake's Debt to Antiquity," 421. Pedersen, *Israel*, I, 115, 123. O'Flaherty, *Unity and Language*, 69–70. McLuhan, *Gutenberg Galaxy*, 67.

Intercourse is what goes on in the sentence. In every sentence the little word "is" is the copula, the penis or bridge; in every sentence magically, with a word, the two one flesh. The little word "is" is the hallmark of Eros, even as, Freud said, the little word "no" is the hallmark of Death. Every sentence is dialectics, an act of love.

Cf. Richard, *Mallarmé* 424–425, 543. Freud, "Negation," 182.

> So they lov'd as love in twain
> Had the essence but in one,
> Two distincts, division none:
> Number there in love was slain.
>
> Reason, in itself confounded,
> Saw division grow together;
> To themselves yet either neither,
> Simple were so well compounded;
>
> That it cried, "How true a twain
> Seemeth this concordant one!
> Love hath reason, reason none,
> If what parts can so remain."

Shakespeare, "The Phoenix and the Turtle."

Dismembered, remembered. Symbolism is not the apprehension of another world of archetypes, but the transfiguration of this world; and the transfiguration of this world is its reunification. Symbolism, says Freud, is the vestige and signpost of a former (a prehistoric) identity: *ein Rest und Merkzeichen einstiger Identität.* The Fall is into Division, and the Resurrection is to Unity. Symbolism is the erotic, or Dionysian, sense of reality; restoring union.

Freud, *Gesammelte Schriften* III, 68; "Interpretation of Dreams," 370. Blake, *Night* I, 21.

In freedom is fusion. Pentecostal freedom, Pentecostal fusion. Speaking with tongues: many tongues, many meanings. The Babylonian confusion of tongues redeemed in the Pentecostal fusion. Many meanings dwelling together in unity; because it is the unspoken meaning that they mean. Real unification is in the unseen unity, unity at the unconscious level, at the level of symbolism. Pentecostal spirit is a principle of unspoken, unconscious unity, behind the diversity of conscious tongues; a unity which is impersonal or supra-personal, a unity in which personality is dissolved. Literal meaning is conscious meaning, a possession of the ego, a personal thing, a matter of personal self-assertion; contentious, divisive; opinion, dogma. To seek unity through univocation is to assure disunity. The blessing of multiplicity rejected returns as a curse: heresies and sects come from the literal sense of scripture. Instead of the Pentecostal fusion, the Babylonian confusion, the battle of books.

Cf. Franck in Williams, *The Radical Reformation,* 460.

Fusion: the distinction between inner self and outside world, between subject and object, overcome. To the enlightened man, the universe becomes his body: "You never enjoy the world aright till the Sea itself floweth in your veins, till you are clothed with the heavens and crowned with the stars." *Anima est quodammodo omnia,* as in schizophrenia: what happens to the person's own body is identified with what happens in the universe.

Traherne, *Centuries of Meditations* I, no. 29.
Cf. Govinda, *Foundations of Tibetan Mysticism,* 225. Storch, *Primitive Archaic Forms,* 4, 86–87.

Fusion, mystical participation. Primitive animism is suffused with the unconscious identification of subject and object: *participation mystique.* Civilized objectivity is non-participating consciousness, consciousness as separation, as dualism, distance, definition; as property and prison: consciousness ruled by negation, which is from the death instinct. Symbolical consciousness, the erotic sense of reality, is a return to the principle of ancient animistic science, mystical participation, but now for the first time freely; instead of religion, poetry.

Cf. Ferenczi, "The Scientific Significance of Freud's Three Essays," 256; *Thalassa,* 2–4.

Psychoanalysis began as a further advance of civilized (scientific) objectivity; to expose remnants of primitive participation, to eliminate them; studying the world of dreams, of primitive magic, of madness, but not participating in dreams or magic, or madness. But the outcome of psychoanalysis is the discovery that magic and madness are everywhere, and dreams is what we are made of. The goal cannot be the elimination of magical thinking, or madness; the goal can only be conscious magic, or conscious madness; conscious mastery of these fires. And dreaming while awake.

Cf. Roheim, *Magic and Schizophrenia,* 83.

There is a marriage (in heaven) between psychoanalysis and the mystical tradition; combining to make us conscious of our unconscious participation in the creation of the phenomenal world. "Neither nature nor man will ever be understood, though certainly physical nature—and perhaps physical man, too—may in the meantime be very skillfully *manipulated,* until we accept that nature is the reflected image of man's conscious and unconscious self." To become conscious of our participation in the creation of the phenomenal world is to pass from passive experience—perception as impressions on a passive mind—to conscious creation, and creative freedom. Every perception is a creation—"when we see physical objects we are makers or poets." Or gods; the world is our creation.

Turbayne, *Myth of Metaphor,* 135. Barfield, "The Meaning of the Word 'Literal,' " 56. Cf. Barfield, *Saving the Appearances,* 88–89, 100–101, 126–131.

All flesh shall see it together. Apocalypse is the dissolution of the group as numerical series, as in representative democracy, and its replacement by the group as fusion, as communion. As in totemism, we participate in each other as we participate in the object.

Cf. Sartre, *Critique de la raison dialectique,* 391; cf. 386–395.

Sleepers, awake. Sleep is separateness; the cave of solitude is the cave of dreams, the cave of the passive spectator. To be awake is to participate, carnally and not in fantasy, in the feast; the great communion.

EPICURUS

(341-270 B.C.)

To participate carnally in the feast as Brown urges us sounds very much like some form of hedonism. Does Brown have Epicureanism in mind? Much of our attitude toward the body derives from the favor or disfavor into which various philosophic movements have fallen. The philosophy of Epicurus has not received much attention in recent years, and consequently many of us who recognize his name associate it only with an ill-formed concept of playboy-pleasure seeking. Perhaps that concept is unjust. We need to take a new look at Epicureanism because the philosophy of body, in its currently primitive state, lacks an ethics. If Epicurus does in fact share many points of view with contemporary thought, both his own work and that of his critics will help us develop the concept of an incarnate consciousness.

A point-by-point comparison between Epicurus' thought and the previous selections would be worth the reader's time. Here are some interesting parallels between Epicurus' situation and our own. Hegel and others developed the insight that the philosophies of both the Stoics and the Epicureans are characterized by a withdrawal of the self from a society perceived to be corrupt and alien. During the decline of Athens from its height in the fifth century B.C., social tumult provoked a withdrawal into self-sufficiency. Where previous philosophers had optimistically charted utopian schemes for social salvation, the loss of the Peloponnesian War, the death of Socrates, and other events marking the decline of the Athenian culture provoked a turn within, a turn toward paths of individual enlightenment, through one's individual body or one's soul, or through the unity of the two.

Does the historical setting of Epicureanism show a possible link between interest in the body and the new interest in mysticism and cosmic consciousness? If Hegel is right, both interests stem from the same source; Epicurus praises "independence of desire" as a "great good," a teaching reminiscent of Buddhist thought. But the Hegelian insight into the history of Epicureanism casts a shadow across any contemporary enthusiasm. And so it should. Enthusiasm is no substitute for reflection, and without reflection we can expect a contemporary Epicureanism to pass the way of its predecessor: into decadence followed by just the Christian asceticism despised by Nietzsche. So let us reflect: What is the original form of Epicureanism? Do we see its recurrence in contemporary thought? If so, what is the meaning of that recurrence?

Letter to Menoeceus

Let no one when young delay to study philosophy, nor when he is old grow weary of his study. For no one can come too early or too late to secure the health of his soul. And the man who says that the age for philosophy has either not yet come or has gone by is like the man who says that the age for happiness is not yet come to him, or has passed away. Wherefore both when young and old a man must study philosophy, that as he grows old he may be young in blessings through the grateful recollection of what has been, and that in youth he may be old as well, since he will know no fear of what is to come. We must then meditate on the things that make our happiness, seeing that when that is with us we have all, but when it is absent we do all to win it.

The things which I used unceasingly to commend to you, these do and practise, considering them to be the first principles of the good life. First of all believe that god is a being immortal and blessed, even as the common idea of a god is engraved on men's minds, and do not assign to him any-

LETTER TO MENOECEUS From *Epicurus, the Extant Remains,* translated by Cyril Bailey, Copyright 1926, pp. 83–93. By permission of The Clarendon Press (original edition), Oxford, and Random House.

thing alien to his immortality or ill-suited to his blessedness: but believe about him everything that can uphold his blessedness and immortality. For gods there are, since the knowledge of them is by clear vision. But they are not such as the many believe them to be: for indeed they do not consistently represent them as they believe them to be. And the impious man is not he who denies the gods of the many, but he who attaches to the gods the beliefs of the many. For the statements of the many about the gods are not conceptions derived from sensation, but false suppositions, according to which the greatest misfortunes befall the wicked and the greatest blessings the good by the gift of the gods. For men being accustomed always to their own virtues welcome those like themselves, but regard all that is not of their nature as alien.

Become accustomed to the belief that death is nothing to us. For all good and evil consists in sensation, but death is deprivation of sensation. And therefore a right understanding that death is nothing to us makes the mortality of life enjoyable, not because it adds to it an infinite span of time, but because it takes away the craving for immortality. For there is nothing terrible in life for the man who has truly comprehended that there is nothing terrible in not living. So that the man speaks but idly who says that he fears death not because it will be painful when it comes, but because it is painful in anticipation. For that which gives no trouble when it comes, is but an empty pain in anticipation. So death, the most terrifying of ills, is nothing to us, since so long as we exist death is not with us; but when death comes, then we do not exist. It does not then concern either the living or the dead, since for the former it is not, and the latter are no more.

But the many at one moment shun death as the greatest of evils, at another yearn for it as a respite from the evils in life. But the wise man neither seeks to escape life nor fears the cessation of life, for neither does life offend him nor does the absence of life seem to be any evil. And just as with food he does not seek simply the larger share and nothing else, but rather the most pleasant, so he seeks to enjoy not the longest period of time, but the most pleasant.

And he who counsels the young man to live well, but the old man to make a good end, is foolish, not merely because of the desirability of life, but also because it is the same training which teaches to live well and to die well. Yet much worse still is the man who says it is good not to be born, but 'once born make haste to pass the gates of Death' (Theognis, 427). For if he says this from conviction why does he not pass away out of life? For it is open to him to do so, if he had firmly made up his mind to this. But if he speaks in jest, his words are idle among men who cannot receive them.

We must then bear in mind that the future is neither ours, not yet wholly not ours, so that we may not altogether expect it as sure to come, nor abandon hope of it, as if it will certainly not come.

We must consider that of desires some are natural, others vain, and of the natural some are necessary and others merely natural; and of the necessary some are necessary for happiness, others for the repose of the body, and others for very life. The right understanding of these facts enables us to refer all choice and avoidance to the health of the body and the soul's freedom from disturbance, since this is the aim of the life of blessedness. For it is to obtain this end that we always act, namely, to avoid pain and fear. And when this is once secured for us, all the tempest of the soul is dispersed, since the living creature has not to wander as though in search of something that is missing, and to look for some other thing by which he can fulfill the good of the soul and the good of the body. For it is then that we have need of pleasure, when we feel pain owing to the absence of pleasure; but when we do not feel pain, we no longer need pleasure. And for this cause we call pleasure the beginning and end of the blessed life. For we recognize pleasure as the first good innate in us, and from pleasure we begin every act of choice and avoidance, and to pleasure we return again, using the feeling as the standard by which we judge every good.

And since pleasure is the first good and natural to us, for this very reason we do not choose every pleasure, but sometimes we pass over many pleasures, when greater discomfort accrues to us as the result of them: and similarly we think many pains better than pleasures, since a greater pleasure comes to us when we have endured pains for a long time. Every pleasure then because of its natural kinship to us is good, yet not every pleasure is to be chosen: even as every pain also is an evil, yet not all are always of a nature to be avoided. Yet by a scale of comparison and by the consideration of advantages and disadvantages we must form our judgement on all these matters. For the good on certain occasions we treat as bad, and conversely the bad as good.

And again independence of desire we think a great good—not that we may at all times enjoy but a few things, but that, if we do not possess many, we may enjoy the few in the genuine persuasion that those have the sweetest pleasure in luxury who least need it, and that all that is natural is easy to be obtained, but that which is superfluous is hard. And so plain savours bring us a pleasure equal to a luxurious diet, when all the pain due to want is removed; and bread and water produce the highest pleasure, when one who needs them puts them to his lips. To grow accustomed therefore to simple and not luxurious diet gives us health to the full, and makes a man alert for the needful employments of life, and when after long intervals we approach luxuries, disposes us better towards them, and fits us to be fearless of fortune.

When, therefore, we maintain that pleasure is the end, we do not mean the pleasures of profligates and those that consist in sensuality, as is supposed by some who are either ignorant or disagree with us or do not understand, but freedom from pain in the body and from trouble in the mind. For it is not continuous drinkings and revellings, nor the satisfaction of lusts, nor the enjoyment of fish and other luxuries of the wealthy table, which produce a pleasant life, but sober reasoning, searching out the motives for all choice and avoidance, and banishing mere opinions, to which are due the greatest disturbance of the spirit.

Of all this the beginning and the greatest good is prudence. Wherefore prudence is a more precious thing even than philosophy: for from prudence are sprung all the other virtues, and it teaches us that it is not possible to live pleasantly without living prudently and honourably and justly, nor, again, to live a life of prudence, honour, and justice without living pleasantly. For the virtues are by nature bound up with the pleasant life, and the pleasant life is inseparable from them. For indeed who, think you, is a better man than he who holds reverent opinions concerning the gods, and is at all times free from fear of death, and has reasoned out the end ordained by nature? He understands that the limit of good things is easy to fulfil and easy to attain, whereas the course of ills is either short in time or slight in pain: he laughs at destiny, whom some have introduced as the mistress of all things. He thinks that with us lies the chief power in determining events, some of which happen by necessity and some by chance, and some are within our control; for while necessity cannot be called to account, he sees that chance is inconstant, but that which is in our control is subject to no master, and to it are naturally attached praise and blame. For, indeed, it were better to follow the myths about the gods than to become a slave to the destiny of the natural philosophers: for the former suggests a hope of placating the gods by worship, whereas the latter involves a necessity which knows no placation. As to chance, he does not regard it as a god as most men do (for in a god's acts there is no disorder), nor as an uncertain cause of all things: for he does not believe that good and evil are given by chance to man for the framing of a blessed life, but that opportunities for great good and great evil are afforded by it. He therefore thinks it better to be unfortunate in reasonable action than to prosper in unreason. For it is better in a man's actions that what is well chosen should fail, rather than that what is ill chosen should be successful owing to chance.

Meditate therefore on these things and things akin to them night and day by yourself, and with a companion like to yourself, and never shall you be disturbed waking or asleep, but you shall live like a god among men. For a man who lives among immortal blessings is not like a mortal being.

Transition: Epistemology and Interpersonal Perception

Just as the preceding selections show that the self is not a ghost in a machine, not a self **connected to** a body, so the following thinkers suggest that neither is the self an originally self-constituted entity that **then** comes into contact with other selves.

The selection from Sartre concluded, "We have to deal with human reality as a being which is what it is not and which is not what it is." In terms of the traditional opposition between essence and existence—the distinction between what a thing **is** (in its very essence) and what it **does** (how it happens to exist)—we could say that human reality is constituted through its existence, not given through an original essence. Human reality is not what it is (essentially), rather it is what it is not; it is what it becomes; it is what it is not now but what it comes to be through its existence. Hence the name 'Existentialism' for a philosophy that argues the primacy of existence to essence.

The following selections hold that the existence of the self is largely constituted by its relations to other selves. You may object that you don't cease to exist as a self when you go off into the woods away from other selves. And, where did the first self come from if it needed other selves to become a self? To the first objection: the reason you don't cease to exist apart from other selves is that selves, once constituted, do not decompose that quickly. A mountain lake does not disappear as soon as the rain stops; yet the water level is clearly not independent of the rainfall. A complex ecology relates the lake to the weather: without sun no trees would grow, no roots would hold the soil, and erosion might empty the mountain lake into the plains below. Both rain and sun preserve the lake, just as society and solitude nourish the self. The relation between the self and others is more complex than a simple moment-to-moment dependence for preservation, and your survival in the woods alone does not discount the possibility that your self depends for its existence on the existence of other selves. So much for the first objection.

But what about the other selves? To return to the second objection, if each self depends on other selves, where did the first self come from? This objection is in a way more difficult but less damaging. After all, if we know that selves are interdependent **now,** why must we speculate on how they got that way? To argue from the lack of an account of the first self to the independence of contemporary selves is like arguing that since we cannot describe the first language user we can claim that contemporary language users do not learn from others but make up their language all by themselves. Though we lack an accurate account of its first beginnings, it is clearly possible for selfhood, as well as language, to have a distinctively social genesis.

If, nevertheless, we want a theory of the first beginnings of selfhood, we can turn to Hegel, who posits the mutual genesis of self-conscious selves in a life-and-death struggle ending in a master-slave relationship. Without going into the details of his analysis, suffice it to say that for the struggle that issues in selfhood, it takes at least two to play. No one can do it alone. **Utterly** alone they are "no one." This is not a sentimental point; it is an ontological point (**ontos,** Greek for "being"; **logos,** "logic" or "science"; hence ontology as the science of being). The being of the self is constituted by its relations to others, just as they in turn are constituted in their being by their relations.

Let us pause on a structural point concerning the relationship of whole to part, and the ways we often misconstrue that relationship. Because we must focus on parts, because we need to identify particular instances in their individuality if we are to get along at all, we often tend to overemphasize their individuality, their apparent self-sufficiency and nonrelatedness. I want to know Charlie "as he really is" and not merely as I sometimes see him, or as Jane sees him. Rather than deal with the impossible complexity of acknowledging that Charlie "as he really is" is a complexity of countless relationships other than his relationships to me and Jane, I tend to distinguish between his relatedness to me and Jane on the one hand, and an autonomous Charlie-as-he-really-is on the other. And once again a false dichotomization suggests that if relatedness qualifies one term of the distinction, then nonrelatedness must qualify the other, whereas in fact Charlie as independent of me and Jane is simply (or rather very complexly) Charlie as dependently related to whole slews of other entities, animate and inanimate. Failing to see this, I absolutize Charlie the particular and lose sight of Charlie as related to the whole. I absolutize a relative. I make a simple substance out of what is really a complex nexus of relations.

We frequently simplify by drawing false dichotomies between the relative and some absolute, and philosophical inquiry often turns out to be a struggle against our absolutizings. The specific form of absolutizing with respect to part and whole often goes something like this: we see the part out of relation to the whole, and then, when it comes to talking about the whole, see it as a mere sum of the parts, or think about it the same way we think about the parts. Knowing that it makes sense to infer from some parts to other parts, we think we can infer from part to whole. For example, knowing what it means to say that the desk is upside-down, we can infer what it would mean for the whole room to be upside-down: not just the desk, but everything in the room, including the walls, would be topsy-turvy. Extrapolating beyond the inference from desk to room, I might think that the following question makes sense: "What if **everything** were upside down?" But a little reflection will show that this question makes no sense at all since the concept 'upside-down' is a relational concept: desk relative to room, or room in relation to the rest of the house or the earth. Because we are able to attribute upside-downness without explicitly or consciously referring to that in relation to which something is upside-down, we slip into thinking of upside-downness as nonrelational, and then imagine that we can attribute it to anything. But our error becomes apparent when we try to attribute upside-downness to the whole—everything—for there is nothing else relative to which everything together could be said to be upside-down.

Nor will it do to say everything is upside down relative to space. **If** space were absolutized into a self-subsistent thing, relative to which everything **else** could be upside-down, we must include that thing called space in the "everything" that gets turned upside-down. But space is not a thing, even though 'space' is a noun. Rather, spatiality is something about the relations among things. Indeed, the nonabsolute character of space is a key doctrine of **relativity** theory in physics.

The following selections are steps toward a relativity theory in philosophy. The comparison with Einstein's theory is apt, for it helps forestall misplaced fears about relativism. When people object to the horrors of so-called modern relativism, they may be objecting to the position I would describe as **subjective** relativism: a position that says I can say whatever I like, and you can say whatever you like, and what I say is true only relative to me, and what you say is true only for you, and so on. A totally subjective relativism reduces to absurdity: truth presupposes intersubjective validity, so the concept of 'true for me' is empty. If there be no intersubjectively shared criteria for truth, then truth becomes indistinguishable from mere opinion. So subjective relativism is a total skepticism in which there is no truth, only a vast multiplicity of opinions, none better than any other.

But one can evade the skepticism of subjective relativism without recourse to a positing of absolutes. Einstein's relativity theory rests on more than Einstein's opinion. Similarly a philosophy that exposes the structures relating part to part and part to whole may qualify as what I would call an **objective** relativism. We understand parts of our experience by their relationships to other parts. We understand ourselves not only **through** our relationships to others, but **as being** our relationships to others.

GEORGE HERBERT MEAD
(1863-1931)

George Herbert Mead joins reflections on the body with a careful appraisal of how a consciousness of self depends on our cognitive reactions to those around us. Less Dionysian in spirit and style than Nietzsche or Brown, Mead develops a measured critique of the theory that the origins of the self can be found in affective experiences involving self-feeling. He addresses his remarks specifically to William James, whose essay, "Does 'Consciousness' Exist?" ends with a discussion of the significance of the sensation of one's own breathing. Mead's remarks are not so much critical of James as they are supplementary. As one of America's greatest thinkers in philosophy and social psychology Mead was always aware of the need to supplement one perspective with another: not the isolated mind alone makes the self, nor the body alone, but an incarnate consciousness in a context of relationships with both intimate friends and a larger society. Pay particular attention to Mead's discussion of the "conversation of gestures," for his remarks on this topic serve as a good introduction to the following essays by Polanyi and Goffman.

THE SOCIAL ORIGINS OF THE SELF

The process out of which the self arises is a social process which implies interaction of individuals in the group, implies the pre-existence of the group.[1] It implies also certain co-operative activities in which the different members of the group are involved. It implies, further, that out of this process there may in turn develop a more elaborate organization than that out of which the self has arisen, and that the selves may be the organs, the essential parts at least, of this more elaborate social organization within which these selves arise and exist. Thus, there is a social process out of which selves arise and within

THE SOCIAL ORIGINS OF THE SELF   From George H. Mead, *Mind, Self & Society.* Published by the University of Chicago Press. Copyright 1934 by the University of Chicago. Reprinted by permission.

[1] The relation of individual organisms to the social whole of which they are members is analogous to the relation of the individual cells of a multi-cellular organism to the organism as a whole.

which further differentiation, further evolution, further organization, take place.

It has been the tendency of psychology to deal with the self as a more or less isolated and independent element, a sort of entity that could conceivably exist by itself. It is possible that there might be a single self in the universe if we start off by identifying the self with a certain feeling-consciousness. If we speak of this feeling as objective, then we can think of that self as existing by itself. We can think of a separate physical body existing by itself, we can assume that it has these feelings or conscious states in question, and so we can set up that sort of a self in thought as existing simply by itself.

Then there is another use of "consciousness" with which we have been particularly occupied, denoting that which we term thinking or reflective intelligence, a use of consciousness which always has, implicitly at least, the reference to an "I" in it. This use of consciousness has no necessary connection with the other; it is an entirely different conception. One usage has to do with a certain mechanism, a certain way in which an organism acts. If an organism is endowed with sense organs then there are objects in its environment, and among those objects will be parts of its own body.[2] It is true that if the organism did not have a retina and a central nervous system there would not be any objects of vision. For such objects to exist there have to be certain physiological conditions, but these objects are not in themselves necessarily related to a self. When we reach a self we reach a certain sort of conduct, a certain type of social process which involves the interaction of different individuals and yet implies individuals engaged in some sort of co-operative activity. In that process a self, as such, can arise.

We want to distinguish the self as a certain sort of structural process in the conduct of the form, from what we term consciousness of objects that are experienced. The two have no necessary relationship. The aching tooth is a very important element. We have to pay attention to it. It is identified in a certain sense with the self in order that we may control that sort of experience. Occasionally we have experiences which we say belong to the atmosphere. The whole world seems to be depressed, the sky is dark, the weather is unpleasant, values that we are interested in are sinking. We do not necessarily identify such a situation with the self; we simply feel a cer-

---

[2] Our constructive selection of our environment is what we term "consciousness," in the first sense of the term. The organism does not project sensuous qualities—colors, for example—into the environment to which it responds; but it endows this environment with such qualities, in a sense similar to that in which an ox endows grass with the quality of being food, or in which—speaking more generally—the relation between biological organisms and certain environmental contents give rise to food objects. If there were no organisms with particular sense organs there would be no environment, in the proper or usual sense of the term. An organism constructs (in the selective sense) its environment; and consciousness often refers to the character of the environment in so far as it is determined or constructively selected by our human organisms, and depends upon the relationship between the former (as thus selected or constructed) and the latter.

tain atmosphere about us. We come to remember that we are subject to such sorts of depression, and find that kind of an experience in our past. And then we get some sort of relief, we take aspirin, or we take a rest, and the result is that the world changes its character. There are other experiences which we may at all times identify with selves. We can distinguish, I think, very clearly between certain types of experience, which we call subjective because we alone have access to them, and that experience which we call reflective.

It is true that reflection taken by itself is something to which we alone have access. One thinks out his own demonstration of a proposition, we will say in Euclid, and the thinking is something that takes place within his own conduct. For the time being it is a demonstration which exists only in his thought. Then he publishes it and it becomes common property. For the time being it was accessible only to him. There are other contents of this sort, such as memory images and the play of the imagination, which are accessible only to the individual. There is a common character that belongs to these types of objects which we generally identify with consciousness and this process which we call that of thinking, in that both are, at least in certain phases, accessible only to the individual. But, as I have said, the two sets of phenomena stand on entirely different levels. This common feature of accessibility does not necessarily give them the same metaphysical status. I do not now want to discuss metaphysical problems, but I do want to insist that the self has a sort of structure that arises in social conduct that is entirely distinguishable from this so-called subjective experience of these particular sets of objects to which the organism alone has access—the common character of privacy of access does not fuse them together.

The self to which we have been referring arises when the conversation of gestures is taken over into the conduct of the individual form. When this conversation of gestures can be taken over into the individual's conduct so that the attitude of the other forms can affect the organism, and the organism can reply with its corresponding gesture and thus arouse the attitude of the other in its own process, then a self arises. Even the bare conversation of gestures that can be carried out in lower forms is to be explained by the fact that this conversation of gestures has an intelligent function. Even there it is a part of social process. If it is taken over into the conduct of the individual it not only maintains that function but acquires still greater capacity. If I can take the attitude of a friend with whom I am going to carry on a discussion, in taking that attitude I can apply it to myself and reply as he replies, and I can have things in very much better shape than if I had not employed that conversation of gestures in my own conduct. The same is true of him. It is good for both to think out the situation in advance. Each individual has to take also the attitude of the community, the generalized attitude. He has to be ready to act with reference to his own conditions just as any individual in the community would act.

One of the greatest advances in the development of the community arises when this reaction of the community on the individual takes on what we call an institutional form. What we mean by that is that the whole community acts toward the individual under certain circumstances in an identical way. It makes no difference, over against a person who is stealing your property, whether it is Tom, Dick, or Harry. There is an identical response on the part of the whole community under these conditions. We call that the formation of the institution.

There is one other matter which I wish briefly to refer to now. The only way in which we can react against the disapproval of the entire community is by setting up a higher sort of community which in a certain sense outvotes the one we find. A person may reach a point of going against the whole world about him; he may stand out by himself over against it. But to do that he has to speak with the voice of reason to himself. He has to comprehend the voices of the past and of the future. That is the only way in which the self can get a voice which is more than the voice of the community. As a rule we assume that this general voice of the community is identical with the larger community of the past and the future; we assume that an organized custom represents what we call morality. The things one cannot do are those which everybody would condemn. If we take the attitude of the community over against our own responses, that is a true statement, but we must not forget this other capacity, that of replying to the community and insisting on the gesture of the community changing. We can reform the order of things; we can insist on making the community standards better standards. We are not simply bound by the community. We are engaged in a conversation in which what we say is listened to by the community and its response is one which is affected by what we have to say. This is especially true in critical situations. A man rises up and defends himself for what he does; he has his "day in court"; he can present his views. He can perhaps change the attitude of the community toward himself. The process of conversation is one in which the individual has not only the right but the duty of talking to the community of which he is a part, and bringing about those changes which take place through the interaction of individuals. That is the way, of course, in which society gets ahead, by just such interactions as those in which some person thinks a thing out. We are continually changing our social system in some respects, and we are able to do that intelligently because we can think.

Such is the reflective process within which a self arises; and what I have been trying to do is to distinguish this kind of consciousness from consciousness as a set of characters determined by the accessibility to the organism of certain sorts of objects. It is true that our thinking is also, while it is just thinking, accessible only to the organism. But that common character of being accessible only to the organism does not make either thought or the self something which we are to identify with a group of objects which simply are accessible. We cannot identify the self with what is commonly called consciousness, that is, with the private or subjective thereness of the characters of objects.

There is, of course, a current distinction between consciousness and self-consciousness: consciousness answering to certain experiences such as those of pain or pleasure, self-consciousness referring to a recognition of appearance of a self as an object. It is, however, very generally assumed that these other conscious contents carry with them also a self-consciousness—that a pain is always somebody's pain, and that if there were not this reference to some individual it would not be pain. There is a very definite element of truth in this, but it is far from the whole story. The pain does have to belong to an individual; it has to be your pain if it is going to belong to you. Pain can belong to anybody, but if it did belong to everybody it would be comparatively unimportant. I suppose it is conceivable that under an anesthetic what takes place is the dissociation of experiences so that the suffering, so to speak, is no longer your suffering. We have illustrations of that, short of the anesthetic dissociation, in an experience of a disagreeable thing which loses its power over us because we give our attention to something else. If we can get, so to speak, outside of the thing, dissociating it from the eye that is regarding it, we may find that it has lost a great deal of its unendurable character. The unendurableness of pain is a reaction against it. If you can actually keep yourself from reacting against suffering you get rid of a certain content in the suffering itself. What takes place in effect is that it ceases to be your pain. You simply regard it objectively. Such is the point of view we are continually impressing on a person when he is apt to be swept away by emotion. In that case what we get rid of is not the offense itself, but the reaction against the offense. The objective character of the judge is that of a person who is neutral, who can simply stand outside of a situation and assess it. If we can get that judicial attitude in regard to the offenses of a person against ourselves, we reach the point where we do not resent them but understand them, we get the situation where to understand is to forgive. We remove much of experience outside of our own self by this attitude. The distinction and natural attitude against another is a resentment of an offense, but we now have in a certain sense passed beyond that self and become a self with other attitudes. There is a certain technique, then, to which we subject ourselves in enduring suffering or any emotional situation, and which consists in partially separating one's self from the experience so that it is no longer the experience of the individual in question.

If, now, we could separate the experience entirely, so that we should not remember it, so that we should not have to take it up continually into the self from day to day, from moment to moment, then it would not exist any longer so far as we are concerned. If we had no memory which identifies experiences with the self, then they would certainly disappear so far as their relation to the self is concerned, and yet they might continue as sensuous or sensible experiences without being taken up into a self. That sort of a situation is presented in the pathological case of a multiple personality in which an individual loses the memory of a certain phase of his existence. Everything connected with that phase of his existence is gone and he becomes a different personality. The past has a reality whether in the experience or not, but here it is not identified with the self—it does not go to make up the self. We take an attitude of that sort, for example, with reference to others when a person has committed some sort of an offense which leads to a statement of the situation, an admission, and perhaps regret, and then is dropped. A person who forgives but does not forget is an unpleasant companion; what goes with forgiving is forgetting, getting rid of the memory of it.

There are many illustrations which can be brought up of the loose relationship of given contents to a self in defense of our recognition of them as having a certain value outside of the self. At the least, it must be granted that we can approach the point where something which we recognize as a content is less and less essential to the self, is held off from the present self, and no longer has the value for that self which it had for the former self. Extreme cases seem to support the view that a certain portion of such contents can be entirely cut off from the self. While in some sense it is there ready to appear under specific conditions, for the time being it is dissociated and does not get in above the threshold of our self-consciousness.

Self-consciousness, on the other hand, is definitely organized about the social individual, and that, as we have seen, is not simply because one is in a social group and affected by others and affects them, but because (and this is a point I have been emphasizing) his own experience as a self is one which he takes over from his action upon others. He becomes a self in so far as he can take the attitude of another and act toward himself as others act. In so far as the conversation of gestures can become part of conduct in the direction and control of experience, then a self can arise. It is the social process of influencing others in a social act and then taking the attitude of the others aroused by the stimulus, and then reacting in turn to this response, which constitutes a self.

Our bodies are parts of our environment; and it is possible for the individual to experience and be conscious of his body, and of bodily sensations, without being conscious or aware of himself—without, in other words, taking the attitude of the other toward himself. According to the social theory of consciousness, what we mean by consciousness is that peculiar character and aspect of the environment of individual human experience which is due to human society, a society of other individual selves who take the attitude of the other toward themselves. The physiological conception or theory of consciousness is by itself inadequate; it requires supplementation from the socio-psychological point of view. The taking or feeling of the attitude of the other toward yourself is what constitutes self-consciousness, and not mere organic sensations of which the individual is aware and which he experiences. Until the rise of his self-consciousness in the process of social experience, the individual experiences his body—its feelings and sensations—merely as an immediate part of his environment, not as his own, not in terms of self-consciousness. The self and self-consciousness have first to arise, and then these experiences can be identified peculiarly with the self, or appropriated by the self; to enter, so to speak, into this heritage of experience, the self has first to develop within the social process in which this heritage is involved.

Through self-consciousness the individual organism enters in some sense into its own environmental field; its own body becomes a part of the set of environmental stimuli to which it responds or reacts. Apart from the context of the social process at its higher levels—those at which it involves conscious communication, conscious conversations of gestures, among the individual organisms interacting with it—the individual organism does not set itself as a whole over against its environment; it does not as a whole become an object to itself (and hence is not self-conscious); it is not as a whole a stimulus to which it reacts. On the contrary, it responds only to parts or separate aspects of itself, and regards them, not as parts or aspects of itself at all, but simply as parts or aspects of its environment in general. Only within the social process at its higher levels, only in terms of the more developed forms of the social environment or social situation, does the total individual organism become an object to itself, and hence self-conscious; in the social process at its lower, non-conscious levels, and also in the merely psychophysiological environment or situation which is logically antecedent to and presupposed by the social process of experience and behavior, it does not thus become an object to itself. In such experience or behavior as may be called self-conscious, we act and react particularly with reference to ourselves, though also with reference to other individuals; and to be self-conscious is essentially to become an object to one's self in virtue of one's social relations to other individuals.

Emphasis should be laid on the central position of thinking when considering the nature of the self. Self-consciousness, rather than affective experience with its motor accompaniments, provides the core and primary structure of the self, which is thus essentially a cognitive rather than an emotional phenomenon. The thinking or intellectual process—the internalization and inner dramatization, by the individual, of the external conversation of significant gestures which constitutes his chief mode of interaction with other individuals belonging to the same society—is the earliest experiential phase in the genesis and development of the self. Cooley and James, it is true, endeavor to find the basis of the self in reflexive affective experiences, i.e., experiences involving "self-feeling"; but the theory that the nature of the self is to be found in such experiences does not account for the origin of the self, or of the self-feeling which is supposed to characterize such experiences. The individual need not take the attitudes of others toward himself in these experiences, since these experiences merely in themselves do not necessitate his doing so, and unless he does so, he cannot develop a self; and he will not do so in these experiences unless his self has already originated otherwise, namely, in the way we have been describing. The essence of the self, as we have said, is cognitive: it lies in the internalized conversation of gestures which constitutes thinking, or in terms of which thought or reflection proceeds. And hence the origin and foundations of the self, like those of thinking, are social.

MICHAEL POLANYI
(1891-   )

Michael Polanyi is a contemporary scientist turned philosopher. In **The Tacit Dimension,** he shows that we can know more than we can tell. Here I wish to stress only three of the many ways his thesis is relevant to our concerns. First, we need an epistemology of interpersonal perception. Mead suggested the importance of gestural communication; Goffman's essay places such stress on the subtlety of communication that we must first be convinced that we can master that subtlety before we can take Goffman seriously. Polanyi establishes an epistemological foundation for the claim that we need not know **that** we are projecting messages about ourselves or **how** we do so in order to be able to project those messages. Similarly, we may be able to read all sorts of things from the behavior of others without being able to say how it is that we read their behavior.

Second, Polanyi's essay is one of the many essays in this volume bearing on the question of women's liberation. Although he does not make the case explicit himself, his argument begs for interpretation as an analysis of so-called women's intuition. In Polanyi's analysis women's intuition is no myth; rather it is a natural capacity available to any human being who does not constrain himself to know only what he can tell. As Polanyi points out, and Germaine Greer will underscore, "an unbridled lucidity can destroy our understanding of complex matters."

Third, and finally, Polanyi articulates the role of personal investment in inquiry. He argues that the ideal of objectivity can be a mistake. This is a complex point whose ramifications may remain tacit for the moment, but I urge the reader to ruminate on Polanyi's remarks until they may surface with at least some lucidity in the introduction to Laing's "Politics of Experience," and again in the debate between Rogers and Skinner.

HOW I KNOW OTHERS

Some of you may know that I turned to philosophy as an afterthought to my career as a scientist. I would like to tell you what I was after in making this change, for it will also explain the general task to which my present lecture should introduce us.

I first met questions of philosophy when I came up against the Soviet ideology under Stalin which denied justification to the pursuit of science. I remember a conversation I had with Bukharin in Moscow in 1935. Though he was heading toward his fall and execution three years later, he was still a leading theoretician of the Communist party. When I asked him about the pursuit of pure science in Soviet Russia, he said that pure science was a morbid symptom of a class society; under socialism the conception of science pursued for its own sake would disappear, for the interests of scientists would spontaneously turn to problems of the current Five-Year Plan.

I was struck by the fact that this denial of the very existence of independent scientific thought came from a socialist theory which derived its tremendous persuasive power from its claim to scientific certainty. The scientific outlook appeared to have produced a mechanical conception of man and history in which there was no place for science itself. This conception denied altogether any intrinsic power to thought and thus denied also any grounds for claiming freedom of thought.

I saw also that this self-immolation of the mind was actuated by powerful moral motives. The mechanical course of history was to bring universal justice. Scientific skepticism would trust only material necessity for achieving universal brotherhood. Skepticism and utopianism had thus fused into a new skeptical fanaticism.

It seemed to me then that our whole civilization was pervaded by the dissonance of an extreme critical lucidity and an intense moral conscience, and that this combination had generated both our tight-lipped modern revolutions and the tormented self-doubt of modern man outside revolutionary movement. So I resolved to inquire into the roots of this condition.

My search has led me to a novel idea of human knowledge from which a harmonious view of thought and existence, rooted in the universe, seems to emerge.

I shall reconsider human knowledge by starting from the fact that *we can know more than we can tell*. This fact seems obvious enough; but it is not easy to say exactly what it means. Take an example. We know a person's face, and can recognize it among a thousand, indeed among a million. Yet we usually cannot tell how we recognize a face we know. So most of

HOW I KNOW OTHERS   From the book *The Tacit Dimension* by Michael Polanyi, Copyright © 1966 by Michael Polanyi. Reprinted by permission of Doubleday & Company, Inc.

this knowledge cannot be put into words. But the police have recently introduced a method by which we can communicate much of this knowledge. They have made a large collection of pictures showing a variety of noses, mouths, and other features. From these the witness selects the particulars of the face he knows, and the pieces can then be put together to form a reasonably good likeness of the face. This may suggest that we can communicate, after all, our knowledge of a physiognomy, provided we are given adequate means for expressing ourselves. But the application of the police method does not change the fact that previous to it we did know more than we could tell at the time. Moreover, we can use the police method only by knowing how to match the features we remember with those in the collection, and we cannot tell how we do this. This very act of communication displays a knowledge that we cannot tell.

There are many other instances of the recognition of a characteristic physiognomy—some commonplace, others more technical—which have the same structure as the identification of a person. We recognize the moods of the human face, without being able to tell, except quite vaguely, by what signs we know it. At the universities great efforts are spent in practical classes to teach students to identify cases of diseases and specimens of rocks, of plants and animals. All descriptive sciences study physiognomies that cannot be fully described in words, nor even by pictures.

But can it not be argued, once more, that the possibility of teaching these appearances by practical exercises proves that we can tell our knowledge of them? The answer is that we can do so only by relying on the pupil's intelligent co-operation for catching the meaning of the demonstration. Indeed, any definition of a word denoting an external thing must ultimately rely on pointing at such a thing. This naming-cum-pointing is called "an ostensive definition"; and this philosophic expression conceals a gap to be bridged by an intelligent effort on the part of the person to whom we want to tell what the word means. Our message had left something behind that we could not tell, and its reception must rely on it that the person addressed will discover that which we have not been able to communicate.

Gestalt psychology has demonstrated that we may know a physiognomy by integrating our awareness of its particulars without being able to identify these particulars, and my analysis of knowledge is closely linked to this discovery of Gestalt psychology. But I shall attend to aspects of Gestalt which have been hitherto neglected. Gestalt psychology has assumed that perception of a physiognomy takes place through the spontaneous equilibration of its particulars impressed on the retina or on the brain. However, I am looking at Gestalt, on the contrary, as the outcome of an active shaping of experience performed in the pursuit of knowledge. This shaping or integrating I hold to be the great and indispensable tacit power by which all knowledge is discovered and, once discovered, is held to be true.

The structure of Gestalt is then recast into a logic of tacit thought, and this changes the range and perspective of the whole subject. The highest forms of integration loom largest now. These are manifested in the tacit power of scientific and artistic genius. The art of the expert diagnostician may be listed next, as a somewhat impoverished form of discovery, and we may put in the same class the performance of skills, whether artistic, athletic, or technical. We have here examples of knowing, both of a more intellectual and more practical kind; both the *"wissen"* and *"können"* of the Germans, or the "knowing what" and the "knowing how" of Gilbert Ryle. These two aspects of knowing have a similar structure and neither is ever present without the other. This is particularly clear in the art of diagnosing, which intimately combines skillful testing with expert observation. I shall always speak of "knowing," therefore, to cover both practical and theoretical knowledge. We can, accordingly, interpret the use of tools, of probes, and of pointers as further instances of the art of knowing, and may add to our list also the denotative use of language, as a kind of verbal pointing.

Perception, on which Gestalt psychology centered its attention, now appears as the most impoverished form of tacit knowing. As such it will be shown to form the bridge between the higher creative power of man and the bodily processes which are prominent in the operations of perception.

Some recent psychological experiments have shown in isolation the principal mechanism by which knowledge is tacitly acquired. Many of you have heard of these experiments as revealing the diabolical machinery of hidden persuasion. Actually, they are but elementary demonstrations of the faculty by which we apprehend the relation between two events, both of which we know, but only one of which we can tell.

Following the example set by Lazarus and McCleary in 1949, psychologists call the exercise of this faculty a process of "subception."[1] These

---

[1] Lazarus, R. S., and McCleary, R. A., *Journal of Personality* (Vol. 18, 1949), p. 191, and *Psychological Review* (Vol. 58, 1951), p. 113. These results were called in question by Eriksen, C. W., *Psychological Review* (Vol. 63, 1956), p. 74 and defended by Lazarus, *Psychological Review* (Vol. 63, 1956), p. 343. But in a later paper surveying the whole field—*Psychological Review* (Vol. 67, 1960), p. 279—Eriksen confirmed the experiments of Lazarus and McCleary, and accepted them as evidence of subception.

I am relying on subception only as a confirmation of tacit knowing in an elementary form, capable of quantitative experimental demonstration. For me it is the mechanism underlying the formation of Gestalt, from which I first derived my conception of tacit knowing in *Personal Knowledge*. Strangely enough, the connection of subception with Gestalt has been hardly noticed by psychologists in the course of their controversies on the validity of subception. I could find only one place alluding to it, in a paper by Klein, George S., "On Subliminal Activation," *Journal of Nervous Mental Disorders* (Vol. 128, 1959), pp. 293–301. He observes: "It requires no experimental demonstration to say confidently that we are not aware of all the stimuli which we use in behavior."

I have said already basically in *Personal Knowledge* and have continued to emphasize since then, that it is a mistake to identify subsidiary awareness with unconscious awareness, or with the Jamesian fringe of awareness. What makes an awareness subsidiary is the *function it fulfills;* it can have any degree of consciousness, so long as it functions as a clue to the object of our focal attention. Klein supports this by saying that subliminal activation is but a special case of *transient or incidental stimuli* of all kinds. It is not the subliminal status that matters but authors presented a person with a large number of nonsense syllables, and after showing certain of the syllables, they administered an electric shock. Presently the person showed symptoms of anticipating the shock at the sight of "shock syllables"; yet, on questioning, he could not identify them. He had come to know when to expect a shock, but he could not tell what made him expect it. He had acquired a knowledge similar to that which we have when we know a person by signs which we cannot tell.

Another variant of this phenomenon was demonstrated by Eriksen and Kuethe in 1958.[2] They exposed a person to a shock whenever he happened to utter associations to certain "shock words." Presently, the person learned to forestall the shock by avoiding the utterance of such associations, but, on questioning, it appeared that he did not know he was doing this. Here the subject got to know a practical operation, but could not tell how he worked it. This kind of subception has the structure of a skill, for a skill combines elementary muscular acts which are not identifiable, according to relations that we cannot define.

These experiments show most clearly what is meant by saying that one can know more than one can tell. For the experimental arrangement wards off the suspicion of self-contradiction, which is not easy to dispel when anyone speaks of things he knows and cannot tell. This is prevented here by the division of roles between the subject and the observer. The experimenter observes that another person has a certain knowledge that he cannot tell, and so no one speaks of a knowledge he himself has and cannot tell.

We may carry forward, then, the following result. In both experiments that I have cited, subception was induced by electric shock. In the first series the subject was shocked after being shown certain nonsense syllables,

---

"the meanings and properties [a stimulus] acquires at the periphery of thought and action."

Eriksen and Kuethe, whose observation of not consciously identified avoidance I have quoted as a kind of subception, have called this avoidance a defense mechanism, thus affiliating it to Freudian conceptions. This practice is widespread and has caused *Psychological Abstracts* to divide the subject matter into subception and defense mechanism.

Yet another fragmentation of this matter occurred by taking due notice of Otto Pötzl's observations going back to 1917. A survey of his work and of that of his direct successors has appeared in *Psychological Issues* (Vol. II, No. 3, 1960) under the title "Preconscious Stimulation in Dreams, Associations, and Images" by Otto Pötzl, Rudolf Allers, and Jacob Teler, International Universities Press, New York 11, N.Y. An introduction to this monograph by Charles Fisher links these observations to recent studies and notes the present uncertainty about the status of stimuli of which we become conscious only in terms of their contribution to subsequent experience. "The matter needs to be settled," writes Fisher on p. 33, "because the issue of subliminality has important implications for theories of perception." I believe that this matter has actually much wider implications and must be generally subsumed under the logical categories of tacit knowing.

[2] Eriksen, C. W., and Kuethe, J. L., "Avoidance Conditioning of Verbal Behavior Without Awareness: A Paradigm of Repression," *Journal of Abnormal and Social Psychology* (Vol. 53, 1956), pp. 203–09.

and he learned to expect this event. In the second series he learned to suppress the uttering of certain associations, which would evoke the shock. In both cases the shock-producing particulars remained tacit. The subject could not identify them, yet he relied on his awareness of them for anticipating the electric shock.

Here we see the basic structure of tacit knowing. It always involves two things, or two kinds of things. We may call them the two terms of tacit knowing. In the experiments the shock syllables and shock associations formed the first term, and the electric shock which followed them was the second term. After the subject had learned to connect these two terms, the sight of the shock syllables evoked the expectation of a shock and the utterance of the shock associations was suppressed in order to avoid shock. Why did this connection remain tacit? It would seem that this was due to the fact that the subject was riveting his attention on the electric shock. He was relying on his awareness of the shock-producing particulars only in their bearing on the electric shock. We may say that he learned to rely on his awareness of these particulars for the purpose of attending to the electric shock.

Here we have the basic definition of the logical relation between the first and second term of a tacit knowledge. It combines two kinds of knowing. We know the electric shock, forming the second term, by attending to it, and hence the subject is *specifiably* known. But we know the shock-producing particulars only by relying on our own awareness of them for attending to something else, namely the electric shock, and hence our knowledge of them remains *tacit*. This is how we come to know these particulars, without becoming able to identify them. Such is the *functional relation* between the two terms of tacit knowing : *we know the first term only by relying on our awareness of it for attending to the second.*

In his book on freedom of the will, Austin Farrar has spoken at one point of *disattending from* certain things for attending *to* others. I shall adopt a variant of this usage by saying that in an act of tacit knowing we *attend from* something for attending *to* something else; namely, *from* the first term *to* the second term of the tacit relation. In many ways the first term of this relation will prove to be nearer to us, the second further away from us. Using the language of anatomy, we may call the first term *proximal,* and the second term *distal.* It is the proximal term, then, of which we have a knowledge that we may not be able to tell.

In the case of a human physiognomy, I would now say that we rely on our awareness of its features for attending to the characteristic appearance of a face. We are attending *from* the features *to* the face, and thus may be unable to specify the features. And I would say, likewise, that we are relying on our awareness of a combination of muscular acts for attending to the performance of a skill. We are attending *from* these elementary movements *to* the achievement of their joint purpose, and hence are usually unable to specify these elementary acts. We may call this the *functional structure* of tacit knowing.

But we may ask: does not the *appearance* of the experimental setting —composed of the nonsense syllables and the electric shocks—undergo some change when we learn to anticipate a shock at the sight of certain syllables? It does, and in a very subtle way. The expectation of a shock, which at first had been vague and unceasing, now becomes sharply fluctuating; it suddenly rises at some moments and drops between them. So we may say that even though we do not learn to recognize the shock syllables as distinct from other syllables, we do become aware of facing a shock syllable in terms of the apprehension it evokes in us. In other words, we are aware of seeing these syllables in terms of that on which we are focusing our attention, which is the probability of an electric shock. Applying this to the case of a physiognomy, we may say that we are aware of its features in terms of the physiognomy to which we are attending. In the exercise of a skill, we are aware of its several muscular moves in terms of the performance to which our attention is directed. We may say, in general, that we are aware of the proximal term of an act of tacit knowing in the appearance of its distal term; we are aware of that *from* which we are attending *to* another thing, in the *appearance* of that thing. We may call this the *phenomenal structure* of tacit knowing.

But there is a significance in the relation of the two terms of tacit knowing which combines its functional and phenomenal aspects. When the sight of certain syllables makes us expect an electric shock, we may say that they *signify* the approach of a shock. This is their *meaning* to us. We could say, therefore, that when shock syllables arouse an apprehension in us, without our being able to identify the syllables which arouse it, we know these syllables only in terms of their meaning. It is their meaning to which our attention is directed. It is in terms of their meaning that they enter into the appearance of that *to* which we are attending *from* them.

We could say, in this sense, that a characteristic physiognomy is the meaning of its features; which is, in fact, what we do say when a physiognomy expresses a particular mood. To identify a physiognomy would then amount to relying on our awareness of its features for attending to their joint meaning. This may sound far-fetched, because the meaning of the features is observed at the same spot where the features are situated, and hence it is difficult to separate mentally the features from their meaning. Yet, the fact remains that the two are distinct, since we may know a physiognomy without being able to specify its particulars.

To see more clearly the separation of a meaning from that which has this meaning, we may take the example of the use of a probe to explore a cavern, or the way a blind man feels his way by tapping with a stick. For here the separation of the two is wide, and we can also observe here the process by which this separation gradually takes place. Anyone using a probe for the first time will feel its impact against his fingers and palm. But as we learn to use a probe, or to use a stick for feeling our way, our awareness of its impact on our hand is transformed into a sense of its point touching the objects we are exploring. This is how an interpretative effort transposes meaningless feelings into meaningful ones, and places these at some distance from the original feeling. We become aware of the feelings in our hand in terms of their meaning located at the tip of the probe or stick to which we are attending. This is so also when we use a tool. We are attending to the meaning of its impact on our hands in terms of its effect on the things to which we are applying it. We may call this the *semantic aspect* of tacit knowing. All meaning tends to be displaced *away from ourselves,* and that is in fact my justification for using the terms "proximal" and "distal" to describe the first and second terms of tacit knowing.

From the three aspects of tacit knowing that I have defined so far— the functional, the phenomenal, and the semantic—we can deduce a fourth aspect; which tells us what tacit knowing is a knowledge of. This will represent its *ontological* aspect. Since tacit knowing establishes a meaningful relation between two terms, we may identify it with the *understanding* of the comprehensive entity which these two terms jointly constitute. Thus the proximal term represents the *particulars* of this entity, and we can say, accordingly, that we comprehend the entity by relying on our awareness of its particulars for attending to their joint meaning.

This analysis can be applied with interesting results to the case of visual perception. Physiologists long ago established that the way we see an object is determined by our awareness of certain efforts inside our body, efforts which we cannot feel in themselves. We are aware of these things going on inside our body in terms of the position, size, shape, and motion of an object, to which we are attending. In other words we are attending *from* these internal processes *to* the qualities of things outside. These qualities are what those internal processes *mean* to us. The transposition of bodily experiences into the perception of things outside may now appear, therefore, as an instance of the transposition of meaning away from us, which we have found to be present to some extent in all tacit knowing.

But it may be said that the feelings transposed by perception differ from those transposed by the use of tools or probes, by being hardly noticeable in themselves previous to their transposition. An answer to this—or at least part of an answer to it—is to be found in experiments extending subception to subliminal stimuli. Hefferline and collaborators have observed that when spontaneous muscular twitches, unfelt by the subject—but observable externally by a million-fold amplification of their action currents —were followed by the cessation of an unpleasant noise, the subject responded by increasing the frequency of the twitches and thus silencing the noise much of the time.[3] Tacit knowing is seen to operate here on an

[3] Hefferline, Ralph F., Keenan, Brian, and Harford, Richard A., "Escape and Avoidance Conditioning in Human Subjects Without Their Observation of the Response," *Science* (Vol. 130, November 1959), pp. 1338–39. Hefferline, Ralph F., and Keenan, Brian, "Amplitude-Induction Gradient of a Small Human Operant in an Escape-Avoidance Situation," *Journal of the Experimental Analysis of Behavior* (Vol. 4, January 1961), pp. 41–43. Hefferline, Ralph F., and Perera, Thomas B., "Proprio-

internal action that we are quite incapable of controlling or even feeling in itself. We become aware of our operation of it only in the silencing of a noise. This experimental result seems closely analogous to the process by which we become aware of subliminal processes inside our body in the perception of objects outside.

This view of perception, that it is an instance of the transposition of feelings which we found in the use of probes and in the process of subception, is borne out by the fact that the capacity to see external objects must be acquired, like the use of probes and the feats of subception, by a process of learning which can be laborious.

Modern philosophers have argued that perception does not involve projection, since we are not previously aware of the internal processes which we are supposed to have projected into the qualities of things perceived. But we have now established that projection of this very kind is present in various instances of tacit knowing. Moreover, the fact that we do not originally sense the internal processes in themselves now appears irrelevant. We may venture, therefore, to extend the scope of tacit knowing to include neural traces in the cortex of the nervous system. This would place events going on inside our brain on the same footing as the subliminal twitches operated by Hefferline's subjects.[4]

This brings us to the point at which I hinted when I first mentioned perception as an instance of tacit knowing. I said that by elucidating the way our bodily processes participate in our perceptions we will throw light on the bodily roots of all thought, including man's highest creative powers. Let me show this now.

Our body is the ultimate instrument of all our external knowledge, whether intellectual or practical. In all our waking moments we are *relying* on our awareness of contacts of our body with things outside for *attending* to these things. Our own body is the only thing in the world which we normally never experience as an object, but experience always in terms of the world to which we are attending from our body. It is by making this

---

ceptive Discrimination of a Covert Operant Without Its Observation by the Subject," *Science* (Vol. 139, March 1963), pp. 834–35. Hefferline, Ralph F., and Keenan, Brian, "Amplitude-Induction Gradient of a Small Scale (Covert) Operant," *Journal of the Experimental Analysis of Behavior* (Vol. 6, July 1963), pp. 307–15. See also general conclusions in Hefferline, Ralph F., "Learning Theory and Clinical Psychology—An Eventual Symbiosis?" from *Experimental Foundations of Clinical Psychology,* ed. Arthur J. Bachrach (1962).

Note also that numerous Russian observations, reported by Razran, G., "The Observable Unconscious and the Inferable Conscious," *Psychological Review* (Vol. 68, 1961), p. 81, have established the conditioning of intestinal stimuli, having a similar covert character as Hefferline's muscular twitches.

[4] Such a hypothesis does not explain how perceived sights, or any other state of consciousness, arise in conjunction with neural processes. It merely applies the principle that wherever some process in our body gives rise to consciousness in us, our tacit knowing of the process will make sense of it in terms of an experience to which we are attending.

intelligent use of our body that we feel it to be our body, and not a thing outside.

I have described how we learn to feel the end of a tool or a probe hitting things outside. We may regard this as the transformation of the tool or probe into a sentient extension of our body, as Samuel Butler has said. But our awareness of our body for attending to things outside it suggests a wider generalization of the feeling we have of our body. Whenever we use certain things for attending *from* them to other things, in the way in which we always use our own body, these things change their appearance. They appear to us now in terms of the entities to which we are attending *from* them, just as we feel our own body in terms of the things outside to which we are attending *from* our body. In this sense we can say that when we make a thing function as the proximal term of tacit knowing, we incorporate it in our body—or extend our body to include it—so that we come to dwell in it.

The full range of this generalization can only be hinted at here. Indications of its scope may be seen by recalling that, at the turn of the last century, German thinkers postulated that indwelling, or empathy, is the proper means of knowing man and the humanities. I am referring particularly to Dilthey[5] and Lipps.[6] Dilthey taught that the mind of a person can be understood only by reliving its workings; and Lipps represented aesthetic appreciation as an entering into a work of art and thus dwelling in the mind of its creator. I think that Dilthey and Lipps described here a striking form of tacit knowing as applied to the understanding of man and of works of art, and that they were right in saying that this could be achieved only by indwelling. But my analysis of tacit knowing shows that they were mistaken in asserting that this sharply distinguished the humanities from the natural sciences. Indwelling, as derived from the structure of tacit knowing, is a far more precisely defined act than is empathy, and it underlies all observations, including all those described previously as indwelling.

We meet with another indication of the wide functions of indwelling when we find acceptance to moral teachings described as their *interiorization*. To interiorize is to identify ourselves with the teachings in question, by making them function as the proximal term of a tacit moral knowledge, as applied in practice. This establishes the tacit framework for our moral acts and judgments. And we can trace this kind of indwelling to logically similar acts in the practice of science. To rely on a theory for understanding nature is to interiorize it. For we are attending from the theory to things seen in its light, and are aware of the theory, while thus using it, in terms of the spectacle that it serves to explain. This is why mathematical theory

[5] Dilthey, W., *Gesammelte Schriften* (Vol. VII, Leipzig and Berlin, 1914–36), pp. 213–16; [Translation by H. A. Hodges, *Wilhelm Dilthey* (New York, Oxford University Press, 1944), pp. 121–24].

[6] Lipps, T., *Ästhetik* (Hamburg, 1903).

can be learned only by practicing its application: its true knowledge lies in our ability to use it.

The identification of tacit knowing with indwelling involves a shift of emphasis in our conception of tacit knowing. We had envisaged tacit knowing in the first place as a way to know more than we can tell. We identified the two terms of tacit knowing, the proximal and the distal, and recognized the way we attend *from* the first *to* the second, thus achieving an integration of particulars to a coherent entity to which we are attending. Since we were not attending to the particulars in themselves, we could not identify them: but if we now regard the integration of particulars as an interiorization, it takes on a more positive character. It now becomes a means of making certain things function as the proximal terms of tacit knowing, so that instead of observing them in themselves, we may be aware of them in their bearing on the comprehensive entity which they constitute. It brings home to us that it is not by looking at things, but by dwelling in them, that we understand their joint meaning.

We can see now how an unbridled lucidity can destroy our understanding of complex matters. Scrutinize closely the particulars of a comprehensive entity and their meaning is effaced, our conception of the entity is destroyed. Such cases are well known. Repeat a word several times, attending carefully to the motion of your tongue and lips, and to the sound you make, and soon the word will sound hollow and eventually lose its meaning. By concentrating attention on his fingers, a pianist can temporarily paralyze his movement. We can make ourselves lose sight of a pattern or physiognomy by examining its several parts under sufficient magnification.

Admittedly, the destruction can be made good by interiorizing the particulars once more. The word uttered again its proper context, the pianist's fingers used again with his mind on his music, the features of a physiognomy and the details of a pattern glanced at once more from a distance: they all come to life and recover their meaning and their comprehensive relationship.

But it is important to note that this recovery never brings back the original meaning. It may improve on it. Motion studies, which tend to paralyze a skill, will improve it when followed by practice. The meticulous dismembering of a text, which can kill its appreciation, can also supply material for a much deeper understanding of it. In these cases, the detailing of particulars, which by itself would destroy meaning, serves as a guide to their subsequent integration and thus establishes a more secure and more accurate meaning of them.

But the damage done by the specification of particulars may be irremediable. Meticulous detailing may obscure beyond recall a subject like history, literature, or philosophy. Speaking more generally, the belief that, since particulars are more tangible, their knowledge offers a true conception of things is fundamentally mistaken.

Of course, tacit reintegration of particulars is not the only way to recover their meaning, destroyed by focusing our attention on them. The destructive analysis of a comprehensive entity can be counteracted in many cases by explicitly stating the relation between its particulars. Where such explicit integration is feasible, it goes far beyond the range of tacit integration. Take the case of a machine. One can learn to use it skillfully, without knowing exactly how it works. But the engineer's understanding of its construction and operation goes much deeper. We possess a practical knowledge of our own body, but the physiologist's theoretical knowledge of it is far more revealing. The formal rules of prosody may deepen our understanding of so delicate a thing as a poem.

But my examples show clearly that, in general, an explicit integration cannot replace its tacit counterpart. The skill of a driver cannot be replaced by a thorough schooling in the theory of the motorcar; the knowledge I have of my own body differs altogether from the knowledge of its physiology; and the rules of rhyming and prosody do not tell me what a poem told me, without any knowledge of its rules.

We are approaching here a crucial question. The declared aim of modern science is to establish a strictly detached, objective knowledge. Any falling short of this ideal is accepted only as a temporary imperfection, which we must aim at eliminating. But suppose that tacit thought forms an indispensable part of all knowledge, then the ideal of eliminating all personal elements of knowledge would, in effect, aim at the destruction of all knowledge. The ideal of exact science would turn out to be fundamentally misleading and possibly a source of devastating fallacies.

I think I can show that the process of formalizing all knowledge to the exclusion of any tacit knowing is self-defeating. For, in order that we may formalize the relations that constitute a comprehensive entity, for example, the relations that constitute a frog, this entity, i.e., the frog, must be first identified informally by tacit knowing; and, indeed, the meaning of a mathematical theory of the frog lies in its continued bearing on this still tacitly known frog. Moreover, the act of bringing a mathematical theory to bear on its subject is itself a tacit integration of the kind we have recognized in the use of a denotative word for designating its object. And we have seen also that a true knowledge of a theory can be established only after it has been interiorized and extensively used to interpret experience. Therefore: a mathematical theory can be constructed only by relying on *prior* tacit knowing and can function as a theory only *within* an act of tacit knowing, which consists in our attending *from* it to the previously established experience on which it bears. Thus the ideal of a comprehensive mathematical theory of experience which would eliminate all tacit knowing is proved to be self-contradictory and logically unsound.

But I must not rest my case on such an abstract argument. Let me finish this lecture, therefore, by presenting you with a most striking concrete example of an experience that cannot possibly be represented by any exact theory. It is an experience within science itself: the experience of seeing a problem, as a scientist sees it in his pursuit of discovery.

It is a commonplace that all research must start from a problem. Research can be successful only if the problem is good; it can be original only if the problem is original. But how can one see a problem, any problem, let alone a good and original problem? For to see a problem is to see something that is hidden. It is to have an intimation of the coherence of hitherto not comprehended particulars. The problem is good if this intimation is true; it is original if no one else can see the possibilities of the comprehension that we are anticipating. To see a problem that will lead to a great discovery is not just to see something hidden, but to see something of which the rest of humanity cannot have even an inkling. All this is a commonplace; we take it for granted, without noticing the clash of self-contradiction entailed in it. Yet Plato has pointed out this contradiction in the *Meno*. He says that to search for the solution of a problem is an absurdity; for either you know what you are looking for, and then there is no problem; or you do not know what you are looking for, and then you cannot expect to find anything.

The solution which Plato offered for this paradox was that all discovery is a remembering of past lives. This explanation has hardly ever been accepted, but neither has any other solution been offered for avoiding the contradiction. So we are faced with the fact that, for two thousand years and more, humanity has progressed through the efforts of people solving difficult problems, while all the time it could be shown that to do this was either meaningless or impossible. We have here the classical case of Poe's *Purloined Letter,* of the momentous document lying casually in front of everybody, and hence overlooked by all. For the *Meno* shows conclusively that if all knowledge is explicit, i.e., capable of being clearly stated, then we cannot know a problem or look for its solution. And the *Meno* also shows, therefore, that if problems nevertheless exist, and discoveries can be made by solving them, we can know things, and important things, that we cannot tell.

The kind of tacit knowledge that solves the paradox of the *Meno* consists in the intimation of something hidden, which we may yet discover. There exists another important manifestation of these mental powers. We are often told that great scientific discoveries are marked by their fruitfulness; and this is true. But how can we recognize truth by its fruitfulness? Can we recognize that a statement is true by appreciating the wealth of its yet undiscovered consequences? This would of course be nonsensical, if we had to know explicitly what was yet undiscovered. But it makes sense if we admit that we can have a tacit foreknowledge of yet undiscovered things. This is indeed the kind of foreknowledge the Copernicans must have meant to affirm when they passionately maintained, against heavy pressure, during one hundred and forty years before Newton proved the point, that the heliocentric theory was not merely a convenient way of computing the paths of planets, but was really true.

It appears, then, that to know that a statement is true is to know more than we can tell and that hence, when a discovery solves a problem, it is itself fraught with further intimations of an indeterminate range, and that furthermore, when we accept the discovery as true, we commit ourselves to a belief in all these as yet undisclosed, perhaps as yet unthinkable, consequences.

Since we have no explicit knowledge of these unknown things, there can also be no explicit justification of a scientific truth. But as we can know a problem, and feel sure that it is pointing to something hidden behind it, we can be aware also of the hidden implications of a scientific discovery, and feel confident that they will prove right. We feel sure of this, because in contemplating the discovery we are looking at it not only in itself but, more significantly, as a clue to a reality of which it is a manifestation. The pursuit of discovery is conducted from the start in these terms; all the time we are guided by sensing the presence of a hidden reality toward which our clues are pointing; and the discovery which terminates and satisfies this pursuit is still sustained by the same vision. It claims to have made contact with reality: a reality which, being real, may yet reveal itself to future eyes in an indefinite range of unexpected manifestations.

We have here reached our main conclusions. Tacit knowing is shown to account (1) for a valid knowledge of a problem, (2) for the scientist's capacity to pursue it, guided by his sense of approaching its solution, and (3) for a valid anticipation of the yet indeterminate implications of the discovery arrived at in the end.

Such indeterminate commitments are necessarily involved in any act of knowing based on indwelling. For such an act relies on interiorizing particulars to which we are not attending and which, therefore, we may not be able to specify, and relies further on our attending from these unspecifiable particulars to a comprehensive entity connecting them in a way we cannot define. This kind of knowing solves the paradox of the *Meno* by making it possible for us to know something so indeterminate as a problem or a hunch, but when the use of this faculty turns out to be an indispensable element of all knowing, we are forced to conclude that all knowledge is of the same kind as the knowledge of a problem.

This is in fact our result. We must conclude that the paradigmatic case of scientific knowledge, in which all the faculties that are necessary for finding and holding scientific knowledge are fully developed, is the knowledge of an approaching discovery.

To hold such knowledge is an act deeply committed to the conviction that there is something there to be discovered. It is personal, in the sense of involving the personality of him who holds it, and also in the sense of being, as a rule, solitary; but there is no trace in it of self-indulgence. The discoverer is filled with a compelling sense of responsibility for the pursuit of a hidden truth, which demands his services for revealing it. His act of knowing exercises a personal judgment in relating evidence to an external reality, an aspect of which he is seeking to apprehend.

The anticipation of discovery, like discovery itself, may turn out to be a delusion. But it is futile to seek for strictly impersonal criteria of its validity, as positivistic philosophies of science have been trying to do for the past eighty years or so. To accept the pursuit of science as a reasonable and successful enterprise is to share the kind of commitments on which scientists enter by undertaking this enterprise. You cannot formalize the act of commitment, for you cannot express your commitment non-committally. To attempt this is to exercise the kind of lucidity which destroys its subject matter. Hence the failure of the positivist movement in the philosophy of science. The difficulty is to find a stable alternative to its ideal of objectivity. This is indeed the task for which the theory of tacit knowing should prepare us.

ERVING GOFFMAN

(1922-   )

In recent years Erving Goffman has made several significant contributions to the psychology and sociology of face-to-face encounters. In his studies of social institutions, from mental asylums to the simple handshake, Goffman has unlocked the codes we use to communicate more than we say. Though he does not make explicit mention of Polanyi's ideas, Goffman's chief concern in this essay is to show how we use our tacit knowledge in our face-to-face encounters with others. Using the metaphor of theater and stage he argues that we create ourselves through the progressive refinement of our performances. Just as a performer cannot completely articulate all the methods he uses for projecting a character through gestures and inflections, so our knowledge of our performances is only tacit. Further, because we value honesty and sincerity we have a stake in letting that knowledge remain tacit. We do not even want to know that we know how to perform. Goffman cuts through this self-imposed veil of illusion and in the process exposes an interesting dialectic of appearance and reality: really to **be** a certain sort of person in a social context entails that one **appear** to be that sort of person, otherwise that **being** is lost on others and they cannot assist in the social construction of one's self. Yet the success of the appearance partly hinges on socially defined rules for what it takes to be that sort of person. Here we have a specific case of what I dubbed earlier the "onion theory of reality": reality does not lie beneath appearances, rather it is the progressive construction of the totality of appearances. Without an appreciation of this metaphysical point the reader runs the risk of rejecting Goffman's analysis as a rationale for a very simple form of dishonesty. Try to read Goffman's analysis as an account of the dynamics of those rich situations when, together with a few friends in comfortable surroundings, you are aware of a tremendous amount of communication but perhaps unsure of precisely what is happening.

HOW OTHERS KNOW ME

When an individual enters the presence of others, they commonly seek to acquire information about him or to bring into play information about him already possessed. They will be interested in his general socio-economic status, his conception of self, his attitude toward them, his competence, his trustworthiness, etc. Although some of this information seems to be sought almost as an end in itself, there are usually quite practical reasons for acquiring it. Information about the individual helps to define the situation, enabling others to know in advance what he will expect of them and what they may expect of him. Informed in these ways, the others will know how best to act in order to call forth a desired response from him.

For those present, many sources of information become accessible and many carriers (or "sign-vehicles") become available for conveying this information. If unacquainted with the individual, observers can glean clues from his conduct and appearance which allow them to apply their previous experience with individuals roughly similar to the one before them or, more important, to apply untested stereotypes to him. They can also assume from past experience that only individuals of a particular kind are likely to be found in a given social setting. They can rely on what the individual says about himself or on documentary evidence he provides as to who and what he is. If they know, or know of, the individual by virtue of experience prior to the interaction, they can rely on assumptions as to the persistence and generality of psychological traits as a means of predicting his present and future behavior.

However, during the period in which the individual is in the immediate presence of the others, few events may occur which directly provide the others with the conclusive information they will need if they are to direct wisely their own activity. Many crucial facts lie beyond the time and place of interaction or lie concealed within it. For example, the "true" or "real" attitudes, beliefs, and emotions of the individual can be ascertained only indirectly, through his avowals or through what appears to be involuntary expressive behavior. Similarly, if the individual offers the others a product or service, they will often find that during the interaction there will be no time and place immediately available for eating the pudding that the proof can be found in. They will be forced to accept some events as conventional or natural signs of something not directly available to the senses. In Ichheiser's terms,[1] the individual will have to act so that he intentionally or unintentionally *expresses* himself, and the others will in turn have to be *impressed* in some way by him.

The expressiveness of the individual (and therefore his capacity to give impressions) appears to involve two radically different kinds of sign activity: the expression that he *gives,* and the expression that he *gives off.* The first involves verbal symbols or their substitutes which he uses admittedly and solely to convey the information that he and the others are known to attach to these symbols. This is communication in the traditional and narrow sense. The second involves a wide range of action that others can treat as symptomatic of the actor, the expectation being that the action was performed for reasons other than the information conveyed in this way. As we shall have to see, this distinction has an only initial validity. The individual does of course intentionally convey misinformation by means of both of these types of communication, the first involving deceit, the second feigning.

Taking communication in both its narrow and broad sense, one finds that when the individual is in the immediate presence of others, his activity will have a promissory character. The others are likely to find that they must accept the individual on faith, offering him a just return while he is present before them in exchange for something whose true value will not be established until after he has left their presence. (Of course, the others also live by inference in their dealings with the physical world, but it is only in the world of social interaction that the objects about which they make inferences will purposely facilitate and hinder this inferential process.) The security that they justifiably feel in making inferences about the individual will vary, of course, depending on such factors as the amount of information they already possess about him, but no amount of such past evidence can entirely obviate the necessity of acting on the basis of inferences. As William I. Thomas suggested:

> It is also highly important for us to realize that we do not as a matter of fact lead our lives, make our decisions, and reach our goals in everyday life either statistically or scientifically. We live by inference. I am, let us say, your guest. You do not know, you cannot determine scientifically, that I will not steal your money or your spoons. But inferentially I will not, and inferentially you have me as a guest.[2]

---

[1] Gustav Ichheiser, "Misunderstandings in Human Relations," Supplement to *The American Journal of Sociology,* LV (September, 1949), pp. 6–7.

[2] Quoted in E. H. Volkart, editor, *Social Behavior and Personality,* Contributions of W. I. Thomas to Theory and Social Research (New York: Social Science Research Council, 1951), p. 5.

Let us now turn from the others to the point of view of the individual who presents himself before them. He may wish them to think highly of him, or to think that he thinks highly of them, or to perceive how in fact he feels toward them, or to obtain no clear-cut impression; he may wish to ensure sufficient harmony so that the interaction can be sustained, or to defraud, get rid of, confuse, mislead, antagonize, or insult them. Regardless of the particular objective which the individual has in mind and of his motive for having this objective, it will be in his interests to control the conduct of the others, especially their responsive treatment of him.[3] This control is achieved largely by influencing the definition of the situation which the others come to formulate, and he can influence this definition by expressing himself in such a way as to give them the kind of impression that will lead them to act voluntarily in accordance with his own plan. Thus, when an individual appears in the presence of others, there will usually be some reason for him to mobilize his activity so that it will convey an impression to others which it is in his interests to convey. Since a girl's dormitory mates will glean evidence of her popularity from the calls she receives on the phone, we can suspect that some girls will arrange for calls to be made, and Willard Waller's finding can be anticipated:

> It has been reported by many observers that a girl who is called to the telephone in the dormitories will often allow herself to be called several times, in order to give all the other girls ample opportunity to hear her paged.[4]

Of the two kinds of communication—expressions given and expressions given off—this report will be primarily concerned with the latter, with the more theatrical and contextual kind, the non-verbal, presumably unintentional kind, whether this communication be purposely engineered or not. As an example of what we must try to examine, I would like to cite at length a novelistic incident in which Preedy, a vacationing Englishman, makes his first appearance on the beach of his summer hotel in Spain:

> But in any case he took care to avoid catching anyone's eye. First of all, he had to make it clear to those potential companions of his holiday that they were of no concern to him whatsoever. He stared through them, round them, over them—eyes lost in space. The beach might have been empty. If by chance a ball was thrown his way, he looked surprised; then let a smile of amusement lighten his face (Kindly Preedy), looked

---

[3] Here I owe much to an unpublished paper by Tom Burns of the University of Edinburgh. He presents the argument that in all interaction a basic underlying theme is the desire of each participant to guide and control the responses made by the others present. A similar argument has been advancd by Jay Haley in a recent unpublished paper, but in regard to a special kind of control, that having to do with defining the nature of the relationship of those involved in the interaction.

[4] Willard Waller, "The Rating and Dating Complex," *American Sociological Review*, II, p. 730.

round dazed to see that there *were* people on the beach, tossed it back with a smile to himself and not a smile *at* the people, and then resumed carelessly his nonchalant survey of space.

But it was time to institute a little parade, the parade of the Ideal Preedy. By devious handlings he gave any who wanted to look a chance to see the title of his book—a Spanish translation of Homer, classic thus, but not daring, cosmopolitan too—and then gathered together his beach-wrap and bag into a neat sand-resistant pile (Methodical and Sensible Preedy), rose slowly to stretch at ease his huge frame (Big-Cat Preedy), and tossed aside his sandals (Carefree Preedy, after all).

The marriage of Preedy and the sea! There were alternative rituals. The first involved the stroll that turns into a run and a dive straight into the water, thereafter smoothing into a strong splashless crawl towards the horizon. But of course not really to the horizon. Quite suddenly he would turn on to his back and thrash great white splashes with his legs, somehow thus showing that he could have swum further had he wanted to, and then would stand up a quarter out of water for all to see who it was.

The alternative course was simpler, it avoided the cold-water shock and it avoided the risk of appearing too high-spirited. The point was to appear to be so used to the sea, the Mediterranean, and this particular beach, that one might as well be in the sea as out of it. It involved a slow stroll down and into the edge of the water—not even noticing his toes were wet, land and water all the same to *him!*—with his eyes up at the sky gravely surveying portents, invisible to others, of the weather (Local Fisherman Preedy).[5]

The novelist means us to see that Preedy is improperly concerned with the extensive impressions he feels his sheer bodily action is giving off to those around him. We can malign Preedy further by assuming that he has acted merely in order to give a particular impression, that this is a false impression, and that the others present receive either no impression at all, or, worse still, the impression that Preedy is affectedly trying to cause them to receive this particular impression. But the important point for us here is that the kind of impression Preedy thinks he is making is in fact the kind impression that others correctly and incorrectly glean from someone in their midst.

I have said that when an individual appears before others his actions will influence the definition of the situation which they come to have. Sometimes the individual will act in a thoroughly calculating manner, expressing himself in a given way solely in order to give the kind of impression to others that is likely to evoke from them a specific response he is concerned to obtain. Sometimes the individual will be calculating in his activity but be relatively unaware that this is the case. Sometimes he will intentionally and consciously express himself in a particular way, but chiefly because the tradition of his group or social status require this kind of expression and

[5] William Sansom, *A Contest of Ladies* (London: Hogarth, 1956), pp. 230–32.

not because of any particular response (other than vague acceptance or approval) that is likely to be evoked from those impressed by the expression. Sometimes the traditions of an individual's role will lead him to give a well-designed impression of a particular kind and yet he may be neither consciously nor unconsciously disposed to create such an impression. The others, in their turn, may be suitably impressed by the individual's efforts to convey something, or may misunderstand the situation and come to conclusions that are warranted neither by the individual's intent nor by the facts. In any case, in so far as the others act *as if* the individual had conveyed a particular impression, we may take a functional or pragmatic view and say that the individual has "effectively" projected a given definition of the situation and "effectively" fostered the understanding that a given state of affairs obtains. [. . .]

Reality and Contrivance

In our own Anglo-American culture there seems to be two common-sense models according to which we formulate our conceptions of behavior: the real, sincere, or honest performance; and the false one that thorough fabricators assemble for us, whether meant to be taken unseriously, as in the work of stage actors, or seriously, as in the work of confidence men. We tend to see real performances as something not purposely put together at all, being an unintentional product of the individual's unself-conscious response to the facts in his situation. And contrived performances we tend to see as something painstakingly pasted together, one false item on another, since there is no reality to which the items of behavior could be a direct response. It will be necessary to see now that these dichotomous conceptions are by way of being the ideology of honest performers, providing strength to the show they put on, but a poor analysis of it.

First, let it be said that there are many individuals who sincerely believe that the definition of the situation they habitually project is the real reality. In this report I do not mean to question their proportion in the population but rather the structural relation of their sincerity to the performances they offer. If a performance is to come off, the witnesses by and large must be able to believe that the performers are sincere. This is the structural place of sincerity in the drama of events. Performers may be sincere—or be insincere but sincerely convinced of their own sincerity—but this kind of affection for one's part is not necessary for its convincing performance. There are not many French cooks who are really Russian spies, and perhaps there are not many women who play the part of wife to one man and mistress to another; but these duplicities do occur, often being sustained successfully for long periods of time. This suggests that while persons usually are what they appear to be, such appearances could still have been managed. There is, then, a statistical relation between appearances and reality, not an intrinsic or necessary one. In fact, given the unanticipated threats that play upon a performance, and given the need (later to be discussed) to maintain solidarity with one's fellow performers and some distance from the witnesses, we find that a rigid incapacity to depart from one's inward view of reality may at times endanger one's performance. Some performances are carried off successfully with complete dishonesty, others with complete honesty; but for performances in general neither of these extremes is essential and neither, perhaps, is dramaturgically advisable.

The implication here is that an honest, sincere, serious performance is less firmly connected with the solid world than one might first assume. And this implication will be strengthened if we look again at the distance usually placed between quite honest performances and quite contrived ones. In this connection take, for example, the remarkable phenomenon of stage acting. It does take deep skill, long training, and psychological capacity to become a good stage actor. But this fact should not blind us to another one: that almost anyone can quickly learn a script well enough to give a charitable audience some sense of realness in what is being contrived before them. And it seems this is so because ordinary social intercourse is itself put together as a scene is put together, by the exchange of dramatically inflated actions, counteractions, and terminating replies. Scripts even in the hands of unpracticed players can come to life because life itself is a dramatically enacted thing. All the world is not, of course, a stage, but the crucial ways in which it isn't are not easy to specify.

The recent use of "psychodrama" as a therapeutic technique illustrates a further point in this regard. In these psychiatrically staged scenes patients not only act out parts with some effectiveness, but employ no script in doing so. Their own past is available to them in a form which allows them to stage a recapitulation of it. Apparently a part once played honestly and in earnest leaves the performer in a position to contrive a showing of it later. Further, the parts that significant others played to him in the past also seem to be available, allowing him to switch from being the person that he was to being the persons that others were for him. This capacity to switch enacted roles when obliged to do so could have been predicted; everyone apparently can do it. For in learning to perform our parts in real life we guide our own productions by not too consciously maintaining an incipient familiarity with the routine of those to whom we will address ourselves. And when we come to be able properly to manage a real routine we are able to do this in part because of "anticipatory socialization,"[6] having already been schooled in the reality that is just coming to be real for us.

When the individual does move into a new position in society and obtains a new part to perform, he is not likely to be told in full detail how to conduct himself, nor will the facts of his new situation press sufficiently on him from the start to determine his conduct without his further giving

[6] See R. K. Merton, *Social Theory and Social Structure* (Glencoe: The Free Press, revised and enlarged edition, 1957), p. 265 ff.

thought to it. Ordinarily he will be given only a few cues, hints, and stage directions, and it will be assumed that he already has in his repertoire a large number of bits and pieces of performances that will be required in the new setting. The individual will already have a fair idea of what modesty, deference, or righteous indignation looks like, and can make a pass at playing these bits when necessary. He may even be able to play out the part of a hypnotic subject[7] or commit a "compulsive" crime[8] on the basis of models for these activities that he is already familiar with.

A theatrical performance or a staged confidence game requires a thorough scripting of the spoken content of the routine; but the vast part involving "expression given off" is often determined by meager stage directions. It is expected that the performer of illusions will already know a good deal about how to manage his voice, his face, and his body, although he—as well as any person who directs him—may find it difficult indeed to provide a detailed verbal statement of this kind of knowledge. And in this, of course, we approach the situation of the straightforward man in the street. Socialization may not so much involve a learning of the many specific details of a single concrete part—often there could not be enough time or energy for this. What does seem to be required of the individual is that he learn enough pieces of expression to be able to "fill in" and manage, more or less, any part that he is likely to be given. The legitimate performances of everyday life are not "acted" or "put on" in the sense that the performer knows in advance just what he is going to do, and does this solely because of the effect it is likely to have. The expressions it is felt he is giving off will be especially "inaccessible" to him.[9] But as in the case of less legitimate performers, the incapacity of the ordinary individual to formulate in advance the movements of his eyes and body does not mean that he will not express himself through these devices in a way that is dramatized and pre-formed in his repertoire of actions. In short, we all act better than we know how.

When we watch a television wrestler gouge, foul, and snarl at his opponent we are quite ready to see that, in spite of the dust, he is, and knows he is, merely playing at being the "heavy," and that in another match he may be given the other role, that of clean-cut wrestler, and perform this with equal verve and proficiency. We seem less ready to see, however, that while such details as the number and character of the falls may be fixed beforehand, the details of the expressions and movements used do not

---

[7] This view of hypnosis is neatly presented by T. R. Sarbin, "Contributions to Role-Taking Theory. I: Hypnotic Behavior," *Psychological Review,* 57, pp. 255–70.

[8] See D. R. Cressey, "The Differential Association Theory and Compulsive Crimes," *Journal of Criminal Law, Criminology and Police Science,* 45, pp. 29–40.

[9] This concept derives from T. R. Sarbin, "Role Theory," in Gardner Lindzey, *Handbook of Social Psychology* (Cambridge: Addison-Wesley, 1954), Vol. 1, pp. 235–36.

come from a script but from command of an idiom, a command that is exercised from moment to moment with little calculation or forethought.

In reading of persons in the West Indies who become the "horse" or the one possessed of a voodoo spirit,[10] it is enlightening to learn that the person possessed will be able to provide a correct portrayal of the god that has entered him because of "the knowledge and memories accumulated in a life spent visiting congregations of the cult,"[11] that the person possessed will be in just the right social relation to those who are watching; that possession occurs at just the right moment in the ceremonial undertakings, the possessed one carrying out his ritual obligations to the point of participating in a kind of skit with persons possessed at the time with other spirits. But in learning this, it is important to see that this contextual structuring of the horse's role still allows participants in the cult to believe that possession is a real thing and that persons are possessed at random by gods whom they cannot select.

And when we observe a young American middle-class girl playing dumb for the benefit of her boy friend, we are ready to point to items of guile and contrivance in her behavior. But like herself and her boy friend, we accept as an unperformed fact that this performer *is* a young American middle-class girl. But surely here we neglect the greater part of the performance. It is commonplace to say that different social groupings express in different ways such attributes as age, sex, territory, and class status, and that in each case these bare attributes are elaborated by means of a distinctive complex cultural configuration of proper ways of conducting oneself. To *be* a given kind of person, then, is not merely to possess the required attributes, but also to sustain the standards of conduct and appearance that one's social grouping attaches thereto. The unthinking ease with which performers consistently carry off such standard-maintaining routines does not deny that a performance has occurred, merely that the participants have been aware of it.

A status, a position, a social place is not a material thing, to be possessed and then displayed; it is a pattern of appropriate conduct, coherent, embellished, and well articulated. Performed with ease or clumsiness, awareness or not, guile or good faith, it is none the less something that must be enacted and portrayed, something that must be realized. Sartre, here, provides a good illustration:

> Let us consider this waiter in the café. His movement is quick and forward, a little too precise, a little too rapid. He comes toward the patrons with a step a little too quick. He bends forward a little too eagerly; his voice, his eyes express an interest a little too solicitous for the order of

[10] See, for example, Alfred Métraux, "Dramatic Elements in Ritual Possession," *Diogenes,* 11, pp. 18–36.

[11] *Ibid.,* p. 24.

the customer. Finally there he returns, trying to imitate in his walk the inflexible stiffness of some kind of automaton while carrying his tray with the recklessness of a tightrope-walker by putting it in a perpetually unstable, perpetually broken equilibrium which he perpetually re-establishes by a light movement of the arm and hand. All his behavior seems to us a game. He applies himself to changing his movements as if they were mechanisms, the one regulating the other; his gestures and even his voice seem to be mechanisms; he gives himself the quickness and pitiless rapidity of things. He is playing, he is amusing himself. But what is he playing? We need not watch long before we can explain it: he is playing at being a waiter in a café. There is nothing there to surprise us. The game is a kind of marking out and investigation. The child plays with his body in order to explore it, to take inventory of it; the waiter in the café plays with his condition in order to *realize* it. This obligation is not different from that which is imposed on all tradesmen. Their condition is wholly one of ceremony. The public demands of them that they realize it as a ceremony; there is the dance of the grocer, of the tailor, of the auctioneer, by which they endeavor to persuade their clientele that they are nothing but a grocer, an auctioneer, a tailor. A grocer who dreams is offensive to the buyer, because such a grocer is not wholly a grocer. Society demands that he limit himself to his function as a grocer, just as the soldier at attention makes himself into a soldier-thing with a direct regard which does not see at all, which is not longer meant to see, since it is the rule and not the interest of the moment which determines the point he must fix his eyes on (the sight "fixed at ten paces"). There are indeed many precautions to imprison a man in what he is, as if we lived in perpetual fear that he might escape from it, that he might break away and suddenly elude his condition.[12] [. . .]

The Role of Expression Is Conveying Impressions of Self

Perhaps a moral note can be permitted at the end. In this report the expressive component of social life has been treated as a source of impressions given to or taken by others. Impression, in turn, has been treated as a source of information about unapparent facts and as a means by which the recipients can guide their response to the informant without having to wait for the full consequences of the informant's actions to be felt. Expression, then, has been treated in terms of the communicative role it plays during social interaction and not, for example, in terms of consummatory or tension-release function it might have for the expresser.[13]

[12] Sartre, *Being and Nothingness,* translated by Hazel E. Barnes (New York: Philosophical Library, 1956), p. 59.

[13] A recent treatment of this kind may be found in Talcott Parsons, Robert F. Bales, and Edward A. Shils, *Working Papers in the Theory of Action* (Glencoe, Ill.: The Free Press, 1953), Chap. II, "The Theory of Symbolism in Relation to Action."

Underlying all social interaction there seems to be a fundamental dialectic. When one individual enters the presence of others, he will want to discover the facts of the situation. Were he to possess this information, he could know, and make allowances for, what will come to happen and he could give the others present as much of their due as is consistent with his enlightened self-interest. To uncover fully the factual nature of the situation, it would be necessary for the individual to know all the relevant social data about the others. It would also be necessary for the individual to know the actual outcome or end product of the activity of the others during the interaction, as well as their innermost feelings concerning him. Full information of this order is rarely available; in its absence, the individual tends to employ substitutes—cues, tests, hints, expressive gestures, status symbols, etc.—as predictive devices. In short, since the reality that the individual is concerned with is unperceivable at the moment, appearances must be relied upon in its stead. And, paradoxically, the more the individual is concerned with the reality that is not available to perception, the more must he concentrate his attention on appearances.

The individual tends to treat the others present on the basis of the impression they give now about the past and the future. It is here that communicative acts are translated into moral ones. The impressions that the others give tend to be treated as claims and promises they have implicitly made, and claims and promises tend to have a moral character. In his mind the individual says: "I am using these impressions of you as a way of checking up on you and your activity, and you ought not to lead me astray." The peculiar thing about this is that the individual tends to take this stand even though he expects the others to be unconscious of many of their expressive behaviors and even though he may expect to exploit the others on the basis of the information he gleans about them. Since the sources of impression used by the observing individual involve a multitude of standards pertaining to politeness and decorum, pertaining both to social intercourse and task-performance, we can appreciate afresh how daily life is enmeshed in moral lines of discrimination.

Let us shift now to the point of view of the others. If they are to be gentlemanly, and play the individual's game, they will give little conscious heed to the fact that impressions are being formed about them but rather act without guile or contrivance, enabling the individual to receive valid impressions about them and their efforts. And if they happen to give thought to the fact that they are being observed, they will not allow this to influence them unduly, content in the belief that the individual will obtain a correct impression and give them their due because of it. Should they be concerned with influencing the treatment that the individual gives them, and this is properly to be expected, then a gentlemanly means will be available to them. They need only guide their action in the present so that its future consequences will be the kind that would lead a just individual to treat them now in a way they want to be treated; once this is done, they have only to rely on the perceptiveness and justness of the individual who observes them.

Sometimes those who are observed do, of course, employ these proper means of influencing the way in which the observer treats them. But there is another way, a shorter and more efficient way, in which the observed can influence the observer. Instead of allowing an impression of their activity to arise as an incidental by-product of their activity, they can reorient their frame of reference and devote their efforts to the creation of desired impressions. Instead of attempting to achieve certain ends by acceptable means, they can attempt to achieve the impression that they are achieving certain ends by acceptable means. It is always possible to manipulate the impression the observer uses as a substitute for reality because a sign for the presence of a thing, not being that thing, can be employed in the absence of it. The observer's need to rely on representations of things itself creates the possibility of misrepresentation.

There are many sets of persons who feel they could not stay in business, whatever their business, if they limited themselves to the gentlemanly means of influencing the individual who observes them. At some point or other in the round of their activity they feel it is necessary to band together and directly manipulate the impression that they give. The observed become a performing team and the observers become the audience. Actions which appear to be done on objects become gestures addressed to the audience. The round of activity becomes dramatized.

We come now to the basic dialectic. In their capacity as performers, individuals will be concerned with maintaining the impression that they are living up to the many standards by which they and their products are judged. Because these standards are so numerous and so pervasive, the individuals who are performers dwell more than we might think in a moral world. But, *qua* performers, individuals are concerned not with the moral issue of realizing these standards, but with the amoral issue of engineering a convincing impression that these standards are being realized. Our activity, then, is largely concerned with moral matters, but as performers we do not have a moral concern with them. As performers we are merchants of morality. Our day is given over to intimate contact with the goods we display and our minds are filled with intimate understandings of them; but it may well be that the more attention we give to these goods, then the more distant we feel from them and from those who are believing enough to buy them. To use a different imagery, the very obligation and profitability of appearing always in a steady moral light, of being a socialized character, forces one to be the sort of person who is practiced in the ways of the stage.

Staging and the Self

The general notion that we make a presentation of ourselves to others is hardly novel; what ought to be stressed in conclusion is that the very structure of the self can be seen in terms of how we arrange for such performances in our Anglo-American society.

In this report, the individual was divided by implication into two basic parts: he was viewed as a *performer,* a harried fabricator of impressions involved in the all-too-human task of staging a performance; he was viewed as a *character,* a figure, typically a fine one, whose spirit, strength, and other sterling qualities the performance was designed to evoke. The attributes of a performer and the attributes of a character are of a different order, quite basically so, yet both sets have their meaning in terms of the show that must go on.

First, character. In our society the character one performs and one's self are somewhat equated, and this self-as-character is usually seen as something housed within the body of its possessor, especially the upper parts thereof, being a nodule, somehow, in the psychobiology of personality. I suggest that this view is an implied part of what we are all trying to present, but provides, just because of this, a bad analysis of the presentation. In this report the performed self was seen as some kind of image, usually creditable, which the individual on stage and in character effectively attempts to induce others to hold in regard to him. While this image is entertained *concerning* the individual, so that a self is imputed to him, this self itself does not derive from its possessor, but from the whole scene of his action, being generated by that attribute of local events which renders them interpretable by witnesses. A correctly staged and performed scene leads the audience to impute a self to a performed character, but this imputation —this self—is a *product* of a scene that comes off, and is not a *cause* of it. The self, then, as a performed character, is not an organic thing that has a specific location, whose fundamental fate is to be born, to mature, and to die; it is a dramatic effect arising diffusely from a scene that is presented, and the characteristic issue, the crucial concern, is whether it will be credited or discredited.

In analyzing the self then we are drawn from its possessor, from the person who will profit or lose most by it, for he and his body merely provide the peg on which something of collaborative manufacture will be hung for a time. And the means for producing and maintaining selves do not reside inside the peg; in fact these means are often bolted down in social establishments. There will be a back region with its tools for shaping the body, and a front region with its fixed props. There will be a team of persons whose activity on stage in conjunction with available props will constitute the scene from which the performed character's self will emerge, and another team, the audience, whose interpretive activity will be necessary for this emergence. The self is a product of all of these arrangements, and in all of its parts bears the marks of this genesis.

The whole machinery of self-production is cumbersome, of course, and sometimes breaks down, exposing its separate components: back region control; team collusion; audience tact; and so forth. But, well oiled, impressions will flow from it fast enough to put us in the grips of one of our types of reality—the performance will come off and the firm self accorded each performed character will appear to emanate intrinsically from its performer.

Let us turn now from the individual as character performed to the individual as performer. He has a capacity to learn, this being exercised in the task of training for a part. He is given to having fantasies and dreams, some that pleasurably unfold a triumphant performance, others full of anxiety and dread that nervously deal with vital discreditings in a public front region. He often manifests a gregarious desire for teammates and audiences, a tactful considerateness for their concerns; and he has a capacity for deeply felt shame, leading him to minimize the chances he takes of exposure.

These attributes of the individual *qua* performer are not merely a depicted effect of particular performances; they are psychobiological in nature, and yet they seem to arise out of intimate interaction with the contingencies of staging performances.

And now a final comment. In developing the conceptual framework employed in this report, some language of the stage was used. I spoke of performers and audiences; of routines and parts; of performances coming off or falling flat; of cues, stage settings and backstage; of dramaturgical needs, dramaturgical skills, and dramaturgical strategies. Now it should be admitted that this attempt to press a mere analogy so far was in part a rhetoric and a maneuver.

The claim that all the world's a stage is sufficiently commonplace for readers to be familiar with its limitations and tolerant of its presentation, knowing that at any time they will easily be able to demonstrate to themselves that it is not to be taken too seriously. An action staged in a theater is a relatively contrived illusion and an admitted one; unlike ordinary life, nothing real or actual can happen to the performed characters—although at another level of course something real and actual can happen to the reputation of performers *qua* professionals whose everyday job is to put on theatrical performances.

And so here the language and mask of the stage will be dropped. Scaffolds, after all, are to build other things with, and should be erected with an eye to taking them down. This report is not concerned with aspects of theater that creep into everyday life. It is concerned with the structure of social encounters—the structure of those entities in social life that come into being whenever persons enter one another's immediate physical presence. The key factor in this structure is the maintenance of a single definition of the situation, this definition having to be expressed, and this expression sustained in the face of a multitude of potential disruptions.

A character staged in a theater is not in some ways real, nor does it have the same kind of real consequences as does the thoroughly contrived character performed by a confidence man; but the *successful* staging of either of these types of false figures involves use of *real* techniques—the same techniques by which everyday persons sustain their real social situations. Those who conduct face to face interaction on a theater's stage must meet the key requirement of real situations; they must expressively sustain a definition of the situation: but this they do in circumstances that have facilitated their developing an apt terminology for the interactional tasks that all of us share.

R. D. LAING

(1927-   )

Despite the fact that Goffman takes down the scaffolding he erected, namely, the metaphor of the stage, we are still inclined to ask, "Why all the acting?" Once we become aware that we do perform, once our tacit knowledge becomes explicit, our first inclination is to close the curtain and examine the script. We want to believe that when the curtain goes up again we will have purged the performance of all contrivance, and in place of an actor whose very essence is to deceive we appear **ourselves,** not as performers of a script written for purposes of social approval.

Granted that who we are is not uniquely determined prior to our contact with society. Granted that "A correctly staged and performed scene leads the audience to impute a self to a performed character, but this imputation—this self—is a **product** of a scene that comes off, and is not a cause of it." Still there must be room for questioning the extent to which we want to let the audience (society) participate in constructing the role played by the self. There is a difference between self creation **with** others and self creation **for** others; the latter amounts to pandering. The playwright may know formulas for getting an audience to clap, but is applause all we are after in real life? Perhaps so for those who have an unalloyed respect for the audience, but for those of us who see certain contradictions in society, for those of us who would prefer to improve on the usual lot rather than perpetuate the contradictions and the unhappiness they produce, applause may be a guarantee that one is not achieving what one set out to achieve. Naturally, the distrust of applause can be inflated to a pathological fear of stepping out on stage at all, and Goffman is right to point to how we do perform, like it or not. But if it is necessary to underscore the possibility of questioning the criteria for judging the performance, Laing's essay does just that. In several of his books Erik Erikson repeatedly returns to his thesis that great men are

those who feel most deeply the contradictions plaguing their generation. Their achievement stems from their attempt to grapple
with and solve the contradictions given to a generation by its particular place in history. Similarly, the way to understand Laing and
his work is to look at both in terms of the contradictions and
crosscurrents that beset our time: loneliness or community; common sense or a higher state of consciousness. Laing is looking for
"a way out" of the contradictions, and his path takes him through
many of the themes treated in this volume.

Both his personal and his theoretical approaches to the problems of the self are dominated by a view that takes the **context** of
the self as all-important. He found it necessary to take up resi-
dency in a ward for schizophrenics before he felt he had any insight into their self-structure. Through his experiential learning,
as well as through his theoretical researches, he came to see the
development of the self in terms of the solutions evolved for dealing with different transactions with other people. When others exert contradictory pressures, the self can find no way out; at this
point the self is in what Gregory Bateson called a "double bind."
According to Laing's view behavior labeled as schizophrenic may
be seen as a rational solution to a double-bind situation. Thus
schizophrenia may not be the irrational behavior pattern of an internally confused self but the rational and even predictable outcome of a nexus of contradictory influences exerted by other selves
and their situations.

Laing's insights are closely tied to the philosophical tradition
culminating in Sartre; with his colleague David Cooper, Laing published a book (**Reason and Violence,** 1964) devoted exclusively to
Sartre's philosophy. (Here it is worth pointing out the connection
between Laing's work and the problem of violence treated later on
by Fanon and Arendt. Sartre wrote a preface to Fanon's work, and
Arendt comments on both Sartre and Laing.)

Laing's latest voyages have taken him into the realms of eastern
religion and mysticism. He left his psychiatric practice in England
for a journey to the East so that he could, as he said, "get on with
it." Where Laing's explorations will take him, who can say? Some
think him mad already; no wonder, they say, he has such insights
into the world of the schizophrenic. But Laing's own works force us
to hear an echo to Pontius Pilate's "What is truth?" Through
Laing's thought we see that "madness" may be the only "sane"
reaction to the many double binds wrought by the contemporary
world, and the reversal of roles indicated by the quotation marks
forces us to hear the echo, "What is madness?" Laing is none too
ready to let contemporary society define the distinction between
madness and sanity on the basis of the socially accepted view of
the distinction between reality and unreality. As I suggested ear-

lier, Laing accepts the importance of social determinants upon the self, but he finds room for criticizing the finality of the norms used by contemporary society.

Laing's attitude toward madness is not unlike Alan Watt's attitude toward psychedelics. What some regard as a mental breakdown might be for others a breakthrough to a transcendent[1] reality, from whose perspective our ordinary affairs look petty and inconsequential if not downright dishonest. But the romance of the breakthrough poses the same problem faced by drug users: as Laing says, "not everyone comes back to us again." Even if madness does introduce some to a reality that seems more real than everyday life, isn't something lost if they are unable to return to everyday life? Laing is aware of the problem, but does he have an answer?

Laing is also familiar with recent philosophical efforts to expunge the ghost in the machine. Note how in the first few pages he manages to argue for a certain inaccessibility of one self to another self without basing that inaccessibility on any myth of an 'inner' self hidden from the observation of the 'outer.' His distinction between experience and behavior is not a distinction between what is present to the inner self and what is evident to the senses, but has rather more to do with James' different lines of relational determination. My experience is mine to the extent that it stands in continuous relation to my historical development, not to an inner me that is present but hidden. Laing's argument for the inaccessibility of another's experience can be interpreted as acknowledging that two different histories do not bring the same past to the now where they intersect. Consequently, while both overcome the subject-object gap in their unities with a third line representing, say, a landscape both are looking at, there is no likelihood that the two unities are qualitatively the same. This further complexity introduced into the idea of taking a given experience "two times over," both subjectively and objectively, actually strengthens James' argument: the subject-subject gap introduced by Laing shows why it is that, despite the numerical identity between an event and my particular experience of that event, still my experience of that event is not "merely objective" in the sense of being independent of my way of looking at things. The subject-subject gap denies literal objectivity to reality by showing how the numerical unity of subjectivity and objectivity can express itself as many times over as there are different subjects present. Objectivity becomes, as Brown would put it, polymorphous; or as Polanyi might put it, the quest for an objectivity independent of

---

[1] Laing uses the term 'transcendental' to refer to the transcendent. For the Kantian distinction, which maintains a different meaning for these two related terms, see pp. 141–42.

subjectivity is a mistake. Subjectivity in this context is not equivalent to a falsifying bias. Once the inner ghost has been expunged each subjective identity can be regarded as a particular sequence of thoroughly objective and manifest events, a world-line, as it were, of continuous relatedness. Of course a given subject **can** falsify his perceptions if, for example, some of those objective events in his past embody objective contradictions that distort his vision. Here we are back to Laing and the problem of the double bind.

THE POLITICS OF EXPERIENCE

Persons and Experience

. . . that great and true Amphibian whose nature is disposed to live, not only like other creatures in divers elements, but in divided and distinguished worlds.
SIR THOMAS BROWNE, *Religio Medici*

Even facts become fictions without adequate ways of seeing "the facts." We do not need theories so much as the experience that is the source of the theory. We are not satisfied with faith, in the sense of an implausible hypothesis irrationally held: we demand to experience the "evidence."

We can see other people's behavior, but not their experience. This has led some people to insist that psychology has nothing to do with the other person's experience, but only with his behavior.

The other person's behavior is an experience of mine. My behavior is an experience of the other. The task of social phenomenology is to relate my experience of the other's behavior to the other's experience of my behavior. Its study is the relation between experience and experience: its true field is *interexperience*.

I see you, and you see me. I experience you, and you experience me. I see your behavior. You see my behavior. But I do not and never have and never will see your *experience* of me. Just as you cannot "see" my experience of you. My experience of you is not "inside" me. It is simply you, as I experience you. And I do not experience you as inside me. Similarly, I take it that you do not experience me as inside you.

"My experience of you" is just another form of words for "you-as-I-

THE POLITICS OF EXPERIENCE From R. D. Laing, *The Politics of Experience*. Published by Penguin Books, Ltd. Copyright © R. D. Laing, 1967. Reprinted by permission of Penguin Books, Ltd.

experience-you," and "your experience of me" equals "me-as-you-experience-me." Your experience of me is not inside you and my experience of you is not inside me, but *your experience of me is invisible to me and my experience of you is invisible to you.*

I cannot experience your experience. You cannot experience my experience. We are both invisible men. All men are invisible to one another. Experience is man's invisibility to man. Experience used to be called the Soul. Experience as invisibility of man to man is at the same time more evident than anything. *Only* experience is evident. Experience is the *only* evidence. [. . .]

Can human beings be persons today? Can a man be his actual self with another man or woman? Before we can ask such an optimistic question as, "What is a personal relationship?," we have to ask if a personal relationship is possible, or, *are persons possible* in our present situation? We are concerned with the possibility of man. This question can be asked only through its facets. Is love possible? Is freedom possible?

Whether or not all, or some, or no human beings are persons, I wish to define a person in a twofold way: in terms of experience, as a center of orientation of the objective universe; and in terms of behavior, as the origin of actions. Personal experience transforms a given field into a field of intention and action: only through action can our experience be transformed. It is tempting and facile to regard "persons" as only separate objects in space, who can be studied as any other natural objects can be studied. But just as Kierkegaard remarked that one will never find consciousness by looking down a microscope at brain cells or anything else, so one will never find persons by studying persons as though they were only objects. A person is the me or you, he or she, whereby an object is experienced. Are these centers of experience and origins of actions living in entirely unrelated worlds of their own composition? Everyone must refer here to their own experience. My own experience as a center of experience and origin of action tells me that this is not so. My experience and my action occur in a social field of reciprocal influence and interaction. I experience myself, identifiable as Ronald Laing by myself and others, as experienced by and acted upon by others, who refer to that person I call "me" as "you" or "him," or grouped together as "one of us" or "one of them" or "one of you."

This feature of personal relations does not arise in the correlation of the behavior of nonpersonal objects. Many social scientists deal with their embarrassment by denying its occasion. Nevertheless, the natural scientific world is complicated by the presence of certain identifiable entities, re-identifiable reliably over periods of years, whose behavior is either the manifestation or a concealment of a view of the world equivalent in ontological status to that of the scientist.

People may be observed to sleep, eat, walk, talk, etc. in relatively predictable ways. We must not be content with observation of this kind alone. Observation of behavior must be extended by inference to attributions about experience. Only when we can begin to do this can we really construct the experiential-behavioral system that is the human species.

It is quite possible to study the visible, audible, smellable effulgences of human bodies, and much study of human behavior has been in those terms. One can lump together very large numbers of units of behavior and regard them as a statistical population, in no way different from the multiplicity constituting a system of nonhuman objects. But one will not be studying persons. In a science of persons, I shall state as axiomatic that: behavior is a function of experience; and both experience and behavior are always in relation to someone or something other than self.

When two (or more) persons are in relation, the behavior of each towards the other is mediated by the experience by each of the other, and the experience of each is mediated by the behavior of each. There is no contiguity between the behavior of one person and that of the other. Much human behavior can be seen as a unilateral or bilateral *attempt* to eliminate experience. A person may treat another *as though* he were not a person, and he may act himself *as though* he were not a person. There is no contiguity between one person's experience and another's. My experience of you is always mediated through your *behavior*. Behavior that is the direct consequence of impact, as of one billiard ball hitting another, or experience directly transmitted to experience, as in the possible cases of extrasensory perception, is not personal. [. . .]

Fantasy as a Mode of Experience

The "surface" experience of self and other emerges from a less differentiated experiential matrix. Ontogenetically the very early experiential schemata are unstable and are surmounted, but never entirely. To a greater or lesser extent, the first ways in which the world has made sense to us continue to underpin our whole subsequent experience and actions. Our first way of experiencing the world is largely what psychoanalysts have called fantasy. This modality has its own validity, its own rationality. Infantile fantasy may become a closed enclave, a dissociated undeveloped "unconscious," but this need not be so. This eventuality is another form of alienation. Fantasy as encountered in many people today is split off from what the person regards as his mature, sane, rational, adult experience. We do not then see fantasy in its true function but experienced merely as an intrusive, sabotaging infantile nuisance.

For most of our social life, we largely gloss over this underlying fantasy level of our relationship.

Fantasy is a particular way of relating to the world. It is part of, sometimes the essential part of, the meaning or sense (*le sens:* Merleau-Ponty) implicit in action. As relationship we may be dissociated from it; as meaning we may not grasp it; as experience it may escape our notice in different ways. That is, it is possible to speak of fantasy being "unconscious," if this general statement is always given specific connotations.

However, although fantasy can be unconscious—that is, although we may be unaware of experience in this mode, or refuse to admit that our behavior implies an experiential relationship or a relational experience that gives it a meaning, often apparent to others if not to ourselves—fantasy need not be thus split from us, whether in terms of its content or modality.

Fantasy, in short, as I am using the term, is always experiential and meaningful; and, if the person is not dissociated from it, relational in a valid way.

Two people sit talking. The one (Peter) is making a point to the other (Paul). He puts his point of view in different ways to Paul for some time, but Paul does not understand.

Let us *imagine* what may be going on, in the sense that I mean by fantasy. Peter is trying to get through to Paul. He feels that Paul is being needlessly closed up against him. It becomes increasingly important to him to soften or get into Paul. But Paul seems hard, impervious and cold. Peter feels he is beating his head against a brick wall. He feels tired, hopeless, progressively more empty as he sees he is failing. Finally he gives up.

Paul feels, on the other hand, that Peter is pressing too hard. He feels he has to fight him off. He doesn't understand what Peter is saying but feels that he has to defend himself from an assault.

The dissociation of each from his fantasy, and the fantasy of the other, betokens the lack of relationship of each to himself and each to the other. They are both more and less related to each other "in fantasy" than each pretends to be to himself and the other.

Here, two roughly complementary fantasy experiences wildly belie the calm manner in which two men talk to each other, comfortably ensconced in their armchairs.

It is mistaken to regard the above description as merely metaphorical.

The Negation of Experience

There seems to be no agent more effective than another person in bringing a world for oneself alive, or, by a glance, a gesture, or a remark, shriveling up the reality in which one is lodged.[1]

The physical environment unremittingly offers us possibilities of experience, or curtails them. The fundamental human significance of architecture stems from this. The glory of Athens, as Pericles so lucidly stated, and the horror of so many features of the modern megalopolis is that the former enhanced and the latter constricts man's consciousness.

Here, however, I am concentrating upon what we do to ourselves and to each other.

Let us take the simplest possible interpersonal scheme. Consider Jack and Jill in relation. Then Jack's behavior towards Jill is experienced by

---

[1] Erving Goffman; *Encounters: Two Studies in the Sociology of Interaction* (Indianapolis: Bobbs-Merrill, 1961), page 41.

Jill in particular ways. How she experiences him affects considerably how she behaves towards him. How she behaves towards him influences (without by any means totally determining) how he experiences her. And his experience of her contributes to his way of behaving towards her, which in turn . . . etc.

Each person may take two fundamentally distinguishable forms of action in this interpersonal system. Each may act on his own experience or upon the other person's experience, *and there is no other form of personal action possible within this system.* That is to say, as long as we are considering personal action of self to self or self to other, the only way one can ever act is on one's own experience or on the other's experience.

Personal action can either open out possibilities of enriched experience or it can shut off possibilities. Personal action is either predominantly validating, confirming, encouraging, supportive, enhancing, or it is invalidating, denying, discouraging, undermining and constricting. It can be creative or destructive.

In a world where the normal condition is one of alienation, most personal action must be destructive both of one's own experience and of that of the other. I shall outline here some of the ways this can be done. I leave the reader to consider from his own experience how pervasive these kinds of action are.

Under the heading of "defense mechanisms," psychoanalysis describes a number of ways in which a person becomes alienated from himself. For example, repression, denial, splitting, projection, introjection. These "mechanisms" are often described in psychoanalytic terms as themselves "unconscious," that is, the person himself appears to be unaware that he is doing this to himself. Even when a person develops sufficient insight to see that "splitting," for example, is going on, he usually experiences this splitting as indeed a mechanism, an impersonal process, so to speak, which has taken over and which he can observe but cannot control or stop.

There is thus some phenomenological validity in referring to such "defenses" by the term "mechanism." But we must not stop there. They have this mechanical quality because the person as he experiences himself is dissociated from them. He appears to himself and to others to suffer from them. They seem to be processes he undergoes, and as such he experiences himself as a patient, with a particular psychopathology.

But this is so only from the perspective of his own alienated experience. As he becomes de-alienated he is able first of all to become aware of them, if he has not already done so, and then to take the second, even more crucial, step of progressively realizing that these are things he does or has done to himself. Process becomes converted back to praxis, the patient becomes an agent.

Ultimately it is possible to regain the ground that has been lost. These defense mechanisms are actions taken by the person on his own experience. On top of this he has dissociated himself from his own action. The end product of this twofold violence is a person who no longer experiences himself fully as a person, but as a part of a person, invaded by destructive psychopathological "mechanisms" in the face of which he is a relatively helpless victim.

These "defenses" are action on oneself. But "defenses" are not only intrapersonal, they are *transpersonal*. I act not only on myself, I can act upon you. And you act not only on yourself, you act upon me. In each case, on *experience*.[2]

If Jack succeeds in forgetting something, this is of little use if Jill continues to remind him of it. He must induce her not to do so. The safest way would be not just to make her keep quiet about it, but to induce her to forget it also.

Jack may act upon Jill in many ways. He may make her feel guilty for keeping on "bringing it up." He may *invalidate* her experience. This can be done more or less radically. He can indicate merely that it is unimportant or trivial, whereas it is important and significant to her. Going further, he can shift the *modality* of her experience from memory to imagination: "It's all in your imagination." Further still, he can invalidate the *content:* "It never happened that way." Finally, he can invalidate not only the significance, modality and content, but her very capacity to remember at all, and make her feel guilty for doing so into the bargain.

This is not unusual. People are doing such things to each other all the time. In order for such transpersonal invalidation to work, however, it is advisable to overlay it with a thick patina of mystification. For instance, by denying that this is what one is doing, and further invalidating any perception that it is being done by ascriptions such as "How can you think such a thing?" "You must be paranoid." And so on. [. . .]

Transcendental Experience

We are living in an age in which the ground is shifting and the foundations are shaking. I cannot answer for other times and places. Perhaps it has always been so. We know it is true today.

In these circumstances, we have every reason to be insecure. When the ultimate basis of our world is in question, we run to different holes in the ground, we scurry into roles, statuses, identities, interpersonal relations. We attempt to live in castles that can only be in the air because there is no

[2] For developments of my theory of *transpersonal defenses,* see R. D. Laing, H. Phillipson and A. R. Lee, *Interpersonal Perception: A Theory and a Method of Research* (London: Tavistock Publications, 1966; New York, Springer, 1966).

firm ground in the social cosmos on which to build. We are all witnesses to this state of affairs. Each sometimes sees the same fragment of the whole situation differently; often our concern is with different presentations of the original catastrophe. [. . .]

Experience may be judged as invalidly mad or as validly mystical. The distinction is not easy. In either case, from a social point of view, such judgements characterize different forms of behavior, regarded in our society as deviant. People behave in such ways because their experience of themselves is different. It is on the existential meaning of such unusual experience that I wish to focus.

Psychotic experience goes beyond the horizons of our common, that is, our communal, sense.

What regions of experience does this lead to? It entails a loss of the usual foundations of the "sense" of the world that we share with one another. Old purposes no longer seem viable; old meanings are senseless; the distinctions between imagination, dream, external perceptions often seem no longer to apply in the old way. External events may seem magically conjured up. Dreams may seem to be direct communications from others; imagination may seem to be objective reality.

But most radical of all, the very ontological foundations are shaken. The being of phenomena shifts and the phenomenon of being may no longer present itself to us as before. There are no supports, nothing to cling to, except perhaps some fragments from the wreck, a few memories, names, sounds, one or two objects, that retain a link with a world long lost. This void may not be empty. It may be peopled by visions and voices, ghosts, strange shapes and apparitions. No one who has not experienced how insubstantial the pageant of external reality can be, how it may fade, can fully realize the sublime and grotesque presences that can replace it, or that can exist alongside it.

When a person goes mad, a profound transposition of his place in relation to all domains of being occurs. His center of experience moves from ego to self. Mundane time becomes merely anecdotal, only the eternal matters. The madman is, however, confused. He muddles ego with self, inner with outer, natural and supernatural. Nevertheless, he can often be to us, even through his profound wretchedness and disintegration, the hierophant of the sacred. An exile from the scene of being as we know it, he is an alien, a stranger signaling to us from the void in which he is foundering, a void which may be peopled by presences that we do not even dream of. They used to be called demons and spirits, and they used to be known and named. He has lost his sense of self, his feelings, his place in the world as we know it. He tells us he is dead. But we are distracted from our cosy security by this mad ghost who haunts us with his visions and voices which seem so senseless and of which we feel impelled to rid him, cleanse him, cure him.

Madness need not be all breakdown. It may also be breakthrough. It is potentially liberation and renewal as well as enslavement and existential death. [. . .]

Certain *transcendental experiences* seem to me to be the original wellspring of all religions. Some psychotic people have transcendental experiences. Often (to the best of their recollection), they have never had such experiences before, and frequently they will never have them again. I am not saying, however, that psychotic experience necessarily contains this element more manifestly than sane experience.

We experience in different modes. We perceive external realities, we dream, imagine, have semiconscious reveries. Some people have visions, hallucinations, experience faces transfigured, see auras and so on. Most people most of the time experience themselves and others in one or another way that I shall call *egoic*. That is, centrally or peripherally, they experience the world and themselves in terms of a consistent identity, a me-here over against a you-there, within a framework of certain ground structures of space and time shared with other members of their society.

This identity-anchored, space-and-time-bound experience has been studied philosophically by Kant, and later by the phenomenologists, e.g. Husserl, Merleau-Ponty. Its historical and ontological relativity should be fully realized by any contemporary student of the human scene. Its cultural, socioeconomic relativity has become a commonplace among anthropologists and a platitude to the Marxists and neo-Marxists. And yet, with the consensual and interpersonal confirmation it offers, it gives us a sense of ontological security, whose validity we *experience* as self-validating, although metaphysically-historically-ontologically-socioeconomically-culturally we know its apparent absolute validity as an illusion.

In fact all religious and all existential philosophies have agreed that such *egoic experience* is a preliminary illusion, a veil, a film of *maya*—a dream to Heraclitus, and to Lao Tzu, the fundamental illusion of all Buddhism, a state of sleep, of death, of socially accepted madness, a womb state to which one has to die, from which one has to be born.

The person going through ego-loss or transcendental experiences may or may not become in different ways confused. Then he might legitimately be regarded as mad. But to be mad is not necessarily to be ill, notwithstanding that in our culture the two categories have become confused. It is assumed that if a person is mad (whatever that means) then *ipso facto* he is ill (whatever that means). The experience that a person may be absorbed in, while to others he appears simply ill-mad, may be for him veritable manna from heaven. The person's whole life may be changed, but it is difficult not to doubt the validity of such vision. Also, not everyone comes back to us again.

Are these experiences simply the effulgence of a pathological process or of a particular alienation? I do not think they are.

In certain cases, a man blind from birth may have an operation performed which gives him his sight. The result—frequently misery, confusion, disorientation. The light that illumines the madman is an unearthly light. It is not always a distorted refraction of his mundane life situation. He may be irradiated by light from other worlds. It may burn him out. [. . .]

As it is, the secular psychotherapist is often in the role of the blind leading the half-blind.

The fountain has not played itself out, the frame still shines, the river still flows, the spring still bubbles forth, the light has not faded. But between *us* and It, there is a veil which is more like fifty feet of solid concrete. *Deus absconditus.* Or we have absconded.

Already everything in our time is directed to categorizing and segregating this reality from objective facts. This is precisely the concrete wall. Intellectually, emotionally, interpersonally, organizationally, intuitively, theoretically, we have to blast our way through the solid wall, even if at the risk of chaos, madness and death. For from *this* side of the wall, this is the risk. There are no assurances, no guarantees.

Many people are prepared to have faith in the sense of scientifically indefensible belief in an untested hypothesis. Few have trust enough to test it. Many people make-believe what they experience. Few are made to believe by their experience. Paul of Tarsus was picked up by the scruff of the neck, thrown to the ground and blinded for three days. This direct experience was self-validating.

We live in a secular world. To adapt to this world the child abdicates its ecstasy. (*"L'enfant abdique son extase":* Mallarmé.) Having lost our experience of the spirit, we are expected to have faith. But this faith comes to be a belief in a reality which is not evident. There is a prophecy in Amos that a time will come when there will be a famine in the land, "not a famine for bread, nor a thirst for water, but of *hearing* the words of the Lord." That time has now come to pass. It is the present age.

From the alienated starting point of our pseudo-sanity, everything is equivocal. Our sanity is not "true" sanity. Their madness is not "true" madness. The madness of our patients is an artifact of the destruction wreaked on them by us and by them on themselves. Let no one suppose that we meet "true" madness any more than that we are truly sane. The madness that we encounter in "patients" is a gross travesty, a mockery, a grotesque caricature of what the natural healing of that estranged integration we call sanity might be. True sanity entails in one way or another the dissolution of the normal ego, that false self competently adjusted to our alienated social reality; the emergence of the "inner" archetypal mediators of divine power, and through this death a rebirth, and the eventual reestablishment of a new kind of ego-functioning, the ego now being the servant of the divine, no longer its betrayer.

4 **From Family to Society**

Introduction:
The Patriarchy
in Microcosm
and Macrocosm

Though Plato's **Republic** presents itself most obviously as a tract in utopian political philosophy, its picture of justice in the state is meant to serve as a large-scale model of justice in the individual. Throughout the **Republic** and the **Timaeus** Plato develops an interlocking metaphorical structure linking the self, the state, and the cosmos. The present section looks at a single link in that metaphorical chain. In moving from self-creation to social and political philosophy, it is helpful to locate these issues in their microcosmic form, namely, the family. Patriarchy, or father rule, has its biological roots in the family. Because the family has often been taken as the rudimentary model of social and political organization, its sexual structure is significant. The family is not just any small group; it is a biological unit joining old and young, male and female. To the extent that the male dominates the family, patriarchy is the appropriate form of political organization.

But patriarchy is under fire, both from the women's liberation movement and the many third-world movements seeking independence from colonial rule. Not surprisingly, the political and sexual assault on patriarchy comes when there is much talk of the "decline of the family." Some seek alternatives to restrictive monogamy; and the communal movement testifies to a quest for alternative forms of microcosmic social organization. How are we to understand these transformations in our culture? How are we to understand these transformations in ourselves? Social scientists of the mass media are fond of unearthing single, clearly definable causes: the cultural revolution is the result of drugs, or of the industrial and technological revolution that takes children out of the home, or of the decline and death of the great Father in the sky, God. But understanding these issues adequately depends no more on locating a single cause than understanding personal identity depended on locating a single substance at the core of the self. A philosophical approach requires a comprehensive, totalizing understanding, which sees how the various dimensions of patriarchy both influence and reflect the other dimensions. While it may be clear that historically patriarchy is on the decline, the meaning of that decline will not be clear until we have reflected on all its ramifications, political, social, sexual, and personal. To cite but one of the problems: Norman O. Brown points out that brotherhood is easy when there is a father, but without a father, how is brotherhood possible? What is brotherhood without a father?

In citing this problem I do not intend, any more than Brown intends, to hold back history; I do not wish to support patriarchy in all its forms. We are not "going too fast." But recent years make it perfectly clear that we have to drive a little more carefully, put on our windshield wipers to clear our vision when the sun ceases to shine. I am reminded of the choice of songs at the Bangladesh concert, a festive occasion, but one in which the reality of tragedy was acknowledged: "A Hard Rain's Gonna Fall," and "It Don't Come Easy." The first flush of optimism in the counter culture has passed. Woodstock was followed by Altamont. Some communes have made it, but many have failed.

To those who say a new more peaceful life style cannot be accomplished, I say, just watch. But to those who say it's easy, I would answer that it takes a good deal more understanding than most of us have mastered at this stage in history. And we can hardly hope to liberate ourselves from the chains of patriarchy if we have no understanding of its many links.

JOHN LOCKE

(1632-1704)

John Locke's **Two Treatises on Civil Government** played a powerful role in the centuries-long decline of patriarchy. The first treatise was written primarily to refute Sir Robert Filmer's **Patriarcha,** which had argued that the state's patriarchal power derives from a divine right of sovereignty inherited from Adam. We can thank Locke for liberating many of his contemporaries from this thesis, including the founding fathers who drafted the Declaration of Independence and the Constitution. Considering Locke's influence on the minds of those men who hammered out the political structure of the United States, it is hard to overestimate his effect on our lives hundreds of years later. If we are to uncover and understand our own roots, the right place to dig is in the writings of John Locke.

Locke both grants and limits the jurisdiction of parents over their children, and he places duties upon the parent as well as the child: the parent is responsible for the child's proper care and education. Given the important relationship between jurisdiction and the transition to the "state of maturity," no wonder Peter Marin's essay stressed the need for a rite of passage to make the transition clear.

While Locke carefully defines the differences separating paternal power from state power, his limits on the extent of paternal power prefigure his limits on the extent of state power. Locke saw that in neither case is power absolute. Consequently he took pains to compare and distinguish the different kinds of power. In reading the following passage, try to see just how far Locke's discussion of the family anticipates the limits of authority of the state over the individual and how far he attempts to dissociate and distinguish his discussion of the family from his remarks on civil government. Where absolutes have been foresworn relative differences become important.

ON PATERNAL POWER AND CIVIL SOCIETY

Of Paternal Power

(52) It may perhaps be censured as an impertinent criticism, in a discourse of this nature, to find fault with words and names, that have obtained in the world: and yet possibly it may not be amiss to offer new ones, when the old are apt to lead men into mistakes, as this of paternal power probably has done; which seems so to place the power of parents over their children wholly in the father, as if the mother had no share in it: whereas, if we consult reason or revelation, we shall find she hath an equal title. This may give one reason to ask, whether this might not be more properly called parental power? for whatever obligation nature and the right of generation lays on children, it must certainly bind them equally to both concurrent causes of it. And accordingly we see the positive law of God every where joins them together, without distinction, when it commands the obedience of children: "Honour thy father

THE FAMILY AND POLITICS   Reprinted from Chapters VI and VII of Locke's *Concerning Civil Government, Second Essay*. Paragraph numbers correspond to the original.

and thy mother," Exod. xx. 12. "Whosoever curseth his father or his mother," Lev. xx. 9. "Ye shall fear every man his mother and his father," Lev. xix. 5. "Children, obey your parents," &c. Eph. vi. 1. is the style of the Old and New Testament.

(53) Had but this one thing been well considered, without looking any deeper into the matter, it might perhaps have kept men from running into those gross mistakes they have made, about this power of parents; which, however it might, without any great harshness, bear the name of absolute dominion, and regal authority, when under the title of paternal power it seemed appropriated to the father; would yet have founded but oddly, and in the very name shown the absurdity, if this supposed absolute power over children had been called parental; and thereby have discovered, that it belonged to the mother too: for it will but very ill serve the turn of those men, who contend so much for the absolute power and authority of the fatherhood, as they call it, that the mother should have any share in it; and it would have but ill supported the monarchy they contend for, when by the very name it appeared that that fundamental authority, from whence they would derive their government of a single person only, was not placed in one, but two persons jointly. But to let this of names pass.

(54) Though I have said above, chap. ii. "That all men by nature are equal," I cannot be supposed to understand all sorts of equality: age or virtue may give men a just precedency: excellency of parts and merit may place others above the common level: birth may subject some, and alliance or benefits others, to pay an observance to those whom nature, gratitude, or other respects, may have made it due: and yet all this conflicts with the equality, which all men are in, in respect of jurisdiction or dominion one over another; which was the equality I there spoke of, as proper to the business in hand, being that equal right, that every man hath, to his natural freedom, without being subjected to the will or authority of any other man.

(55) Children, I confess, are not born in the state of equality, though they are born to it. Their parents have a sort of rule and jurisdiction over them, when they come into the world, and for some time after; but it is but a temporary one. The bonds of this subjection are like the swaddling clothes they are wrapt up in, and supported by, in the weakness of their infancy: age and reason, as they grow up, loosen them, till at length they drop quite off, and leave a man at his own free disposal.

(56) Adam was created a perfect man, his body and mind in full possession of their strength and reason, and so was capable from the first instant of his being to provide for his own support and preservation; and govern his actions according to the dictates of the law of reason which God had implanted in him. From him the world is peopled with his descendants, who are all born infants, weak and helpless, without knowledge or understanding: but to supply the defects of this imperfect state, till the improvement of growth and age hath removed them, Adam and Eve, and after them all parents were, by the law of nature, "under an obligation to

preserve, nourish, and educate the children," they had begotten; not as their own workmanship, but the workmanship of their own maker, the Almighty, to whom they were to be accountable for them.

(57) The law, that was to govern Adam, was the same that was to govern all his posterity, the law of reason. But his offspring having another way of entrance into the world, different from him, by a natural birth, that produced them ignorant and without the use of reason, they were not presently under that law; for nobody can be under a law, which is not promulgated to him; and this law being promulgated or made known by reason only, he that is not come to the use of his reason, cannot be said to be under this law; and Adam's children, being not presently as soon as born under this law of reason, were not presently free: for law, in its true notion, is not so much the limitation, as the direction of the free and intelligent agent to his proper interest, and prescribes no farther than is for the general good of those under that law: could they be happier without it, the law, as an useless thing, would of itself vanish; and that ill deserves the name of confinement which hedges us in only from bogs and precipices. So that, however it may be mistaken, the end of law is not to abolish or restrain, but to preserve and enlarge freedom: for in all the states of created beings capable of laws, "where there is no law, there is no freedom;" for liberty is to be free from restraint and violence from others; which cannot be where there is not law: but freedom is not, as we are told, "a liberty for every man to do what he lists:" (for who could be free, when every other man's humour might domineer over him?) but a liberty to dispose, and order as he lists, his person, actions, possessions, and his whole property, within the allowance of those laws under which he is, and therein not to be subject to the arbitrary will of another, but freely follow his own.

(58) The power, then, that parents have over their children, arises from that duty which is incumbent on them, to take care of their offspring, during the imperfect state of childhood. To inform the mind, and govern the actions of their yet ignorant nonage, till reason shall take its place, and ease them of that trouble, is what the children want, and the parents are bound to: for God having given man an understanding to direct his actions, has allowed him a freedom of will, and liberty of acting, as properly belonging thereunto, within the bounds of that law he is under. But whilst he is in an estate, wherein he has not understanding of his own to direct his will, he is not to have any will of his own to follow: he that understands for him, must will for him too; he must prescribe to his will, and regulate his actions; but when he comes to the estate that made his father a freeman, the son is a freeman too.

(59) This holds in all the laws a man is under, whether natural or civil. Is a man under the law of nature? What made him free of that law? what gave him a free disposing of his property, according to his own will, within the compass of that law? I answer, a state of maturity, wherein he might be supposed capable to know that law, that so he might keep his actions within the bounds of it. When he has acquired that state, he is presumed to

know how far that law is to be his guide, and how far he may make use of his freedom, and so comes to have it; till then, somebody else must guide him, who is presumed to know how far the law allows a liberty. If such a state of reason, such an age of discretion made him free, the same shall make his son free too. Is a man under the law of England? What made him free of that law? that is, to have the liberty to dispose of his actions and possessions according to his own will, within the permission of that law? A capacity of knowing that law; which is supposed by that law, at the age of one and twenty years, and in some cases sooner. If this made the father free, it shall make the son free too. Till then we see the law allows the son to have no will, but he is to be guided by the will of his father or guardian, who is to understand for him. And if the father die, and fail to substitute a deputy in his trust; if he hath not provided a tutor, to govern his son, during his minority, during his want of understanding; the law takes care to do it; some other must govern him, and be a will to him, till he hath attained to a state of freedom, and his understanding be fit to take the government of his will. But after that, the father and son are equally free as much as tutor and pupil after non-age; equally subjects of the same law together, without any dominion left in the father over the life, liberty, or estate of his son. [. . .]

(63) The freedom then of man, and liberty of acting according to his own will, is grounded on his having reason, which is able to instruct him in that law he is to govern himself by, and make him know how far he is left to the freedom of his own will. To turn him loose to an unrestrained liberty, before he has reason to guide him, is not the allowing him the privilege of his nature to be free; but to thrust him out amongst brutes, and abandon him to a state as wretched, and as much beneath that of a man, as their's. This is that which puts the authority into the parents hands to govern the minority of their children. God hath made it their business to employ this care on their offspring, and hath placed in them suitable inclinations of tenderness and concern to temper this power, to apply it, as his wisdom designed it, to the children's good, as long as they should need to be under it.

(64) But what reason can hence advance this care of the parents due to their offspring into an absolute arbitrary dominion of the father, whose power reaches no farther than, by such a discipline as he finds most effectual, to give such strength and health to their bodies, such vigour and rectitude to their minds, as may best fit his children to be most useful to themselves and others; and, if it be necessary to his condition, to make them work, when they are able, for their own subsistence. But in this power the mother too has her share with the father.

(65) Nay, this power so little belongs to the father by any peculiar right of nature, but only as he is guardian of his children, that when he quits his care of them, he loses his power over them, which goes along with their nourishment and education, to which it is inseparably annexed; and it belongs as much to the foster father of an exposed child, as to the

natural father of another. So little power does the bare act of begetting give a man over his issue; if all his care ends there, and this be all the title he hath to the name and authority of a father. And what will become of this paternal power in that part of the world where one woman hath more than one husband at a time? or in those parts of America, where, when the husband and wife part, which happens frequently, the children are all left to the mother, follow her, and are wholly under her care and provision? If the father die whilst the children are young, do they not naturally every where owe the same obedience to their mother, during their minority, as to their father were he alive; and will any one say, that the mother hath a legislative power over her children? that she can make standing rules, which shall be of perpetual obligation, by which they ought to regulate all the concerns of their property, and bound their liberty all the course of their lives? or can she enforce the observation of them with capital punishments? for this is the proper power of the magistrate, of which the father hath not so much as the shadow. His command over his children is but temporary, and reaches not their life or property: it is but a help to the weakness and imperfection of their nonage, a discipline necessary to their education: and though a father may dispose of his own possessions as he pleases, when his children are out of danger of perishing for want, yet his power extends not to the lives or goods, which either their own industry, or another's bounty has made their's; nor to their liberty neither, when they are once arrived to the infranchisement of the years of discretion. The father's empire then ceases, and can from thenceforwards no more dispose of the liberty of his son, than that of any other man: and it must be far from an absolute or perpetual jurisdiction, from which a man may withdraw himself, having licence from divine authority to "leave father and mother, and cleave to his wife."

(66) But though there be a time when a child comes to be as free from subjection to the will and command of his father, as the father himself is free from subjection to the will of any body else, and they are each under no other restraint, but that which is common to them both, whether it be the law of nature, or municipal law of their country; yet this freedom exempts not a son from that honour which he ought, by the law of God and nature, to pay his parents. God having made the parents instruments in his great design of continuing the race of mankind, and the occasions of life to their children; as he hath laid on them an obligation to nourish, preserve, and bring up their offspring; so he has laid on the children a perpetual obligation of honouring their parents, which containing in it an inward esteem and reverence to be shown by all outward expressions, ties up the child from any thing that may ever injure or affront, disturb or endanger, the happiness or life of those from whom he received his; and engages him in all actions of defence, relief, assistance and comfort of those, by whose means he entered into being, and has been made capable of any enjoyments of life: from this obligation no state, no freedom can absolve children. But this is very far from giving parents a power of command over

their children, or authority to make laws and dispose as they please of their lives and liberties. It is one thing to owe honour, respect, gratitude, and assistance; another to require an absolute obedience and submission. The honour due to parents, a monarch in his throne owes his mother; and yet this lessens not his authority, nor subjects him to her government.

(67) The subjection of a minor, places in the father a temporary government, which terminates with the minority of the child: and the honour due from a child, places in the parents perpetual right to respect, reverence, support and compliance too, more or less, as the father's care, cost, and kindness in his education, have been more or less. This ends not with minority, but holds in all parts and conditions of a man's life. The want of distinguishing these two powers, *viz.* that which the father hath in the right of tuition, during minority, and the right of honour all his life, may perhaps have caused a great part of the mistakes about this matter: for, to speak properly of them, the first of these is rather the privilege of children, and duty of parents, than any prerogative of paternal power. [. . .]

(69) The first part then of paternal power, or rather duty, which is education, belongs so to the father, that it terminates at a certain season; when the business of education is over, it ceases of itself, and is also alienable before: for a man may put the tuition of his son in other hands; and he that has made his son an apprentice to another, has discharged him, during that time, of a great part of his obedience both to himself and to his mother. But all the duty of honour, the other part, remains nevertheless entire to them; nothing can cancel that: it is so inseparable from them both, that the father's authority cannot dispossess the mother of this right, nor can any man discharge his son from honouring her that bore him. But both these are very far from a power to make laws, and enforcing them with penalties that may reach estate, liberty, limbs and life. The power of commanding ends with nonage; and though after that, honour and respect, support and defence, and whatsoever gratitude can oblige a man to, for the highest benefits he is naturally capable of, be always due from a son to his parents; yet all this puts no sceptre into the father's hand, no sovereign power of commanding. He has no dominion over his son's property, or actions; nor any right that his will should prescribe to his son's in all things; however it may become his son in many things, not very inconvenient to him and his family, to pay a deference to it.

(70) A man may owe honour and respect to an ancient, or wise man; defence to his child or friend; relief and support to the distressed; and gratitude to a benefactor, to such a degree, that all he has, all he can do, cannot sufficiently pay it: but all these give no authority, no right to any one, of making laws over him from whom they are owing. And it is plain, all this is due not only to the bare title of father; not only because, as has been said, it is owing to the mother too, but because these obligations to parents, and the degrees of what is required of children, may be varied by the different care and kindness, trouble and expence, which are often employed upon one child more than another.

(71) This shows the reason how it comes to pass, that parents in societies, where they themselves are subjects, retain a power over their children, and have as much right to their subjection as those who are in the state of nature. Which could not possibly be, if all political power were only paternal, and that in truth they were one and the same thing: for then, all paternal power being in the prince, the subject could naturally have none of it. But these two powers, political and paternal, are so perfectly distinct and separate, are built upon so different foundations, and given to so different ends, that every subject that is a father, has as much a paternal power over his children, as the prince has over his: and every prince, that has parents, owes them as much filial duty and obedience, as the meanest of his subjects due to their's; and cannot therefore contain any part or degree of that kind of dominion which a prince or magistrate has over his subjects. [. . .]

(74) To conclude then, though the father's power of commanding extends no farther than the minority of his children, and to a degree only fit for the discipline and government of that age; and though that honour and respect, and all that which the Latins called piety, which they indispensibly owe to their parents all their life-time, and in all estates, with all that support and defence which is due to them, gives the father no power of governing, *i.e.* making laws and enacting penalties on his children; though by all this he has no dominion over the property or actions of his son: yet it is obvious to conceive how casy it was, in the first ages of the world, and in places still, where the thinness of people gives families leave to separate into unpossessed quarters, and they have room to remove or plant themselves in yet vacant habitations, for the father of the family to become the prince[1] of it; he had been a ruler from the beginning of the infancy of his children: and since without some government it would be hard for them to live together, it was likeliest it should, by the express or tacit consent of the children when they were grown up, be in the father, where it seemed without any change barely to continue; when indeed nothing more was required to it, than the permitting the father to exercise alone, in his family, that executive power of the law of nature, which every free man naturally hath, and by that permission resigning up to him a monarchical power,

---

[1] It is no improbable opinion therefore, which the arch-philosopher was of, "That the chief person in every household was always, as it were, a king: so when numbers of households joined themselves in civil societies together, kings were the first kind of governors amongst them, which is also, as it seemeth, the reason why the name of fathers continued still in them, who, of fathers, were made rulers; as also the ancient custom of governors to do as Melchizedeck, and being kings, to exercise the office of priests, which fathers did at the first, grew perhaps by the same occasion. Howbeit, this is not the only kind of regiment that has been received in the world. The inconveniencies of one kind have caused sundry others to be devised; so that, in a word, all public regiment, of what kind soever, seemeth evidently to have risen from the deliberate advice, consultation, and composition between men, judging it convenient and behoveful; there being no impossibility in nature considered by itself, but that man might have lived without any public regiment." (Hooker's Eccl. P. lib. i. sect. 10.)

whilst they remained in it. But that this was not by any paternal right, but only by the consent of his children, is evident from hence, that nobody doubts, but if a stranger, whom chance or business had brought to his family, had there killed any of his children, or committed any other act, he might condemn and put him to death, or otherwise punish him, as well as any of his children: which it was impossible he should do by virtue of any paternal authority over one who was not his child, but by virtue of that executive power of the law of nature, which, as a man, he had a right to: and he alone could punish him in his family, where the respect of his children had laid by the exercise of such a power, to give way to the dignity and authority they were willing should remain in him, above the rest of his family.

(75) Thus it was easy, and almost natural for children, by a tacit, and scarce avoidable consent, to make way for the father's authority and government. They had been accustomed in their childhood to follow his direction, and to refer their little differences to him; and when they were men, who fitter to rule them? Their little properties, and less covetousness, seldom afforded greater controversies; and when any should arise, where could they have a fitter umpire than he, by whose care they had every one been sustained and brought up, and who had a tenderness for them all? It is no wonder that they made no distinction betwixt minority and full age; nor looked after one and twenty, or any other age that might make them the free disposers of themselves and fortunes, when they could have no desire to be out of their pupilage: the government they had been under during it, continued still to be more their protection than restraint: and they could no-where find a greater security to their peace, liberties, and fortunes, than in the rule of a father.

(76) Thus the natural fathers of families by an insensible change became the politic monarchs of them too: and as they chanced to live long, and leave able and worthy heirs, for several successions, or otherwise; so they laid the foundations of hereditary, or elective kingdoms, under several constitutions and manners, according as chance, contrivance, or occasions happened to mould them. But if princes have their titles in their fathers right, and it be a sufficient proof of the natural right of fathers to political authority, because they commonly were those in whose hands we find, de facto, the exercise of government: I say, if this argument be good, it will as strongly prove, that all princes, nay princes only, ought to be priests, since it is as certain, that in the beginning, "the father of the family was priest, as that he was ruler in his own household."

Of Political or
Civil Society

(77) God having made man such a creature, that in his own judgment, it was not good for him to be alone, put him under strong obligations of necessity, convenience, and inclination, to drive him into society, as well as fitted him with understanding and language to continue and enjoy it. The first society was between man and wife, which gave beginning to that between parents and children; to which, in time, that between master and servant came to be added: and though all these might, and commonly did meet together, and make up but one family, wherein the master or mistress of it had some sort of rule proper to a family; each of these, or all together, come short of political society, as we shall see, if we consider the different ends, ties, and bounds of each of these.

(78) Conjugal society is made by a voluntary compact between man and woman; and though it consist chiefly in such a communion and right in one another's bodies as is necessary to its chief end, procreation; yet it draws with it mutual support and assistance, and a communion of interests too, as necessary not only to unite their care and affection, but also necessary to their common offspring, who have a right to be nourished and maintained by them, till they are able to provide for themselves.

(79) For the end of conjunction between male and female being not barely procreation, but the continuation of the species; this conjunction betwixt male and female ought to last, even after procreation, so long as is necessary to the nourishment and support of the young ones, who are to be sustained by those that got them, till they are able to shift and provide for themselves. This rule, which the infinite wise Maker hath set to the works of his hands, we find the inferior creatures steadily obey. In those viviparous animals which feed on grass, the conjunction between male and female lasts no longer than the very act of copulation; because the teat of the dam being sufficient to nourish the young, till it be able to feed on grass, the male only begets, but concerns not himself for the female or young, to whose sustenance he can contribute nothing. But in beasts of prey the conjunction lasts longer: because the dam not being able well to subsist herself, and nourish her numerous offspring by her own prey alone, a more laborious, as well as more dangerous way of living, than by feeding on grass; the assistance of the male is necessary to the maintenance of their common family, which cannot subsist till they are able to prey for themselves, but by the joint care of male and female. The same is to be observed in all birds, (except some domestic ones, where plenty of food excuses the cock from feeding, and taking care of the young brood) whose young needing food in the nest, the cock and hen continue mates, till the young are able to use their wing, and provide for themselves.

(80) And herein I think lies the chief, if not the only reason, "why

the male and female in mankind are tied to a longer conjunction" than other creatures, viz. because the female is capable of conceiving, and de facto is commonly with child again, and brings forth to a new birth, long before the former is out of a dependency for support on his parents help, and able to shift for himself, and has all the assistance that is due to him from his parents: whereby the father, who is bound to take care for those he hath begot, is under an obligation to continue in conjugal society with the same woman longer than other creatures, whose young being able to subsist of themselves before the time of procreation returns again, the conjugal bond dissolves of itself and they are at liberty, till Hymen at his usual anniversary season summons them again to choose new mates. Wherein one cannot but admire the wisdom of the great Creator, who having given to man foresight, and an ability to lay up for the future, as well as to supply the present necessity, hath made it necessary, that society of man and wife should be more lasting, than of male and female amongst other creatures; that so their industry might be encouraged, and their interest better united, to make provision and lay up goods for their common issue, which uncertain mixture, or easy and frequent solutions of conjugal society, would mightily disturb.

(81) But though these are ties upon mankind, which make the conjugal bonds more firm and lasting in man, than the other species of animals; yet it would give one reason to inquire, why this compact, where procreation and education are secured, and inheritance taken care for, may not be made determinable, either by consent, or at a certain time, or upon certain conditions, as well as any other voluntary compacts, there being no necessity in the nature of the thing, nor to the ends of it, that it should always be for life; I mean, to such as are under no restraint of any positive law, which ordains all such contracts to be perpetual.

(82) But the husband and wife, though they have but one common concern, yet having different understandings, will unavoidably sometimes have different wills too; it therefore being necessary that the last determination, i.e. the rule, should be placed somewhere; it naturally falls to the man's share, as the abler and the stronger. But this reaching but to the things of their common interest and property, leaves the wife in the full and free possession of what by contract is her peculiar right, and gives the husband no more power over her life than she has over his; the power of the husband being so far from that of an absolute monarch, that the wife has in many cases a liberty to separate from him, where natural right or their contract allows it; whether that contract be made by themselves in the state of nature, or by the customs or laws of the country they live in; and the children upon such separation fall to the father's or mother's lot, as such contract does determine.

(83) For all the ends of marriage being to be obtained under politic government, as well as in the state of nature, the civil magistrate doth not abridge the right or power of either naturally necessary to those ends, viz. procreation and mutual support and assistance whilst they are together;

but only decides any controversy that may arise between man and wife about them. If it were otherwise, and that absolute sovereignty and power of life and death naturally belonged to the husband, and were necessary to the society between man and wife, there could be no matrimony in any of those countries where the husband is allowed no such absolute authority. But the ends of matrimony requiring no such power in the husband, the condition of conjugal society put it not in him, it being not at all necessary to that state. Conjugal society could subsist and attain its ends without it; nay, community of goods, and the power over them, mutual assistance and maintenance, and other things belonging to conjugal society, might be varied and regulated by that contract which unites man and wife in that society, as far as many consist with procreation and the bringing up of children till they could shift for themselves; nothing being necessary to any society, that is not necessary to the ends for which it is made.

(84) The society betwixt parents and children, and the distinct rights and powers belonging respectively to them, I have treated of so largely, in the foregoing chapter, that I shall not here need to say any thing of it. And I think it is plain, that it is far different from a politic society.

(85) Master and servant are names as old as history, but given to those of far different condition; for a freeman makes himself a servant to another, by selling him, for a certain time, the service he undertakes to do, in exchange for wages he is to receive: and though this commonly puts him into the family of his master, and under the ordinary discipline thereof: yet it gives the master but a temporary power over him, and no greater than what is contained in the contract between them. But there is another sort of servants, which by a peculiar name we call slaves, who being captives taken in a just war, are by the right of nature subjected to the absolute dominion and arbitrary power of their masters. These men having, as I say, forfeited their lives, and with it their liberties, and lost their estates; and being in the state of slavery, not capable of any property; cannot in that state be considered as any part of civil society; the chief end whereof is the preservation of property.

(86) Let us therefore consider a master of a family with all these subordinate relations of wife, children, servants, and slaves, united under the domestic rule of a family; which, what resemblance soever it may have in its order, offices, and number too, with a little commonwealth, yet is very far from it, both in its constitution, power, and end: or if it must be thought a monarchy, and the paterfamilias the absolute monarch in it, absolute monarchy will have but a very shattered and short power, when it is plain, by what has been said before, that the master of the family has a very distinct and differently limited power, both as to time and extent, over those several persons that are in it: for excepting the slave (and the family is as much a family, and his power as paterfamilias as great, whether there be any slaves in his family or no) he has no legislative power of life and death over any of them, and none too but what a mistress of a family may have as well as he. And he certainly can have no absolute power over the

whole family, who has but a very limited one over every individual in it. But how a family, or any other society of men, differ from that which is properly political society, we shall best see by considering wherein political society itself consists.

(87) Man being born, as has been proved, with a title to perfect freedom, and uncontrolled enjoyment of all the rights and privileges of the law of nature, equally with any other man, or number of men in the world, hath by nature a power, not only to preserve his property, that is, his life, liberty, and estate, against the injuries and attempts of other men; but to judge of and punish the breaches of that law in others, as he is persuaded the offence deserves, even with death itself, in crimes where the heinousness of the fact, in his opinion, requires it. But because no political society can be, nor subsist, without having in itself the power to preserve the property, and, in order thereunto, punish the offences of all those of that society; there, and there only is political society, where every one of the members hath quitted this natural power, resigned it up into the hands of the community in all cases that excludes him not from appealing for protection to the law established by it. And thus all private judgment of every particular member being excluded, the community comes to be umpire, by settled standing rules, indifferent, and the same to all parties: and by men having authority from the community, for the execution of those rules, decides all the differences that may happen between any members of that society concerning any matter of right; and punishes those offences which any member hath committed against the society, with such penalties as the law has established: whereby it is easy to discern, who are, and who are not, in political society together. Those who are united into one body, and have a common established law and judicature to appeal to, with authority to decide controversies between them, and punish offenders, are in civil society one with another: but those who have no such common appeal, I mean on earth, are still in the state of nature, each being, where there is no other, judge for himself, and executioner: which is, as I have before showed it, the perfect state of nature.

(88) And thus the commonwealth comes by a power to set down what punishment shall belong to the several transgressions which they think worthy of it, committed amongst the members of that society, (which is the power of making laws) as well as it has the power to punish any injury done unto any of its members, by any one that is not of it, (which is the power of war and peace;) and all this for the preservation of the property of all the members of that society, as far as is possible. But though every man who has entered into civil society, and is become a member of any commonwealth, has thereby quitted his power to punish offences against the law of nature, in prosecution of his own private judgment; yet with the judgment of offences, which he has given up to the legislative in all cases, where he can appeal to the magistrate, he has given a right to the commonwealth to employ his force, for the execution of the judgments of the commonwealth, whenever he shall be called to it; which indeed are his own

judgments, they being made by himself, or his representative. And herein we have the original of the legislative and executive power of civil society, which is to judge by standing laws, how far offences are to be punished, when committed within the commonwealth; and also to determine, by occasional judgments founded on the present circumstances of the fact, how far injuries from without are to be vindicated; and in both these to employ all the force of all the members, when there shall be need.

(89) Whenever therefore any number of men are so united into one society, as to quit every one his executive power of the law of nature, and to resign it to the public, there and there only is a political, or civil society.

WILHELM REICH

(1897-1957)

Wilhelm Reich was one of the first in this century to integrate psychoanalytic insights and political theory. During the 1920's and 1930's he wrote several books seeking a synthesis of Freudian and Marxist theory, a synthesis since made popular by Herbert Marcuse and Norman O. Brown. Time and again rejected by both the Freudian and Communist establishments for his devotion to a synthesis they both branded as theoretically impure eclecticism, Reich emigrated to the United States where his claims for psychotherapeutic cures were branded fraudulent. He was sentenced to prison where he died in 1957. The bizarre conclusion of Reich's career detracted considerably from his influence for some time after his death, but recent years have seen a renaissance in Reichian theory and an appreciation for Reich's original contributions to the synthesis of Freud and Marx.

In the following section from his important book, **The Sexual Revolution,** Reich examines the apparent conflict between the demands of nature and the demands of culture. Freud, particularly in **Civilization and Its Discontents,** had concluded that these opposing sets of demands were perhaps irreconcilable. The civilizing demands of culture seemed to require that the natural instincts of both sexuality and aggression be denied, or at best sublimated (redirected), so that their energies would dissipate in cultural endeavors like art and commerce. But Freud was pessimistic; he saw civilized man buying security at the price of losing happiness. When men collectively decided to "quit every one his executive power of the law of nature," as Locke put it, they gave up the right to the immediate gratification of their instinctual drives, and that, according to Freud, amounts to giving up happiness. Either individual happiness or the securities of civilization: the opposition seemed absolute in Freud's eyes. But just as Locke relativized the concept of authority, so Reich relativizes the concept of instinctual gratification and thereby discovers a way out of the apparently absolute contradiction. His way out consists in man's ability to influence the unconscious historically. Just as a single man's life is not the playing out of an original and permanent essence but a process of self-creation, so mankind as a whole can alter the ingredients in its store of resources, both conscious and unconscious.

The Sexual Revolution

Freud's cultural philosophical standpoint was always that culture owes its existence to instinctual repression and renunciation. The basic idea is that cultural achievements are the result of sublimated sexual energy; from this it follows logically that sexual suppression and repression are an indispensable factor in the cultural process. There is historical evidence of the incorrectness of this formulation; there are in existence highly cultured societies without any sexual suppression and a completely free sex life.

What is correct in this theory is only that sexual suppression forms the mass-psychological basis for a *certain* culture, namely, the *patriarchal authoritarian* one, in all of its forms. What is incorrect is the formulation that sexual suppression is the basis of culture in general. How did Freud arrive at this concept? Certainly not for conscious reasons of politics or Weltanschauung [world view]. On the contrary: early works such as that on "cultural sexual morals" point definitely in the direction of a criticism of culture in the sense of a sexual revolution. Freud never followed this path; on the contrary, he was adverse to any attempts in this direction and once called them "not being in the middle of the road of psychoanalysis." It was exactly my early attempts at a sex policy involving criticism of culture which led to the first serious differences of opinion between Freud and me.

In analyzing the psychic mechanisms, Freud found the unconscious filled with antisocial impulses. Everyone using the psychoanalytic method can confirm these findings. Every man has phantasies of murdering his father and of taking the father's place with his mother. In everyone, sadistic impulses, inhibited by more or less conscious guilt feelings, are found. In most women, violent impulses to castrate men, to acquire the penis, e.g., by swallowing it, can be found. The inhibition of such impulses, which con-

THE SEXUAL REVOLUTION Reprinted with the permission of Farrar, Straus & Giroux, Inc. from *The Sexual Revolution,* Fourth Edition, Revised by Wilhelm Reich. Copyright © 1945, 1962, 1969 by Mary Boyd Higgins as trustee of the Wilhelm Reich Infant Trust Fund.

tinue to work in the unconscious, results not only in social adjustment, but also in all kinds of disturbances (as, for example, hysterical vomiting). The man's sadistic phantasies of hurting or piercing the woman in the sexual act lead to various kinds of impotence if they are inhibited by anxiety and guilt feelings; if they are not, they may lead to perverse activities or sex murder. Such unconscious desires as that of eating feces can be found in a great many individuals, regardless of their social class. Such psychoanalytic discoveries as that the oversolicitude of a mother for her child or of a woman for her husband corresponds to the intensity of her unconscious phantasies of murder were highly inconvenient for the ideological champions of "sacred mother love" or of the "sacrament of marriage"; nevertheless, they are correct. Such examples could be multiplied indefinitely; but let us return to our subject. These contents of the unconscious were shown to be remnants of infantile attitudes toward parents, siblings, etc. In order to exist and to fit into our culture, the children have to suppress these impulses. The price they pay for it is the acquisition of a neurosis, that is, a reduction of their ability to work and of their sexual potency.

The finding of the antisocial nature of the unconscious was correct; so was the finding of the necessity of instinctual renunciation for the purpose of adjustment to social existence. However, two facts are at variance: On the one hand, the child has to suppress its instincts in order to become capable of cultural adjustment. On the other hand, it acquires, in this very process, a neurosis which in turn makes it incapable of cultural development and adjustment and in the end makes it antisocial. In order to make natural instinctual gratification possible, one has to eliminate the repression and to liberate the instincts. This is the prerequisite of cure, although not as yet the cure itself as Freud's early statements would have it. What, then, should take the place of instinctual repression? Certainly not the repressed instincts themselves, because, according to psychoanalytic theory, that would mean the impossibility of existing in this culture.

In many places in psychoanalytic literature we find the statement that the uncovering of the unconscious, that is, the affirmation of its existence, does by no means imply an affirmation of the corresponding action. The analyst lays down a law here which applies for life as well as for the treatment session: "You are allowed and supposed to *say* what you want; but that does not mean that you also can *do* what you want."

However, the responsible analyst was—and always is—confronted with the question as to what is to happen to the previously repressed and now liberated instincts. The psychoanalytic answer was: *sublimation* and *rejection*. Since, however, only the fewest patients prove capable of sublimation to a sufficient degree, the only other way out is renunciation through rejection of the instinct. Repression comes to be replaced by rejection. This demand was justified by the following formulation: The child faced its instincts with a weak, undeveloped ego and thus had no other choice but that of repression; the adult faces his instincts with a strong, adult ego which is capable of handling the instincts by way of rejection. Though this formulation contradicts clinical experience, it became—and still is—the accepted one. This point of view also dominates psychoanalytic pedagogy, as represented, for example, by Anna Freud.

Since, according to this concept, the individual becomes capable of culture as a result of instinctual renunciation instead of repression, and since society is regarded as behaving like the individual, it follows from this concept that culture is based on instinctual renunciation.

The whole construction seems unobjectionable and enjoys the approval not only of the majority of analysts but of the representatives of an abstract concept of culture in general. This substitution of renunciation and rejection for repression seems to banish the ghost which raised its threatening head when Freud confronted the world with his early findings. These findings showed unequivocally that sexual repression makes people not only sick but also incapable of work and cultural achievement. The whole world began to rage against Freud because of the threat to morals and ethics, and reproached Freud with preaching the "living out," with threatening culture, etc. Freud's alleged antimoralism was one of the most potent weapons of his early opponents. This ghost did not begin to vanish until the theory of rejection was propounded; Freud's earlier assurance that he was affirming "culture," that his discoveries constituted no threat to it, had made little impression. This was shown by the never-ending talk about "pansexualism." Then, after the new formulation of rejection, the previous enmity was replaced by partial acceptance. For just as long as the instincts were not lived out, it did not make any difference, from a "cultural point of view," whether it was the mechanism of instinctual rejection or that of repression which played the Cerberus keeping the shadows of the underworld from emerging to the surface. One was even able to register progress: that from the unconscious repression of evil to the voluntary renunciation of instinctual gratification. Since ethics does not consist in being asexual but, on the contrary, in resisting sexual temptations, everybody could now agree with everybody. Psychoanalysis, previously condemned, had now itself become capable of culture—unfortunately by way of "renunciation of the instinct," that is, the renunciation of its own theory of the instincts.

I regret to have to destroy some illusions. The whole system contains a miscalculation which is easily demonstrable. Not by any means in the sense that the psychoanalytic findings on which these conclusions are based are incorrect. On the contrary, they are quite correct; only, they are incomplete, and many of the formulations are abstract and thus distract from the real conclusions.

Instinctual Gratification and Instinctual Renunciation

Those German psychoanalysts who attempted a "Gleichschaltung" [unified revision] of psychoanalysis tried to justify their unscientific behavior by quotations from Freud's writings. They contain, in fact, formulations which nullify the revolutionary character of clinical psychoanalytic findings and which clearly demonstrate the contradiction between the scientist and the middle-class cultural philosopher in Freud. One such quotation runs:

> It is a bad misunderstanding, explained only by ignorance, if people say that psychoanalysis expects the cure of neurotic illness from the free "living out" of sexuality. On the contrary, the making conscious of the repressed sexual desires makes possible their *control* [italics mine. W.R.], a control which could not have been achieved by the repression. It would be more correct to say that the analysis liberates the neurotic from the shackles of his sexuality.
> (Freud, *Ges. Schriften,* Bd. XI [*Collected Writings,* Vol. XI], p. 217f.)

If, for example, the 17-year-old daughter of a National Socialist dignitary suffers from hysterical attacks as a result of a repressed desire for sexual intercourse, this desire, in the psychoanalytic treatment, will be recognized, to begin with, as an incestuous desire, and will be rejected as such. So far so good. But what happens to the sexual need? According to the above-quoted formulation, the girl is "liberated" from the shackles of her sexuality. Clinically, however, it looks like this: When the girl, with the aid of the analysis, frees herself from her father, she liberates herself only from the toils of her incest wish, *but not from her sexuality as such.* Freud's formulation neglects this basic fact. The scientific dispute about the role of genitality took its origin precisely from this clinical problem; it is the central point of divergence between the sex-economic and the revised psychoanalytic formulation. Freud's formulation postulates a renunciation on the part of the girl of all sexual life. In this form, psychoanalysis is acceptable even to the Nazi dignitary and becomes, in the hands of analysts like Müller-Braunschweig, an instrument for the "breeding of the heroic human." This form of psychoanalysis, however, has nothing in common with that psychoanalysis contained in the books which Hitler had burned. The latter kind of psychoanalysis, not hide-bound by reactionary prejudice states unequivocally that the girl can get well only if she transfers the genital desires from the father to a friend with whom she satisfies them. But just this is at variance with the total Nazi ideology and inexorably brings up the whole question of the social sexual order. Because, in order to be able to live sex-economically, it is not sufficient that the girl have a free genital sexuality; she needs, in addition, an undisturbed room, proper contraceptives, a friend who is capable of love, that is, not a National Socialist with a sex-negative structure; she needs understanding parents and a sex-affirmative social atmosphere; these needs are all the greater the less she is in a financial situation which would allow her to break through the social barriers of adolescent sex life.

The replacement of sexual repression by renunciation or rejection would be a simple matter were it not for the fact that these latter mechanisms are also dependent on the economy of instinctual life. Renunciation of the instinct is possible only under definite sex-economic conditions. The same is true of sublimation. Character-analytic experience shows clearly that lasting renunciation of a pathological or antisocial impulse is possible only when the sexual economy is in order, that is, if there is no sexual stasis which provides energy for the impulse which is to be renounced. *An ordered sex-economy, however, is possible only in the presence of such sexual gratification as corresponds to any given age.* Which means that an adult can give up infantile and pathogenic desires only if he experiences full genital gratification. The perverse and neurotic modes of gratification against which society should be protected are in themselves only substitutes for genital gratification and arise only if genital gratification is disturbed or made impossible. This fact makes it clear that we cannot speak of instinctual gratification or renunciation in general. We must ask concretely: the gratification of *what* instinct, the renunciation of *what* instinct? If analytic therapy sees its job in eliminating repressions and not in preaching morals, then it can bring about the renunciation only of *one* kind of gratification; that which does not correspond to the respective age or stage of development. Thus, it will bring a girl to the renunciation of her infantile fixation to her father by nothing else but making this fixation conscious. But that does not imply a renunciation of sexual desires as such, because the sexual energy continues to urge toward discharge. While it is easy to make her give up her sexual desires for her father, she cannot be brought to renounce her sexual gratification with a boy her age except by moralistic arguments; to do this, however, is at variance with therapeutic principles and possibilities of cure. On the other hand, she can really dissolve her fixation to her father only under one condition: when her sexuality finds another, normal object and *actual gratification*. Unless this is the case, the infantile fixation is not dissolved, or there occurs a regression to other infantile instinctual goals, and the basic problem continues to exist.

The same is true of *any* case of neurotic disease. If a woman is dissatisfied in her marriage, she will unconsciously reactivate infantile sexual demands; these she can give up only if her sexuality finds another satisfactory outlet. True, the rejection of the infantile sexual desires is a prerequisite for the establishment of a normal sexuality; but the establishment of a normal sex life with actual gratification is also an indispensable prerequisite for the final relinquishing of the infantile instinctual goals. A sexual pervert or criminal, such as a sex murderer, can be cured of his pathological impulses only if he finds his way into a biologically normal sex life. The alternative, thus, is not instinctual renunciation or instinctual living out, but renunciation of *what* impulses, and gratification of *what* impulses?

In speaking abstractly of the evil nature of the repressed unconscious, one obscures the most fundamental facts not only of the therapy and prevention of the neuroses, but of education as well. Freud made the discovery that the unconscious of the neurotics—that is, the vast majority of people in our civilization—contains essentially infantile, cruel, antisocial impulses.

This finding is correct. But it obscured another fact, the fact, namely, that the unconscious also contains many impulses which represent natural biological demands, such as the sexual desire of adolescents or of people tied down in an unhappy marriage. The intensity of the later infantile and antisocial impulses derives, historically and economically, from the non-gratification of these natural demands; the damned-up libidinal energy partly reinforces primitive infantile impulses, partly creates entirely new ones, mostly of an antisocial nature, such as the desire for exhibitionism or impulses to sex murder. Ethnological research shows that such impulses are absent in primitive peoples up to a definite point of economic development and begin to make their appearance only after social repression of normal love life has become an established feature.

These antisocial impulses, which result from social repression of normal sexuality and which have to be repressed because society—rightly—does not allow them to be satisfied, these impulses are considered *biological facts* by psychoanalysis. This concept is closely related to that of Hirschfeld that exhibitionism is due to special exhibitionistic hormones. This naive mechanistic biologism is so difficult to unmask because it serves a definite function in our society: that of shifting the problem from the sociological to the biological realm where nothing can be done about it.

There is such a thing as a *sociology of the unconscious* and of antisocial sexuality, that is, a social history of the unconscious impulses, with regard to their intensity as well as their contents. Not only is repression itself a sociological phenomenon, but also that which causes the repression. The study of the "partial impulses" will have to take pointers from ethnological findings such as the fact that in certain matriarchal societies there is little if any of the anal phase of libidinal development which in our society is considered a normal stage between the oral and the genital phase. This is so because in these societies the children are nursed until the third or fourth year when they immediately enter a phase of intensive genital play activities.

The psychoanalytic concept of antisocial impulses is an absolute one and thus leads to conclusions which are at variance with the facts. If, on the other hand, one realizes the *relative* character of the antisocial impulses, one arrives at basically different conclusions regarding not only psychotherapy but especially sociology and sex-economy. The anal activities of a child of one or two have nothing whatsoever to do with "social" or "antisocial." If, however, one adheres to the abstract view that these anal impulses are antisocial, one will institute a regime designed to make the child "capable of culture" as early as the 6th month of life; the later result is exactly the opposite, namely, incapacity for anal sublimation and the development of anal-neurotic disturbances. The mechanistic concept of the absolute antithesis between sexuality and culture makes even analytically trained parents take measures against infantile masturbation, at least in the form of "mild diversions." As far as I know, none of the writings of Anna Freud mention what in private conversation she admitted to be an inevitable conclusion from psychoanalytic findings: that infantile masturbation is a physiological manifestation and should *not* be inhibited. If one adheres to the concept that that which is repressed and unconscious is also anti-social, one will, for example, condemn the genital demands of the adolescent. This is substantiated by such phrases as that the "reality principle" requires the postponement of instinctual gratification.

The fact that this reality principle is *itself relative,* that it is determined by an authoritarian society and serves its purposes, this decisive fact goes carefully unmentioned; to mention this, they say, is "politics," and science has nothing to do with politics. They refuse to see the fact that not to mention it is also politics. Such attitudes have seriously endangered analytic progress; not only have they prevented the discovery of certain facts, but, more important, they have hindered the practical application of definitely established facts by misinterpreting them in terms of conservative cultural concepts. Since psychoanalysis constantly deals with the influences exerted upon the individual by society as well as with judgments as to what is healthy or sick, social or antisocial, and at the same time is unaware of the revolutionary character of its method and findings, it moves around in a tragic circle: it finds that sexual repression endangers culture and at the same time that it is a necessary prerequisite of culture.

Let us summarize the facts which psychoanalysis has overlooked and which are at variance with the psychoanalytic concept of culture:

The unconscious itself is—quantitatively as well as qualitatively—socially determined;

The giving up of infantile and antisocial impulses presupposes the gratification of the normal physiological sexual needs;

Sublimation, as the essential cultural achievement of the psychic apparatus, is possible only in the absence of sexual repression; in the adult, it applies only to the *pregenital,* but not to the *genital* impulses;

Genital gratification—the decisive sex-economic factor in the prevention of neuroses and establishment of social achievement—is at variance, in every respect, with present-day laws and with every patriarchal religion;

The elimination of sexual repression—introduced by psychoanalysis as a therapy as well as a sociologically important factor—is strictly at variance with all those cultural elements in our society which are based just on this repression.

To the extent to which psychoanalysis maintains its cultural standpoint, it does so at the expense of the very results of its own work. The conflict between the cultural concepts of the analytic investigators on the one hand and the scientific results which militate against this culture on the other hand is solved by them in favor of the patriarchal Weltanschauung. When psychoanalysis does not dare to accept the consequences of its findings, it points to the allegedly non-political (unpragmatic) character of science, while, in fact, every step of psychoanalytic theory and practice deals with political (pragmatic) issues.

If one investigates ecclesiastical, fascist and other reactionary ideologies for their unconscious content, one finds that they are essentially defense reactions. They are formed for fear of the unconscious inferno which everyone carries within himself. From this, one could deduce a justification of an ascetic morality only if the unconscious antisocial impulses were absolute and biologically given; if that were so, the political reaction would be correct, and any attempt to eliminate sexual misery would be senseless. Then, the conservative world could correctly point out that the destruction of "the higher qualities," "the central values," the "divine" and the "moral" in the human would lead to sexual and ethical chaos. This is what people mean unconsciously when they talk of "Kulturbolschewismus." The revolutionary movement—except for the sex-political wing—does not know this connection; in fact, it often finds itself on the same front with the political reaction when it comes to basic questions of sex-economy. True, it turns against sex-economic principles for different reasons than does the political reaction: it does not know these principles and their implications. It also believes in the biological and absolute nature of the antisocial impulses and consequently in the necessity of moral inhibition and regulation. It overlooks, like its opponents, the fact that the moral regulation of instinctual life creates exactly what it pretends to master: antisocial impulses.

Sex-economic investigation, on the other hand, shows that the antisocial unconscious impulses—as far as they are really antisocial and not just regarded as such by the moralists—are a result of moral regulation and will continue to exist as long as that regulation exists. Sex-economic regulation alone can eliminate the antithesis between culture and nature; with the elimination of sexual repression, the perverse and antisocial impulses will also be eliminated.

R. D. LAING
(1927-   )

Once again it is time to meet R. D. Laing's radical doubt. And once again I wish to liken Laing's strengths and weaknesses to Descartes'. In the following essay the similarity is even more striking than in **The Politics of Experience,** where Laing invoked madness to propel us into a space that makes our ordinary lives look like the playing out of so many games of appearance. In **The Politics of the Family** Laing explicitly challenges us to regard our ordinary wakefulness as a kind of posthypnotic trance induced in early childhood by our elders who, themselves unconscious of what they were doing, used all the subtle tools of verbal and nonverbal communication to convey us into a world of safety, sickness, and sterility. Laing's argument is powerful. He warns us of the dangers of letting others know we have awoken from the trance.

I cannot help issuing a warning myself, for each time I reread this essay I am staggered by its force and implications, yet also distressed by the extent to which Laing seems to despise this ordinary life. He wishes to discard the skin of the orange symbolizing the veil of illusion once he has peeled it away. And who would not prefer to bite into that tender fruit rather than peel and keep all the successive layers of an onion. But what if—just to use the Cartesian-Laingian doubt to its utmost extent—what if in that orange peel were treasures to which our haste and excitement blinded us? What then?

Or, to return to another criticism made against Descartes, how are we to know when we have peeled far enough? Laing ingeniously uncovers the ingenuity with which society covers its tracks on its path toward repression. But his analysis is so powerful, the Cartesian drill so sharp, that it becomes difficult to know when you have reached rock-bottom in the series of nested rules for doing society's bidding. The drill keeps cutting through the bedrock it is seeking. Once you have understood Laing's analysis, once you have seen how it is possible to be under a spell without knowing it, then ask yourself, "If I were in Heaven, or in the best conceivable social setting, would it not still be both necessary and possible to impose a doubt about whether my happiness were not the product of a clever illusion?"

Laing is at a midpoint in his writing career. It is presumptuous to make a prediction but nonetheless I prophesy a subtle change in Laing's future writings (if there are any; Laing warned in **The Politics of Experience** that "not everyone comes back to us again."). He will not foreswear the necessity for breaking through appearances to see another reality, but his residence in that other reality will lead him to a deeper understanding of the nature and necessity of the rules he has uncovered, and then he will exhibit a greater compassion for the keepers of those rules, conscious or unconscious as they may be.

We return to these themes at the end of the book, when we meet the mystic tradition Laing has gone off to find. For now read Laing and try to break through to that 'laborious wakefulness' Descartes spoke of. But do not imagine that with such a breakthrough the path has come to an end. Do not prejudge what is there on the "other side." What if you burn your bridges and find that the "other side" was this side all along only you didn't know it? An unlikely turn of events, you say. But I answer, with Descartes and Laing, "What if . . . ?" Cross the bridge, but do not burn it.

The Politics of
the Family

The most common situation I en-
counter in families is when what *I* think is going on bears almost no resemblance to what anyone in the family experiences or thinks is happening,
whether or not this coincides with common sense. Maybe no one knows
what is happening. However, one thing is often clear to an outsider: there
is concerted family *resistance* to discovering what is going on, and there are
complicated stratagems to keep everyone in the dark, and in the dark they
are in the dark.

We would know more of what is going on if we were not forbidden to do
so, and forbidden to realize that we are forbidden to do so.

Between truth and lie are images and ideas we imagine and think are
real, that paralyze our imagination and our thinking in our efforts to con-
serve them.

Each generation projects onto the next, elements derived from a product
of at least three factors: what was (1) *projected* onto it by prior generations, (2) *induced* in it by prior generations, and (3) its response to this
projection and induction.

If I project element x from set A onto element y of set B, and if we call
the operation of projection or mapping ϕ, then y is the image of x under ϕ.

As we say, Johnny is the 'image' of his grandfather.

There is always a projection or a mapping of one *set* of relations onto
another *set* of relations. These are relations in time as well as space. In this
type of projection or mapping, the *temporal* sequence may be retained or
altered.

Projection (like other operations we shall consider later) is usually unknown to the people who are involved. Different mappings go on simultaneously.

Pure projection is not enough. As images of ghostly relations under the
operation of projection, we induce others, and are ourselves induced, to
embody them: to enact, unbeknown to ourselves, a shadow play, as images
of images of images . . . of the dead, who have in their turn embodied
and enacted such dramas projected upon them, and induced in them, by
those before them.

One way to get someone to *do* what one wants, is to give an order. To
get someone to *be* what one wants him to be, or supposes he is or is afraid
he is (whether or not this is what one wants), that is, to get him to embody
one's projections, is another matter. In a hypnotic (or similar) context,
one does not tell him what *to be,* but tells him what he is. Such *attributions,*
in context, are many times more powerful than orders (or other forms of

coercion or persuasion). An instruction need not be defined as an instruction. It is my impression that we receive most of our earliest and most lasting instructions in the form of attributions. We are told such and such is the case. One is, say, told one *is* a good or a bad boy or girl, not only instructed *to be* a good or bad boy or girl. One may be subject to both, but if one *is* (this or that), it is not necessary to be told to be what one has already been 'given to understand' one is. The key medium for communication of this kind is probably not verbal language. When attributions have the function of instructions or injunctions, this function may be denied, giving rise to one type of *mystification,* akin to, or identical with, hypnotic suggestion. Hypnosis may be an experimental model of a naturally occurring phenomenon in many families. In the family situation, however, the hypnotists (the parents) are already hypnotized (by their parents) and are carrying out their instructions, by bringing their children up to bring their children up . . . in such a way, which includes not realizing that one is carrying out instructions: since one instruction is not to think that one is thus instructed. This state is easily induced under hypnosis.

One may tell someone to feel something and not to remember he has been told. Simply tell him he feels it. Better still, tell a third party, in front of him, that he feels it.

Under hypnosis, he feels it; and does not know that he has been hypnotized to feel it. How much of what we ordinarily feel, is what we have all been hypnotized to feel? How much of who we are, is what we have been hypnotized to be?

Your word is my command. A relationship of one to another may be of such power that you become what I take you to be, at my glance, at my touch, at my cough. I do not need to say anything. An attribution, as I am using the term, may be kinetic, tactile, olfactory, visual. Such an attribution is equivalent to an instruction to be obeyed 'implicitly'.

So, if I hypnotize you, I do not say, 'I order you to feel cold.' I indicate it is cold. You immediately *feel* cold. I think many children begin *in* a state like this.

We indicate to them how it is: they take up their positions in the space we define. They may then choose to become a fragment of that fragment of their possibilities we indicate they are.

What we explicitly *tell* them is, I suspect, of less account.

What we indicate they are, is, in effect, an instruction for a drama: a scenario.

For example, a naughty child is a role in a particular family drama. Such a drama is a continuous production. His parents tell him he *is* naughty, because he does not do what they tell him. What they tell him he *is,* is *induction,* far more potent than what they tell him to do. Thus through the attribution: 'You are naughty', they are effectively telling him *not to do* what they are ostensibly telling him to do. We are likely to find that such words as: 'You are naughty', are the least of it. One is likely to find that the child is being induced to behave as he is by tactile–kinetic–olfactory–

visual signals: and that this is part of a 'secret' communications network, dissociated from the official verbal communiqués.

These signals do not tell him to be naughty; they define what he does *as* naughty. In this way, he learns that he *is* naughty, and *how* to be naughty in his particular family: it is a learned skill. Some children have a special aptitude for it.

I do not mean that this is the only way a child becomes 'naughty', but it is one way.

Thus:

Not: Do what I tell you *to* do
But: You will do what I indicate you *are* doing
You see what I say you see
Not: Be what I tell you to be
But: You are what I indicate you are.

The clinical hypnotist *knows* what he is doing; the family hypnotist almost never. A few parents have described this technique to me as a deliberate stratagem.

More often parents are themselves confused by a child who does *x,* when they tell him to *do y* and indicate he is *x.*

'I'm always trying to get him to make more friends, but he is so self-conscious. Isn't that right, dear?'

'He's so naughty. He never does what I tell him. Do you?'

'I keep telling him to be more careful, but he's so careless, aren't you?'

When such indications or attributions[1] and instructions are discrepant, the two systems A and B are evident. If there is a smooth 'normal' state of affairs, the structure is less evident, but not essentially different. Moreover, if it all seems to work, no one is likely to want to see how it works:

'He knows right from wrong himself: I've never had to tell him not to do these things.'

'He does it without me having to ask him.'

'He knows himself when he has had enough.'

The smoothly working family system is much more difficult to study than one that is in difficulties.

---

[1] All the media of communication may carry these quasi-hypnotic indicators (attributions). The way things are said (paralinguistics) rather than the 'content' (linguistics). The movements we use (kinesics and para kinesics). And touch, taste, smell. The most intensive systematic study of kinesics has been conducted for some years by Professor Birdwhistell of Eastern Pennsylvanian Psychiatric Institute, and his associates. No systematic data, as far as I know, has been gathered on taste and smell. At the University of Florida Professor Jourard has made a beginning of a study of our touching habits (Jourard, 1968), but so far has not carried his studies into families. Dr. Harry Wiener of New York Medical College has published a series of highly suggestive speculations on the way our social conduct may be partially controlled by external chemical messengers (ECM) or *ecto*-hormones, as we know the intricate social coordination of some insects to be, opening up a vast and hitherto almost entirely unexplored field of human studies: the relation of ecto-hormones to social behaviour in man (Wiener, 1966, 1967, 1968).

There are usually great resistances against the process of mapping the past onto the future coming to light, in any circumstances. If anyone in a family begins to realize he is a shadow of a puppet, he will be wise to exercise the greatest precautions as to whom he imparts this information to.

It is not 'normal' to realize such things. There are a number of psychiatric names, and a variety of treatments, for such realizations.

I consider many adults (including myself) are or have been, more or less, in a hypnotic trance, induced in early infancy: we remain in this state until—when we dead awaken, as Ibsen makes one of his characters say—we shall find that we have never lived.

Attempts to wake before our time are often punished, especially by those who love us most. Because they, bless them, are asleep. They think anyone who wakes up, or who, still asleep, realizes that what is taken to be real is a 'dream' is going crazy. Anyone in this transitional state is likely to be confused. To indicate that this confusion is a sign of illness, is a quick way to create psychosis. The person who realizes that 'this is all a nightmare' is afraid he is going crazy. A psychiatrist who professes to be a healer of souls, but who keeps people asleep, treats them for waking up, and drugs them asleep again (increasingly effectively as this field of technology sharpens its weapons), helps to drive them crazy.

The most awake people I have met are most aware of this. They are few. They are not necessarily psychotic, nor well-known intellectuals. A celebrated philosopher told me he reckons he did not awaken from this post-infancy hypnotic state till over fifty, when he had already written most of the works for which he is renowned. [. . .]

When I was thirteen, I had a very embarrassing experience. I shall not embarrass you by recounting it. About two minutes after it happened, I caught myself in the process of putting it out of my mind. I had already more than half forgotten it. To be more precise, I was in the process of sealing off the whole operation by forgetting that I had forgotten it. How many times I had done this before I cannot say. It may have been many times because I cannot remember many embarrassing experiences before that one, and I have no memory of such an *act* of forgetting I was forgetting before thirteen. I am sure this was not the first time I had done that trick, and not the last, but most of these occasions, so I believe, are still so effectively repressed that I have still forgotten that I have forgotten them.

This is repression. It is not a simple operation. We forget something. And forget that we have forgotten it. As far as we are subsequently concerned, there is nothing we have forgotten.

A clean-cut operation of repression achieves a *cut-off,* so that

a. we forget X
b. we are unaware that there is an X that we have forgotten
c. we are unaware that we have *forgotten* X
d. and unaware that we are unaware that we have forgotten we have forgotten X.

Repression is the annihilation, not only *from* the memory of, but *of* the memory of, a part of E, *together with,* the annihilation of the experience of the operation. It is a product of at least three operations.

When we consider any actual instance of any operations, we find that it is almost impossible to find a pure example of a single operation in isolation. This is what we might expect. It does not mean, because a baby moves all the fingers of one hand at once, that it has not five fingers. Denial and displacement form a common operation product. 'It's not *my* fault. It's your fault.' Denial and displacement can equal projection.

Wish-fulfilment and idealization are varieties of operation entailing projection and denial. All projection involves some measure of denial of the range of E. I am unhappy. I am *not* unhappy (denial). I am *not* denying that I am unhappy (denial of denial).

I take the principal function of all these operations to be: the production and maintenance of E that is at best desired, at least tolerated, in the family by the family in the first place.

The operations I have alluded to are operations on one's own experience. They are done by one person to himself or herself. But they would be unnecessary unless the rules of the family required them: and ineffectual unless others cooperated. Denial is demanded by the others: it is part of a *transpersonal system of collusion,* whereby we comply with the others, and they comply with us. For instance, one requires collusion to play 'Happy Families'. Individually, I am unhappy. I deny I am to *myself;* I deny I am denying anything to *myself* and to the others. They must do the same. I must collude with their denial and collusion, and they must collude with mine.

So we are a happy family and we have no
secrets from one another.
If we are unhappy/we have to keep it a secret/
and we are unhappy that we have to keep it a secret
and unhappy *that* we have to keep secret/the fact/that we
have to keep it a secret
and that we *are* keeping all that secret.
But since we are a happy family you can see
this difficulty does not arise.

Repression of much infant sexuality is sanctioned, the act of repression is itself denied, and repression, its sanction, and the denial of repression, are denied. Nothing has happened. 'I don't know what you're talking about.' For instance, who ever heard of a good boy, and a normal man, *ever,* having wanted to suck his father's penis? It is quite normal, at one time, to have wanted to suck his mother's breast. However, it is on the whole best not to connect mother's breast and girl friend's breast, or, if one is a woman, woman's breast with boy friend's genitals. It is safest, on the whole, to keep these sets of relations in separate partitions (splitting), and *repress,* to be even more on the safe side, *all infantile desires* in case they were too 'perverse', since they antedate partitioning and repression, etc., *and* to deny the existence of any such operations of partitioning and repression, and to deny this denial. The product arrived at is the outcome of many rules without which it could not be generated or maintained, but to admit the rules would be to admit what the rules and operations are attempting to render nonexistent.

One is expected to be capable of passion, once married, but not to have experienced too much passion (let alone acted upon it) too much before. If this is too difficult, one has to pretend first not to feel the passion one really feels, then, to pretend to passion one does *not* really feel, and to pretend that certain passionate upsurges of resentment, hatred, envy, are unreal, or don't happen, or are something else. This requires false realizations, false de-realizations, and a cover-story (rationalization). After this almost complete holocaust of one's experience on the altar of conformity, one is liable to feel somewhat empty, but one can try to fill one's emptiness up with money, consumer goods, position, respect, admirations, envy of one's fellows for their business, professional, social success. These together with a repertoire of distractions, permitted or compulsory, serve to distract one from one's own distraction: and if one finds oneself overworked, under too great a strain, there are perfectly approved additional lines of defence, concoctions to taste of, narcotics, stimulants, sedatives, tranquillizers to depress one further so that one does not know how depressed one is and to help one to over-eat and over-sleep. And there are lines of defence beyond *that,* to electroshocks, to the (almost) final solution of simply removing sections of the offending body, especially the central nervous system. This last solution is necessary, however, only if the *normal social* lobotomy does not work, and chemical lobotomy has also failed.

I can think of no way of generating a 'normal' product from the stuff of our original selves except in some such way: once we arrive at our matrix of distinctions, we have rules for combining and partitioning them into sets and subsets. The 'normal' product requires that these operations themselves are denied. We like the food served up elegantly before us: we do not want to know about the animal factories, the slaughterhouses, and what goes on in the kitchen. Our own cities are our own animal factories; families, schools, churches are the slaughterhouses of our children; colleges and other places are the kitchens. As adults in marriages and business, we eat the product. [. . .]

If my view is right, we at this moment may not know we have *rules against knowing about certain rules.*

Some of you sense that you have rules about rules, but perhaps have never thought about it in these terms.

Some of you are clear this far. You will have to bear with me, for a little, before I get to where you are at, if I can.

I want to talk about the rules that we cannot talk about—just enough to convince any of you who are not sure what I am talking about that this is a very important issue, which I cannot talk about more directly.

There is a law against murder. We can talk about murder, and about the law about murder.

There is a law against incest. We can talk about the law against incest, rather more freely than we can talk about incest: commonly there is a rule against talking about incest, in front of the children especially: but not an absolute rule against talking about whether or not there is a law against incest.

It used to be obvious to many (including Lévy-Bruhl) that when incest does not happen it is because there is a 'natural' revulsion against it. To many, it may now seem equally obvious that it does not occur more frequently because there are rules against it.

Many people used to be scandalized by this view, for it seems to imply that, if there were not such rules, people might do what was prohibited. Many people felt, and some no doubt still do, that to admit that there were rules against incest would be to admit that parents and children, and brothers and sisters, might *want* to have sexual relations with each other. Why should there be a rule against what no one 'naturally' wants to do? Freud's view was that what people think they 'naturally' don't want to do *may* be a product of repression, and other operations, at the behest of rules against even thinking much less doing it. The desire, even the thought, *and* the rule against the desire or thought, are all eliminated from our awareness, so that the product of these operations on oneself is a 'normal' state of awareness, whereby one is unaware of the desire, the thought *and* the rules, and the operations.

One tends to assume that every negative rule (such as that against incest) implies a prior desire, impulse, propensity, instinct, tendency to do it. Don't do that, implies that one would be inclined to if not forbidden.

There is treasure at the bottom of the tree. You will find it. Only remember not to think of a white monkey. The moment you do, the treasure will be lost to you forever. (A favourite story of Francis Huxley.)

We can, by direct experiment, verify that some negative injunctions have a paradoxical effect, to induce one to do what one has been told not to, *especially if one did not,* and does not, in fact, wish to.

'I would never have thought of it until I was told that I must not.'

Negative rules may themselves generate actions they prohibit. If you want people not to do something they are not doing, do not forbid it. There is a better chance that I will not think what I have not yet thought, if you do not tell me *not* to.

In this last minute, I have not been trying to establish whether or not incest is ruled out by social rules or natural law, or both. I have wished only to demonstrate that there is not a rule against talking *about* whether or not there are such rules or such a natural law.

A family has a rule that little Johnny should not think filthy thoughts. Little Johnny is a good boy: he does not have to be told not to think filthy thoughts. They never have *taught* him *not* to think filthy thoughts. He never has.

So, according to the family, and even little Johnny, there is no rule against filthy thoughts, because there is no need to have a rule against what never happens. Moreover, we do not talk in the family about a rule against filthy thoughts, because since there are no filthy thoughts, and no rule against them, there is no need to talk about this dreary, abstract, irrelevant, or even vaguely filthy subject. There is no rule against talking about a nonexistent rule about nonexistent filthy thoughts: and no rule against talking about nonexistent talk about a nonexistent rule about something that is nonexistent.

Perhaps no one outside such a family rule system could knowingly embrace it—

Rule A: Don't. Rule A1: Rule A does not exist. Rule A2: Rule A1 does not exist.

This type of ruling applies only to some rules. One can talk about certain rules (when one can cross the street). But there are others that one cannot talk about without breaking the rule that one should not talk about them.

If you obey these rules, you will not know that they exist. There is no rule against talking about putting one's finger into one's own mouth, one's brother's, sister's, mother's, father's, anyone's mouth. No rule against *talking* about putting one's finger into the custard pie, though there *is* a rule about putting one's finger into the custard pie. No rule against recognizing the rule: don't put your finger into the fire. Why not? Because you will burn yourself. There is no rule against *talking* about it and giving reasons for it.

But, I may say, I have never put my finger into a number of . . . (unmentionable) places.[2] What places? I can't mention them. Why not? When one cannot talk about a rule about which one cannot talk, we have reached a limit to what we can talk about.

I have thought about the problem of how not to think a thought one is not supposed to think. I cannot think of any way to do so except, in some peculiar way, to 'think' what one must not think in order to ensure that one does not think it.

'Of course', it never would even occur to a perfectly brainwashed person to think certain unmentionably filthy thoughts. Such cleanliness, however, requires constant vigilance: vigilance against what? The answer is strictly unthinkable. To have clean memories, reveries, desires, dreams, imagination, one must keep clean company, and guard all senses against pollution. If one only overhears someone else talking filthy, one has been polluted. Even if one can forget one ever heard it, right away. But one has to remem-

---

[2] 'Unmentionable' only in relation to what cannot be related to it (my finger) in this particular context.

ber to continue to forget and remember to remember to avoid that person in future.

Many such rules about rules apply to what parts of whose body can be 'thought' of in relation to whom.

Rules apply to what kinds of sensations one is supposed to have where and when in one's own body, in relation to whom.

What are the funny places where funny feelings go on? Where do they come from? Where do they go to?

One seeks to avoid painful feelings, but there are many pleasurable feelings many people are forbidden to experience, imagine, remember, dream about, and they are definitely forbidden to talk about the fact that they are forbidden to talk about them. This is easy if one has already obeyed the injunction not even to 'think' of what I can possibly be talking about.

One has then got to the position in which one cannot think *that* one cannot think about what one cannot think about because there is a rule against thinking about X, and a rule against thinking that there is a rule against thinking that one must *not* think about *not* thinking about certain things.

If some thoughts cannot be thought: and among the thoughts that cannot be thought is the thought that there are certain thoughts that cannot be thought, including the aforementioned thought, then: he who had complied with this calculus of antithoughts will not be aware he is not aware that he is obeying a rule not to think that he is obeying a rule not to think about X. So he is not aware of X and not aware that he is not aware of the rule against being not aware of X. By obeying a rule not to realize he is obeying a rule, he will deny that there is any rule he is obeying.

When one does no more than scratch the surface of the structure of one of the varieties of Western 'conscience', one must marvel at its ingenuity. It must constitute one of the biggest knots in which man has ever tied himself. One of its many peculiar features is that the more tied in the knot, the less aware are we that we are tied in it.

Anyone fully caught in the full anticalculus of this kind cannot possibly avoid being bad in order to be good. In order to comply with the rules, rules have to be broken. Even if one could wash out one's brain three times a day, part of one's self must be aware of what one is not supposed to know in order to assure the continuance of those paradoxical states of multiplex ignorance, spun in the paradoxical spiral that the more we comply with the law, the more we break the law: the more righteous we become the deeper in sin: our *righteousness* is as filthy rags.

Transition:
Authority
and the
Individual

The title of John Stuart Mill's essay, "Of the Limits to the Authority of Society over the Individual," nicely states the problem that liberal democratic political theory hopes to solve. Theorists within that tradition, from Locke and Mill on through David Riesman, presuppose a picture of the individual as the basic unit from which various social systems may or may not be built and in terms of which various social systems are to be judged. Whether or not the "state of nature" ever actually existed (and a sympathetic reading of Locke, Hobbes, Rousseau, and others allows them to use the concept of a state of nature as a theoretical construct rather than as a description of unknown past ages), the role played by the state of nature in political philosophy shows that it implies a theory of the individual according to which the self is **not** constituted by a social context. The self is ontologically self-sufficient. The self **is,** as a human self, whether in society or in the state of nature. But the ontological self-sufficiency of the self does not imply a factual self-sufficiency: the individual in the state of nature may be a fully developed human self, but he may not last very long. As Hobbes put it, life in the state of nature is "solitary, poor, nasty, brutish, and short." Hence each separate and struggling Robinson Crusoe concludes that he'd be better off in his struggle with nature and other men if he joined others. As Locke describes: "Whenever therefore any number of men are so united into one society, as to quit every one his executive power of the law of nature, and to resign it to the public, there and there only is a political, or civil society." The individual pays a price: he quits his executive power of the law of nature. He cannot kill and plunder in civil society as he killed and plundered in the state of nature. The question of political theory then becomes how high a price must the individual pay, or, "the limits to the authority of society over the individual."

Political science may be regarded as the science of calculating the various degrees of security that can be bought for various prices—a scientific cost analysis in the market of freedom and authority, as it were. But political philosophy is concerned with a more radical analysis, not in the sense of being leftist or revolutionary, but radical in going to the roots of the problem (**radix:** "root"). While political science may entertain different answers to Mill's question, political philosophy will entertain different questions. Is the formulation of the question correct? Are there "individuals" in the sense presupposed by the liberal democratic tradition, or is the sense of individuality rather a result of a high state of social organization, specialization, and hence individuation? If the primordial individual suffers the same fate as the underlying subject did, that is, if the "individual" presupposed by liberal political theory turns out to be a "ghost in the machine" (Ryle) or a result rather than a cause (Nietzsche), the question of political theory will have to be reformulated.

The following essays presuppose, implicitly or explicitly, different theories of the individual, and a proper reading should examine those different presuppositions rather than assume that each author answers Mill's question differently.

PLATO

(428-347 B.C.)

Plato sees the individual as fostered by the state, though his argument does not imply that the individual can never oppose the state. Even though Socrates refused to oppose the state's laws by agreeing to escape from prison, the **Crito** finds Socrates in prison as a result of his perpetual questioning of the authority of certain individuals and institutions in ancient Athens. The apparent conflict between the antiauthoritarian tenor of the **Apology** and the argument for subservience in the **Crito** might lead us to convict Plato of self-contradiction were we not aware of his subtle powers of thought and writing. Though Plato taught the importance of **generalized** absolutes, such as beauty, justice, and virtue, he saw how wrong it can be to seek absolute answers to **specific** questions, such as, "Does the state have a legitimate authority over the individual?" His answer is neither an unequivocal yes nor an unequivocal no. Does that mean he equivocates? I think not.

Careful Plato scholarship has shown that the seemingly incidental opening lines of many of the dialogues do more than provide a dramatic introduction to the scene. In his manifold vision Plato was able to see each event many times over in all its varied significances. And he expected the same of his careful readers. Consequently he often used the first few lines to introduce the central themes of a dialogue. Take a moment now to read the opening exchanges and then think about them as saying more than might first appear. Then, if you can tear yourself away from the dialogue, return to the rest of these introductory remarks.

At a crucial point in the argument Socrates states a major premise, that a man ought to do what he admits to be right, whatever harmful consequences might befall him, and he asks, "But if this is true, what is the application?" Socrates then considers the implicit contract he has with the state of Athens by his having lived within her walls and derived benefits from her people and laws. But throughout his discussion of his debt to Athens we want to know, is his argument so strong that it would forbid any and all civil disobedience? Carefully read, the dialogue answers no, but neither does it give absolute justification for civil disobedience. The leading premises dictate that we not harm others, even where we have been unjustly treated. The application of that premise is a difficult matter, however. One almost always does greater harm in breaking the laws than in keeping them. Indeed, it is because the greatest harm usually comes from breaking the laws that the argument of the **Crito** is so strong. But sometimes the laws are wrong. Plato could certainly imagine times when keeping the laws would do the greater harm. But it is hard to know just when those times are. Even if we possess standards of justice, applying them is a difficult business depending on the details of the historical matters at hand. Rather than give an absolute answer to the specific question of the authority of the state over the individual, Plato's **Crito** makes an important and appropriately strong argument for the authority of the state, combined with a subtler discourse on the applicability of absolute principles. There might just be a time for civil disobedience. Socrates wishes to know, "What is the exact time?"

Crito

Persons of the Dialogue

SOCRATES   CRITO

SCENE: The Prison of Socrates

Socrates—[43] Why have you come at this hour, Crito? it must be quite early?

Crito—Yes, certainly.

Soc.—What is the exact time?

Cr.—The dawn is about to break.

Soc.—I wonder that the keeper of the prison would let you in.

Cr.—He knows me, because I often come, Socrates; moreover, I have done him a kindness.

Soc.—And are you only just arrived?

Cr.—No, I came some time ago.

Soc.—Then why did you sit and say nothing, instead of at once awakening me?

Cr.—Awaken you, Socrates? Certainly not! I wish I were not myself so sleepless and full of sorrow. I have been watching with amazement your peaceful slumbers; and I deliberately refrained from awaking you, because I wished time to pass for you as happily as might be. Often before during the course of your life I have thought you fortunate in your disposition; but never did I see anything like the easy, tranquil manner in which you bear this calamity.

Soc.—Why, Crito, when a man has reached my age he ought not to be repining at the approach of death.

Cr.—And yet other old men find themselves in similar misfortunes, and age does not prevent them from repining.

Soc.—That is true. But you do not say why you come so early.

Cr.—I come to bring you a painful message; not, as I believe, to yourself, but painful and grievous to all of us who are your friends, and most grievous of all to me.

Soc.—What? Has the ship come from Delos, on the arrival of which I am to die?

Cr.—No, the ship has not actually arrived, but she will probably be here today, as persons who have come from Sunium tell me that they left her there; and therefore tomorrow, Socrates, must be the last day of your life.

Soc.—Very well, Crito; if such is the will of God, I am willing; but my belief is that there will be a delay of a day.

Cr.—[44] Why do you think so?

Soc.—I will tell you. I am to die on the day after the arrival of the ship.

Cr.—Yes; that is what the authorities say.

Soc.—But I do not think that the ship will be here until tomorrow; this I infer from a vision which I had last night, or rather only just now, when you fortunately allowed me to sleep.

Cr.—And what was the nature of the vision?

Soc.—There appeared to me the likeness of a woman, fair and comely, clothed in bright raiment, who called to me and said: "O Socrates, 'The third day hence to fertile Phthia shalt thou come.'[1]"

Cr.—What a singular dream, Socrates!

Soc.—There can be no doubt about the meaning, Crito, I think.

Cr.—Yes; the meaning is only too clear. But, oh! my beloved Socrates, let me entreat you once more to take my advice and escape. For if you die I shall not only lose a friend who can never be replaced, but there is another evil: people who do not know you and me will believe that I might have saved you if I had been willing to spend money, but that I did not care. Now, can there be a worse disgrace than this—that I should be

---

[1] Homer, *Il.* ix. 363.

thought to value money more than the life of a friend? For the many will not be persuaded that I wanted you to escape, and that you refused.

Soc.—But why, my dear Crito, should we care about the opinion of the many? The best men, and they are the only persons who are worth considering, will think of these things truly as they occurred.

Cr.—But you see, Socrates, that the opinion of the many must be regarded, for what is now happening shows of itself that they can do the greatest evil to anyone who has lost their good opinion.

Soc.—I only wish it were so, Crito, and that the many could do the greatest evil; for then they would also be able to do the greatest good—and what a fine thing this would be! But in reality they can do neither; for they cannot make a man either wise or foolish, and they do not care what they make of him.

Cr.—Well, I will not dispute with you; but please to tell me, Socrates, whether you are not acting out of regard to me and your other friends: are you not afraid that if you escape from prison we may get into trouble with the informers for having stolen you away, and lose either the whole or a great part of our [45] property; or that even a worse evil may happen to us? Now, if you fear on our account, be at ease; for in order to save you, we ought surely to run this, or even a greater risk; be persuaded, then, and do as I say.

Soc.—Yes, Crito, that is one fear which you mention, but by no means the only one.

Cr.—Fear not—there are persons who are willing to get you out of prison at no great cost; and as for the informers, you know that they are far from being exorbitant in their demands—a little money will satisfy them. My means, which are certainly ample, are at your service, and if out of regard for my interests you have a scruple about spending my money, here are strangers who will give you the use of theirs; and one of them, Simmias the Theban, has brought a large sum for this very purpose; and Cebes and many others are prepared to spend their money in helping you to escape. I say, therefore, do not shirk the effort on our account, and do not say, as you did in the court, that you will have a difficulty in knowing what to do with yourself anywhere else. For men will love you in other places to which you may go, and not in Athens only; there are friends of mine in Thessaly, if you like to go to them, who will value and protect you, and no Thessalian will give you any trouble. Nor can I think that you are at all justified, Socrates, in betraying your own life when you might be saved; in acting thus you are working to bring on yourself the very fate which your enemies would and did work to bring on you, your own destruction. And further I should say that you are deserting your own children; for you might bring them up and educate them; instead of which you go away and leave them, and they will have to take their chance; and if they do not meet with the usual fate of orphans, there will be small thanks to you. No man should bring children into the world who is unwilling to persevere to the end in their nurture and education. But you appear to be choosing the easier part, not the better and manlier, which would have been more be-coming in one who professes to care for virtue in all his life, like yourself. And indeed, I am ashamed not only of you, but of us who are your friends, when I reflect that the whole business may be attributed entirely to our want of courage. The trial need never have come on, or might have been managed differently; and this last opportunity will seem (crowning futility of it all) to have escaped us through our own incompetence and cowardice, who might [46] have saved you if we had been good for anything, and you might have saved yourself; for there was no difficulty at all. See now, Socrates, how discreditable as well as disastrous are the consequences, both to us and you. Make up your mind then, or rather have your mind already made up, for the time of deliberation is over, and there is only one thing to be done, which must be done this very night, and if we delay at all will be no longer practicable or possible; I beseech you therefore, Socrates, be persuaded by me, and do not say me nay.

Soc.—Dear Crito, your zeal is invaluable, if a right one; but if wrong, the greater the zeal the greater the danger; and therefore we ought to con-sider whether I shall or shall not do as you say. For I am and always have been one of those natures who must be guided by reason, whatever the rea-son may be which upon reflection appears to me to be the best; and now that this chance has befallen me, I cannot repudiate my own doctrines, which seem to me as sound as ever: the principles which I have hitherto honoured and revered I still honour, and unless we can at once find other and better principles, I am certain not to agree with you; no, not even if the power of the multitude could let loose upon us many more imprison-ments, confiscations, deaths, frightening us like children with hobgoblin terrors. What will be the fairest way of considering the question? Shall I return to your old argument about the opinions of men?—we were saying that some of them are to be regarded, and others not. Now were we right in maintaining this before I was condemned? And has the argument which was once good now proved to be talk for the sake of talking—mere child-ish nonsense? That is what I want to consider with your help, Crito:— whether, under my present circumstances, the argument will appear to me in any way different or not; and whether we shall dismiss or accept it. That argument, which, as I believe, is maintained by many persons of authority, was to the effect, as I was saying, that the opinions of some men are to be regarded, and of other men not to be regarded. Now you, Crito, are not going to die tomorrow—at least, there is no [47] human probability of this —and therefore you are disinterested and not liable to be deceived by the circumstances in which you are placed. Tell me then, I beg you, whether I am right in saying that some opinions, and the opinions of some men only, are to be valued, and that others are to be disregarded. Is not this true?

Cr.—Certainly.

Soc.—The good opinions are to be regarded, and not the bad?

Cr.—Yes.

Soc.—And the opinions of the wise are good, and the opinions of the unwise are evil?

Cr.—Certainly.

Soc.—And what was said about another matter? Does the pupil who devotes himself to the practice of gymnastics attend to the praise and blame and opinion of any and every man, or of one man only—his physician or trainer, whoever he may be?

Cr.—Of one man only.

Soc.—And he ought to fear the censure and welcome the praise of that one only, and not of the many?

Cr.—Clearly so.

Soc.—And he ought to act and train, and eat and drink in the way which seems good to his single master who has understanding, rather than according to the opinion of all other men put together?

Cr.—True.

Soc.—And if he disobeys and disregards the opinion and approval of the one, and regards the opinion of the many who have no understanding, will he not suffer evil?

Cr.—Certainly he will.

Soc.—And what will the evil be, whither tending and what affecting, in the disobedient person?

Cr.—Clearly, affecting the body; that is what is ruined by the evil.

Soc.—Very good; and is not this true, Crito, of other things which we need not separately enumerate? In questions of just and unjust, fair and foul, good and evil, which are the subjects of our present consultation, ought we to follow the opinion of the many and to fear them; or the opinion of the one man who has understanding? ought we not to fear and reverence him more than all the rest of the world, and if we desert him shall we not corrupt and outrage that principle in us which may be assumed to be improved by justice and deteriorated by injustice?—there is such a principle?

Cr.—Certainly there is, Socrates.

Soc.—Take a parallel instance:—if, acting against the advice of those who have understanding, we ruin that which is improved by health and is corrupted by disease, would life be worth having? And that which has been corrupted is—the body?

Cr.—Yes.

Soc.—Is our life worth living, with an evil and corrupted body?

Cr.—Certainly not.

Soc.—And will it be worth living, if that higher part of man be corrupted which is improved by justice and depraved by injustice? Do we suppose that principle, whatever it may be in [48] man, which has to do with justice and injustice, to be inferior to the body?

Cr.—Certainly not.

Soc.—More honourable than the body?

Cr.—Far more.

Soc.—Then, my friend, we must not particularly regard what the many say of us: but what he, the one man who has understanding of just and unjust, will say, and what the truth will say. And therefore you begin in error when you advise that we should regard the opinion of the many about just and unjust, good and evil, honourable and dishonourable.—'Well,' someone will say, 'but the many can kill us.'

Cr.—That will clearly be the answer, Socrates; you are right there.

Soc.—But still, my excellent friend, I find that the old argument is unshaken as ever. And I should like to know whether I may say the same of another proposition—that not life, but a good life, is to be chiefly valued?

Cr.—Yes, that also remains unshaken.

Soc.—And a good life is equivalent to a just and honourable one—that holds also?

Cr.—Yes, it does.

Soc.—From these premises I proceed to argue the question whether it is or is not right for me to try and escape without the consent of the Athenians: and if it is clearly right, then I will make the attempt; but if not, I will abstain. The other considerations which you mention, of money and loss of character and the duty of educating one's children, are, I fear, only the doctrines of the multitude, who would restore people to life, if they were able, as thoughtlessly as they put them to death—and with as little reason. But now, since the argument has carried us thus far, the only question which remains to be considered is, whether we shall do rightly, I by escaping and you by helping me, and by paying the agents of my escape in money and thanks; or whether in reality we shall not do rightly; and if the latter, then death or any other calamity which may ensue on my remaining quietly here must not be allowed to enter into the calculation.

Cr.—I think that you are right, Socrates; how then shall we proceed?

Soc.—Let us consider the matter together, and do you either refute me if you can, and I will be convinced; or else cease, my dear friend, from repeating to me that I ought to escape against the wishes of the Athenians: for I am very eager that what I do should be done with your approval. And now please [49] to consider my first position, and try how you can best answer me.

Cr.—I will.

Soc.—Are we to say that we are never intentionally to do wrong, or that in one way we ought and in another way we ought not to do wrong, or is doing wrong always evil and dishonourable, as has already been often acknowledged by us? Are all the admissions we have made within these last few days to be thrown over? And have we, at our age, been earnestly discoursing with one another all our life long only to discover that we are no better than children? Or, in spite of the opinion of the many, and in spite of all consequences whether for the better or the worse, shall we insist on the truth of what was then said, that injustice is always an evil and dishonour to him who acts unjustly? Shall we say so or not?

Cr.—Yes.

Soc.—Then we must do no wrong?

Cr.—Certainly not.

Soc.—Nor when injured injure in return, as the many imagine; for we must injure no one at all?

Cr.—Clearly not.

Soc.—Again, Crito, may we do evil?

Cr.—Surely not, Socrates.

Soc.—And what of doing evil in return for evil, which is the morality of the many—is that just or not?

Cr.—Not just.

Soc.—For doing evil to another is the same as injuring him?

Cr.—Very true.

Soc.—Then we ought not to retaliate or render evil for evil to anyone, whatever evil we may have suffered from him. But I would have you consider, Crito, whether you really mean what you are saying. For this opinion has never been held, and never will be held, by any considerable number of persons; and those who are agreed and those who are not agreed upon this point have no common ground, and can only despise one another when they see how widely they differ. Tell me, then, whether you agree with and assent to my first principle, that neither injury nor retaliation nor warding off evil by evil is ever right. And shall that be the premiss of our argument? Or do you decline and dissent from this? For so I have ever thought, and continue to think; but, if you are of another opinion, let me hear what you have to say. If, however, you remain of the same mind as formerly, I will proceed to the next step.

Cr.—You may proceed, for I have not changed my mind.

Soc.—Then I will go on to the next point, which may be put in the form of a question:—Ought a man to do what he admits to be right, or ought he to betray the right?

Cr.—He ought to do what he thinks right.

Soc.—But if this is true, what is the application? In leaving [50] the prison against the will of the Athenians, do I wrong any? or rather do I not wrong those whom I ought least to wrong? Do I not desert the principles which were acknowledged by us to be just—what do you say?

Cr.—I cannot answer your question, Socrates; for I do not understand it.

Soc.—Then consider the matter in this way:—Imagine that I am about to run away (you may call the proceeding by any name which you like), and the laws and the state appear to me and interrogate me: 'Tell us, Socrates,' they say; 'what are you about? are you not going by an act of yours to bring us to ruin—the laws, and the whole state, as far as in you lies? Do you imagine that a state can subsist and not be overthrown, in which the decisions of law have no power, but are set aside and trampled upon by individuals?' What will be our answer, Crito, to these and the like words? Anyone, and especially a rhetorician, will have a good deal to say against the subversion of the law which requires a sentence to be carried out. Shall we reply, 'Yes; but the state has injured us and given an unjust sentence.' Suppose we say that?

Cr.—Very good, Socrates.

Soc.—'And was that our agreement with you?' the law would answer; 'or were you to abide by the sentence of the state?' And if we were to express our astonishment at their words, the law would probably add: 'Answer, Socrates, instead of opening your eyes—you are in the habit of asking and answering questions. Tell us,—What complaint have you to make against us which justifies you in attempting to ruin us and the state? In the first place did we not bring you into existence? Your father married your mother by our aid and begat you. Say whether you have any objection to urge against those of us who regulate marriage?' None, I should reply. 'Or against those of us who after birth regulate the nurture and education of children, in which you also were trained? Were not the laws, which have the charge of education, right in commanding your father to train you in music and gymnastic?' Right, I should reply. 'Well then, since you were brought into the world and nurtured and educated by us, can you deny in the first place that you are our child and slave, as your fathers were before you? And if this is true you cannot suppose that you are on equal terms with us in matters of right and wrong, or think that you have a right to do to us what we are doing to you. Would you have any right to strike or revile or do any other evil to your father or your master, if you had one, because you have [51] been struck or reviled by him, or received some other evil at his hands?—you would not say this? And because we think right to destroy you, do you think that you have any right to destroy us in return, and your country as far as in you lies? Will you, O professor of true virtue, pretend that you are justified in this? Has a philosopher like you failed to discover that our country is more precious and higher and holier far than mother or father or any ancestor, and more to be regarded in the eyes of the gods and of men of understanding? also to be soothed, and gently and reverently entreated when angry, even more than a father, and either to be persuaded, or if not persuaded, to be obeyed? And when we are punished by her, whether with imprisonment or stripes, the punishment is to be endured in silence; and if she lead us to wounds or death in battle, thither we follow as is right; neither may anyone yield or retreat or leave his rank, but whether in battle or in a court of law, or in any other place, he must do what his city and his country order him; or he must change their view of what is just: and if he may do no violence to his father or mother, much less may he do violence to his country.' What answer shall we make to this, Crito? Do the laws speak truly, or do they not?

Cr.—I think that they do.

Soc.—Then the laws will say: 'Consider, Socrates, if we are speaking truly that in your present attempt you are going to do us a wrong. For, having brought you into the world, and nurtured and educated you, and given you and every other citizen a share in every good which we had to give, we further proclaim to any Athenian by the liberty which we allow him, that if he does not like us, the laws, when he has become of age and has seen the ways of the city, and made our acquaintance, he may go where he pleases and take his goods with him. None of us laws will forbid him or interfere with anyone who does not like us and the city, and who wants to emigrate to a colony or to any other city; he may go where he likes, with his property. But he who has experience of the manner in which we order justice and administer the state, and still remains, has by so doing entered into an implied contract that he will do as we command him. And he who disobeys us is, as we maintain, thrice wrong; first, because in disobeying us he is disobeying his parents; secondly, because we are the authors of his education; thirdly, because having made an agreement with us that he will duly obey our commands, he neither obeys them nor convinces us that our [52] commands are unjust; although we do not roughly require unquestioning obedience, but give him the alternative of obeying or convincing us;—that is what we offer, and he does neither.

'These are the sort of accusations to which, as we were saying, you, Socrates, will be exposed if you accomplish your intentions; you, above all other Athenians.' Suppose now I ask, why I rather than anybody else? no doubt they will justly retort upon me that I above all other Athenians have acknowledged the agreement. 'There is clear proof,' they will say, 'Socrates, that we and the city were not displeasing to you. Of all Athenians you have been the most constant resident in the city, which, as you never leave, you may be supposed to love. For you never went out of the city either to see the games, except once when you went to the Isthmus, or to any other place unless when you were on military service; nor did you travel as other men do. Nor had you any curiosity to know other states or their laws: your affections did not go beyond us and our state; we were your special favourites, and you acquiesced in our government of you; and here in this city you begat your children, which is a proof of your satisfaction. Moreover, you might in the course of the trial, if you had liked, have fixed the penalty at banishment; you might then have done with the state's assent what you are now setting out to do without it. But you pretended that you preferred death to exile, and that you were not unwilling to die. And now you have forgotten these fine sentiments, and pay no respect to us the laws, of whom you are the destroyer; and are doing what only a miserable slave would do, running away and turning your back upon the compacts and agreements of your citizenship which you made with us. And first of all answer this very question: Are we right in saying that you agreed to live under our government in deed, and not in word only? Is that true or not?' How shall we answer, Crito? Must we not assent?

Cr.—We cannot help it, Socrates.

Soc.—Then will they not say: 'You, Socrates, are breaking the covenants and agreements which you made with us at your leisure, not under any compulsion or deception or in enforced haste, but after you have had seventy years to think of them, during which time you were at liberty to leave the city, if we were not to your mind or if our covenants appeared to you to be unfair. You had your choice, and might have gone either to Lacedaemon or Crete, both which states are often praised by you for their good government, or to some other Hellenic or [53] foreign state. Whereas you, above all other Athenians, seemed to be so fond of the state, and obviously therefore of us her laws (for who would care about a state without its laws?), that you never stirred out of her; the halt, the blind, the maimed were not more stationary in her than you were. And now you refuse to abide by your agreements. Not so, Socrates, if you will take our advice; do not make yourself ridiculous by leaving the city.

'For just consider, if you transgress and err in this sort of way, what good will you do either to yourself or to your friends? That your friends will be in danger of being driven into exile and deprived of citizenship, or of losing their property, is tolerably certain; and you yourself, if you fly to one of the neighbouring cities, as, for example, Thebes or Megara, both of which are well governed, will come to them as an enemy of their government and all patriotic citizens will look askance at you as a subverter of the laws, and you will confirm in the minds of the judges the justice of their own condemnation of you. For he who is a corrupter of the laws is more than likely to be a corrupter of the young and foolish portion of mankind. Will you then flee from well-ordered cities and virtuous men? and is existence worth having on these terms? Or will you go to them without shame, and talk to them, saying—what will you say to them? What you say here about virtue and justice and institutions and laws being the best things among men? Would that be decent of Socrates? Surely not. But if you go away from well-governed states to Crito's friends in Thessaly, where there is great disorder and licence, they will be charmed to hear the tale of your escape from prison, set off with ludicrous particulars of the manner in which you were wrapped in a goatskin or some other disguise, and metamorphosed as the manner is of runaways; but will there be no one to remind you that in your old age, when little time was left to you, you were not ashamed to violate the most sacred laws from a greedy desire of life? Perhaps not, if you keep them in a good temper; but if they are out of temper you will hear many degrading things. You will live, but how?— fawning upon all men, and the servant of all men; and doing what?—faring sumptuously in Thessaly, having gone abroad in order that you may get a dinner. And where will be your fine sentiments about justice [54] and virtue? Say that you wish to live for the sake of your children—you want to bring them up and educate them—will you take them into Thessaly and deprive them of Athenian citizenship? Is this the benefit which you will confer upon them? Or are you under the impression that they will be better cared for and educated here if you are still alive, although absent from them; for your friends will take care of them? Do you fancy that if you have left Athens for Thessaly they will take care of them, but if you have left it for the other world that they will not take care of them? Nay; but if they who call themselves friends are good for anything, they will—to be sure they will.

'Listen, then, Socrates, to us who have brought you up. Think not of life and children first, and of justice afterwards, but of justice first, that you may so vindicate yourself before the princes of the world below. For neither will you nor any that belong to you be happier or holier or juster in this life, or happier in another, if you do as Crito bids. Now you depart, if it must be so, in innocence, a sufferer and not a doer of evil; a victim, not of the laws but of men. But if you leave the city, basely returning evil for evil and injury for injury, breaking the covenants and agreements which you have made with us, and wronging those whom you ought least of all to wrong, that is to say, yourself, your friends, your country, and us, we shall be angry with you while you live, and our brethren, the laws in the world below, will give you no friendly welcome; for they will know that you have done your best to destroy us. Listen, then, to us and not to Crito.'

This, dear Crito, is the voice which I seem to hear murmuring in my ears, like the sound of the flute in the ears of the mystic; that voice, I say, is humming in my ears, and prevents me from hearing any other. Be assured, then, that anything more which you may say to shake this my faith will be said in vain. Yet speak, if you have anything to say.

Cr.—I have nothing to say.

Soc.—It is enough then, Crito. Let us fulfil the will of God, and follow whither He leads.

JOHN STUART MILL
(1806-1873)

In his essay **On Liberty,** written in 1859, John Stuart Mill makes as strong a case for political individualism as I think can be made. Not altogether unlike his fellow Britisher a century later, R. D. Laing, Mill argues against society's meddling in affairs that are properly personal. He endorses a charitable interpretation of the contemporary slogan, "Do your own thing." And his discourse on the particular example of Prohibition of alcoholic drinks will likely be heralded as a precursor to a philosophical defense for legalizing marijuana.

But before we are swept away with enthusiasm for Mill's noble defense of the rights of the individual, let us recall Slater's analysis of the price paid for individualism of the sort that Mill espouses. Slater has good reasons for wondering whether Mill is right when he says of the freely acting individual, "All errors which he is likely to commit against advice and warning are far outweighed by the evil of allowing others to constrain him to what they deem his good." Mill is not here speaking of dangers to others but of dangers to the individual himself. And Mill is not simply wrong, even if the considerations Slater and others adduce tip the balance away from individualism (note Mill's use of the term, "outweighed"). Nor is he simply right, because, as the metaphor of the scale indicates, we are dealing here with a question of varying degrees. Mill describes real ills liable to befall the society with insufficient respect for the dignity of the individual, and his case must be heard and understood if we are to weigh the question of individualism today.

Of the Limits to the Authority of Society Over the Individual

What, then, is the rightful limit to the sovereignty of the individual over himself? Where does the authority of society begin? How much of human life should be assigned to individuality, and how much to society?

Each will receive its proper share, if each has that which more particularly concerns it. To individuality should belong the part of life in which it is chiefly the individual that is interested; to society, the part which chiefly interests society.

Though society is not founded on a contract, and though no good purpose is answered by inventing a contract in order to deduce social obligations from it, everyone who receives the protection of society owes a return for the benefit, and the fact of living in society renders it indispensable that each should be bound to observe a certain line of conduct towards the rest. This conduct consists, *first,* in not injuring the interests of one another; or rather certain interests, which, either by express legal provision or by tacit understanding, ought to be considered as rights; and *secondly,* in each person's bearing his share (to be fixed on some equitable principle) of the labors and sacrifices incurred for defending the society or its members from injury and molestation. These conditions society is justified in enforcing, at all costs to those who endeavor to withhold fulfillment. Nor is this all that society may do. The acts of an individual may be hurtful to others, or wanting in due consideration for their welfare, without going to the length of violating any of their constituted rights. The offender may then

OF THE LIMITS TO THE AUTHORITY OF SOCIETY OVER THE INDIVIDUAL From John Stuart Mill, *On Liberty.*

be justly punished by opinion, though not by law. As soon as any part of a person's conduct affects prejudicially the interests of others, society has jurisdiction over it, and the question whether the general welfare will or will not be promoted by interfering with it, becomes open to discussion. But there is no room for entertaining any such question when a person's conduct affects the interests of no persons besides himself, or need not affect them unless they like (all the persons concerned being of full age, and the ordinary amount of understanding). In all such cases, there should be perfect freedom, legal and social, to do the action and stand the consequences.

It would be a great misunderstanding of this doctrine to suppose that it is one of selfish indifference, which pretends that human beings have no business with each other's conduct in life, and that they should not concern themselves about the well-doing or well-being of one another, unless their own interest is involved. Instead of any diminution, there is need of a great increase of disinterested exertion to promote the good of others. But disinterested benevolence can find other instruments to persuade people to their good than whips and scourges, either of the literal or the metaphorical sort. I am the last person to undervalue the self-regarding virtues: they are only second in importance, if even second, to the social. It is equally the business of education to cultivate both. But even education works by conviction and persuasion as well as by compulsion, and it is by the former only that, when the period of education is passed, the self-regarding virtues should be inculcated. Human beings owe to each other help to distinguish the better from the worse, and encouragement to choose the former and avoid the latter. They should be forever stimulating each other to increased exercise of their higher faculties, and increased direction of their feelings and aims towards wise instead of foolish, elevating instead of degrading, objects and contemplations. But neither one person, nor any number of persons, is warranted in saying to another human creature of ripe years, that he shall not do with his life for his own benefit what he chooses to do with it. He is the person most interested in his own well-being: the interest which any other person, except in cases of strong personal attachment, can have in it, is trifling, compared with that which he himself has; the interest which society has in him individually (except as to his conduct to others) is fractional, and altogether indirect; while with respect to his own feelings and circumstances, the most ordinary man or woman has means of knowledge immeasurably surpassing those that can be possessed by anyone else. The interference of society to overrule his judgment and purposes in what only regards himself must be grounded on general presumptions; which may be altogether wrong, and even if right, are as likely as not to be misapplied to individual cases, by persons no better acquainted with the circumstances of such cases than those are who look at them merely from without. In this department, therefore, of human affairs, individuality has its proper field of action. In the conduct of human beings towards one another it is necessary that general rules should for the most part be observed, in order that people may know what they have to expect; but in each person's own concerns his individual spontaneity is entitled to free exercise. Considerations to aid his judgment, exhortations to strengthen his will, may be offered to him, even obtruded on him, by others: but he himself is the final judge. All errors which he is likely to commit against advice and warning are far outweighed by the evil of allowing others to constrain him to what they deem his good.

I do not mean that the feelings with which a person is regarded by others ought not to be in any way affected by his self-regarding qualities or deficiencies. This is neither possible nor desirable. If he is eminent in any of the qualities which conduce to his own good, he is, so far, a proper object of admiration. He is so much the nearer to the ideal perfection of human nature. If he is grossly deficient in those qualities, a sentiment the opposite of admiration will follow. There is a degree of folly, and a degree of what may be called (though the phrase is not unobjectionable) lowness or depravation of taste, which, though it cannot justify doing harm to the person who manifests it, renders him necessarily and properly a subject of distaste, or, in extreme cases, even of contempt: a person could not have the opposite qualities in due strength without entertaining these feelings. Though doing no wrong to anyone, a person may so act as to compel us to judge him, and feel to him, as a fool, or as a being of an inferior order; and since this judgment and feeling are a fact which he would prefer to avoid, it is doing him a service to warn him of it beforehand, as of any other disagreeable consequence to which he exposes himself. It would be well, indeed, if this good office were much more freely rendered than the common notions of politeness at present permit, and if one person could honestly point out to another that he thinks him in fault, without being considered unmannerly or presuming. We have a right, also, in various ways, to act upon our unfavorable opinion of anyone, not to the oppression of his individuality, but in the exercise of ours. We are not bound, for example, to seek his society; we have a right to avoid it (though not to parade the avoidance), for we have a right to choose the society most acceptable to us. We have a right, and it may be our duty, to caution others against him, if we think his example or conversation likely to have a pernicious effect on those with whom he associates. We may give others a preference over him in optional good offices, except those which tend to his improvement. In these various modes a person may suffer very severe penalties at the hands of others for faults which directly concern only himself; but he suffers these penalties only in so far as they are the natural and, as it were, the spontaneous consequences of the faults themselves, not because they are purposely inflicted on him for the sake of punishment. A person who shows rashness, obstinacy, self-conceit—who cannot live within moderate means—who cannot restrain himself from hurtful indulgences—who pursues animal pleasures at the expense of those of feeling and intellect —must expect to be lowered in the opinion of others, and to have a less share of their favorable sentiments; but of this he has no right to complain, unless he has merited their favor by special excellence in his social relations, and has thus established a title to their good offices, which is not affected by his demerits towards himself.

What I contend for is, that the inconveniences which are strictly inseparable from the unfavorable judgment of others, are the only ones to which a person should ever be subjected for that portion of his conduct and character which concerns his own good, but which does not affect the interest of others in their relations with him. Acts injurious to others require a totally different treatment. Encroachment on their rights; infliction on them of any loss or damage not justified by his own rights; falsehood or duplicity in dealing with them; unfair or ungenerous use of advantages over them; even selfish abstinence from defending them against injury—these are fit objects of moral reprobation, and, in grave cases, of moral retribution and punishment. And not only these acts, but the dispositions which lead to them, are properly immoral, and fit subjects of disapprobation which may rise to abhorrence. Cruelty of disposition; malice and ill-nature; that most antisocial and odious of all passions, envy; dissimulation and insincerity, irascibility on insufficient cause, and resentment disproportioned to the provocation; the love of domineering over others; the desire to engross more than one's share of advantages (the πλεονεξία [greediness, arrogance] of the Greeks); the pride which derives gratification from the abasement of others; the egotism which thinks self and its concerns more important than everything else, and decides all doubtful questions in its own favor;—these are moral vices, and constitute a bad and odious moral character: unlike the self-regarding faults previously mentioned, which are not properly immoralities, and to whatever pitch they may be carried, do not constitute wickedness. They may be proofs of any amount of folly, or want of personal dignity and self-respect; but they are only a subject of moral reprobation when they involve a breach of duty to others, for whose sake the individual is bound to have care for himself. What are called duties to ourselves are not socially obligatory, unless circumstances render them at the same time duties to others. The term 'duty to oneself,' when it means anything more than prudence, means self-respect or self-development, and for none of these is anyone accountable to his fellow-creatures, because for none of them is it for the good of mankind that he be held accountable to them.

The distinction between the loss of consideration which a person may rightly incur by defect of prudence or of personal dignity, and the reprobation which is due to him for an offense against the rights of others, is not a merely nominal distinction. It makes a vast difference both in our feelings and in our conduct towards him whether he displeases us in things in which we think we have a right to control him, or in things in which we know that we have not. If he displeases us, we may express our distaste, and we may stand aloof from a person as well as from a thing that displeases us; but we shall not therefore feel called on to make his life uncomfortable. We shall reflect that he already bears, or will bear, the whole penalty of his error; if he spoils his life by mismanagement, we shall not, for that reason, desire to spoil it still further: instead of wishing to punish him, we shall rather endeavor to alleviate his punishment, by showing him how he may avoid or cure the evils his conduct tends to bring upon him. He may be to us an object of pity, perhaps of dislike, but not of anger or resentment; we shall not treat him like an enemy of society: the worst we shall think ourselves justified in doing is leaving him to himself, if we do not interfere benevolently by showing interest or concern for him. It is far otherwise if he has infringed the rules necessary for the protection of his fellow-creatures, individually or collectively. The evil consequences of his acts do not then fall on himself, but on others; and society, as the protector of all its members, must retaliate on him; must inflict pain on him for the express purpose of punishment, and must take care that it be sufficiently severe. In the one case, he is an offender at our bar, and we are called on not only to sit in judgment on him, but, in one shape or another, to execute our own sentence: in the other case, it is not our part to inflict any suffering on him, except what may incidentally follow from our using the same liberty in the regulation of our own affairs, which we allow to him in his.

The distinction here pointed out between the part of a person's life which concerns only himself, and that which concerns others, many persons will refuse to admit. How (it may be asked) can any part of the conduct of a member of society be a matter of indifference to the other members? No person is an entirely isolated being; it is impossible for a person to do anything seriously or permanently hurtful to himself, without mischief reaching at least to his near connections, and often far beyond them. If he injures his property, he does harm to those who directly or indirectly derived support from it, and usually diminishes, by a greater or less amount, the general resources of the community. If he deteriorates his bodily or mental faculties, he not only brings evil upon all who depended on him for any portion of their happiness, but disqualifies himself for rendering the services which he owes to his fellow-creatures generally; perhaps becomes a burden on their affection or benevolence; and if such conduct were very frequent, hardly an offense that is committed would detract more from the general sum of good. Finally, if by his vices or follies a person does no direct harm to others, he is nevertheless (it may be said) injurious by his example; and ought to be compelled to control himself, for the sake of those whom the sight or knowledge of his conduct might corrupt or mislead.

And even (it will be added) if the consequences of misconduct could be confined to the vicious or thoughtless individual, ought society to abandon to their own guidance those who are manifestly unfit for it? If protection against themselves is confessedly due to children and persons under age, is not society equally bound to afford it to persons of mature years who are equally incapable of self-government? If gambling, or drunkenness, or incontinence, or idleness, or uncleanliness, are as injurious to happiness, and as great a hindrance to improvement, as many or most of the acts prohibited by law, why (it may be asked) should not law, so far as is consistent with practicability and social convenience, endeavor to repress these also? And as a supplement to the unavoidable imperfections of law, ought not opinion at least to organize a powerful police against these vices, and visit rigidly with social penalties those who are known to practice them? There is no question here (it may be said) about restricting individuality, or impeding the trial of new and original experiments in living. The only things it is sought to prevent are things which have been tried and condemned from the beginning of the world until now; things which experience has shown not to be useful or suitable to any person's individuality. There must be some length of time and amount of experience after which a moral or prudential truth may be regarded as established: and it is merely desired to prevent generation after generation from falling over the same precipice which has been fatal to their predecessors.

I fully admit that the mischief which a person does to himself may seriously affect, both through their sympathies and their interests, those nearly connected with him and, in a minor degree, society at large. When, by conduct of this sort, a person is led to violate a distinct and assignable obligation to any other person or persons, the case is taken out of the self-regarding class, and becomes amenable to moral disapprobation in the proper sense of the term. If, for example, a man, through intemperance or extravagance, becomes unable to pay his debts, or, having undertaken the moral responsibility of a family, becomes from the same cause incapable of supporting or educating them, he is deservedly reprobated, and might be justly punished; but it is for the breach of duty to his family or creditors, not for the extravagance. If the resources which ought to have been devoted to them, had been diverted from them for the most prudent investment, the moral culpability would have been the same. George Barnwell murdered his uncle to get money for his mistress, but if he had done it to set himself up in business, he would equally have been hanged. Again, in the frequent case of a man who causes grief to his family by addiction to bad habits, he deserves reproach for his unkindness or ingratitude; but so he may for cultivating habits not in themselves vicious, if they are painful to those with whom he passes his life, or who from personal ties are dependent on him for their comfort. Whoever fails in the consideration generally due to the interests and feelings of others, not being compelled by some more imperative duty, or justified by allowable self-preference, is a subject of moral disapprobation for that failure, but not for the cause of it, nor for the errors, merely personal to himself, which may have remotely led to it. In like manner, when a person disables himself, by conduct purely self-regarding, from the performance of some definite duty incumbent on him to the public, he is guilty of a social offense. No person ought to be punished simply for being drunk; but a soldier or a policeman should be punished for being drunk on duty. Whenever, in short, there is a definite damage, or a definite risk of damage, either to an individual or to the public, the case is taken out of the province of liberty, and placed in that of morality or law.

But with regard to the merely contingent, or, as it may be called, constructive injury which a person causes to society, by conduct which neither violates any specific duty to the public, nor occasions perceptible hurt to any assignable individual except himself, the inconvenience is one which society can afford to bear, for the sake of the greater good of human freedom. If grown persons are to be punished for not taking proper care of themselves, I would rather it were for their own sake, than under pretense of preventing them from impairing their capacity of rendering to society benefits which society does not pretend it has a right to exact. But I cannot consent to argue the point as if society had no means of bringing its weaker members up to its ordinary standard of rational conduct, except waiting till they do something irrational, and then punishing them, legally or morally, for it. Society has had absolute power over them during all the early portion of their existence: it has had the whole period of childhood and nonage in which to try whether it could make them capable of rational conduct in life. The existing generation is master both of the training and the entire circumstances of the generation to come; it cannot indeed make them perfectly wise and good, because it is itself so lamentably deficient in goodness and wisdom; and its best efforts are not always, in individual cases, its most successful ones; but it is perfectly well able to make the rising generation, as a whole, as good as, and a little better than, itself. If society lets any considerable number of its members grow up mere children, incapable of being acted on by rational consideration of distant motives, society has itself to blame for the consequences. Armed not only with all the powers of education, but with the ascendency which the authority of a received opinion always exercises over the minds who are least fitted to judge for themselves; and aided by the *natural* penalties which cannot be prevented from falling on those who incur the distaste or the contempt of those who know them; let not society pretend that it needs, besides all this, the power to issue commands and enforce obedience in the personal concerns of individuals, in which, on all principles of justice and policy, the decision ought to rest with those who are to abide the consequences. Nor is there anything which tends more to discredit and frustrate the better means of influencing conduct than a resort to the worse. If there be among those whom it is attempted to coerce into prudence or temperance any of the material of which vigorous and independent characters are made, they will infallibly rebel against the yoke. No such person will ever feel that others have a right to control him in his concerns, such as they have to prevent him from injuring them in theirs; and it easily comes to be considered a mark of spirit and courage to fly in the face of such usurped authority, and do with ostentation the exact opposite of what it enjoins; as in the fashion of grossness which succeeded, in the time of Charles II, to the fanatical moral intolerance of the Puritans. With respect to what is said of the necessity of protecting society from the bad example set to others by the vicious or the self-indulgent, it is true that bad example may have a pernicious effect, especially the example of doing wrong to others with impunity to the wrong-doer. But we are now speaking of conduct which, while it does no wrong to others, is supposed to do great harm to the agent himself: and I do not see how those who believe this can think otherwise than that the example, on the whole, must be more salutary than hurtful; since, if it displays the misconduct, it displays also the painful or degrading consequences which, if the conduct is justly censured, must be supposed to be in all or most cases attendant on it.

But the strongest of all the arguments against the interference of the public with purely personal conduct is that, when it does interfere, the odds are that it interferes wrongly, and in the wrong place. On questions of social morality, of duty to others, the opinion of the public, that is, of an overruling majority, though often wrong, is likely to be still oftener right; because on such questions they are only required to judge of their own interests; of the manner in which some mode of conduct, if allowed to be practiced, would affect themselves. But the opinion of a similar majority, imposed as a law on the minority, on questions of self-regarding conduct, is quite as likely to be wrong as right; for in these cases public opinion means, at the best, some people's opinion of what is good or bad for other people; while very often it does not even mean that; the public, with the most perfect indifference, passing over the pleasure or convenience of those whose conduct they censure, and considering only their own preference. There are many who consider as an injury to themselves any conduct which they have a distaste for, and resent it as an outrage to their feelings; as a religious bigot, when charged with disregarding the religious feelings of others, has been known to retort that they disregard his feelings, by persisting in their abominable worship or creed. But there is no parity between the feeling of a person for his own opinion, and the feeling of another who is offended at his holding it; no more than between the desire of a thief to take a purse, and the desire of the right owner to keep it. And a person's taste is as much his own peculiar concern as his opinion or his purse. It is easy for anyone to imagine an ideal public which leaves the freedom and choice of individuals in all uncertain matters undisturbed, and only requires them to abstain from modes of conduct which universal experience has condemned. But where has there been seen a public which set any such limit to its censorship? or when does the public trouble itself about universal experience? In its interferences with personal conduct it is seldom thinking of anything but the enormity of acting or feeling differently from itself; and this standard of judgment, thinly disguised, is held up to mankind as the dictate of religion and philosophy, by nine-tenths of all moralists and speculative writers. These teach that things are right because they are right; because we feel them to be so. They tell us to search in our own minds and hearts for laws of conduct binding on ourselves and on all others. What can the poor public do but apply these instructions, and make their own personal feelings of good and evil, if they are tolerably unanimous in them, obligatory on all the world?

The evil here pointed out is not one which exists only in theory; and it may perhaps be expected that I should specify the instances in which the public of this age and country improperly invests its own preferences with the character of moral laws. I am not writing an essay on the aberrations of existing moral feeling. That is too weighty a subject to be discussed parenthetically, and by way of illustration. Yet examples are necessary to show that the principle I maintain is of serious and practical moment, and that I am not endeavoring to erect a barrier against imaginary evils. And it is not difficult to show, by abundant instances, that to extend the bounds of what may be called moral police, until it encroaches on the most unquestionably legitimate liberty of the individual, is one of the most universal of all human propensities.

As a first instance, consider the antipathies which men cherish on no better grounds than that persons whose religious opinions are different from theirs do not practice their religious observances, especially their religious abstinences. To cite a rather trivial example, nothing in the creed or practice of Christians does more to envenom the hatred of Mohammedans against them than the fact of their eating pork. There are few acts which Christians and Europeans regard with more unaffected disgust than Mussulmans regard this particular mode of satisfying hunger. It is, in the first place, an offense against their religion; but this circumstance by no means explains either the degree or the kind of their repugnance; for wine also is forbidden by their religion, and to partake of it is by all Mussulmans accounted wrong, but not disgusting. Their aversion to the flesh of the "unclean beast" is, on the contrary, of that peculiar character, resembling an instinctive antipathy, which the idea of uncleanness, when once it thoroughly sinks into the feelings, seems always to excite even in those whose personal habits are anything but scrupulously cleanly, and of which the sentiment of religious impurity, so intense in the Hindoos, is a remarkable example. Suppose now that in a people, of whom the majority were Mussulmans, that majority should insist upon not permitting pork to be eaten within the limits of the country. This would be nothing new in Mohammedan countries.[1] Would it be a legitimate exercise of the moral authority of public opinion? and if not, why not? The practice is really revolting to such a public. They also sincerely think that it is forbidden and abhorred by the Deity. Neither could the prohibition be censured as religious persecution. It might be religious in its origin, but it would not be persecution for religion, since nobody's religion makes it a duty to eat pork. The only tenable ground of condemnation would be that with the personal tastes and

---

[1] The case of the Bombay Parsees is a curious instance in point. When this industrious and enterprising tribe, the descendants of the Persian fire-worshipers, flying from their native country before the Caliphs, arrived in Western India, they were admitted to toleration by the Hindoo sovereigns, on condition of not eating beef. When those regions afterwards fell under the dominion of Mohammedan conquerors, the Parsees obtained from them a continuance of indulgence, on condition of refraining from pork. What was at first obedience to authority became a second nature, and the Parsees to this day abstain both from beef and pork. Though not required by their religion, the double abstinence has had time to grow into a custom of their tribe; and custom, in the East, is a religion.

self-regarding concerns of individuals the public has no business to interfere.

To come somewhat nearer home: the majority of Spaniards consider it a gross impiety, offensive in the highest degree to the Supreme Being, to worship him in any other manner than the Roman Catholic; and no other public worship is lawful on Spanish soil. The people of all Southern Europe look upon a married clergy as not only irreligious, but unchaste, indecent, gross, disgusting. What do Protestants think of these perfectly sincere feelings, and of the attempt to enforce them against non-Catholics? Yet, if mankind are justified in interfering with each other's liberty in things which do not concern the interests of others, on what principle is it possible consistently to exclude these cases? or who can blame people for desiring to suppress what they regard as a scandal in the sight of God and man? No stronger case can be shown for prohibiting anything which is regarded as a personal immorality, than is made out for suppressing these practices in the eyes of those who regard them as impieties; and unless we are willing to adopt the logic of persecutors, and to say that we may persecute others because we are right, and that they must not persecute us because they are wrong, we must beware of admitting a principle of which we should resent as a gross injustice the application to ourselves.

The preceding instances may be objected to, although unreasonably, as drawn from contingencies impossible among us: opinion, in this country, not being likely to enforce abstinence from meats, or to interfere with people for worshiping, and for either marrying or not marrying, according to their creed or inclination. The next example, however, shall be taken from an interference with liberty which we have by no means passed all danger of.

Wherever the Puritans have been sufficiently powerful, as in New England, and in Great Britain at the time of the Commonwealth, they have endeavored, with considerable success, to put down all public, and nearly all private amusements: especially music, dancing, public games, or other assemblages for purposes of diversion, and the theater. There are still in this country large bodies of persons by whose notions of morality and religion these recreations are condemned; and those persons belonging chiefly to the middle class, who are the ascendant power in the present social and political condition of the kingdom, it is by no means impossible that persons of these sentiments may at some time or other command a majority in Parliament. How will the remaining portion of the community like to have the amusements that shall be permitted to them regulated by the religious and moral sentiments of the stricter Calvinists and Methodists? Would they not, with considerable peremptoriness, desire these intrusively pious members of society to mind their own business? This is precisely what should be said to every government and every public, who have the pretension that no person shall enjoy any pleasure which they think wrong. But if the principle of the pretension be admitted, no one can reasonably object to its being acted on in the sense of the majority, or other preponderating power in the country; and all persons must be ready to conform to the idea of a Christian commonwealth, as understood by the early settlers in New England, if a religious profession similar to theirs should ever succeed in regaining its lost ground, as religions supposed to be declining have so often been known to do.

To imagine another contingency, perhaps more likely to be realized than the one last mentioned. There is confessedly a strong tendency in the modern world towards a democratic constitution of society, accompanied or not by popular political institutions. It is affirmed that in the country where this tendency is most completely realized—where both society and the government are most democratic—the United States—the feeling of the majority, to whom any appearance of a more showy or costly style of living than they can hope to rival is disagreeable, operates as a tolerably effectual sumptuary law, and that in many parts of the Union it is really difficult for a person possessing a very large income to find any mode of spending it which will not incur popular disapprobation. Though such statements as these are doubtless much exaggerated as a representation of existing facts, the state of things they describe is not only a conceivable and possible, but a probable result of democratic feeling, combined with the notion that the public has a right to a veto on the manner in which individuals shall spend their incomes. We have only further to suppose a considerable diffusion of Socialist opinions, and it may become infamous in the eyes of the majority to possess more property than some very small amount, or any income not earned by manual labor. Opinions similar in principle to these already prevail widely among the artisan class, and weigh oppressively on those who are amenable to the opinion chiefly of that class, namely, its own members. It is known that the bad workmen who form the majority of the operatives in many branches of industry, are decidedly of opinion that bad workmen ought to receive the same wages as good, and that no one ought to be allowed, through piecework or otherwise, to earn by superior skill or industry more than others can without it. And they employ a moral police, which occasionally becomes a physical one, to deter skillful workmen from receiving, and employers from giving, a larger remuneration for a more useful service. If the public have any jurisdiction over private concerns, I cannot see that these people are in fault, or that any individual's particular public can be blamed for asserting the same authority over his individual conduct which the general public asserts over people in general.

But, without dwelling upon supposititious cases, there are, in our own day, gross usurpations upon the liberty of private life actually practiced, and still greater ones threatened with some expectation of success, and opinions propounded which assert an unlimited right in the public not only to prohibit by law everything which it thinks wrong, but, in order to get at what it thinks wrong, to prohibit a number of things which it admits to be innocent.

Under the name of preventing intemperance, the people of one English colony, and of nearly half the United States, have been interdicted by law from making any use whatever of fermented drinks, except for medical purposes: for prohibition of their sale is in fact, as it is intended to be, prohibition of their use. And though the impracticability of executing the law has caused its repeal in several of the States which had adopted it, including the one from which it derives its name, an attempt has notwithstanding been commenced, and is prosecuted with considerable zeal by many of the professed philanthropists, to agitate for a similar law in this country. The association, or "Alliance" as it terms itself, which has been formed for this purpose, has acquired some notoriety through the publicity given to a correspondence between its secretary and one of the very few English public men who hold that a politician's opinions ought to be founded on principles. Lord Stanley's share in this correspondence is calculated to strengthen the hopes already built on him, by those who know how rare such qualities as are manifested in some of his public appearances unhappily are among those who figure in political life. The organ of the Alliance, who would "deeply deplore the recognition of any principle which could be wrested to justify bigotry and persecution," undertakes to point out the "broad and impassable barrier" which divides such principles from those of the association. "All matters relating to thought, opinion, conscience, appear to me," he says "to be without the sphere of legislation; all pertaining to social act, habit, relation, subject only to a discretionary power vested in the State itself, and not in the individual, to be within it." No mention is made of a third class, different from either of these, viz., acts and habits which are not social, but individual; although it is to this class, surely, that the act of drinking fermented liquors belongs. Selling fermented liquors, however, is trading, and trading is a social act. But the infringement complained of is not on the liberty of the seller, but on that of the buyer and consumer; since the State might just as well forbid him to drink wine as purposely make it impossible for him to obtain it. The secretary, however, says, "I claim, as a citizen, a right to legislate whenever my social rights are invaded by the social act of another." And now for the definition of these 'social rights.' "If anything invades my social rights, certainly the traffic in strong drink does. It destroys my primary right of security, by constantly creating and stimulating social disorder. It invades my right of equality, by deriving a profit from the creation of a misery I am taxed to support. It impedes my right to free moral and intellectual development, by surrounding my path with dangers, and by weakening and demoralizing society, from which I have a right to claim mutual aid and intercourse." A theory of 'social rights' the like of which probably never before found its way into distinct language: being nothing short of this— that it is the absolute social right of every individual, that every other individual shall act in every respect exactly as he ought; that whosoever fails thereof in the smallest particular violates my social right, and entitles me to demand from the legislature the removal of the grievance. So monstrous a principle is far more dangerous than any single interference with liberty; there is no violation of liberty which it would not justify; it acknowledges no right to any freedom whatever, except perhaps to that of holding opinions in secret, without ever disclosing them: for, the moment an opinion which I consider noxious passes anyone's lips, it invades all the 'social rights' attributed to me by the Alliance. The doctrine ascribes to all mankind a vested interest in each other's moral, intellectual, and even physical perfection, to be defined by each claimant according to his own standard.

Another important example of illegitimate interference with the rightful liberty of the individual, not simply threatened, but long since carried into triumphant effect, is Sabbatarian legislation. Without doubt, abstinence on one day in the week, so far as the exigencies of life permit, from the usual daily occupation, though in no respect religiously binding on any except Jews, is a highly beneficial custom. And inasmuch as this custom cannot be observed without a general consent to that effect among the industrious classes, therefore, in so far as some persons by working may impose the same necessity on others, it may be allowable and right that the law should guarantee to each the observance by others of the custom, by suspending the greater operations of industry on a particular day. But this justification, grounded on the direct interest which others have in each individual's observance of the practice, does not apply to the self-chosen occupations in which a person may think fit to employ his leisure; nor does it hold good, in the smallest degree, for legal restrictions on amusements. It is true that the amusement of some is the day's work of others; but the pleasure, not to say the useful recreation, of many, is worth the labor of a few, provided the occupation is freely chosen, and can be freely resigned. The operatives are perfectly right in thinking that if all worked on Sunday, seven days' work would have to be given for six days' wages; but so long as the great mass of employments are suspended, the small number who for the enjoyment of others must still work, obtain a proportional increase of earnings; and they are not obliged to follow those occupations if they prefer leisure to emolument. If a further remedy is sought, it might be found in the establishment by custom of a holiday on some other day of the week for those particular classes of persons. The only ground, therefore, on which restrictions on Sunday amusements can be defended, must be that they are religiously wrong; a motive of legislation which can never be too earnestly protested against. *"Deorum injuriae Diis curae."* It remains to be proved that society or any of its officers holds a commission from on high to avenge any supposed offense to Omnipotence, which is not also a wrong to our fellow-creatures. The notion that it is one man's duty that another should be religious, was the foundation of all the religious persecutions ever perpetrated, and, if admitted, would fully justify them. Though the feeling which breaks out in the repeated attempts to stop railways traveling on Sunday, in the resistance to the opening of museums, and the like, has not the cruelty of the old persecutors, the state of mind indicated by it is fundamentally the same. It is a determination not to tolerate others in doing what is permitted by their religion, because it is not permitted by the persecutor's religion. It is a belief that God not only abominates the act of the misbeliever, but will not hold us guiltless if we leave him unmolested.

I cannot refrain from adding to these examples of the little account commonly made of human liberty, the language of downright persecution which breaks out from the press of this country whenever it feels called on to notice the remarkable phenomenon of Mormonism. Much might be said on the unexpected and instructive fact that an alleged new revelation, and a religion founded on it, the product of palpable imposture, not even supported by the *prestige* of extraordinary qualities in its founder, is believed by hundreds of thousands, and has been made the foundation of a society, in the age of newspapers, railways, and the electric telegraph. What here concerns us is, that this religion, like other and better religions, has its martyrs: that its prophet and founder was, for his teaching, put to death by a mob; that others of its adherents lost their lives by the same lawless violence; that they were forcibly expelled, in a body, from the country in which they first grew up; while, now that they have been chased into a solitary recess in the midst of a desert, many in this country openly declare that it would be right (only that it is not convenient) to send an expedition against them, and compel them by force to conform to the opinions of other people. The article of the Mormonite doctrine which is the chief provocative to the antipathy which thus breaks through the ordinary restraints of religious tolerance, is its sanction of polygamy; which, though permitted to Mohammedans, and Hindoos, and Chinese, seems to excite unquenchable animosity when practiced by persons who speak English and profess to be a kind of Christians. No one has a deeper disapprobation than I have of this Mormon institution; both for other reasons, and because, far from being in any way countenanced by the principle of liberty, it is a direct infraction of that principle, being a mere riveting of the chains of one half of the community, and an emancipation of the other from reciprocity of obligation towards them. Still, it must be remembered that this relation is as much voluntary on the part of the women concerned in it, and who may be deemed the sufferers by it, as is the case with any other form of the marriage institution; and however surprising this fact may appear, it has its explanation in the common ideas and customs of the world, which teaching women to think marriage the one thing needful, make it intelligible that many a woman should prefer being one of several wives, to not being a wife at all. Other countries are not asked to recognize such unions, or release any portion of their inhabitants from their own laws on the score of Mormonite opinions. But when the dissentients have conceded to the hostile sentiments of others far more than could justly be demanded; when they have left the countries to which their doctrines were unacceptable, and established themselves in a remote corner of the earth, which they have been the first to render habitable to human beings; it is difficult to see on what principles but those of tyranny they can be prevented from living there under what laws they please, provided they commit no aggression on other nations, and allow perfect freedom of departure to those who are dissatisfied with their ways. A recent writer, in some respects of considerable merit, proposes (to use his own words) not a crusade, but a *civilisade,* against this polygamous community, to put an end to what seems to him a retrograde step in civilization. It also appears so to me, but I am not aware that any community has a right to force another to be civilized. So long as the sufferers by the bad law do not invoke assistance from other communities, I cannot admit that persons entirely unconnected with them ought to step in and require that a condition of things with which all who are directly interested appear to be satisfied, should be put an end to because it is a scandal to persons some thousands of miles distant, who have no part or concern in it. Let them send missionaries, if they please, to preach against it; and let them, by any fair means (of which silencing the teachers is not one), oppose the progress of similar doctrines among their own people. If civilization has got the better of barbarism when barbarism had the world to itself, it is too much to profess to be afraid lest barbarism, after having been fairly got under, should revive and conquer civilization. A civilization that can thus succumb to its vanquished enemy, must first have become so degenerate, that neither its appointed priests and teachers, nor anybody else, has the capacity, or will take the trouble, to stand up for it. If this be so, the sooner such a civilization receives notice to quit the better. It can only go on from bad to worse, until destroyed and regenerated (like the Western Empire) by energetic barbarians.

KARL MARX

(1818-1883)

Karl Marx's philosophy rejects the individualism found in the writing of Locke and Mill. Yet unlike the Stalinist practices carried out under his name, Marx himself did not wish to sacrifice the individual to the interests of the state. Indeed, he diagnoses the ills suffered by alienated individuals when the state functions improperly. Marx's essay prompts us to ask whether individualism is not itself a social product of alienation. If, as Mead and others have shown, the origin of the self is truly social, then perhaps it is only a sick society that individuates the self so thoroughly that the self forgets its origins and fancies itself utterly autonomous. How could this happen?

One of the basic Marxian insights can be explicated in terms of a dialectic of means and ends: men use their agreements with one another and their development of technology in order to better the lot of each and every individual. The political-economic machinery is first conceived as a tool to further the ends of man. But as the political-economic machinery undergoes historical development, it may reach a point at which, like the Frankenstein monster, it runs amok. Though the economic rampage is less dramatically visible than Frankenstein's, especially if you are shielded from poverty, the effects are similar: what was first conceived as a tool for the ends of mankind transforms itself into an autonomous force that turns on man and often uses men as its own tools. Man comes to serve the machine rather than the reverse. In this subservient state people naturally become alienated.

Marx details four forms of alienation: the individual's alienation from nature, from himself, from his species being, and from other men. Marx's analysis of alienation from species being (**Gattungs-wesen**) is perhaps the most difficult to understand, yet it is most important as Marx's reply to individualism. The other three forms of alienation can be understood and experienced within the context of individualism, but from that starting point the very idea of species being sounds somewhat obscure if not mystical. The concept of species being is an alternative to individualism. Marx is talking about feeling oneself a part of a whole rather than an atomic unit standing against the whole, or even joined to the whole by some artificial contract. This sense of being part of a whole is very important to Marx's argument, and his analysis of the third form of alienation is also an analysis of why we may find his argument difficult to comprehend. The following paragraph contains a closer explication to which you may want to return if Marx's text remains obscure.

Marx develops the third form of alienation from the first two: "In estranging from man (1) nature, and (2) himself, his own active functions, his life-activity, estranged labour estranges the **species** from man. It turns for him the **life of the species** into a means of individual life." The concept of species being has its origins in the theology of Ludwig Feuerbach and the social philosophy of Moses Hess. Feuerbach used the idea in arguing that religion is the result of man's projection of his own perfections upon another being he chooses to call God; because no single man represents all human perfections, the collective projection is the species being of man. Hess, on the other hand, argued the specifically social connotations of the concept of species being: to be truly human, man must see himself not as an isolated individual but as a collaborator in a common task of working together in a productive community. Marx combines the ideas of Feuerbach and Hess: "First it [estranged labor] estranges the life of the species and individual life, and secondly it makes individual life in its abstract form [as isolated and atomic] the purpose of the life of the species, likewise in its abstract and estranged form [namely, as a mere totality or aggregate of those atoms]." The first point derives from Feuerbach's analysis of man's separation of the life of the species from individual life through the projection of man's species being upon God; the second from Hess' social analysis of the concept of species-being. The two strands of the concept correspond to their immediate genesis from the first two aspects of alienation: man's alienation from nature corresponds to the spiritualization of man in religion, to which Feuerbach objected; second, man's alienation from himself turns out to be his failure to attain that social existence which, Hess and Marx both say, constitutes the true essence of man. To the extent that man is trapped in estranged labor, he is no better than an animal who works only to satisfy his own, immediate, individual needs. In a nonalienated society, however, men should be able to realize their species being in two senses. First, they will work together in "the working up of the objective world," a sensuous, concrete process that marks man's return from the alienation of a religion that worships a transcendent God. Second, the process of working up inorganic nature differs from animal effort in that each member of the community sees his effort as serving the conscious ends of the whole community. Finally, the two points with their two sets of two origins attain a uniquely Marxian synthesis in the idea: "Through and because of this production, nature appears as **his** work and his reality. The object of labour is, therefore, the **objectification of man's species life:** for he duplicates himself not only, as in consciousness, intellectually, but also actively, in reality, and therefore he contemplates himself in a world that he has created."

Marx saw man as potentially inhabiting a world of his own creation, a world from which he would not be alienated, a world in which he and his products would constitute a historical dialectic of human self-creation and self-expression. For Marx the historical development of social relations meant the historical development of man, for, as he put it in his theses on Feuerbach, "the human essence is no abstraction inherent in each single individual. In its reality it is the ensemble of social relations." This historicist view of man is analogous to the existentialist philosophy of the individual man as self-creative. But for Marx the creative subject must be mankind and not individual man. It is just this view of mankind as historically creative that underlies such ideas as Wilhelm Reich's theory of the historical development of the human unconscious.

ON ALIENATION

We have proceeded from the premises of political economy. We have accepted its language and its laws. We presupposed private property, the separation of labour, capital and land, and of wages, profit of capital and rent of land—likewise division of labour, competition, the concept of exchange-value, etc. On the basis of political economy itself, in its own words, we have shown that the worker sinks to the level of a commodity and becomes indeed the most wretched of commodities; that the wretchedness of the worker is in inverse proportion to the power and magnitude of his production; that the necessary result of competition is the accumulation of capital in a few hands, and thus the restoration of monopoly in a more terrible form; that finally the distinction between capitalist and land-rentier, like that between the tiller of the soil and the factory-worker, disappears and that the whole of society must fall apart into the two classes—the property-*owners* and the propertiless *workers*.

Political economy proceeds from the fact of private property, but it does not explain it to us. It expresses in general, abstract formulae the *material* process through which private property actually passes, and these formulae it then takes for *laws*. It does not *comprehend* these laws—i.e., it does not demonstrate how they arise from the very nature of private property. Political economy does not disclose the source of the division between labour and capital, and between capital and land. When, for example, it defines the relationship of wages to profit, it takes the interest of the capitalists to be the ultimate cause; i.e., it takes for granted what it is supposed to evolve. Similarly, competition comes in everywhere. It is explained from external circumstances. As to how far these external and apparently fortuitous circumstances are but the expression of a necessary course of development, political economy teaches us nothing. We have seen how, to it, exchange itself appears to be a fortuitous fact. The only wheels which political economy sets in motion are *avarice* and the *war amongst the avaricious—competition*.

Precisely because political economy does not grasp the connections within the movement, it was possible to counterpose, for instance, the doctrine of competition to the doctrine of monopoly, the doctrine of craft-liberty to the doctrine of the corporation, the doctrine of the division of landed property to the doctrine of the big estate—for competition, craft-liberty and the division of landed property were explained and comprehended only as fortuitous, premeditated and violent consequences of monopoly, the corporation, and feudal property, not as their necessary, inevitable and natural consequences.

Now, therefore, we have to grasp the essential connection between pri-

ON ALIENATION From Karl Marx, *The Economic and Philosophic Manuscripts of 1844,* Foreign Languages Publishing House, Moscow.

vate property, avarice, and the separation of labour, capital and landed property; between exchange and competition, value and the devaluation of men, monopoly and competition, etc.; the connection between this whole estrangement and the *money*-system.

Do not let us go back to a fictitious primordial condition as the political economist does, when he tries to explain. Such a primordial condition explains nothing. He merely pushes the question away into a grey nebulous distance. He assumes in the form of fact, of an event, what he is supposed to deduce—namely, the necessary relationship between two things—between, for example, division of labour and exchange. Theology in the same way explains the origin of evil by the fall of man: that is, it assumes as a fact, in historical form, what has to be explained.

We proceed from an *actual* economic fact.

The worker becomes all the poorer the more wealth he produces, the more his production increases in power and range. The worker becomes an ever cheaper commodity the more commodities he creates. With the *increasing value* of the world of things proceeds in direct proportion the *devaluation* of the world of men. Labour produces not only commodities: it produces itself and the worker as a *commodity*—and does so in the proportion in which it produces commodities generally.

This fact expresses merely that the object which labour produces—labour's product—confronts it as *something alien,* as a *power independent* of the producer. The product of labour is labour which has been congealed in an object, which has become material: it is the *objectification* of labour. Labour's realisation is its objectification. In the conditions dealt with by political economy this realisation of labour appears as *loss of reality* for the workers; objectification as *loss of the object* and *object-bondage;* appropriation as *estrangement,* as *alienation.*[1]

So much does labour's realisation appear as loss of reality that the worker loses reality to the point of starving to death. So much does objectification appear as loss of the object that the worker is robbed of the objects most necessary not only for his life but for his work. Indeed, labour itself becomes an object which he can get hold of only with the greatest effort and with the most irregular interruptions. So much does the appropriation of the object appear as estrangement that the more objects the worker produces the fewer can he possess and the more he falls under the dominion of his product, capital.

All these consequences are contained in the definition that the worker is related to the *product of his labour* as to an *alien* object. For on this premise it is clear that the more the worker spends himself, the more powerful the alien objective world becomes which he creates over-against himself, the poorer he himself—his inner world—becomes, the less belongs to him

---

[1] Marx uses two terms, *Entfremdung* and *Entäusserung,* both of which are often translated simply as "alienation." The present translation has the merit of distinguishing between the two, translating *Entfremdung* quite literally as "estrangement" and *Entäusserung* as "alienation."—J.A.O.

as his own. It is the same in religion. The more man puts into God, the less he retains in himself. The worker puts his life into the object; but now his life no longer belongs to him but to the object. Hence, the greater this activity, the greater is the worker's lack of objects. Whatever the product of his labour is, he is not. Therefore the greater this product, the less is he himself. The *alienation* of the worker in his product means not only that his labour becomes an object, an *external* existence, but that it exists *outside him,* independently, as something alien to him, and that it becomes a power on its own confronting him; it means that the life which he has conferred on the object confronts him as something hostile and alien.

Let us now look more closely at the *objectification,* at the production of the worker; and therein at the *estrangement,* the *loss* of the object, his product.

The worker can create nothing without *nature,* without the *sensuous external world.* It is the material on which his labour is manifested, in which it is active, from which and by means of which it produces.

But just as nature provides labour with the *means of life* in the sense that labour cannot *live* without objects on which to operate, on the other hand, it also provides the *means of life* in the more restricted sense—i.e., the means for the physical subsistence of the *worker* himself.

Thus the more the worker by his labour *appropriates* the external world, sensuous nature, the more he deprives himself of *means of life* in the double respect: first, that the sensuous external world more and more ceases to be an object belonging to his labour—to be his labour's *means of life;* and secondly, that it more and more ceases to be *means of life* in the immediate sense, means for the physical subsistence of the worker.

Thus in this double respect the worker becomes a slave of his object, first, in that he receives an *object of labour,* i.e., in that he receives *work;* and secondly, in that he receives *means of subsistence.* Therefore, it enables him to exist, first, as a *worker;* and, second, as a *physical subject.* The extremity of this bondage is that it is only as a *worker* that he continues to maintain himself as a *physical subject,* and that it is only as a *physical subject* that he is a *worker.*

(The laws of political economy express the estrangement of the worker in his object thus: the more the worker produces, the less he has to consume; the more values he creates, the more valueless, the more unworthy he becomes; the better formed his product, the more deformed becomes the worker; the more civilised his object, the more barbarous becomes the worker; the mightier labour becomes, the more powerless becomes the worker; the more ingenious labour becomes, the duller becomes the worker and the more he becomes nature's bondsman).

Political economy conceals the estrangement inherent in the nature of labour by not considering the direct relationship between the worker (labour) *and production.* It is true that labour produces for the rich wonderful things—but for the worker it produces privation. It produces palaces—but for the worker, hovels. It produces beauty—but for the worker, deformity. It replaces labour by machines—but some of the workers it throws back to a barbarous type of labour, and the other workers it turns into machines. It produces intelligence—but for the worker idiocy, cretinism.

The direct relationship of labour to its produce is the relationship of the worker to the objects of his production. The relationship of the man of means to the objects of production and to production itself is only a *consequence* of this first relationship—and confirms it. We shall consider this other aspect later.

When we ask, then, what is the essential relationship of labour we are asking about the relationship of the *worker* to production.

Till now we have been considering the estrangement, the alienation of the worker only in one of its aspects, i.e., the worker's *relationship to the products of his labour*. But the estrangement is manifested not only in the result but in the *act of production*—within the *producing activity* itself. How would the worker come to face the product of his activity as a stranger, were it not that in the very act of production he was estranging himself from himself? The product is after all but the summary of the activity, of production. If then the product of labour is alienation, production itself must be active alienation, the alienation of activity, the activity of alienation. In the estrangement of the object of labour is merely summarised the estrangement, the alienation, in the activity of labour itself.

What, then, constitutes the alienation of labour?

First, the fact that labour is *external* to the worker, i.e., it does not belong to his essential being; that in his work, therefore, he does not affirm himself but denies himself, does not feel content but unhappy, does not develop freely his physical and mental energy but mortifies his body and ruins his mind. The worker therefore only feels himself outside his work, and in his work feels outside himself. He is at home when he is not working, and when he is working he is not at home. His labour is therefore not voluntary, but coerced; it is *forced labour*. It is therefore not the satisfaction of a need; it is merely a *means* to satisfy needs external to it. Its alien character emerges clearly in the fact that as soon as no physical or other compulsion exists, labour is shunned like the plague. External labour, labour in which man alienates himself, is a labour of self-sacrifice, of mortification. Lastly, the external character of labour for the worker appears in the fact that it is not his own, but someone else's, that it does not belong to him, that in it he belongs, not to himself, but to another. Just as in religion the spontaneous activity of the human imagination, of the human brain and the human heart, operates independently of the individual—that is, operates on him as an alien, divine or diabolical activity—in the same way the worker's activity is not his spontaneous activity. It belongs to another; it is the loss of his self.

As a result, therefore, man (the worker) no longer feels himself to be freely active in any but his animal functions—eating, drinking, procreating, or at most in his dwelling and in dressing-up, etc.; and in his human functions he no longer feels himself to be anything but an animal. What is animal becomes human and what is human becomes animal.

Certainly eating, drinking, procreating, etc., are also genuinely human functions. But in the abstraction which separates them from the sphere of all other human activity and turns them into sole and ultimate ends, they are animal.

We have considered the act of estranging practical human activity, labour, in two of its aspects. (1) The relation of the worker to the *product of labour* as an alien object exercising power over him. This relation is at the same time the relation to the sensuous external world, to the objects of nature as an alien world antagonistically opposed to him. (2) The relation of labour to the *act of production* within the *labour* process. This relation is the relation of the worker to his own activity as an alien activity not belonging to him; it is activity as suffering, strength as weakness, begetting as emasculating, the worker's *own* physical and mental energy, his personal life or what is life other than activity—as an activity which is turned against him, neither depends on nor belongs to him. Here we have *self-estrangement,* as we had previously the estrangement of the *thing.*

We have yet a third aspect of *estranged labour* to deduce from the two already considered.

Man is a species being, not only because in practice and in theory he adopts the species as his object (his own as well as those of other things), but—and this is only another way of expressing it—but also because he treats himself as the actual, living species; because he treats himself as a *universal* and therefore a free being.

The life of the species, both in man and in animals, consists physically in the fact that man (like the animal) lives on inorganic nature; and the more universal man is compared with an animal, the more universal is the sphere of inorganic nature on which he lives. Just as plants, animals, stones, the air, light, etc., constitute a part of human consciousness in the realm of theory, partly as objects of natural science, partly as objects of art—his spiritual inorganic nature, spiritual nourishment which he must first prepare to make it palatable and digestible—so too in the realm of practice they constitute a part of human life and human activity. Physically man lives only on these products of nature, whether they appear in the form of food, heating, clothes, a dwelling, or whatever it may be. The universality of man is in practice manifested precisely in the universality which makes all nature his *inorganic* body—both inasmuch as nature is (1) his direct means of life, and (2) the material, the object, and the instrument of his life-activity. Nature is man's *inorganic body*—nature, that is, in so far as it is not itself the human body. Man *lives* on nature—means that nature is his *body,* with which he must remain in continuous intercourse if he is not to die. That man's physical and spiritual life is linked to nature means simply that nature is linked to itself, for man is a part of nature.

In estranging from man (1) nature, and (2) himself, his own active functions, his life-activity, estranged labour estranges the *species* from man. It turns for him the *life of the species* into a means of individual life. First it estranges the life of the species and individual life, and secondly it makes individual life in its abstract form the purpose of the life of the species, likewise in its abstract and estranged form.

For in the first place labour, *life-activity, productive life* itself, appears to man merely as a *means* of satisfying a need—the need to maintain the physical existence. Yet the productive life is the life of the species. It is life-engendering life. The whole character of a species—its species character —is contained in the character of its life-activity; and free, conscious activity is man's species character. Life itself appears only as a *means to life.*

The animal is immediately identical with its life-activity. It does not distinguish itself from it. It is *its life-activity.* Man makes his life-activity itself the object of his will and of his consciousness. He has conscious life-activity. It is not a determination with which he directly merges. Conscious life-activity directly distinguishes man from animal life-activity. It is just because of this that he is a species being. Or it is only because he is a species being that he is a Conscious Being, i.e., that his own life is an object for him. Only because of that is his activity free activity. Estranged labour reverses this relationship, so that it is just because man is a conscious being that he makes his life-activity, his *essential* being, a mere means to his *existence.*

In creating an *objective world* by his practical activity, in *working-up* inorganic nature, man proves himself a conscious species being, i.e., as a being that treats the species as its own essential being, or that treats itself as a species being. Admittedly animals also produce. They build themselves nests, dwellings, like the bees, beavers, ants, etc. But an animal only produces what it immediately needs for itself or its young. It produces onesidedly, whilst man produces universally. It produces only under the dominion of immediate physical need, whilst man produces even when he is free from physical need and only truly produces in freedom therefrom. An animal produces only itself, whilst man reproduces the whole of nature. An animal's product belongs immediately to its physical body, whilst man freely confronts his product. An animal forms things in accordance with the standard and the need of the species to which it belongs, whilst man knows how to produce in accordance with the standard of every species, and knows how to apply everywhere the inherent standard to the object. Man therefore also forms things in accordance with the laws of beauty.

It is just in the working-up of the objective world, therefore, that man first really proves himself to be a *species being.* This production is his active species life. Through and because of this production, nature appears as *his* work and his reality. The object of labour is, therefore, the *objectification of man's species life:* for he duplicates himself not only, as in consciousness, intellectually, but also actively, in reality, and therefore he contemplates himself in a world that he has created. In tearing away from man the object of his production, therefore, estranged labour tears from him his *species life,* his real species objectivity, and transforms his advantage over animals into the disadvantage that his inorganic body, nature, is taken from him.

Similarly, in degrading spontaneous activity, free activity, to a means, estranged labour makes man's species life a means to his physical existence.

The consciousness which man has of his species is thus transformed by estrangement in such a way that the species life becomes for him a means.

Estranged labour turns thus:

(3) *Man's species being,* both nature and his spiritual species property, into a being *alien* to him, into a *means* to his *individual existence.* It estranges man's own body from him, as it does external nature and his spiritual essence, his *human* being.

(4) An immediate consequence of the fact that man is estranged from the product of his labour, from his life-activity, from his species being is the *estrangement of man* from *man.* If a man is confronted by himself, he is confronted by the *other* man. What applies to a man's relation to his work, to the product of his labour and to himself, also holds of a man's relation to the other man, and to the other man's labour and object of labour.

In fact, the proposition that man's species nature is estranged from him means that one man is estranged from the other, as each of them is from man's essential nature.[2]

---

[2] Species nature (and earlier species being)—*Gattungswesen:* man's essential nature—*menschlichen Wesen.*

The following short passages from Feuerbach's *Essence of Christianity* may help readers to understand the ideological background to this part of Marx's thought, and, incidentally, to see how Marx accepted but infused with new content concepts made current by Feuerbach as well as by Hegel and the political economists:

"What is this essential difference between man and the brute? . . . Consciousness—but consciousness in the strict sense; for the consciousness implied in the feeling of self as an individual in discrimination by the senses, in the perception and even judgment of outward things according to definite sensible signs, cannot be denied to the brutes. Consciousness in the strictest sense is present only in a being to whom his species, his essential nature, is an object of thought. The brute is indeed conscious of himself as an individual—and he has accordingly the feeling of self as the common centre of successive sensations—but not as a species. . . . In practical life we have to do with individuals; in science, with species. . . . But only a being to whom his own species, his own nature, is an object of thought, can make the essential nature of other things or beings an object of thought. . . . The brute has only a simple, man a twofold life; in the brute, the inner life is one with the outer. Man has both an inner and an outer life. The inner life of man is the life which has relation to his species—to his general, as distinguished from his individual nature. . . . The brute can exercise no function which has relation to its species without another individual external to itself; but man can perform the functions of thought and speech, which strictly imply such a relation, apart from another individual. . . . Man is in fact at once I and Thou; he can put himself in the place of another, for this reason, that to him his species, his essential nature, and not merely his individuality, is an object of thought. . . . An object to which a subject essentially, necessarily relates, is nothing else than this subject's own, but objective nature. . . .

"The relation of the sun to the earth is, therefore, at the same time a relation of the earth to itself, or to its own nature, for the measure of the size and of the intensity of light which the sun possesses as the object of the earth, is the measure

The estrangement of man, and in fact every relationship in which man stands to himself, is first realised and expressed in the relationship in which a man stands to other men.

Hence within the relationship of estranged labour each man views the other in accordance with the standard and the position in which he finds himself as a worker.

We took our departure from a fact of political economy—the estrangement of the worker and his production. We have formulated the concept of this fact—*estranged, alienated* labour. We have analysed this concept—hence analysing merely a fact of political economy.

Let us now see, further, how in real life the concept of estranged, alienated labour must express and present itself.

If the product of labour is alien to me, if it confronts me as an alien power, to whom, then, does it belong?

If my own activity does not belong to me, if it is an alien, a coerced activity, to whom, then, does it belong?

To a being *other* than me.

Who is this being?

The *gods?* To be sure, in the earliest times the principal production (for example, the building of temples, etc., in Egypt, India and Mexico) appears to be in the service of the gods, and the product belongs to the gods. However, the gods on their own were never the lords of labour. No more was *nature.* And what a contradiction it would be if, the more man subjugated nature by his labour and the more the miracles of the gods were rendered superfluous by the miracles of industry, the more man were to renounce the joy of production and the enjoyment of the produce in favour of these powers.

The *alien* being, to whom labour and the produce of labour belongs, in whose service labour is done and for whose benefit the produce of labour is provided, can only be *man* himself.

If the product of labour does not belong to the worker, if it confronts him as an alien power, this can only be because it belongs to some *other man than the worker.* If the worker's activity is a torment to him, to another it must be *delight* and his life's joy. Not the gods, not nature, but only man himself can be this alien power over man.

We must bear in mind the above-stated proposition that man's relation to himself only becomes *objective* and *real* for him through his relation to the other man. Thus, if the product of his labour, his labour *objectified,* is for him an *alien,* hostile, powerful object independent of him, then his position towards it is such that someone else is master of this object, some-

---

of the distance, which determines the peculiar nature of the earth. . . . In the object which he contemplates, therefore, man becomes acquainted with himself. . . . The power of the object over him is therefore the power of his own nature."

(*The Essence of Christianity,* by Ludwig Feuerbach, translated from the second German edition by Marian Evans, London, 1854, pp. 1–5.)—*Ed.*

one who is alien, hostile, powerful, and independent of him. If his own activity is to him an unfree activity, then he is treating it as activity performed in the service, under the dominion, the coercion and the yoke of another man.

Every self-estrangement of man from himself and from nature appears in the relation in which he places himself and nature to men other than and differentiated from himself. For this reason religious self-estrangement necessarily appears in the relationship of the layman to the priests, or again to a mediator, etc., since we are here dealing with the intellectual world. In the real practical world self-estrangement can only become manifest through the real practical relationship to other men. The medium through which estrangement takes place is itself *practical*. Thus through estranged labour man not only engenders his relationship to the object and to the act of production as to powers that are alien and hostile to him; he also engenders the relationship in which other men stand to his production and to his product, and the relationship in which he stands to these other men. Just as he begets his own production as the loss of his reality, as his punishment; just as he begets his own product as a loss, as a product not belonging to him; so he begets the dominion of the one who does not produce over production and over the product. Just as he estranges from himself his own activity, so he confers to the stranger activity which is not his own.

Till now we have only considered this relationship from the standpoint of the worker and later we shall be considering it also from the standpoint of the non-worker.

Through *estranged, alienated labour,* then, the worker produces the relationship to this labour of a man alien to labour and standing outside it. The relationship of the worker to labour engenders the relation to it of the capitalist, or whatever one chooses to call the master of labour. *Private property* is thus the product, the result, the necessary consequence, of *alienated labour,* of the external relation of the worker to nature and to himself.

Private property thus results by analysis from the concept of *alienated labour*—i.e., of *alienated man,* of estranged labour, of estranged life, of *estranged* man.

True, it is as a result of the *movement of private property* that we have obtained the concept of *alienated labour (of alienated life)* from political economy. But on analysis of this concept it becomes clear that though private property appears to be the source, the cause of alienated labour, it is really its consequence, just as the gods *in the beginning* are not the cause but the effect of man's intellectual confusion. Later this relationship becomes reciprocal.

Only at the very culmination of the development of private property does this, its secret, re-emerge, namely, that on the one hand it is the *product* of alienated labour, and that secondly it is the *means* by which labour alienates itself, the *realisation of this alienation.*

This exposition immediately sheds light on various hitherto unsolved conflicts.

(1) Political economy starts from labour as the real soul of production; yet to labour it gives nothing, and to private property everything. From this contradiction Proudhon has concluded in favour of labour and against private property. We understand, however, that this apparent contradiction is the contradiction of *estranged labour* with itself, and that political economy has merely formulated the laws of estranged labour.

We also understand, therefore, that *wages* and *private property* are identical: where the product, the object of labour pays for labour itself, the wage is but a necessary consequence of labour's estrangement, for after all in the wage of labour, labour does not appear as an end in itself but as the servant of the wage. We shall develop this point later, and meanwhile will only deduce some conclusions.

A *forcing-up of wages* (disregarding all other difficulties, including the fact that it would be by force, too, that the higher wages, being an anomaly, could be maintained) would therefore be nothing but *better payment for the slave,* and would not conquer either for the worker or for labour their human status and dignity.

Indeed, even the *equality of wages* demanded by Proudhon only transforms the relationship of the present-day worker to his labour into the relationship of all men to labour. Society is then conceived as an abstract capitalist.

Wages are a direct consequence of estranged labour, and estranged labour is the direct cause of private property. The downfall of the one aspect must therefore mean the downfall of the other.

(2) From the relationship of estranged labour to private property it further follows that the emancipation of society from private property, etc., from servitude, is expressed in the *political* form of the *emancipation of the workers;* not that *their* emancipation alone was at stake but because the emancipation of the workers contains universal human emancipation—and it contains this, because the whole of human servitude is involved in the relation of the worker to production, and every relation of servitude is but a modification and consequence of this relation.

Just as we have found the concept of *private property* from the concept of *estranged, alienated labour* by *analysis,* in the same way every *category* of political economy can be evolved with the help of these two factors; and we shall find again in each category, e.g., trade, competition, capital, money, only a *definite* and *developed expression* of the first foundations.

Before considering this configuration, however, let us try to solve two problems.

(1) To define the general *nature of private property,* as it has arisen as a result of estranged labour, in its relation to *truly human, social property.*

(2) We have accepted the *estrangement of labour,* its *alienation,* as a fact, and we have analysed this fact. How, we now ask, does *man* come to *alienate,* to estrange, *his labour?* How is this estrangement rooted in the nature of human development? We have already gone a long way to the solution of this problem by *transforming* the question as to the *origin of*

private property into the question as to the relation of *alienated labour* to the course of humanity's development. For when one speaks of *private property*, one thinks of being concerned with something external to man. When one speaks of labour, one is directly concerned with man himself. This new formulation of the question already contains its solution.

As to (1): The general nature of private property and its relation to truly human property.

Alienated labour has resolved itself for us into two elements which mutually condition one another, or which are but different expressions of one and the same relationship. *Appropriation* appears as *estrangement*, as *alienation;* and *alienation* appears as *appropriation, estrangement* as true *enfranchisement.*

We have considered the one side—*alienated* labour—in relation to the *worker* himself, i.e., the *relation of alienated labour to itself.* The *property-relation of the non-worker to the worker and to labour* we have found as the product, the necessary outcome of this relation of alienated labour. *Private property,* as the material, summary expression of alienated labour, embraces both relations—the *relation of the worker to work, to the product of his labour and to the non-worker,* and the relation of the *non-worker to the worker and to the product of his labour.*

Having seen that in relation to the worker who *appropriates* nature by means of his labour, this appropriation appears as estrangement, his own spontaneous activity as activity for another and as activity of another, vitality as a sacrifice of life, production of the object as loss of the object to an alien power, to an *alien* person—we shall now consider the relation to the worker, to labour and its object of this person who is *alien* to labour and the worker.

First it has to be noticed, that everything which appears in the worker as an *activity of alienation, of estrangement,* appears in the non-worker as a *state of alienation, of estrangement.*

Secondly, that the worker's *real, practical attitude* in production and to the product (as a state of mind) appears in the non-worker confronting him as a *theoretical* attitude.

Thirdly, the non-worker does everything against the worker which the worker does against himself; but he does not do against himself what he does against the worker.

Let us look more closely at these three relations.[3]

---

[3] At this point the first manuscript breaks off unfinished.

CARL ROGERS and B. F. SKINNER
(1902-   )   (1904-   )

The Marxist challenge to the modern world charges that the means of production have alienated men from themselves, nature, and other men. Since technology has played an increasing role in defining the means of production, technology, and less directly science, have been tools in the alienation of men. According to the Marxist analysis, technology helps make men feel isolated. Yet in his discussion of technology, Fromm declared that "requirements of maximal efficiency lead as a consequence to the requirement of minimal individuality." Erich Fromm and Carl Rogers are both contemporary psychologists in the humanist tradition. They both wish to see man a free, self-actualizing being. Is their humanism equivalent to a libertarian individualism? I think not, but the boundaries are not easy to see. Here, as elsewhere in philosophy, we must guard against a false dichotomy: "monolithic technological state" on the one hand opposed to "free individual" on the other. There is a tendency, if one abhors the dehumanizing influence of a technological monolith, to think that the only defense is a flight into individualism. But if Mead and Marx are right, this flight is only an alienated reaction and not a creative, human response. So rather than simply opposing the individual to the technological state, we must distinguish between the socially situated but free man and the isolated, alienated, technologically determined individual; conversely we must distinguish between social-technological institutions that use rather than serve human beings, and healthy communities that enable the self-actualization of the socially situated person.

Distinctions like these are necessary because otherwise we shall not be able to tell our enemies from our friends. Skinnerian psychology may be an enemy that looks like a friend, precisely because Skinner is so close to the truth that he attracts us, yet far enough away that we may be led down the garden path into a profound historical error. He sees the ills, the high price of modern libertarian individualism. Further, he sees in an unsentimental, detached, and truthful way that men are far more manipulable than they would like to believe. Yet his answer to the ills of individualism lies in manipulating men in nicer ways rather than trying to set them free. The title to his recent and highly publicized book tells all: **Beyond Freedom and Dignity.**

Aside from continuing the debates on technology and on the individual and the state, the following exchange continues the obviously related controversy over freedom and determinism. By this time, after reading Goffman and Laing, the reader should be quite ready to believe what Skinner has to say about the possibility of psychological determinism. Indeed, it is worth asking whether or not Skinner and Rogers are not fighting at the barn door after the horses have fled. They are debating the **possibility** of psychological determinism; Goffman and Laing come close to arguing its present and past actuality. The question then becomes not whether psychological techniques are to be used in manipulating behavior, but whether society at large should remain the master of those techniques of reinforcement or should their control and application rest in the hands of a small part of society, namely, the master psychologists who would replace Plato's philosopher-king at the head of the Republic. This question posed by the following debate is difficult because undoubtedly history has shown that society at large is capable of making some awful blunders. Should we perhaps let some intelligent men help society along on its wayward trek? But who shall they be? How are we to judge their intelligence? Do they embrace the right values, whatever they are? Rogers accuses Skinner of valuing states of being rather than the process of becoming. No matter how ideal a state of being may appear, the denial of becoming amounts to a denial of freedom, that process of self-creation described by Sartre and Marx. Or, to go back to St. Augustine and the predictability of freedom, what would it mean for Skinner to posit freedom as the goal toward which his scientific psychology aimed?

Some Issues Concerning the Control of Human Behavior A Symposium

SKINNER

Science is steadily increasing our power to influence, change, mold—in a word, control—human behavior. It has extended our "understanding" (whatever that may be) so that we deal more successfully with people in nonscientific ways, but it has also identified conditions or variables which can be used to predict and control behavior in a new, and increasingly rigorous, technology. The broad disci-

SOME ISSUES CONCERNING THE CONTROL OF HUMAN BEHAVIOR: A SYMPOSIUM "Some Issues Concerning the Control of Human Behavior: A Symposium," Carl Rogers and B. F. Skinner, in *Science*, Vol. 124, pp. 1057–66, November 30, 1956. Reprinted by permission.

plines of government and economics offer examples of this, but there is special cogency in those contributions of anthropology, sociology, and psychology which deal with individual behavior. Carl Rogers has listed some of the achievements to date in a recent paper.[1]

Those of his examples which show or imply the control of the single organism are primarily due, as we should expect, to psychology. It is the experimental study of behavior which carries us beyond awkward or inaccessible "principles," "factors," and so on, to variables which can be directly manipulated.

It is also, and for more or less the same reasons, the conception of human behavior emerging from an experimental analysis which most directly challenges traditional views. Psychologists themselves often do not seem to be aware of how far they have moved in this direction. But the change is not passing unnoticed by others. Until only recently it was customary to deny the possibility of a rigorous science of human behavior by arguing, either that a lawful science was impossible because man was a free agent, or that merely statistical predictions would always leave room for personal freedom. But those who used to take this line have become most vociferous in expressing their alarm at the way these obstacles are being surmounted.

Now, the control of human behavior has always been unpopular. Any undisguised effort to control usually arouses emotional reactions. We hesitate to admit, even to ourselves, that we are engaged in control, and we may refuse to control, even when this would be helpful, for fear of criticism. Those who have explicitly avowed an interest in control have been roughly treated by history. Machiavelli is the great prototype. As Macaulay said of him, "Out of his surname they coined an epithet for a knave and out of his Christian name a synonym for the devil." There were obvious reasons. The control that Machiavelli analyzed and recommended, like most political control, used techniques that were aversive to the controllee. The threats and punishments of the bully, like those of the government operating on the same plan, are not designed—whatever their success—to endear themselves to those who are controlled. Even when the techniques themselves are not aversive, control is usually exercised for the selfish purposes of the controller and, hence, has indirectly punishing effects upon others.

Man's natural inclination to revolt against selfish control has been exploited to good purpose in what we call the philosophy and literature of democracy. The doctrine of the rights of man has been effective in arousing individuals to concerted action against governmental and religious tyranny. The literature which has had this effect has greatly extended the number of terms in our language which express reactions to the control of men. But the ubiquity and ease of expression of this attitude spells trouble for any science which may give birth to a powerful technology of behavior. Intelligent men and women, dominated by the humanistic philosophy of the past

[1] C. R. Rogers, *Teachers College Record* 57, 316 (1956).

two centuries, cannot view with equanimity what Andrew Hacker has called "the specter of predictable man."[2] Even the statistical or actuarial prediction of human events, such as the number of fatalities to be expected on a holiday weekend, strikes many people as uncanny and evil, while the prediction and control of individual behavior is regarded as little less than the work of the devil. I am not so much concerned here with the political or economic consequences for psychology, although research following certain channels may well suffer harmful effects. We ourselves, as intelligent men and women, and as exponents of Western thoughts, share these attitudes. They have already interfered with the free exercise of a scientific analysis, and their influence threatens to assume more serious proportions.

Three broad areas of human behavior supply good examples. The first of these—*personal control*—may be taken to include person-to-person relationships in the family, among friends, in social and work groups, and in counseling and psychotherapy. Other fields are *education* and *government*. A few examples from each will show how nonscientific preconceptions are affecting our current thinking about human behavior.

Personal Control

People living together in groups come to control one another with a technique which is not inappropriately called "ethical." When an individual behaves in a fashion acceptable to the group, he receives admiration, approval, affection, and many other reinforcements which increase the likelihood that he will continue to behave in that fashion. When his behavior is not acceptable, he is criticized, censured, blamed, or otherwise punished. In the first case the group calls him "good"; in the second, "bad." This practice is so thoroughly ingrained in our culture that we often fail to see that it is a technique of control. Yet we are almost always engaged in such control, even though the reinforcements and punishments are often subtle.

The practice of admiration is an important part of a culture, because behavior which is otherwise inclined to be weak can be set up and maintained with its help. The individual is especially likely to be praised, admired, or loved when he acts for the group in the face of greater danger, for example, or sacrifices himself or his possessions, or submits to prolonged hardship, or suffers martyrdom. These actions are not admirable in any absolute sense, but they require admiration if they are to be strong. Similarly, we admire people who behave in original or exceptional ways, not because such behavior is itself admirable, but because we do not know how to encourage original or exceptional behavior in any other way. The group acclaims independent, unaided behavior in part because it is easier to reinforce than to help.

2 A. Hacker, *Antioch Rev.* 14, 195 (1954).

As long as this technique of control is misunderstood, we cannot judge correctly an environment in which there is less need for heroism, hardship, or independent action. We are likely to argue that such an environment is itself less admirable or produces less admirable people. In the old days, for example, young scholars often lived in undesirable quarters, ate unappetizing or inadequate food, performed unprofitable tasks for a living or to pay for necessary books and materials or publication. Older scholars and other members of the group offered compensating reinforcement in the form of approval and admiration for these sacrifices. When the modern graduate student receives a generous scholarship, enjoys good living conditions, and has his research and publication subsidized, the grounds for evaluation seem to be pulled from under us. Such a student no longer *needs* admiration to carry him over a series of obstacles (no matter how much he may need it for other reasons), and, in missing certain familiar objects of admiration, we are likely to conclude that such *conditions* are less admirable. Obstacles to scholarly work may serve as a useful measure of motivation —and we may go wrong unless some substitute is found but we can scarcely defend a deliberate harassment of the student for this purpose. The productivity of any set of conditions can be evaluated only when we have freed ourselves of the attitudes which have been generated in us as members of an ethical group.

A similar difficulty arises from our use of punishment in the form of censure or blame. The concept of responsibility and the related concepts of foreknowledge and choice are used to justify techniques of control using punishment. Was So-and-So aware of the probable consequences of his action, and was the action deliberate? If so, we are justified in punishing him. But what does this mean? It appears to be a question concerning the efficacy of the contingent relations between behavior and punishing consequences. We punish behavior because it is objectionable to us or the group, but in a minor refinement of rather recent origin we have come to withhold punishment when it cannot be expected to have any effect. If the objectionable consequences of an act were accidental and not likely to occur again, there is no point in punishing. We say that the individual was not "aware of the consequences of his action" or that the consequences were not "intentional." If the action could not have been avoided—if the individual "had no choice"—punishment is also withheld, as it is if the individual is incapable of being changed by punishment because he is of "unsound mind." In all these cases—different as they are—the individual is held "not responsible" and goes unpunished.

Just as we say that it is "not fair" to punish a man for something he could not help doing, so we call it "unfair" when one is rewarded beyond his due or for something he could not help doing. In other words, we also object to wasting *reinforcers* where they are not needed or will do no good. We make the same point with the words *just* and *right*. Thus we have no right to punish the irresponsible, and a man has no right to reinforcers he does not earn or deserve. But concepts of choice, responsibility, justice, and so on, provide a most inadequate analysis of efficient reinforcing and punishing contingencies because they carry a heavy semantic cargo of a quite different sort, which obscures any attempt to clarify controlling practices or to improve techniques. In particular, they fail to prepare us for techniques based on other than aversive techniques of control. Most people would object to forcing prisoners to serve as subjects of dangerous medical experiments, but few object when they are induced to serve by the offer of return privileges—even when the reinforcing effect of these privileges has been created by forcible deprivation. In the traditional scheme the right to refuse guarantees the individual against coercion or an unfair bargain. But to what extent *can* a prisoner refuse under such circumstances?

We need not go so far afield to make the point. We can observe our own attitude toward personal freedom in the way we resent any interference with what we want to do. Suppose we want to buy a car of a particular sort. Then we may object, for example, if our wife urges us to buy a less expensive model and to put the difference into a new refrigerator. Or we may resent it if our neighbor questions our need for such a car or our ability to pay for it. We would certainly resent it if it were illegal to buy such a car (remember Prohibition); and if we find we cannot actually afford it, we may resent governmental control of the price through tariffs and taxes. We resent it if we discover that we cannot get the car because the manufacturer is holding the model in deliberately short supply in order to push a model we do not want. In all this we assert our democratic right to buy the car of our choice. We are well prepared to do so and to resent any restriction on our freedom.

But why do we not ask *why* it is the car of our choice and resent the forces which made it so? Perhaps our favorite toy as a child was a car, of a very different model, but nevertheless bearing the name of the car we now want. Perhaps our favorite TV program is sponsored by the manufacturer of that car. Perhaps we have seen pictures of many beautiful or prestigeful persons driving it—in pleasant or glamorous places. Perhaps the car has been designed with respect to our motivational patterns: the device on the hood is a phallic symbol; or the horsepower has been stepped up to please our competitive spirit in enabling us to pass other cars swiftly (or, as the advertisements say, "safely"). The concept of freedom that has emerged as part of the cultural practice of our group makes little or no provision for recognizing or dealing with these kinds of control. Concepts like "responsibility" and "rights" are scarcely applicable. We are prepared to deal with coercive measures, but we have no traditional recourse with respect to other measures which in the long run (and especially with the help of science) may be much more powerful and dangerous.

Education

The techniques of education were once frankly aversive. The teacher was usually older and stronger than his pupils and was able to "make them learn." This meant that they were not actually taught but were surrounded by a threatening world from which they could escape only by learning. Usually they were left to their own resources in discovering how to do so. Claude Coleman has published a grimly amusing reminder of these older practices.[3] He tells of a school-teacher who published a careful account of his services during 51 years of teaching, during which he administered: ". . . 911,527 blows with a cane; 124,010 with a rod; 20,989 with a ruler; 136,715 with the hand; 10,295 over the mouth; 7,905 boxes on the ear; [and] 1,115,800 slaps on the head. . . ."

Progressive education was a humanitarian effort to substitute positive reinforcement for such aversive measures, but in the search for useful human values in the classroom it has never fully replaced the variables it abandoned. Viewed as a branch of behavioral technology, education remains relatively inefficient. We supplement it, and rationalize it, by admiring the pupil who learns *for himself;* and we often attribute the learning process, or knowledge itself, to something *inside* the individual. We admire behavior which seems to have inner sources. Thus we admire one who *recites* a poem more than one who simply *reads* it. We admire one who *knows* the answer more than one who *knows where to look it up.* We admire the *writer* rather than the *reader.* We admire the arithmetician who can do a problem in his head rather than with a slide rule or calculating machine, or in "original" ways rather than by a direct application of rules. In general we feel that any aid or "crutch"—except those aids to which we are now thoroughly accustomed—reduces the credit due. In Plato's *Phaedrus,* Thamus, the king, attacks the invention of the alphabet on similar grounds! He is afraid "it will produce forgetfulness in the minds of those who learn to use it, because they will not practice their memories. . . ." In other words, he holds it more admirable to remember than to use a memorandum. He also objects that pupils "will read many things without instruction . . . [and] will therefore seem to know many things when they are for the most part ignorant." In the same vein we are today sometimes contemptuous of book learning, but, as educators, we can scarcely afford to adopt this view without reservation.

By admiring the student for knowledge and blaming him for ignorance, we escape some of the responsibility of teaching him. We resist any analysis of the educational process which threatens the notion of inner wisdom or questions the contention that the fault of ignorance lies with the student. More powerful techniques which bring about the same changes in behavior by manipulating *external* variables are decried as brainwashing or thought control. We are quite unprepared to judge *effective* educational measures. As long as only a few pupils learn much of what is taught, we do not worry about uniformity or regimentation. We do not fear the feeble technique; but we should view with dismay a system under which every student

---

[3] C. Coleman, *Bull. Am. Assoc. Univ. Professors* 39, 457 (1953).

learned everything listed in a syllabus—although such a condition is far from unthinkable. Similarly, we do not fear a system which is so defective that the student must *work* for an education; but we are loath to give credit for anything learned without effort—although this could well be taken as an ideal result—and we flatly refuse to give credit if the student already knows what a school teaches.

A world in which people are wise and good without trying, without "having to be," without "choosing to be," could conceivably be a far better world for everyone. In such a world we should not have to "give anyone credit"—we should not need to admire anyone—for being wise and good. From our present point of view we cannot believe that such a world would be admirable. We do not even permit ourselves to imagine what it would be like.

Government

Government has always been the special field of aversive control. The state is frequently defined in terms of the power to punish, and jurisprudence leans heavily upon the associated notion of personal responsibility. Yet it is becoming increasingly difficult to reconcile current practice and theory with these earlier views. In criminology, for example, there is a strong tendency to drop the notion of responsibility in favor of some such alternative as capacity or controllability. But no matter how strongly the facts, or even practical expedience, support such a change, it is difficult to make the change in a legal system designed on a different plan. When governments resort to other techniques (for example, positive reinforcement), the concept of responsibility is no longer relevant and the theory of government is no longer applicable.

The conflict is illustrated by two decisions of the Supreme Court in the 1930's which dealt with, and disagreed on, the definition of control or coercion.[4] The Agricultural Adjustment Act proposed that the Secretary of Agriculture make "rental or benefit payments" to those farmers who agreed to reduce production. The government agreed that the Act would be unconstitutional if the farmer had been *compelled* to reduce production but was not, since he was merely *invited* to do so. Justice Roberts[5] expressed the contrary majority view of the court that "The power to confer or withhold unlimited benefits is the power to coerce or destroy." This recognition of positive reinforcement was withdrawn a few years later in another case in which Justice Cardozo[6] wrote "To hold that motive or temptation is equivalent to coercion is to plunge the law in endless difficulties." We may agree with him, without implying that the proposition is therefore wrong.

[4] P. A. Freund *et al., Constitutional Law: Cases and Other Problems,* vol. I, p. 233 (Little, Brown, Boston, 1954).

[5] *Ibid.*

[6] *Ibid.,* p. 244.

Sooner or later the law must be prepared to deal with all possible techniques of governmental control.

The uneasiness with which we view government (in the broadest possible sense) when it does not use punishment is shown by the reception of my utopian novel, *Walden Two*.[7] This was essentially a proposal to apply a behavioral technology to the construction of a workable, effective, and productive pattern of government. It was greeted with wrathful violence. *Life* magazine called it "a travesty on the good life," and "a menace . . . a triumph of mortmain or the dead hand not envisaged since the days of Sparta . . . a slur upon a name, a corruption of an impulse." Joseph Wood Krutch devoted a substantial part of his book, *The Measure of Man*,[8] to attacking my views and those of the protagonist, Frazier, in the same vein, and Morris Viteles has recently criticized the book in a similar manner in *Science*.[9]—Perhaps the reaction is best expressed in quotation from *The Quest for Utopia* by Negley and Patrick[10]:

"Halfway through this contemporary utopia, the reader may feel sure, as we did, that this is a beautifully ironic satire on what has been called 'behavioral engineering.' The longer one stays in this better world of the psychologist, however, the plainer it becomes that the inspiration is not satiric, but messianic. This is indeed the behaviorally engineered society, and while it was to be expected that sooner or later the principle of psychological conditioning would be made the basis of a serious construction of utopia—Brown anticipated it in *Limanora*—yet not even the effective satire of Huxley is adequate preparation for the shocking horror of the idea when positively presented. Of all the dictatorships espoused by utopists, this is the most profound, and incipient dictators might well find in this utopia a guidebook of political practice."

One would scarcely guess that the authors are talking about a world in which there is food, clothing, and shelter for all, where everyone chooses his own work and works on the average only four hours a day, where music and the arts flourish, where personal relationships develop under the most favorable circumstances, where education prepares every child for the social and intellectual life which lies before him, where—in short—people are truly happy, secure, productive, creative, and forward-looking. What is wrong with it? Only one thing: someone "planned it that way." If these critics had come upon a society in some remote corner of the world which boasted similar advantages, they would undoubtedly have hailed it as providing a pattern we all might well follow—provided that it was clearly the result of a natural process of cultural evolution. Any evidence that intelligence had been used in arriving at this version of the good life would, in

[7] B. F. Skinner, *Walden Two* (Macmillan, New York, 1948).

[8] J. W. Krutch, *The Measure of Man* (Bobbs-Merrill, Indianapolis, 1953).

[9] M. Viteles, *Science* 122, 1167 (1955).

[10] G. Negley and J. M. Patrick, *The Quest for Utopia* (Schuman, New York, 1952).

their eyes, be a serious flaw. No matter if the planner of *Walden Two* diverts none of the proceeds of the community to his own use, no matter if he has no current control or is, indeed, unknown to most of the other members of the community (he planned that, too), somewhere back of it all he occupies the position of prime mover. And this, to the child of the democratic tradition, spoils it all.

The dangers inherent in the control of human behavior are very real. The possibility of the misuse of scientific knowledge must always be faced. We cannot escape by denying the power of a science of behavior or arresting its development. It is no help to cling to familiar philosophies of human behavior simply because they are more reassuring. As I have pointed out elsewhere,[11] the new techniques emerging from a science of behavior must be subject to the explicit countercontrol which has already been applied to earlier and cruder forms. Brute force and deception, for example, are now fairly generally suppressed by ethical practices and by explicit governmental and religious agencies. A similar countercontrol of scientific knowledge in the interests of the group is a feasible and promising possibility. Although we cannot say how devious the course of its evolution may be, a cultural pattern of control and countercontrol will presumably emerge which will be most widely supported because it is most widely reinforcing.

If we cannot foresee all the details of this (as we obviously cannot), it is important to remember that this is true of the critics of science as well. The dire consequences of new techniques of control, the hidden menace in original cultural designs—these need some proof. It is only another example of my present point that the need for proof is so often overlooked. Man has got himself into some pretty fixes, and it is easy to believe that he will do so again. But there is a more optimistic possibility. The slow growth of the methods of science, now for the first time being applied to human affairs, *may* mean a new and exciting phase of human life to which historical analogies will not apply and in which earlier political slogans will not be appropriate. If we are to use the knowledge that a science of behavior is now making available with any hope of success, we must look at human nature as it is brought into focus through the methods of science rather than as it has been presented to us in a series of historical accidents.

If the advent of a powerful science of behavior causes trouble, it will not be because science itself is inimical to human welfare but because older conceptions have not yielded easily or gracefully. We expect resistance to new techniques of control from those who have heavy investments in the old, but we have no reason to help them preserve a series of principles that are not ends in themselves but rather outmoded means to an end. What is needed is a new conception of human behavior which is compatible with the implications of a scientific analysis. All men control and are controlled. The question of government in the broadest possible sense is not how freedom is to be preserved but what kinds of control are to be used and to what

[11] B. F. Skinner, *Trans. N.Y. Acad. Sci.* 17, 547 (1955).

ends. Control must be analyzed and considered in its proper proportions. No one, I am sure, wishes to develop new master-slave relationships or bend the will of the people to despotic rulers in new ways. These are patterns of control appropriate to a world without science. They may well be the first to go when the experimental analysis of behavior comes into its own in the design of cultural practices.

ROGERS

There are, I believe, a number of matters in connection with this important topic on which the authors of this article, and probably a large majority of psychologists, are in agreement. These matters then are not issues as far as we are concerned, and I should like to mention them briefly in order to put them to one side.

Points of Agreement

I am sure we agree that men—as individuals and as societies—have always endeavored to understand, predict, influence, and control human behavior—their own behavior and that of others.

I believe we agree that the behavioral sciences are making and will continue to make increasingly rapid progress in the understanding of behavior, and that as a consequence the capacity to predict and to control behavior is developing with equal rapidity.

I believe we agree that to deny these advances, or to claim that man's behavior cannot be a field of science, is unrealistic. Even though this is not an issue for us, we should recognize that many intelligent men still hold strongly to the view that the actions of men are free in some sense such that scientific knowledge of man's behavior is impossible. Thus Reinhold Niebuhr, the noted theologian, heaps scorn on the concept of psychology as a science of man's behavior and even says, "In any event, no scientific investigation of past behavior can become the basis of predictions of future behavior."[12] So, while this is not an issue for psychologists, we should at least notice in passing that it is an issue for many people.

I believe we are in agreement that the tremendous potential power of a science which permits the production and control of behavior may be misused, and that the possibility of such misuse constitutes a serious threat.

Consequently Skinner and I are in agreement that the whole question of the scientific control of human behavior is a matter with which psychologists and the general public should concern themselves. As Robert Oppenheimer told the American Psychological Association last year[13] the

[12] R. Niebuhr, *The Self and the Dramas of History* (Scribner, New York, 1955), p. 47.

[13] R. Oppenheimer, *Am. Psychol.* 11, 127 (1956).

problems that psychologists will pose for society by their growing ability to control behavior will be much more grave than the problems posed by the ability of physicists to control the reactions of matter. I am not sure whether psychologists generally recognize this. My impression is that by and large they hold a laissez-faire attitude. Obviously Skinner and I do not hold this laissez-faire view, or we would not have written this article.

Points at Issue

With these several points of basic and important agreement, are there then any issues that remain on which there are differences? I believe there are. They can be stated very briefly: Who will be controlled? Who will exercise control? What type of control will be exercised? Most important of all, toward what end or what purpose, or in the pursuit of what value, will control be exercised?

It is on questions of this sort that there exist ambiguities, misunderstandings, and probably deep differences. These differences exist among psychologists, among members of the general public in this country, and among various world cultures. Without any hope of achieving a final resolution of these questions, we can, I believe, put these issues in clearer form.

Some Meanings

To avoid ambiguity and faulty communication, I would like to clarify the meanings of some of the terms we are using.

Behavioral science is a term that might be defined from several angles but in the context of this discussion it refers primarily to knowledge that the existence of certain describable conditions in the human being and/or in his environment is followed by certain describable consequences in his actions.

Prediction means the prior identification of behaviors which then occur. Because it is important in some things I wish to say later, I would point out that one may predict a highly specific behavior, such as an eye blink, or one may predict a class of behaviors. One might correctly predict "avoidant behavior," for example, without being able to specify whether the individual will run away or simply close his eyes.

The word *control* is a very slippery one, which can be used with any one of several meanings. I would like to specify three that seem most important for our present purposes. *Control* may mean: (i) The setting of conditions by B for A, A having no voice in the matter, such that certain predictable behaviors then occur in A. I refer to this as external control. (ii) The setting of conditions by B for A, A giving some degree of consent to these conditions, such that certain predictable behaviors then occur in A. I refer to this as the influence of B on A. (iii) The setting of conditions by A such that certain predictable behaviors then occur in himself. I refer to this as internal control. It will be noted that Skinner lumps together the first two meanings, external control and influence, under the concept of control. I find this confusing.

Usual Concept of Control
of Human Behavior

With the underbrush thus cleared away (I hope), let us review very briefly the various elements that are involved in the usual concept of the control of human behavior as mediated by the behavioral sciences. I am drawing here on the previous writings of Skinner, on his present statements, on the writings of others who have considered in either friendly or antagonistic fashion the meanings that would be involved in such control. I have not excluded the science fiction writers, as reported recently by Vandenberg,[14] since they often show an awareness of the issues involved, even though the methods described are as yet fictional. These then are the elements that seem common to these different concepts of the application of science to human behavior.

1. There must first be some sort of decision about goals. Usually desirable goals are assumed, but sometimes, as in George Orwell's book *1984*, the goal that is selected is an aggrandizement of individual power with which most of us would disagree. In a recent paper Skinner suggests that one possible set of goals to be assigned to the behavioral technology is this: "Let men be happy, informed, skillful, well-behaved and productive."[15] In the first draft of his part of this article, which he was kind enough to show me, he did not mention such definite goals as these, but desired "improved" educational practices, "wiser" use of knowledge in government, and the like. In the final version of his article he avoids even these value-laden terms, and his implicit goal is the very general one that scientific control of behavior is desirable, because it would perhaps bring "a far better world for everyone."

Thus the first step in thinking about the control of human behavior is the choice of goals, whether specific or general. It is necessary to come to terms in some way with the issue, "For what purpose?"

2. A second element is that, whether the end selected is highly specific or is a very general one such as wanting "a better world," we proceed by the methods of science to discover the means to these ends. We continue through further experimentation and investigation to discover more effective means. The method of science is self-correcting in thus arriving at increasingly effective ways of achieving the purpose we have in mind.

3. The third aspect of such control is that as the conditions or methods are discovered by which to reach the goal, some person or some group establishes these conditions and uses these methods, having in one way or another obtained the power to do so.

[14] S. G. Vandenberg, *Am. Psychol.* 11, 339 (1956).

[15] B. F. Skinner, *Am. Scholar* 25, 47 (1955–56).

4. The fourth element is the exposure of individuals to the prescribed conditions, and this leads, with a high degree of probability, to behavior which is in line with the goals desired. Individuals are now happy, if that has been the goal, or well-behaved, or submissive, or whatever it has been decided to make them.

5. The fifth element is that if the process I have described is put in motion then there is a continuing social organization which will continue to produce the types of behavior that have been valued.

Some Flaws

Are there any flaws in this way of viewing the control of human behavior? I believe there are. In fact the only element in this description with which I find myself in agreement is the second. It seems to me quite incontrovertibly true that the scientific method is an excellent way to discover the means by which to achieve our goals. Beyond that, I feel many sharp differences, which I will try to spell out.

I believe that in Skinner's presentation here and in his previous writings, there is a serious underestimation of the problem of power. To hope that the power which is being made available by the behavioral sciences will be exercised by the scientist, or by a benevolent group, seems to me a hope little supported by either recent or distant history. It seems far more likely that behavioral scientists, holding their present attitudes, will be in the position of the German rocket scientists specializing in guided missiles. First they worked devotedly for Hitler to destroy the U.S.S.R. and the United States. Now, depending on who captured them, they work devotedly for the U.S.S.R. in the interest of destroying the United States, or devotedly for the United States in the interest of destroying the U.S.S.R. If behavioral scientists are concerned solely with advancing their science, it seems most probable that they will serve the purposes of whatever individual or group has the power.

But the major flaw I see in this review of what is involved in the scientific control of human behavior is the denial, misunderstanding, or gross underestimation of the place of ends, goals or values in their relationship to science. This error (as it seems to me) has so many implications that I would like to devote some space to it.

Ends and Values
in Relation to Science

In sharp contradiction to some views that have been advanced, I would like to propose a two-pronged thesis: (i) In any scientific endeavor—whether "pure" or applied science—there is a prior subjective choice of the purpose or value which that scientific work is perceived as serving. (ii) This subjective value choice which brings the scientific endeavor into being must always lie outside of that endeavor and can never become a part of the science involved in that endeavor.

Let me illustrate the first point from Skinner himself. It is clear that in his earlier writing it is recognized that a prior value choice is necessary, and it is specified as the goal that men are to become happy, well-behaved, productive, and so on. I am pleased that Skinner has retreated from the goals he then chose, because to me they seem to be stultifying values. I can only feel that he was choosing these goals for others, not for himself. I would hate to see Skinner become "well-behaved," as that term would be defined for him by behavioral scientists. His recent article in the *American Psychologist*[16] shows that he certainly does not want to be "productive" as that value is defined by most psychologists. And the most awful fate I can imagine for him would be to have him constantly "happy." It is the fact that he is very unhappy about many things which makes me prize him.

In the first draft of his part of this article, he also included such prior value choices, saying for example, "We must decide how we are to use the knowledge which a science of human behavior is now making available." Now he has dropped all mention of such choices, and if I understand him correctly, he believes that science can proceed without them. He has suggested this view in another recent paper, stating that "We must continue to experiment in cultural design . . . testing the consequences as we go. Eventually the practices which make for the greatest biological and psychological strength of the group will presumably survive."[17]

I would point out, however, that to choose to experiment is a value choice. Even to move in the direction of perfectly random experimentation is a value choice. To test the consequences of an experiment is possible only if we have first made a subjective choice of a criterion value. And implicit in his statement is a valuing of biological and psychological strength. So even when trying to avoid such choice, it seems inescapable that a prior subjective value choice is necessary for any scientific endeavor, or for any application of scientific knowledge.

I wish to make it clear that I am not saying that values cannot be included as a subject of science. It is not true that science deals only with certain classes of "facts" and that these classes do not include values. It is a bit more complex than that, as a simple illustration or two may make clear.

If I value knowledge of the "three R's" as a goal of education, the methods of science can give me increasingly accurate information on how this goal may be achieved. If I value problem-solving ability as a goal of education, the scientific method can give me the same kind of help.

Now, if I wish to determine whether problem-solving ability is "better" than knowledge of the three R's, then scientific method can also study those two values but *only*—and this is very important—in terms of some

16 ——, *Am. Psychol.* 11, 221 (1956).

17 B. F. Skinner, *Trans. N.Y. Acad. Sci.* 17, 549 (1955).

other value which I have subjectively chosen. I may value college success. Then I can determine whether problem-solving ability or knowledge of the three R's is most closely associated with that value. I may value personal integration or vocational success or responsible citizenship. I can determine whether problem-solving ability or knowledge of the three R's is "better" for achieving any one of these values. But the value or purpose that gives meaning to a particular scientific endeavor must always lie outside of that endeavor.

Although our concern in this symposium is largely with applied science, what I have been saying seems equally true of so-called "pure" science. In pure science the usual prior subjective value choice is the discovery of truth. But this is a subjective choice, and science can never say whether it is the best choice, save in the light of some other value. Geneticists in the U.S.S.R., for example, had to make a subjective choice of whether it was better to pursue truth or to discover facts which upheld a governmental dogma. Which choice is "better"? We could make a scientific investigation of those alternatives but only in the light of some other subjectively chosen value. If, for example, we value the survival of a culture, then we could begin to investigate with the methods of science the question of whether pursuit of truth or support of governmental dogma is most closely associated with cultural survival.

My point then is that any endeavor in science, pure or applied, is carried on in the pursuit of a purpose or value that is subjectively chosen by persons. It is important that this choice be made explicit, since the particular value which is being sought can never be tested or evaluated, confirmed or denied, by the scientific endeavor to which it gives birth. The initial purpose or value always and necessarily lies outside the scope of the scientific effort which it sets in motion.

Among other things this means that if we choose some particular goal or series of goals for human beings and then set out on a large scale to control human behavior to the end of achieving those goals, we are locked in the rigidity of our initial choice, because such a scientific endeavor can never transcend itself to select new goals. Only subjective human persons can do that. Thus if we chose as our goal the state of happiness for human beings (a goal deservedly ridiculed by Aldous Huxley in *Brave New World*), and if we involved all of society in a successful scientific program by which people became happy, we would be locked in a colossal rigidity in which no one would be free to question this goal, because our scientific operations could not transcend themselves to question their guiding purposes. And without laboring this point, I would remark that colossal rigidity, whether in dinosaurs or dictatorships, has a very poor record of evolutionary survival.

If, however, a part of our scheme is to set free some "planners" who do not have to be happy, who are not controlled, and who are therefore free to choose other values, this has several meanings. It means that the purpose we have chosen as our goal is not a sufficient and a satisfying one for human beings but must be supplemented. It also means that if it is necessary to set up an elite group which is free, then this shows all too clearly that the great majority are only the slaves—no matter by what high-sounding name we call them—of those who select the goals.

Perhaps, however, the thought is that a continuing scientific endeavor will evolve its own goals; that the initial findings will alter the directions, and subsequent findings will alter them still further, and that science somehow develops its own purpose. Although he does not clearly say so, this appears to be the pattern Skinner has in mind. It is surely a reasonable description, but it overlooks one element in this continuing development, which is that subjective personal choice enters in at every point at which the direction changes. The findings of a science, the results of an experiment, do not and never can tell us what next scientific purpose to pursue. Even in the purest of science, the scientist must decide what the findings mean and must subjectively choose what next step will be most profitable in the pursuit of his purpose. And if we are speaking of the application of scientific knowledge, then it is distressingly clear that the increasing scientific knowledge of the structure of the atom carries with it no necessary choice as to the purpose to which this knowledge will be put. This is a subjective personal choice which must be made by many individuals.

Thus I return to the proposition with which I began this section of my remarks—and which I now repeat in different words. Science has its meaning as the objective pursuit of a purpose which has been subjectively chosen by a person or persons. This purpose or value can never be investigated by the particular scientific experiment or investigation to which it has given birth and meaning. Consequently, any discussion of the control of human beings by the behavioral sciences must first and most deeply concern itself with the subjectively chosen purposes which such an application of science is intended to implement.

Is the Situation Hopeless?

The thoughtful reader may recognize that, although my remarks up to this point have introduced some modifications in the conception of the processes by which human behavior will be controlled, these remarks may have made such control seem, if anything, even more inevitable. We might sum it up this way: Behavioral science is clearly moving forward; the increasing power for control which it gives will be held by someone or some groups; such an individual or group will surely choose the values or goals to be achieved; and most of us will then be increasingly controlled by means so subtle that we will not even be aware of them as controls. Thus, whether a council of wise psychologists (if this is not a contradiction in terms), or a Stalin, or a Big Brother has the power, and whether the goal is happiness, or productivity, or resolution of the Oedipus complex, or submission, or love of Big Brother, we will inevitably find ourselves moving toward the chosen goal and probably thinking that we ourselves desire it. Thus, if this line of reasoning is correct, it appears that some form of *Walden Two* or of *1984* (and at a deep philosophic level they seem indistinguishable) is coming. The fact that it would surely arrive piecemeal, rather than all at once, does not greatly change the fundamental issues. In any event, as Skinner has indicated in his writings, we would then look back upon the concepts of human freedom, the capacity for choice, the responsibility for choice, and the worth of the human individual as historical curiosities which once existed by cultural accident as values in a prescientific civilization.

I believe that any person observant of trends must regard something like the foregoing sequence as a real possibility. It is not simply a fantasy. Something of that sort may even be the most likely future. But is it an inevitable future? I want to devote the remainder of my remarks to an alternative possibility.

Alternative Set of Values

Suppose we start with a set of ends, values, purposes, quite different from the type of goals we have been considering. Suppose we do this quite openly, setting them forth as a possible value choice to be accepted or rejected. Suppose we select a set of values that focuses on fluid elements of process rather than static attributes. We might then value: man as a process of becoming, as a process of achieving worth and dignity through the development of his potentialities; the individual human being as a self-actualizing process, moving on to more challenging and enriching experiences; the process by which the individual creatively adapts to an ever-new and changing world; the process by which knowledge transcends itself, as, for example, the theory of relativity transcended Newtonian physics, itself to be transcended in some future day by a new perception.

If we select values such as these we turn to our science and technology of behavior with a very different set of questions. We will want to know such things as these: Can science aid in the discovery of new modes of richly rewarding living? more meaningful and satisfying modes of interpersonal relationships? Can science inform us on how the human race can become a more intelligent participant in its own evolution—its physical, psychological and social evolution? Can science inform us on ways of releasing the creative capacity of individuals, which seem so necessary if we are to survive in this fantastically expanding atomic age? Oppenheimer has pointed out[18] that knowledge, which used to double in millennia or centuries, now doubles in a generation or a decade. It appears that we must discover the utmost in release of creativity if we are to be able to adapt effectively. In short, can science discover the methods by which man can most readily become a continually developing and self-transcending proc-

---

[18] R. Oppenheimer, *Roosevelt University Occasional Papers* 2 (1956).

ess, in his behavior, his thinking, his knowledge? Can science predict and release an essentially "unpredictable" freedom?

It is one of the virtues of science as a method that it is as able to advance and implement goals and purposes of this sort as it is to serve static values, such as states of being well-informed, happy, obedient. Indeed we have some evidence of this.

Small Example

I will perhaps be forgiven if I document some of the possibilities along this line by turning to psychotherapy, the field I know best.

Psychotherapy, as Meerloo[19] and others have pointed out, can be one of the most subtle tools for the control of *A* by *B*. The therapist can subtly mold individuals in imitation of himself. He can cause an individual to become a submissive and conforming being. When certain therapeutic principles are used in extreme fashion, we call it brainwashing, an instance of the disintegration of the personality and a reformulation of the person along lines desired by the controlling individual. So the principles of therapy can be used as an effective means of external control of human personality and behavior. Can psychotherapy be anything else?

Here I find the developments going on in client-centered psychotherapy[20] an exciting hint of what a behavioral science can do in achieving the kinds of values I have stated. Quite aside from being a somewhat new orientation in psychotherapy, this development has important implications regarding the relation of a behavioral science to the control of human behavior. Let me describe our experience as it relates to the issues of this discussion.

In client-centered therapy, we are deeply engaged in the prediction and influencing of behavior, or even the control of behavior. As therapists, we institute certain attitudinal conditions, and the client has relatively little voice in the establishment of these conditions. We predict that if these conditions are instituted, certain behavioral consequences will ensue in the client. Up to this point this is largely external control, no different from what Skinner has described, and no different from what I have discussed in the preceding sections of this article. But here any similarity ceases.

The conditions we have chosen to establish predict such behavioral consequences as these: that the client will become self-directing, less rigid, more open to the evidence of his senses, better organized and integrated, more similar to the ideal which he has chosen for himself. In other words, we have established by external control conditions which we predict will be followed by internal control by the individual, in pursuit of internally chosen goals. We have set the conditions which predict various classes of behaviors—self-directing behaviors, sensitivity to realities within and with-

[19] J. A. M. Meerloo, *J. Nervous Mental Disease* 122, 353 (1955).

[20] C. R. Rogers, *Client-Centered Therapy* (Houghton-Mifflin, Boston, 1951).

out, flexible adaptiveness—which are by their very nature unpredictable in their specifics. Our recent research[21] indicates that our predictions are to a significant degree corroborated, and our commitment to the scientific method causes us to believe that more effective means of achieving these goals may be realized.

Research exists in other fields—industry, education, group dynamics—which seems to support our own findings. I believe it may be conservatively stated that scientific progress has been made in identifying those conditions in an interpersonal relationship which, if they exist in *B,* are followed in *A* by greater maturity in behavior, less dependence on others, an increase in expressiveness as a person, an increase in variability, flexibility and effectiveness of adaptation, an increase in self-responsibility and self-direction. And, quite in contrast to the concern expressed by some, we do not find that the creatively adaptive behavior which results from such self-directed variability of expression is a "happy accident" which occurs in "chaos." Rather, the individual who is open to his experience, and self-directing, is harmonious not chaotic, ingenious rather than random, as he orders his responses imaginatively toward the achievement of his own purposes. His creative actions are no more a "happy accident" that was Einstein's development of the theory of relativity.

Thus we find ourselves in fundamental agreement with John Dewey's statement: "Science has made its way by releasing, not by suppressing, the elements of variation, of invention and innovation, of novel creation in individuals."[22] Progress in personal life and in group living is, we believe, made in the same way.

Possible Concept
of the Control of Human Behavior

It is quite clear that the point of view I am expressing is in sharp contrast to the usual conception of the relationship of the behavioral sciences to the control of human behavior. In order to make this contrast even more blunt, I will state this possibility in paragraphs parallel to those used before.

1. It is possible for us to choose to value man as a self-actualizing process of becoming; to value creativity, and the process by which knowledge becomes self-transcending.

2. We can proceed, by the methods of science, to discover the conditions which necessarily precede these processes and, through continuing experimentation, to discover better means of achieving these purposes.

3. It is possible for individuals or groups to set these conditions, with a

[21] —— and R. Dymond, Eds., *Psychotherapy and Personality Change* (Univ. of Chicago Press, Chicago, 1954).

[22] J. Ratner, Ed., *Intelligence in the Modern World: John Dewey's Philosophy* (Modern Library, New York, 1939), p. 359.

minimum of power or control. According to present knowledge, the only authority necessary is the authority to establish certain qualities of inter-personal relationship.

4. Exposed to these conditions, present knowledge suggests that indi-viduals become more self-responsible, make progress in self-actualization, become more flexible, and become more creatively adaptive.

5. Thus such an initial choice would inaugurate the beginnings of a social system or subsystem in which values, knowledge, adaptive skills, and even the concept of science would be continually changing and self-transcending. The emphasis would be upon man as a process of becoming.

I believe it is clear that such a view as I have been describing does not lead to any definable utopia. It would be impossible to predict its final outcome. It involves a step-by-step development, based on a continuing subjective choice of purposes, which are implemented by the behavioral sciences. It is in the direction of the "open society," as that term has been defined by Popper,[23] where individuals carry responsibility for personal deci-sions. It is at the opposite pole from his concept of the closed society, of which *Walden Two* would be an example.

I trust it is also evident that the whole emphasis is on process, not on end-states of being. I am suggesting that it is by choosing to value certain qualitative elements of the process of becoming that we can find a pathway toward the open society.

The Choice

It is my hope that we have helped to clarify the range of choice which will lie before us and our children in regard to the behavioral sciences. We can choose to use our growing knowledge to enslave people in ways never dreamed of before, deperson-alizing them, controlling them by means so carefully selected that they will perhaps never be aware of their loss of personhood. We can choose to utilize our scientific knowledge to make men happy, well-behaved, and productive, as Skinner earlier suggested. Or we can insure that each person learns all the syllabus which we select and set before him, as Skinner now suggests. Or at the other end of the spectrum of choice we can choose to use the behavioral sciences in ways which will free, not control; which will bring about constructive variability, not conformity; which will develop creativity, not contentment; which will facilitate each person in his self-directed process of becoming; which will aid individuals, groups, and even the con-cept of science to become self-transcending in freshly adaptive ways of meeting life and its problems. The choice is up to us, and, the human race being what it is, we are likely to stumble about, making at times some

[23] K. R. Popper, *The Open Society and Its Enemies* (Rutledge and Kegan Paul, London, 1945).

nearly disastrous value choices and at other times highly constructives ones.

I am aware that to some, this setting forth of a choice is unrealistic, because a choice of values is regarded as not possible. Skinner has stated: "Man's vaunted creative powers . . . his capacity to choose and our right to hold him responsible for his choice—none of these is conspicuous in this new self-portrait (provided by science). Man, we once believed, was free to express himself in art, music, and literature, to inquire into nature, to seek salvation in his own way. He could initiate action and make spontaneous and capricious changes of course. . . . But science insists that action is initiated by forces impinging upon the individual, and that caprice is only another name for behavior for which we have not yet found a cause."[24]

I can understand this point of view, but I believe that it avoids looking at the great paradox of behavioral science. Behavior, when it is examined scientifically, is surely best understood as determined by prior causation. This is one great fact of science. But responsible personal choice, which is the most essential element in being a person, which is the core experience in psychotherapy, which exists prior to any scientific endeavor, is an equally prominent fact in our lives. To deny the experience of responsible choice is, to me, as restricted a view as to deny the possibility of a behavioral science. That these two important elements of our experience appear to be in contradiction has perhaps the same significance as the contradiction between the wave theory and the corpuscular theory of light, both of which can be shown to be true, even though incompatible. We cannot profitably deny our subjective life, any more than we can deny the objective description of that life.

In conclusion then, it is my contention that science cannot come into being without a personal choice of the values we wish to achieve. And these values we choose to implement will forever lie outside of the science which implements them; the goals we select, the purposes we wish to follow, must always be outside of the science which achieves them. To me this has the encouraging meaning that the human person, with his capacity of subjective choice, can and will always exist, separate from and prior to any of his scientific undertakings. Unless as individuals and groups we choose to relinquish our capacity of subjective choice, we will always remain persons, not simply pawns of a self-created science.

SKINNER

                    I cannot quite agree that the practice of science *requires* a prior decision about goals or a prior choice of values. The metallurgist can study the properties of steel and the engineer can design a bridge without raising the question of whether a bridge is to

[24] B. F. Skinner, *Am. Scholar* 25, 52–53 (1955–56).

be built. But such questions are certainly frequently raised and tentatively answered. Rogers wants to call the answers "subjective choices of values." To me, such an expression suggests that we have had to abandon more rigorous scientific practices in order to talk about our own behavior. In the experimental analysis of other organisms I would use other terms, and I shall try to do so here. Any list of values is a list of reinforcers—conditioned or otherwise. We are so constituted that under certain circumstances food, water, sexual contact, and so on, will make any behavior which produces them more likely to occur again. Other things may acquire this power. We do not need to say that an organism chooses to eat rather than to starve. If you answer that it is a very different thing when a man chooses to starve, I am only too happy to agree. If it were not so, we should have cleared up the question of choice long ago. An organism can be reinforced by—can be made to "choose"—almost any given state of affairs.

Rogers is concerned with choices that involve multiple and usually conflicting consequences. I have dealt with some of these elsewhere[25] in an analysis of self-control. Shall I eat these delicious strawberries today if I will then suffer an annoying rash tomorrow? The decision I am to make used to be assigned to the province of ethics. But we are now studying similar combinations of positive and negative consequences, as well as collateral conditions which affect the result, in the laboratory. Even a pigeon can be taught some measure of self-control! And this work helps us to understand the operation of certain formulas—among them value judgments—which folk-wisdom, religion, and psychotherapy have advanced in the interests of self-discipline. The observable effect of any statement of value is to alter the relative effectiveness of reinforcers. We may no longer enjoy the strawberries for thinking about the rash. If rashes are made sufficiently shameful, illegal, sinful, maladjusted, or unwise, we may glow with satisfaction as we push the strawberries aside in a grandiose avoidance response which would bring a smile to the lips of Murray Sidman.

People behave in ways which, as we say, conform to ethical, governmental, or religious patterns because they are reinforced for doing so. The resulting behavior may have far-reaching consequences for the survival of the pattern to which it conforms. And whether we like it or not, survival is the ultimate criterion. This is where, it seems to me, science can help—not in choosing a goal, but in enabling us to predict the survival value of cultural practices. Man has too long tried to get the kind of world he wants by glorifying some brand of immediate reinforcement. As science points up more and more of the remoter consequences, he may begin to work to strengthen behavior, not in a slavish devotion to a chosen value, but with respect to the ultimate survival of mankind. Do not ask me why I want mankind to survive. I can tell you why only in the sense in which the physi-

---

[25] B. F. Skinner, *Science and Human Behavior* (Macmillan, New York, 1953).

ologist can tell you why I want to breathe. Once the relation between a given step and the survival of my group has been pointed out, I will take that step. And it is the business of science to point out just such relations.

The values I have occasionally recommended (and Rogers has not led me to recant) are transitional. Other things being equal, I am betting on the group whose practices make for healthy, happy, secure, productive, and creative people. And I insist that the values recommended by Rogers are transitional, too, for I can ask him the same kind of question. Man as a process of becoming—*what?* Self-actualization—for what? Inner control is no more a goal than external.

What Rogers seems to me to be proposing, both here and elsewhere,[26] is this: Let us use our increasing power of control to create individuals who will not need and perhaps will no longer respond to control. Let us solve the problem of our power by renouncing it. At first blush this seems as implausible as a benevolent despot. Yet power has occasionally been foresworn. A nation has burned its Reichstag, rich men have given away their wealth, beautiful women have become ugly hermits in the desert, and psychotherapists have become nondirective. When this happens, I look to other possible reinforcements for a plausible explanation. A people relinquish democratic power when a tyrant promises them the earth. Rich men give away wealth to escape the accusing finger of their fellowmen. A woman destroys her beauty in the hope of salvation. And a psychotherapist relinquishes control because he can thus help his client more effectively.

The solution that Rogers is suggesting is thus understandable. But is he correctly interpreting the result? What evidence is there that a client ever becomes truly *self*-directing? What evidence is there that he ever makes a truly *inner* choice of ideal or goal? Even though the therapist does not do the choosing, even though he encourages "self-actualization"—he is not out of control as long as he holds himself ready to step in when occasion demands—when, for example, the client chooses the goal of becoming a more accomplished liar or murdering his boss. But supposing the therapist does withdraw completely or is no longer necessary—what about all the other forces acting upon the client? Is the self-chosen goal independent of his early ethical and religious training? of the folk-wisdom of his group? of the opinions and attitudes of others who are important to him? Surely not. The therapeutic situation is only a small part of the world of the client. From the therapist's point of view it may appear to be possible to relinquish control. But the control passes, not to a "self," but to forces in other parts of the client's world. The solution of the therapist's problem of power cannot be our solution, for we must consider *all* the forces acting upon the individual.

The child who must be prodded and nagged is something less than a fully developed human being. We want to see him hurrying to his appointment,

26 C. R. Rogers, *Teachers College Record* 57, 316 (1956).

not because each step is taken in response to verbal reminders from his mother, but because certain temporal contingencies, in which dawdling has been punished and hurrying reinforced, have worked a change in his behavior. Call this a state of better organization, a greater sensitivity to reality, or what you will. The plain fact is that the child passes from a temporary verbal control exercised by his parents to control by certain inexorable features of the environment. I should suppose that something of the same sort happens in successful psychotherapy. Rogers seems to me to be saying this: Let us put an end, as quickly as possible, to any pattern of master-and-slave, to any direct obedience to command, to the submissive following of suggestions. Let the individual be free to adjust himself to more rewarding features of the world about him. In the end, let his teachers and counselors "wither away," like the Marxist state. I not only agree with this as a useful ideal, I have constructed a fanciful world to demonstrate its advantages. It saddens me to hear Rogers say that "at a deep philosophic level" *Walden Two* and George Orwell's *1984* "seem indistinguishable." They could scarcely be more unlike—at any level. The book *1984* is a picture of immediate aversive control for vicious selfish purposes. The founder of *Walden Two,* on the other hand, has built a community in which neither he nor any other person exerts any *current* control. His achievement lay in his original *plan,* and when he boasts of this ("It is enough to satisfy the thirstiest tyrant") we do not fear him but only pity him for his weakness.

Another critic of *Walden Two,* Andrew Hacker[27] has discussed this point in considering the bearing of mass conditioning upon the liberal notion of autonomous man. In drawing certain parallels between the Grand Inquisition passage in Dostoevsky's *Brothers Karamazov,* Huxley's *Brave New World,* and *Walden Two,* he attempts to set up a distinction to be drawn in any society between conditioners and conditioned. He assumes that "the conditioner can be said to be autonomous in the traditional liberal sense." But then he notes: "Of course the conditioner has been conditioned. But he has not been conditioned by the conscious manipulation of another *person.*" But how does this affect the resulting behavior? Can we not soon forget the origins of the "artificial" diamond which is identical with the real thing? Whether it is an "accidental" cultural pattern, such as is said to have produced the founder of *Walden Two,* or the engineered environment which is about to produce his successors, we are dealing with sets of conditions generating human behavior which will ultimately be measured by their contribution to the strength of the group. We look to the future, not the past, for the test of "goodness" or acceptability.

If we are worthy of our democratic heritage we shall, of course, be ready to resist any tyrannical use of science for immediate or selfish purposes. But if we value the achievements and goals of democracy we must not refuse to apply science to the design and construction of cultural patterns,

27 A. Hacker, *J. Politics* 17, 590 (1955).

even though we may then find ourselves in some sense in the position of controllers. Fear of control, generalized beyond any warrant, has led to a misinterpretation of valid practices and the blind rejection of intelligent planning for a better way of life. In terms which I trust Rogers will approve, in conquering this fear we shall become more mature and better organized and shall, thus, more fully actualize ourselves as human beings.

5 Politics

Introduction:
Community
and the
New Anarchism

In answer to the traditional problem of liberal political theory—the limits to the authority of society over the individual—the traditional anarchist answers: "Society has no authority over me." This is essentially Robert Paul Wolff's argument in his recent book **In Defense of Anarchism.** Faced with the traditional problem of political theory, he honestly and unabashedly confesses that he is unable to find any valid and persuasive argument justifying the authority claimed for the state. Consequently, the individual is left as both the alpha and omega of social theory. The old anarchy is the kingdom of the unrestrained individual, free of social contracts binding him to a particular form of government. The old anarchism is an essentially individualistic response to the problem of political philosophy.

But a new anarchism is now emerging. Some of today's anarchists take an approach that bypasses traditional political theory by starting from different premises and a different question. The new anarchism is not individualistic but communal or tribal (see Snyder's title, "Why Tribe"). Consequently the new anarchists are not interested in how the **individual** relates to the state, for the new anarchists are not political theorists, but people already living a "tribal" existence. To find out why they live as they do we need to go outside political theory for the determinants of their life style. This is not to say that the anarchic life style will not have influences on political realities which must be analyzed from the perspective of political theory. But the new anarchism functions as a **cause** in the political matrix rather than as a **result** of a line of argument in political theory. Traditional anarchist literature saw anarchism as a result and tried to show why it would be desirable. I wish to distinguish a newer approach that simply takes anarchistic life styles as a fact, and then seeks to explore the origins and significance of that fact.

The origins of the new anarchism can be seen in a peculiar twist on the traditional problem of political theory: where the problem once was to see how an individual could preserve himself from "the state of nature" by joining with other individuals, now the problem is to see how groups can preserve themselves from their ancestors' success at fleeing the state of nature. Mankind inserted technology and political organization between itself and nature; the new anarchists are trying to protect themselves from technology and the dominant forms of political organization. Where liberal political theory saw individuals using technology to carve out livable spaces in an alien natural environment, the new anarchism is looking for ways that groups can carve out livable spaces in an alien technological-political environment. This does not mean that the new anarchists intend to forswear technology any more than political-technological man forswore nature: he used rivers to drive his mills and natural resources to stoke his fires, just as "post-scarcity anarchists" (Bookchin's term) use technological know-how to carve out spaces free from the ills of technology, namely the **Whole Earth Catalogue.**

Analyzing the genesis of contemporary anarchism as arising from classical political and technological solutions, we might conclude that the basic insight underlying the new anarchism is just this: as a maker of his own history, man continually risks subjugating himself to the solutions of his previous problems. First his problem was nature in her infelicities, but he solved that problem through political organization and technology. Now his problem is precisely the political organization and technology that constituted the solution to his previous problem. This sort of historical analysis of the new anarchism suggests that there might never be an eternal solution to the "problem of political theory." As a maker of his own history, man guarantees that the nature of his problems keep changing. The guarantee is reflected in the anarchist's preference for the primacy of **practice** to theory, and that preference goes a long way toward accounting for the general lack of first-rank political theorists in the anarchist tradition, a lack that Barber takes as diminishing the credibility of anarchists.

While the old anarchist may be a political theorist who believes that a radically individualistic answer to the problem of politics offers the key to the solution of man's ills, the new anarchist does not believe that **any** political answer is a key. The new anarchist is philosophically interesting for the radicalism of his nonanswer to the political question. Rather than proffer an answer, he undermines the question. He may be living as an anarchist because of religious views rather than political convictions. (Here Snyder's and Krishnamurti's writings are most indicative.) The new anarchist is thus a political atheist: he simply does not believe in the reality of political power. He sees national (but not local) politics as essentially mythical: Washington as Mount Olympus, elections as tribal rites without any discernible efficacy. However meticulously one performs the rites, life goes on much as before, whether it be too little rain or too little peace.

Such views will arouse indignation, the same indignation aroused by religious heresies when everybody believed in God and the Church. Hence the title of "political atheist" for the new anarchist. He is not a political theorist among other political theorists any more than Nietzsche was a theologian among theologians. But just as Nietzsche brought the radicalism of philosophical critique to the questions theologians were dealing with, so the new anarchists, by their deeds as much as their words, bring the radicalism of philosophical critique into the domain of political theory.

MARTIN BUBER

(1878-1965)

Martin Buber, one of the foremost religious philosophers in the twentieth century, was no stranger to social and political issues. At the time he was writing his book **Paths in Utopia,** completed in 1945, the term 'anarchism' still suffered under the connotation of violence; it was known more as a tactic than a political philosophy. Anarchists were considered renegades who, instead of participating in party strategies, preferred to promote their political causes, whatever they might be, by acts of individual terror and violence. Consequently, Buber was careful not to refer to his political philosophy as anarchism, but his main subjects—the ideas of men like Proudhon, Kropotkin, and Landauer—are generally recognized to be central to the old anarchist tradition.

Yet Buber's essay anticipates quite remarkably many of the tenets of the new anarchism, and in a philosophically respectable way. He sees that the problem of the individual and society is not an either-or question but, as he says, "a question of the right line of demarcation that has to be drawn ever anew." His call for a decentralization of politics is not the cry of a political conservative, as is clear from his declaration "in favor of a rebirth of the commune." Of course it is difficult these days to know just what is politically "conservative" ever since Paul Goodman, an old-time radical who was active in the contemporary scene, described himself as a radical conservative. Many of our current labels are not only confusing but even damaging to the extent that they lead us to think in either-or terms. Where a false dichotomy is the only dichotomy with a label, both sides may be wrong. Sometimes one needs to cut across old distinctions with new distinctions. As I suggested in the transition to the epistemology of interpersonal perception, the distinction between subjective relativism and absolutism inhibits our thinking of an objective relativism. There, as in the present case, careful thought requires an analysis of both sides of an easily labeled dichotomy. We needn't abandon relativism in our haste to escape the chaos of subjectivism. Why throw out the baby with the bath water? Here too we want to avoid locating anarchism on one side of the false distinction between radicalism and conservatism. Just as we can be objective relativists, and Paul Goodman can be a radical conservative, so the anarchist may fall into none of the neatly labeled camps generated by the usual partisan disputes.

UTOPIAN COMMUNITIES

In the Midst of Crisis

For the last three decades we have felt that we were living in the initial phases of the greatest crisis humanity has ever known. It grows increasingly clear to us that the tremendous happenings of the past years, too, can be understood only as symptoms of this crisis. It is not merely the crisis of one economic and social system being superseded by another, more or less ready to take its place; rather all systems, old and new, are equally involved in the crisis. What is in question, therefore, is nothing less than man's whole existence in the world.

Ages ago, far beyond our calculation, this creature "Man" set out on his journey; from the point of view of Nature a well-nigh incomprehensible anomaly; from the point of view of the spirit an incarnation hardly less incomprehensible, perhaps unique; from the point of view of both a being whose very essence it was to be threatened with disaster every instant, both from within and without, exposed to deeper and deeper crises. During the ages of his early journey man has multiplied what he likes to call his "power over Nature" in increasingly rapid tempo, and he has borne what he likes to call the "creations of his spirit" from triumph to triumph. But at the same time he has felt more and more profoundly, as one crisis succeeded another, how fragile all his glories are; and in moments of clairvoyance he has come to realize that in spite of everything he likes to call "progress" he is not travelling along the high-road at all, but is picking his precarious way along a narrow ledge between two abysses. The graver the crisis becomes the more earnest and consciously responsible is the knowledge demanded of us; for although what is demanded is a deed, only that deed which is born of knowledge will help to overcome the crisis. In a time of great crisis it is not enough to look back to the immediate past in order to bring the enigma of the present nearer to solution: we have to bring the stage of the journey we have now reached face to face with its beginnings, so far as we can picture them.

The essential thing among all those things which once helped man to emerge from Nature and, notwithstanding his feebleness as a natural being, to assert himself—more essential even than the making of a "technical" world out of things expressly formed for the purpose—was this: that he banded together with his own kind for protection and hunting, food gathering and work; and did so in such a way that from the very beginning and thereafter to an increasing degree he faced the others as more or less independent entities and communicated with them as such, addressing and being addressed by them in that manner. This creation of a "social" world out of persons at once mutually dependent and independent differed in kind from all similar undertakings on the part of animals, just as the technical work of man differed in kind from all the animals' works. Apes, too, make use of some stick they happen to have found, as a lever, a digging-tool or a weapon; but that is an affair of chance only: they cannot conceive and produce a tool as an object constituted so and not otherwise and having an existence of its own. And again, many of the insects live in societies built up on a strict division of labour; but it is just this division of labour that governs absolutely their relations with one another; they are all as it were tools; only, their own society is the thing that makes use of them for its "instinctive" purposes; there is no improvisation, no degree, however modest, of mutual independence, no possibility of "free" regard for one another, and thus no person-to-person relationship. Just as the specific technical creations of man mean the conferring of independence on things, so his specific social creation means the conferring of independence on beings of his own kind. It is in the light of this specifically human idiosyncrasy that we have to interpret man's journey with all its ups and downs, and so also the point we have reached on this journey, our great and particular crisis.

In the evolution of mankind hitherto this, then, is the line that predominates: the forming and re-forming of communities on the basis of growing personal independence, their mutual recognition and collaboration on that basis. The two most important steps that the man of early times took on the road to human society can be established with some certainty. The first is that inside the individual clan each individual, through an extremely primitive form of division of labour, was recognized and utilized in his special capacity, so that the clan increasingly took on the character of an ever-renewed association of persons each the vehicle of a different function. The second is that different clans would, under certain conditions, band together in quest of food and for campaigns, and consolidated their mutual help as customs and laws that took firmer and firmer root; so that as once between individuals, so now between communities people discerned and acknowledged differences of nature and function. Wherever genuine human society has since developed it has always been on this same basis of functional autonomy, mutual recognition and mutual responsibility, whether individual or collective. Power-centres of various kinds have split off, organizing and guaranteeing the common order and security of all; but to the political sphere in the stricter sense, the State with its police-system and its bureaucracy, there was always opposed the organic, functionally organized society as such, a great society built up of various societies, the great society in which men lived and worked, competed with one another and helped one another; and in each of the big and little societies composing it, in each of these communes and communities the individual human being, despite all the difficulties and conflicts, felt himself at home as once in the clan, felt himself approved and affirmed in his functional independence and responsibility.

All this changed more and more as the centralistic political principle subordinated the de-centralistic social principle. The crucial thing here was not that the State, particularly in its more or less totalitarian forms, weakened and gradually displaced the free associations, but that the political principle with all its centralistic features percolated into the associations themselves, modifying their structure and their whole inner life, and thus politicized society to an ever-increasing extent. Society's assimilation in the State was accelerated by the fact that, as a result of modern industrial development and its ordered chaos, involving the struggle of all against all for access to raw materials and for a larger share of the world-market, there grew up, in place of the old struggles between States, struggles between whole societies. The individual society, feeling itself threatened not only by its neighbours' lust for aggression but also by things in general, knew no way of salvation save in complete submission to the principle of centralized power; and, in the democratic forms of society no less than in its totalitarian forms, it made this its guiding principle. Everywhere the only thing of importance was the minute organization of power, the unquestioning observance of slogans, the saturation of the whole of society with the real or supposed interests of the State. Concurrently with this there is an internal development. In the monstrous confusion of modern life, only thinly disguised by the reliable functioning of the economic and State-apparatus, the individual clings desperately to the collectivity. The little society in which he was embedded cannot help him; only the great collectivities, so he thinks, can do that, and he is all too willing to let himself be deprived of personal responsibility: he only wants to obey. And the most valuable of all goods—the life between man and man—gets lost in the process; the autonomous relationships become meaningless, personal relationships wither; and the very spirit of man hires itself out as a functionary. The personal human being ceases to be the living member of a social body and becomes a cog in the "collective" machine. Just as his degenerate technology is causing man to lose the feel of good work and proportion, so the degrading social life he leads is causing him to lose the feel of community—just when he is so full of the illusion of living in perfect devotion to his community.

A crisis of this kind cannot be overcome by struggling back to an earlier stage of the journey, but only by trying to master the problems as they are, without minimizing them. There is no going back for us, we have to go through with it. But we shall only get through if we know *where* we want to go.

We must begin, obviously, with the establishment of a vital peace which will deprive the political principle of its supremacy over the social principle. And this primary objective cannot in its turn be reached by any devices of political organization, but only by the resolute will of all peoples to cultivate the territories and raw materials of our planet and govern its inhabitants, *together*. At this point, however, we are threatened by a danger greater than all the previous ones: the danger of a gigantic centralization of power covering the whole planet and devouring all free community. Everything depends on not handing the work of planetary management over to the political principle.

Common management is only possible as socialistic management. But if the fatal question for contemporary man is: Can he or can he not decide in favour of, and educate himself up to, a common socialistic economy? then the propriety of the question lies in an inquiry into Socialism itself: what sort of Socialism is it to be, under whose aegis the common economy of man is to come about, if at all?

The ambiguity of the terms we are employing is greater here than anywhere else. People say, for instance, that Socialism is the passing of the control of the means of production out of the hands of the entrepreneurs into the hands of the collectivity; but again, it all depends on what you mean by "collectivity." If it is what we generally call the "State," that is to say, an institution in which a virtually unorganized mass allows its affairs to be conducted by "representation," as they call it, then the chief change in a socialistic society will be this: that the workers will feel themselves represented by the holders of power. But what is representation? Does not the worst defect of modern society lie precisely in everybody letting himself be represented *ad libitum?* And in a "socialistic" society will there not, on top of this passive political representation, be added a passive economic representation, so that, with everybody letting himself be represented by everybody else, we reach a state of practically unlimited representation and hence, ultimately, the reign of practically unlimited centralist accumulation of power? But the more a human group lets itself be represented in the management of its common affairs, and the more it lets itself be represented from outside, the less communal life there is in it and the more impoverished it becomes as a community. For community—not the primitive sort, but the sort possible and appropriate to modern man—declares itself primarily in the common and active management of what it has in common, and without this it cannot exist.

The primary aspiration of all history is a genuine community of human beings—genuine because it is *community all through*. A community that failed to base itself on the actual and communal life of big and little groups living and working together, and on their mutual relationships, would be fictitious and counterfeit. Hence everything depends on whether the collectivity into whose hands the control of the means of production passes will facilitate and promote in its very structure and in all its institutions the genuine common life of the various groups composing it—on whether, in fact, these groups themselves become proper foci of the productive process; therefore on whether the masses are so organized in their separate organizations (the various "communities") as to be as powerful as the common economy of man permits; therefore on whether centralist representation only goes as far as the new order of things absolutely demands. The fatal question does not take the form of a fundamental Either-Or: it is only a question of the right line of demarcation that has to be drawn ever anew— the thousandfold system of demarcation between the spheres which must of necessity be centralized and those which can operate in freedom; between the degree of government and the degree of autonomy; between the law of unity and the claims of community. The unwearying scrutiny of conditions in terms of the claims of community, as something continually exposed to the depredations of centralist power—the *custody of the true boundaries,* ever changing in accordance with changing historical circumstances: such would be the task of humanity's spiritual conscience, a Supreme Court unexampled in kind, the right true representation of a living idea. A new incarnation is waiting here for Plato's "custodians."

Representation of an idea, I say: not of a rigid principle but of a living form that wants to be shaped in the daily stuff of this earth. Community should not be made into a principle; it, too, should always satisfy a situation rather than an abstraction. The realization of community, like the realization of any idea, cannot occur once and for all time: always it must be the moment's answer to the moment's question, and nothing more.

In the interests of its vital meaning, therefore, the idea of community must be guarded against all contamination by sentimentality or emotionalism. Community is never a mere attitude of mind, and if it is *feeling* it is an inner disposition that is felt. Community is the inner disposition or constitution of a life in common, which knows and embraces in itself hard "calculation," adverse "chance," the sudden access of "anxiety." It is community of tribulation and only because of that community of spirit; community of toil and only because of that community of salvation. Even those communities which call the spirit their master and salvation their Promised Land, the "religious" communities, are community only if they serve their lord and master in the midst of simple, unexalted, unselected reality, a reality not so much chosen by them as sent to them just as it is; they are community only if they prepare the way to the Promised Land through the thickets of this pathless hour. True, it is not "works" that count, but the work of faith does. A community of faith truly exists only when it is a community of work.

The real essence of community is to be found in the fact—manifest or otherwise—that is has a centre. The real beginning of a community is when its members have a common relation to the centre overriding all other relations: the circle is described by the radii, not by the points along its circumference. And the originality of the centre cannot be discerned unless it is discerned as being transpicuous to the light of something divine. All this is true; but the more earthly, the more creaturely, the more attached the centre is, the truer and more transpicuous it will be. This is where the "social" element comes in. Not as something separate, but as the all-pervading realm where man stands the test; and it is here that the truth of the centre is proved. The early Christians were not content with the community that existed alongside or even above the world, and they went into the desert so as to have no more community save with God and no more disturbing world. But it was shown them that God does not wish man to be alone with him; and above the holy impotence of the hermit there rose the Brotherhood. Finally, going beyond St. Benedict, St. Francis entered into alliance with all creatures.

Yet a community need not be "founded." Wherever historical destiny had brought a group of men together in a common fold, there was room for the growth of a genuine community; and there was no need of an altar to the city deity in the midst when the citizens knew they were united round—and by—the Nameless. A living togetherness, constantly renewing itself, was already there, and all that needed strengthening was the immediacy of relationships. In the happiest instances common affairs were deliberated and decided not through representatives but in gatherings in the market-place; and the unity that was felt in public permeated all personal contacts. The danger of seclusion might hang over the community, but the communal spirit banished it; for here this spirit flourished as nowhere else and broke windows for itself in the narrow walls, with a large view of people, mankind and the world.

All this, I may be told, has gone irrevocably and for ever. The modern city has no agora and the modern man has no time for negotiations of which his elected representatives can very well relieve him. The pressure of numbers and the forms of organization have destroyed any real togetherness. Work forges other personal links than does leisure, sport again others than politics, the day is cleanly divided and the soul too. These links are material ones; though we follow our common interests and tendencies together, we have no use for "immediacy." The collectivity is not a warm, friendly gathering but a great link-up of economic and political forces inimical to the play of romantic fancies, only understandable in terms of quantity, expressing itself in actions and effects—a thing which the individual has to belong to with no intimacies of any kind but all the time conscious of his energetic contribution. Any "unions" that resist the inevitable trend of events must disappear. There is still the family, of course, which, as a domestic community, seems to demand and guarantee a modicum of communal life; but it too will either emerge from the crisis in which it is involved, as an association for a common purpose, or else it will perish.

Faced with this medley of correct premises and absurd conclusions I declare in favour of a rebirth of the commune. A rebirth—not a bringing back. It cannot in fact be brought back, although I sometimes think that every touch of helpful neighbourliness in the apartment-house, every wave of warmer comradeship in the lulls and "knock-offs" that occur even in the most perfectly "rationalized" factory, means an addition to the world's community-content; and although a rightly constituted village commune sometimes strikes me as being a more real thing than a parliament; but it cannot be brought back. Yet whether a rebirth of the commune will ensue from the "water and spirit" of the social transformation that is imminent— on this, it seems to me, hangs the whole fate of the human race. An organic commonwealth—and only such commonwealths can join together to form a shapely and articulated race of men—will never build itself up out of individuals but only out of small and ever smaller communities: a nation is a community to the degree that it is a community of communities. If the family does not emerge from the crisis which to-day has all the appearance of a disintegration, purified and renewed, then the State will be nothing more than a machine stoked with the bodies of generations of men. The community that would be capable of such a renewal exists only as a residue. If I speak of its rebirth I am not thinking of a permanent world-situation but an altered one. By the new communes—they might equally well be called the new Co-operatives—I mean the subjects of a changed economy: the collectives into whose hands the control of the means of production is to pass. Once again, everything depends on whether they will be ready.

Just how much economic and political autonomy—for they will of necessity be economic and political units at once—will have to be conceded to them is a technical question that must be asked and answered over and over again; but asked and answered beyond the technical level, in the knowledge that the internal authority of a community hangs together with its external authority. The relationship between centralism and decentralization is a problem which, as we have seen, cannot be approached in principle, but, like everything to do with the relationship between idea and reality, only with great spiritual tact, with the constant and tireless weighing and measuring of the right proportion between them. Centralization— but only so much as is indispensable in the given conditions of time and place. And if the authorities responsible for the drawing and re-drawing of lines of demarcation keep an alert conscience, the relations between the base and the apex of the power-pyramid will be very different from what they are now, even in States that call themselves Communist, i.e. struggling for community. There will have to be a system of representation, too, in the sort of social pattern I have in mind; but it will not, as now, be composed of the pseudorepresentatives of amorphous masses of electors but of representatives well tested in the life and work of the communes. The represented will not, as they are to-day, be bound to their representatives by some windy abstraction, by the mere phraseology of a party-programme, but concretely, through common action and common experience.

The essential thing, however, is that the process of community-building shall run all through the relations of the communes with one another. Only a community of communities merits the title of Commonwealth.

The picture I have hastily sketched will doubtless be laid among the documents of "Utopian Socialism" until the storm turns them up again. Just as I do not believe in Marx's "gestation" of the new form, so I do not believe either in Bakunin's virgin-birth from the womb of Revolution. But I do believe in the meeting of idea and fate in the creative hour.

MURRAY BOOKCHIN

(1921-   )

Murray Bookchin, editor of **Anarchos** magazine, is perhaps the most articulate of the new anarchists. In the title essay from his recent book, **Post-Scarcity Anarchism,** Bookchin argues that the New Left has made some bad mistakes in its attempts to liberate "the people" from oppressive political forms. While agreeing with much of Marx's analysis of the ills of classical capitalist society, Bookchin sees the present state of society as qualitatively different from the nineteenth-century society Marx took as his text. Consequently, new ideas are in order.

Bookchin derives his new ideas from multiple sources. Moving from ecology and the psychology of sexuality to reflections on the counterculture, his argument synthesizes many of the points made by Slater, Marin, and Reich. They would surely endorse Bookchin's description of nature as a model for building collective stability through individuation and diversity rather than simplification and uniformity. Interested readers can find out more about Bookchin's ideas on ecology from his essay "Ecology and Revolutionary Thought," also in **Post-Scarcity Anarchism.**

In analyzing the merits of Bookchin's case one is struck by how frequently an argument rests on factual claims rather than conceptual analysis. Bookchin's argument is historical, as the title of his book proclaims. He presents us with an avowedly utopian picture of an anarchistic society that is just around the corner if we but liberate ourselves and see. The positive picture, based as it is on appealing philosophical, psychological, and social concepts, can hardly help but arouse our hopes and enthusiasm, just as Plato's ideas of Beauty and Justice fill us with admiration. But here again, as with the **Crito,** we are faced with a difficult question of applicability, of timing, which is just what Bookchin's essay is all about. He claims that the time is ripe. Now is the time for the anarchist revolution. Is he right?

While all too ready to commit myself on many issues, I'm not so sure about this one. The final cogency of Bookchin's argument rests on claims of historical fact and not on conceptual analysis. **Are** we just around the corner from revolution? **Is** the groundswell of discontent as widespread as Bookchin claims? Are the basic economic resources really at hand?

Whether or not his grasp of the historical situation is correct, however, Bookchin's contribution to utopian theory is valuable. Without a utopian dimension in social and political thinking we lose the power to step outside existing conditions to get a perspective on the present. Plato's **Republic** was not intended as a model to be actualized, but as a thought experiment allowing its readers to gain a breadth of perspective on their actual situation, social and personal. Bookchin's essay, though clearly intended as a call to immediate action, can also serve the aims of reflection.

Post-Scarcity Anarchism

Preconditions and Possibilities

All the successful revolutions of the past have been particularistic revolutions of minority classes seeking to assert their specific interests over those of society as a whole. The great bourgeois revolutions of modern times offered an ideology of sweeping political reconstitution, but in reality they merely certified the social dominance of the bourgeoisie, giving formal political expression to the economic ascendancy of capital. The lofty notions of the "nation," the "free citizen," of "equality before the law," concealed the mundane reality of the centralized state, the atomized isolated man, the dominance of bourgeois interest. Despite their sweeping ideological claims, the particularistic revolutions replaced the rule of one class by another, one system of exploitation by another, one system of toil by another, and one system of psychological repression by another.

What is unique about our era is that the particularistic revolution has now been subsumed by the possibility of the generalized revolution—complete and totalistic. Bourgeois society, if it achieved nothing else, revolutionized the means of production on a scale unprecedented in history. This technological revolution, culminating in cybernation, has created the objective, quantitative basis for a world without class rule, exploitation, toil or material want. The means now exist for the development of the rounded man, the total man, freed of guilt and the workings of authoritarian modes of training, and given over to desire and the sensuous apprehension of the marvelous. It is now possible to conceive of man's future experience in terms of a coherent process in which the bifurcations of thought and activity, mind and sensuousness, discipline and spontaneity, individuality and community, man and nature, town and country, education and life, work and play are all resolved, harmonized, and organically wedded in a qualitatively new realm of freedom. Just as the particularized revolution produced a particularized, bifurcated society, so the generalized revolution can produce an organically unified, many-sided community. The great wound opened by propertied society in the form of the "social question" can now be healed.

That freedom must be conceived of in human terms, not in animal terms —in terms of life, not of survival—is clear enough. Men do not remove their ties of bondage and become fully human merely by divesting themselves of social domination and obtaining freedom in its *abstract* form. They must also be free *concretely*: free from material want, from toil, from the burden of devoting the greater part of their time—indeed, the greater part of their lives—to the struggle with necessity. To have seen these material preconditions for human freedom, to have emphasized that freedom presupposes free time and the material abundance for abolishing free time as a social privilege, is the great contribution of Karl Marx to modern revolutionary theory.

By the same token, the *preconditions* for freedom must not be mistaken for the *conditions* of freedom. The *possibility* of liberation does not constitute its *reality*. Along with its positive aspects, technological advance has a distinctly negative, socially regressive side. If it is true that technological progress enlarges the historical potentiality for freedom, it is also true that the bourgeois control of technology reinforces the established organization of society and everyday life. Technology and the resources of abundance furnish capitalism with the means for assimilating large sections of society to the established system of hierarchy and authority. They provide the system with the weaponry, the detecting devices and the propaganda media for the threat as well as the reality of massive repression. By their centralistic nature, the resources of abundance reinforce the monopolistic, centralistic and bureaucratic tendencies in the political apparatus. In short, they furnish the state with historically unprecedented means for manipulating and mobilizing the entire environment of life—and for perpetuating hierarchy, exploitation and unfreedom.

It must be emphasized, however, that this manipulation and mobilization of the environment is extremely problematical and laden with crises. Far from leading to pacification (one can hardly speak, here, of harmonization), the attempt of bourgeois society to control and exploit its environment, natural as well as social, has devastating consequences. Volumes have been written on the pollution of the atmosphere and waterways, on the destruction of tree cover and soil, and on toxic materials in foods and liquids. Even more threatening in their final results are the pollution and destruction of the very ecology required for a complex organism like man. The concentration of radioactive wastes in living things is a menace to the health and genetic endowment of nearly all species. Worldwide contamination by pesticides that inhibit oxygen production in plankton or by the near-toxic level of lead from gasoline exhaust are examples of an enduring pollution that threatens the biological integrity of all advanced lifeforms—including man.

No less alarming is the fact that we must drastically revise our traditional notions of what constitutes an environmental pollutant. A few decades ago it would have been absurd to describe carbon dioxide and heat as pollutants in the customary sense of the term. Yet both may well rank among the most serious sources of future ecological imbalance and may pose major threats to the viability of the planet. As a result of industrial and domestic combustion activities, the quantity of carbon dioxide in the atmosphere has increased by roughly twenty-five percent in the past one hundred years, and may well double by the end of the century. The famous "greenhouse effect" which the increasing quantity of the gas is expected to produce has been widely discussed in the media; eventually, it is supposed, the gas will inhibit the dissipation of the world's heat into space, causing a rise in over-all temperatures which will melt the polar ice caps and result in the inundation of vast coastal areas. Thermal pollution, the result mainly of warm water discharged by nuclear and conventional power plants, has had disastrous effects on the ecology of lakes, rivers and estuaries. Increases in water temperature not only damage the physiological and reproductive activities of the fish, they also promote the great blooms of algae that have become such formidable problems in waterways.

Ecologically, bourgeois exploitation and manipulation are undermining the very capacity of the earth to sustain advanced forms of life. The crisis is being heightened by massive increases in air and water pollution; by a mounting accumulation of nondegradable wastes, lead residues, pesticide residues and toxic additives in food; by the expansion of cities into vast urban belts; by increasing stresses due to congestion, noise and mass living;

and by the wanton scarring of the earth as a result of mining operations, lumbering, and real estate speculation. As a result, the earth has been despoiled in a few decades on a scale that is unprecedented in the entire history of human habitation of the planet.

Socially, bourgeois exploitation and manipulation have brought everyday life to the most excruciating point of vacuity and boredom. As society has been converted into a factory and a marketplace, the very rationale of life has been reduced to production for its own sake—and consumption for its own sake.[1]

The Redemptive Dialectic

Is there a redemptive dialectic that can guide the social development in the direction of an anarchic society where people will attain full control over their daily lives? Or does the social dialectic come to an end with capitalism, its possibilities sealed off by the use of a highly advanced technology for repressive and co-optative purposes?

We must learn here from the limits of Marxism, a project which, understandably in a period of material scarcity, anchored the social dialectic and the contradictions of capitalism in the economic realm. Marx, it has been emphasized, examined the *preconditions for* liberation, not the *conditions of* liberation. The Marxian critique is rooted in the past, in the era of material want and relatively limited technological development. Even its humanistic theory of alienation turns primarily on the issue of work and man's alienation from the product of his labor. Today, however, capitalism is a parasite on the future, a vampire that survives on the technology and resources of freedom. The industrial capitalism of Marx's time organized its commodity relations around a prevailing system of material scarcity; the state capitalism of our time organizes its commodity relations around a prevailing system of material abundance. A century ago, scarcity had to be endured; today, it has to be enforced—hence the importance of the state in the present era. It is not that modern capitalism has resolved its contradictions[2] and annulled the social dialectic, but rather that the social dialectic and the contradictions of capitalism have expanded from the economic to the hierarchical realms of society, from the abstract "historic" domain to

[1] It is worth noting here that the emergence of the "consumer society" provides us with remarkable evidence of the difference between the industrial capitalism of Marx's time and state capitalism today. In Marx's view, capitalism as a system organized around "production for the sake of production" results in the economic immiseration of the proletariat. "Production for the sake of production" is paralleled today by "consumption for the sake of consumption," in which immiseration takes a spiritual rather than an economic form—it is starvation of life.

[2] The economic contradictions of capitalism have not disappeared, but the system can plan to such a degree that they no longer have the explosive characteristics they had in the past.

the concrete minutiae of everyday experience, from the arena of survival to the arena of life.

The dialectic of bureaucratic state capitalism originates in the contradiction between the repressive character of commodity society and the enormous potential freedom opened by technological advance. This contradiction also opposes the exploitative organization of society to the natural world—a world that includes not only the natural environment, but also man's "nature"—his Eros-derived impulses. The contradiction between the exploitative organization of society and the natural environment is beyond co-optation: the atmosphere, the waterways, the soil and the ecology required for human survival are not redeemable by reforms, concessions, or modifications of strategic policy. There is no technology that can reproduce atmospheric oxygen in sufficient quantities to sustain life on this planet. There is no substitute for the hydrological systems of the earth. There is no technique for removing massive environmental pollution by radioactive isotopes, pesticides, lead and petroleum wastes. Nor is there the faintest evidence that bourgeois society will relent at any time in the foreseeable future in its disruption of vital ecological processes, in its exploitation of natural resources, in its use of the atmosphere and waterways as dumping areas for wastes, or in its cancerous mode of urbanization and land abuse.

Even more immediate is the contradiction between the exploitative organization of society and man's Eros-derived impulses—a contradiction that manifests itself as the banalization and impoverishment of experience in a bureaucratically manipulated, impersonal mass society. The Eros-derived impulses in man can be repressed and sublimated, but they can never be eliminated. They are renewed with every birth of a human being and with every generation of youth. It is not surprising today that the young, more than any economic class or stratum, articulate the life-impulses in humanity's nature—the urgings of desire, sensuousness, and the lure of the marvelous. Thus, the biological matrix, from which hierarchical society emerged ages ago, reappears at a new level with the era that marks the end of hierarchy, only now this matrix is saturated with social phenomena. Short of manipulating humanity's germ plasm, the life-impulses can be annulled only with the annihilation of man himself.

The contradictions within bureaucratic state capitalism permeate all the hierarchical forms developed and overdeveloped by bourgeois society. The hierarchical forms which nurtured propertied society for ages and promoted its development—the state, city, centralized economy, bureaucracy, patriarchal family, and marketplace—have reached their historic limits. They have exhausted their social functions as modes of stabilization. It is not a question of whether these hierarchical forms were ever "progressive" in the Marxian sense of the term. As Raoul Vaneigem has observed: "Perhaps it isn't enough to say that hierarchical power has preserved humanity for thousands of years as alcohol preserves a fetus, by arresting either growth or decay."[3] Today these forms constitute the target of all the revolutionary forces that are generated by modern capitalism, and whether one sees their outcome as nuclear catastrophe or ecological disaster *they now threaten the very survival of humanity.*

With the development of hierarchical forms into a threat to the very existence of humanity, the social dialectic, far from being annulled, acquires a new dimension. It poses the "social question" in an entirely new way. If man had to acquire the conditions of survival in order to live (as Marx emphasized), now he must acquire the conditions of life in order to survive. By this inversion of the relationship between survival and life, revolution acquires a new sense of urgency. No longer are we faced with Marx's famous choice of socialism or barbarism; we are confronted with the more drastic alternatives of anarchism or annihilation. The problems of necessity and survival have become congruent with the problems of freedom and life. They cease to require any theoretical mediation, "transitional" stages, or centralized organizations to bridge the gap between the existing and the possible. The possible, in fact, is all that can exist. Hence, the problems of "transition," which occupied the Marxists for nearly a century, are eliminated not only by the advance of technology, but by the social dialectic itself. The problems of social reconstruction have been reduced to practical tasks that can be solved spontaneously by self-liberatory acts of society.

Revolution, in fact, acquires not only a new sense of urgency, but a new sense of promise. In the hippies' tribalism, in the drop-out lifestyles and free sexuality of millions of youth, in the spontaneous affinity groups of the anarchists, we find forms of affirmation that follow from acts of negation. With the inversion of the "social question" there is also an inversion of the social dialectic; a "yea" emerges automatically and simultaneously with a "nay."

The solutions take their point of departure from the problems. When the time has arrived in history that the state, the city, bureaucracy, the centralized economy, the patriarchal family and the marketplace have reached their historic limits, what is posed is no longer a change in form but the absolute negation of *all* hierarchical forms *as such*. The absolute negation of the state is anarchism—a situation in which men liberate not only "history," but all the immediate circumstances of their everyday lives. The absolute negation of the city is community—a community in which the social environment is decentralized into rounded, ecologically balanced communes. The absolute negation of bureaucracy is immediate as distinguished from mediated relations—a situation in which representation is replaced by face-to-face relations in a general assembly of free individuals. The absolute negation of the centralized economy is regional ecotechnology—a situation in which the instruments of production are molded to the resources of an ecosystem. The absolute negation of the patriarchal family is liberated

---

[3] Raoul Vaneigem, "The Totality for Kids" (International Situationist pamphlet; London, n.d.), p. 1.

sexuality—in which all forms of sexual regulation are transcended by the spontaneous, untrammeled expression of eroticism among equals. The absolute negation of the marketplace is communism—in which collective abundance and cooperation transform labor into play and need into desire.

Spontaneity and Utopia

It is not accidental that at a point in history when hierarchical power and manipulation have reached their most threatening proportions, the very concepts of hierarchy, power and manipulation are being brought into question. The challenge to these concepts comes from a rediscovery of the importance of spontaneity—a rediscovery nourished by ecology, by a heightened conception of self-development, and by a new understanding of the revolutionary process in society.

What ecology has shown is that balance in nature is achieved by organic variation and complexity, not by homogeneity and simplification. For example, the more varied the flora and fauna of an ecosystem, the more stable the population of a potential pest. The more environmental diversity is diminished, the greater will the population of a potential pest fluctuate, with the probability that it will get out of control. Left to itself, an ecosystem tends spontaneously toward organic differentiation, greater variety of flora and fauna, and diversity in the number of prey and predators. This does not mean that interference by man must be avoided. The need for a productive agriculture—itself a form of interference with nature—must always remain in the foreground of an ecological approach to food cultivation and forest management. No less important is the fact that man can often produce changes in an ecosystem that would vastly improve its ecological quality. But these efforts require insight and understanding, not the exercise of brute power and manipulation.

This concept of management, this new regard for the importance of spontaneity, has far-reaching applications for technology and community—indeed, for the social image of man in a liberated society. It challenges the capitalist ideal of agriculture as a factory operation, organized around immense, centrally controlled land-holdings, highly specialized forms of monoculture, the reduction of the terrain to a factory floor, the substitution of chemical for organic processes, the use of gang-labor, etc. If food cultivation is to be a mode of cooperation with nature rather than a contest between opponents, the agriculturist must become thoroughly familiar with the ecology of the land; he must acquire a new sensitivity to its needs and possibilities. This presupposes the reduction of agriculture to a human scale, the restoration of moderate-sized agricultural units, and the diversification of the agricultural situation; in short, it presupposes a decentralized, ecological system of food cultivation.

The same reasoning applies to pollution control. The development of giant factory complexes and the use of single- or dual-energy sources are responsible for atmospheric pollution. Only by developing small industrial units and diversifying energy sources by the extensive use of clean power (solar, wind and water power) will it be possible to reduce industrial pollution. The means for this radical technological change are now at hand. Technologists have developed miniaturized substitutes for large-scale industrial operation—small versatile machines and sophisticated methods for converting solar, wind and water energy into power usable in industry and the home. These substitutes are often more productive and less wasteful than the large-scale facilities that exist today.

The implications of small-scale agriculture and industry for a community are obvious: if humanity is to use the principles needed to manage an ecosystem, the basic communal unit of social life must itself become an ecosystem—an ecocommunity. It too must become diversified, balanced and well-rounded. By no means is this concept of community motivated exclusively by the need for a lasting balance between man and the natural world; it also accords with the utopian ideal of the rounded man, the individual whose sensibilities, range of experience, and life style are nourished by a wide range of stimuli, by a diversity of activities, and by a social scale that always remains within the comprehension of a single human being. Thus the means and conditions of survival become the means and conditions of life; need becomes desire and desire becomes need. The point is reached where the greatest social decomposition provides the source of the highest form of social integration, bringing the most pressing ecological necessities into a common focus with the highest utopian ideals.

If it is true, as Guy Debord observes, that "daily life is the measure of everything: of the fulfillment or rather the non-fulfillment of human relationships, of the use we make of our time,"[4] a question arises: Who are "we" whose daily lives are to be fulfilled? And how does the liberated self emerge that is capable of turning time into life, space into community, and human relationships into the marvelous?

The liberation of the self involves, above all, a social process. In a society that has shriveled the self into a commodity—into an object manufactured for exchange—there can be no fulfilled self. There can only be the beginnings of selfhood, the *emergence* of a self that seeks fulfillment—a self that is largely defined by the obstacles it must overcome to achieve realization. In a society whose belly is distended to the bursting point with revolution, whose chronic state is an unending series of labor pains, whose real condition is a mounting emergency, only one thought and act is relevant—giving birth. Any environment, private or social, that does not make this fact the center of human experience is a sham and diminishes whatever self remains to us after we have absorbed our daily poison of everyday life in bourgeois society.

It is plain that the goal of revolution today must be the liberation of daily life. Any revolution that fails to achieve this goal is counterrevolution.

---

[4] Guy Debord, "Perspectives for Conscious Modification of Daily Life," mimeographed translation from *Internationale Situationiste*, no. 6 (n.p., n.d.), p. 2.

Above all, it is *we* who have to be liberated, *our* daily lives, with all their moments, hours and days, and not universals like "History" and "Society."[5] The self must always be *identifiable* in the revolution, not overwhelmed by it. The self must always be *perceivable* in the revolutionary process, not submerged by it. There is no word that is more sinister in the "revolutionary" vocabulary than "masses." Revolutionary liberation must be a self-liberation that reaches social dimensions, not "mass liberation" or "class liberation" behind which lurks the rule of an elite, a hierarchy and a state. If a revolution fails to produce a new society by the self-activity and self-mobilization of revolutionaries, if it does not involve the forging of a self in the revolutionary process, the revolution will once again circumvent those whose lives are to be lived every day and leave daily life unaffected. Out of the revolution must emerge a self that takes full possession of daily life, not a daily life that once again takes full possession of the self. The most advanced form of class consciousness thus becomes self-consciousness—the concretization in daily life of the great liberating universals.

If for this reason alone, the revolutionary movement is profoundly concerned with lifestyle. It must try to *live* the revolution in all its totality, not only participate in it. It must be deeply concerned with the way the revolutionist lives, his relations with the surrounding environment, and his degree of self-emancipation. In seeking to change society, the revolutionist cannot avoid changes in himself that demand the reconquest of his own being. Like the movement in which he participates, the revolutionist must try to reflect the conditions of the society he is trying to achieve—at least to the degree that this is possible today.

The treacheries and failures of the past half century have made it axiomatic that there *can be no separation of the revolutionary process from the revolutionary goal.* A society whose fundamental aim is self-administration in all facets of life can be achieved only by self-activity. This implies a mode of administration that is always possessed by the self. The power of man over man can be destroyed only by the very process in which man acquires power over his own life and in which he not only "discovers" himself but, more meaningfully, in which he formulates his self-hood in all its social dimensions.

A libertarian society can be achieved only by a libertarian revolution. Freedom cannot be "delivered" to the individual as the "end-product" of a "revolution"; the assembly and community cannot be legislated or decreed into existence. A revolutionary group can seek, purposively and consciously, to promote the creation of these forms, but if assembly and community are not allowed to emerge organically, if their growth is not matured by the process of demassification, by self-activity and by self-realization, they will

---

[5] Despite its lip service to the dialectic, the traditional left has yet to take Hegel's "concrete universal" seriously and see it not merely as a philosophical concept but as a social program. This has been done only in Marx's early writings, in the writings of the great utopians (Fourier and William Morris) and, in our time, by the drop-out youth.

remain nothing but forms, like the soviets in postrevolutionary Russia. Assembly and community must arise within the revolutionary process; indeed, the revolutionary process must *be* the formation of assembly and community, and also the destruction of power, property, hierarchy and exploitation.

Revolution as self-activity is not unique to our time. It is the paramount feature of all the great revolutions in modern history. It marked the *journées* of the *sans-culottes* [poor people's march] in 1792 and 1793, the famous "Five Days" of February 1917 in Petrograd, the uprising of the Barcelona proletariat in 1936, the early days of the Hungarian Revolution in 1956, and the May-June events in Paris in 1968. Nearly every revolutionary uprising in the history of our time has been initiated spontaneously by the self-activity of "masses"—often in flat defiance of the hesitant policies advanced by the revolutionary organizations. Every one of these revolutions has been marked by extraordinary individuation, by a joyousness and solidarity that turned everyday life into a festival. This surreal dimension of the revolutionary process, with its explosion of deep-seated libidinal forces, grins irascibly through the pages of history like the face of a satyr on shimmering water. It is not without reason that the Bolshevik commissars smashed the wine bottles in the Winter Palace on the night of November 7, 1917.

The puritanism and work ethic of the traditional left stem from one of the most powerful forces opposing revolution today—the capacity of the bourgeois environment to infiltrate the revolutionary framework. The origins of this power lie in the commodity nature of man under capitalism, a quality that is almost automatically transferred to the organized group—and which the group, in turn, reinforces in its members. As the late Josef Weber emphasized, all organized groups "have the tendency to render themselves autonomous, i.e, to alienate themselves from their original aim and to become an end in themselves in the hands of those administering them."[6] This phenomenon is as true of revolutionary organizations as it is of state and semi-state institutions, official parties and trade unions.

The problem of alienation can never be completely resolved apart from the revolutionary process itself, but it can be guarded against by an acute awareness that the problem exists, and partly solved by a voluntary but drastic remaking of the revolutionary and his group. This remaking can only begin when the revolutionary group recognizes that it is a catalyst in the revolutionary process, not a "vanguard." The revolutionary group must clearly see that its goal is not the seizure of power but the dissolution of power—indeed, it must see that the entire problem of power, of control from below and control from above, can be solved only if there is no above or below.

Above all, the revolutionary group must divest itself of the forms of power—statutes, hierarchies, property, prescribed opinions, fetishes, paraphernalia, official etiquette—and of the subtlest as well as the most obvious

[6] Josef Weber, "The Great Utopia," *Contemporary Issues,* vol. 2, no. 5 (1950), p. 12.

of bureaucratic and bourgeois traits that consciously and unconsciously reinforce authority and hierarchy. The group must remain open to public scrutiny not only in its formulated decisions but also in their very formulation. It must be coherent in the profound sense that its theory is its practice and its practice its theory. It must do away with all commodity relations in its day-to-day existence and constitute itself along the decentralizing organizational principles of the very society it seeks to achieve—community, assembly, spontaneity. It must, in Josef Weber's superb words, be "marked always by simplicity and clarity, always thousands of unprepared people can enter and direct it, always it remains *transparent* to and controlled by all."[7] Only then, when the revolutionary movement is congruent with the decentralized community it seeks to achieve, can it avoid becoming another elitist obstacle to the social development and dissolve into the revolution like surgical thread into a healing wound.

Prospect

The most important process going on in America today is the sweeping de-institutionalization of the bourgeois social structure. A basic, far-reaching disrespect and a profound disloyalty are developing toward the values, the forms, the aspirations and, above all, the institutions of the established order. On a scale unprecedented in American history, millions of people are shedding their commitment to the society in which they live. They no longer believe in its claims. They no longer respect its symbols. They no longer accept its goals, and, most significantly, they refuse almost intuitively to live by its institutional and social codes.

This growing refusal runs very deep. It extends from an opposition to war into a hatred of political manipulation in all its forms. Starting from a rejection of racism, it brings into question the very existence of hierarchical power as such. In its detestation of middle-class values and lifestyles it rapidly evolves into a rejection of the commodity system; from an irritation with environmental pollution, it passes into a rejection of the American city and modern urbanism. In short, it tends to transcend every particularistic critique of the society and to evolve into a generalized opposition to the bourgeois order on an ever broadening scale.

In this respect, the period in which we live closely resembles the revolutionary Enlightenment that swept through France in the eighteenth century —a period that completely reworked French consciousness and prepared the conditions for the Great Revolution of 1789. Then as now, the old institutions were slowly pulverized by molecular action from below long before they were toppled by mass revolutionary action. This molecular movement creates an atmosphere of general lawlessness: a growing personal day-to-day disobedience, a tendency not to "go along" with the existing system, a seemingly "petty" but nevertheless critical attempt to circumvent restric-

---

[7] Ibid., p. 19 (my emphasis—M.B.).

tion in every facet of daily life. The society, in effect, becomes disorderly, undisciplined, Dionysian—a condition that reveals itself most dramatically in an increasing rate of official crimes. A vast critique of the system develops—the actual Enlightenment itself, two centuries ago, and the sweeping critique that exists today—which seeps downward and accelerates the molecular movement at the base. Be it an angry gesture, a "riot" or a conscious change in lifestyle, an ever-increasing number of people—who have no more of a commitment to an organized revolutionary movement than they have to society itself—begin spontaneously to engage in their own defiant propaganda of the deed.

In its concrete details, the disintegrating social process is nourished by many sources. The process develops with all the unevenness, indeed with all the contradictions, that mark every revolutionary trend. In eighteenth century France, radical ideology oscillated between a rigid scientism and a sloppy romanticism. Notions of freedom were anchored in a precise, logical ideal of self-control, and also a vague, instinctive norm of spontaneity. Rousseau stood at odds with d'Holbach, Diderot at odds with Voltaire, yet in retrospect we can see that one not only transcended but also presupposed the other in a *cumulative* development toward revolution.

The same uneven, contradictory and cumulative development exists today, and in many cases it follows a remarkably direct course. The "beat" movement created the most important breach in the solid, middle-class values of the 1950s, a breach that was widened enormously by the illegalities of pacifists, civil-rights workers, draft resisters and longhairs. Moreover, the merely reactive response of rebellious American youth has produced invaluable forms of libertarian and utopian affirmation—the right to make love without restriction, the goal of community, the disavowal of money and commodities, the belief in mutual aid, and a new respect for spontaneity. Easy as it is for revolutionaries to criticize certain pitfalls within this orientation of personal and social values, the fact remains that it has played a preparatory role of decisive importance in forming the present atmosphere of indiscipline, spontaneity, radicalism and freedom.

A second parallel between the revolutionary Enlightenment and our own period is the emergence of the crowd, the so-called "mob," as a major vehicle of social protest. The typical institutionalized forms of public dissatisfaction—in our own day, they are orderly elections, demonstration and mass meetings—tend to give way to direct action by crowds. This shift from predictable, highly organized protests within the institutionalized framework of the existing society to sporadic, spontaneous, near-insurrectionary assaults from outside (and even against) socially acceptable forms reflects a profound change in popular psychology. The "rioter" has begun to break, however partially and intuitively, with those deep-seated norms of behavior which traditionally weld the "masses" to the established order. He actively sheds the internalized structure of authority, the long-cultivated body of conditioned reflexes, and the pattern of submission sustained by guilt that tie one to the system even more effectively than any fear of police violence and juridical reprisal. Contrary to the views of social psychologists, who see in these modes of direct action the submission of the individual to a terrifying collective entity called the "mob," the truth is that "riots" and crowd actions represent the first gropings of the mass toward individuation. The mass tends to become demassified in the sense that it begins to assert itself against the really massifying automatic responses produced by the bourgeois family, the school and the mass media. By the same token, crowd actions involve the rediscovery of the streets and the effort to liberate them. Ultimately, it is in the streets that power must be dissolved: for the streets, where daily life is endured, suffered and eroded, and where power is confronted and fought, must be turned into the domain where daily life is enjoyed, created and nourished. The rebellious crowd marked the beginning not only of a spontaneous transmutation of private into social revolt, but also of a return from the abstractions of social revolt to the issues of everyday life.

Finally, as in the Enlightenment, we are seeing the emergence of an immense and ever-growing stratum of *déclassés,* a body of lumpenized individuals drawn from every stratum of society. The chronically indebted and socially insecure middle classes of our period compare loosely with the chronically insolvent and flighty nobility of prerevolutionary France. A vast flotsam of educated people emerged then as now, living at loose ends, without fixed careers or established social roots. At the bottom of both structures we find a large number of chronic poor—vagabonds, drifters, people with part-time jobs or no jobs at all, threatening, unruly *sans-culottes* —surviving on public aid and on the garbage thrown off by society, the poor of the Parisian slums, the blacks of the American ghettoes.

But here all the parallels end. The French Enlightenment belongs to a period of revolutionary transition from feudalism to capitalism—both societies based on economic scarcity, class rule, exploitation, social hierarchy and state power. The day-to-day popular resistance which marked the eighteenth century and culminated in open revolution was soon disciplined by the newly emerging industrial order—as well as by naked force. The vast mass of *déclassés* and *sans-culottes* was largely absorbed into the factory system and tamed by industrial discipline. Formerly rootless intellectuals and footloose nobles found secure places in the economic, political, social and cultural hierarchy of the new bourgeois order. From a socially and culturally fluid condition, highly generalized in its structure and relations, society hardened again into rigid, particularized class and institutional forms—the classical Victorian era appeared not only in England but, to one degree or another, in all of Western Europe and America. Critique was consolidated into apologia, revolt into reform, *déclassés* into clearly defined classes and "mobs" into political constituencies. "Riots" became the well-behaved processionals we call "demonstrations," and spontaneous direct action turned into electoral rituals.

Our own era is also a transitional one, but with a profound and new difference. In the last of their great insurrections, the *sans-culottes* of the French Revolution rose under the fiery cry: "Bread and the Constitution of '93!" The black *sans-culottes* of the American ghettoes rise under the slogan: "Black is beautiful!" Between these two slogans lies a development of unprecedented importance. The *déclassés* of the eighteenth century were formed during a slow transition from an agricultural to an industrial era; they were created out of a pause in the historical transition from one regime of toil to another. The demand for bread could have been heard at any time in the evolution of propertied society. The new *déclassés* of the twentieth century are being created as a result of the bankruptcy of all social forms based on toil. They are the end products of the process of propertied society itself and of the social problems of material survival. In the era when technological advances and cybernation have brought into question the exploitation of man by man, toil, and material want in any form whatever, the cry "Black is beautiful" or "Make love, not war" marks the transformation of the traditional demand for survival into a historically new demand for life.[8] What underpins every social conflict in the United States today is the demand for the realization of all human potentialities in a fully rounded, balanced, totalistic way of life. In short, the potentialities for revolution in America are now anchored in the potentialities of man himself.

What we are witnessing is the breakdown of a century and a half of embourgeoisement and a pulverization of all bourgeois institutions *at a point in history when the boldest concepts of utopia are realizable.* And there is nothing that the present bourgeois order can substitute for the destruction of its traditional institutions but bureaucratic manipulation and state capitalism. This process is unfolding most dramatically in the United States. Within a period of little more than two decades, we have seen the collapse of the "American Dream," or what amounts to the same thing, the steady destruction in the United States of the myth that material abundance, based on commodity relations between men, can conceal the inherent poverty of bourgeois life. Whether this process will culminate in revolution or in annihilation will depend in great part on the ability of revolutionists to extend social consciousness and defend the spontaneity of the revolutionary development from authoritarian ideologies, both of the "left" and of the right.

New York
Oct. 1967–Dec. 1968

[8] The above lines were written in 1966. Since then, we have seen the graffiti on the walls of Paris, during the May–June revolution: "All power to the imagination"; "I take my desires to be reality, because I believe in the reality of my desires"; "Never work"; "The more I make love, the more I want to make revolution"; "Life without dead times"; "The more you consume, the less you live"; "Culture is the inversion of life"; "One does not buy happiness, one steals it"; "Society is a carnivorous flower." These are not graffiti, they are a program for life and desire.

BENJAMIN BARBER
(1939-   )

Benjamin Barber is a new phenomenon on the literary scene. Having already established a dual career as a playwright and political philosopher at age thirty-two, he will undoubtedly have more to say before many years have passed. In the present piece, from his book **Superman and Common Men,** Barber attacks the anarchist tradition with insight and blistering prose. As I suggested in introducing Bookchin's essay, a crucial question for the viability of anarchism is the breadth and popularity of its principles. Barber addresses himself to the question of why anarchism has never gained great popularity. He places part of the blame on its unsuccessful popularizers. The anarchist, he claims, is "a proselytizing aristocrat who, possessed by a **noblesse oblige** of the apocalyptic, is driven to share his own transfiguration with the people. He is an egalitarian elitist dedicated to the notion that all men can be made superior."

While Barber presents enough evidence to show that his case surely applies to **some** anarchists, a real question remains as to whether it applies equally well to **all** anarchists. Specifically, we want to know whether it applies to Bookchin, or to Gary Snyder, whose short essay follows Barber's. Is there a new anarchism, and if so, has Barber appreciated its difference from the old? For example, his very first piece of evidence has backfired. He cites James Joll as acknowledging in 1964 in **The Anarchists** that the movement he is writing about has failed and "no longer exists as a significant historical force." Yet in 1971 Joll and David Apter edited a book of essays with the title **Anarchism Today.** Joll concludes the book with the sentence, "At least, as the essays in this volume clearly show, the international experience of the past few years has proved that, in one form or another, anarchism is, in the second half of the 20th century, still very much a living tradition." So the historical accuracy of Barber's account remains as much in doubt as Bookchin's historical judgment.

But just as Bookchin's essay serves the philosophical function of reflecting a utopian dimension in social thought, so Barber's essay includes an interesting argument showing why certain forms of anarchism are bound to be unsuccessful. He speaks of the anarchists' penchant for standing the naturalistic fallacy on its head. The so-called naturalistic fallacy is to claim that things **ought** to be as they **are** naturally; for example, an extreme form would be the old idea that if man were meant to fly he'd have wings, so since he does not have wings, "by nature" he ought not to fly. Barber is saying that anarchists reverse the naturalistic fallacy when they see man only as he ought to be and not as he is. Barber also tries to show why anarchists are inclined to obscure their own historical vision.

But who is correct? It seems to me that the new anarchists are correct about what man **could** be, but the call for political action depends for its cogency on the claim that enough men already conform to the anarchist vision. Otherwise, as Barber suggests, premature and abortive movements end only in reaction: a more repressive, less liberated existence. Taking Bookchin and Barber together one hears the voice of the visionary tempered by a vision of insistent actuality. But it is not as simple as that either. What **is** actual?

Poetry and Revolution: The Anarchist as Reactionary

There, where the state ceaseth—pray look thither my brethren! Do you not see it, the rainbow and the bridges of the Superman?

NIETZSCHE, *Thus Spake Zarathustra*

Now all bonds are burst that bound me.
Now my flag shall wave around me
Though none follow where I lead.

IBSEN, *Brand*

Anarchism is dead. Certification papers can be found in any number of recent histories and biographies.[1] Nevertheless, anarchism lives: in the banners and slogans of the French Student Movement, in New York townhouse laboratories where amateur chemists forge weapons of terror at the risk of their lives, in the syncretic vision of the anti-authoritarian young Left, and in the street theater and comic braggadocio of the Yippies.

The typologies which have been manufactured to divide anarchists into individualists and collectivists, rationalists and irrationalists, pacifists and terrorists, nationalists and humanists, or progressives and Luddites may suffice in the dissection of anarchism's historical corpse, but they leave the

POETRY AND REVOLUTION: THE ANARCHIST AS REACTIONARY   From Benjamin R. Barber, *Superman and Common Men*. Published by Praeger Publishers, Inc. Copyright 1971 by Praeger Publishers, Inc., New York.

[1] In *The Anarchists* (Boston, 1964), James Joll devotes the greater part of his introduction to a defense of why he is writing the history of a movement which has failed and no longer exists as a significant historical force.

more practical mysteries of the movement unresolved and thus are remarkably unhelpful in dealing with the minuscule anarchist renaissance which has attended the birth of the 1970's.

To comprehend anarchism as a historical force and as a potentially significant contemporary movement requires the focusing of attention on a different order of questions. Why has anarchism been a movement of poets rather than first-order philosophers? Of saints rather than social scientists? Of exemplary rebels rather than successful revolutionaries? Of theatrical eccentrics rather than systematic reformers? Of legends rather than accomplishments? Peruse the list of notables: Godwin, Shelley, Proudhon, Stirner, Tolstoy, Courbet, Kropotkin, Bakunin, Nechayev, Pissaro, Ravachol, Sorel, Cafiero, Makhno, Seurat, Durruti—aristocrats, dilettantes, visionaries, adventurers, literati, poets, and madmen. Where are the circumspect philosophers? The careful students of the social system? The dedicated representatives of the public will? The Hobbeses, the Webers, the Castros of anarchism are nowhere to be found.

But this is not the only puzzle. The anarchists are not only a strange breed of revolutionaries, they are a tribe of failures. Their failure lies less in their inability to liberate any sizable collectivity of men from the tyranny of authority than in their inability to attract any significant number of men to their peculiar vision of liberation. The question is not so much why they failed to vanquish the exploiters as why they failed to move the exploited. Where nationalism, liberal democracy, syndicalism (unionism), and Marxism succeeded, anarchism failed. Alone among nineteenth-century movements for change, it won no permanent victories, secured no trustworthy allies, and attracted no large-scale support. Only in Spain in the 1930's did it enjoy a brief encounter with success. But Spanish anarcho-syndicalism, deeply enmeshed in union organization, military planning, and peasant communalism, was an anomaly whose features are not easily reconciled with anarchism elsewhere. And even in Spain, the movement finally failed—even less able to contend with Communism than with Fascism.

These two puzzles—the peculiarities of anarchism's leaders, its failure to secure a mass following—fit together to form a picture which raises fundamental questions about the viability of anarchism as a philosophy of revolution. If there is any unity at all to be found among the anarchists it is in their common antipathy to political order (whether established or disestablished) and their concomitant dedication not merely to the eventual achievement of radical alternatives, but to the necessity for a revolutionary (though not always violent or cataclysmic) overthrow of present order to reach their goals. Anarchism is, then, a doctrine of revolution, and anarchists are always rebels (whatever else they may be).

It is critical that anarchism be defined as a doctrine of action rather than as a passive metaphysic, because it is in the problems raised by revolutionary strategy and tactics that the beginnings of an answer to our questions are to be found.

The anarchists have never satisfactorily reconciled their multiple and disparate visions of man and society as they conceive them following the revolutionary overthrow of authority with the actual requisites of successful revolutionary activity. Although they have often propounded the inseparability of means and ends—as, for example, in Bakunin's rejection of central organization and political action in the First International[2]—they have never managed to translate the doctrine into a consistent and effective instrument of revolution. Deterred by their fierce sense of mission from adopting a posture of utopian isolationism that would permit them to depict alternative futures without taking responsibility for developing the strategies required for their realization,[3] they nevertheless have not been able to bring themselves to treat strategy in terms divorced from utopia. Not even those among them possessed of a Godwinean mildness can be labeled gradualist, but neither can the most impatient and venomous be called a master strategist. For the inseparability of means and ends makes compromise a sin; and though they are not content to be mere "visionary utopians"[4] they are equally unwilling to accommodate themselves to the realities upon which successful revolutions depend. As Andrew Hacker has written, "quite clearly anarchists wish to have it all ways at once."[5] The purity of utopia but the impact of revolution. And so, hanging somewhere between the ideal and the real, between their vision for the future and their aspirations for the present, the anarchists end by treating the men upon whom they wish to foist a revolution as figments of their own utopian ideals. Utopia becomes an operations' plan, men as they actually exist are treated as if they had already become that which the revolution aspires to make them. Bound by convention and shackled by authority, men are nonetheless entreated to behave like Shelley's Prometheus Unbound:

> Sceptreless, free, uncircumscribed—but man:
> Equal, unclassed, tribeless, and nationless,
> Exempt from awe, worship, degree, the king
> Over himself . . .

Through a confluence of their visionary utopianism and their proselytizing zeal, the anarchists manage to stand the naturalistic fallacy on its head: not that natural man, as he is, is what he ought to be; but that utopian man, as the anarchist conceives he ought to be, is in fact what man is—the evi-

[2] For a sharply critical discussion of the controversy from Marx's position see Engels's *Letter to T. Cuno* dated January 24, 1872 in Marx/Engels, *Selected Works,* II (Moscow, 1951).

[3] I have in mind the utopias of such thinkers as Plato or More or Swift, which were not intended to be taken as doctrinaire programs for revolutionary action.

[4] As Paul Avrich misleadingly calls them in his *The Russian Anarchists* (Princeton, 1967), p. 253.

[5] "Anarchism," *International Encyclopedia of Social Sciences* (New York, 1968).

dence of history and psychology notwithstanding. The realists mistake a limited but empirical portrait of man as he can be described under specified circumstances for man as he ought to be. The anarchist mistakes man as he ought to be in the ideal unauthoritarian society, for man as he is in actual authoritarian societies. Prince Kropotkin thus constructs an ingenious argument to demonstrate that natural selection favors cooperation (mutualism) rather than competition, at least within discrete species.[6] While Huxley and the Social Darwinists try to read a normative lesson on competition *out* of the empirical data assembled by Darwin, Kropotkin tries to read a normative lesson on cooperation *into* those same data, as annotated by his own Siberian research. Similarly, while for Hobbes the laws of justice are but artifices of man and the laws of nature but a codification of how men attuned to their own interest must behave in the state of nature, for Proudhon "the system of the laws of justice is the same as the system of the laws of the world, and they are present in the human soul not only as ideas or concepts but as emotions or feelings."[7] Once again, the difference is between reading laws, *a posteriori,* out of actual behavior, and thus justifying imperatives with naturalistic descriptions, and reading laws rooted in *a priori* reasoning into actual men, thus creating a "real" man at variance with observable behavior patterns.

In light of these observations, it can be no surprise that the anarchist sees the real verichrome world in strange, monochrome hues. It is a world of infinite mutability, a world without power where the limits of revolution are circumscribed only by the rebel's imagination, where the liberation of the masses becomes an impassioned exercise in exhortation. The communist-anarchist Senex warns his individualist comrades that "political sovereignty can be attenuated but cannot be conjured out of existence by a revolutionary fiat,"[8] but most anarchists remain, in Paul Avrich's characterization, neither "able or even willing to come to terms with the inescapable realities of political power."[9] The anarchist revolutionary camp is thus strewn with rhetoric, a living theater of intentional deceptions. (The blurring of the distinction between illusion and reality, which is the special virtue of theater, is remarkably well suited to the anarchist's collapse of the distinction be-

---

[6] "Happily enough, competition is not the rule either in the animal world or in mankind. It is limited among animals to exceptional periods, and natural selection finds better fields for its activity. Better conditions are created by the *elimination of competition* by means of mutual aid and support. . . . 'Don't compete!' . . . That is the tendency of nature, not always realized in full, but always present." P. Kropotkin, *Mutual Aid: A Factor of Evolution* (New York, 1904), p. 74.

[7] Pierre-Joseph Proudhon, *Selected Writings* (New York, 1969), p. 230.

[8] Senex, "Decentralization and Socialism," *Vanguard,* IV, no. 4 (July, 1938), p. 10. Lenin makes the same argument: "The majority of anarchists think and write about the future without understanding the present." Cited by L. Schapiro, *The Origin of the Communist Autocracy* (New York, 1955), p. 182.

[9] Avrich, *loc. cit.*

tween utopian possibilities and revolutionary realities.) Political strategy
with its endless subtleties, its stultifying caveats, is abandoned in favor of
"propaganda by the deed" (*le propagande par la fait*) which turns out,
however, to consist neither in suasive propaganda nor in relevant political
deeds but in a species of spectacular terror that, except for the bloodshed,
might easily be taken as vaudeville. Bombs and slogans become inter-
changeable props in an interminable theatric. The more gentle anarchists—
like Dostoyevsky's *Idiot*—live not only as saints in the world but as if they
lived in a world of saints.[10] And among the violent, enthusiasm is confused
with success, zeal with victory. In the manner that Bakunin once fantasized
about a host of international, conspiratorial anarchist societies bringing Europe to the brink of cataclysm, Jerry Rubin today fantasizes about hordes
of "niggers, and longhair scum invading white middle-class homes, fucking
on the living room floor, crashing on the chandeliers, spewing sperm on the
Jesus pictures, breaking the furniture and smashing Sunday school napalm-
blood Amerika forever."[11] Both Bakunin and Rubin confound iconoclasm
with revolution. Rubin wants to "outrage Amerika until the bourgeoisie
dies of apoplexy,"[12] but systems of power, not being susceptible to coron-
aries, have not been known to expire and collapse in the face of profanity.
In fact, underlying the profanity of the Yippies and the iconoclastic rhetoric
of nihilistic anarchists like Nechayev is a profound innocence about what
moves men and regimes to action. In their naiveté, the anarchists are blind
to the truly profane element in politics—the struggle for power among
ambitious and competitive interest-oriented beings. Marx speaks of the profane in this sense when he berates Proudhon for missing the "profane origin
and the profane history of the categories which he deifies."[13]

For all the anarchists' profanity, their view of actual men is wildly ro-
manticized. Hunger, greed, ambition, avarice, the will to power, to glory, to
honor, and to security which have played some role in all traditional eth-
nologies find no place in the anarchist portrait of man. Max Stirner, the
turgid, darkly romantic early nineteenth-century anarchist, may appear as

[10] A telling difference between white radicals and black militants is the realism with
which the blacks size up their opponents; Julius Lester notes that the enemies of the
nineteenth-century abolitionist Garrison "were thieves and murderers, not candidates
for sainthood." *Look Out Whitey! Black Power's Gon' Get Your Mama* (New York,
1969), p. 41.

[11] Jerry Rubin, *Do It!* (New York, 1970), p. 111.

[12] *Ibid.*, p. 112. The metamorphosis of politics into theatrics is reflected in popular
journals that increasingly treat "political" events in their theater sections. "Is Abbie
Hoffman the Will Shakespeare of the 1970's?" asks a recent Sunday *New York Times*
theater columnist (October 11, 1970). (He isn't.)

[13] Marx, *Letter to P. V. Annekov*, Appendix to *The Poverty of Philosophy* (New
York, 1963), p. 192. I do not mean to make a brief for the realist view of politics,
which suggests that power is *all* there is to politics.

an irrationalist, but his argument for the disenthrallment of Ego is neither an invitation to the exploiters to widen their dominion nor a justification of crass, animal competition. It is a selective call to men to respond to the *unique* in themselves, to throw off the constraints with which society and religion have affected to contain their real selves. Stirner despises the mind —that same reason upon which the eighteenth-century English rationalist Godwin relies for the salvation of man—but his ultimate enemy is Godwin's enemy too: the hierarchy of authority, the dominion of constraint. But where for Godwin dominion and hierarchy are products of ignorance, for Stirner they are products of reason: "Hierarchy is the dominion of thought, the dominion of mind."[14] Both seek autonomy and individuality; they differ only in where they think to have discovered them: Godwin, in the rational mind, Stirner in the unbridled Ego.[15]

Whether the thrust is toward puritanical constraint (as in Godwin or Proudhon) or toward psychic liberation (as in Stirner, Nietzsche, or the Yippies), the anarchist vision does not encompass the mundane species of placid, compromising men who for the most part inhabit the globe. Anarchists of every variety have forever gone among the people as prophets, with Zarathustra's proverb "Man is Something to be Surpassed" on their lips.[16] Reaching downward toward the primitive or upward toward the sublime, they have remained strangers to the middle regions where men live out their daily lives. They have been aggressors rather than interlocutors, prosyletizers not listeners. The distinction between politics and ethics, between collective revolution and personal conversion, has escaped them in the search for what Emma Goldman (an American anarchist of the early part of the century) called a *"fundamental transvaluation of values."*[17] The anarchist becomes a "great TEACHER of the NEW ETHICS."[18]

No revolutionaries can compromise with their enemies and survive, but the anarchists are unwilling to compromise with their followers. They expect men to endure a physical hunger in the struggle to quench a spiritual

---

[14] Max Stirner, *The Ego and His Own* (New York, 1907), p. 95.

[15] Stirner's "Ego" is every bit as vague and indeterminate as the humanist's "man" which Stirner criticizes as "not a person, but an ideal, a spook." (*Ibid.*, p. 101.) It is in fact the particular device of his inverted naturalism noted above. Stirner's naturalism is assailed by Marx in *The German Ideology*.

[16] Friedrich Nietzsche, *Thus Spake Zarathustra,* in *The Philosophy of Nietzsche* (New York: Modern Library), p. 36.

[17] Emma Goldman, "My Further Disillusionment in Russia," in L. I. Krimerman and L. Perry, eds., *Patterns of Anarchy* (Garden City, N.Y., 1966), p. 111. (Emphasis in original.) The use of Nietzsche's phrase "transvaluation of values" (*Umwertung aller Werte*) is of course no mere coincidence.

[18] *Ibid.*, p. 113. (Emphasis in original.)

thirst. "I think," advises Tolstoy, "that the efforts of those who wish to improve our social life should be directed towards the liberation of themselves."[19] The enemy is within, not without, and so the anarchist posture must be one of unceasing exhortation: "Surpass Thyselves!" Like the preacher Brand in Ibsen's most austere play, the anarchist is driven by a fervent passion, both holy and profane, to lead the people out of the Egypt of their unseeing, apathetic lives into a promised land of redemptive liberation:

> Come thou, young man—fresh and free—
> Let a life-breeze lighten thee
> From this dim vault's clinging dust.
> Conquer with me! For thou must
> One day waken, one day rise,
> Nobly break with compromise;—
> Up, and fly the evil days,
> Fly the maze of middle ways,
> Strike the foreman full and fair,
> Battle to the death declare.

The revolution becomes a taking of vows;[20] not a promise to the people that they shall receive but a demand that they sacrifice; not rest to their bodies but spiritual travail and the searing transfiguration of their souls. Eventual salvation, but apocalypse and purgatory first.[21]

The cleansing by fire advocated by the violent anarchists seems intended not only to purge the enemy but to sanctify the revolutionary masses as well: "It is to violence," cries Sorel, "that Socialism owes those high ethical values by means of which it brings *salvation* to the modern world."[22] "The revolutionist is a doomed man," prophesizes Nechayev in the bleak opening paragraph of his grim *Revolutionary Catechism:* "He has no personal interests, no affairs, sentiments, attachments, property, not even a name of his own. Everything in him is absorbed by one exclusive interest, one thought,

[19] Cited by George Woodcock, *Anarchism: A History of Libertarian Ideas and Movements* (New York, 1962), p. 225.

[20] Gandhi, though an anarchist more in spirit than in practice, exacted from the followers of his program of discipline vows of Truthfulness, Nonviolence, Celibacy, Control of the Palate, Nonthieving, and Nonpossession, among others.

[21] The peasants of Andalusia who tried to establish village communes on the ascetic blueprint of the anarchist leader Durruti experienced a period of trial and torment rather than liberation, and Durruti's success in the Spanish Civil War—like Makhno's in the Bolshevik campaigns against the White Forces, in which his anarchist units participated—was due primarily to his military prowess. For an account of an anarchist commune during the Spanish Civil War see Franz Borkenau, *The Spanish Cockpit* (London, 1937).

[22] Georges Sorel, *Reflections on Violence* (New York, 1950), p. 249. (Emphasis in original.) Sorel's language is typically anarchistic in its messianic tone.

one passion—the revolution."[23] Like Brand, Nechayev can promise only a crown of thorns; his way is hard, his dedication total. The man of the middle regions can look on in awe, but can he follow? Anarchism speaks no simple dialect; it rants, in the language of the possessed, of redemption through nihilism, rebirth through sacrifice.[24] It commences mildly enough with the ascetic rationalism of a Godwin asking only that men contain their passion and "propagate their species, not because a certain sensible pleasure is annexed to this action, but because it is right that the species should be propagated," and that the "manner in which they exercise this function . . . be regulated by the dictates of reason and duty."[25] It culminates in Nechayev's renunciation of everything save the revolution: "Surpass Thyselves O Men!"

But revolutions, though they may require renunciation, are fired by the spirit of appropriation. They may produce that "intoxication" which Stirner saw as essential to their success,[26] but they are produced by desperation and sustained by the foresight of the lifting of burdens. George Woodcock praises the more saintly anarchists for calling "on us to stand on our own moral feet like a generation of princes,"[27] but the revolutionary masses are not princes in search of Grace; they are mere men, hungry and oppressed, in search of subsistence, security, and perhaps a modicum of individual autonomy (liberty).

The anarchist remains, however, a proselytizing aristocrat who, possessed by a *noblesse oblige* of the apocalyptic, is driven to share his own transfiguration with the people. He is an egalitarian elitist dedicated to the notion that all men can be made superior. Like the artist, he perceives a larger world; like the prophet, a more enriching plain of experience; like the utopian, a more humane form of community. But unlike these visionaries, he is an impatient social activist, a driving revolutionary who would embody his perceptions in the real world, *now*. He is the *Uebermensch* [overman] of the underdogs. [. . .]

In his *Anarchism and Socialism,* the Russian Marxist Plekhanov draws a biased but suggestive picture of the relationship between the anarchist's ideals, his hatred of compromise, and his acquiescence to terror:

[23] Cited by Philip Pomper, *The Russian Revolutionary Intelligentsia* (New York, 1970), p. 95.

[24] Dostoyevsky's novel about the nihilist-anarchist movement in the early part of the nineteenth century is titled *The Possessed.*

[25] William Godwin, *An Enquiry Concerning Political Justice,* 2 vols. (Philadelphia, 1796), vol. 2, Book VIII, chap. 6.

[26] "For every [revolutionary] effort arrives at reaction when it comes to discreet reflection, and storms forward in the original action only so long as it is an *intoxication.*" *Op. cit.,* p. 144.

[27] Woodcock, *op. cit.,* p. 476.

Whenever the proletariat makes an attempt to somewhat ameliorate its economic position, "large-hearted people," vowing they love the proletariat most tenderly, rush in from all points of the compass . . . put spokes in the wheel of the movement, do their utmost to prove the movement is useless. . . . When the proletariat takes no notice of this, and pursues its "immediate economic" aims undisturbed . . . the same "large-hearted people" re-appear upon the scene armed with bombs. . . .

An Anarchist will have nothing to do with "parliamentarism," since it only lulls the people to sleep . . . [no] "reforms," since reforms are but so many compromises with the possessing classes. He wants a revolution, a "full, complete, immediate and immediately economic" revolution. To attain this end he arms himself with a saucepan full of explosive materials and throws it amongst the public in a theatre or a cafe.

Plekhanov's conclusion is overblown, but it helps to explain why the reactionary right has found such succor in certain anarchist traditions:

Thus, in the name of revolution, the Anarchists serve the cause of reaction; in the name of morality they approve the most immoral acts; in the name of liberty they trample underfoot all the rights of their fellows.

The ambivalence of anarchism toward the people as a revolutionary collective is compounded by the historical circumstances in which the nineteenth-century movement sprang up. The philosophical core of anarchism consists of a rejection of all authority—particularly those oppressive forms of authority which manifested themselves in a statist coercion. Yet by the nineteenth century, the more tyrannical and arbitrary forms of statist authority had already been deposed by liberal and democratic theory—in theory if not in fact. The very concept of legitimacy had been articulated precisely to discriminate between acceptable and unacceptable varieties of authority. Though initially grounded in natural law reasoning, it had by the nineteenth century come to be seen as a function of consent—either explicitly (majoritarianism) or implicitly (the social contract). Though liberals were careful to limit the sphere of action of legitimate authority, they concurred in the general recognition that authority was a prerequisite of civilized life and that justifications for authority were necessary. Rousseau and Kant further solidified the notion of legitimate authority by exploring the relationship between individual autonomy and obedience to law.

The upshot of these developments in political philosophy was that anarchist theory—already disposed against the pliant, yielding masses by its aristocratic temper—found itself face to face not with the abstract notion of authority but with the concrete democratic justification of legitimacy. Of the traditional arguments for authority, only the one rooted in consent survived and flourished into the nineteenth century. Godwin had clearly perceived this at the end of the eighteenth century. "The Voice of the People is not . . . 'the voice of Truth and of God,' " he warns; "consent cannot convert right into wrong."[28] Proudhon was, by the beginning of the nineteenth, to be far more blunt: "Universal Suffrage is the Counterrevolution" became a lasting slogan of the movement.

The anarchists saw, much more clearly than liberals like Tocqueville and Mill (who shared their elitism), that authority blessed by numbers was far less tractable than authority consecrated by papal benediction and upheld by royalty. The more stentorian the voice, the more numerous the people, the more dangerous the enemy! Max Stirner cautioned:

> The monarch in the person of the "royal master" has been a paltry monarch compared with the new monarch, the "sovereign nation." This *monarchy* was a thousand times severer, stricter, and more consistent. Against the new monarch there was no longer any right, any privilege at all; how limited the "absolute king" of the *ancient regime* looks in comparison! The revolution effected the transformation of *limited monarchy* into *absolute monarchy.*[29]

Finally, anarchist theory has no choice but to reject the entire mode of discourse by which degrees and kinds of justice and injustice are distinguished in the political realm; it must reject political theory itself in favor of poetry and revelation. Like Herbert Read, it can see nothing to choose between fascism and democracy, between a Hitler and a Churchill.[30] Indeed, like Read, it must view the "incursions of democracy [as] far more dangerous because they are far more deceitful."[31] And so the contemporary anarchist not only sees nothing in the choice between Humphrey and Nixon (it is not at all clear that there is anything in this choice), but also sees nothing in the choice between Wallace and Julian Bond. They are all tainted, all politicians playing the power game whether for or against the people.

Robert Paul Wolff represents the philosophical extreme of the rejection of political discourse: "On the basis of a lengthy reflection upon the concept of *de jure* legitimate authority," he relates with characteristic understatement, "I have come to the conclusion that philosophical anarchism is true. That is to say, I believe that there is not, and there could not be, a state that has a right to command and whose subjects have a binding obli-

[28] *Op. cit.,* Book II, chap. 5.

[29] *Op. cit.,* p. 132.

[30] "I am concerned to show that from a certain point of view there is nothing to choose between fascism and democracy." Herbert Read, *To Hell with Culture* (New York, 1964), p. 49. Also see p. 46.

[31] *Ibid.,* p. 49.

gation to obey."[32] If authority is to be sent into exile, it is legitimacy that must be banished. The temperamental predilection of the anarchists for elitism thus finds its philosophical analog in the need to rebut the claims not simply of democratic theory, but of political theory generally. At the same time, anarchist arguments combating democracy confirm the anarchist's temperamental disdain for the people and seem to justify his refusal to articulate revolutionary goals appropriate to the practical needs of men.

Our questions then answer themselves—for the answers are in the asking; the puzzle is solved. Anarchism has attracted no social scientists because its concerns are not with social realities; it has intrigued no first order philosophers because it is riddled with paradox, stranded between its lust for revolution and its penchant for utopia. It has attracted no followers because it has had leaders who would lead where men cannot or will not follow. It disdains the men it would liberate. At the crucial moment it prefers its own visions to their needs.

In the anarchist hierarchy of values, it is the primacy of the aesthetic that is most evident. The anarchist poet Laurent Tailhade speaks at least a little for all anarchists when he writes, "What matter the victims provided the gesture is beautiful?" Anarchism is a movement of the imagination—real men, mundane needs, come second.

The lesson for the contemporary anarchist ripple—it hardly qualifies as a movement—is obvious enough. Those who would save society must first face some difficult choices. They must choose between the solipsistic imagination and the realities of exploitation and human misery; between the theatrics of grand tragedy and the dull desperate plight of uninteresting prisoners of poverty, ignorance, and mediocrity; between pristine ideals and the possibilities of actual change. Not all good things mix: ultimately, they may have to choose between poetry and revolution.

GARY SNYDER

(1930-   )

Gary Snyder would seem to be a prime candidate for Barber's attack: he is a poet. Yet his short and elegant statement is included for several reasons. First, Snyder shows the nonpolitical origins and intentions of a certain type of anarchism. Second, his gentle voice speaks its own reply to Barber's rhetorical charges. (And who is the greater proselytizer?)

---

[32] "On Violence," *Journal of Philosophy*, LXVI, no. 19 (1969), p. 607. See also his *In Defense of Anarchism* (New York, 1970) in which he elaborates his assault on classical democratic theory. Wolff's crisis of conscience is the subject of further analysis in the third essay in this volume.

Snyder offers only a description of the tribe, no manifesto. He apparently accepts the idea that this movement may always remain on the margins of society, yet he shows none of the arrogance of elitism. No one will be kept out of the tribe. You may simply take it or leave it; it's up to you. Third, note his interest in the question, "What is Consciousness?" Philosophy can help here.

Fourth, and finally, his incredibly compact statement: the tribe "has recognized that for one to 'follow the grain' it is necessary to look exhaustively into the negative and demonic potentials of the Unconscious, and by recognizing these powers—symbolically acting them out—one releases himself from these forces. By this profound exorcism and ritual drama, the Great Subculture destroys the one credible claim of Church and State to a necessary function." Though exorcism may sound like a ridiculous solution to today's problems, the Unconscious as a phenomenon is a well-entrenched feature of modern scientific psychology. We cannot afford to ignore it, as Reich and Marin among others recognize. If you are intrigued by Snyder's references to the symbolic quest for the potentials of the Unconscious, I recommend you read C. G. Jung. Some of his writings are not easy, and it is especially difficult to find a short statement introducing his work; hence the absence of Jung from this anthology. But if you are willing to attempt a longer piece, Jung's autobiography, **Memories, Dreams and Reflections,** is an ideal introduction to his thought.

Why Tribe

We use the term Tribe because it suggests the type of new society now emerging within the industrial nations. In America of course the word has associations with the American Indians, which we like. This new subculture is in fact more similar to that ancient and successful tribe, the European Gypsies—a group without nation or territory which maintains its own values, its language and religion, no matter what country it may be in.

The Tribe proposes a totally different style: based on community houses, villages and ashrams; tribe-run farms or workshops or companies; large open families; pilgrimages and wanderings from center to center. A synthesis of Gandhian "village anarchism" and I.W.W. syndicalism. Interesting visionary pamphlets along these lines were written several years ago by Gandhians Richard Gregg and Appa Patwardhan. The Tribe proposes personal responsibilities rather than abstract centralized government, taxes and advertising-agency-plus-Mafia type international brainwashing corporations.

In the United States and Europe the Tribe has evolved gradually over the last fifty years—since the end of World War I—in response to the increasing insanity of the modern nations. As the number of alienated intellectuals, creative types and general social misfits grew, they came to recognize each other by various minute signals. Much of this energy was channeled into Communism in the thirties and early forties. All the anarchists and left-deviationists—and many Trotskyites—were tribesmen at heart. After World War II, another generation looked at Communist rhetoric with a fresh eye and saw that within the Communist governments (and states of mind) there are too many of the same things as are wrong with "capitalism"—too much anger and murder. The suspicion grew that perhaps the whole Western Tradition, of which Marxism is but a (Millennial Protestant) part, is off the track. This led many people to study other major civilizations—India and China—to see what they could learn.

It's an easy step from the dialectic of Marx and Hegel to an interest in the dialectic of early Taoism, the *I Ching,* and the yin-yang theories. From Taoism it is another easy step to the philosophies and mythologies of India—vast, touching the deepest areas of the mind, and with a view of the ultimate nature of the universe which is almost identical with the most sophisticated thought in modern physics—that truth, whatever it is, which is called "The Dharma."

Next comes a concern with deepening one's understanding in an experiential way: abstract philosophical understanding is simply not enough. At this point many, myself included, found in the Buddha-Dharma a practical method for clearing one's mind of the trivia, prejudices and false values that our conditioning had laid on us—and more important, an approach to the basic problem of how to penetrate to the deepest non-self Self. Today we have many who are exploring the Ways of Zen, Vajrayāna, Yoga, Shamanism, Psychedelics. The Buddha-Dharma is a long, gentle, human dialog—2,500 years of quiet conversation—on the nature of human nature and the eternal Dharma—and practical methods of realization.

In the course of these studies it became evident that the "truth" in Buddhism and Hinduism is not dependent in any sense on Indian or Chinese culture; and that "India" and "China"—as societies—are as burdensome to human beings as any others; perhaps more so. It became clear that "Hinduism" and "Buddhism" as social institutions had long been accomplices of the State in burdening and binding people, rather than serving to liberate them. Just like the other Great Religions.

At this point, looking once more quite closely at history both East and West, some of us noticed the similarities in certain small but influential heretical and esoteric movements. These schools of thought and practice were usually suppressed, or diluted and made harmless, in whatever society they appeared. Peasant witchcraft in Europe, Tantrism in Bengal, Quakers in England, Tachikawa-ryū in Japan, Ch'an in China. These are all outcroppings of the Great Subculture which runs underground all through history. This is the tradition that runs without break from Paleo-Siberian Shamanism and Magdalenian cave-painting; through megaliths and Mysteries, astronomers, ritualists, alchemists and Albigensians; gnostics and vagantes, right down to Golden Gate Park.

The Great Subculture has been attached in part to the official religions but is different in that it transmits a community style of life, with an ecstatically positive vision of spiritual and physical love; and is opposed for very fundamental reasons to the Civilization Establishment.

It has taught that man's natural being is to be trusted and followed; that we need not look to a model or rule imposed from outside in searching for the center; and that in following the grain, one is being truly "moral." It has recognized that for one to "follow the grain" it is necessary to look exhaustively into the negative and demonic potentials of the Unconscious, and by recognizing these powers—symbolically acting them out—one releases himself from these forces. By this profound exorcism and ritual drama, the Great Subculture destroys the one credible claim of Church and State to a necessary function.

All this is subversive to civilization: for civilization is built on hierarchy and specialization. A ruling class, to survive, must propose a Law: a law to work must have a hook into the social psyche—and the most effective way to achieve this is to make people doubt their natural worth and instincts, especially sexual. To make "human nature" suspect is also to make Nature—the wilderness—the adversary. Hence the ecological crisis of today.

We came, therefore, (and with many Western thinkers before us) to suspect that civilization may be overvalued. Before anyone says "This is ridiculous, we all know civilization is a necessary thing," let him read some cultural anthropology. Take a look at the lives of South African Bushmen, Micronesian navigators, the Indians of California; the researches of Claude Lévi-Strauss. Everything we have thought about man's welfare needs to be rethought. The tribe, it seems, is the newest development in the Great Subculture. We have almost unintentionally linked ourselves to a transmission of gnosis, a potential social order, and techniques of enlightenment, surviving from prehistoric times.

The most advanced developments of modern science and technology have come to support some of these views. Consequently the modern Tribesman, rather than being old-fashioned in his criticism of civilization, is the most relevant type in contemporary society. Nationalism, warfare, heavy industry and consumership, are already outdated and useless. The next great step of mankind is to step into the nature of his own mind—the real question is "just what is consciousness?"—and we must make the most intelligent and creative use of science in exploring these questions. The man of wide international experience, much learning and leisure—luxurious product of our long and sophisticated history—may with good reason wish to live simply, with few tools and minimal clothes, close to nature.

The Revolution has ceased to be an ideological concern. Instead, people are trying it out right now—communism in small communities, new family organization. A million people in America and another million in England and Europe. A vast underground in Russia, which will come out in the open four or five years hence, is now biding. How do they recognize each other? Not always by beards, long hair, bare feet or beads. The signal is a bright and tender look; calmness and gentleness, freshness and ease of manner. Men, women and children—all of whom together hope to follow the timeless path of love and wisdom, in affectionate company with the sky, winds, clouds, trees, waters, animals and grasses—this is the tribe.

Transition:
Dialectics
of Oppression
and Liberation

Part of the new politics has been the proliferation of liberation fronts. The National Liberation Front in Vietnam, the various Third World and women's liberation movements are not unconnected. They do not form a conspiracy; they do not hold secret meetings to coordinate strategy and ideology. But the roughly simultaneous emergence of these movements suggests that even in their ideological variety and geographical distance from each other they nevertheless share a common origin in the history that spawned them, and consequently they share some common problems, at least at a formal level.

In the 1960's many different groups of people collectively banded together (albeit in different bands) to say, "No, absolutely not! We will not have it go on any more the way it is now." The various liberation movements all seemed to come of age at once, following a latent period in the fifties. They all decided to have done with patriarchy, whether it be the paternalism of the United States represented in the Diem regime in Vietnam, or the paternalism of an outright colonial power like Portugal in Angola, or the paternalism of resident whites in South Africa descended from those proud British who were ready to carry the "white man's burden," or the paternalism of the male sex toward the female sex.

In citing paternalism as a common issue I hardly intend to claim that all oppressors act like fathers, or that all fathers are oppressors. The accusation of paternalism usually implies that someone is demanding the prerogatives of fatherhood in an inappropriate context or without accepting its obligations. Locke emphasized the duties that attend the privileges of fatherhood, but even accepting those duties elicits the accusation of paternalism where the claim to fatherhood is inappropriate. Despite the inappropriateness of the claim, however, that the oppressed experience their oppression as paternalism suggests that they are fighting some of the same battles fought by children against parents. Once again this is not to demean liberation movements as childish; we are only exploring the analogy between the struggle of the oppressed and the struggle of growth. The keys to the analogy are the concepts of internalization, identification, and dynamic development. After seeing the meaning of these concepts in the context of the family, we shall test their validity in the very different context of liberation struggles.

Freud describes a son as wavering back and forth between wishing to be like his father in every way and harboring animosity toward his father, occasioned partly by knowing that, unlike his father, he cannot possess his mother. A son becomes who he is partially by internalizing his father's values, yet he cannot identify completely, as the ancient taboo against incest with the mother symbolizes. So man born of woman is to a certain extent unlike other living things, which reproduce true to type. A son cannot be exactly like his father. Yet the son's differentiation, his success in consolidating his own identity, does not consist merely in opposition or negation. Instead, Freud unfolds a dynamic development of identification and rejection: "the great task of detaching himself from his parents" is not a one-shot operation but a series of interactions including "reconciling himself with his father if he has remained antagonistic to him, or in freeing himself from his domination if, in the reaction to the infantile revolt, he has lapsed into subservience to him."[1]

The more one has internalized from and identified with a paternal power, the more the pain of liberation is a function of how much one is trying to cut away from a part of oneself. Liberation is not simply the good guys wresting control from the bad guys. It often represents an internal struggle, difficult precisely because we are fighting a part of ourselves. I am who I am partly through the process of identification with my father. When I detach myself from my father, as I must do, I detach myself from part of myself; and that part of myself may not like it. Hence the perpetual fear of "Uncle Tomism" in the liberation movements. Some people seem happy, like Uncle Tom, with their subservience to a paternalistic master. And those people are a threat to every liberationist, because he or she knows the extent to which he or she too shares some of the same feelings. How could it be otherwise? We are who we are partly as a result of the paternalism we are in the midst of

---

[1] Sigmund Freud, *Complete Introductory Lectures on Psychoanalysis*, ed. and trans. James Strachey, Standard Edition 16, 1917, p. 337.

rejecting, even if the effort of rejection makes us temporarily blind to those similarities.

Another formal feature shared by aptly named liberation **movements** is their developmental character. We can hardly overlook the various stages of liberation movements, for example, from the militant rejection and rioting, through accommodating schemes of blacks and whites working together, to nonmilitant black separatist movements, and so on. A similar dynamic attends the women's liberation movement, though in both movements claims to a strict linearity of stages must be tempered by the confusing evidence of different people in different stages at the same time. Yet it seems safe to say that individuals do tend to recapitulate historical movements in their attempts to come to terms with the liberation struggle. A young black in 1972 may not actually engage in a riot the way his older brother did five years before, but he may feel the rage of militancy in a way quite different from his father of a generation before. Even though his experience is like his father's in that he doesn't riot, he has felt a new rage as the result of his vicarious experience of history, a history he has internalized in a way his father could not. So the stages do get lived by individuals, and often in the same order as history displays for the movement as a whole.

To summarize: First, the struggle is often with a real part of ourselves, since we were partially created by that from which we now wish liberation. Second, the task of liberation is a dynamic process involving a dialectical development of rejection and identification. Now these two ideas fit together with many of the ideas developed in earlier essays: the process of identification is encouraged by all the subtleties discussed by Goffman, Laing, and Skinner. Through various kinds of attribution, positive reinforcement, applause, and so on, our parents and our peers aid in the constitution of the self and its identity. Further, the existentialist, historicist view of the self as a process of development argues even more strongly than Freud ever did that we are what we become.

If we combine the formal features of the dialectics of liberation with the ideas just mentioned, we get the following picture. Assuming that one feels the necessity of saying no to some forces of oppression, one must then acknowledge that the forces are not all without; many are within. The external enemy is the more oppressive the more it can condition the oppressed to accept a negative self-image. But then the more oppressive a force is, the more it has placed the enemy within. If racism were not effective at making oppressed races think poorly of themselves then racism would not be so oppressive. But a large part of racism in the United States is the subtle reinforcement of a negative self-image. Hence the importance of 'black is beautiful' as a stage in the dialectic. If sexism were not effective at making women feel inferior, then sexism would not really be very oppressive. But it does make women feel that the sexist claims are true. Consequently—and here is the import of historicism—oppression has an uncanny way of generating its own "truth": if you convince people in subtle and deepseated ways that they are lazy or stupid, chances are that attribution may stick, not because they **are** (essentially) lazy or stupid, but because people are capable of **becoming** any number of things with enough social reinforcement. With a certain "coming of age" a person or a people may somehow become aware of other possibilities. Perhaps I might become different from what I have become. I may in fact come to despise what I have become, and I may blame others for making me become what I have become. But one point remains distressingly clear from the arguments combined so far: I will get nowhere in becoming something else until I acknowledge how much I am, at least for now, what I have become up to now. I say "distressingly clear" because it is much easier to believe that the righteousness of a liberation front derives from the simple mistakenness of the current enemy, as if sexists and racists and nationalists were simply wrong and had to be shown the error of their ways. Like a son struggling for his identity, each movement must struggle with its identification with the oppressor. The struggle is difficult because it arouses self-doubt: what I am fighting is in me, perhaps even to the extent that the form of my struggle is dictated by what has been done to me; perhaps it is even silly to imagine that I could ever fight my way out if the fight itself is part of my conditioning—if, for example, I'm only proving them true when they say I am surly and rebellious. And around and around it goes: the awareness of the reality of identification engenders a distrust in one's ability to detach oneself from the parents, and the distrust itself gets blamed on the "parents," from whom one then wants detachment all the more. It is easier to ignore the reality of identification. But to view the dialectics of liberation philosophically requires that we put aside the doctrinaire mongering of simple slogans that locate the entire problem in someone else's consciousness and actions. The quest for self-knowledge requires an uncovering of our own racism and sexism toward ourselves. In short, we need a little consciousness raising.

ARTHUR SCHOPENHAUER

(1788-1860)

Arthur Schopenhauer was a pessimist, yet his thought is so full of paradox that sometimes it reflects an irrepressible hope. A fundamental tenet of his philosophy is that life, even the examined life, is fundamentally not worth living. Life is a series of sorrows, or, less sentimentally and more in Schopenhauer's style, an unpleasant chore of balancing occasional peace against the heavier weights of boredom and pain. Yet the energy of his writing belies the ascetic resignation that should follow from his pessimism.

A taste for paradox complements the sources of his thought. By his own declaration Schopenhauer acknowledged that his philosophy contains very little that is new. Rather, it grew from a synthesis of Kant's philosophy and the long tradition of Indian philosophy going back to the Vedanta scriptures about 2500–2000 B.C. Kant's claim that we know appearances rather than things in themselves is interpreted by Schopenhauer in terms of the Indian doctrine of **maya,** or illusion. We live most of our lives in a world of illusion; the best we can do is deny the reality of the illusion, which amounts to denying what most people regard as life. Hence the implication of ascetic withdrawal and indifference that pervades much of Schopenhauer's writing. Yet his very indifference sometimes gives him the clarity of one who has no stake in the matter, no interests to protect. Schopenhauer is free of the need to bolster his picture of reality with convenient, optimistic truths, because he has already resigned himself to the possibility that each inquiry will demonstrate anew the intolerability of life. And that very resignation sometimes allows him, more than others, to penetrate to the truths that set one free. Sometimes his pessimism colors the object of his inquiry, but often it merely removes the rosy glasses that keep others from seeing true colors. Reading Schopenhauer presents the difficult task of deciding whether his pessimism allows a perspective on the truth or gets in the way of the truth. His essay on women is a case in point.

Schopenhauer demolishes women. He is the ultimate "male chauvinist pig." He accuses women of being deficient in intellect and the arts. According to him, they are somewhere between children and fully developed men. They are experts only in such things as dissimulation and child rearing; they are not to be trusted with important matters like handling property or capital; and so on. Now in suggesting that Schopenhauer's essay be taken even the least bit seriously the point is that we are all male chauvinists by our very birth into modern western civilization. Most women are male chauvinists, even those champions of women's rights (those who claim that there are no important differences between men and women). They have been brainwashed with the idea that to be fully human is to be like a man, so they deny that they are in any significant way different from men, and to deny differences is to limit chances of their proper evaluation.

Schopenhauer's essay is helpful in trying to ferret out the realities of our chauvinism, for we cannot help admitting that on many points his words ring true: many women are as Schopenhauer describes them. If we refuse to accept this fact we can hardly begin to liberate ourselves, for how can you liberate yourself from what is unacknowledged. Only when we recognize that things are as bad as Schopenhauer says they are can we know the realities well enough to change them.

I hardly endorse everything Schopenhauer has to say. I find it necessary to distinguish between the descriptive and the evaluative in his essay. After accurately describing some differences between men and women, he unjustifiably values everything masculine and devalues everything feminine. But we can learn from his descriptions without agreeing with his evaluations. Simply to deny the differences he describes is to agree with his evaluations: if you insist that men and women are equally suited to both child rearing and high finance, and do so in order to gain jobs for women in "more important posts," then chances are you think economics is to be valued more than child rearing. But that is a male chauvinist evaluation. Am I claiming that women are better suited to rear children and that this natural endowment should be honored above their desires to do other things such as pursue careers? No. I am not arguing that everything is as it ought to be in some sort of natural scheme of allotted endowments or essences. Aside from biological considerations, women have been socially conditioned to their affinity with children. But we must not lose sight of the reality of this social conditioning. Many women are as Schopenhauer describes them, not by nature, but because they are believed to be that way, and this widely held belief has its historical influence on social reality. We cannot change that reality until we acknowledge that it is indeed reality.

So read Schopenhauer's essay carefully. Try to distinguish the truly male chauvinist evaluations from the descriptions his pessimism allows him to acknowledge. And finally, try to be pessimistically honest about the depths of your own chauvinism. This is consciousness raising.

On Women

Schiller's poem in honour of women, *Würde der Frauen,* is the result of much careful thought, and it appeals to the reader by its antithetic style and its use of contrast; but as an expression of the true praise which should be accorded to them, it is, I think, in-

ON WOMEN From Arthur Schopenhauer, originally appeared in Schopenhauer's *Parerga und Paralipomena,* 1851. The translation is by Thomas Bailey Saunders (1860–1928).

ferior to these few words of Jouy's: *Without women the beginning of our life would be helpless; the middle, devoid of pleasure; and the end, of consolation.* The same thing is more feelingly expressed by Byron in *Sardanapalus:*—

> The very first
> Of human life must spring from women's breast,
> Your first small words are taught you from her lips,
> Your first tears quench'd by her, and your last sighs
> Too often breathed out in a woman's hearing,
> When men have shrunk from the ignoble care
> Of watching the last hour of him who led them.
> (Act I. Scene 2.)

These two passages indicate the right standpoint for the appreciation of women.

You need only look at the way in which she is formed to see that woman is not meant to undergo great labour, whether of the mind or of the body. She pays the debt of life not by what she does but by what she suffers; by the pains of childbearing and care for the child, and by submission to her husband, to whom she should be a patient and cheering companion. The keenest sorrows and joys are not for her, nor is she called upon to display a great deal of strength. The current of her life should be more gentle, peaceful and trivial than man's, without being essentially happier or unhappier.

Women are directly fitted for acting as the nurses and teachers of our early childhood by the fact that they are themselves childish, frivolous and short-sighted; in a word, they are big children all their life long—a kind of intermediate stage between the child and the full-grown man, who is man in the strict sense of the word. See how a girl will fondle a child for days together, dance with it and sing to it; and then think what a man, with the best will in the world, could do if he were put in her place.

With young girls Nature seems to have had in view what, in the language of the drama, is called a *coup de théâtre.* For a few years she dowers them with a wealth of beauty and is lavish in her gift of charm, at the expense of the rest of their life, in order that during those years they may capture the fantasy of some man to such a degree that he is hurried into undertaking the honourable care of them, in some form or other, as long as they live —a step for which there would not appear to be any sufficient warranty if reason only directed his thoughts. Accordingly Nature has equipped woman, as she does all her creatures, with the weapons and implements requisite for the safeguarding of her existence, and for just as long as it is necessary for her to have them. Here, as elsewhere, Nature proceeds with her usual economy; for just as the female ant, after fecundation, loses her wings, which are then superfluous, nay, actually a danger to the business of breeding; so, after giving birth to one or two children, a woman generally loses her beauty; probably, indeed, for similar reasons.

And so we find that young girls, in their hearts, look upon domestic affairs or work of any kind as of secondary importance, if not actually as a mere jest. The only business that really claims their earnest attention is love, making conquests, and everything connected with this—dress, dancing, and so on.

The nobler and more perfect a thing is, the later and slower it is in arriving at maturity. A man reaches the maturity of his reasoning powers and mental faculties hardly before the age of twenty-eight; a woman, at eighteen. And then, too, in the case of woman, it is only reason of a sort —very niggard in its dimensions. That is why women remain children their whole life long; never seeing anything but what is quite close to them, cleaving to the present moment, taking appearance for reality, and preferring trifles to matters of the first importance. For it is by virtue of his reasoning faculty that man does not live in the present only, like the brute, but looks about him and considers the past and the future; and this is the origin of prudence, as well as of that care and anxiety which so many people exhibit. Both the advantages and the disadvantages which this involves, are shared in by the woman to a smaller extent because of her weaker power of reasoning. She may, in fact, be described as intellectually shortsighted, because, while she has an intuitive understanding of what lies quite close to her, her field of vision is narrow and does not reach to what is remote: so that things which are absent or past or to come have much less effect upon women than upon men. This is the reason why women are more often inclined to be extravagant, and sometimes carry their inclination to a length that borders upon madness. In their hearts women think that it is men's business to earn money and theirs to spend it—if possible during their husband's life, but, at any rate, after his death. The very fact that their husband hands them over his earnings for purposes of housekeeping strengthens them in this belief.

However many disadvantages all this may involve, there is at least this to be said in its favour: that the woman lives more in the present than the man, and that, if the present is at all tolerable, she enjoys it more eagerly. This is the source of that cheerfulness which is peculiar to woman, fitting her to amuse man in his hours of recreation, and, in case of need, to console him when he is borne down by the weight of his cares.

It is by no means a bad plan to consult women in matters of difficulty, as the Germans used to do in ancient times; for their way of looking at things is quite different from ours, chiefly in the fact that they like to take the shortest way to their goal, and, in general, manage to fix their eyes upon what lies before them; while we, as a rule, see far beyond it, just because it is in front of our noses. In cases like this, we need to be brought back to the right standpoint, so as to recover the near and simple view.

Then, again, women are decidedly more sober in their judgment than we are, so that they do not see more in things than is really there; whilst, if our passions are aroused, we are apt to see things in an exaggerated way, or imagine what does not exist.

The weakness of their reasoning faculty also explains why it is that women show more sympathy for the unfortunate than men do, and so treat them with more kindness and interest; and why it is that, on the contrary, they are inferior to men in point of justice, and less honourable and conscientious. For it is just because their reasoning power is weak that present circumstances have such a hold over them, and those concrete things which lie directly before their eyes exercise a power which is seldom counteracted to any extent by abstract principles of thought, by fixed rules of conduct, firm resolutions, or, in general, by consideration for the past and the future, or regard for what is absent and remote. Accordingly, they possess the first and main elements that go to make a virtuous character, but they are deficient in those secondary qualities which are often a necessary instrument in the formation of it.

Hence it will be found that the fundamental fault of the female character is that it has *no sense of justice*. This is mainly due to the fact, already mentioned, that women are defective in the powers of reasoning and deliberation; but it is also traceable to the position which Nature has assigned to them as the weaker sex. They are dependent, not upon strength, but only craft; and hence their instinctive capacity for cunning, and their ineradicable tendency to say what is not true. For as lions are provided with claws and teeth, and elephants and boars with tusks, bulls with horns, and the cuttle fish with its cloud of inky fluid, so Nature has equipped woman, for her defence and protection, with the arts of dissimulation; and all the power which Nature has conferred upon man in the shape of physical strength and reason has been bestowed upon women in this form. Hence dissimulation is innate in woman, and almost as much a quality of the stupid as of the clever. It is as natural for them to make use of it on every occasion as it is for those animals to employ their means of defence when they are attacked; they have a feeling that in doing so they are only within their rights. Therefore a woman who is perfectly truthful and not given to dissimulation is perhaps an impossibility, and for this very reason they are so quick at seeing through dissimulation in others that it is not a wise thing to attempt it with them. But this fundamental defect which I have stated, with all that it entails, gives rise to falsity, faithlessness, treachery, ingratitude, and so on. Perjury in a court of justice is more often committed by women than by men. It may, indeed, be generally questioned whether women ought to be sworn at all. From time to time one finds repeated cases everywhere of ladies, who want for nothing, taking things from shop-counters when no one is looking and making off with them.

Nature has appointed that the propagation of the species shall be the business of men who are young, strong and handsome; so that the race may not degenerate. This is the firm will and purpose of Nature in regard to the species, and it finds its expression in the passions of women. There is no law that is older or more powerful than this. Woe, then, to the man who sets up claims and interests that will conflict with it; whatever he may say and do, they will be unmercifully crushed at the first serious encounter. For the innate rule that governs women's conduct, though it is secret and unformulated, nay, unconscious in its working, is this: *We are justified in deceiving those who think they have acquired rights over the species by paying little attention to the individual, that is, to us. The constitution and, therefore, the welfare of the species have been placed in our hands and committed to our care, through the control we obtain over the next generation, which proceeds from us; let us discharge our duties conscientiously.* But women have no abstract knowledge of this leading principle; they are conscious of it only as a concrete fact; and they have no other method of giving expression to it than the way in which they act when the opportunity arrives. And then their conscience does not trouble them so much as we fancy; for in the darkest recesses of their heart they are aware that, in committing a breach of their duty towards the individual, they have all the better fulfilled their duty towards the species, which is infinitely greater.

And since women exist in the main solely for the propagation of the species, and are not destined for anything else, they live, as a rule, more for the species than for the individual, and in their hearts take the affairs of the species more seriously than those of the individual. This gives their whole life and being a certain levity; the general bent of their character is in a direction fundamentally different from that of man; and it is this which produces that discord in married life which is so frequent, and almost the normal state.

The natural feeling between men is mere indifference, but between women it is actual enmity. The reason of this is that trade-jealousy which, in the case of men, does not go beyond the confines of their own particular pursuit but with women embraces the whole sex; since they have only one kind of business. Even when they meet in the street women look at one another like Guelphs and Ghibellines. And it is a patent fact that when two women make first acquaintance with each other they behave with more constraint and dissimulation than two men would show in a like case; and hence it is that an exchange of compliments between two women is a much more ridiculous proceeding than between two men. Further, whilst a man will, as a general rule, always preserve a certain amount of consideration and humanity in speaking to others, even to those who are in a very inferior position, it is intolerable to see how proudly and disdainfully a fine lady will generally behave towards one who is in a lower social rank (I do not mean a woman who is in her service), whenever she speaks to her. The reason of this may be that, with women, differences of rank are much more precarious than with us; because, while a hundred considerations carry weight in our case, in theirs there is only one, namely, with which man they have found favour; as also that they stand in much nearer relations with one another than men do, in consequence of the one-sided nature of their calling. This makes them endeavour to lay stress upon differences of rank.

It is only the man whose intellect is clouded by his sexual impulses that could give the name of *the fair sex* to that undersized, narrow-shouldered, broad-hipped, and short-legged race: for the whole beauty of the sex is bound up with this impulse. Instead of calling them beautiful, there would be more warrant for describing women as the unæsthetic sex. Neither for music, nor for poetry, nor for fine art, have they really and truly any sense or susceptibility; it is a mere mockery if they make a pretence of it in order to assist their endeavour to please. Hence, as a result of this, they are incapable of taking a *purely objective interest* in anything; and the reason of it seems to me to be as follows. A man tries to acquire *direct* mastery over things, either by understanding them or by forcing them to do his will. But a woman is always and everywhere reduced to obtaining this mastery *indirectly,* namely through a man; and whatever direct mastery she may have is entirely confined to him. And so it lies in woman's nature to look upon everything only as a means for conquering man; and if she takes an interest in anything else it is simulated—a mere roundabout way of gaining her ends by coquetry and feigning what she does not feel. Hence even Rousseau declared: *"Women have, in general, no love of any art; they have no proper knowledge of any; and they have no genius.*[1]

No one who sees at all below the surface can have failed to remark the same thing. You need only observe the kind of attention women bestow upon a concert, an opera, or a play—the childish simplicity, for example, with which they keep on chattering during the finest passages in the greatest masterpieces. If it is true that the Greeks excluded women from their theatres, they were quite right in what they did; at any rate you would have been able to hear what was said upon the stage. In our day, besides, or in lieu of saying, *Let a woman keep silence in the church,* it would be much to the point to say, *Let a woman keep silence in the theatre.* This might, perhaps, be put up in big letters on the curtain.

And you cannot expect anything else of women if you consider that the most distinguished intellects among the whole sex have never managed to produce a single achievement in the fine arts that is really great, genuine, and original; or given to the world any work of permanent value in any sphere. This is most strikingly shown in regard to painting, where mastery of technique is at least as much within their power as within ours—and hence they are diligent in cultivating it; but still, they have not a single great painting to boast of, just because they are deficient in that objectivity of mind which is so directly indispensable in painting. They never get beyond a subjective point of view. It is quite in keeping with this that ordinary women have no real susceptibility for art at all; for Nature proceeds in strict sequence—*non facit saltum.* The case is not altered by particular and partial exceptions; taken as a whole, women are, and remain, thoroughgoing philistines, and quite incurable. Hence, with that absurd arrangement which allows them to share the rank and title of their husbands, they are a constant stimulus to his ignoble ambitions. And, further, it is just because they are philistines that modern society, where they take the lead and set the tone, is in such a bad way. Napoleon's saying—that *women have no*

---

[1] Lettre à d'Alembert. Note xx.

rank—should be adopted as the right standpoint in determining their position in society; and as regards their other qualities Chamfort makes the very true remark:

> They are made to trade with our own weaknesses and our follies, but not with our reason. The sympathies that exist between them and men are skin-deep only, and do not touch the mind or the feelings or the character.

They form the *sexus sequior*—the second sex, inferior in every respect to the first; their infirmities should be treated with consideration; but to show them great reverence is extremely ridiculous, and lowers us in their eyes. When Nature made two divisions of the human race, she did not draw the line exactly through the middle. These divisions are polar and opposed to each other, it is true; but the difference between them is not qualitative merely, it is also quantitative.

This is just the view which the ancients took of woman, and the view which people in the East take now; and their judgment as to her proper position is much more correct than ours, with our old French notions of gallantry and our preposterous system of reverence—that highest product of Teutonico-Christian stupidity. These notions have served only to make women more arrogant and overbearing; so that one is occasionally reminded of the holy apes in Benares, who in the consciousness of their sanctity and inviolable position think they can do exactly as they please.

But in the West the woman, and especially the *lady,* finds herself in a false position; for woman, rightly called by the ancients *sexus sequior,* is by no means fit to be the object of our honour and veneration, or to hold her head higher than man and be on equal terms with him. The consequences of this false position are sufficiently obvious. Accordingly it would be a very desirable thing if this Number Two of the human race were in Europe also relegated to her natural place, and an end put to that lady-nuisance, which not only moves all Asia to laughter but would have been ridiculed by Greece and Rome as well. It is impossible to calculate the good effects which such a change would bring about in our social, civil and political arrangements. There would be no necessity for the Salic law: it would be a superfluous truism. In Europe the *lady,* strictly so-called, is a being who should not exist at all; she should be either a housewife or a girl who hopes to become one; and she should be brought up, not to be arrogant, but to be thrifty and submissive. It is just because there are such people as *ladies* in Europe that the women of the lower classes, that is to say, the great majority of the sex, are much more unhappy than they are in the East. And even Lord Byron says:

> Thought of the state of women under the ancient Greeks—convenient enough. Present state, a remnant of the barbarism of the chivalric and the feudal ages—artificial and unnatural. They ought to mind home—and be well fed and clothed—but not mixed in society. Well educated, too, in

religion—but to read neither poetry nor politics—nothing but books of
piety and cookery. Music—drawing—dancing—also a little gardening and
ploughing now and then. I have seen them mending the roads in Epirus
with good success. Why not, as well as haymaking and milking?

The laws of marriage prevailing in Europe consider the woman as the
equivalent of the man—start, that is to say, from a wrong position. In our
part of the world where monogamy is the rule, to marry means to halve
one's rights and double one's duties. Now when the laws gave women equal
rights with man, they ought to have also endowed her with a masculine intellect. But the fact is that, just in proportion as the honours and privileges
which the laws accord to women exceed the amount which Nature gives,
there is a diminution in the number of women who really participate in
these privileges; and all the remainder are deprived of their natural rights
by just so much as is given to the others over and above their share. For the
institution of monogamy, and the laws of marriage which it entails, bestow
upon the woman an unnatural position of privilege, by considering her
throughout as the full equivalent of the man, which is by no means the case;
and seeing this men who are shrewd and prudent very often scruple to
make so great a sacrifice and to acquiesce in so unfair an arrangement.

Moreover, the bestowal of unnatural rights upon women has imposed
upon them unnatural duties, and nevertheless a breach of these duties makes
them unhappy. Let me explain. A man may often think that his social or
financial position will suffer if he marries, unless he makes some brilliant
alliance. His desire will then be to win a woman of his own choice under
conditions other than those of marriage, such as will secure her position
and that of the children. However fair, reasonable, fit and proper these conditions may be, if the woman consents by foregoing that undue amount of
privilege which marriage alone can bestow, she to some extent loses her
honour, because marriage is the basis of civic society; and she will lead an
unhappy life, since human nature is so constituted that we pay an attention
to the opinion of other people which is out of all proportionate to its value.
On the other hand, if she does not consent, she runs the risk either of having to be given in marriage to a man whom she does not like, or of being
landed high and dry as an old maid; for the period during which she has a
chance of being settled for life is very short. And in view of this aspect of
the institution of monogamy, Thomasius' profoundly learned treatise *On
Concubinage* is well worth reading; for it shows that, amongst all nations
and in all ages, down to the Lutheran Reformation, concubinage was permitted; nay, that it was an institution which was to a certain extent actually
recognised by law, and attended with no dishonour. It was only the Lutheran Reformation that degraded it from this position. It was seen to be a
further justification for the marriage of the clergy; and then, after that, the
Catholic Church did not dare to remain behindhand in the matter.

The first love of a mother for her child is, with the lower animals as with
men, of a purely *instinctive* character, and so it ceases when the child is no

longer in a physically helpless condition. After that, the first love should give way to one that is based on habit and reason; but this often fails to make its appearance, especially where the mother did not love the father. The love of a father for his child is of a different order, and more likely to last; because it has its foundation in the fact that in the child he recognises his own inner self; that is to say, his love for it is metaphysical in its origin.

In almost all nations, whether of the ancient or the modern world, even amongst the Hottentots, property is inherited by the male descendants alone; it is only in Europe that a departure has taken place; but not amongst the nobility, however. That the property which has cost men long years of toil and effort, and been won with so much difficulty, should afterwards come into the hands of women, who then, in their lack of reason, squander it in a short time, or otherwise fool it away, is a grievance and a wrong, as serious as it is common, which should be prevented by limiting the right of women to inherit. In my opinion the best arrangement would be that by which women, whether widows or daughters, should never receive anything beyond the interest for life on property secured by mortgage, and in no case the property itself, or the capital, except where all male descendants fail. The people who make money are men, not women; and it follows from this that women are neither justified in having unconditional possession of it, nor fit persons to be entrusted with its administration. When wealth, in any true sense of the word, that is to say, funds, houses or land, is to go to them as an inheritance, they should never be allowed the free disposition of it. In their case a guardian should always be appointed; and hence they should never be given the free control of their own children, wherever it can be avoided. The vanity of women, even though it should not prove to be greater than that of men, has this much danger in it that it takes an entirely material direction. They are vain, I mean, of their personal beauty, and then of finery, show and magnificence. That is just why they are so much in their element in society. It is this, too, which makes them so inclined to be extravagant, all the more as their reasoning power is low. But with men vanity often takes the direction of non-material advantages, such as intellect, learning, courage.

That woman is by nature meant to obey may be seen by the fact that every woman who is placed in the unnatural position of complete independence, immediately attaches herself to some man, by whom she allows herself to be guided and ruled. It is because she needs a lord and master. If she is young, it will be a lover; if she is old, a priest.

GERMAINE GREER

(1939-   )

Among the many manifestoes of the women's liberation movement, Germaine Greer's **The Female Eunuch** is one of the best, partly because it is least like a manifesto. Greer feels **and** thinks. She does not simplify for the sake of polemics. She does not argue a simple sameness of men and women. Instead she acknowledges descriptive differences and then attacks the chauvinist evaluations of those differences. Inferiority does not follow from difference. Indeed, Greer's essay links together with many of the essays in this volume in a way that suggests a superiority of traditionally "female" virtues. Faced with the claim that men often possess stronger egos, she challenges their tenacity to a rigid sense of identity. Here support can be found in Ryle, Hume, Nietzsche, and James. She explicitly refers to Brown's call for "an erotic sense of reality," in which a connectedness with one's environment would replace a rigid, atomic individualism. The very characteristics for which women have often been chided turn out to be the traits that would characterize the wise man as his picture emerges from many of the essays in this volume. For example, 'women's intuition' turns out to be no more than an openness and sensitivity to the riches of communication discussed by Laing, Goffman, and Polanyi. And the political attack on patriarchy is hardly irrelevant to women's liberation. In short, at least half the essays in this volume have a direct bearing on Greer's "Womanpower."

Womanpower

The failure of specially designed tests to reveal any specifically sexual difference in intellectual capacity between males and females is irrelevant as far as those who challenge women's fitness for certain responsibilities and work are concerned. They think that the tests reflect more upon the testers and the method of testing than they do upon male and female. Dr. Leavis believed that he could identify a woman writer by her style, even though necessarily all that she wrote must have been a parody of some man's superior achievement. After all, there was not much wrong with Virginia Woolf except that she was a woman. It could be argued that the tests were specially contoured in an attempt to counter-act the effect of sexual conditioning, while real women in the real world are continually conditioned. No adjustment of our theoretical opinion of their basic capacity can alter the nature of their achievement. Men complain that they cannot handle women, that arguments with women must be avoided at all costs because they always get the last word mostly by foul means. How "like a woman" they sigh, and all agree. The detection of sex in mind is not only the privilege of the most eminent literary pundits from Dr. Leavis to Norman Mailer,[1] it extends to the lowest levels of illiteracy—the schoolboy muttering about "bloody girls." Because the difference is so wholeheartedly believed in, it is also experienced. As a conviction it becomes a motive for behavior and a continuing cause of the phenomenon itself. It is not to be put aside by rational means. There is of course no reason why women should limit themselves to logic: we might perversely decide to *exploit* the Ovarian Theory of Mind.[2]

One of the fullest statements of the theory of the female soul was set out in *Sex and Character,* a remarkably rigorous and committed book by a mere boy, Otto Weininger, who committed suicide some years after its pub-lication. His brilliant, neurotic life can be taken as an illustration of what dimorphism must eventually accomplish. By disintegrating human nature and building boundaries between warring halves, Weininger condemned

---

Women tend to make their emotions perform the functions they exist to serve, and hence remain mentally much healthier than men.

Ashley Montagu,
The Natural Superiority of Women, 1953

---

himself to perversion, guilt, and early death. He began by identifying women with the body, with unconscious sexuality, and thereafter with pas-sive animalism. As a rational male he condemned such a bestial element. "No men who think really deeply about women retain a high opinion of them; men either despise women or they have never thought seriously about them."[3]

Like Freud, with whom he had much more in common, he thought of women as castrated by nature; because he thought so highly of the penis he thought women did too:

An absolute nude female figure in life leaves an impression of something

---

[1] See Mary Ellman, *Thinking About Women* (New York, 1968), *passim.* Mailer explains his concept of the novel as the Great Bitch and how women cannot be said to get a piece of her in "Some Children of the Goddess," *Cannibals and Christians* (New York, 1966).

[2] The term is culled from Cynthia Ozick, "The Demise of the Dancing Dog," *Motive,* March–April 1969.

[3] Otto Weininger, *Sex and Character* (London, 1906), p. 236.

wanting, an incompleteness which is incompatible with beauty . . .[4]
The qualities that appeal to a woman are the signs of a developed sexuality; those that repel her are the qualities of the higher mind. Woman is essentially a phallus worshipper . . .[5]

Weininger thought the dimorphism of the sexes right through, and discovered that, given such a polarity, men could have no real communion with women, only a highly compromised shared hypocrisy. Valerie Solanas performed the same exercise for women, and found that men covet all that women are, seeking degradation and effeminization at their hands.[6] She retaliated by shooting Andy Warhol in the chest. Weininger more honestly made his attempt upon himself and succeeded. Just as Solanas despises men as they present themselves to be and in their failure to live up to their own stereotype, Weininger despises women both because their image is passive and animalistic, and because they are not genuinely so. Their pretense is brought about by the exigency of the sexual situation which they exploit, hence the duplicity and mendacity which characterize all their actions. Because woman lives vicariously she need take no moral responsibility for her behavior: because she has no responsibility she has no morality and no ego. Because of the lack of ego and the variety of roles that women manipulate, they have no identity, as one may guess from their willingness to give up their names. Woman is never genuine at any period of her life.[7]

Political and civic equality of the sexes implies moral equality. It implies the perfectly appalling logical consequence that the morals of women shall in future be the same as those of respectable Christian Victorian man—at best. That, of course, means the total collapse of Christian morality.

Robert Briffault, *Sin and Sex,* 1931, p. 132

The most chastening reflection is that Weininger was simply describing what he saw in female behavior around him. He could not see that these deformities were what women would one day clamor to be freed from. As far as he could see, women were like that and he did not know what came first, their condition or their character. He assumed that it must have been the latter, because he could not explain their condition any other way.

All the moral deficiencies Weininger detected masqueraded in Victorian

[4] *Ibid.,* p. 241.

[5] *Ibid.,* p. 250.

[6] Valerie Solanas, *The S.C.U.M. Manifesto* (New York, 1968), p. 73.

[7] Weininger (*op. cit.*), p. 274. The claim that deceitfulness is a secondary sexual characteristic of the female mind has been made by many observers, including feminists like Mary Wollstonecraft who saw it as an essential consequence of female degradation and B. L. Hutchins, *Conflicting Ideals: Two Sides of the Woman Question* (London, 1913), "Girls have been brought up on intensely insincere ideals" (p. 30).

society as virtues. Weininger is to be credited with describing them properly. Nevertheless his concepts of ego, identity, logic and morality were formed from observation of this same undesirable status quo, and women today might well find that what Weininger describes as defects might be in fact *freedoms* which they might do well to promote. For example:

> With women thinking and feeling are identical, for man they are in opposition. The woman has many of her mental experiences as henids (undifferentiated perceptions) whilst in man these have passed through a process of clarification.[8]

"Definitio est negatio." We might argue that clarification is tantamount to falsification: if you want to know what happened in a particular situation you would be better off asking someone who had perceived the whole and remembered all of it, not just some extrapolated clarification. How sad it is for men to have feeling and thought in opposition! Eliot argued that the seventeenth century had seen a dissociation of sensibility, so that intelligence no longer served as a direct index of the intensity of feeling but rather undermined it.[9] Can it be that women have survived the process which debilitated the rest of male-dominated western culture? If we can make anything of such a seductive possibility, we must reflect that most educated women have simply been admitted to the masculine academic culture, and have lost their power to perceive in henids. According to Antonin Artaud, Anaïs Nin might have survived even that:

> I brought many people, men and women, to see the beautiful canvas, but it is the first time I ever saw artistic emotion make a human being palpitate like love. Your senses trembled and I realized that the mind and body are formidably linked in you, because such a pure spiritual could unleash such a powerful storm in your organism. But in that universal marriage it is the mind that lords over the body and dominates it, and it must end up by dominating it in every way. I feel that there is a world of things in you that are begging to be born should it find its exorcist.[10]

Most of this is nonsense. We might expect the inventor of the theater of cruelty to see the phenomenon of unified sensibility and spend a paragraph trying to prove the domination of the mind to the point of implying that she

---

[8] Weininger (*op. cit.*), p. 100. The assumptions that women perceive differently from men, are subjective rather than men and so on, despite the failure of testing to indicate any justification for them, are taken on trust by psychologists who deal with femininity. Deutsch luxuriates in extolling the value of women's subjective, intuitive perception as the desirable complement to male objectivity and mental aggression.

[9] T. S. Eliot, "The Metaphysical Poets," *Selected Essays* (New York, 1950).

[10] Antonin Artaud, "Letters to Anais Nin," translated by Mary Beach, *International Times*, No. 16. Letter of June 14 or 15, 1933.

needed an exorcist! Artaud's manicheism prevented him from seeing that the stimulus of the painting was sensual in the first instance. All that happened was that Nin responded with both mind and body to a sensible and intelligent stimulus. The painting was one and her response was equally integrated.

If women retain their experience in their original unclassified form they may escape the great limitation of scientific thought, which was pointed out by A. N. Whitehead in *Adventures of Ideas.*

> In the study of ideas it is necessary to remember that insistence on hard-headed clarity issues from sentimental feeling, as it were a mist, cloaking the complexities of fact. Insistence on clarity at all costs is based on sheer superstition as to the mode in which human intelligence functions. Our reasonings grasp at straws for premises and float on gossamers for deductions.[11]

At a banal level this functioning difference in male and female thought is easily demonstrated: we have only to think of Father mocking Mother for keeping the salt in a box marked Sago, or the frequently celebrated female intuition, which is after all only a faculty for observing tiny insignificant aspects of behavior and forming an empirical conclusion which cannot be syllogistically examined. Now that most information is not disseminated in argumentative form on the printed page, but is assimilated in various non-verbal ways from visual and aural media, clarification and the virtues of disputation are more and more clearly seen to be simply alternative ways of knowing and not the only or the principal ones. The take-over by computers of much vertical thinking has placed more and more emphasis on the creative propensities of human thought. The sudden increase in political passion in the last decade, especially among the generation which has absorbed most of its education in this undifferentiated form, bears witness to a reintegration of thought and feeling happening on a wide scale. In the circumstances any such peculiarity of the female mind could well become a strength.

Unfortunately my own arguments have all the faults of an insufficient regard for logic and none of its strengths, the penalty after all for a Cartesian education. So much for privilege. Here I am, a Negro who cannot do the lindyhop or sing the Blues! Nowadays education itself is changing so that creative thought does not decline with the inculcation of mental disciplines, which are now not taught as ends but simply as means to other ends. Unfortunately, the chief result of the change so far seems to be the reluctance

---

[11] This quotation appears in Marshall McLuhan, *The Medium Is the Massage* (New York, 1967), ascribed to A. N. Whitehead, and a book called *Adventures in Ideas.* I cannot recall seeing it in *Adventures of Ideas* but it does catch the drift of much that Whitehead did say, e.g., "The Anatomy of Some Scientific Ideas," in *The Organisation of Thought* (London, 1917), pp. 134–90 *passim,* or *Science and the Modern World* (Cambridge, 1927), Chap. V, "The Romantic Reaction" (pp. 93–118), *passim,* or indeed *Adventures of Ideas* (Cambridge, 1933), pp. 150–1, 173, 184–5.

of children to study science, but eventually science itself will become a complete study.

Weininger has more serious charges though:

> A woman cannot grasp that one must act from principle; as she has no continuity she does not experience the necessity for logical support of her mental processes . . . she may be regarded as "logically insane."[12]

It is true that women often refuse to argue logically. In many cases they simply do not know how to, and men may dazzle them with a little pompous sophistry. In some cases they are intimidated and upset before rationalization begins. But it is also true that in most situations logic is simply rationalization of an infralogical aim. Women know this; even the best educated of them know that arguments with their menfolk are disguised realpolitik. It is not a contest of mental agility with the right as the victor's spoils, but a contest of wills. The rules of logical discourse are no more relevant than the Marquess of Queensberry's are to a pub brawl. Female hardheadedness rejects the misguided masculine notion that men are rational animals. Male logic can only deal with simple issues: women, because they are passive and condemned to observe and react rather than initiate, are more aware of complexity. Men have been forced to suppress their receptivity, in the interests of domination. One of the possible advantages of infantilization of women is that they might after all become, in the words of Lao-Tse, "a channel drawing all the world towards it" so that they "will not be severed from the eternal virtue" and "can return again to the state of infancy."[13] If only the state of women were infancy, and not what we have reduced infancy itself to, new possibilities might be closer to realization than they seem. When Schopenhauer described the state of women as *moral infancy,* he was reflecting not only his prejudice against women, but also against babies. The failure of women to take logic seriously has serious consequences for their morality. Freud adds the gloss to Weininger's text:

> I cannot evade the notion (though I hesitate to give it expression) that for women the level of what is ethically normal is different from what it is in men. Their superego is never so inexorable, so impersonal, so independent of its emotional origins as we require it to be in men. Character-traits which critics of every epoch have brought up against women—that they show less sense of justice than men, that they are less ready to submit to the great exigencies of life, that they are more often influenced in their judgements by their feelings of affection or hostility—all these would be amply accounted for in the modification of the formation of their superego. . . . We must not allow ourselves to be deflected from such conclu-

---

[12] Weininger (*op. cit.*), p. 149.

[13] J. Needham, *Science and Civilisation in China* (Cambridge, 1954), Vol. II, p. 58.

sions by the denial of the feminists, who are anxious to force us to regard the two sexes as completely equal in position and worth.[14]

The circularity of this utterance is quite scary. After all, are the sexes equal in position and worth or not? What is position? What is worth? He promises to explain unsubstantiated deficiencies in the female character by an unsubstantiated modification in an unsubstantiated entity, the superego: if physiology is destiny Freud is anxious to invent a physiology of the mind. If judgment had not been separated from feeling so unnaturally in the Nazi officers presumably they would not have carried out orders so crisply. What kind of criticism is it to say that women are less stoical than men? After two world wars stoicism seems to have outlived its value. If women have been denied moral responsibility by male "justice" and dubbed angels while they were treated with contempt, it is likely that they will have formed their own conclusions about the monstrous superego and illusory morality of men. Protestant Europe has set for itself an unattainable morality of integrity in defiance of heavenly mercy, the unaided conscience bowed by full and unending responsibility for all actions, despite the partiality of knowledge and infirmity of will which characterize human action. Freud saw the results in his own community but he could not postulate an alternative to guilt and neurosis. The chief mainstay of such religion is the capacity of the ego to continue repression. Women may be bad at keeping up the cycle of the organism punishing itself, but that too may be an advantage which involves less delusion than its opposite.

> The feeling of identity in all circumstances is quite wanting in the true woman, because her memory, even if exceptionally good, is devoid of continuity . . . women, if they look back on their earlier lives, never understand themselves.[15]

> My colleague Nathan Leites, Ph.D., has concluded after a review of the literature that the term "identity" has little use other than as a fancy dress in which to disguise vagueness, ambiguity, tautologies, lack of clinical data, and poverty of explanation.
>
> Robert Stoller, *Sex and Gender,* 1968, p. x

On Weininger's evidence the ego is ersatz, consisting of the memory of the self which exists at any particular time. He remarks with horror that if you ask a woman about herself, she understands it to be her body. She does not seek to define herself by asserting her image of her merit, her behavior. Man has a temporal notion of identity, which is falsifiable, woman a simple spatial one. "Here you are," said the white buttons Yoko Ono gave away

---

[14] S. Freud, *Some Psychic Consequences of the Anatomical Distinction Between the Sexes,* Complete Works, Vol. XIX, pp. 257–8.

[15] Weininger (*op. cit.*), p. 146.

at her exhibition. It seems important after all. Perhaps woman, like the child, retains some power of connecting freely with external reality. Weininger seemed to think so. "The absolute female has no ego."[16]

> The primal act of the human ego is a negative one—not to accept reality, specifically the separation of the child's body from the mother's body . . . this negative posture blossoms into negation of self (repression) and negation of the environment (aggression).[17]

What a blossoming! If women had no ego, if they had no sense of separation from the rest of the world, no repression and no regression, how nice that would be! What need would there be of justice if everyone felt no aggression but infinite compassion! Of course I am taking advantage of the masters of psychology, bending and selecting their words like this, but what else can they be for? We cannot allow them to define what must be or change would be impossible. Whitehead and Needham looked forward to a new kind of knowledge which would correct the insanity of pure intelligence, "a science based on an erotic sense of reality, rather than an aggressive dominating attitude to reality."[18] If wisdom might not be incompatible with a low sense of ego, then charity seems in the mystical definitions of it to be dependent upon such a corrosion of separateness: the greatest myth of Christianity is that of the mystical body.

> To heal is to make whole, as in wholesome; to make one again; to unify. or reunify; this is Eros in action. Eros is the instinct that makes for union, or unification, and Thanatos, the death instinct, is the instinct that makes for separation or division.[19]

Weininger's disgust for Eros and his devotion to Thanatos drive him to state women's comprehensiveness more fully. Believing him we might think we had been saved already:

> This sense of continuity with the rest of mankind is a sexual character of the female, and displays itself in the desire to touch, to be in contact with the object of her pity; the mode in which her tenderness expresses itself is a kind of animal sense of contact. It shows an absence of that sharp line that separates one real personality from another.[20]

[16] *Ibid.*, p. 186.

[17] Norman O. Brown, *Life Against Death.*

[18] *Ibid.*, p. 276.

[19] Norman O. Brown, *Love's Body* (New York, 1966), p. 80.

[20] Weininger (*op. cit.*), p. 198.

Poor Weininger finally cut himself off altogether in a last act of fealty to death. The immorality of individualism is obvious in an age when loneliness is the most pernicious disease of our overcrowded metropolises. The results of parceling families in tiny slivers living in self-contained dwellings has defaced our cities and created innumerable problems of circulation and cohabitation. The sense of separateness is vainly counteracted by the pressure for conformity without community. In most of the big cities of the world the streets are dangerous to walk upon. Woman's oceanic feeling for the race has little opportunity for expression; it is grotesquely transmogrified in organized works of charity, where her genius for touching and soothing has dwindled into symbolic attitudinizing. Weininger's repugnance for animal contact is still universal among the northern races. Even crushed against his brother in the Tube the average Englishman pretends desperately that he is alone. Psychoanalysis, the most obscenely intimate contact of all, is not hallowed by any physical contact. Latterly, special classes form in church halls in arty suburbs, so that men and women can recover their sense of reassurance by touch. Too late for Weininger.

The intellectual pressure to make the whole world whole again has come from mystics like Lao-Tse, scientists like Whitehead and Needham and Merleau-Ponty, and as brilliant speculation from Norman O. Brown, Herbert Marcuse, Borges. Their words were not specifically addressed to women, because all of them felt that the polarity of the sexes was the basic alienation of man from himself, but none of them would reject the idea that their words were a special encouragement to women to undertake the work of saving mankind. Perhaps my treatment of their highly sophisticated arguments has been brutal, but reverence before authority has never accomplished much in the way of changing things. In inventing a new mythology one must plunder all sources, letting the situation into which the ideas fall

---

Might the cleavage between the subjective and objective have been badly made; might the opposition between a universe of science—entirely outside of self—and a universe of consciousness—defined by the total presence of self to self—be untenable? And if realistic analysis fails will biology find its method in an ideal analysis of the psychomathematical type, in Spinozistic intellection? Or might not value and signification be intrinsic determinations of the organism which could only be accessible to a new mode of "comprehension"?

Maurice Merleau-Ponty,
The Structure of Behaviour, p. 10

---

serve as their crucible. Most of the defects pointed out by critics of women are simply the results of their having been sheltered from the subtler and more effective types of enculturation which their society lavished upon its male leaders. The strengths they have are of sheer ignorance.

Dominant ideas need not always be so obvious for them to exert just as powerful an organizing influence on the way a person thinks and approaches a problem. Old and adequate ideas, like old and adequate cities, come to polarize everything around them. All organization is based on them, all things are referred to them. Minor alterations can be made on the outskirts, but it is impossible to change the whole structure radically and very difficult to shift the centre of organization to a different place.[21]

Facing this problem, Edward de Bono devised a series of exercises to develop the faculty he called lateral thinking. Lateral thought is the kind which produces ideas and inventions, rather than demonstrable solutions to specific problems. It is the kind of problem-solving which would not get you good marks for method in an examination, and is nevertheless right. It cannot be duplicated by a computer, which only has to learn what it is fed and a method to deal with it. In fact lateral thinking is a one-dimensional analogue of the child's modes of thought. A woman might claim to retain some of the child's faculties, although very limited and diffused, simply because she has not been encouraged to learn methods of thought and develop a disciplined mind. As long as education remains largely induction, ignorance will retain these advantages over learning and it is time that women impudently put them to work.

The prevailing criticism of the female soul can best be explained by the male battle to repress certain faculties in their own mental functioning. Women possessed in abundance those qualities which civilized men strove to repress in themselves, just as children and savages did. The value of such criticism is in the degree to which it reveals the severity of the contouring

---

> For a Tear is an Intellectual thing,
> And a Sigh is the Sword of an Angel King,
> And the bitter groan of a Martyr's woe
> Is an Arrow from the Almightie's Bow.
>
> Blake, *Jerusalem,* pl. 52

---

of the ideal personality, that is to say, male criticism of the female mind is revealing only of the male himself. Men in our culture crippled themselves by setting up an impossible standard of integrity: women were not given the chance to fool themselves in this way. Women have been charged with deviousness and duplicity since the dawn of civilization so they have never been able to pretend that their masks were anything but masks. It is a slender case but perhaps it does mean that women have always been in closer contact with reality than men: it would seem to be the just recompense for being deprived of idealism.

If women understand by emancipation the adoption of the masculine role then we are lost indeed. If women can supply no counterbalance to the blindness of male drive the aggressive society will run to its lunatic extremes at

---

[21] Edward De Bono, *New Think: The Use of Lateral Thinking in the Generation of New Ideas* (New York, 1968); *cf.* A. N. Whitehead, *An Introduction to Mathematics* (London, 1911), p. 138, and William James, *Some Problems in Philosophy,* Chap. X.

ever-escalating speed. Who will safeguard the despised animal faculties of compassion, empathy, innocence and sensuality? What will hold us back from Weininger's fate? Most women who have arrived at positions of power in a men's world have done so by adopting masculine methods which are not incompatible with the masquerade of femininity. They still exploit the sado-masochistic hook-up of the sexes, in which "we have only the choice of being hammer or anvil."[22] Wanda wore feminine clothes to add poig-

---

There is much to suggest that when human beings acquired the powers of conscious attention and rational thought they became so fascinated with these new tools that they forgot all else, like chickens hypnotized with their beaks to a chalk line. Our total sensitivity became identified with these partial functions so that we lost the ability to feel nature from the inside, and more, to feel the seamless unity of ourselves and the world. Our philosophy of action falls into the alternatives of voluntarism and determinism, because we have no sense of the wholeness of the endless knot and of the identity of its actions and ours.

A. E. Watts, *Nature, Man and Woman*, 1958, p. 12

---

nancy to her torture of Gregor, just as Mrs. Castle made sure that she looked attractive when she went to berate the workers as a criminal and irresponsible element in society. It is up to women to develop a form of genuine womanpower against which the Omnipotent Administrator in frilly knickers cannot prevail.

Womanpower means the self-determination of women, and that means that all the baggage of paternalistic society will have to be thrown overboard. Woman must have room and scope to devise a morality which does not disqualify her from excellence, and a psychology which does not condemn her to the status of a spiritual cripple. The penalties for such delinquency may be terrible for she must explore the dark without any guide. It may seem at first that she merely exchanges one mode of suffering for another, one neurosis for another. But she may at last claim to have made a definite choice which is the first prerequisite of moral action. She may never herself see the ultimate goal, for the fabric of society is not unraveled in a single lifetime, but she may state it as her belief and find hope in it.

The great renewal of the world will perhaps consist in this, that man and maid, freed from all false feeling and aversion, will seek each other not as opposites, but as brother and sister, as neighbours, and will come together as human beings.[23]

[22] Leopold Von Sacher-Masoch, *Venus in Furs* (London, 1969), p. 160.

[23] Rainer Maria Rilke, *Letters to a Young Poet* (Edinburgh, 1945), p. 23.

FRANZ FANON

(1925-1961)

Black thinkers are divided on whether color is skin deep or deeper—that is, does color make no difference or a difference that blacks and whites alike should esteem rather than disvalue. For those who see differences to be valued, many of the issues discussed in relation to women are equally important concerning blacks: if we reject the dominant character traits of the white male as exclusively defining what it is to be a human, then what are the dominant black character traits that add to the rich plurality of ways to be human?

But stressing differences, even where they are esteemed, runs the risk of justifying injustices. Despite differences in ways of being human, men, women, blacks, whites, indians, and aryans all share a common humanity, and deserve equality from any of man's laws. Fanon's **Wretched of the Earth** chronicles the results of a systematic denial of basic human equality.

Despite his importance to Third World liberation movements, Fanon's insights into revolution do not derive from the political practice that informs the writings of revolutionaries like Che Guevara. Fanon is a psychoanalyst. From his clinical practice, particularly with patients who had suffered the horrors of the Algerian struggle with French colonial rule, he discovered ways that oppression works through the capacity of the oppressed to internalize the values of the oppressors. Or to recall an earlier formulation, Fanon explored the **identification** of part of the oppressed personality with the attributions and reinforcements encouraged by the oppressor. Fanon sees this process as being so thorough that violence may be required to break the spell of identification. Greer's closing paragraph suggests that "all the baggage of paternalistic society will have to be thrown overboard." Though Greer does not draw out the implications of the violence of her metaphor, Fanon is concerned precisely with throwing out the baggage of paternalistic society and is explicit about the violence of the metaphor. He sees violence as a purgatory a colonialized people may have to pass through before they can achieve a fresh sense of their own identity, distinct from internalized colonial values.

The pain of apocalypse is a general theme in the dialectics of oppression and liberation. Recall yet once again Plato's description of the person forced to turn his eyes away from the images on the cave wall. And think again of the formal similarities running through all the dialectics of liberation: just as it is possible to extrapolate from the women's movement to the importance of

esteeming differences in fighting racist evaluations of color differences, so reflect on how the blacks' struggle for basic human
equality before the law may shed light on women's liberation.
What violence may women have to perpetrate to free themselves
from the yoke of their own identification with male chauvinist
values? Fanon's reflections do not extol violence as either a legitimate or even a successful means of vanquishing an external
enemy. His argument, based as it is on the dynamics of internalization and identification, has far more to do with the role of violence in regard to the enemy within.

VIOLENCE AND LIBERATION

The settler makes history and is con-
scious of making it. And because he constantly refers to the history of his
mother country, he clearly indicates that he himself is the extension of that
mother country. Thus the history which he writes is not the history of the
country which he plunders but the history of his own nation in regard to all
that she skims off, all that she violates and starves.

The immobility to which the native is condemned can only be called in
question if the native decides to put an end to the history of colonization—
the history of pillage—and to bring into existence the history of the nation
—the history of decolonization.

A world divided into compartments, a motionless, Manicheistic world, a
world of statues: the statue of the general who carried out the conquest, the
statue of the engineer who built the bridge; a world which is sure of itself,
which crushes with its stones the backs flayed by whips: this is the colonial
world. The native is a being hemmed in; apartheid is simply one form of
the division into compartments of the colonial world. The first thing which
the native learns is to stay in his place, and not to go beyond certain limits.
This is why the dreams of the native are always of muscular prowess; his
dreams are of action and of aggression. I dream I am jumping, swimming,
running, climbing; I dream that I burst out laughing, that I span a river in
one stride, or that I am followed by a flood of motorcars which never catch
up with me. During the period of colonization, the native never stops
achieving his freedom from nine in the evening until six in the morning.

The colonized man will first manifest this aggressiveness which has been
deposited in his bones against his own people. This is the period when the
niggers beat each other up, and the police and magistrates do not know

VIOLENCE AND LIBERATION From Franz Fanon, *The Wretched of the Earth*. Reprinted by permission of Grove Press, Inc. Copyright © 1963 by Présence Africaine.

which way to turn when faced with the astonishing waves of crime in North Africa. We shall see later how this phenomenon should be judged. When the native is confronted with the colonial order of things, he finds he is in a state of permanent tension. The settler's world is a hostile world, which spurns the native, but at the same time it is a world of which he is envious. We have seen that the native never ceases to dream of putting himself in the place of the settler—not of becoming the settler but of substituting himself for the settler. This hostile world, ponderous and aggressive because it fends off the colonized masses with all the harshness it is capable of, represents not merely a hell from which the swiftest flight possible is desirable, but also a paradise close at hand which is guarded by terrible watchdogs.

The native is always on the alert, for since he can only make out with difficulty the many symbols of the colonial world, he is never sure whether or not he has crossed the frontier. Confronted with a world ruled by the settler, the native is always presumed guilty. But the native's guilt is never a guilt which he accepts; it is rather a kind of curse, a sort of sword of Damocles, for, in his innermost spirit, the native admits no accusation. He is overpowered but not tamed; he is treated as an inferior but he is not convinced of his inferiority. He is patiently waiting until the settler is off his guard to fly at him. The native's muscles are always tensed. You can't say that he is terrorized, or even apprehensive. He is in fact ready at a moment's notice to exchange the role of the quarry for that of the hunter. The native is an oppressed person whose permanent dream is to become the persecutor. The symbols of social order—the police, the bugle calls in the barracks, military parades and the waving flags—are at one and the same time inhibitory and stimulating: for they do not convey the message "Don't dare to budge"; rather, they cry out "Get ready to attack." And, in fact, if the native had any tendency to fall asleep and to forget, the settler's hauteur and the settler's anxiety to test the strength of the colonial system would remind him at every turn that the great showdown cannot be put off indefinitely. That impulse to take the settler's place implies a tonicity of muscles the whole time; and in fact we know that in certain emotional conditions the presence of an obstacle accentuates the tendency toward motion.

The settler-native relationship is a mass relationship. The settler pits brute force against the weight of numbers. He is an exhibitionist. His preoccupation with security makes him remind the native out loud that there he alone is master. The settler keeps alive in the native an anger which he deprives of outlet; the native is trapped in the tight links of the chains of colonialism. But we have seen that inwardly the settler can only achieve a pseudo petrification. The native's muscular tension finds outlet regularly in bloodthirsty explosions—in tribal warfare, in feuds between septs, and in quarrels between individuals.

Where individuals are concerned, a positive negation of common sense is evident. While the settler or the policeman has the right the livelong day to strike the native, to insult him and to make him crawl to them, you will see the native reaching for his knife at the slightest hostile or aggressive glance cast on him by another native; for the last resort of the native is to defend his personality vis-à-vis his brother. Tribal feuds only serve to perpetuate old grudges buried deep in the memory. By throwing himself with all his force into the vendetta, the native tries to persuade himself that colonialism does not exist, that everything is going on as before, that history continues. Here on the level of communal organizations we clearly discern the well-known behavior patterns of avoidance. It is as if plunging into a fraternal blood bath allowed them to ignore the obstacle, and to put off till later the choice, nevertheless inevitable, which opens up the question of armed resistance to colonialism. Thus collective autodestruction in a very concrete form is one of the ways in which the native's muscular tension is set free. All these patterns of conduct are those of the death reflex when faced with danger, a suicidal behavior which proves to the settler (whose existence and domination is by them all the more justified) that these men are reasonable human beings. In the same way the native manages to by-pass the settler. A belief in fatality removes all blame from the oppressor; the cause of misfortunes and of poverty is attributed to God: He is Fate. In this way the individual accepts the disintegration ordained by God, bows down before the settler and his lot, and by a kind of interior restabilization acquires a stony calm.

Meanwhile, however, life goes on, and the native will strengthen the inhibitions which contain his aggressiveness by drawing on the terrifying myths which are so frequently found in underdeveloped communities. There are maleficent spirits which intervene every time a step is taken in the wrong direction, leopard-men, serpent-men, six-legged dogs, zombies— a whole series of tiny animals or giants which create around the native a world of prohibitions, of barriers and of inhibitions far more terrifying than the world of the settler. This magical superstructure which permeates native society fulfills certain well-defined functions in the dynamism of the libido. One of the characteristics of underdeveloped societies is in fact that the libido is first and foremost the concern of a group, or of the family. The feature of communities whereby a man who dreams that he has sexual relations with a woman other than his own must confess it in public and pay a fine in kind or in working days to the injured husband or family is fully described by ethnologists. We may note in passing that this proves that the so-called prehistoric societies attach great importance to the unconscious.

The atmosphere of myth and magic frightens me and so takes on an undoubted reality. By terrifying me, it integrates me in the traditions and the history of my district or of my tribe, and at the same time it reassures me, it gives me a status, as it were an identification paper. In underdeveloped countries the occult sphere is a sphere belonging to the community which is entirely under magical jurisdiction. By entangling myself in this inextricable network where actions are repeated with crystalline inevitability, I find the everlasting world which belongs to me, and the perenniality which is thereby affirmed of the world belonging to us. Believe me, the zombies are more terrifying than the settlers; and in consequence the problem is no longer that of keeping oneself right with the colonial world and its barbed-wire entanglements, but of considering three times before urinating, spitting, or going out into the night.

The supernatural magical powers reveal themselves as essentially personal; the settler's powers are infinitely shrunken, stamped with their alien origin. We no longer really need to fight against them since what counts is the frightening enemy created by myths. We perceive that all is settled by a permanent confrontation on the phantasmic plane.

It has always happened in the struggle for freedom that such a people, formerly lost in an imaginary maze, a prey to unspeakable terrors yet happy to lose themselves in a dreamlike torment, such a people becomes unhinged, reorganizes itself, and in blood and tears gives birth to very real and immediate action. Feeding the *moudjahidines,*[1] posting sentinels, coming to the help of families which lack the bare necessities, or taking the place of a husband who has been killed or imprisoned: such are the concrete tasks to which the people is called during the struggle for freedom.

In the colonial world, the emotional sensitivity of the native is kept on the surface of his skin like an open sore which flinches from the caustic agent; and the psyche shrinks back, obliterates itself and finds outlet in muscular demonstrations which have caused certain very wise men to say that the native is a hysterical type. This sensitive emotionalism, watched by invisible keepers who are however in unbroken contact with the core of the personality, will find its fulfillment through eroticism in the driving forces behind the crisis' dissolution.

On another level we see the native's emotional sensibility exhausting itself in dances which are more or less ecstatic. This is why any study of the colonial world should take into consideration the phenomena of the dance and of possession. The native's relaxation takes precisely the form of a muscular orgy in which the most acute aggressivity and the most impelling violence are canalized, transformed, and conjured away. The circle of the dance is a permissive circle: it protects and permits. At certain times on certain days, men and women come together at a given place, and there, under the solemn eye of the tribe, fling themselves into a seemingly unorganized pantomime, which is in reality extremely systematic, in which by various means—shakes of the head, bending of the spinal column, throwing of the whole body backward—may be deciphered as in an open book the huge effort of a community to exorcise itself, to liberate itself, to explain itself. There are no limits—inside the circle. The hillock up which you have toiled as if to be nearer to the moon; the river bank down which you slip as if to show the connection between the dance and ablutions, cleansing and purification—these are sacred places. There are no limits—for in reality your purpose in coming together is to allow the accumulated libido, the

---

[1] Highly-trained soldiers who are completely dedicated to the Moslem cause.—*Trans.*

hampered aggressivity, to dissolve as in a volcanic eruption. Symbolical killings, fantastic rides, imaginary mass murders—all must be brought out. The evil humors are undammed, and flow away with a din as of molten lava.

One step further and you are completely possessed. In fact, these are actually organized séances of possession and exorcism; they include vampirism, possession by djinns, by zombies, and by Legba, the famous god of the voodoo. This disintegrating of the personality, this splitting and dissolution, all this fulfills a primordial function in the organism of the colonial world. When they set out, the men and women were impatient, stamping their feet in a state of nervous excitement; when they return, peace has been restored to the village; it is once more calm and unmoved.

During the struggle for freedom, a marked alienation from these practices is observed. The native's back is to the wall, the knife is at his throat (or, more precisely, the electrode at his genitals): he will have no more call for his fancies. After centuries of unreality, after having wallowed in the most outlandish phantoms, at long last the native, gun in hand, stands face to face with the only forces which contend for his life—the forces of colonialism. And the youth of a colonized country, growing up in an atmosphere of shot and fire, may well make a mock of, and does not hesitate to pour scorn upon the zombies of his ancestors, the horses with two heads, the dead who rise again, and the djinns who rush into your body while you yawn. The native discovers reality and transforms it into the pattern of his customs, into the practice of violence and into his plan for freedom.

We have seen that this same violence, though kept very much on the surface all through the colonial period, yet turns in the void. We have also seen that it is canalized by the emotional outlets of dance and possession by spirits; we have seen how it is exhausted in fratricidal combats. Now the problem is to lay hold of this violence which is changing direction. When formerly it was appeased by myths and exercised its talents in finding fresh ways of committing mass suicide, now new conditions will make possible a completely new line of action. [. . .]

But let us return to that atmosphere of violence, that violence which is just under the skin. We have seen that in its process toward maturity many leads are attached to it, to control it and show it the way out. Yet in spite of the metamorphoses which the colonial regime imposes upon it in the way of tribal or regional quarrels, that violence makes its way forward, and the native identifies his enemy and recognizes all his misfortunes, throwing all the exacerbated might of his hate and anger into this new channel. But how do we pass from the atmosphere of violence to violence in action? What makes the lid blow off? There is first of all the fact that this development does not leave the settler's blissful existence intact. The settler who "understands" the natives is made aware by several straws in the wind showing that something is afoot. "Good" natives become scarce; silence falls when the oppressor approaches; sometimes looks are black, and attitudes and remarks openly aggressive. The nationalist parties are astir, they hold a great many meetings, the police are increased and reinforcements of soldiers are brought in. The settlers, above all the farmers isolated on their land, are the first to become alarmed. They call for energetic measures.

The authorities do in fact take some spectacular measures. They arrest one or two leaders, they organize military parades and maneuvers, and air force displays. But the demonstrations and warlike exercises, the smell of gunpowder which now fills the atmosphere, these things do not make the people draw back. Those bayonets and cannonades only serve to reinforce their aggressiveness. The atmosphere becomes dramatic, and everyone wishes to show that he is ready for anything. And it is in these circumstances that the guns go off by themselves, for nerves are jangled, fear reigns and everyone is trigger-happy. A single commonplace incident is enough to start the machine-gunning: Sétif in Algeria, the Central Quarries in Morocco, Moramanga in Madagascar.

The repressions, far from calling a halt to the forward rush of national consciousness, urge it on. Mass slaughter in the colonies at a certain stage of the embryonic development of consciousness increases that consciousness, for the hecatombs are an indication that between oppressors and oppressed everything can be solved by force. It must be remarked here that the political parties have not called for armed insurrection, and have made no preparations for such an insurrection. All these repressive measures, all those actions which are a result of fear are not within the leaders' intentions: they are overtaken by events. At this moment, then, colonialism may decide to arrest the nationalist leaders. But today the governments of colonized countries know very well that it is extremely dangerous to deprive the masses of their leaders; for then the people, unbridled, fling themselves into *jacqueries,* mutinies, and "brutish murders." The masses give free rein to their "bloodthirsty instincts" and force colonialism to free their leaders, to whom falls the difficult task of bringing them back to order. The colonized people, who have spontaneously brought their violence to the colossal task of destroying the colonial system, will very soon find themselves with the barren, inert slogan "Release X or Y."[2] Then colonialism will release these men, and hold discussions with them. The time for dancing in the streets has come.

In certain circumstances, the party political machine may remain intact. But as a result of the colonialist repression and of the spontaneous reaction of the people the parties find themselves out-distanced by their militants. The violence of the masses is vigorously pitted against the military forces of the occupying power, and the situation deteriorates and comes to a head. Those leaders who are free remain, therefore, on the touchline. They have suddenly become useless, with their bureaucracy and their reasonable demands; yet we see them, far removed from events, attempting the crowning imposture—that of "speaking in the name of the silenced nation." As a

[2] It may happen that the arrested leader is in fact the authentic mouthpiece of the colonized masses. In this case colonialism will make use of his period of detention to try to launch new leaders.

general rule, colonialism welcomes this godsend with open arms, transforms these "blind mouths" into spokesmen, and in two minutes endows them with independence, on condition that they restore order.

So we see that all parties are aware of the power of such violence and that the question is not always to reply to it by a greater violence, but rather to see how to relax the tension.

What is the real nature of this violence? We have seen that it is the intuition of the colonized masses that their liberation must, and can only, be achieved by force. By what spiritual aberration do these men, without technique, starving and enfeebled, confronted with the military and economic might of the occupation, come to believe that violence alone will free them? How can they hope to triumph?

It is because violence (and this is the disgraceful thing) may constitute, in so far as it forms part of its system, the slogan of a political party. The leaders may call on the people to enter upon an armed struggle. This problematical question has to be thought over. When militarist Germany decides to settle its frontier disputes by force, we are not in the least surprised; but when the people of Angola, for example, decide to take up arms, when the Algerian people reject all means which are not violent, these are proofs that something has happened or is happening at this very moment. The colonized races, those slaves of modern times, are impatient. They know that this apparent folly alone can put them out of reach of colonial oppression. A new type of relations is established in the world. The underdeveloped peoples try to break their chains, and the extraordinary thing is that they succeed. It could be argued that in these days of sputniks it is ridiculous to die of hunger; but for the colonized masses the argument is more down-to-earth. The truth is that there is no colonial power today which is capable of adopting the only form of contest which has a chance of succeeding, namely, the prolonged establishment of large forces of occupation.

HANNAH ARENDT
(1906-   )

Hannah Arendt's appearance in this section serves a double purpose: aside from the specific content of her essay on violence, she contributes an outstanding example of what women can, in fact, do with their brains. For decades Arendt has been one of the finest philosophically trained minds in the field of social commentary and contemporary history, as her books **The Origins of Totalitarianism; Eichmann in Jerusalem;** and particularly **The Human Condition** show. The past several years she has been teaching advanced seminars at both The New School for Social Research in New York City and at the University of Chicago.

In the following essay, a slightly altered version of a lecture she delivered at Yale and then published in the **New York Review of Books,** Arendt notes the changed climate of current reflections on violence, referring explicitly to Fanon and to Sartre's introduction to Fanon's book. She then draws a series of important distinctions among the concepts of violence, power, force, strength, and authority. Violence, she argues, is not the necessary means to power but quite the contrary of power. Violence is used as a last resort where power is lacking. Because power and violence are contraries, however, violence cannot lead to power; it can lead only to the destruction of power.

On Violence

The more dubious and uncertain an instrument violence has become in international relations, the more it has gained in reputation and appeal in domestic affairs, specifically in the matter of revolution. The strong Marxist rhetoric of the New Left coincides with the steady growth of the entirely non-Marxian conviction, proclaimed by Mao Tse-tung, that "Power grows out of the barrel of a gun." To be sure, Marx was aware of the role of violence in history, but this role was to him secondary; not violence but the contradictions inherent in the old society brought about its end. The emergence of a new society was preceded, but not caused, by violent outbreaks, which he likened to the labor pangs that precede, but of course do not cause, the event of organic birth. In the same vein he regarded the state as an instrument of violence in the command of the ruling class; but the actual power of the ruling class did not consist of or rely on violence. It was defined by the role the ruling class played in society, or, more exactly, by its role in the process of production. It has often been noticed, and sometimes deplored, that the revolutionary Left under the influence of Marx's teachings ruled out the use of violent means; the "dictatorship of the proletariat"—openly repressive in Marx's writings—came after the revolution and was meant, like the Roman dictatorship, to last a strictly limited period. Political assassination, except for a few acts of individual terror perpetrated by small groups of anarchists, was mostly the prerogative of the Right, while organized armed uprisings remained the specialty of the military. The Left remained convinced "that all conspiracies are not only useless but harmful. They [knew] only too well that the revolutions are not made intentionally and arbitrarily, but that they

ON VIOLENCE © 1970 by Hannah Arendt. From "On Violence" in *Crises of the Republic* by Hannah Arendt, by permission of Harcourt Brace Jovanovich, Inc.

were always and everywhere the necessary result of circumstances entirely independent of the will and guidance of particular parties and whole classes."[1]

On the level of theory there were a few exceptions. Georges Sorel, who at the beginning of the century tried to combine Marxism with Bergson's philosophy of life—the result, though on a much lower level of sophistication, is oddly similar to Sartre's current amalgamation of existentialism and Marxism—thought of class struggle in military terms; yet he ended by proposing nothing more violent than the famous myth of the general strike, a form of action which we today would think of as belonging rather to the arsenal of nonviolent politics. Fifty years ago even this modest proposal earned him the reputation of being a fascist, notwithstanding his enthusiastic approval of Lenin and the Russian Revolution. Sartre, who in his preface to Fanon's *The Wretched of the Earth* goes much farther in his glorification of violence than Sorel in his famous *Reflections on Violence* —farther than Fanon himself, whose argument he wishes to bring to its conclusion—still mentions "Sorel's fascist utterances." This shows to what extent Sartre is unaware of his basic disagreement with Marx on the question of violence, especially when he states that "irrepressible violence . . . is man recreating himself," that it is through "mad fury" that "the wretched of the earth" can "become men." These notions are all the more remarkable because the idea of man creating himself is strictly in the tradition of Hegelian and Marxian thinking; it is the very basis of all leftist humanism. But according to Hegel man "produces" himself through thought,[2] whereas for Marx, who turned Hegel's "idealism" upside down, it was labor, the human form of metabolism with nature, that fulfilled this function. And though one may argue that all notions of man creating himself have in common a rebellion against the very factuality of the human condition—nothing is more obvious than that man, whether as member of the species or as an individual, does *not* owe his existence to himself—and that therefore what Sartre, Marx, and Hegel have in common is more relevant than the particular activities through which this non-fact should presumably have come about, still it cannot be denied that a gulf separates the essentially peaceful activities of thinking and laboring from all deeds of violence. "To shoot down a European is to kill two birds with one stone . . . there remain a dead man and a free man," says Sartre in his preface. This is a sentence Marx could never have written.

I quoted Sartre in order to show that this new shift toward violence in the thinking of revolutionaries can remain unnoticed even by one of their most representative and articulate spokesmen, and it is all the more note-

[1] I owe this early remark of Engels, in a manuscript of 1847, to Jacob Barion, *Hegel und die marxistische Staatslehre,* Bonn, 1963.

[2] It is quite suggestive that Hegel speaks in this context of *"Sichselbstproduzieren."* See *Vorlesungen über die Geschichte der Philosophie,* ed. Hoffmeister, p. 114, Leipzig, 1938.

worthy for evidently not being an abstract notion in the history of ideas. (If one turns the "idealistic" *concept* of thought upside down, one might arrive at the "materialistic" *concept* of labor; one will never arrive at the notion of violence.) No doubt all this has a logic of its own, but it is one springing from experience, and this experience was utterly unknown to any generation before.

The pathos and the *élan* of the New Left, their credibility, as it were, are closely connected with the weird suicidal development of modern weapons; this is the first generation to grow up under the shadow of the atom bomb. They inherited from their parents' generation the experience of a massive intrusion of criminal violence into politics: they learned in high school and in college about concentration and extermination camps, about genocide and torture,[3] about the wholesale slaughter of civilians in war without which modern military operations are no longer possible even if restricted to "conventional" weapons. Their first reaction was a revulsion against every form of violence, an almost matter-of-course espousal of a politics of nonviolence. The very great successes of this movement, especially in the field of civil rights, were followed by the resistance movement against the war in Vietnam, which has remained an important factor in determining the climate of opinion in this country. But it is no secret that things have changed since then, that the adherents of nonviolence are on the defensive, and it would be futile to say that only the "extremists" are yielding to a glorification of violence and have discovered—like Fanon's Algerian peasants—that "only violence pays."[4] [. . .]

It is, I think, a rather sad reflection on the present state of political science that our terminology does not distinguish among such key words as "power," "strength," "force," "authority," and, finally, "violence"—all of which refer to distinct, different phenomena and would hardly exist unless they did. (In the words of d'Entrèves, "might, power, authority: these are all words to whose exact implications no great weight is attached in current speech; even the greatest thinkers sometimes use them at random. Yet it is fair to presume that they refer to different properties, and their meaning should therefore be carefully assessed and examined. . . . The correct use of these words is a question not only of logical grammar, but of historical

---

[3] Noam Chomsky rightly notices among the motives for open rebellion the refusal "to take one's place alongside the 'good German' we have all learned to despise." *American Power and the New Mandarins* (New York, 1969), p. 368.

[4] Frantz Fanon, *The Wretched of the Earth* (1961), Grove Press edition, 1968, p. 61. I am using this work because of its great influence on the present student generation. Fanon himself, however, is much more doubtful about violence than his admirers. It seems that only the book's first chapter, "Concerning Violence," has been widely read. Fanon knows of the "unmixed and total brutality [which], if not immediately combatted, invariably leads to the defeat of the movement within a few weeks" (p. 147).

For the recent escalation of violence in the student movement, see the instructive series "Gewalt" in the German news magazine *Der Spiegel* (February 10, 1969 ff.), and the series "Mit dem Latein am Ende" (Nos. 26 and 27, 1969).

perspective.")[5] To use them as synonyms not only indicates a certain deafness to linguistic meanings, which would be serious enough, but it has also resulted in a kind of blindness to the realities they correspond to. In such a situation it is always tempting to introduce new definitions, but—though I shall briefly yield to temptation—what is involved is not simply a matter of careless speech. Behind the apparent confusion is a firm conviction in whose light all distinctions would be, at best, of minor importance: the conviction that the most crucial political issue is, and always has been, the question of Who rules Whom? Power, strength, force, authority, violence— these are but words to indicate the means by which man rules over man; they are held to be synonyms because they have the same function. It is only after one ceases to reduce public affairs to the business of dominion that the original data in the realm of human affairs will appear, or, rather, reappear, in their authentic diversity.

These data, in our context, may be enumerated as follows:

Power corresponds to the human ability not just to act but to act in concert. Power is never the property of an individual; it belongs to a group and remains in existence only so long as the group keeps together. When we say of somebody that he is "in power" we actually refer to his being empowered by a certain number of people to act in their name. The moment the group, from which the power originated to begin with (*potestas in populo,* without a people or group there is no power), disappears, "his power" also vanishes. In current usage, when we speak of a "powerful man" or a "powerful personality," we already use the word "power" metaphorically; what we refer to without metaphor is "strength."

Strength unequivocally designates something in the singular, an individual entity; it is the property inherent in an object or person and belongs to its character, which may prove itself in relation to other things or persons, but is essentially independent of them. The strength of even the strongest individual can always be overpowered by the many, who often will combine for no other purpose than to ruin strength precisely because of its peculiar independence. The almost instinctive hostility of the many toward the one has always, from Plato to Nietzsche, been ascribed to resentment, to the envy of the weak for the strong, but this psychological interpretation misses the point. It is in the nature of a group and its power to turn against independence, the property of individual strength.

Force, which we often use in daily speech as a synonym for violence, especially if violence serves as a means of coercion, should be reserved, in terminological language, for the "forces of nature" or the "force of cir-

---

[5] P. D'Entrèves, *The Notion of the State, An Introduction to Political Theory* (Oxford, 1967), p. 7. Cf. also p. 171, where, discussing the exact meaning of the words "nation" and "nationality," he rightly insists that "the only competent guides in the jungle of so many different meanings are the linguists and the historians. It is to them that we must turn for help." And in distinguishing authority and power, he turns to Cicero's *potestas in populo, auctoritas in senatu.*

cumstances" (*la force des choses*), that is, to indicate the energy released by physical or social movements.

Authority, relating to the most elusive of these phenomena and therefore, as a term, most frequently abused,[6] can be vested in persons—there is such a thing as personal authority, as, for instance, in the relation between parent and child, between teacher and pupil—or it can be vested in offices, as, for instance, in the Roman senate (*auctoritas in senatu*) or in the hierarchical offices of the Church (a priest can grant valid absolution even though he is drunk). Its hallmark is unquestioning recognition by those who are asked to obey; neither coercion nor persuasion is needed. (A father can lose his authority either by beating his child or by starting to argue with him, that is, either by behaving to him like a tyrant or by treating him as an equal.) To remain in authority requires respect for the person or the office. The greatest enemy of authority, therefore, is contempt, and the surest way to undermine it is laughter.[7]

Violence, finally, as I have said, is distinguished by its instrumental character. Phenomenologically, it is close to strength, since the implements of violence, like all other tools, are designed and used for the purpose of multiplying natural strength until, in the last stage of their development, they can substitute for it.

It is perhaps not superfluous to add that these distinctions, though by no means arbitrary, hardly ever correspond to watertight compartments in the real world, from which nevertheless they are drawn. Thus institutionalized power in organized communities often appears in the guise of authority, demanding instant, unquestioning recognition; no society could function

---

[6] There is such a thing as authoritarian government, but it certainly has nothing in common with tyranny, dictatorship, or totalitarian rule. For a discussion of the historical background and political significance of the term, see my "What is Authority?" in *Between Past and Future: Exercises in Political Thought,* New York, 1968, and Part I of Karl-Heinz Lübke's valuable study, *Auctoritas bei Augustin,* Stuttgart, 1968, with extensive bibliography.

[7] Wolin and Schaar, in "Berkeley: The Battle of People's Park" (*New York Review of Books,* June 19, 1969), are entirely right: "The rules are being broken because University authorities, administrators and faculty alike, have lost the respect of many of the students." They then conclude, "When authority leaves, power enters." This too is true, but, I am afraid, not quite in the sense they meant it. What entered first at Berkeley was student power, obviously the strongest power on every campus simply because of the students' superior numbers. It was in order to break this power that authorities resorted to violence, and it is precisely because the university is essentially an institution based on authority, and therefore in need of respect, that it finds it so difficult to deal with power in nonviolent terms. The university today calls upon the police for protection exactly as the Catholic church used to do before the separation of state and church forced it to rely on authority alone. It is perhaps more than an oddity that the severest crisis of the church as an institution should coincide with the severest crisis in the history of the university, the only secular institution still based on authority. Both may indeed be ascribed to "the progressing explosion of the atom 'obedience' whose stability was allegedly eternal," as Heinrich Böll remarked of the crisis in the churches. See "Es wird immer später," in *Antwort an Sacharow,* Zürich, 1969.

without it. (A small, and still isolated, incident in New York shows what can happen if authentic authority in social relations has broken down to the point where it cannot work any longer even in its derivative, purely functional form. A minor mishap in the subway system—the doors on a train failed to operate—turned into a serious shutdown on the line lasting four hours and involving more than fifty thousand passengers, because when the transit authorities asked the passengers to leave the defective train, they simply refused.)[8] Moreover, nothing, as we shall see, is more common than the combination of violence and power, nothing less frequent than to find them in their pure and therefore extreme form. From this, it does not follow that authority, power, and violence are all the same.

Still it must be admitted that it is particularly tempting to think of power in terms of command and obedience, and hence to equate power with violence, in a discussion of what actually is only one of power's special cases —namely, the power of government. Since in foreign relations as well as domestic affairs violence appears as a last resort to keep the power structure intact against individual challengers—the foreign enemy, the native criminal—it looks indeed as though violence were the prerequisite of power and power nothing but a façade, the velvet glove which either conceals the iron hand or will turn out to belong to a paper tiger. On closer inspection, though, this notion loses much of its plausibility. For our purpose, the gap between theory and reality is perhaps best illustrated by the phenomenon of revolution.

Since the beginning of the century theoreticians of revolution have told us that the chances of revolution have significantly decreased in proportion to the increased destructive capacities of weapons at the unique disposition of governments.[9] The history of the last seventy years, with its extraordinary record of successful and unsuccessful revolutions, tells a different story. Were people mad who even tried against such overwhelming odds? And, leaving out instances of full success, how can even a temporary success be explained? The fact is that the gap between state-owned means of violence and what people can muster by themselves—from beer bottles to Molotov cocktails and guns—has always been so enormous that technical improvements make hardly any difference. Textbook instructions on "how

[8] See the New York *Times,* January 4, 1969, pp. 1 and 29.

[9] Thus Franz Borkenau, reflecting on the defeat of the Spanish revolution, states: "In this tremendous contrast with previous revolutions one fact is reflected. Before these latter years, counter-revolution usually depended upon the support of reactionary powers, which were technically and intellectually inferior to the forces of revolution. This has changed with the advent of fascism. Now, every revolution is likely to meet the attack of the most modern, most efficient, most ruthless machinery yet in existence. It means that the age of revolutions free to evolve according to their own laws is over." This was written more than thirty years ago (*The Spanish Cockpit,* London, 1937; Ann Arbor, 1963, pp. 288–289) and is now quoted with approval by Chomsky (*op. cit.,* p. 310). He believes that American and French intervention in the civil war in Vietnam proves Borkenau's prediction accurate, "with substitution of 'liberal imperialism' for 'fascism.' " I think that this example is rather apt to prove the opposite.

to make a revolution" in a step-by-step progression from dissent to conspiracy, from resistance to armed uprising, are all based on the mistaken notion that revolutions are "made." In a contest of violence against violence the superiority of the government has always been absolute; but this superiority lasts only as long as the power structure of the government is intact—that is, as long as commands are obeyed and the army or police forces are prepared to use their weapons. When this is no longer the case, the situation changes abruptly. Not only is the rebellion not put down, but the arms themselves change hands—sometimes, as in the Hungarian revolution, within a few hours. (We should know about such things after all these years of futile fighting in Vietnam, where for a long time, before getting massive Russian aid, the National Liberation Front fought us with weapons that were made in the United States.) Only after this has happened, when the disintegration of the government in power has permitted the rebels to arm themselves, can one speak of an "armed uprising," which often does not take place at all or occurs when it is no longer necessary. Where commands are no longer obeyed, the means of violence are of no use; and the question of this obedience is not decided by the command-obedience relation but by opinion, and, of course, by the number of those who share it. Everything depends on the power behind the violence. The sudden dramatic breakdown of power that ushers in revolutions reveals in a flash how civil obedience—to laws, to rulers, to institutions—is but the outward manifestation of support and consent.

Where power has disintegrated, revolutions are possible but not necessary. We know of many instances when utterly impotent regimes were permitted to continue in existence for long periods of time—either because there was no one to test their strength and reveal their weakness or because they were lucky enough not to be engaged in war and suffer defeat. Disintegration often becomes manifest only in direct confrontation; and even then, when power is already in the street, some group of men prepared for such an eventuality is needed to pick it up and assume responsibility. We have recently witnessed how it did not take more than the relatively harmless, essentially nonviolent French students' rebellion to reveal the vulnerability of the whole political system, which rapidly disintegrated before the astonished eyes of the young rebels. Unknowingly they had tested it; they intended only to challenge the ossified university system, and down came the system of governmental power, together with that of the huge party bureaucracies—*"une sorte de désintégration de toutes les hiérarchies."*[10] It was a textbook case of a revolutionary situation[11] that did not develop into

[10] Raymond Aron, *La Révolution Introuvable,* 1968, p. 41.

[11] Stephen Spender, in *The Year of the Young Rebels* (New York, 1969), p. 56, disagrees: "What was so much more apparent than the revolutionary situation [was] the nonrevolutionary one." It may be "difficult to think of a revolution taking place when . . . everyone looks particularly good humoured," but this is what usually happens in the beginning of revolutions—during the early great ecstasy of fraternity.

a revolution because there was nobody, least of all the students, prepared to seize power and the responsibility that goes with it. Nobody except, of course, de Gaulle. Nothing was more characteristic of the seriousness of the situation than his appeal to the army, his journey to see Massu and the generals in Germany, a walk to Canossa, if there ever was one, in view of what had happened only a few years before. But what he sought and received was support, not obedience, and the means were not commands but concessions. If commands had been enough, he would never have had to leave Paris.

No government exclusively based on the means of violence has ever existed. Even the totalitarian ruler, whose chief instrument of rule is torture, needs a power basis—the secret police and its net of informers. Only the development of robot soldiers, which, as previously mentioned, would eliminate the human factor completely and, conceivably, permit one man with a push button to destroy whomever he pleased, could change this fundamental ascendancy of power over violence. Even the most despotic domination we know of, the rule of master over slaves, who always outnumbered him, did not rest on superior means of coercion as such, but on a superior organization of power—that is, on the organized solidarity of the masters.[12] Single men without others to support them never have enough power to use violence successfully. Hence, in domestic affairs, violence functions as the last resort of power against criminals or rebels —that is, against single individuals who, as it were, refuse to be overpowered by the consensus of the majority. And as for actual warfare, we have seen in Vietnam how an enormous superiority in the means of violence can become helpless if confronted with an ill-equipped but well-organized opponent who is much more powerful. This lesson, to be sure, was there to be learned from the history of guerrilla warfare, which is at least as old as the defeat in Spain of Napoleon's still-unvanquished army.

To switch for a moment to conceptual language: Power is indeed of the essence of all government, but violence is not. Violence is by nature instrumental; like all means, it always stands in need of guidance and justification through the end it pursues. And what needs justification by something else cannot be the essence of anything. The end of war—end taken in its twofold meaning—is peace or victory; but to the question And what is the end of peace? there is no answer. Peace is an absolute, even though in recorded history periods of warfare have nearly always outlasted periods of peace. Power is in the same category; it is, as they say, "an end in itself." (This, of course, is not to deny that governments pursue policies and employ their power to achieve prescribed goals. But the power structure itself precedes and outlasts all aims, so that power, far from being the means to an end, is actually the very condition enabling a group of people to think and act

---

[12] In ancient Greece, such an organization of power was the polis, whose chief merit, according to Xenophon, was that it permitted the "citizens to act as bodyguards to one another against slaves and criminals so that none of the citizens may die a violent death." (*Hiero,* IV, 3.)

in terms of the means-end category.) And since government is essentially organized and institutionalized power, the current question What is the end of government? does not make much sense either. The answer will be either question-begging—to enable men to live together—or dangerously utopian —to promote happiness or to realize a classless society or some other non-political ideal, which if tried out in earnest cannot but end in some kind of tyranny.

Power needs no justification, being inherent in the very existence of political communities; what it does need is legitimacy. The common treatment of these two words as synonyms is no less misleading and confusing than the current equation of obedience and support. Power springs up whenever people get together and act in concert, but it derives its legitimacy from the initial getting together rather than from any action that then may follow. Legitimacy, when challenged, bases itself on an appeal to the past, while justification relates to an end that lies in the future. Violence can be justifiable, but it never will be legitimate. Its justification loses in plausibility the farther its intended end recedes into the future. No one questions the use of violence in self-defense, because the danger is not only clear but also present, and the end justifying the means is immediate.

Power and violence, though they are distinct phenomena, usually appear together. Wherever they are combined, power, we have found, is the primary and predominant factor. The situation, however, is entirely different when we deal with them in their pure states—as, for instance, with foreign invasion and occupation. We saw that the current equation of violence with power rests on government's being understood as domination of man over man by means of violence. If a foreign conqueror is confronted by an impotent government and by a nation unused to the exercise of political power, it is easy for him to achieve such domination. In all other cases the difficulties are great indeed, and the occupying invader will try immediately to establish Quisling governments, that is, to find a native power base to support his dominion. The head-on clash between Russian tanks and the entirely nonviolent resistance of the Czechoslovak people is a textbook case of a confrontation between violence and power in their pure states. But while domination in such an instance is difficult to achieve, it is not impossible. Violence, we must remember, does not depend on numbers or opinions, but on implements, and the implements of violence, as I mentioned before, like all other tools, increase and multiply human strength. Those who oppose violence with mere power will soon find that they are confronted not by men but by men's artifacts, whose inhumanity and destructive effectiveness increase in proportion to the distance separating the opponents. Violence can always destroy power; out of the barrel of a gun grows the most effective command, resulting in the most instant and perfect obedience. What never can grow out of it is power.

In a head-on clash between violence and power, the outcome is hardly in doubt. If Gandhi's enormously powerful and successful strategy of nonviolent resistance had met with a different enemy—Stalin's Russia, Hitler's

Germany, even prewar Japan, instead of England—the outcome would not have been decolonization, but massacre and submission. However, England in India and France in Algeria had good reasons for their restraint. Rule by sheer violence comes into play where power is being lost; it is precisely the shrinking power of the Russian government, internally and externally, that became manifest in its "solution" of the Czechoslovak problem—just as it was the shrinking power of European imperialism that became manifest in the alternative between decolonization and massacre. To substitute violence for power can bring victory, but the price is very high; for it is not only paid by the vanquished, it is also paid by the victor in terms of his own power. This is especially true when the victor happens to enjoy domestically the blessings of constitutional government. Henry Steele Commager is entirely right: "If we subvert world order and destroy world peace we must inevitably subvert and destroy our own political institutions first."[13] The much-feared boomerang effect of the "government of subject races" (Lord Cromer) on the home government during the imperialist era meant that rule by violence in faraway lands would end by affecting the government of England, that the last "subject race" would be the English themselves. The recent gas attack on the campus at Berkeley, where not just tear gas but also another gas, "outlawed by the Geneva Convention and used by the Army to flush out guerrillas in Vietnam," was laid down while gas-masked Guardsmen stopped anybody and everybody "from fleeing the gassed area," is an excellent example of this "backlash" phenomenon. It has often been said that impotence breeds violence, and psychologically this is quite true, at least of persons possessing natural strength, moral or physical. Politically speaking, the point is that loss of power becomes a temptation to substitute violence for power—in 1968 during the Democratic convention in Chicago we could watch this process on television—and that violence itself results in impotence. Where violence is no longer backed and restrained by power, the well-known reversal in reckoning with means and ends has taken place. The means, the means of destruction, now determine the end—with the consequence that the end will be the destruction of all power.

Nowhere is the self-defeating factor in the victory of violence over power more evident than in the use of terror to maintain domination, about whose weird successes and eventual failures we know perhaps more than any generation before us. Terror is not the same as violence; it is, rather, the form of government that comes into being when violence, having destroyed all power, does not abdicate but, on the contrary, remains in full control. It has often been noticed that the effectiveness of terror depends almost entirely on the degree of social atomization. Every kind of organized opposition must disappear before the full force of terror can be let loose. This atomization—an outrageously pale, academic word for the horror it implies—is maintained and intensified through the ubiquity of the informer, who can be literally omnipresent because he no longer is merely a profes-

---

[13] "Can We Limit Presidential Power?" in *The New Republic,* April 6, 1968.

sional agent in the pay of the police but potentially every person one comes into contact with. How such a fully developed police state is established and how it works—or, rather, how nothing works where it holds sway—can now be learned in Aleksandr I. Solzhenitsyn's *The First Circle,* which will probably remain one of the masterpieces of twentieth-century literature and certainly contains the best documentation on Stalin's regime in existence. The decisive difference between totalitarian domination, based on terror, and tyrannies and dictatorships, established by violence, is that the former turns not only against its enemies but against its friends and supporters as well, being afraid of all power, even the power of its friends. The climax of terror is reached when the police state begins to devour its own children, when yesterday's executioner becomes today's victim. And this is also the moment when power disappears entirely. There exist now a great many plausible explanations for the de-Stalinization of Russia—none, I believe, so compelling as the realization by the Stalinist functionaries themselves that a continuation of the regime would lead, not to an insurrection, against which terror is indeed the best safeguard, but to paralysis of the whole country.

To sum up: politically speaking, it is insufficient to say that power and violence are not the same. Power and violence are opposites; where the one rules absolutely, the other is absent. Violence appears where power is in jeopardy, but left to its own course it ends in power's disappearance. This implies that it is not correct to think of the opposite of violence as nonviolence; to speak of nonviolent power is actually redundant. Violence can destroy power; it is utterly incapable of creating it. Hegel's and Marx's great trust in the dialectial "power of negation," by virtue of which opposites do not destroy but smoothly develop into each other because contradictions promote and do not paralyze development, rests on a much older philosophical prejudice: that evil is no more than a privative *modus* of the good, that good can come out of evil; that, in short, evil is but a temporary manifestation of a still-hidden good. Such time-honored opinions have become dangerous. They are shared by many who have never heard of Hegel or Marx, for the simple reason that they inspire hope and dispel fear—a treacherous hope used to dispel legitimate fear. By this, I do not mean to equate violence with evil; I only want to stress that violence cannot be derived from its opposite, which is power, and that in order to understand it for what it is, we shall have to examine its roots and nature.

6 Tradition and Upheaval: Esthetics and Education

Introduction:
Education
and
Society

Before I introduce the next two authors, let us examine the general trend of the argument uniting the preceding essays with the six that follow. We are moving around a curve that is continuous with the previous sections on politics and liberation, through the related issues of student power and pedagogy, to the actual anatomy of the classroom situation where the quality of the immediate experience is important. Freire emphasizes the importance of the teacher-student relationship, Dewey notes the unfortunate loss of physicality and concreteness in many classrooms, and Leonard, with explicit reference to Dewey, takes a close look at the esthetics of the classroom. Leonard wants to make us aware of the felt quality, the texture, the potential beauty of the classroom experience. He talks about it much as one talks about the experience of a work of art—which brings us to esthetics as the philosophy of art. Plato, Breton, and Marcuse all talk about art, but each, in his separate way, leads the discussion of esthetics back to politics so that the curve of topical progression recrosses itself.

The essays naturally lend themselves to this arrangement because the so-called branches of philosophy are not in fact separable or separate. Rubrics like 'esthetics,' 'education,' 'politics' tend to make us think we are dealing with clearly distinguishable species of the genus philosophy. Rather than thinking in terms of the 'branches' of philosophy—a natural metaphor that corresponds well to the logical separateness of species in a "tree" of genus-species distinctions—we do better to regard philosophy as an even more organic whole that can be dissected only at the risk of death. Each part of the organism is in a living relationship with every other, and a sense of their connectedness is as important as a knowledge of each part. Let us move now from politics and education to education and esthetics, from there to esthetics and art, and thence to art and politics.

Thinkers from Plato to Norman O. Brown have drawn on the analogy between the dynamics of the self and the structure of the state. The same idea finds application in speaking of **repression** of parts of the self and political **repression** of classes of people deemed less than equal. This analogy has been played out in the arena of education. The New Politics—the slightly anarchistic politics that finds the meaning of politics elsewhere than in elections and parliamentary procedures—the politics that has grown visibly on the campus, I shall refer to from now on as metapolitics. The educational reform movement has gone through many changes, and many of them correspond to the dialectics of oppression and liberation. For example, we hear less nowadays about "student power" than in the 1960's when it was a goal conceived according to the old politics. People still believed in hierarchic structures, and the point was to get some "student representatives" high in the hierarchy. To the extent that the hierarchies remain, that kind of infiltration may still be necessary, but more and more students are simply fed up with playing the hierarchies game. How can you build a community of equals if the rules and structure of the game dictate from the outset that some must be on top and some on the bottom? Who cares if you win when you are playing a game where winning means losing the goal you started with?

Some of the fight has gone out of the student movement, some of the militancy, some of the violence. At least in 1973 (and who knows how these words will look in five years?) some of us wonder what happened to the student movement that flared so hot during the sixties. Some may think "things have settled down" and education will proceed once more with the quietness of the 1950's. But a definite change in self-consciousness among students has occurred, which is not a regression to apathy and a refusal to "see" (although there is some of that too). Rather a truly metapolitical consciousness is at work in student politics, and because it is metapolitical it is postmilitant. If war is politics by other means, then war must pass with the demise of traditional power politics. Militancy is irrelevant to the new politics on the campus level. When students felt used by the educational system, they revolted, and militancy seemed appropriate. But instead of feeling manipulated by the campus, students are now beginning to use the campus to build a new consciousness much broader than the "maturity" sought during the fifties and early sixties. By the definition of the word, the metapolitical ("after politics") student has lived aware of the pressure of political issues. If the metapolitical student is not as much an activist as his older brother who preceded him by five years, it is not because he has lapsed into the political unconsciousness and blissful ignorance of fifteen years ago. Rather, political consciousness is frustrated by the apparent lack of appropriate avenues of expression. Whether you "win" or "lose," activism in the old political context just keeps the competitive, hierarchic context going. So students look around for modes of political behavior unlike the traditional and very visible student activism.

A large part of nonactivist action has taken the form of community organizing: food co-ops, health clinics, crisis centers, and so on, but even these manifestations are too visible to serve as the best evidence of metapolitical consciousness on campus. What I am talking about is the all-but-invisible shared awareness of political realities, the tacit agreements among so many students about where they stand with respect to the "system." Not that these agreements are all that clear; often they lie precisely in the quality of doubt about both the dominant political order and those who oppose it with such confident militancy. Where the mass of nonactive students were once just apathetic or ignorant or scared, now the nonactive majority seems more aware and more critical of the established roads to success within the "system" and the established methods of opposition to the "system." The student movement has grown from a stage of uncritical identification and acceptance of a hierarchic system, through a violent rejection of that system, into a posture of militancy with its own conventions and hierarchies, and finally toward a latent period in which both the traditional acceptance and conventional rejection appear as equally familiar and equally questionable extremes. This, then, is a particularly apt time for the pursuit of philosophy. Now seems to be the time when more and more students wish to gain their own awareness of their situation in a social-educational-political order, an awareness that can be shared among a vast majority rather than bought from the few political heavyweights who always seemed at the hub of the action during the really political stages of the student movement. In my own experience I can recall the contradiction between the fact of leadership by a few and an explicit awareness that we were seeking broad-based, participatory, nonhierarchic modes of organization and action. There was the active vanguard whose task it was to rouse the apathetic masses, yet all the majority had to do was listen to the **content** of what the few were saying in order to see that the **form**—many listening to a few—was inappropriate to the goal. The few were talking about participatory democracy and community, but in a most nonparticipatory, noncommunal manner.

But many got the message. They may have resisted pressure to man the barricades in militant activism, but they got the message about alternative styles of social organization and education. And now they want to learn more, understand more, so they can build a truly broad-based, participatory, metapolitical culture. And the campus can be used to gain that understanding. Naturally there will be regressions and exceptions; surely not everyone is already completely self-conscious and knows precisely what is happening. My intention is to acknowledge a confusion and ambivalence, a latent period in the dialectic when things are not as clear as when one extreme dominates. I am trying to clarify the fact of confusion and openness.

The following essays help clarify the confusion. Though they hardly represent anything like the full range of issues in the philosophy of education, they at least show how some of them relate to other circles of self-awareness. Much of the confusion about what is going on in education derives from the fact that we fail to make those connections. Just as our schools are in many cases physically separated from the community, so we tend to separate family life from education and education from society. But these separations are to some extent artificial, however expedient they may sometimes be. If we think about education from the perspective of the home or the society, we achieve insights that rarely surface in the classroom where education is supposed to be happening. But those insights, those connections that constitute the web of self-awareness, **can** surface in the classroom, especially where there is a philosophical inquiry into fundamentals.

For instance, Why education? A simple question, but one that is rarely asked except perhaps in the less radical form of, Why education for me? Why go to college? Actually these questions seem radical when they are first confronted. If we have always assumed that going to college is the thing to do, it is radical to wonder **why** it is the thing to do. Parents say you go to college to get an education, but that leads us again to, Why education? For the individual the answer may have to do with getting a better job. But why do we demand so much education of those who usually do not use much of their classroom training in their jobs anyway? We could probably dole out the jobs and get just as much done without using the vast clearinghouse of higher education. What other reasons might there be for the major role that education plays in modern society?

To be most blunt—a bluntness that will be refined in a dialectical development of this initially extreme view—perhaps education is central to modern society not to increase people's self-awareness but rather to decrease it in favor of a social awareness. That is, perhaps the role of education is to socialize people in the negative sense of regimenting them into a manipulable order. Ever think of that? Of course, I take this view to be just one moment, one extreme, in the dialectic. If this book increases your self-awareness, and if you are reading it in the context of the educational system, then the negative charge cannot be entirely true. We will then want to distinguish between good education and bad education rather than speak of the function of education in general. The next two essays speak about good education and bad education in relation to social systems.

PAOLO FREIRE
(1921-   )

Among those who have been thinking, writing, and reading about educational reform in recent years, one of the most talked-about books has been Paolo Freire's **Pedagogy of the Oppressed.** Though Freire's experience has been mostly in South America, what he has to say is frequently applicable to our own educational framework. In the following essay— Chapter 2 from his book—Freire opposes what he calls the "banking" concept of education to the "problem posing" concept of education. In the former the students are passive receptacles for knowledge possessed initially only by the teacher. In the latter the teacher-student relationship is infused with the dynamism of a group of human beings inquiring together into the problems posed by their ever changing historical situation.

Freire's ideas relate to the rest of this volume, both in their form and their content. The contemporary situation is the starting point of this volume, and the here and now of self-knowledge is the stated goal for each reader. The form of the book follows the historical and personal quest for consciousness. The contents include some of the sources that are also central to Freire's picture of man as dynamic, changing, and historical. Yet an essay like Freire's makes me realize that even this book could be used in a classroom that follows the banking concept of education, could be regarded (mistakenly) as a body of information to be deposited in the student's mind. Freire's essay cannot help but raise the issue of the teacher-student relationship in the classes where this book is used. For those who have not yet looked at the teacher-student relationship, for those to whom the following essay may sound like a condemnation, a few words of special introduction may be helpful.

It is never too late to withdraw from the banking concept of education. Let us pose, right now, a problem to students and teachers alike: say you read the following essay and find you are participating in what Freire regards as the stultifying banking-concept classroom. Both students **and** teachers face this problem, and the first step in solving the problem is to see that they do indeed face it **together** and not against each other, that they get beyond blaming the other side for keeping the bank functioning as a bank. Students blame teachers for subjecting them to hours of deposits to be held in storage until the exam. Teachers blame students for not participating, for asking to be entertained and regaled with riches of information. The problem is **our** problem.

We all come to the classroom programmed by years of banking education, and it is not easy to change. The story is the same in rural high schools and the most elite colleges. Many of the students at universities are there precisely because their talents at banking got them through the rigorous admissions competition. If the university teacher ceases to make the deposits, they get upset; they are not getting the goods they paid for.

Both teachers and students are victimized by a tradition manifested in the following education study: Kindergarten teachers were asked what they conceived their job to be. What were they doing for their children? Most answered that they were preparing them for first grade. The first grade teachers by and large said they were preparing their children for second grade. Grammar school teachers prepare their students for high school. High school teachers prepare their students for college. Many college professors tend to favor those students they can train for graduate school in their fields of expertise. And finally, graduate schools train their students to be teachers. The circle is so tight that once again it remains possible to traverse the entire circle without ever asking, Why education? The teacher who receives a classroom of students trained in this circle will not have an easy time breaking out of it, and sooner or later may stop trying, however noble his first intentions. After all, who can put up with all the anxiety produced when a whole classroom of students suddenly, perhaps for the first time, feels the pain of being wrenched away from the images on the wall of the cave? It is much easier to become an expert on the images, a narrator for the story everyone is used to hearing. Students often like best the teachers most talented at tying them to the images on the wall of the cave; and many of us like to be liked.

So the problem is not easy. To liberate the teacher-student relationship from the shackles of past programming requires ongoing and cumulative interaction. The first attempts usually fail. I remember when I had just finished graduate school I was determined to avoid the banking concept; I would learn from my students. But my concept of learning was dominated by the way I learned in graduate school. Consequently, I found myself disappointed and resentful that my students were not teaching me anything, since, of course, they were not teaching me the way my teachers in graduate school had. So then I started teaching, and lo and behold, as I got feedback on what I had to say, I began to learn—a very obscure process that took several years to unravel, and the end of the ball of twine is hardly in sight.

Perhaps these special introductory remarks are unnecessary. I make them in hopes that mutual understanding and compassion might take the place of animosity or disrespect. The problem of teacher-student relationships is always **our** problem, and it is one of the most difficult that a problem-posing education can pose.

The Pedagogy
of the Oppressed

A careful analysis of the teacher-student relationship at any level, inside or outside the school, reveals its fundamentally *narrative* character. This relationship involves a narrating Subject (the teacher) and patient, listening objects (the students). The contents, whether values or empirical dimensions of reality, tend in the process of being narrated to become lifeless and petrified. Education is suffering from narration sickness.

The teacher talks about reality as if it were motionless, static, compartmentalized, and predictable. Or else he expounds on a topic completely alien to the existential experience of the students. His task is to "fill" the students with the contents of his narration—contents which are detached from reality, disconnected from the totality that engendered them and could give them significance. Words are emptied of their concreteness and become a hollow, alienated, and alienating verbosity.

The outstanding characteristic of this narrative education, then, is the sonority of words, not their transforming power. "Four times four is sixteen; the capital of Pará is Belém." The student records, memorizes, and repeats these phrases without perceiving what four times four really means, or realizing the true significance of "capital" in the affirmation "the capital of Pará is Belém," that is, what Belém means for Pará and what Pará means for Brazil.

Narration (with the teacher as narrator) leads the students to memorize mechanically the narrated content. Worse yet, it turns them into "containers," into "receptacles" to be "filled" by the teacher. The more completely he fills the receptacles, the better a teacher he is. The more meekly the receptacles permit themselves to be filled, the better students they are.

Education thus becomes an act of depositing, in which the students are the depositories and the teacher is the depositor. Instead of communicating, the teacher issues communiqués and makes deposits which the students patiently receive, memorize, and repeat. This is the "banking" concept of education, in which the scope of action allowed to the students extends only as far as receiving, filing, and storing the deposits. They do, it is true, have the opportunity to become collectors or cataloguers of the things they store.

THE PEDAGOGY OF THE OPPRESSED　From Paolo Freire, *The Pedagogy of the Oppressed*. Published by Herder & Herder. Copyright © 1970 by Paolo Freire. Reprinted by permission of Herder & Herder.

But in the last analysis, it is men themselves who are filed away through the lack of creativity, transformation, and knowledge in this (at best) misguided system. For apart from inquiry, apart from the praxis, men cannot be truly human. Knowledge emerges only through invention and re-invention, through the restless, impatient, continuing, hopeful inquiry men pursue in the world, with the world, and with each other.

In the banking concept of education, knowledge is a gift bestowed by those who consider themselves knowledgeable upon those whom they consider to know nothing. Projecting an absolute ignorance onto others, a characteristic of the ideology of oppression, negates education and knowledge as processes of inquiry. The teacher presents himself to his students as their necessary opposite; by considering their ignorance absolute, he justifies his own existence. The students, alienated like the slave in the Hegelian dialectic, accept their ignorance as justifying the teacher's existence—but, unlike the slave, they never discover that they educate the teacher.

The *raison d'être* of libertarian education, on the other hand, lies in its drive towards reconciliation. Education must begin with the solution of the teacher-student contradiction, by reconciling the poles of the contradiction so that both are simultaneously teachers *and* students.

This solution is not (nor can it be) found in the banking concept. On the contrary, banking education maintains and even stimulates the contradiction through the following attitudes and practices, which mirror oppressive society as a whole:

    a. the teacher teaches and the students are taught;
    b. the teacher knows everything and the students know nothing;
    c. the teacher thinks and the students are thought about;
    d. the teacher talks and the students listen—meekly;
    e. the teacher disciplines and the students are disciplined;
    f. the teacher chooses and enforces his choice, and the students comply;
    g. the teacher acts and the students have the illusion of acting through the action of the teacher;
    h. the teacher chooses the program content, and the students (who were not consulted) adapt to it;
    i. the teacher confuses the authority of knowledge with his own professional authority, which he sets in opposition to the freedom of the students;
    j. the teacher is the Subject of the learning process, while the pupils are mere objects.

It is not surprising that the banking concept of education regards men as adaptable, manageable beings. The more students work at storing the deposits entrusted to them, the less they develop the critical consciousness which would result from their intervention in the world as transformers of that world. The more completely they accept the passive role imposed on them, the more they tend simply to adapt to the world as it is and to the fragmented view of reality deposited in them.

The capability of banking education to minimize or annul the students' creative power and to stimulate their credulity serves the interests of the oppressors, who care neither to have the world revealed nor to see it transformed. The oppressors use their "humanitarianism" to preserve a profitable situation. Thus they react almost instinctively against any experiment in education which stimulates the critical faculties and is not content with a partial view of reality but always seeks out the ties which link one point to another and one problem to another.

Indeed, the interests of the oppressors lie in "changing the consciousness of the oppressed, not the situation which oppresses them";[1] for the more the oppressed can be led to adapt to that situation, the more easily they can be dominated. To achieve this end, the oppressors use the banking concept of education in conjunction with a paternalistic social action apparatus, within which the oppressed receive the euphemistic title of "welfare recipients." They are treated as individual cases, as marginal men who deviate from the general configuration of a "good, organized, and just" society. The oppressed are regarded as the pathology of the healthy society, which must therefore adjust these "incompetent and lazy" folk to its own patterns by changing their mentality. These marginals need to be "integrated," "incorporated" into the healthy society that they have "forsaken."

The truth is, however, that the oppressed are not "marginals," are not men living "outside" society. They have always been "inside"—inside the structure which made them "beings for others." The solution is not to "integrate" them into the structure of oppression, but to transform that structure so that they can become "beings for themselves." Such transformation, of course, would undermine the oppressors' purposes; hence their utilization of the banking concept of education to avoid the threat of student *conscientização* [the deepening awareness of social, political, and economic contradictions inherent in one's own situation].

The banking approach to adult education, for example, will never propose to students that they critically consider reality. It will deal instead with such vital questions as whether Roger gave green grass to the goat, and insist upon the importance of learning that, on the contrary, *Roger* gave green grass to the *rabbit*. The "humanism" of the banking approach masks the effort to turn men into automatons—the very negation of their ontological vocation to be more fully human.

Those who use the banking approach, knowingly or unknowingly (for there are innumerable well-intentioned bank-clerk teachers who do not realize that they are serving only to dehumanize), fail to perceive that the deposits themselves contain contradictions about reality. But, sooner or later, these contradictions may lead formerly passive students to turn against

---

[1] Simone de Beauvoir, *La Pensée de Droite, Aujourd'hui* (Paris); ST, *El Pensamiento político de la Derecha* (Buenos Aires, 1963), p. 34.

their domestication and the attempt to domesticate reality. They may discover through existential experience that their present way of life is irreconcilable with their vocation to become fully human. They may perceive through their relations with reality that reality is really a *process,* undergoing constant transformation. If men are searchers and their ontological vocation is humanization, sooner or later they may perceive the contradiction in which banking education seeks to maintain them, and then engage themselves in the struggle for their liberation.

But the humanist, revolutionary educator cannot wait for this possibility to materialize. From the outset, his efforts must coincide with those of the students to engage in critical thinking and the quest for mutual humanization. His efforts must be imbued with a profound trust in men and their creative power. To achieve this, he must be a partner of the students in his relations with them.

The banking concept does not admit to such partnership—and necessarily so. To resolve the teacher-student contradiction, to exchange the role of depositor, prescriber, domesticator, for the role of student among students would be to undermine the power of oppression and serve the cause of liberation.

Implicit in the banking concept is the assumption of a dichotomy between man and the world: man is merely *in* the world, not *with* the world or with others; man is spectator, not re-creator. In this view, man is not a conscious being (*corpo consciente*); he is rather the possessor of *a* consciousness: an empty "mind" passively open to the reception of deposits of reality from the world outside. For example, my desk, my books, my coffee cup, all the objects before me—as bits of the world which surrounds me—would be "inside" me, exactly as I am inside my study right now. This view makes no distinction between being accessible to consciousness and entering consciousness. The distinction, however, is essential: the objects which surround me are simply accessible to my consciousness, not located within it. I am aware of them, but they are not inside me.

It follows logically from the banking notion of consciousness that the educator's role is to regulate the way the world "enters into" the students. His task is to organize a process which already occurs spontaneously, to "fill" the students by making deposits of information which he considers to constitute true knowledge.[2] And since men "receive" the world as passive entities, education should make them more passive still, and adapt them to the world. The educated man is the adapted man, because he is better "fit" for the world. Translated into practice, this concept is well suited to the purposes of the oppressors, whose tranquility rests on how well men fit the world the oppressors have created, and how little they question it.

The more completely the majority adapt to the purposes which the domi-

---

[2] This concept corresponds to what Sartre calls the "digestive" or "nutritive" concept of education, in which knowledge is "fed" by the teacher to the students to "fill them out." See Jean-Paul Sartre, "Une idée fondamentale de la phénoménologie de Husserl: L'intentionalité," *Situations I* (Paris, 1947).

nant minority prescribe for them (thereby depriving them of the right to their own purposes), the more easily the minority can continue to prescribe. The theory and practice of banking education serve this end quite efficiently. Verbalistic lessons, reading requirements,[3] the methods for evaluating "knowledge," the distance between the teacher and the taught, the criteria for promotion: everything in this ready-to-wear approach serves to obviate thinking.

The bank-clerk educator does not realize that there is no true security in his hypertrophied role, that one must seek to live *with* others in solidarity. One cannot impose oneself, nor even merely co-exist with one's students. Solidarity requires true communication, and the concept by which such an educator is guided fears and proscribes communication.

Yet only through communication can human life hold meaning. The teacher's thinking is authenticated only by the authenticity of the students' thinking. The teacher cannot think for his students, nor can he impose his thought on them. Authentic thinking, thinking that is concerned about *reality,* does not take place in ivory tower isolation, but only in communication. If it is true that thought has meaning only when generated by action upon the world, the subordination of students to teachers becomes impossible.

Because banking education begins with a false understanding of men as objects, it cannot promote the development of what Fromm calls "biophily," but instead produces its opposite: "necrophily."

> While life is characterized by growth in a structured, functional manner, the necrophilous person loves all that does not grow, all that is mechanical. The necrophilous person is driven by the desire to transform the organic into the inorganic, to approach life mechanically, as if all living persons were things. . . . Memory, rather than experience; having, rather than being, is what counts. The necrophilous person can relate to an object —a flower or a person—only if he possesses it; hence a threat to his possession is a threat to himself; if he loses possession he loses contact with the world. . . . He loves control, and in the act of controlling he kills life.[4]

Oppression—overwhelming control—is necrophilic; it is nourished by love of death, not life. The banking concept of education, which serves the interests of oppression, is also necrophilic. Based on a mechanistic, static, naturalistic, spatialized view of consciousness, it transforms students into receiving objects. It attempts to control thinking and action, leads men to adjust to the world, and inhibits their creative power.

When their efforts to act responsibly are frustrated, when they find them-

---

[3] For example, some professors specify in their reading lists that a book should be read from pages 10 to 15—and do this to "help" their students!

[4] Erich Fromm, *The Heart of Man* (New York, 1966), p. 41.

selves unable to use their faculties, men suffer. "This suffering due to impotence is rooted in the very fact that the human equilibrium has been disturbed."[5] But the inability to act which causes men's anguish also causes them to reject their impotence, by attempting

> . . . to restore [their] capacity to act. But can [they], and how? One way is to submit to and identify with a person or group having power. By this symbolic participation in another person's life, [men have] the illusion of acting, when in reality [they] only submit to and become a part of those who act.[6]

Populist manifestations perhaps best exemplify this type of behavior by the oppressed, who, by identifying with charismatic leaders, come to feel that they themselves are active and effective. The rebellion they express as they emerge in the historical process is motivated by that desire to act effectively. The dominant elites consider the remedy to be more domination and repression, carried out in the name of freedom, order, and social peace (that is, the peace of the elites). Thus they can condemn—logically, from their point of view—"the violence of a strike by workers and [can] call upon the state in the same breath to use violence in putting down the strike."[7]

Education as the exercise of domination stimulates the credulity of students, with the ideological intent (often not perceived by educators) of indoctrinating them to adapt to the world of oppression. This accusation is not made in the naïve hope that the dominant elites will thereby simply abandon the practice. Its objective is to call the attention of true humanists to the fact that they cannot use banking educational methods in the pursuit of liberation, for they would only negate that very pursuit. Nor may a revolutionary society inherit these methods from an oppressor society. The revolutionary society which practices banking education is either misguided or mistrusting of men. In either event, it is threatened by the specter of reaction.

Unfortunately, those who espouse the cause of liberation are themselves surrounded and influenced by the climate which generates the banking concept, and often do not perceive its true significance or its dehumanizing power. Paradoxically, then, they utilize this same instrument of alienation in what they consider an effort to liberate. Indeed, some "revolutionaries" brand as "innocents," "dreamers," or even "reactionaries" those who would challenge this educational practice. But one does not liberate men by alienating them. Authentic liberation—the process of humanization—is not another deposit to be made in men. Liberation is a praxis: the action and

---

[5] *Ibid.,* p. 31.

[6] *Ibid.*

[7] Reinhold Niebuhr, *Moral Man and Immoral Society* (New York, 1960), p. 130.

reflection of men upon their world in order to transform it. Those truly committed to the cause of liberation can accept neither the mechanistic concept of consciousness as an empty vessel to be filled, nor the use of banking methods of domination (propaganda, slogans—deposits) in the name of liberation.

Those truly committed to liberation must reject the banking concept in its entirety, adopting instead a concept of men as conscious beings, and consciousness as consciousness intent upon the world. They must abandon the educational goal of deposit-making and replace it with the posing of the problems of men in their relations with the world. "Problem-posing" education, responding to the essence of consciousness—*intentionality*—rejects communiqués and embodies communication. It epitomizes the special characteristic of consciousness: being *conscious of,* not only as intent on objects but as turned in upon itself in a Jasperian "split"—consciousness as consciousness *of* consciousness.

Liberating education consists in acts of cognition, not transferrals of information. It is a learning situation in which the cognizable object (far from being the end of the cognitive act) intermediates the cognitive actors —teacher on the one hand and students on the other. Accordingly, the practice of problem-posing education entails at the outset that the teacher-student contradiction be resolved. Dialogical relations—indispensable to the capacity of cognitive actors to cooperate in perceiving the same cognizable object—are otherwise impossible.

Indeed, problem-posing education, which breaks with the vertical patterns characteristic of banking education, can fulfill its function as the practice of freedom only if it can overcome the above contradiction. Through dialogue, the teacher-of-the-students and the students-of-the-teacher cease to exist and a new term emerges: teacher-student with students-teachers. The teacher is no longer merely the-one-who-teaches, but one who is himself taught in dialogue with the students, who in turn while being taught also teach. They become jointly responsible for a process in which all grow. In this process, arguments based on "authority" are no longer valid; in order to function, authority must be *on the side of* freedom, not *against* it. Here, no one teaches another, nor is anyone self-taught. Men teach each other, mediated by the world, by the cognizable objects which in banking education are "owned" by the teacher.

The banking concept (with its tendency to dichotomize everything) distinguishes two stages in the action of the educator. During the first, he cognizes a cognizable object while he prepares his lessons in his study or his laboratory; during the second, he expounds to his students about that object. The students are not called upon to know, but to memorize the contents narrated by the teacher. Nor do the students practice any act of cognition, since the object towards which that act should be directed is the property of the teacher rather than a medium evoking the critical reflection of both teacher and students. Hence in the name of the "preservation of culture and knowledge" we have a system which achieves neither true knowledge nor true culture.

The problem-posing method does not dichotomize the activity of the teacher-student: he is not "cognitive" at one point and "narrative" at another. He is always "cognitive," whether preparing a project or engaging in dialogue with the students. He does not regard cognizable objects as his private property, but as the object of reflection by himself and the students. In this way, the problem-posing educator constantly re-forms his reflections in the reflection of the students. The students—no longer docile listeners— are now critical co-investigators in dialogue with the teacher. The teacher presents the material to the students for their consideration, and re-considers his earlier considerations as the students express their own. The role of the problem-posing educator is to create, together with the students, the conditions under which knowledge at the level of the *doxa* [opinion] is superseded by true knowledge, at the level of the *logos* [science].

Whereas banking education anesthetizes and inhibits creative power, problem-posing education involves a constant unveiling of reality. The former attempts to maintain the *submersion* of consciousness; the latter strives for the *emergence* of consciousness and *critical intervention* in reality.

Students, as they are increasingly posed with problems relating to themselves in the world and with the world, will feel increasingly challenged and obliged to respond to that challenge. Because they apprehend the challenge as interrelated to other problems within a total context, not as a theoretical question, the resulting comprehension tends to be increasingly critical and thus constantly less alienated. Their response to the challenge evokes new challenges, followed by new understandings; and gradually the students come to regard themselves as committed.

Education as the practice of freedom—as opposed to education as the practice of domination—denies that man is abstract, isolated, independent, and unattached to the world; it also denies that the world exists as a reality apart from men. Authentic reflection considers neither abstract man nor the world without men, but men in their relations with the world. In these relations consciousness and world are simultaneous: consciousness neither precedes the world nor follows it.

> La conscience et le monde sont dormés d'un même coup: extérieur par essence à la conscience, le monde est, par essence relatif à elle.[8]

In one of our culture circles in Chile, the group was discussing (based on a codification) the anthropological concept of culture. In the midst of the discussion, a peasant who by banking standards was completely ignorant said: "Now I see that without man there is no world." When the educator

---

[8] Sartre, *op. cit.,* p. 32.

responded: "Let's say, for the sake of argument, that all the men on earth were to die, but that the earth itself remained, together with trees, birds, animals, rivers, seas, the stars . . . wouldn't all this be a world?" "Oh no," the peasant replied emphatically. "There would be no one to say: 'This is a world'."

The peasant wished to express the idea that there would be lacking the consciousness of the world which necessarily implies the world of consciousness. *I* cannot exist without a *not-I*. In turn, the *not-I* depends on that existence. The world which brings consciousness into existence becomes the world *of* that consciousness. Hence, the previously cited affirmation of Sartre: *"La conscience et le monde sont dormés d'un même coup."*

As men, simultaneously reflecting on themselves and on the world, increase the scope of their perception, they begin to direct their observations towards previously inconspicuous phenomena:

> In perception properly so-called, as an explicit awareness [*Gewahren*], I am turned towards the object, to the paper, for instance. I apprehend it as being this here and now. The apprehension is a singling out, every object having a background in experience. Around and about the paper lie books, pencils, ink-well, and so forth, and these in a certain sense are also "perceived", perceptually there, in the "field of intuition"; but whilst I was turned towards the paper there was no turning in their direction, nor any apprehending of them, not even in a secondary sense. They appeared and yet were not singled out, were not posited on their own account. Every perception of a thing has such a zone of background intuitions or background awareness, if "intuiting" already includes the state of being turned towards, and this also is a "conscious experience", or more briefly a "consciousness of" all indeed that in point of fact lies in the co-perceived objective background.[9]

That which had existed objectively but had not been perceived in its deeper implications (if indeed it was perceived at all) begins to "stand out," assuming the character of a problem and therefore of challenge. Thus, men begin to single out elements from their "background awarenesses" and to reflect upon them. These elements are now objects of men's consideration, and, as such, objects of their action and cognition.

In problem-posing education, men develop their power to perceive critically *the way they exist* in the world *with which* and *in which* they find themselves; they come to see the world not as a static reality, but as a reality in process, in transformation. Although the dialectical relations of men with the world exist independently of how these relations are perceived (or whether or not they are perceived at all), it is also true that the form of action men adopt is to a large extent a function of how they perceive themselves in the world. Hence, the teacher-student and the students-teachers

[9] Edmund Husserl, *Ideas—General Introduction to Pure Phenomenology* (London, 1969), pp. 105–106.

reflect simultaneously on themselves and the world without dichotomizing this reflection from action, and thus establish an authentic form of thought and action.

Once again, the two educational concepts and practices under analysis come into conflict. Banking education (for obvious reasons) attempts, by mythicizing reality, to conceal certain facts which explain the way men exist in the world; problem-posing education sets itself the task of demythologizing. Banking education resists dialogue; problem-posing education regards dialogue as indispensable to the act of cognition which unveils reality. Banking education treats students as objects of assistance; problem-posing education makes them critical thinkers. Banking education inhibits creativity and domesticates (although it cannot completely destroy) the *intentionality* of consciousness by isolating consciousness from the world, thereby denying men their ontological and historical vocation of becoming more fully human. Problem-posing education bases itself on creativity and stimulates true reflection and action upon reality, thereby responding to the vocation of men as beings who are authentic only when engaged in inquiry and creative transformation. In sum: banking theory and practice, as immobilizing and fixating forces, fail to acknowledge men as historical beings; problem-posing theory and practice take man's historicity as their starting point.

Problem-posing education affirms men as beings in the process of *becoming*—as unfinished, uncompleted beings in and with a likewise unfinished reality. Indeed, in contrast to other animals who are unfinished, but not historical, men know themselves to be unfinished; they are aware of their incompletion. In this incompletion and this awareness lie the very roots of education as an exclusively human manifestation. The unfinished character of men and the transformational character of reality necessitate that education be an ongoing activity.

Education is thus constantly remade in the praxis. In order to *be,* it must *become*. Its "duration" (in the Bergsonian meaning of the word) is found in the interplay of the opposites *permanence* and *change*. The banking method emphasizes permanence and becomes reactionary; problem-posing education—which accepts neither a "well-behaved" present nor a predetermined future—roots itself in the dynamic present and becomes revolutionary.

Problem-posing education is revolutionary futurity. Hence it is prophetic (and, as such, hopeful). Hence, it corresponds to the historical nature of man. Hence, it affirms men as beings who transcend themselves, who move forward and look ahead, for whom immobility represents a fatal threat, for whom looking at the past must only be a means of understanding more clearly what and who they are so that they can more wisely build the future. Hence, it identifies with the movement which engages men as beings aware of their incompletion—an historical movement which has its point of departure, its Subjects and its objective.

The point of departure of the movement lies in men themselves. But since men do not exist apart from the world, apart from reality, the movement must begin with the men-world relationship. Accordingly, the point of departure must always be with men in the "here and now," which constitutes the situation within which they are submerged, from which they emerge, and in which they intervene. Only by starting from this situation —which determines their perception of it—can they begin to move. To do this authentically they must perceive their state not as fated and unalterable, but merely as limiting—and therefore challenging.

Whereas the banking method directly or indirectly reinforces men's fatalistic perception of their situation, the problem-posing method presents this very situation to them as a problem. As the situation becomes the object of their cognition, the naïve or magical perception which produced their fatalism gives way to perception which is able to perceive itself even as it perceives reality, and can thus be critically objective about that reality.

A deepened consciousness of their situation leads men to apprehend that situation as an historical reality susceptible of transformation. Resignation gives way to the drive for transformation and inquiry, over which men feel themselves to be in control. If men, as historical beings necessarily engaged with other men in a movement of inquiry, did not control that movement, it would be (and is) a violation of men's humanity. Any situation in which some men prevent others from engaging in the process of inquiry is one of violence. The means used are not important; to alienate men from their own decision-making is to change them into objects.

This movement of inquiry must be directed towards humanization— man's historical vocation. The pursuit of full humanity, however, cannot be carried out in isolation or individualism, but only in fellowship and solidarity; therefore it cannot unfold in the antagonistic relations between oppressors and oppressed. No one can be authentically human while he prevents others from being so. Attempting *to be more* human, individualistically, leads to *having more,* egotistically: a form of dehumanization. Not that it is not fundamental *to have* in order *to be* human. Precisely because it *is* necessary, some men's *having* must not be allowed to constitute an obstacle to others' *having,* must not consolidate the power of the former to crush the latter.

Problem-posing education, as a humanist and liberating praxis, posits as fundamental that men subjected to domination must fight for their emancipation. To that end, it enables teachers and students to become Subjects of the educational process by overcoming authoritarianism and an alienating intellectualism; it also enables men to overcome their false perception of reality. The world—no longer something to be described with deceptive words—becomes the object of that transforming action by men which results in their humanization.

Problem-posing education does not and cannot serve the interests of the oppressor. No oppressive order could permit the oppressed to begin to question: Why? While only a revolutionary society can carry out this education in systematic terms, the revolutionary leaders need not take full power before they can employ the method. In the revolutionary process, the leaders cannot utilize the banking method as an interim measure, justified on grounds of expediency, with the intention of *later* behaving in a genuinely revolutionary fashion. They must be revolutionary—that is to say, dialogical—from the outset.

JOHN DEWEY

(1859-1952)

Much of John Dewey's inquiry revolved around **experience** as a central category. In this he was like William James, and both were known as pragmatists, along with the third member of the triumvirate of American pragmatism, Charles Sanders Peirce (1839–1914). Pragmatist philosophy is characterized by the double role of experience: first, as the source of the real-life problem that gives rise to an inquiry, and second, as the ultimate court of appeals for the solution to any intellectual problem. The pragmatists were not inclined to begin an inquiry for inquiry's sake as more scholastic-minded philosophers might. Nor were they inclined to settle on a solution that was elegant in theory but lacked any conceivable validation in practice. Experience was the key, both at the beginning and end of inquiry. Dewey quite agrees with Freire in the value of problem-posing education situated in current historical experience. He further agrees that a repressive stratification in a class society inhibits the aims of education. But Dewey's perspective on the inhibitions induced by class society is different from Freire's and, I think, nicely complementary. Dewey regrets the ills of stratification from the side of the oppressor rather than the oppressed. He does not say so explicitly, but you can read his essay as arguing that the way the oppressors educate their heirs dehumanizes them by distancing them from the full range of experience. Because stratification defines a labor class and a leisure class, and different educational tracks are intended to reproduce that stratification, each class is excluded from some of the experiences needed to render education whole and appropriately human. But Dewey's main concern seems to be the nonexperiential, overintellectual education awarded to the leisure class.

Dewey's contributions to the philosophy of education are immense. Aside from several books that have profoundly influenced American education, his personal influence and energy contributed to countless experiments in educational reform. Dewey carries the influence of social stratification into personal stratification among the parts of the self, and his insights anticipate a good deal of contemporary thinking in social psychology. Dewey's respect for the body, for a full integration of all the parts of a fully human self, make him as contemporary now as he was when he was writing fifty years ago.

Labor and Leisure

The Origin of the Opposition

The isolation of aims and values which we have been considering leads to opposition between them. Probably the most deep-seated antithesis which has shown itself in educational history is that between education in preparation for useful labor and education for a life of leisure. The bare terms "useful labor" and "leisure" confirm the statement already made that the segregation and conflict of values are not self-inclosed, but reflect a division within social life. Were the two functions of gaining a livelihood by work and enjoying in a cultivated way the opportunities of leisure, distributed equally among the different members of a community, it would not occur to any one that there was any conflict of educational agencies and aims involved. It would be self-evident that the question was how education could contribute most effectively to both. And while it might be found that some materials of instruction chiefly accomplished one result and other subject matter the other, it would be evident that care must be taken to secure as much overlapping as conditions permit; that is, the education which had leisure more directly in view should indirectly reënforce as much as possible the efficiency and the enjoyment of work, while that aiming at the latter should produce habits of emotion and intellect which would procure a worthy cultivation of leisure.

These general considerations are amply borne out by the historical development of educational philosophy. The separation of liberal education from professional and industrial education goes back to the time of the Greeks, and was formulated expressly on the basis of a division of classes into those who had to labor for a living and those who were relieved from this necessity. The conception that liberal education, adapted to men in the latter class, is intrinsically higher than the servile training given to the former class reflected the fact that one class was free and the other servile in its social status. The servile class labored not only for its own subsistence, but also for the means which enabled the superior class to live without personally engaging in occupations taking almost all the time and not of a nature to engage or reward intelligence.

LABOR AND LEISURE   From John Dewey, *Democracy and Education.*

That a certain amount of labor must be engaged in goes without saying. Human beings have to live and it requires work to supply the resources of life. Even if we insist that the interests connected with getting a living are only material and hence intrinsically lower than those connected with enjoyment of time released from labor, and even if it were admitted that there is something engrossing and insubordinate in material interests which leads them to strive to usurp the place belonging to the higher ideal interests, this would not—barring the fact of socially divided classes—lead to neglect of the kind of education which trains men for the useful pursuits. It would rather lead to scrupulous care for them, so that men were trained to be efficient in them and yet to keep them in their place; education would see to it that we avoided the evil results which flow from their being allowed to flourish in obscure purlieus of neglect. Only when a division of these interests coincides with a division of an inferior and a superior social class will preparation for useful work be looked down upon with contempt as an unworthy thing: a fact which prepares one for the conclusion that the rigid identification of work with material interests, and leisure with ideal interests is itself a social product.

The educational formulations of the social situation made over two thousand years ago have been so influential and give such a clear and logical recognition of the implications of the division into laboring and leisure classes, that they deserve especial note. According to them, man occupies the highest place in the scheme of animate existence. In part, he shares the constitution and functions of plants and animals—nutritive, reproductive, motor or practical. The *distinctively* human function is reason existing for the sake of beholding the spectacle of the universe. Hence the truly human end is the fullest possible of this distinctive human prerogative. The life of observation, meditation, cogitation, and speculation pursued as an end in itself is the proper life of man. From reason moreover proceeds the proper control of the lower elements of human nature—the appetites and the active, motor, impulses. In themselves greedy, insubordinate, lovers of excess, aiming only at their own satiety, they observe moderation—the law of the mean—and serve desirable ends as they are subjected to the rule of reason.

Such is the situation as an affair of theoretical psychology and as most adequately stated by Aristotle. But this state of things is reflected in the constitution of classes of men and hence in the organization of society. Only in a comparatively small number is the function of reason capable of operating as a law of life. In the mass of people, vegetative and animal functions dominate. Their energy of intelligence is so feeble and inconstant that it is constantly overpowered by bodily appetite and passion. Such persons are not truly ends in themselves, for only reason constitutes a final end. Like plants, animals and physical tools, they are means, appliances, for the attaining of ends beyond themselves, although unlike them they have enough intelligence to exercise a certain discretion in the execution of the tasks committed to them. Thus by nature, and not merely by social convention, there are those who are slaves—that is, means for the ends of others.[1] The great body of artisans are in one important respect worse off than even slaves. Like the latter they are given up to the service of ends external to themselves; but since they do not enjoy the intimate association with the free superior class experienced by domestic slaves they remain on a lower plane of excellence. Moreover, women are classed with slaves and craftsmen as factors among the animate instrumentalities of production and reproduction of the means for a free or rational life.

Individually and collectively there is a gulf between merely living and living worthily. In order that one may live worthily he must first live, and so with collective society. The time and energy spent upon mere life, upon the gaining of subsistence, detracts from that available for activities that have an inherent rational meaning; they also unfit for the latter. Means are menial, the serviceable is servile. The true life is possible only in the degree in which the physical necessities are had without effort and without attention. Hence slaves, artisans, and women are employed in furnishing the means of subsistence in order that others, those adequately equipped with intelligence, may live the life of leisurely concern with things intrinsically worth while.

To these two modes of occupation, with their distinction of servile and free activities (or "arts") correspond two types of education: the base or mechanical and the liberal or intellectual. Some persons are trained by suitable practical exercises for capacity in *doing* things, for ability to use the mechanical tools involved in turning out physical commodities and rendering personal service. This training is a mere matter of habituation and technical skill; it operates through repetition and assiduity in application, not through awakening and nurturing thought. Liberal education aims to train intelligence for its proper office: to know. The less this knowledge has to do with practical affairs, with making or producing, the more adequately it engages intelligence. So consistently does Aristotle draw the line between menial and liberal education that he puts what are now called the "fine" arts, music, painting, sculpture, in the same class with menial arts so far as their practice is concerned. They involve physical agencies, assiduity of practice, and external results. In discussing, for example, education in music he raises the question how far the young should be practiced in the playing of instruments. His answer is that such practice and proficiency may be tolerated as conduce to appreciation; that is, to understanding and enjoyment of music when played by slaves or professionals. When professional power is aimed at, music sinks from the liberal to the professional level. One might then as well teach cooking, says Aristotle. Even a liberal concern with the works of fine art depends upon the existence of a hireling class of practitioners who have subordinated the development of their own

[1] Aristotle does not hold that the class of actual slaves and of natural slaves necessarily coincide.

personality to attaining skill in mechanical execution. The higher the activity the more purely mental is it; the less does it have to do with physical things or with the body. The more purely mental it is, the more independent or self-sufficing is it.

These last words remind us that Aristotle again makes a distinction of superior and inferior even within those living the life of reason. For there is a distinction in ends and in free action, according as one's life is merely accompanied by reason or as it makes reason its own medium. That is to say, the free citizen who devotes himself to the public life of his community, sharing in the management of its affairs and winning personal honor and distinction, lives a life accompanied by reason. But the thinker, the man who devotes himself to scientific inquiry and philosophic speculation, works, so to speak, *in* reason, not simply *by* it. Even the activity of the citizen in his civic relations, in other words, retains some of the taint of practice, of external or merely instrumental doing. This infection is shown by the fact that civic activity and civic excellence need the help of others; one cannot engage in public life all by himself. But all needs, all desires imply, in the philosophy of Aristotle, a material factor; they involve lack, privation; they are dependent upon something beyond themselves for completion. A purely intellectual life, however, one carries on by himself, in himself; such assistance as he may derive from others is accidental, rather than intrinsic. In *knowing,* in the life of theory, reason finds its own full manifestation; knowing for the sake of knowing irrespective of any application is alone independent, or self-sufficing. Hence only the education that makes for power to know as an end in itself, without reference to the practice of even civic duties, is truly liberal or free.

The Present Situation

If the Aristotelian conception represented just Aristotle's personal view, it would be a more or less interesting historical curiosity. It could be dismissed as an illustration of the lack of sympathy or the amount of academic pedantry which may coexist with extraordinary intellectual gifts. But Aristotle simply described without confusion and without that insincerity always attendant upon mental confusion, the life that was before him. That the actual social situation has greatly changed since his day there is no need to say. But in spite of these changes, in spite of the abolition of legal serfdom, and the spread of democracy, with the extension of science and of general education (in books, newspapers, travel, and general intercourse as well as in schools), there remains enough of a cleavage of society into a learned and an unlearned class, a leisure and a laboring class, to make his point of view a most enlightening one from which to criticize the separation between culture and utility in present education. Behind the intellectual and abstract distinction as it figures in pedagogical discussion, there looms a social distinction between those whose pursuits involve a minimum of self-directive thought and aesthetic appreciation, and those who are concerned more directly with things of the intelligence and with the control of the activities of others.

Aristotle was certainly permanently right when he said that "any occupation or art or study deserves to be called mechanical if it renders the body or soul or intellect of free persons unfit for the exercise and practice of excellence." The force of the statement is almost infinitely increased when we hold, as we nominally do at present, that all persons, instead of a comparatively few, are free. For when the mass of men and all women were regarded as unfree by the very nature of their bodies and minds, there was neither intellectual confusion nor moral hypocrisy in giving them only the training which fitted them for mechanical skill, irrespective of its ulterior effect upon their capacity to share in a worthy life. He was permanently right also when he went on to say that "all mercenary employments as well as those which degrade the condition of the body are mechanical, since they deprive the intellect of leisure and dignity,"—permanently right, that is, if gainful pursuits as matter of fact deprive the intellect of the conditions of its exercise and so of its dignity. If his statements are false, it is because they identify a phase of social custom with a natural necessity. But a different view of the relations of mind and matter, mind and body, intelligence and social service, is better than Aristotle's conception only if it helps render the old idea obsolete in fact—in the actual conduct of life and education.

Aristotle was permanently right in assuming the inferiority and subordination of mere skill in performance and mere accumulation of external products to understanding, sympathy of appreciation, and the free play of ideas. If there was an error, it lay in assuming the necessary separation of the two: in supposing that there is a natural divorce between efficiency in producing commodities and rendering service, and self-directive thought; between significant knowledge and practical achievement. We hardly better matters if we just correct his theoretical misapprehension, and tolerate the social state of affairs which generated and sanctioned his conception. We lose rather than gain in change from serfdom to free citizenship if the most prized result of the change is simply an increase in the mechanical efficiency of the human tools of production. So we lose rather than gain in coming to think of intelligence as an organ of control of nature through action, if we are content that an unintelligent, unfree state persists in those who engage directly in turning nature to use, and leave the intelligence which controls to be the exclusive possession of remote scientists and captains of industry. We are in a position honestly to criticize the division of life into separate functions and of society into separate classes only so far as we are free from responsibility for perpetuating the educational practices which train the many for pursuits involving mere skill in production, and the few for a knowledge that is an ornament and a cultural embellishment. In short, ability to transcend the Greek philosophy of life and education is not secured by a mere shifting about of the theoretical symbols meaning free, rational, and worthy. It is not secured by a change of sentiment regarding the dignity of labor, and the superiority of a life of service to that of an aloof self-sufficing independence. Important as these theoretical and emotional changes are, their importance consists in their being turned to account in the development of a truly democratic society, a society in which all share in useful service and all enjoy a worthy leisure. It is not a mere change in the concepts of culture—or a liberal mind—and social service which requires an educational reorganization; but the educational transformation is needed to give full and explicit effect to the changes implied in social life. The increased political and economic emancipation of the "masses" has shown itself in education; it has effected the development of a common school system of education, public and free. It has destroyed the idea that learning is properly a monopoly of the few who are predestined by nature to govern social affairs. But the revolution is still incomplete. The idea still prevails that a truly cultural or liberal education cannot have anything in common, directly at least, with industrial affairs, and that the education which is fit for the masses must be a useful or practical education in a sense which opposes useful and practical to nurture of appreciation and liberation of thought.

As a consequence, our actual system is an inconsistent mixture. Certain studies and methods are retained on the supposition that they have the sanction of peculiar liberality, the chief content of the term liberal being uselessness for practical ends. This aspect is chiefly visible in what is termed the higher education—that of the college and of preparation for it. But it has filtered through into elementary education and largely controls its processes and aims. But, on the other hand, certain concessions have been made to the masses who must engage in getting a livelihood and to the increased rôle of economic activities in modern life. These consessions are exhibited in special schools and courses for the professions, for engineering, for manual training and commerce in vocational and prevocational courses; and in the spirit in which certain elementary subjects, like the three R's, are taught. The result is a system in which both "cultural" and "utilitarian" subjects exist in an inorganic composite where the former are not by dominant purpose socially serviceable and the latter not liberative of imagination or thinking power.

In the inherited situation, there is a curious intermingling, in even the same study, of concession to usefulness and a survival of traits once exclusively attributed to preparation for leisure. The "utility" element is found in the motives assigned for the study, the "liberal" element in methods of teaching. The outcome of the mixture is perhaps less satisfactory than if either principle were adhered to in its purity. The motive popularly assigned for making the studies of the first four or five years consist almost entirely of reading, spelling, writing, and arithmetic, is, for example, that ability to read, write, and figure accurately is indispensable to getting ahead. These studies are treated as mere instruments for entering upon a gainful employment or of later progress in the pursuit of learning, according as pupils do not or do remain in school. This attitude is reflected in the emphasis put upon drill and practice for the sake of gaining automatic skill. If we turn to Greek schooling, we find that from the earliest years the acquisition of skill was subordinated as much as possible to acquisition of literary content possessed of aesthetic and moral significance. Not getting a tool for subsequent use but present subject matter was the emphasized thing. Nevertheless the isolation of these studies from practical application, their reduction to purely symbolic devices, represents a survival of the idea of a liberal training divorced from utility. A thorough adoption of the idea of utility would have led to instruction which tied up the studies to situations in which they were directly needed and where they were rendered immediately and not remotely helpful. It would be hard to find a subject in the curriculum within which there are not found evil results of a compromise between the two opposed ideals. Natural science is recommended on the ground of its practical utility, but is taught as a special accomplishment in removal from application. On the other hand, music and literature are theoretically justified on the ground of their culture value and are then taught with chief emphasis upon forming technical modes of skill.

If we had less compromise and resulting confusion, if we analyzed more carefully the respective meanings of culture and utility, we might find it easier to construct a course of study which should be useful and liberal at the same time. Only superstition makes us believe that the two are necessarily hostile so that a subject is illiberal because it is useful and cultural because it is useless. It will generally be found that instruction which, in aiming at utilitarian results, sacrifices the development of imagination, the refining of taste and the deepening of intellectual insight—surely cultural values—also in the same degree renders what is learned limited in its use. Not that it makes it wholly unavailable but that its applicability is restricted to routine activities carried on under the supervision of others. Narrow modes of skill cannot be made useful beyond themselves; any mode of skill which is achieved with deepening of knowledge and perfecting of judgment is readily put to use in new situations and is under personal control. It was not the bare fact of social and economic utility which made certain activities seem servile to the Greeks but the fact that the activities directly connected with getting a livelihood were not, in their days, the expression of a trained intelligence nor carried on because of a personal appreciation of their meaning. So far as farming and the trades were rule-of-thumb occupations and so far as they were engaged in for results external to the minds of agricultural laborers and mechanics, they were illiberal—but only so far. The intellectual and social context has now changed. The elements in industry due to mere custom and routine have become subordinate in most economic callings to elements derived from scientific inquiry. The most important occupations of today represent and depend upon applied mathematics, physics, and chemistry. The area of the human world influenced by economic production and influencing consumption has been so indefinitely widened that geographical and political considerations of an almost infinitely wide scope enter in. It was natural for Plato to deprecate the learning of geometry and arithmetic for practical ends, because as matter of fact the practical uses to which they were put were few, lacking in content and mostly mercenary in quality. But as their social uses have increased and enlarged, their liberalizing or "intellectual" value and their practical value approach the same limit.

Doubtless the factor which chiefly prevents our full recognition and employment of this identification is the conditions under which so much work is still carried on. The invention of machines has extended the amount of leisure which is possible even while one is at work. It is a commonplace that the mastery of skill in the form of established habits frees the mind for a higher order of thinking. Something of the same kind is true of the introduction of mechanically automatic operations in industry. They may release the mind for thought upon other topics. But when we confine the education of those who work with their hands to a few years of schooling devoted for the most part to acquiring the use of rudimentary symbols at the expense of training in science, literature, and history, we fail to prepare the minds of workers to take advantage of this opportunity. More fundamental is the fact that the great majority of workers have no insight into the social aims of their pursuits and no direct personal interest in them. The results actually achieved are not the ends of *their* actions, but only of their employers. They do what they do, not freely and intelligently, but for the sake of the wage earned. It is this fact which makes the action illiberal, and which will make any education designed simply to give skill in such undertakings illiberal and immoral. The activity is not free because not freely participated in.

Nevertheless, there is already an opportunity for an education which, keeping in mind the larger features of work, will reconcile liberal nurture with training in social serviceableness, with ability to share efficiently and happily in occupations which are productive. And such an education will of itself tend to do away with the evils of the existing economic situation. In the degree in which men have an active concern in the ends that control their activity, their activity becomes free or voluntary and loses its externally enforced and servile quality, even though the physical aspect of behavior remain the same. In what is termed politics, democratic social organization makes provision for this direct participation in control: in the economic region, control remains external and autocratic. Hence the split between inner mental action and outer physical action of which the traditional distinction between the liberal and the utilitarian is the reflex. An education which should unify the disposition of the members of society would do much to unify society itself.

Summary

Of the segregations of educational values discussed in the last chapter, that between culture and utility is probably the most fundamental. While the distinction is often thought to be intrinsic and absolute, it is really historical and social. It originated, so far as conscious formulation is concerned, in Greece, and was based upon the fact that the truly human life was lived only by a few who subsisted upon the results of the labor of others. This fact affected the psychological doctrine of the relation of intelligence and desire, theory and practice. It was embodied in a political theory of a permanent division of human beings into those capable of a life of reason and hence having their own ends, and those capable only of desire and work, and needing to have their ends provided by others. The two distinctions, psychological and political, translated into educational terms, effected a division between a liberal education, having to do with the self-sufficing life of leisure devoted to knowing for its own sake, and a useful, practical training for mechanical occupations, devoid of intellectual and aesthetic content. While the present situation is radically diverse in theory and much changed in fact, the factors of the older historic situation still persist sufficiently to maintain the educational distinction, along with compromises which often reduce the efficacy of the educational measures. The problem of education in a democratic society is to do away with the dualism and to construct a course of studies which makes thought a guide of free practice for all and which makes leisure a reward of accepting responsibility for service, rather than a state of exemption from it.

Transition:
Esthetic
Education

Freire argues that the best education awakens students to their own interests and the systematic denial of those interests by political oppression. Dewey argues the importance of experiential immediacy in education. Both are saying that education should meet real needs rather than induce false needs. Erikson, Mead, Goffman, and Laing all agree that the socially constituted self is manipulable even to the extent of denying the reality of some of its most immediate needs. Indeed the very concept of false need becomes questionable if we regard the self as wholly constituted by its social context: whatever needs are induced, even the need for the conspicuous consumption of status symbols, may be real if society is the ultimate creator of selves and conspicuous consumption serves the ends of society as a whole. But clearly society is not the sole creator, and equally clearly many products in a waste economy do not gratify genuinely human needs. If society is not the sole creator of the self, however, how can we correct the social standards of real and false needs? What other criteria are available, and where may we find them?

Traditionally, philosophers and theologians have found it easy to contrast human creation and divine creation. If man was created in God's image, one had only to appeal to the divine image of man for a criterion of needs transcending the historical flux of human society. But modern historicist and existentialist philosophers have undermined belief in an eternal transcendent standard. Man makes himself. Herein lies the hope of modern man to solve his problems. As Reich argued, even the unconscious, that repository of man's most basic instinctual desires, is subject to historical modification. But how are we to judge whether the historical development of man's needs is for the better or for the worse? Who is to say what counts as a false need, and why?

Here esthetics comes into the picture as more than just the philosophical basis of art criticism. As the science of sensibility esthetics deals with minimally cognitive reactions to stimuli. If we withdraw connotations of eternal essence from the term 'natural,' we can say that esthetics deals with our more natural, less artificial, less societally influenced reactions. Esthetics, then, is the way out of the dilemma between accepting all of society's historical meanderings as creating true needs or appealing to an eternal standard of human nature for identifying all created needs as false. Some true needs are historically generated; some true needs—for example, the instinct for aggression—may be outgrown in human history. We need a criterion for distinguishing true from false needs, a criterion that does not define the true as the natural and the natural as the anthropologically original. Esthetics offers a way of putting us in touch with natural man who is still historical man. Esthetic education not only educates the student to the man-made products of his cultural tradition; it also quickens his sensitivity to his own felt needs for a balanced and whole human existence. Wholeness is an elusive standard when the parts of human existence keep changing with the flux of history. A fixed inventory of human capacities no more functions as a checklist for wholeness than a list of colors tells a painter when he has completed a picture. The point is not to use each of the colors or human capacities. We need an esthetic sensibility to tell us whether man's most recent creations of himself cohere in a healthy pattern of wholeness or fall apart into schizoid decadence. Esthetic sensibility becomes the arbiter of true and false needs.

GEORGE LEONARD
(1931-   )

Just as Freire's **Pedagogy of the Oppressed** and Dewey's "Labor and Leisure" make us aware of the political dimension of education, George Leonard's recent book, **Education and Ecstasy,** emphasizes the esthetic dimension of education. Leonard extends Dewey's insights into the experience of education in its sensuous immediacy. Actually, the word 'sensuous' does not capture the full range of experiences that qualify as ecstatic, just as 'art' does not define the full range of experiences that qualify as esthetic. We take the sensuous and the artistic as paradigms for the immediate experience of a very rich joy. But as the greatest thinkers have always known, the joy associated with art and sensuousness can also be felt in experiencing nonartistic objects and exercising faculties other than taste, smell, and touch.

Leonard's inroad into the importance of immediacy certainly came through the senses. Before devoting himself to research and writing on education he helped establish the Esalen Institute at Big Sur in California. In the inviting context of hot springs, sea, and sunlight, Leonard and others developed the techniques of sensitivity training. For some years now Esalen has been running workshops in the many methods of awakening people to the immediate quality of their experience—how one feels one's body, one's sensations, and one's emotions. While the Esalen mystique has tended to lead some of its followers to a total and one-sided condemnation of "head-tripping," it has given others the opportunity for discovering an immediacy that can be intellectual as well as sensuous. Leonard even claims that "solving an elegant mathematical problem and making love are different classes in the same order of things, sharing common ecstasy."

Some of Leonard's critics find him overoptimistic precisely to the extent that his vision is restricted to the esthetics of education and excludes the political dimension. As appealing and persuasive as are Leonard's descriptions of classrooms where teachers and students alike cultivate an intense and ecstatic awareness about every aspect of their pedagogical environment, Leonard's critics ask how the consciousness of the student can develop such esthetic-intellectual sensitivity when the world outside the classroom insists on bludgeoning him back into insensitivity. Leonard's classroom is utopian, they claim, and cannot survive or function in the context of the present social order.

This criticism echoes an argument developed nearly two hundred years ago by Friedrich Schiller, an amazingly talented and prolific German poet, playwright, and philosopher. In his **Letters on the Aesthetic Education of Man** (1795), Schiller spells out the almost paradoxical relationship between esthetics and politics in the quest for liberation. After describing the same specialization and divisions Dewey found in contemporary education, Schiller asks whether we can expect the state to solve the problem of the fragmentation of man. He answers no, "for the State, as it is now constituted, has brought about the evil; and the rationally conceived State, instead of being able to establish this better humanity, must first be itself established by it." Yet Schiller acknowledges, along with Leonard's critics, that the "esthetic education of man" is a difficult enterprise in a hostile political environment. We seem to need esthetic education to develop a better society, yet a better society seems to be a condition for the possibility of an education. Where to begin? Part of Leonard's clarity derives from his unequivocal claim that we can break into the circle of politics, education, esthetics, art, and politics at the point where education and esthetics meet. For a less optimistic and less clear statement of a position very close to Leonard's, recall Marin's essay. While he called for changes fully as cataclysmic as Leonard's, Marin was passionately frustrated by the problems facing contemporary education. With Schiller he saw that a partial reform movement limited to the space of the classroom could neither survive within the present society nor develop the consciousnesses of the children of the present society. Because Marin uses the social and political dimensions beyond the very important esthetic dimension of the classroom, he almost despairs at tackling a problem so immense, as if one must simultaneously alter every arc on the circle of politics-education-esthetics-art-and-politics again.

Education and Ecstasy

There are no neutral moments. Even in those classrooms where the education some of us might hope for is impossible, a kind of shadowy, negative learning is going on. Some pupils learn how to daydream; others, how to take tests. Some learn the petty deceptions involved in cheating; others, the larger deceptions of playing the school game absolutely straight (the well-kept notebook, the right answer, the senior who majors in good grades). Most learn that the symbolic tricks their keepers attempt to teach them have little to do with their own deeper

EDUCATION AND ECSTASY From *Education and Ecstasy* by George B. Leonard. Copyright © 1968 by George B. Leonard. Reprinted by permission of the publisher, Delacorte Press.

feelings or anything in the here and now. The activity that masquerades under the ancient and noble name of "education" actually seems to serve as a sort of ransom to the future, a down payment toward "getting ahead"—or at least toward not falling behind. Lifetime-earnings figures are pressed upon potential high-school dropouts. These figures seem to show that giving an acceptable interpretation of "Ode on a Grecian Urn" somehow means you will live in a better suburb and drive a bigger car. A vision of Florida retirement superimposes itself on every diagram in plane geometry. Some students refuse to pay the ransom, and you should not be surprised that these students may be what the society itself calls the "brighter" ones. (According to Dr. Louis Bright, director of research for the U.S. Office of Education, high-school dropouts in large cities where the figures are available have higher IQs than high-school graduates.) But dropouts and graduates alike have had plenty of practice in fragmenting their lives—segregating senses from emotions from intellect, building boxes for art and abstractions, divorcing the self from the reality and the joy of the present moment. No need for obscure psychological explanations for modern man's fragmentation; that is what his schools teach.

Perhaps this has been so ever since education was first formalized. Historian Arnold Toynbee traces the disintegration of the Chinese Empire under the Ts'in and Han Dynasties as well as that of the Roman Empire, in part, to their attempts to extend formal education from the privileged minority to a wider circle. "One reason," Toynbee wrote, "was that the former privileged minority's traditional system of education was impoverished in the process of being disseminated. It degenerated into a formal education in book learning divorced from a spontaneous apprenticeship for life. . . . In fact, the art of playing with words was substituted for the art of living."

In more primitive cultures, the Polynesian, for example, education was sacramental. Every aspect of life, every act of living was related, and life's procedures were learned in a manner simultaneously more intense and more casual than would seem possible in a formal institution. All things were observed and experienced in unity. The educational institutions of Western civilization, on the other hand, have almost always been formalistic and symbolic to the extreme. When the Renaissance academies took the Roman educator Quintilian for their model, they managed to adopt his most negative and stultifying precepts, leading to purely verbal training in ancient literature—even though Quintilian's was a specialized school for orators.

Until relatively recent times, however, only a tiny proportion of the West's population ever saw the inside of an academy. (As recently as 1900, less than ten percent of American sixteen-year-olds were in school.) Education for the vast majority, though less sacramental and ecstatic, resembled that of the Polynesians. Under the tutelage of such stable institutions as the family, the farm, the village, the church and the craft guild, the ordinary young Westerner served his apprenticeship for living—limiting, perhaps, but all of a piece. As for the aristocrat, he lived and learned under the sure guidance of class tradition and accepted formal education primarily as an instrument for fortifying class lines. Better than badges and plumes were Latin and Greek, maintained, under the fiction of teaching "thinking," for centuries after the world's literature was available in translation. (All attempts to prove that the study of Latin improves thinking skills have failed.) A school accent served as well as a school tie in bolstering those barriers between people which seemed so necessary in building and maintaining a militaristic, colonial empire.

The successive historical events we know as the Enlightenment, the process of democratization, the Industrial Revolution and the explosive developments of consumerism and leisure weakened the prime educating institutions of the past (family, farm, village, church, guild), leaving successively more of the younger generation's total education-for-living to the schools and colleges. The young crowded into classrooms and were led away from life.

Reformers tried to stop the fragmentation. The greatest among them was John Dewey. We have at last reached a hillock in time from which we can look across a lot of pointless controversy and view this man's genius with a certain clarity and dispassion. Dewey sought a unity in life. He recognized that education is a process of living and not a preparation for future living. He believed that education is the fundamental method of social progress and reform. He provided a philosophical underpinning for the Progressive Education movement which, simply stated, saved the American public-school system by making it just flexible and forgiving enough to accommodate the children of immigrants, poor farmers and other followers of the American dream.

But Dewey did not provide educators with the hard-honed tools of true reform. Seduced by the psychology of his time, he enjoined teachers to spend more energy helping children form "images" than making them learn certain things. More disabling yet, he was fascinated with the notion of "interests," which he felt would automatically manifest themselves in children when they were *ready* to learn something. This notion, somewhat misinterpreted, led a generation of teachers to wait for children to show signs of "interest" before they moved ahead and thereby woefully to underrate their capacity for learning. Teachers found further justification for just waiting in the work of developmental psychologists who followed Dewey. These good-hearted doubters are still around with stacks of studies to show us precisely what children *cannot* do until this age or that age. Their studies become worthless, as we shall see in the next chapter, when children are placed in learning environments designed to let them crash through all the ceilings erected by the past. Progressive education was a useful, humane and sometimes joyful reform, but it was not the true revolution in education that the times then needed and now demand. The worst of that movement may be summed up in one sentence: It is as cruel to bore a child as to beat him.

Learning eventually involves interaction between learner and environment, and its effectiveness relates to the frequency, variety and intensity of the interaction.

For the most part, the schools have not really changed. They have neither taken up the slack left by the retreat of the past's prime educators nor significantly altered the substance and style of their teaching. The most common mode of instruction today, as in the Renaissance, has a teacher sitting or standing before a number of students in a single room, presenting them with facts and techniques of a verbal-rational nature. Our expectation of what the human animal can learn, can do, can be remains remarkably low and timorous. Our definition of education's root purpose remains shortsightedly utilitarian. Our map of the territory of learning remains antiquated: vocational training, homemaking, driving and other "fringe" subjects, themselves limiting and fragmenting, have invaded the curriculum, but are generally considered outside the central domain of "education." This domain, this venerable bastion, is still a place where people are trained to split their world into separate symbolic systems, the better to cope with and manipulate it. Such "education," suprarationalistic and analytical to the extreme, has made possible colonialism, the production line, space voyaging and the H-bomb. But it has not made people happy or whole, nor does it now offer them ways to change, deep down, in an age that cries out with the urgency of a rocket's flight, "Change or die."

All that goes on in most schools and colleges today is only a thin slice, as we shall see, of what education can become. And yet, our present institutions show a maddening inefficiency even in dealing with this thin slice. In recent years, there has been a small net gain in American students' performance in the basic subjects. But this has been accomplished only at the cost of a large increase in gross effort—more and more homework assigned under threat of more and tougher exams to force students to learn, on their own, what most of today's teachers have long since realized they cannot teach them. A visitor from another planet might conclude that our schools are hellbent on creating—in a society that offers leisure and demands creativity—a generation of joyless drudges.

There are signs the school will not succeed in this drab mission. Already, the seeds of a real change are germinating—on college campuses, in teachers' associations, in laboratories of science, in out-of-the-way places that will be discussed in later chapters. This reform would bypass entirely the patchwork remedial measures (Spanish in second grade, teachers in teams, subject matter updated) that presently pass for reform. It cuts straight to the heart of the educational enterprise, in and out of school, seeking new method, content, idiom, domain, purpose and, indeed, a new definition of education. Far from decrying and opposing an onrushing technology, it sees technology as an ally, a force that can as easily enhance as diminish the human spirit. Avoiding hard-and-fast assumptions of its own, it is rigorous in questioning some of the automatic assumptions of the past. It is a new journey. To join it, you had best leave your awe of history behind, open your mind to unfamiliar or even disreputable solutions if they are the ones that work, look upon all systems of abstractions as strictly tentative and throw out of the window every prior guideline about what human beings can accomplish.

The prospects are exhilarating, though it is becoming dangerous to write about them if only because nowadays it is so hard to stay ahead of reality. Let us assume the future will surprise us; and, so assuming, speculate only about what is already coming to pass. For example, the following prospects are in the realm of possibility:

1. Ways can be worked out to help average students learn whatever is needed of present-day subject matter in a third or less of the present time, pleasurably rather than painfully, with almost certain success. Better yet, the whole superstructure of rational-symbolic knowledge can be rearranged so that these aspects of life's possibilities can be perceived and learned as unity and diversity within change rather than fragmentation within an illusory permanence.

2. Ways can be worked out to provide a new apprenticeship for living, appropriate to a technological age of constant change. Many new types of learning having to do with crucial areas of human functioning that are now neglected or completely ignored can be made a part of the educational enterprise. Much of what will be learned tomorrow does not today have even a commonly accepted name.

3. Ways can be worked out so that almost every day will be a "teachable day," so that almost every educator can share with his students the inspired moments of learning now enjoyed by only the most rare and remarkable.

4. Education in a new and greatly broadened sense can become a lifelong pursuit for everyone. To go on learning, to go on sharing that learning with others may well be considered a purpose worthy of mankind's ever-expanding capacities.

Education, at best, is ecstatic.

If education in the coming age is to be, not just a part of life, but the main purpose of life, then education's purpose will, at last, be viewed as central. What, then, is the purpose, the goal of education? A large part of the answer may well be what men of this civilization have longest feared and most desired: *the achievement of moments of ecstasy.* Not fun, not simply pleasure as in the equation of Bentham and Mill, not the libido pleasure of Freud, but ecstasy, *ananda,* the ultimate delight.

Western civilization, for well-known historical reasons, has traditionally eschewed ecstasy as a threat to goal-oriented control of men, matter and energy—and has suffered massive human unhappiness. Other civilizations, notably that of India, have turned their best energies toward the attainment of ecstasy, while neglecting practical goals—and have suffered massive human unhappiness. Now modern science and technology seem to be preparing a situation where the successful control of practical matters and the attainment of ecstasy can safely coexist; where each reinforces the other;

and, quite possibly, where neither can long exist *without* the other. Abundance and population control already are logically and technologically feasible. At the same time, cybernation, pervasive and instantaneous communication and other feedback devices of increasing speed, range and sensitivity extend and enhance man's sensory apparatus, multiplying the possibilities for understanding and ecstasy as well as for misunderstanding and destruction. The times demand that we choose delight.

Do discipline and mastery of technique stand in opposition to freedom, self-expression and the ecstatic moment? Most Western educators have acted as if they did. Strange, when there exist so many models of the marriage between the two. Take the artistic endeavor: the composer discovers that the soul of creation transcends the body of form only when form is his completely. The violinist arrives as the sublime only through utter mastery of technique. The instruments of living that are now coming into our hands —rich, responsive and diverse—require mastery. The process of mastery itself can be ecstatic, leading to delight that transcends mastery.

The new revolutionaries of education must soothe those who fear techniques no less than those who fear delight. Many a liberal educational reform has foundered on lack of specific tools for accomplishing its purposes —even if a tool may be something as simple as knowing *precisely when* to leave the learner entirely alone. Education must use its most powerful servant, technique, in teaching skills that go far beyond those which submit to academic achievement tests. Even today, as will be seen, specific, systematic ways are being worked out to help people learn to love, to feel deeply, to expand their inner selves, to create, to enter new realms of being.

What is education? The answer may be far simpler than we imagine. Matters of great moment and processes that affect our lives at the very heart are generally less obscure and mysterious than they at first appear. The travels of celestial bodies, once requiring the efforts of a pantheon of gods, now follow a few easy formulas. Chemical reactions explained by essences, vapors, phlogiston became easier to understand when reduced to a single variable: weight. Mankind's most awesome mystery, fire, once understood, could be handled by little children. Throughout history, the way to understanding, control and ecstasy has been a long, sinuous journey toward simplicity and unity.

To learn is to change. Education is a process that changes the learner.

The first part of a simple, operational definition of education calls on the educator to view his work as consequential, not theoretical or formalistic. Looking for *change* in his student (and himself) as a measure, he will discover what is important in his work and what is waste motion. Asking himself, "What has changed in the student, and me, because of this particular experience?," he may have to answer that what has changed is only the student's ability to recite a few more "facts" than he could before the session. He may find that the student has changed in wider and deeper ways. He may have to admit that the student has hardly changed at all or, if so, in a way that no one had intended. In any case, he will not ask himself the *wrong* questions ("Wasn't my presentation brilliant?" "Why are they so dumb?").

Looking for the *direction and further consequences* of the change, he will be forced to ask whether it is for the good of the student, himself and society. In doing this, the educator will discover he has to become sensitive to what is happening to the student at every moment, and thereby will become a feeling participant in the circle of learning. Viewing learning as anything that changes the learner's behavior, the educator will expand his domain a thousandfold, for he will realize that there are hardly any aspects of human life that cannot be changed, educated. He will see clearly that, if the educational enterprise limits itself to what is now ordinarily taught in classrooms, it will be pursuing failure in the coming age.

Learning involves interaction between the learner and his environment, and its effectiveness relates to the frequency, variety and intensity of the interaction.

Guided by this second part of the definition, the educator will pay far closer attention to the learning environment than ever before in education's history. The environment may be a book, a game, a programmed device, a choir, a brainwave feedback mechanism, a silent room, an interactive group of students, even a teacher—but in every case, the educator will turn his attention from mere *presentation* of the environment (a classroom lecture, for example) to the *response* of the learner. He will study and experiment with the learning process, the series of responses, at every step along the way, better to utilize the increasing capacities of environment and learner as each changes. Observing the work of what have been called "master teachers" in this light, he will find that their mysterious, unfathomable "artistry" actually comprises a heightened sensitivity to student responses plus the use of personally developed, specific, flexible techniques. The educator will work out ways to help every teacher become an "artist."

Education, at best, is ecstatic.

The first two parts of the definition need the third, which may be seen as a way of praising learning for its own sake. And yet, it goes further, for the educator of the coming age will not be vague or theoretical about this matter. As he loses his fear of delight, he will become explicit and specific in his pursuit of the ecstatic moment. At its best, its most effective, its most unfettered, the moment of learning is a moment of delight. This essential and obvious truth is demonstrated for us every day by the baby and the preschool child, by the class of the "artist" teacher, by learners of all ages interacting with new learning programs that are designed for success. When joy is absent, the effectiveness of the learning process falls and falls until the human being is operating hesitantly, grudgingly, fearfully at only a tiny fraction of his potential.

The notion that ecstasy is mainly an inward-directed experience testifies to our distrust of our own society, of the outer environment we have created for ourselves. Actually, the varieties of ecstasy are limitless, as will be seen in the coming chapters. The new educator will seek out the possibility of delight in every form of learning. He will realize that solving an elegant mathematical problem and making love are different classes in the same order of things, sharing common ecstasy. He will find that even education now considered nothing more than present drudgery for future payoff—learning the multiplication tables, for example—can become joyful when a skillfully designed learning environment (a programmed game, perhaps) makes the learning quick and easy. Indeed, the skillful pursuit of ecstasy will make the pursuit of excellence, not for the few, but for the many, what it never has been—successful. And yet, make no mistake about it, excellence, as we speak of it today, will be only a byproduct of a greater unity, a deeper delight.

PLATO

(428-347 B.C.)

With Plato we move to another point on the circle of politics-education-esthetics-art-politics: the meeting of esthetics and art. Politics and education are not hard to see in the background: the following selection renews the discussion of education in the ideal state of the **Republic.** Talk of the meeting of esthetics and art may sound redundant to some, as if esthetics were equivalent to the philosophy of fine art. Though the term 'esthetics' is sometimes used to refer to the philosophy of art, Kant, among others, favored its use to cover a wider range of immediate experience.

When Kant titled one of the sections of his **Critique of Pure Reason** the "Transcendental Aesthetic" he appended a footnote bemoaning the use of the term 'esthetic' "in order to signify what others call the critique of taste." He wished instead "to give up using the name in this sense of critique of taste, and to reserve it for that doctrine of sensibility which is true science" (**Critique of Pure Reason,** Axxi/Bxxxv). While it happens to have turned out that Kant's call for linguistic reform went largely unheard, I wish nevertheless to call attention to both senses of 'esthetics': not only are we talking about the philosophy of fine art, we also include under esthetics what Kant referred to as the science of sensibility. We want to know how we look at things other than art objects. Esthetics might then sound very much like epistemology, but with this difference: where epistemology includes the study of knowledge of a logical, rational type, for example, mathematics and science, esthetics is more concerned with the affective dimensions of feeling and sensation. As rough as this distinction is, to refine it any more might give the impression that feelings are in no way rational or that cognition involves no affective elements. As Kant well knew, concepts without percepts are empty, and percepts without concepts are blind. Hence the distinction between esthetics and epistemology, which corresponds to the distinction between percepts and concepts, cannot really separate two discrete kinds of awareness, only two dimensions of the same awareness.

To distinguish between esthetics and the philosophy of art helps in understanding Plato's attitude toward artists. As usual his text contains depths of meaning beneath the surface argument. If we ignore the distinction between esthetics and the philosophy of art and restrict ourselves to a literal reading of the surface level—if, in short, we remain esthetically insensitive to Plato's art—we will see only an outrageous argument condemning artists of untruth in their second-hand imitation of reality. The literal reading compares the things of the realm of becoming (recall the divided line) to their forms in the realm of being; as the former relate to the latter in an imitative way, so the work of art relates to the things in the realm of becoming. The work of art stands at a second remove from reality, and therein lies its falsity and deceptiveness. The outrageousness of the argument lies in the assumption that the function of art is to imitate, as if a painter were trying to be a photographer.

But beneath the literal level we can find more in Plato's text. That Plato could not condemn art is clear from his own artistry. What, then, did he intend as the role of art? At one crucial point in the argument he asks, "Is the man at unity with himself?" Plato cites the multiplicity of "oppositions occurring at the same moment," which cause a man to lose his bearing and act foolishly. Of the good man who suffers the misfortune of losing a son he says, "will he have no sorrow; or shall we say that although he cannot help sorrowing, he will moderate his sorrow?" From a quick reading of Plato's attack on the poets we might have concluded that he attacks them for portraying heroes with any emotions at all, as if a man's unity with himself were to be achieved at the price of eliminating all the stresses and strains of emotions. Yet here Plato praises the good man for sorrowing, so long as his sorrow is moderate, that is, appropriate to the unity and balance of his being. To sorrow not at all would be clearly inappropriate to the loss of a son.

Plato's complaint with artists is that they tend to exploit extremes for the purposes of their art, whereas the proper role for art is in the service of that moderation that brings unity to man. (Moderation, by the way, does not mean stultifying constraint; repression is the other extreme of madness, and moderation is "in between." One can be immoderate in the pursuit of stability as well as in the pursuit of pleasure.) Opposed to those artists who exploit human extremes for their art, Plato exploits art to achieve unity and balance in his dialogues. This is a more difficult task than mimetic or imitative art, since it requires the artist, namely Plato, to know what he is talking about. The imitative artist is like the illustrator of an anatomy book who tries to copy the details of each separate muscle. The true artist is more like the doctor who uses knowledge rather than imitation to restore the functional unity of health to a diseased body; or, as Plato says in his development of the analogy between art and medicine, art should aid us in "always accustoming the soul forthwith to apply a remedy, raising up that which is sickly and fallen, banishing the cry of sorrow by the healing art."

The content of Plato's second-level argument on art[1] shows why he employs the art of writing on different levels. Precisely the people who tend to be most easily moved to extremes by taking seriously the literal meaning of an art work are those who penetrate only the literal level of Plato's dialogue. They need to hear that it is dangerous to trust unquestioningly the written works of poets and tragedians, however highly they may be respected. Those who already know how to question and inquire more deeply, who are less inclined to extremes of feeling, will be more likely to penetrate to a level of the dialogue that endorses appropriate feelings and the potentially healing character of art. Like Socrates, Plato's dialogues measure their words according to the needs of the interlocutor. Plato's deeper argument suggests the role of a "healing art," but different people need different treatments. Consequently the universal elixir in the artistic medium is an art that adapts itself to the needs of its audience, an art that bends to the esthetic sensibility of each reader.

---

[1] I say 'second-level' rather than deepest level argument because I make no claims that the second-level argument represents Plato's final word on art. Deeper levels of interpretation may be available to the careful reader. It may be that, like the Bible, Plato's dialogues defy final interpretation. The "reformation" in Plato scholarship sees attempts to establish orthodoxy as inconsistent with the Socratic flexibility of the Platonic text.

THE CASE AGAINST ART

[595] Of the many excellences which I perceive in the order of our State, there is none which upon reflection pleases me better than the rule about poetry.

To what do you refer?

To the rejection of imitative poetry, which certainly ought not to be received; as I see far more clearly now that the parts of the soul have been distinguished.

What do you mean?

Speaking in confidence, for I should not like to have my words repeated to the tragedians and the rest of the imitative tribe—but I do not mind saying to you, that all poetical imitations are ruinous to the understanding of the hearers, and that the knowledge of their true nature is the only antidote to them.

Explain the purport of your remark.

Well, I will tell you, although I have always from my earliest youth had an awe and love of Homer, which even now makes the words falter on my lips, for he is the great captain and teacher of the whole of that charming tragic company; but a man is not to be reverenced more than the truth, and therefore I will speak out.

Very good, he said.

Listen to me then, or rather, answer me.

Put your question.

Can you tell me what imitation is? for I really do not know.

A likely thing, then, that I should know. [596]

Why not? for the duller eye may often see a thing sooner than the keener.

Very true, he said; but in your presence, even if I had any faint notion, I could not muster courage to utter it. Will you enquire yourself?

Well then, shall we begin the enquiry in our usual manner: Whenever a number of individuals have a common name, we assume them to have also a corresponding idea or form:—do you understand me?

I do.

Let us take any common instance; there are beds and tables in the world —plenty of them, are there not?

Yes.

But there are only two ideas or forms of them—one the idea of a bed, the other of a table.

True.

And the maker of either of them makes a bed or he makes a table for our use, in accordance with the idea—that is our way of speaking in this

THE CASE AGAINST ART   From Plato, *The Dialogues of Plato,* Fourth Edition, Volume II, *The Republic,* from Book X, translated by B. Jowett. Copyright © 1953. Reprinted by permission of the Clarendon Press, Oxford.

and similar instances—but no artificer makes the ideas themselves: how could he?

Impossible.

And there is another artist,—I should like to know what you would say of him.

Who is he?

One who is the maker of all the works of all other workmen.

What an extraordinary man!

Wait a little, and there will be more reason for your saying so. For this is he who is able to make not only vessels of every kind, but plants and animals, himself and all other things—the earth and heaven, and the things which are in heaven or under the earth; he makes the gods also.

He must be a wizard and no mistake.

Oh! you are incredulous, are you? Do you mean that there is no such maker or creator, or that in one sense there might be a maker of all these things but in another not? Do you see that there is a way in which you could make them all yourself?

What way?

An easy way enough; or rather, there are many ways in which the feat might be quickly and easily accomplished, none quicker than that of turning a mirror round and round—you would soon enough make the sun and the heavens, and the earth and yourself, and other animals and plants, and all the other things of which we were just now speaking, in the mirror.

Yes, he said; but they would be appearances only.

Very good, I said, you are coming to the point now. And the painter too is, as I conceive, just such another—a creator of appearances, is he not?

Of course.

But then I suppose you will say that what he creates is untrue. And yet there is a sense in which the painter also creates a bed?

Yes, he said, but not a real bed. [597]

And what of the maker of the bed? were you not saying that he too makes, not the idea which, according to our view, is the essence of the bed, but only a particular bed?

Yes, I did.

Then if he does not make that which exists he cannot make true existence, but only some semblance of existence; and if any one were to say that the work of the maker of the bed, or of any other workman, has real existence, he could hardly be supposed to be speaking the truth.

At any rate, he replied, philosophers would say that he was not speaking the truth.

No wonder, then, that his work too is an indistinct expression of truth.

No wonder.

Suppose now that by the light of the examples just offered we enquire who this imitator is?

If you please.

Well then, here are three beds: one existing in nature, which is made by God, as I think that we may say—for no one else can be the maker?

No.

There is another which is the work of the carpenter?

Yes.

And the work of the painter is a third?

Yes.

Beds, then, are of three kinds, and there are three artists who superintend them: God, the maker of the bed, and the painter?

Yes, there are three of them.

God, whether from choice or from necessity, made one bed in nature and one only; two or more such ideal beds neither ever have been nor ever will be made by God.

Why is that?

Because even if He had made but two, a third would still appear behind them which both of them would have for their idea, and that would be the ideal bed and not the two others.

Very true, he said.

God knew this, and He desired to be the real maker of a real bed, not a particular maker of a particular bed, and therefore He created a bed which is essentially and by nature one only.

So we believe.

Shall we, then, speak of Him as the natural author or maker of the bed?

Yes, he replied; inasmuch as by the natural process of creation He is the author of this and of all other things.

And what shall we say of the carpenter—is not he also the maker of the bed?

Yes.

But would you call the painter a creator and maker?

Certainly not.

Yet if he is not the maker, what is he in relation to the bed?

I think, he said, that we may fairly designate him as the imitator of that which the others make.

Good, I said; then you call him who is third in the descent from nature an imitator?

Certainly, he said.

And the tragic poet is an imitator, and therefore, like all other imitators, he is thrice removed from the king and from the truth?

That appears to be so.

Then about the imitator we are agreed. And what about the painter? [598]—I would like to know whether he may be thought to imitate that which originally exists in nature, or only the creations of artists?

The latter.

As they are or as they appear? you have still to determine this.

What do you mean?

I mean, that you may look at a bed from different points of view, obliquely or directly or from any other point of view, and the bed will appear different, but there is no difference in reality. And the same of all things.

Yes, he said, the difference is only apparent.

Now let me ask you another question: Which is the art of painting designed to be—an imitation of things as they are, or as they appear—of appearance or of reality?

Of appearance.

Then the imitator, I said, is a long way off the truth, and can do all things because he lightly touches on a small part of them, and that part an image. For example: A painter will paint a cobbler, carpenter, or any other artist, though he knows nothing of their arts; and, if he is a good artist, he may deceive children or simple persons, when he shows them his picture of a carpenter from a distance, and they will fancy that they are looking at a real carpenter.

Certainly.

And whenever any one informs us that he has found a man who knows all the arts, and all things else that anybody knows, and every single thing with a higher degree of accuracy than any other man—whoever tells us this, I think that we can only imagine him to be a simple creature who is likely to have been deceived by some wizard or actor whom he met, and whom he thought all-knowing, because he himself was unable to analyse the nature of knowledge and ignorance and imitation.

Most true.

And so, when we hear persons saying that the tragedians, and Homer, who is at their head, know all the arts and all things human, virtue as well as vice, and divine things too, for that the good poet cannot compose well unless he knows his subject, and that he who has not this knowledge can never be a poet, we ought to consider whether here also there may not be a similar illusion. Perhaps they may have come across imitators and been deceived by them; [599] they may not have remembered when they saw their works that these were but imitations thrice removed from the truth, and could easily be made without any knowledge of the truth, because they are appearances only and not realities? Or, after all, they may be in the right, and poets do really know the things about which they seem to the many to speak so well?

The question, he said, should by all means be considered.

Now do you suppose that if a person were able to make the original as well as the image, he would seriously devote himself to the image-making branch? Would he allow imitation to be the ruling principle of his life, as if he had nothing higher in him?

I should say not.

The real artist, who knew what he was imitating, would be interested in realities and not in imitations; and would desire to leave as memorials of himself works many and fair; and, instead of being the author of encomiums, he would prefer to be the theme of them.

Yes, he said, that would be to him a source of much greater honour and profit.

Then, I said, we must put a question to Homer; not about medicine, or any of the arts to which his poems only incidentally refer: we are not going to ask him, or any other poet, whether he has cured patients like Asclepius, or left behind him a school of medicine such as the Asclepiads were, or whether he only talks about medicine and other arts at second-hand; but we have a right to know respecting military tactics, politics, education, which are the chiefest and noblest subjects of his poems, and we may fairly ask him about them. 'Friend Homer,' then we say to him, 'if you are only in the second remove from truth in what you say of virtue, and not in the third—not an image maker or imitator—and if you are able to discern what pursuits make men better or worse in private or public life, tell us what State was ever better governed by your help? The good order of Lacedaemon is due to Lycurgus, and many other cities great and small have been similarly benefited by others; but who says that you have been a good legislator to them and have done them any good? Italy and Sicily boast of Charondas, and there is Solon who is renowned among us; but what city has anything to say about you?' Is there any city which he might name?

I think not, said Glaucon; not even the Homerids themselves pretend that he was a legislator. [600]

Well, but is there any war on record which was carried on successfully by him, or aided by his counsels, when he was alive?

There is not.

Or is there any invention of his, applicable to the arts or to human life, such as Thales the Milesian or Anacharsis the Scythian, and other ingenious men have conceived, which is attributed to him?

There is absolutely nothing of the kind.

But, if Homer never did any public service, was he privately a guide or teacher of any? Had he in his lifetime friends who loved to associate with him, and who handed down to posterity an Homeric way of life, such as was established by Pythagoras who was so greatly beloved for his wisdom, and whose followers are to this day quite celebrated for the order which was named after him?

Nothing of the kind is recorded of him. For surely, Socrates, Creophylus, the companion of Homer, that child of flesh, whose name always makes us laugh, might be more justly ridiculed for his stupidity, if, as is said, Homer was greatly neglected by him and others in his own day when he was alive?

Yes, I replied, that is the tradition. But can you imagine, Glaucon, that if Homer had really been able to educate and improve mankind—if he had possessed knowledge and not been a mere imitator—can you imagine, I say, that he would not have had many followers, and been honoured and loved by them? Protagoras of Abdera, and Prodicus of Ceos, and a host of others, have only to whisper to their contemporaries: 'You will never be able to manage either your own house or your own State until you appoint us to be your ministers of education'—and this ingenious device of theirs has such an effect in making men love them that their companions all but carry them about on their shoulders. And is it conceivable that the contemporaries of Homer, or again of Hesiod, would have allowed either of them to go about as rhapsodists, if they had really been able to make mankind virtuous? Would they not have been as unwilling to part with them as with gold, and have compelled them to stay at home with them? Or, if the master would not stay, then the disciples would have followed him about everywhere, until they had got education enough?

Yes, Socrates, that, I think, is quite true.

Then must we not infer that all these poetical individuals, beginning with Homer, are only imitators; they copy images of virtue and the like, but the truth they never reach? The poet is like a painter who, as we have already observed, will make a likeness of a cobbler though he understands nothing of cobbling; and his picture is good enough for those who know no more than he does, and judge only by colours and figures. [601]

Quite so.

In like manner the poet with his words and phrases[1] may be said to lay on the colours of the several arts, himself understanding their nature only enough to imitate them; and other people, who are as ignorant as he is, and judge only from his words, imagine that if he speaks of cobbling, or of military tactics, or of anything else, in metre and harmony and rhythm, he speaks very well—such is the sweet influence which melody and rhythm by nature have. And I think that you must have observed again and again what a poor appearance the tales of poets make when stripped of the colours which music puts upon them, and recited in simple prose.

Yes, he said.

They are like faces which were never really beautiful, but only blooming; and now the bloom of youth has passed away from them?

Exactly.

Here is another point: The imitator or maker of the image knows nothing of true existence; he knows appearances only. Am I not right?

Yes.

Then let us have a clear understanding, and not be satisfied with half an explanation.

Proceed.

Of the painter we say that he will paint reins, and he will paint a bit?

Yes.

And the worker in leather and brass will make them?

Certainly.

But does the painter know the right form of the bit and reins? Nay, hardly even the workers in brass and leather who make them: only the horseman who knows how to use them—he knows their right form.

Most true.

And may we not say the same of all things?

---

[1] Or, 'with his nouns and verbs.'

What?

That there are three arts which are concerned with all things: one which uses, another which makes, a third which imitates them?

Yes.

And the excellence or beauty or truth of every structure, animate or inanimate, and of every action of man, is relative to the use for which nature or the artist has intended them. [602]

True.

Then the user of them must have the greatest experience of them, and he must indicate to the maker the good or bad qualities which develop themselves in use; for example, the flute-player will tell the flute-maker which of his flutes is satisfactory to the performer; he will tell him how he ought to make them, and the other will attend to his instructions?

Of course.

The one knows and therefore speaks with authority about the goodness and badness of flutes, while the other, confiding in him, will do what he is told by him?

True.

The instrument is the same, but about the excellence or badness of it the maker will only attain to a correct belief; and this he will gain from him who knows, by talking to him and being compelled to hear what he has to say, whereas the user will have knowledge?

True.

But will the imitator have either? Will he know from use whether or no his drawing is correct or beautiful? or will he have right opinion from being compelled to associate with another who knows and gives him instructions about what he should draw?

Neither.

Then he will no more have true opinion than he will have knowledge about the goodness or badness of his imitations?

I suppose not.

The imitative artist will be in a brilliant state of intelligence about his own creations?

Nay, very much the reverse.

And still he will go on imitating without knowing what makes a thing good or bad, and may be expected therefore to imitate only that which appears to be good to the ignorant multitude?

Just so.

Thus far then we are pretty well agreed that the imitator has no knowledge worth mentioning of what he imitates. Imitation is only a kind of play or sport, and the tragic poets, whether they write in Iambic or in Heroic verse, are imitators in the highest degree?

Very true.

And now tell me, I conjure you, has not imitation been shown by us to be concerned with that which is thrice removed from the truth?

Certainly.

And what is the faculty in man to which imitation is addressed?

What do you mean?

I will explain: The body which is large when seen near, appears small when seen at a distance?

True.

And the same object appears straight when looked at out of the water, and crooked when in the water; and the concave becomes convex, owing to the illusion about colours to which the sight is liable. Thus every sort of confusion is revealed within us; and this is that weakness of the human mind on which the art of conjuring and of deceiving by light and shadow and other ingenious devices imposes, having an effect upon us like magic.

True.

And the arts of measuring and numbering and weighing come to the rescue of the human understanding—there is the beauty of them—and the apparent greater or less, or more or heavier, no longer have the mastery over us, but give way before calculation and measure and weight?

Most true.

And this, surely, must be the work of the calculating and rational principle in the soul?

To be sure.

And when this principle measures and certifies that some things are equal, or that some are greater or less than others, there occurs an apparent contradiction?

True.

But were we not saying that such a contradiction is impossible—the same faculty cannot have contrary opinions at the same time about the same thing?

Very true. [603]

Then that part of the soul which has an opinion contrary to measure is not the same with that which has an opinion in accordance with measure?

True.

And the better part of the soul is likely to be that which trusts to measure and calculation?

Certainly.

And that which is opposed to them is one of the inferior principles of the soul?

No doubt.

This was the conclusion at which I was seeking to arrive when I said that painting or drawing, and imitation in general, when doing their own proper work, are far removed from truth, and the companions and friends and associates of a principle within us which is equally removed from reason, and that they have no true or healthy aim.

Exactly.

The imitative art is an inferior who marries an inferior, and has inferior offspring.

Very true.

And is this confined to the sight only, or does it extend to the hearing also, relating in fact to what we term poetry?

Probably the same would be true of poetry.

Do not rely, I said, on a probability derived from the analogy of painting; but let us examine further and see whether the faculty with which poetical imitation is concerned is good or bad.

By all means.

We may state the question thus:—Imitation imitates the actions of men, whether voluntary or involuntary, on which, as they imagine, a good or bad result has ensued, and they rejoice or sorrow accordingly. Is there anything more?

No, there is nothing else.

But in all this variety of circumstances is the man at unity with himself —or rather, as in the instance of sight there was confusion and opposition in his opinions about the same things, so here also is there not strife and inconsistency in his life? Though I need hardly raise the question again, for I remember that all this has been already admitted; and the soul has been acknowledged by us to be full of these and ten thousand similar oppositions occurring at the same moment?

And we were right, he said.

Yes, I said, thus far we were right; but there was an omission which must now be supplied.

What was the omission?

Were we not saying that a good man, who has the misfortune to lose his son or anything else which is most dear to him, will bear the loss with more equanimity than another?

Yes.

But will he have no sorrow, or shall we say that although he cannot help sorrowing, he will moderate his sorrow?

The latter, he said, is the truer statement. [604]

Tell me: will he be more likely to struggle and hold out against his sorrow when he is seen by his equals, or when he is alone?

It will make a great difference whether he is seen or not.

When he is by himself he will not mind saying or doing many things which he would be ashamed of any one hearing or seeing him do?

True.

There is a principle of law and reason in him which bids him resist, as well as a feeling of his misfortune which is forcing him to indulge his sorrow?

True.

But when a man is drawn in two opposite directions, to and from the same object, this, as we affirm, necessarily implies two distinct principles in him?

Certainly.

One of them is ready to follow the guidance of the law?

How do you mean?

The law would say that to be patient under suffering is best, and that we should not give way to impatience, as there is no knowing whether such things are good or evil; and nothing is gained by impatience; also, because no human thing is of serious importance, and grief stands in the way of that which at the moment is most required.

What is most required? he asked.

That we should take counsel about what has happened, and when the dice have been thrown order our affairs in the way which reason deems best; not, like children who have had a fall, keeping hold of the part struck and wasting time in setting up a howl, but always accustoming the soul forthwith to apply a remedy, raising up that which is sickly and fallen, banishing the cry of sorrow by the healing art.

Yes, he said, that is the true way of meeting the attacks of fortune.

Yes, I said; and the higher principle is ready to follow this suggestion of reason?

Clearly.

And the other principle, which inclines us to recollection of our troubles and to lamentation, and can never have enough of them, we may call irrational, useless, and cowardly?

Indeed, we may.

And does not the latter—I mean the rebellious principle—furnish a great variety of materials for imitation? Whereas the wise and calm temperament, being always nearly equable, is not easy to imitate or to appreciate when imitated, especially at a public festival when a promiscuous crowd is assembled in a theatre. For the feeling represented is one to which they are strangers.

Certainly. [605]

Then the imitative poet who aims at being popular is not by nature made, nor is his art intended, to please or to affect the rational principle in the soul; but he will prefer the passionate and fitful temper, which is easily imitated?

Clearly.

And now we may fairly take him and place him by the side of the painter, for he is like him in two ways: first, inasmuch as his creations have an inferior degree of truth—in this, I say, he is like him; and he is also like him in being concerned with an inferior part of the soul; and therefore we shall be right in refusing to admit him into a well-ordered State, because he awakens and nourishes and strengthens the feelings and impairs the reason. As in a city when the evil are permitted to have authority and the good are put out of the way, so in the soul of man, as we maintain, the imitative poet implants an evil constitution, for he indulges the irrational nature which has no discernment of greater and less, but thinks the same thing at one time great and at another small—he is a manufacturer of images and is very far removed from the truth.

Exactly.

But we have not yet brought forward the heaviest count in our accusation:—the power which poetry has of harming even the good (and there are very few who are not harmed), is surely an awful thing?

Yes, certainly, if the effect is what you say.

Hear and judge: The best of us, as I conceive, when we listen to a passage of Homer, or one of the tragedians, in which he represents some pitiful hero who is drawling out his sorrows in a long oration, or weeping, and smiting his breast—the best of us, you know, delight in giving way to sympathy, and are in raptures at the excellence of the poet who stirs our feelings most.

Yes, of course I know.

But when any sorrow of our own happens to us, then you may observe that we pride ourselves on the opposite quality—we would fain be quiet and patient; this is the manly part, and the other which delighted us in the recitation is now deemed to be the part of a woman.

Very true, he said.

Now can we be right in praising and admiring another who is doing that which any one of us would abominate and be ashamed of in his own person?

No, he said, that is certainly not reasonable.

Nay, I said, quite reasonable from one point of view. [606]

What point of view?

If you consider, I said, that when in misfortune we feel a natural hunger and desire to relieve our sorrow by weeping and lamentation, and that this feeling which is kept under control in our own calamities is satisfied and delighted by the poets;—the better nature in each of us, not having been sufficiently trained by reason or habit, allows the sympathetic element to break loose because the sorrow is another's; and the spectator fancies that there can be no disgrace to himself in praising and pitying any one who comes telling him what a good man he is, and making a fuss about his troubles; he thinks that the pleasure is a gain, and why should he be supercilious and lose this and the poem too? Few persons ever reflect, as I should imagine, that from the evil of other men something of evil is communicated to themselves. And so the feeling of sorrow which has gathered strength at the sight of the misfortunes of others is with difficulty repressed in our own.

How very true!

And does not the same hold also of the ridiculous? There are jests which you would be ashamed to make yourself, and yet on the comic stage, or indeed in private, when you hear them, you are greatly amused by them, and are not at all disgusted at their unseemliness;—the case of pity is repeated;—there is a principle in human nature which is disposed to raise a laugh, and this which you once restrained by reason, because you were afraid of being thought a buffoon, is now let out again; and having stimulated the risible faculty at the theatre, you are betrayed unconsciously to yourself into playing the comic poet at home.

Quite true, he said.

And the same may be said of lust and anger and all the other affections, of desire and pain and pleasure, which are held to be inseparable from every action—in all of them poetry feeds and waters the passions instead of drying them up; she lets them rule, although they ought to be controlled, if mankind are ever to increase in happiness and virtue.

I cannot deny it.

Therefore, Glaucon, I said, whenever you meet with any of the eulogists of Homer declaring that has been the educator of Hellas, and that he is profitable for education and for the ordering of human things, and that you should take him up again and again and get to know him and regulate your whole life according to him, we may love and honour those who say these things—they are excellent people, as far as their lights extend; [607] and we are ready to acknowledge that Homer is the greatest of poets and first of tragedy writers; but we must remain firm in our conviction that hymns to the gods and praises of famous men are the only poetry which ought to be admitted into our State. For if you go beyond this and allow the honeyed muse to enter, either in epic or lyric verse, not law and the reason of mankind, which by common consent have ever been deemed best, but pleasure and pain will be the rulers in our State.

That is most true, he said.

And now since we have reverted to the subject of poetry, let this our defence serve to show the reasonableness of our former judgment in sending away out of our State an art having the tendencies which we have described; for reason constrained us. But that she may not impute to us any harshness or want of politeness, let us tell her that there is an ancient quarrel between philosophy and poetry; of which there are many proofs, such as the saying of 'the yelping hound howling at her lord,' or of one 'mighty in the vain talk of fools,' and 'the mob of sages circumventing Zeus,' and the 'subtle thinkers who are beggars after all'; and there are innumerable other signs of ancient enmity between them. Notwithstanding this, let us assure our sweet friend and the sister arts of imitation, that if she will only prove her title to exist in a well-ordered State we shall be delighted to receive her —we are very conscious of her charms; but we may not on that account betray the truth. I dare say, Glaucon, that you are as much charmed by her as I am, especially when she appears in Homer?

Yes, indeed, I am greatly charmed.

Shall I propose, then, that she be allowed to return from exile, but upon this condition only—that she make a defence of herself in lyrical or some other metre?

Certainly.

And we may further grant to those of her defenders who are lovers of poetry and yet not poets the permission to speak in prose on her behalf: let them show not only that she is pleasant but also useful to States and to human life, and we will listen in a kindly spirit; for if this can be proved we shall surely be the gainers—I mean, if there is a use in poetry as well as a delight?

Transition:
Art
and
Politics

Whatever Plato may have intended at the deepest levels of his dialogues, superficial readings contributed to a Platonic-Christian tradition that Norman O. Brown condemned as the spirit of literalism. According to the orthodox tradition (and its legacy, common sense) inquiry and art should aim at picturing the world **as it really is,** not as it appears to be. The orthodox, common-sense view is consistent with what I have dubbed the orange theory of reality: we must penetrate and discard the rind of illusion to reach the fruit of truth. That truth, once revealed, will exhibit Cartesian clarity and a univocity or singleness of meaning that is susceptible to literal representation. In such a view—which amounts to a metaphysics—art plays at least two roles: it may assist in penetrating the rind of illusion, or it may simply amuse. Actually the two roles intertwine: art helps an audience penetrate illusion precisely to the extent that it entertains. We are not inclined to listen to someone if he bores us. Similarly, the role of art may be to render the truth more vivid by translating it into a more intense or more palatable or more entertaining message. In this orthodox or traditional view, art as a medium is in principle distinct from the literal truth or falsity of its message. Plato could complain that art was capable of a powerful transmission of false messages to the extent that it represented the realm of becoming rather than the realm of being.

To understand the upheaval in the arts it is necessary to understand that modern art reflects an upheaval in all our traditions, including orthodox Christian-Platonic metaphysics. In the context of the traditional metaphysics, esthetics consisted largely of developing criteria for judgments concerning the effectiveness with which art represented truth and beauty. Indeed, the subjective experience of beauty was taken by many as an index of the truth of what was represented through the medium of the art work. But the modern upheaval in metaphysics undercuts traditional esthetics because modern art has no final truth to represent, so how can esthetics concern itself with the truthfulness, that is the beauty, of the representation?

But surely modern paintings represent faces or mountains or other objects, however distorted these may be by Impressionism or Expressionism or Cubism. Surely something is represented, and the distortions are intended to make us see in a less literal but more truthful way. But what about abstract art and the various works of so-called antiart: empty canvases, vacant frames, perfectly silent pieces of "music"? A different theory is needed for these most extreme cases; it will not do to say that they remain representational and choose nothingness or silence as their object. They are, instead, commentaries on modern art itself and the nonrepresentational role it plays, an abandonment of the entire Christian-Platonic orthodoxy with its orange theory of metaphysics. Is the onion theory any more helpful? Let us review its features.

If reality is not a clear and distinct bedrock lying beneath a layer of appearances, or, to return to the culinary metaphor, a rich fruit beneath the rind of illusion; if reality is, like the onion, a totality of the layers of "illusion," or the interlocking wholeness of a multiplicity of appearances; if, as Brown says, everything is symbolic and nothing the ultimate, literal source of the symbolism, then art has no literal truth to represent. There is no separate absolute that art may glorify above the relativities of appearance. There is an absolute, but it is not separate; it is the totality of all those relativities the traditional metaphysics discarded as the rind of illusion. But how can art represent the absolute if the absolute is the totality? To represent everything is to represent nothing. I write: **'everything.'** And I have said nothing. Traditional art said **something** to the extent that it could represent a part rather than the whole, namely that part that the artist took to be truth as distinct from error. But the modern artist, to the extent that he reflects the onion theory of metaphysics, cannot reject any part of reality as being less true, less a part of the all-comprehensive absolute, than any other. Hence we find in our art museums everything from empty canvases to piles of junk.

Rather than exploiting esthetic sensibility to represent a truth distinct from appearances, modern art uses appearances to exercise the esthetic sensibility. The esthetic sensibility is important not because it opens a door to a single, literal truth but because it is uniquely suited to perceive the multiplicity of meanings exhibited in every appearance. Art as a medium then comes to be itself the message: art does not represent reality; it is symbolic of reality to the extent that everything is symbolic. Everything is a representation of a representation of a representation of . . . The psychology of Oedipal development represents politics; similarly the politics of nations represents the politics of races; the politics of races represents the politics of sexes, and so on. No one explanation, psychological, political, or physical, represents the final truth.[1] Only art, to the extent that it symbolizes the multiplicity of possi-

<hr>

[1] While many classical theoretical systems claim to describe the fruit of the orange in a reductionistic way—that is, by saying that everything is *nothing but* economics

ble interpretations, reflects the nonreductionist metaphysics of the on-ion theory of reality. Art does not say everything is nothing but art. Art says everything is what it is and symbolic of a lot else besides.

Art is neither a knife cutting through to the fruit of truth from which it is separated as a means to an end, nor is art itself the truth to which other ways of looking at the world must be subordinated. Despite modern art's special role in symbolizing the multiplicity of the whole, art itself is but one more layer of the onion. As such it represents the other layers **and** is represented by them. The next two essays are preoccupied not only with (a) the way in which the upheaval in art reflects an upheaval in the metaphysical tradition, but also (b) how modern art and modern politics mutually represent one another, that is, how each pictures the other while both reciprocally influence each other.

Traditional metaphysics and esthetics described the relationship between art and politics as either nonexistent or at best restricted to the function of propaganda. Contemporary common sense—the legacy of traditional metaphysics—generally takes the former view, that there is **no** important relationship between art and politics, and that artists and philosophers can insist on such a relationship only in the interests of propaganda. Thus art may be removed from its normally innocuous role as entertainment or diversion and serve instead a specific political ideology. One thinks of the heavy-handed works of Soviet painting and architecture under Stalin, the mechanical representations attempting to glorify the workers' struggle. But against this "backward" art one can find artists who see a different relationship between their art and their politics, an often unconscious relationship that others have to uncover. Briefly stated, modern art serves to **effect** liberation rather than **represent** liberation. The best modern art touches the viewer by liberating him from the literal, not by impressing him with a specific truth. Because this liberating effect is so largely negative, classical esthetics is baffled in its attempt to find "the meaning of modern art." Because modern art liberates its audience from the tyranny of single meanings to the multiplicity of all possible meanings, it is fundamentally mistaken to pursue **the meaning** of modern art. But this liberation from univocal meaning is a powerful political force, for no longer will the audience accept the idea of a single order of things. The multiplicity of meanings reflected in art corresponds to the multiplicity of stages in the Hegelian dialectic that moves Marxist revolutions; and the lack of a final order at the core of the onion corresponds to the temporalized version of multiplicity in the modern concept of permanent revolution.

---

or instinctual manifestation or matter in space and time, and consequently everything could be explained by the laws of economics, or the laws of physics—some theorists seem aware of the representative rather than the reductionistic relationships among various theories. Thus psycho-history, in the hands of someone like Erikson, is not so much an attempt to explain history in terms of psychology as it is an attempt to enrich psychology through a mutual representation with history.

Just as the role of art is no longer as a means to an end, a medium separate from a message, so revolution is no longer a means to an end, but an aspect, a layer of a permanent state of becoming. Just as non-representational modern art symbolizes (and is symbolized by) the multiplicity of meanings at a single moment, so the dizzying dispersion of ever newer schools in modern art symbolizes (and is symbolized by) the permanent revolution and dispersion of decentralized metapolitical forms. Permanent flux is multiplicity in time. Modern art generates the consciousness capable of this permanent flux. Rather than representing a particular order of things, modern art bewilders the critics in its capacity for propelling its audience out of the existing order and into a state of flux. Art may use the materials of another order to effect its liberation, but the materials used become the shapeless clouds of a fantasy rather than the iron structures of a utopia to be made real. Consequently the means of artistic creation come to have less to do with the craft required in the careful building of representative structures. From the speedwriting techniques of surrealism to the random or aleatory techniques of modern music and spontaneous theater, the role of craftsmanship has come into question. While both the following essays reflect the modern upheaval in metaphysics, politics, and esthetics, they differ on the role craftsmanship ought to play in works of art.

ANDRÉ BRETON

(1896-1966)

André Breton would undoubtedly be one of the first men exiled from Plato's Republic. He was a poet and an early practitioner of French Surrealism; the very title of which advertises a rejection of the realism implicit in Plato's critique of artists. Breton has no intention of representing the real according to a Platonic scheme of grades of reality and appearance at different removes from reality. He wants to deepen his audience's respect for the dimensions of experience that the Platonic tradition rejects as least real: namely, the dimensions of dream and fantasy in the underworld of the unconscious. Breton's "Manifesto" reflects a radically un-Platonic metaphysics and ontology. His entire essay leads up to the elusive last line, "Existence is elsewhere."

While parts of Breton's esthetics suggest a distance from worldly affairs, he was in fact intensely involved in political disputes. The choice of "Manifesto" for the title reflects Breton's respect for the **Communist Manifesto** by Marx and Engels. As he became more and more embroiled in the turbulence of French politics, the 1924 "Manifesto of Surrealism" reprinted here was followed by a "Second Manifesto of Surrealism" in 1930 and a "Prolegomena to a Third Surrealist Manifesto or Not" in 1942. His struggles with the Communist Party, his collaborations with the anarchist Leon Trotsky, and his lasting dedication to art all reflect a struggle with political minds similar to the battle waged by Murray Bookchin: is the revolutionary trying to liberate souls from the prevailing order or shackle them to a different order?

Manifesto of Surrealism

The mere word "freedom" is the only one that still excites me. I deem it capable of indefinitely sustaining the old human fanaticism. It doubtless satisfies my only legitimate aspiration. Among all the many misfortunes to which we are heir, it is only fair to admit that we are allowed the greatest degree of freedom of thought. It is up to us not to misuse it. To reduce the imagination to a state of slavery —even though it would mean the elimination of what is commonly called happiness—is to betray all sense of absolute justice within oneself. Imagination alone offers me some intimation of what *can be,* and this is enough to remove to some slight degree the terrible injunction; enough, too, to allow me to devote myself to it without fear of making a mistake (as though it were possible to make a bigger mistake). Where does it begin to turn bad, and where does the mind's stability cease? For the mind, is the possibility of erring not rather the contingency of good?

There remains madness, "the madness that one locks up," as it has aptly been described. That madness or another. . . . We all know, in fact, that the insane owe their incarceration to a tiny number of legally reprehensible acts and that, were it not for these acts their freedom (or what we see as their freedom) would not be threatened. I am willing to admit that they are, to some degree, victims of their imagination, in that it induces them not to pay attention to certain rules—outside of which the species feels itself threatened—which we are all supposed to know and respect. But their profound indifference to the way in which we judge them, and even to the various punishments meted out to them, allows us to suppose that they derive a great deal of comfort and consolation from their imagination, that they enjoy their madness sufficiently to endure the thought that its validity

MANIFESTO OF SURREALISM   From André Breton, *Manifestoes of Surrealism,* translated by Richard Seaver and Helen R. Lane. Published by Ann Arbor Paperbacks. Copyright © 1972 by The University of Michigan Press. Reprinted by permission.

does not extend beyond themselves. And, indeed, hallucinations, illusions, etc., are not a source of trifling pleasure. The best controlled sensuality partakes of it, and I know that there are many evenings when I would gladly tame that pretty hand which, during the last pages of Taine's *L'Intelligence,* indulges in some curious misdeeds. I could spend my whole life prying loose the secrets of the insane. These people are honest to a fault, and their naiveté has no peer but my own. Christopher Columbus should have set out to discover America with a boatload of madmen. And note how this madness has taken shape, and endured.

It is not the fear of madness which will oblige us to leave the flag of imagination furled.

The case against the realistic attitude demands to be examined, following the case against the materialistic attitude. The latter, more poetic in fact than the former, admittedly implies on the part of man a kind of monstrous pride which, admittedly, is monstrous, but not a new and more complete decay. It should above all be viewed as a welcome reaction against certain ridiculous tendencies of spiritualism. Finally, it is not incompatible with a certain nobility of thought.

By contrast, the realistic attitude, inspired by positivism, from Saint Thomas Aquinas to Anatole France, clearly seems to me to be hostile to any intellectual or moral advancement. I loathe it, for it is made up of mediocrity, hate, and dull conceit. It is this attitude which today gives birth to these ridiculous books, these insulting plays. It constantly feeds on and derives strength from the newspapers and stultifies both science and art by assiduously flattering the lowest of tastes; clarity bordering on stupidity, a dog's life. The activity of the best minds feels the effects of it; the law of the lowest common denominator finally prevails upon them as it does upon the others. An amusing result of this state of affairs, in literature for example, is the generous supply of novels. Each person adds his personal little "observation" to the whole. As a cleansing antidote to all this, M. Paul Valéry recently suggested that an anthology be compiled in which the largest possible number of opening passages from novels be offered; the resulting insanity, he predicted, would be a source of considerable edification. The most famous authors would be included. Such a thought reflects great credit on Paul Valéry who, some time ago, speaking of novels, assured me that, so far as he was concerned, he would continue to refrain from writing: "The Marquise went out at five." But has he kept his word?

If the purely informative style, of which the sentence just quoted is a prime example, is virtually the rule rather than the exception in the novel form, it is because, in all fairness, the author's ambition is severely circumscribed. The circumstantial, needlessly specific nature of each of their notations leads me to believe that they are perpetrating a joke at my expense. I am spared not even one of the character's slightest vacillations: will he be fairhaired? what will his name be? will we first meet him during the summer? So many questions resolved once and for all, as chance directs; the only discretionary power left me is to close the book, which I am careful to do somewhere in the vicinity of the first page. And the descriptions! There is nothing to which their vacuity can be compared; they are nothing but so many superimposed images taken from some stock catalogue, which the author utilizes more and more whenever he chooses; he seizes the opportunity to slip me his postcards, he tries to make me agree with him about the clichés:

> The small room into which the young man was shown was covered with yellow wallpaper: there were geraniums in the windows, which were covered with muslin curtains; the setting sun cast a harsh light over the entire setting. . . . There was nothing special about the room. The furniture, of yellow wood, was all very old. A sofa with a tall back turned down, an oval table opposite the sofa, a dressing table and a mirror set against the pierglass, some chairs along the walls, two or three etchings of no value portraying some German girls with birds in their hands—such were the furnishings.[1]

I am in no mood to admit that the mind is interested in occupying itself with such matters, even fleetingly. It may be argued that this school-boy description has its place, and that at this juncture of the book the author has his reasons for burdening me. Nevertheless he is wasting his time, for I refuse to go into his room. Others' laziness or fatigue does not interest me. I have too unstable a notion of the continuity of life to equate or compare my moments of depression or weakness with my best moments. When one ceases to feel, I am of the opinion one should keep quiet. And I would like it understood that I am not accusing or condemning lack of originality *as such*. I am only saying that I do not take particular note of the empty moments of my life, that it may be unworthy for any man to crystallize those which seem to him to be so. I shall, with your permission, *ignore* the description of that room, and many more like it.

Not so fast, there; I'm getting into the area of psychology, a subject about which I shall be careful not to joke.

The author attacks a character and, this being settled upon, parades his hero to and fro across the world. No matter what happens, this hero, whose actions and reactions are admirably predictable, is compelled not to thwart or upset—even though he looks as though he is—the calculations of which he is the object. The currents of life can appear to lift him up, roll him over, cast him down, he will still belong to this *readymade* human type. A simple game of chess which doesn't interest me in the least—man, whoever he may be, being for me a mediocre opponent. What I cannot bear are those wretched discussions relative to such and such a move, since winning or losing is not in question. And if the game is not worth the candle, if objective reason does a frightful job—as indeed it does—of serving him

[1] Dostoevski, *Crime and Punishment.*

who calls upon it, is it not fitting and proper to avoid all contact with these categories? "Diversity is so vast that every different tone of voice, every step, cough, every wipe of the nose, every sneeze. . . ."[2] If in a cluster of grapes there are no two alike, why do you want me to describe this grape by the other, by all the others, why do you want me to make a palatable grape? Our brains are dulled by the incurable mania of wanting to make the unknown known, classifiable. The desire for analysis wins out over the sentiments.[3] The result is statements of undue length whose persuasive power is attributed solely to their strangeness and which impress the reader only by the abstract quality of their vocabulary, which moreover is ill-defined. If the general ideas that philosophy has thus far come up with as topics of discussion revealed by their very nature their definitive incursion into a broader or more general area, I would be the first to greet the news with joy. But up till now it has been nothing but idle repartee; the flashes of wit and other niceties vie in concealing from us the true thought in search of itself, instead of concentrating on obtaining successes. It seems to me that every act is its own justification, at least for the person who has been capable of committing it, that it is endowed with a radiant power which the slightest gloss is certain to diminish. Because of this gloss, it even in a sense ceases to happen. It gains nothing to be thus distinguished. Stendhal's heroes are subject to the comments and appraisals—appraisals which are more or less successful—made by that author, which add not one whit to their glory. Where we really find them again is at the point at which Stendhal has lost them.

We are still living under the reign of logic: this, of course, is what I have been driving at. But in this day and age logical methods are applicable only to solving problems of secondary interest. The absolute rationalism that is still in vogue allows us to consider only facts relating directly to our experience. Logical ends, on the contrary, escape us. It is pointless to add that experience itself has found itself increasingly circumscribed. It paces back and forth in a cage from which it is more and more difficult to make it emerge. It too leans for support on what is most immediately expedient, and it is protected by the sentinels of common sense. Under the pretense of civilization and progress, we have managed to banish from the mind everything that may rightly or wrongly be termed superstition, or fancy; forbidden is any kind of search for truth which is not in conformance with accepted practices. It was, apparently, by pure chance that a part of our mental world which we pretended not to be concerned with any longer— and, in my opinion by far the most important part—has been brought back to light. For this we must give thanks to the discoveries of Sigmund Freud. On the basis of these discoveries a current of opinion is finally forming by

[2] Pascal.

[3] Barrès, Proust.

means of which the human explorer will be able to carry his investigations much further, authorized as he will henceforth be not to to confine himself solely to the most summary realities. The imagination is perhaps on the point of reasserting itself, of reclaiming its rights. If the depths of our mind contain within it strange forces capable of augmenting those on the surface, or of waging a victorious battle against them, there is every reason to seize them—first to seize them, then, if need be, to submit them to the control of our reason. The analysts themselves have everything to gain by it. But it is worth noting that no means has been designated a priori for carrying out this undertaking, that until further notice it can be construed to be the province of poets as well as scholars, and that its success is not dependent upon the more or less capricious paths that will be followed.

Freud very rightly brought his critical faculties to bear upon the dream. It is, in fact, inadmissible that this considerable portion of psychic activity (since, at least from man's birth until his death, thought offers no solution of continuity, the sum of the moments of dream, from the point of view of time, and taking into consideration only the time of pure dreaming, that is the dreams of sleep, is not inferior to the sum of the moments of reality, or, to be more precisely limiting, the moments of waking) has still today been so grossly neglected. I have always been amazed at the way an ordinary observer lends so much more credence and attaches so much more importance to waking events than to those occurring in dreams. It is because man, when he ceases to sleep, is above all the plaything of his memory, and in its normal state memory takes pleasure in weakly retracing for him the circumstances of the dream, in stripping it of any real importance, and in dismissing the only *determinant* from the point where he thinks he has left it a few hours before: this firm hope, this concern. He is under the impression of continuing something that is worthwhile. Thus the dream finds itself reduced to a mere parenthesis, as is the night. And, like the night, dreams generally contribute little to furthering our understanding. This curious state of affairs seems to me to call for certain reflections:

1. Within the limits where they operate (or are thought to operate) dreams give every evidence of being continuous and show signs of organization. Memory alone arrogates to itself the right to excerpt from dreams, to ignore the transitions, and to depict for us rather a series of dreams than the *dream itself*. By the same token, at any given moment we have only a distinct notion of realities, the coordination of which is a question of will.[4] What is worth noting is that nothing allows us to presuppose a greater dis-

---

[4] Account must be taken of the *depth* of the dream. For the most part I retain only what I can glean from its most superficial layers. What I most enjoy contemplating about a dream is everything that sinks back below the surface in a waking state, everything I have forgotten about my activities in the course of the preceding day, dark foliage, stupid branches. In "reality," likewise, I prefer to fall.

sipation of the elements of which the dream is constituted. I am sorry to
have to speak about it according to a formula which in principle excludes
the dream. When will we have sleeping logicians, sleeping philosophers? I
would like to sleep, in order to surrender myself to the dreamers, the way
I surrender myself to those who read me with eyes wide open; in order to
stop imposing, in this realm, the conscious rhythm of my thought. Perhaps
my dream last night follows that of the night before, and will be continued
the next night, with an exemplary strictness. *It's quite possible,* as the saying goes. And since it has not been proved in the slightest that, in doing so,
the "reality" with which I am kept busy continues to exist in the state of
dream, that it does not sink back down into the immemorial, why should I
not grant to dreams what I occasionally refuse reality, that is, this value
of certainty in itself which, in its own time, is not open to my repudiation?
Why should I not expect from the sign of the dream more than I expect
from a degree of consciousness which is daily more acute? Can't the dream
also be used in solving the fundamental questions of life? Are these questions the same in one case as in the other and, in the dream, do these questions already exist? Is the dream any less restrictive or punitive than the
rest? I am growing old and, more than that reality to which I believe I subject myself, it is perhaps the dream, the difference with which I treat the
dream, which makes me grow old.

2. Let me come back again to the waking state. I have no choice but to
consider it a phenomenon of interference. Not only does the mind display,
in this state, a strange tendency to lose its bearings (as evidenced by the
slips and mistakes the secrets of which are just beginning to be revealed to
us), but, what is more, it does not appear that, when the mind is functioning normally, it really responds to anything but the suggestions which
come to it from the depths of that dark night to which I commend it. However conditioned it may be, its balance is relative. It scarcely dares express
itself and, if it does, it confines itself to verifying that such and such an
idea, or such and such a woman, has made an impression on it. What impression it would be hard pressed to say, by which it reveals the degree of
its subjectivity, and nothing more. This idea, this woman, disturb it, they
tend to make it less severe. What they do is isolate the mind for a second
from its solvent and spirit it to heaven, as the beautiful precipitate it can
be, that it is. When all else fails, it then calls upon chance, a divinity
even more obscure than the others to whom it ascribes all its aberrations.
Who can say to me that the angle by which that idea which affects it is
offered, that what it likes in the eye of that woman is not precisely what
links it to its dream, binds it to those fundamental facts which, through its
own fault, it has lost? And if things were different, what might it be capable
of? I would like to provide it with the key to this corridor.

3. The mind of the man who dreams is fully satisfied by what happens
to him. The agonizing question of possibility is no longer pertinent. Kill, fly

faster, love to your heart's content. And if you should die, are you not certain of reawaking among the dead? Let yourself be carried along, events will not tolerate your interference. You are nameless. The ease of everything is priceless.

What reason, I ask, a reason so much vaster than the other, makes dreams seem so natural and allows me to welcome unreservedly a welter of episodes so strange that they would confound me now as I write? And yet I can believe my eyes, my ears; this great day has arrived, this beast has spoken.

If man's awaking is harder, if it breaks the spell too abruptly, it is because he has been led to make for himself too impoverished a notion of atonement.

4. From the moment when it is subjected to a methodical examination, when, by means yet to be determined, we succeed in recording the contents of dreams in their entirety (and that presupposes a discipline of memory spanning generations; but let us nonetheless begin by noting the most salient facts), when its graph will expand with unparalleled volume and regularity, we may hope that the mysteries which really are not will give way to the great Mystery. I believe in the future resolution of these two states, dream and reality, which are seemingly so contradictory, into a kind of absolute reality, a *surreality,* if one may so speak. It is in quest of this surreality that I am going, certain not to find it but too unmindful of my death not to calculate to some slight degree the joys of its possession.

A story is told according to which Saint-Pol-Roux, in times gone by, used to have a notice posted on the door of his manor house in Camaret, every evening before he went to sleep, which read: THE POET IS WORKING.

A great deal more could be said, but in passing I merely wanted to touch upon a subject which in itself would require a very long and much more detailed discussion; I shall come back to it. At this juncture, my intention was merely to mark a point by noting the *hate of the marvelous* which rages in certain men, this absurdity beneath which they try to bury it. Let us not mince words: the marvelous is always beautiful, anything marvelous is beautiful, in fact only the marvelous is beautiful. [. . .]

Man proposes and disposes. He and he alone can determine whether he is completely master of himself, that is, whether he maintains the body of his desires, daily more formidable, in a state of anarchy. Poetry teaches him to. It bears within itself the perfect compensation for the miseries we endure. It can also be an organizer, if ever, as the result of a less intimate disappointment, we contemplate taking it seriously. The time is coming when it decrees the end of money and by itself will break the bread of heaven for the earth! There will still be gatherings on the public squares, and *movements* you never dared hope participate in. Farewell to absurd choices, the dreams of dark abyss, rivalries, the prolonged patience, the flight of the seasons, the artificial order of ideas, the ramp of danger, time for everything! May you only take the trouble to *practice* poetry. Is it not incumbent upon us, who are already living off it, to try and impose what we hold to be our case for further inquiry?

It matters not whether there is a certain disproportion between this defense and the illustration that will follow it. It was a question of going back to the sources of poetic imagination and, what is more, of remaining there. Not that I pretend to have done so. It requires a great deal of fortitude to try to set up one's abode in these distant regions where everything seems at first to be so awkward and difficult, all the more so if one wants to try to take someone there. Besides, one is never sure of really being there. If one is going to all that trouble, one might just as well stop off somewhere else. Be that as it may, the fact is that the way to these regions is clearly marked, and that to attain the true goal is now merely a matter of the travelers' ability to endure.

We are all more or less aware of the road traveled. I was careful to relate, in the course of a study of the case of Robert Desnos entitled ENTRÉE DES MÉDIUMS,[5] that I had been led to "concentrate my attention on the more or less partial sentences which, when one is quite alone and on the verge of falling asleep, become perceptible for the mind without its being possible to discover what provoked them." I had then just attempted the poetic adventure with the minimum of risks, that is, my aspirations were the same as they are today but I trusted in the slowness of formulation to keep me from useless contacts, contacts of which I completely disapproved. This attitude involved a modesty of thought certain vestiges of which I still retain. At the end of my life, I shall doubtless manage to speak with great effort the way people speak, to apologize for my voice and my few remaining gestures. The virtue of the spoken word (and the written word all the more so) seemed to me to derive from the faculty of foreshortening in a striking manner the exposition (since there was exposition) of a small number of facts, poetic or other, of which I made myself the substance. I had come to the conclusion that Rimbaud had not proceeded any differently. I was composing, with a concern for variety that deserved better, the final poems of *Mont de piété,* that is, I managed to extract from the blank lines of this book an incredible advantage. These lines were the closed eye to the operations of thought that I believed I was obliged to keep hidden from the reader. It was not deceit on my part, but my love of shocking the reader. I had the illusion of a possible complicity, which I had more and more difficulty giving up. I had begun to cherish words excessively for the space they allow around them, for their tangencies with countless other words that I did not utter. The poem BLACK FOREST derives precisely from this state of mind. It took me six months to write it, and you may take my word

5 See *Les Pas perdus,* published by N. R. F. [Nouvelle Revue Français]

for it that I did not rest a single day. But this stemmed from the opinion I had of myself in those days, which was high, please don't judge me too harshly. I enjoy these stupid confessions. At that point cubist pseudo-poetry was trying to get a foothold, but it had emerged defenseless from Picasso's brain, and I was thought to be as dull as dishwater (and still am). I had a sneaking suspicion, moreover, that from the viewpoint of poetry I was off on the wrong road, but I hedged my bet as best I could, defying lyricism with salvos of definitions and formulas (the Dada phenomena were waiting in the wings, ready to come on stage) and pretending to search for an application of poetry to advertising (I went so far as to claim that the world would end, not with a good book but with a beautiful advertisement for heaven or for hell).

In those days, a man at least as boring as I, Pierre Reverdy, was writing:

The image is a pure creation of the mind.
It cannot be born from a comparison but from a juxtaposition of two more or less distant realities.
The more the relationship between the two juxtaposed realities is distant and true, the stronger the image will be—the greater its emotional power and poetic reality . . .[6]

These words, however sibylline for the uninitiated, were extremely revealing, and I pondered them for a long time. But the image eluded me. Reverdy's aesthetic, a completely a posteriori aesthetic, led me to mistake the effects for the causes. It was in the midst of all this that I renounced irrevocably my point of view.

One evening, therefore, before I fell asleep, I perceived, so clearly articulated that it was impossible to change a word, but nonetheless removed from the sound of any voice, a rather strange phrase which came to me without any apparent relationship to the events in which, my consciousness agrees, I was then involved, a phrase which seemed to me insistent, a phrase, if I may be so bold, *which was knocking at the window*. I took cursory note of it and prepared to move on when its organic character caught my attention. Actually, this phrase astonished me: unfortunately I cannot remember it exactly, but it was something like: "There is a man cut in two by the window," but there could be no question of ambiguity, accompanied as it was by the faint visual image[7] of a man walking cut half

---

[6] *Nord-Sud,* March 1918.

[7] Were I a painter, this visual depiction would doubtless have become more important for me than the other. It was most certainly my previous predispositions which decided the matter. Since that day, I have had occasion to concentrate my attention voluntarily on similar apparitions, and I know that they are fully as clear as auditory phenomena. With a pencil and white sheet of paper to hand, I could easily trace their outlines. Here again it is not a matter of drawing, *but simply of tracing.* I could thus depict a tree, a wave, a musical instrument, all manner of things of which

way up by a window perpendicular to the axis of his body. Beyond the slightest shadow of a doubt, what I saw was the simple reconstruction in space of a man leaning out a window. But this window having shifted with the man, I realized that I was dealing with an image of a fairly rare sort, and all I could think of was to incorporate it into my material for poetic construction. No sooner had I granted it this capacity than it was in fact succeeded by a whole series of phrases, with only brief pauses between them, which surprised me only slightly less and left me with the impression of their being so gratuitous that the control I had then exercised upon myself seemed to me illusory and all I could think of was putting an end to the interminable quarrel raging within me.[8]

Completely occupied as I still was with Freud at that time, and familiar as I was with his methods of examination which I had had some slight occasion to use on some patients during the war, I resolved to obtain from myself what we were trying to obtain from them, namely, a monologue spoken as rapidly as possible without any intervention on the part of the critical faculties, a monologue consequently unencumbered by the slightest inhibition and which was, as closely as possible, akin to *spoken thought*. It

---

I am presently incapable of providing even the roughest sketch. I would plunge into it, convinced that I would find my way again, in a maze of lines which at first glance would seem to be going nowhere. And, upon opening my eyes, I would get the very strong impression of something "never seen." The proof of what I am saying has been provided many times by Robert Desnos: to be convinced, one has only to leaf through the pages of issue number 36 of *Feuilles libres* which contains several of his drawings (*Romeo and Juliet, A Man Died This Morning,* etc.) which were taken by this magazine as the drawings of a madman and published as such.

[8] Knut Hamsum ascribes this sort of revelation to which I had been subjected as deriving from *hunger,* and he may not be wrong. (The fact is I did not eat every day during that period of my life). Most certainly the manifestations that he describes in these terms are clearly the same:

"The following day I awoke at an early hour. It was still dark. My eyes had been open for a long time when I heard the clock in the apartment above strike five. I wanted to go back to sleep, but I couldn't; I was wide awake and a thousand thoughts were crowding through my mind.
Suddenly a few good fragments came to mind, quite suitable to be used in a rough draft, or serialized; all of a sudden I found, quite by chance, beautiful phrases, phrases such as I had never written. I repeated them to myself slowly, word by word; they were excellent. And there were still more coming. I got up and picked up a pencil and some paper that were on a table behind my bed. It was as though some vein had burst within me, one word followed another, found its proper place, adapted itself to the situation, scene piled upon scene, the action unfolded, one retort after another welled up in my mind, I was enjoying myself immensely. Thoughts came to me so rapidly and continued to flow so abundantly that I lost a whole host of delicate details, because my pencil could not keep up with them, and yet I went as fast as I could, my hand in constant motion, I did not lose a minute. The sentences continued to well up within me, I was pregnant with my subject."

Apollinaire asserted that Chirico's first paintings were done under the influence of cenesthesic disorders (migraines, colics, etc.).

had seemed to me, and still does—the way in which the phrase about the man cut in two had come to me is an indication of it—that the speed of thought is no greater than the speed of speech, and that thought does not necessarily defy language, nor even the fast-moving pen. It was in this frame of mind that Philippe Soupault—to whom I had confided these initial conclusions—and I decided to blacken some paper, with a praiseworthy disdain for what might result from a literary point of view. The ease of execution did the rest. By the end of the first day we were able to read to ourselves some fifty or so pages obtained in this manner, and begin to compare our results. All in all, Soupault's pages and mine proved to be remarkably similar: the same overconstruction, shortcomings of a similar nature, but also, on both our parts, the illusion of an extraordinary verve, a great deal of emotion, a considerable choice of images of a quality such that we would not have been capable of preparing a single one in longhand, a very special picturesque quality and, here and there, a strong comical effect. The only difference between our two texts seemed to me to derive essentially from our respective tempers, Soupault's being less static than mine, and, if he does not mind my offering this one slight criticism, from the fact that he had made the error of putting a few words by way of titles at the top of certain pages, I suppose in a spirit of mystification. On the other hand, I must give credit where credit is due and say that he constantly and vigorously opposed any effort to retouch or correct, however slightly, any passage of this kind which seemed to me unfortunate. In this he was, to be sure, absolutely right.[9] It is, in fact, difficult to appreciate fairly the various elements present; one may even go so far as to say that it is impossible to appreciate them at a first reading. To you who write, these elements are, on the surface, *as strange to you as they are to anyone else,* and naturally you are wary of them. Poetically speaking, what strikes you about them above all is their *extreme degree of immediate absurdity,* the quality of this absurdity, upon closer scrutiny, being to give way to everything admissible, everything legitimate in the world: the disclosure of a certain number of properties and of facts no less objective, in the final analysis, than the others.

In homage to Guillaume Apollinaire, who had just died and who, on several occasions, seemed to us to have followed a discipline of this kind, without however having sacrificed to it any mediocre literary means, Soupault and I baptized the new mode of pure expression which we had at our disposal and which we wished to pass on to our friends, by the name of SURREALISM. I believe that there is no point today in dwelling any further

---

[9] I believe more and more in the infallibility of my thought with respect to myself, and this is too fair. Nonetheless, with this *thought-writing,* where one is at the mercy of the first outside distraction, "ebullutions" can occur. It would be inexcusable for us to pretend otherwise. By definition, thought is strong, and incapable of catching itself in error. The blame for these obvious weaknesses must be placed on suggestions that come to it from without.

on this word and that the meaning we gave it initially has generally prevailed over its Apollinarian sense. To be even fairer, we could probably have taken over the word SUPERNATURALISM employed by Gérard de Nerval in his dedication to the *Filles de feu*.[10] It appears, in fact, that Nerval possessed to a tee the spirit with which we claim a kinship, Apollinaire having possessed, on the contrary, naught but *the letter,* still imperfect, of Surrealism, having shown himself powerless to give a valid theoretical idea of it. Here are two passages by Nerval which seem to me to be extremely significant in this respect:

> I am going to explain to you, my dear Dumas, the phenomenon of which you have spoken a short while ago. There are, as you know, certain storytellers who cannot invent without identifying with the characters their imagination has dreamt up. You may recall how convincingly our old friend Nodier used to tell how it had been his misfortune during the Revolution to be guillotined; one became so completely convinced of what he was saying that one began to wonder how he had managed to have his head glued back on.
>
> . . . And since you have been indiscreet enough to quote one of the sonnets composed in this SUPERNATURALISTIC dream-state, as the Germans would call it, you will have to hear them all. You will find them at the end of the volume. They are hardly any more obscure than Hegel's metaphysics or Swedenborg's MEMORABILIA, and would lose their charm if they were explained, if such were possible; at least admit the worth of the expression. . . .[11]

Those who might dispute our right to employ the term SURREALISM in the very special sense that we understand it are being extremely dishonest, for there can be no doubt that this word had no currency before we came along. Therefore, I am defining it once and for all:

SURREALISM, *n.* Psychic automatism in its pure state, by which one proposes to express—verbally, by means of the written word, or in any other manner—the actual functioning of thought. Dictated by thought, in the absence of any control exercised by reason, exempt from any aesthetic or moral concern.

ENCYCLOPEDIA. *Philosophy.* Surrealism is based on the belief in the superior reality of certain forms of previously neglected associations, in the omnipotence of dream, in the disinterested play of thought. It tends to ruin once and for all all other psychic mechanisms and to substitute itself for them in solving all the principal problems of life. [. . .]

[10] And also by Thomas Carlyle in *Sartor Resartus* ([Book III] Chapter VIII, "Natural Supernaturalism"), 1833–34.

[11] See also *L'Idéoréalisme* by Saint-Pol-Roux.

The theater, philosophy, science, criticism would all succeed in finding their bearings there. I hasten to add that future Surrealist techniques do not interest me.

Far more serious, in my opinion[12]—I have intimated it often enough— are the applications of Surrealism to action. To be sure, I do not believe in the prophetic nature of the Surrealist word. "It is the oracle, the things I say."[13] Yes, *as much as I like,* but what of the oracle itself?[14] Men's piety does not fool me. The Surrealist voice that shook Cumae, Dodona, and Delphi is nothing more than the voice which dictates my less irascible speeches to me. My *time* must not be its time, why should this voice help me resolve the childish problem of my destiny? I pretend, unfortunately, to act in a world where, in order to take into account its suggestions, I would be obliged to resort to two kinds of interpreters, one to translate its judgments for me, the other, impossible to find, to transmit to my fellow

[12] Whatever reservations I may be allowed to make concerning responsibility in general and the medico-legal considerations which determine an individual's degree of responsibility—complete responsibility, irresponsibility, limited responsibility (sic)— however difficult it may be for me to accept the principle of any kind of responsibility, I would like to know how the first punishable offenses, the Surrealist character of which will be clearly apparent, will be *judged.* Will the accused be acquitted, or will he merely be given the benefit of the doubt because of extenuating circumstances? It's a shame that the violation of the laws governing the Press is today scarcely repressed, for if it were not we would soon see a trial of this sort: the accused has published a book which is an outrage to public decency. Several of his "most respected and honorable" fellow citizens have lodged a complaint against him, and he is also charged with slander and libel. There are also all sorts of other charges against him, such as insulting and defaming the army, inciting to murder, rape, etc. The accused, moreover, wastes no time in agreeing with the accusers in "stigmatizing" most of the ideas expressed. His only defense is claiming that he does not consider himself to be the author of his book, said book being no more and no less than a Surrealist concoction which precludes any question of merit or lack of merit on the part of the person who signs it; further, that all he has done is copy a document without offering any opinion thereon, and that he is at least as foreign to the accused text as is the presiding judge himself.

What is true for the publication of a book will also hold true for a whole host of other acts as soon as Surrealist methods begin to enjoy widespread favor. When that happens, a new morality must be substituted for the prevailing morality, the source of all our trials and tribulations.

[13] Rimbaud.

[14] Still, STILL. . . . We must absolutely get to the bottom of this. Today, June 8, 1924, about one o'clock, the voice whispered to me: "Béthune, Béthune." What did it mean? I have never been to Béthune, and have only the vaguest notion as to where it is located on the map of France. Béthune evokes nothing for me, not even a scene from *The Three Musketeers.* I should have left for Béthune, where perhaps there was something awaiting me; that would have been too simple, really. Someone told me they had read in a book by Chesterton about a detective who, in order to find someone he is looking for in a certain city, simply scoured from roof to cellar the houses which, from the outside, seemed somehow abnormal to him, were it only in some slight detail. This system is as good as any other.

Similarly, in 1919, Soupault went into any number of impossible buildings to ask the concierge whether Philippe Soupault did in fact live there. He would not have been surprised, I suspect, by an affirmative reply. He would have gone and knocked on his door.

men whatever sense I could make out of them. This world, in which I endure what I endure (don't go see) this modern world, I mean, what the devil do you want me to do with it? Perhaps the Surrealist voice will be stilled, I have given up trying to keep track of those who have disappeared. I shall no longer enter into, however briefly, the marvelous detailed description of my years and my days. I shall be like Nijinski who was taken last year to the Russian ballet and did not realize what spectacle it was he was seeing. I shall be alone, very alone within myself, indifferent to all the world's ballets. What I have done, what I have left undone, I give it to you.

And ever since I have had a great desire to show forbearance to scientific musing, however unbecoming, in the final analysis, from every point of view. Radios? Fine. Syphilis? If you like. Photography? I don't see any reason why not. The cinema? Three cheers for darkened rooms. War? Gave us a good laugh. The telephone? Hello. Youth? Charming white hair. Try to make me say thank you: "Thank you." Thank you. If the common man has a high opinion of things which properly speaking belong to the realm of the laboratory, it is because such research has resulted in the manufacture of a machine or the discovery of some serum which the man in the street views as affecting him directly. He is quite sure that they have been trying to improve his lot. I am not quite sure to what extent scholars are motivated by humanitarian aims, but it does not seem to me that this factor constitutes a very marked degree of goodness. I am, of course, referring to true scholars and not to the vulgarizers and popularizers of all sorts who take out patents. In this realm as in any other, I believe in the pure Surrealist joy of the man who, forewarned that all others before him have failed, refuses to admit defeat, sets off from whatever point he chooses, along any other path save a reasonable one, and arrives whenever he can. Such and such an image, by which he deems it opportune to indicate his progress and which may result, perhaps, in his receiving public acclaim, is to me, I must confess, a matter of complete indifference. Nor is the material with which he must perforce encumber himself; his glass tubes or my metallic feathers . . . As for his method, I am willing to give it as much credit as I do mine. I have seen the inventor of the cutaneous plantar reflex at work; he manipulated his subjects without respite, it was much more than an "examination" he was employing; *it was obvious that he was following no set plan.* Here and there he formulated a remark; distantly, without nonetheless setting down his needle, while his hammer was never still. He left to others the futile task of curing patients. He was wholly consumed by and devoted to that sacred fever.

Surrealism, such as I conceive of it, asserts our complete *nonconformism* clearly enough so that there can be no question of translating it, at the trial of the real world, as evidence for the defense. It could, on the contrary, only serve to justify the complete state of distraction which we hope to achieve here below. Kant's absentmindedness regarding women, Pasteur's absentmindedness about "grapes," Curie's absentmindedness with respect to vehicles, are in this regard profoundly symptomatic. This world is only very relatively in tune with thought, and incidents of this kind are only the most obvious episodes of a war in which I am proud to be participating. Surrealism is the "invisible ray" which will one day enable us to win out over our opponents. "You are no longer trembling, carcass." This summer the roses are blue; the wood is of glass. The earth, draped in its verdant cloak, makes as little impression upon me as a ghost. It is living and ceasing to live that are imaginary solutions. Existence is elsewhere.

HERBERT MARCUSE

(1898-   )

Herbert Marcuse has played a major part in forging an ideology for contemporary liberation movements. The depth and richness of his contributions to current thinking can best be appreciated by a brief review of some of his books. In **Soviet Marxism** (1958) and **Reason and Revolution: Hegel and the Rise of Social Theory** (1941) he explores the contributions of Marx and Hegel in their original intent and as they apply to the twentieth century. In **Eros and Civilization** (1955) Marcuse turned to Freud and the psychoanalytic tradition in an attempt to find theoretical foundations for a utopian image of man that transcends the present order while remaining consistent with a Marxist historical materialism. That is, Marcuse did not merely develop a utopian picture based on modern psychology; he tried to show how contemporary social and economic determinants had paved the way for a new era of human liberation. Toward the end of the 1950's and in the early 1960's, however, Marcuse was gripped by pessimism. In his Preface to the second edition of **Eros and Civilization** (1961) and in his most famous book **One-Dimensional Man** (1964) Marcuse offered an analysis of American society showing its capacity for neutralizing liberation movements. He argued that our advanced industrial society had in effect bought off the potential powers of opposition; revolution had been rendered impossible by the spread of a "happy consciousness" that was nonetheless a "false consciousness," based as it was on the gratification of the "false needs" of a crass materialistic consumerism. But that was before the rise of the youth movements of the late sixties and early seventies, which substantiated Marcuse's analysis by rejecting false needs as indeed false but also somewhat embarrassed Marcuse's analysis, since he in effect argued that the youth movement **could not happen.** Retrenching somewhat on his earlier pessimism, Marcuse then issued his **Essay on Liberation,** in which he returned to the theme of synthesis between Freudian theory and a utopian Marxism based on an analysis of the newer and more hopeful developments in transcending the one-dimensional society. But Marcuse never abandoned the staunchly political perspective of his Marxist training. Consequently he takes issue with Brown's move to metapolitics.

In a review of Brown's **Love's Body** (published with Brown's reply in **Commentary** in 1967 and then reprinted in a book of Marcuse's essays under the title **Negations),** Marcuse rejects the idea that everything is symbolic and condemns Brown for "spiritualizing" both sexuality and politics. At times Marcuse's response sounds almost like Barber's answer to the new anarchists. While arguing for liberation he places little hope in apocalyptic visions that transcend **all** order. Like Barber, he is worried about counterrevolution marching under the banner of revolution. His newest book, from which the following essay is taken, is titled **Counterrevolution and Revolt** (1972).

Marcuse acknowledges the power of art for transforming consciousness, and he does not see art's political role as restricted to a didactic representation of alternative truths, but he refuses to be swept away by the forces of antirationalism. He argues the need for order in transcending what he calls the irrational rationality of the current order.

Art and Revolution

At precisely this stage, the radical effort to sustain and intensify the "power of the negative," the subversive potential of art, must sustain and intensify the *alienating* power of art: the aesthetic form, in which alone the radical force of art becomes communicable.

In his essay "Die Phantasie im Spätkapitalismus und die Kulturrevolution," Peter Schneider calls this recapture of the aesthetic transcendence the "propagandistic function of art":

ART AND REVOLUTION   From Herbert Marcuse, *Counterrevolution and Revolt.* Copyright © 1972 by Herbert Marcuse. Reprinted by permission of Beacon Press. "Die Liebenden" by Bertolt Brecht. Aus *Aufstieg und Fall der Stadt Mahagonny.* Copyright by Suhrkamp Verlag 1955. All rights reserved. Translated by permission of Pantheon Books, a Division of Random House, Inc., the publisher of *Bertolt Brecht: Plays, Poetry & Prose,* edited by Ralph Manheim and John Willett.

Propagandistic art would seek in the recorded dream history [*Wunsch-geschichte*] of mankind the utopian images, would free them from the distorted forms which were imposed upon them by the material conditions of life, and show to these dreams [*Wünschen*] the road to realization which now, finally, has become possible. . . . The aesthetic of this art should be the strategy of dream realization.[1]

This strategy of realization, precisely because it is to be that of a dream, can never be "complete," never be a translation into reality, which would make art into a psychoanalytic process. Realization rather means finding the *aesthetic* forms which can communicate the possibilities of a liberating transformation of the technical and natural environment. But here, too, the distance between art and practice, the dissociation of the former from the latter, remains.

At the time between the two World Wars, where the protest seemed to be directly translatable into action, joined to action, where the shattering of the aesthetic form seemed to be the response to the revolutionary forces in action, Antonin Artaud formulated the program for the abolition of art: "En finir avec les chefs-d'oeuvres"; art must become the concern of the masses (*la foule*), must be an affair of the streets, and above all, of the organism, the body, of nature. Thus, it would *move* men, would move things, for: "il faut que les choses crèvent pour repartir et recommencer." The serpent moves to the tones of the music not because of their "spiritual content" but because their vibrations communicate themselves through the earth to the serpent's entire body. Art has cut off this communication and "deprived a gesture [*un geste*] from its repercussion in the organism": this unity with nature must be restored: "beneath the poetry of text, there is a poetry *tout court,* without form and without text." This natural poetry must be recaptured which is still present in the eternal myths of mankind (such as "beneath the text" in Sophocles' *Oedipus*) and in the magic of the primitives: its rediscovery is prerequisite for the liberation of man. For "we are not free, and the sky can still fall on our head. And the theater is made first of all in order to teach us all this."[2] To attain this goal, the theater must leave the stage and go on the street, to the masses. And it must *shock,* cruelly shock and *shatter* the complacent consciousness and unconscious.

. . . [a theater] where violent physical images crush and hypnotize the sensibility of the spectator, seized in the theater as by a whirlwind of superior forces.

Even at the time when Artaud wrote, the "superior forces" were of a very different kind, and they seized man, not to liberate but rather to en-

[1] G. Warren Nutter, Assistant Secretary of Defense for International Security, *New York Times,* March 23, 1971.

[2] Antonin Artaud, *Le Théâtre et son double* (Paris: Gallimard, 1964), pp. 113, 119, 121, 123, 124, 126 (written in 1933).

slave and destroy him more effectively. And today, what possible language, what possible image can crush and hypnotize minds and bodies which live in peaceful coexistence with (and even profiting from) genocide, torture and poison? And if Artaud wants a "constant sonorization: sounds and noises and cries, first for their quality of vibration and then for that which they represent," we ask: has not the audience, even the "natural" audience on the streets, long since become familiar with the violent noises, cries, which are the daily equipment of the mass media, sports, highways, places of recreation? They do not break the oppressive familiarity with destruction; they reproduce it.

The German writer Peter Handke blasted the "ekelhafte Unwahrheit von Ernsthaftigkeiten im Spielraum [the loathsome untruth of seriousness in play]."[3] This indictment is not an attempt to keep politics out of the theater, but to indicate the form in which it can find expression. The indictment cannot be upheld with respect to Greek tragedy, to Shakespeare, Racine, Kleist, Ibsen, Brecht, Beckett: there, by virtue of the aesthetic form, the "play" creates its own universe of "seriousness" which is *not* that of the given reality, but rather its negation. But the indictment holds for the guerrilla theater of today: it is a *contradictio in adjecto;* altogether different from the Chinese (regardless of whether it was played on or after the Long March); there, the theater did not take place in a "universe of play"; it was part of a revolution in actual process, and established, as an episode, the identity between the players and the fighters: unity of the space of the play and the space of the revolution.

The Living Theatre may serve as an example of self-defeating purpose.[4] It makes a systematic attempt to unite the theater and the Revolution, the play and the battle, bodily and spiritual liberation, individual internal and social external change. But this union is shrouded in mysticism: "the Kabbalah, Tantric and Hasidic teaching, the I Ching, and other sources." The mixture of Marxism and mysticism, of Lenin and Dr. R. D. Laing does not work; it vitiates the political impulse. The liberation of the body, the sexual revolution, becoming a ritual to be performed ("the rite of universal intercourse"), loses its place in the political revolution: if sex is a voyage to God, it can be tolerated even in extreme forms. The revolution of love, the nonviolent revolution, is no serious threat; the powers that be have always been capable of coping with the forces of love. The radical desublimation which takes place in the theater, *as* theater, is organized, arranged, performed desublimation—it is close to turning into its opposite.[5]

[3] Quoted in Yark Karsunke, "Die Strasse und das Theater," in *Kursbuch* 20, 1969, p. 67.

[4] See *Paradise Now: Collective Creation of the Living Theatre,* written down by Judith Malina and Julian Beck (Random House).

[5] In the summer of 1971, the Living Theatre group that had been playing before the wretched of the earth in Brazil was incarcerated by the fascist government. There, in the midst of the terror which is the life of the people, and which precluded any in-

Untruth is the fate of the unsublimated, direct representation. Here, the "illusory" character of art is not abolished but doubled: the players only play the actions they want to demonstrate, and this action itself is unreal, is play.

The distinction between an internal revolution of the aesthetic form and its destruction, between authentic and contrived directness (a distinction based on the tension between art and reality), has also become decisive in the development (and function) of "living music," "natural music." It is as if the cultural revolution had fulfilled Artaud's demand that, in a literal sense, music move the body, thereby drawing nature into the rebellion. Life music has indeed an authentic basis: *black music* as the cry and song of the slaves and the ghettos.[6] In this music, the very life and death of black men and women are lived again: the music *is* body; the aesthetic form is the "gesture" of pain, sorrow, indictment. With the takeover by the whites, a significant change occurs: white "rock" is what its black paradigm is *not,* namely, *performance.* It is as if the crying and shouting, the jumping and playing, now take place in an artificial, organized space; that they are directed toward a (sympathetic) *audience.* What had been part of the permanence of life now becomes a concert, festival, a disc in the making. "The group" becomes a fixed entity (*verdinglicht*), absorbing the individuals; it is "totalitarian" in the way in which it overwhelms individual consciousness and mobilizes a collective unconscious which remains without social foundation.

And as this music loses its radical impact, it tends to massification: the listeners and coperformers in the audience are masses streaming to a spectacle, a performance.

True, in this spectacle, the audience actively participates: the music *moves* their bodies, makes them "natural." But their (literally) electrical excitation often assumes the features of hysteria. The aggressive force of the endlessly repeated hammering rhythm (the variations of which do not open another dimension of music), the squeezing dissonances, the stan-

---

tegration into the established order, even the mystified liberation play seemed a threat to the regimen. I wish to express my solidarity with Judith Malina and Julian Beck and their group; my criticism is fraternal, since we share the same struggle.

[6] Pierre Lere analyzes the dialectic of this black music in his article "Free Jazz: Évolution ou Révolution": ". . . the liberty of the musical forms is only the aesthetic translation of the will to social liberation. Transcending the tonal framework of the theme, the musician finds himself in a position of freedom. This search for freedom is translated into atonal musicality; it defines a modal climate where the Black expresses a new order. The melodic line becomes the medium of communication between an initial order which is rejected and a final order which is hoped for. The frustrating possession of the one, joined with the liberating attainment of the other, establishes a rupture in between the Weft of harmony which gives way to an aesthetic of the cry [*esthétique du cri*]. This cry, the characteristic resonant [*sonore*] element of "free music," born in an exasperated tension, announces the violent rupture with the established white order and translates the advancing [*promotrice*] violence of a new black order" (*Revue d'Esthétique,* vols. 3–4, 1970, pp. 320, 321).

dardized "frozen" distortions, the noise level in general—is it not the force of frustration?[7] And the identical gestures, the twisting and shaking of bodies which rarely (if ever) really touch each other—it seems like treading on the spot, it does not get you anywhere except into a mass soon to disperse. This music is, in a literal sense, *imitation, mimesis* of effective aggression: it is, moreover, another case of *catharsis:* group therapy which, temporarily, removes inhibitions. Liberation remains a private affair.

The tension between art and revolution seems irreducible. Art itself, in practice, cannot change reality, and art cannot submit to the actual requirements of the revolution without denying itself. But art can and will draw its inspirations, and its very form, from the then prevailing revolutionary movement—for revolution is in the substance of art. The historical substance of art asserts itself in all modes of alienation; it precludes any notion that recapturing the aesthetic form today could mean revival of classicism, romanticism or any other traditional form. Does an analysis of the social reality allow any indication as to art forms which would respond to the revolutionary potential in the contemporary world?

According to Adorno, art responds to the total character of repression and administration with total alienation. The highly intellectual, constructivist and at the same time spontaneous-formless music of John Cage, Stockhausen, Pierre Boulez, may be the extreme examples.

But has this effort already reached the point of no return, that is, the point where the *oeuvre* drops out of the dimension of alienation, of *formed* negation and contradiction, and turns into a sound game, language game— harmless and without commitment, shock which no longer shocks, and thus succumbing?

The radical literature which speaks in formless semispontaneity and directness loses with the aesthetic form the political content, while this content erupts in the most highly formed poems of Allen Ginsberg and Ferlinghetti. The most uncompromising, most extreme indictment has found expression in a work which precisely because of its radicalism repels the political sphere: in the work of Samuel Beckett, there is no hope which can be translated into political terms, the aesthetic form excludes all accommodation and leaves literature as literature. And as literature, the work carries one single message: to make an end with things as they are. Similarly, the revolution is in Bertolt Brecht's most perfect lyric rather than in his political plays, and in Alban Berg's *Wozzeck* rather than in today's antifascist opera.

This is the passing of antiart, the reemergence of form. And with it we find a new expression of the inherently subversive qualities of the aesthetic dimension, especially beauty as the sensuous appearance of the idea of

---

[7] The frustration behind the noisy aggression is revealed very neatly in a statement by Grace Slick of the "Jefferson Airplane" group, reported in *The New York Times Magazine* (October 18, 1970): "Our eternal goal in life, Grace says, absolutely deadpan, is to get louder."

freedom. The delight of beauty and the horror of politics; Brecht has condensed it in five lines:

> Within me there is a struggle between
> The delight about the blooming apple tree
> And the horror about a Hitler speech.
> But only the latter
> Forces me to my desk
> 　　　　　[Translated from the German by Reinhard Lettau]

The image of the tree remains present in the poem which is "enforced" by a Hitler speech. The horror of that which is marks the moment of creation, is the origin of the poem which celebrates the beauty of the blooming apple tree. The political dimension remains committed to the other, the aesthetic dimension, which, in turn, assumes political value. This happens not only in the work of Brecht (who is already considered a "classic") but also in some of the radical songs of protest of today—or yesterday, especially in the lyrics and music of Bob Dylan. Beauty returns, the "soul" returns: not the one in food and "on ice" but the old and repressed one, the one that was in the *Lied,* in the melody: *cantabile.* It becomes the form of the subversive content, not as artificial revival, but as a "return of the repressed." The music, in its own development, carries the song to the point of rebellion where the voice, in word and pitch, *halts* the melody, the song, and turns into outcry, shout.

Junction of art and revolution in the aesthetic dimension,[8] in art itself. Art which has bceome capable of being political even in the (apparently) total absence of political content, where nothing remains but the poem— about what? Brecht accomplishes the miracle of making the simplest ordinary language say the unutterable: the poem invokes, for a vanishing moment, the images of a liberated world, liberated nature:

DIE LIEBENDEN
Sieh jene Kraniche in grossem Bogen!
Die Wolken, welche ihnen beigegeben
Zogen mit ihnen schon, als sie entflogen
Aus einem Leben in ein andres Leben.
In gleicher Höhe und mit gleicher Eile

---

[8] One only has to read some of the authentic-sounding poems of young activists (or former activists) in order to see how poetry, remaining poetry, can be political also today. These love poems are political as love poems: not where they are fashionably desublimated, verbal release of sexuality, but on the contrary: where the erotic energy finds sublimated, poetic expression—a poetic language becoming the outcry against that which is done to men and women who love in this society. In contrast, the union of love and subversion, the social liberation inherent in Eros is lost where the poetic language is abandoned in favor of versified (or pseudoversified) pig language. There is such a thing as pornography, namely, the sexual publicity, propaganda with the exhibitionist, marketable Eros. Today, the pig language and the glossy photography of sex have exchange value—not the romantic love poem.

Scheinen sie alle beide nur daneben.
Dass so der Kranich mit der Wolke teile
Den schönen Himmel, den sie kurz befliegen
Dass also keiner länger hier verweile
Und keines andres sehe als das Wiegen
Des andern in dem Wind, den beide spüren
Die jetzt im Fluge beieinander liegen
So mag der Wind sie in das Nichts entführen
Wenn sie nur nicht vergehen und sich bleiben
Solange kann sie beide nichts berühren
Solange kann man sie von jedem Ort vertreiben
Wo Regen drohen oder Schüsse schallen.
So unter Sonn und Monds wenig verschiedenen
       Scheiben
Fliegen sie hin, einander ganz verfallen.
Wohin, ihr?—Nirgend hin.—Von wem davon?—
       Von allen.
Ihr fragt, wie lange sind sie schon beisammen?
Seit kurzem.—Und wann werden sie sich trennen?
       —Bald.
So scheint die Liebe Liebenden ein Halt.[9]

THE LOVERS

Cranes on the wing, what a sight!
And the clouds that follow light as a feather
Drawn along when they first took flight
Out of one life and into another.
Matching height and speed as a pair
They seem to be alone together
If only crane and cloud can share
The beautiful sky where they're winging
Even if neither may linger there
Seeing nothing but the other's swinging
Feeling the wind and one another
Lying close while lightly soaring
If only they last and stay with each other
Seduced by the wind, aware of nothing
Then for a while they can't be bothered
Wherever there's rain or rifles shooting
Then they'll be driven by foul weather
Under the eyes of sun and moon
So they'll fly soaring together.
Where' you going?
       Nowhere.
              Away from whom?
                     From all.

---

[9] *Gedichte,* vol. II (Frankfurt: Suhrkamp, 1960), p. 210. Erich Kahler and Theodor W. Adorno have revealed the significance of this poem. See Adorno, *Aesthetische Theorie* (Frankfurt/Main: Suhrkamp, 1970), p. 123.

How long ago they discovered each other?
Not long.
                When will it be over?
                          Soon.
      That's how love looks to lovers—high noon.
                    [Translation by James A. Ogilvy]

The image of liberation is in the flight of the cranes, through their beautiful sky, with the clouds which accompany them: sky and clouds belong to them—without mastery and domination. The image is in their ability to flee the spaces where they are threatened: the rain and the rifle shots. They are safe as long as they remain themselves, entirely with each other. The image is a vanishing one: the wind can take them into nothingness—they would still be safe: they fly from one life into another life. Time itself matters no longer: the cranes met only a short while ago, and they will leave each other soon. Space is no longer a limit: they fly nowhere, and they flee from everyone, from all. The end is illusion: love *seems* to give duration, to conquer time and space, to evade destruction. But the illusion cannot deny the reality which it invokes: the cranes *are,* in their sky, with their clouds. The end is also denial of the illusion, insistence on its reality, realization. This insistence is in the poem's language which is prose becoming verse and song in the midst of the brutality and corruption of the *Netzestadt* (Mahagonny)—in the dialogue between a whore and a bum. There is no word in this poem which is not prose. But these words are joined to sentences, or parts of sentences which say and show what ordinary language never says and shows. The apparent "protocol statements," which seem to describe things and movements in direct perception, turn into images of that which goes beyond all direct perception: the flight into the realm of freedom which is also the realm of beauty.

Strange phenomenon: beauty as a quality which is in an opera of Verdi as well as in a Bob Dylan song, in a painting of Ingres as well as Picasso, in phrase of Flaubert as well as James Joyce, in a gesture of the Duchess of Guermantes as well as of a hippie girl! Common to all of them is the expression, against its plastic deerotization, of beauty as negation of the commodity world and of the performances, attitudes, looks, gestures, required by it.

The aesthetic form will continue to change as the political practice succeeds (or fails) to build a better society. At the optimum, we can envisage a universe common to art and reality, but in this common universe, art would retain its transcendence. In all likelihood, people would not talk or write or compose poetry; *la prose du monde* would persist. The "end of art" is conceivable only if men are no longer capable of distinguishing between true and false, good and evil, beautiful and ugly, present and future. This would be the state of perfect barbarism at the height of civilization—and such a state is indeed a historical possibility.

Art can do nothing to prevent the ascent of barbarism—it cannot by itself keep open its own domain in and against society. For its own preservation and development, art depends on the struggle for the abolition of the social system which generates barbarism as its own potential stage: potential form of its progress. The fate of art remains linked to that of the revolution. In this sense, it is indeed an internal exigency of art which drives the artist to the streets—to fight for the Commune, for the Bolshevist revolution, for the German revolution of 1918, for the Chinese and Cuban revolutions, for all revolutions which have the historical chance of liberation. But in doing so he leaves the universe of art and enters the larger universe of which art remains an antagonistic part: that of radical practice.

Today's cultural revolution places anew on the agenda the problems of a Marxist aesthetics. In the preceding sections, I tried to make a tentative contribution to this subject; an adequate discussion would require another book. But one specific question must again be raised in this context, namely, the meaning, and the very possibility, of a "proletarian literature" (or working-class literature). In my view, the discussion has never again reached the theoretical level it attained in the twenties and early thirties, especially in the controversy between Georg Lukács, Johannes R. Becher and Andor Gabor on the one side, and Bertolt Brecht, Walter Benjamin, Hanns Eisler and Ernst Bloch on the other. The discussion during this period is recorded and reexamined in Helga Gallas' excellent book *Marxistische Literaturtheorie*.[10]

All protagonists accept the central concept according to which art (the discussion is practically confined to literature) is determined, in its "truth content" as well as in its forms, by the class situation of the author (of course not simply in terms of his personal position and consciousness but of the objective correspondence of his work to the material and ideological position of the class). The conclusion which emerges from this discussion is that at the historical stage where the position of the proletariat alone renders possible insight into the totality of the social process, and into the necessity and direction of radical change (i.e., into "the truth"), only a proletarian literature can fulfill the progressive function of art and develop a revolutionary consciousness: indispensable weapon in the class struggle.

Can such a literature arise in the traditional forms of art, or will it develop new forms and techniques? This is the case of the controversy: while Lukács (and with him the then "official" Communist line) insists on the validity of the (revamped) tradition (especially the great realistic novel of the nineteenth century), Brecht demands radically different forms (such as the "epic theater") and Benjamin calls for the transition from the art form itself to such new technical expressions as the film: "large, closed forms versus small, open forms."

In a sense, the confrontation between closed and open forms seems no longer an adequate expression of the problem: compared with today's

---

[10] (Neuwied: Luchterhand, 1971).

antiart, Brecht's open forms appear as "traditional" literature. The problem is rather the underlying concept of a *proletarian world view* which, by virtue of its (particular) class character, represents the truth which art must communicate if it is to be authentic art. This theory

> presupposes the existence of a proletarian world view. But precisely this presupposition does not stand up to an even tentative [*annähernde*] examination.[11]

This is a statement of fact—and a theoretical insight. If the term "proletarian world view" is to mean the world view that is prevalent among the working class, then it is, in the advanced capitalist countries, a world view shared by a large part of the other classes, especially the middle classes. (In ritualized Marxist language, it would be called petty bourgeois reformist consciousness.) If the term is to designate *revolutionary* consciousness (latent or actual), then it is today certainly not distinctively or even predominantly "proletarian"—not only because the revolution against global monopoly capitalism is more and other than a proletarian revolution, but also because its conditions, prospects and goals cannot be adequately formulated in terms of a proletarian revolution. And if this revolution is to be (in whatever form) present as a goal in literature, such literature could not be typically proletarian.

This is at least the conclusion suggested by Marxian theory. I recall again the dialectic of the universal and the particular in the concept of the proletariat: as a class in but not of capitalist society, its particular interest (its own liberation) is at the same time the general interest: it cannot free itself without abolishing itself as a class, and all classes. This is not an "ideal," but the very dynamic of the socialist revolution. It follows that the goals of the proletariat *as revolutionary class* are self-transcendent: while remaining historical concrete goals, they extend, in their class content, beyond the specific class content. And if such transcendence is an essential quality of all art, it follows that the goals of the revolution may find expression in bourgeois art, and in all forms of art. It seems to be more than a matter of personal preference if Marx had a conservative taste in art and Trotsky, as well as Lenin, was critical of the notion of a "proletarian culture."[12]

It is therefore no paradox, and no exception, when even specifically proletarian contents find their home in "bourgeois literature." They are often accompanied by a kind of linguistic revolution, which replaces the language of the ruling class by that of the proletariat—without exploding the traditional form (of the novel, the drama). Or, conversely, the proletarian revolutionary contents are formed in the "high," stylized language of (tradi-

[11] Ibid., p. 73.

[12] Gallas, Ibid., p. 210 f.

tional) poetry: as in Brecht's *Three Penny Opera* and *Mahagonny* and in the "artistic" prose of his *Galilei.*

The spokesmen for a specifically proletarian literature tried to save this notion by establishing a sweeping criterion that would allow them to reject the "reformist" bourgeois radicals, namely, the appearance, in the work, of the basic laws which govern capitalist society. Lukács himself made this the shibboleth by which to identify authentic revolutionary literature. But precisely this requirement offends the very nature of art. The basic structure and dynamic of society can never find sensuous, aesthetic expression: they are, in Marxian theory, the essence behind the appearance, which can only be attained through scientific analysis, and formulated only in the terms of such an analysis. The "open form" cannot close the gap between the scientific truth and its aesthetic appearance. The introduction, into the play or the novel, of montage, documentation, reportage may well (as in Brecht) become an essential part of the aesthetic form—but it can do so only as a subordinate part.

Art can indeed become a weapon in the class struggle by promoting changes in the prevailing consciousness. However, the cases where a transparent correlation exists between the respective *class* consciousness and the work of art are extremely rare (Molière, Beaumarchais, Defoe). By virtue of its own subversive quality, art is associated with revolutionary consciousness, but to the degree to which the prevailing consciousness of a class is affirmative, integrated, blunted, revolutionary art will be opposed to it. Where the proletariat is nonrevolutionary, revolutionary literature will *not* be proletarian literature. Nor can it be "anchored" in the prevailing ("nonrevolutionary") consciousness: only the *rupture,* the *leap,* can prevent the resurrection of the "false" consciousness in a socialist society.

The fallacies which surround the notion of a revolutionary literature are still aggravated in today's cultural revolution. The antiintellectualism rampant in the New Left champions the demand for a working-class literature which expresses the worker's actual interests and "emotions." For example:

"Intellectual pundits of the Left" are blamed for their "revolutionary aesthetic," and a "certain coterie of talmudists" is taken to task for being more "expert in weighing the many shadings and nuances of a word than involvement in the revolutionary process."[13] Archaic antiintellectualism abhors the idea that the former may be an essential part of the latter, part of that translation of the world into a new language which may communicate the radically new claims of liberation.

Such spokesmen for the proletarian ideology criticize the cultural revolution as a "middle-class trip." The philistine mind is at its very best when it proclaims that this revolution will "become meaningful" only "when it begins to understand the very real cultural meaning that a washing machine, for instance, has for a working class family with small children in diapers." And the philistine mind demands that "the artists of that revolution . . .

13 Irvin Silber, in *Guardian,* December 13, 1969.

tune in on the emotions of that family on the day, after months of debate and planning, that the washing machine is delivered. . . ."[14]

This demand is reactionary not only from an artistic but also from a political point of view. Regressive is, not the emotion of the working-class family, but the idea to make them into a standard for authentic radical and socialist literature: what is proclaimed to be the focal point of a revolutionary new culture is in fact the adjustment to the established one.

To be sure, the cultural revolution must recognize and subvert this atmosphere of the working-class home, but this will not be done by "tuning in" on the emotions aroused by the delivery of a washing machine. On the contrary, such empathy perpetuates the prevailing "atmosphere."

The concept of proletarian literature = revolutionary literature remains questionable even if it is freed from the "tuning in" on *prevailing* emotions, and, instead, related to the most *advanced* working-class consciousness. This would be a political consciousness, and prevalent only among a minority of the working class. If art and literature would reflect such advanced consciousness, they would have to express the actual conditions of the class struggle and the actual prospects of subverting the capitalist system. But precisely these brutally political contents *militate* against their aesthetic transformation—therefore the very valid objection against "pure art." However, these contents also militate against a less pure translation into art, namely, the translation into the concreteness of the daily life and practice. Lukács has, on these grounds, criticized a representative workers' novel of the time: the personages of this novel talk at the dinner table at home the same language as a delegate at a party meeting.[15]

A revolutionary literature in which the working class is the subject-object, and which is the historical heir, the definite negation, of "bourgeois" literature, remains a thing of the future.

But what holds true for the notion of revolutionary art with respect to the working classes in the advanced capitalist countries does not apply to the situation of the racial minorities in these countries, and the majorities in the Third World. I have already referred to black music; there is also a black literature, especially poetry, which may well be called revolutionary: it lends voice to a total rebellion which finds expression in the aesthetic form. It is not a "class" literature, and its particular content is at the same time the universal one: what is at stake in the specific situation of the oppressed racial minority is the most general of all needs, namely, the very existence of the individual and his group as human beings. The most extreme political content does not repel traditional forms.

[14] Irvin Silber, in *Guardian,* December 6, 1969, p. 17.

[15] Gallas, *loc. cit.,* p. 121. A Communist participant in the discussion remarked correctly that in this case one should call things by their name and speak not of art or literature but of propaganda.

7 The Community of Man and Cosmos

Introduction:
On Relating
to the
Divine

A good deal of philosophy of religion deals with various proofs for the existence of God and the philosophical criticism of those proofs. The philosophy is interesting, but as far as the existence of God is concerned, who cares? Blasphemy? Not so. Existence is not the issue, at least not in the sense of whether God exists the way the moon exists—as a particular entity apart from this world, accessible only to some.

Here again the fate of the underlying subject, or the "ghost in the machine," is instructive. In denying the existence of the ghost in the machine Ryle is not denying the existence of selves. Similarly, in denying the existence of God some theologians are not denying the dimension of divinity in our lives. They are simply saying that we have been relating to that divinity in the wrong way. We have been asking the wrong questions and expecting the wrong **kind** of answers. Even in talking about "God" we may be individualizing the dimension of the divine too much, just as we are inclined to simplify the many interrelated processes of the self into a single substance called the "subject." Consequently, a leading twentieth-century theologian, Karl Barth, writes that whenever we use the name "God" we are talking about the not-God. Our use of language fools us. We feel gratitude and we know how to give thanks only when we are giving thanks to someone. But that is **our** shortcoming. So in saying that the existence of God is not the point, contemporary theologians are not denying the appropriateness of the feeling of gratitude, only that we may be confused in the way we **express** our feelings.

Though a theological disinterest in the existence of God would seem to be a correlate of the relatively recent and much publicized "death of God" theology, many modern theologians have denied that the existence of God is a central issue. As Martin Buber put it, after Auschwitz the question is not whether God exists but whether we can pray to him. Here again the question is one of the appropriate expression of our relationship to something divine.

Just as twentieth-century developments in esthetics reflect an upheaval in the Platonic-Christian metaphysical tradition, so twentieth-century theology reflects that same upheaval. If the quest for truth is no longer a quest for a reality that art can find **beneath** the veil of illusion, then theology no longer looks for a God who stands **above and apart from** worldly appearances. Just as Nietzsche anticipates Ryle's purge of the ghost in his claim that the soul is something about the body, so modern theology could claim that God is something about the world. In the language of theology this point is usually put using the terms 'immanence' and 'transcendence': the traditional, transcendent God existed beyond or apart from human experience. To say that God is immanent is to say that he pervades our experience. But the theology of immanence naturally finds it easier to talk about the divine aspect of experience and not about a God whose particularity as a "person" renders the pervasiveness of immanence difficult to conceive.

So rather than worship or thank or pray to a particular, transcendent God, modern theology tends to reflect upon the divine within experience. The so-called death of the transcendent God is not equivalent to a secularization of experience. Quite the contrary. If the transcendent God stood like a single star above the flat horizon of secular existence, the new theology might look to some like an atheism that simply banishes that star from the heavens. A more careful reading shows that the new theology replaces the old picture with a "vertical" existence stretching from the mysteries of demonology to the marvels of the sacred. The theology of immanence transfigures the horizon of secularism into a tower of sacred-profane existence. And this transfiguration has very little to do with the existence of God, except perhaps as a convenient but misleading way of talking about the sacredness of that existence.

This new way of talking about religion renders a continuity with the other issues of philosophy much more plausible. In talking about religion we are not talking about any new entities, but about a new way of seeing the same things we have been talking about all along. It almost sounds like esthetics. And certainly some of the language of the Bible suggests the appropriateness of this new way: "those who have eyes to see . . ." Thus the question of belief or faith becomes a question of the mode of one's relationship to experience and not one of the existence of some object that may or may not be encountered within or beyond experience. Consequently, the whole grammar of the terms 'belief' and 'faith' tends to be misleading, since we usually take belief as belief **in** something and faith as faith **in** something, where the something is just the sort of object which the theology of immanence has rejected. To use Ryle's example of a Category-mistake, if you have seen all the particular buildings of a university and then ask to see the university, must you have faith in the university once you have been told you cannot see it the way you can see its buildings? To relate to the university is to relate to what goes on in its buildings. What about someone who claims to have faith in the university but never goes to classes? How is that person like many who profess belief in God?

The turn to eastern religions is consistent with the new religious spirit because Buddhism and Taoism are in general less preoccupied with God than are the western religions. The eastern religions place a greater emphasis on the self and those states of consciousness and modes of activity that put one in relation to the cosmos. Yet we could hardly accuse the eastern religions of secularism; religious experience is a central element in their path to enlightenment. What is needed is a definition of the religious that does not depend on God for its meaning. Then it will be clear that a denial of transcendent Gods is not a denial of religion.

SØREN KIERKEGAARD

(1813-1855)

Søren Kierkegaard lived and died in Denmark, during the years 1813 to 1855, to be precise. Yet he would be the first to point out the paradox of such precision. What does such objective precision matter, measured against his contemporaneity as perhaps the first truly existentialist philosopher and his quest for an eternal happiness against which historical dates seem irrelevant? Kierkegaard's life was dominated by the most intense experiences of paradox. He broke off an engagement with a girl he loved and then suffered as he saw her quickly take another man. And his writings are filled with images of paradox: the king who loves a peasant girl but knows that he cannot appear to her as the king without foredooming all hopes of a loving relationship; the mother who blackens her breast to wean the baby she cherishes. Always in the background of Kierkegaard's tortured and passionate thought looms the specter of paradox: I must, but I cannot. And this paradox is nowhere more intense than in Kierkegaard's relation to God.

Disgusted by the ease with which his contemporaries paraded into church, Kierkegaard was at pains to point out the follies of popular theology. Kierkegaard believed passionately, which to him was the **only** way to believe. Otherwise one was simply holding opinions about objective truths, and religion has little to do with

objective truths. Kierkegaard held in contempt the calm assurances concerning the completeness of the "system" advertised
by the Danish Hegelians. Against dialectical mediations of extremes, Kierkegaard demanded his readers to face radical choices.
One of his most famous books is titled **Either/Or.**

Reading Kierkegaard is difficult. His language is perfectly intelligible—indeed he is a master stylist—but he poses alternatives
that are difficult to accept, which was precisely his intention. It is
hard to accept the apparent irrationalism of his leap of faith, to
accept a subjectivism that, in the extreme form Kierkegaard develops it, seems a close cousin to a socially and spiritually destructive individualism. Yet I keep reading Kierkegaard and try to
accommodate his insights. I sweep away his objections to the
Danish Hegelians with the Hegelian reflection that Kierkegaard's
thought is the next important turn in the dialectic after Hegel
synthesized its progress up to the advent of Kierkegaard. Kierkegaard then becomes the subjective negation of the objective totality in Hegel's dialectic, symbolizing that part in each of us that
must ask, "So what?" What is it to me, an existing individual, that
all the relationships in the cosmos have been objectively drawn
and understood? How do these "truths" relate to me? And then,
of course, a synthesis between Kierkegaardian subjectivism and
Hegelian objectivism should follow. But before we can proceed to
that synthesis, Kierkegaard is there crying out, "I will not be synthesized! I will not be mediated! If you synthesize me with Hegel
it cannot be me you have synthesized!" So we are thrust back into
Kierkegaard's finality of objective uncertainty. And perhaps this
objective uncertainty is the only legitimate synthesis. Certainly
Kierkegaard is the last one to be offering us objective truths; he
leaves the questions relentlessly up to the reader.

In order to do battle with Kierkegaard's demands, think about
some previous essays as you read Kierkegaard. First is the issue
of individualism raised in the first four essays. Recall the distinction, discussed in connection with Marin's essay, between the kind
of individualism attacked by Slater and the concern for persons as
persons expressed by Marin. Next, on the issue of subjectivism,
review the essays by James and Polanyi, and Laing's "Politics of
Experience." Kierkegaard's essay can help formulate a real difference between possessive individualism on the one hand and what
I still think we can call an objective relativism. Here Kierkegaard's
contribution is to make us see that truths must **relate** to the subject, even if they are relative to more than the subject. Even the
most complete system of self-awareness is always seen from some
perspective. If we lose sight of the perspective, the existing individual, we fall into error.

Truth Is Subjectivity

*When the question of truth is raised
in an objective manner, reflection is directed objectively to the truth, as an
object to which the knower is related. Reflection is not focussed upon the
relationship, however, but upon the question of whether it is the truth to
which the knower is related. If only the object to which he is related is the
truth, the subject is accounted to be in the truth. When the question of the
truth is raised subjectively, reflection is directed subjectively to the nature
of the individual's relationship; if only the mode of this relationship is in
the truth, the individual is in the truth even if he should happen to be thus
related to what is not true.*[1] Let us take as an example the knowledge of
God. Objectively, reflection is directed to the problem of whether this object is the true God; subjectively, reflection is directed to the question
whether the individual is related to a something *in such a manner* that his
relationship is in truth a God-relationship. On which side is the truth now
to be found? Ah, may we not here resort to a mediation, and say: It is on
neither side, but in the mediation of both? Excellently well said, provided
we might have it explained how an existing individual manages to be in a
state of mediation. For to be in a state of mediation is to be finished, while
to exist is to become. Nor can an existing individual be in two places at
the same time—he cannot be an identity of subject and object. When he is
nearest to being in two places at the same time he is in passion; but passion
is momentary, and passion is also the highest expression of subjectivity.

The existing individual who chooses to pursue the objective way enters
upon the entire approximation-process by which it is proposed to bring
God to light objectively. But this is in all eternity impossible, because God
is a subject, and therefore exists only for subjectivity in inwardness. The
existing individual who chooses the subjective way apprehends instantly the
entire dialectical difficulty involved in having to use some time, perhaps a
long time, in finding God objectively; and he feels this dialectical difficulty
in all its painfulness, because every moment is wasted in which he does not
have God.[2] That very instant he has God, not by virtue of any objective

---

TRUTH IS SUBJECTIVITY From Søren Kierkegaard, *Concluding Unscientific Post-
script,* translated by David F. Swenson and Walter Lowrie (Copyright 1941 © 1969
by Princeton University Press; Princeton Paperback, 1968), pp. 178–182, 186–188,
and 218–220. Reprinted by permission of Princeton University Press and the American Scandinavian Foundation.

[1] The reader will observe that the question here is about essential truth, or about the
truth which is essentially related to existence, and that it is precisely for the sake of
clarifying it as inwardness or as subjectivity that this contrast is drawn.

[2] In this manner God certainly becomes a postulate, but not in the otiose manner in
which this word is commonly understood. It becomes clear rather that the only way
in which an existing individual comes into relation with God, is when the dialectical
contradiction brings his passion to the point of despair, and helps him to embrace
God with the "category of despair" (faith). Then the postulate is so far from being

deliberation, but by virtue of the infinite passion of inwardness. The objective inquirer, on the other hand, is not embarrassed by such dialectical difficulties as are involved in devoting an entire period of investigation to finding God—since it is possible that the inquirer may die tomorrow; and if he lives he can scarcely regard God as something to be taken along if convenient, since God is precisely that which one takes *a tout prix,* which in the understanding of passion constitutes the true inward relationship to God.

It is at this point, so difficult dialectically, that the way swings off for everyone who knows what it means to think, and to think existentially; which is something very different from sitting at a desk and writing about what one has never done, something very different from writing *de omnibus dubitandum* [doubt everything] and at the same time being as credulous existentially as the most sensuous of men. Here is where the way swings off, and the change is marked by the fact that while objective knowledge rambles comfortably on by way of the long road of approximation without being impelled by the urge of passion, subjective knowledge counts every delay a deadly peril, and the decision so infinitely important and so instantly pressing that it is as if the opportunity had already passed.

Now when the problem is to reckon up on which side there is most truth, whether on the side of one who seeks the true God objectively, and pursues the approximate truth of the God-idea; or on the side of one who, driven by the infinite passion of his need of God, feels an infinite concern for his own relationship to God in truth (and to be at one and the same time on both sides equally, is as we have noted not possible for an existing individual, but is merely the happy delusion of an imaginary I-am-I): the answer cannot be in doubt for anyone who has not been demoralized with the aid of science. If one who lives in the midst of Christendom goes up to the house of God, the house of the true God, with the true conception of God in his knowledge, and prays, but prays in a false spirit; and one who lives in an idolatrous community prays with the entire passion of the infinite, although his eyes rest upon the image of an idol: where is there most truth? The one prays in truth to God though he worships an idol; the other prays falsely to the true God, and hence worships in fact an idol.

When one man investigates objectively the problem of immortality, and another embraces an uncertainty with the passion of the infinite: where is there most truth, and who has the greater certainty? The one has entered upon a never-ending approximation, for the certainty of immortality lies precisely in the subjectivity of the individual; the other is immortal, and fights for his immortality by struggling with the uncertainty. Let us consider Socrates. Nowadays everyone dabbles in a few proofs; some have several such proofs, others fewer. But Socrates! He puts the question objectively in a problematic manner: *if* there is an immortality. He must therefore be ac-

---

arbitrary that it is precisely a life-necessity. It is then not so much that God is a postulate, as that the existing individual's postulation of God is a necessity.

counted a doubter in comparison with one of our modern thinkers with the three proofs? By no means. On this "if" he risks his entire life, he has the courage to meet death, and he has with the passion of the infinite so determined the pattern of his life that it must be found acceptable—*if* there is an immortality. Is any better proof capable of being given for the immortality of the soul? But those who have the three proofs do not at all determine their lives in conformity therewith; if there is an immortality it must feel disgust over their manner of life: can any better refutation be given of the three proofs? The bit of uncertainty that Socrates had, helped him because he himself contributed the passion of the infinite; the three proofs that the others have do not profit them at all, because they are dead to spirit and enthusiasm, and their three proofs, in lieu of proving anything else, prove just this. A young girl may enjoy all the sweetness of love on the basis of what is merely a weak hope that she is beloved, because she rests everything on this weak hope; but many a wedded matron more than once subjected to the strongest expressions of love, has in so far indeed had proofs, but strangely enough has not enjoyed *quod erat demonstrandum* [that which was to be proven]. The Socratic ignorance, which Socrates held fast with the entire passion of his inwardness, was thus an expression for the principle that the eternal truth is related to an existing individual, and that this truth must therefore be a paradox for him as long as he exists; and yet it is possible that there was more truth in the Socratic ignorance as it was in him, than in the entire objective truth of the System, which flirts with what the times demand and accommodates itself to *Privatdocents*.

The objective accent falls on WHAT is said, the subjective accent on HOW it is said. This distinction holds even in the aesthetic realm, and receives definite expression in the principle that what is in itself true may in the mouth of such and such a person become untrue. In these times this distinction is particularly worthy of notice, for if we wish to express in a single sentence the difference between ancient times and our own, we should doubtless have to say: "In ancient times only an individual here and there knew the truth; now all know it, except that the inwardness of its appropriation stands in an inverse relationship to the extent of its dissemination.[3] Aesthetically the contradiction that truth becomes untruth in this

---

[3] *Stages on Life's Way,* Note on p. 426. Though ordinarily not wishing an expression of opinion on the part of reviewers, I might at this point almost desire it, provided such opinions, so far from flattering me, amounted to an assertion of the daring truth that what I say is something that everybody knows, even every child, and that the cultured know infinitely much better. If it only stands fast that everyone knows it, my standpoint is in order, and I shall doubtless make shift to manage with the unity of the comic and the tragic. If there were anyone who did not know it I might perhaps be in danger of being dislodged from my position of equilibrium by the thought that I might be in a position to communicate to someone the needful preliminary knowledge. It is just this which engages my interest so much, this that the cultured are accustomed to say: that everyone knows what the highest is. This was not the case in paganism, nor in Judaism, nor in the seventeen centuries of Christianity. Hail to the nineteenth century! Everyone knows it. What progress has been made since the time when only a few knew it. To make up for this, perhaps, we must assume that no one nowadays does it.

or that person's mouth, is best construed comically: In the ethico-religious sphere, accent is again on the "how." But this is not to be understood as referring to demeanor, expression, or the like; rather it refers to the relationship sustained by the existing individual, in his own existence, to the content of his utterance. Objectively the interest is focussed merely on the thought-content, subjectively on the inwardness. At its maximum this inward "how" is the passion of the infinite, and the passion of the infinite is the truth. But the passion of the infinite is precisely subjectivity, and thus subjectivity becomes the truth. Objectively there is no infinite decisiveness, and hence it is objectively in order to annul the difference between good and evil; together with the principle of contradiction, and therewith also the infinite difference between the true and the false. Only in subjectivity is there decisiveness, to seek objectivity is to be in error. It is the passion of the infinite that is the decisive factor and not its content, for its content is precisely itself. In this manner subjectivity and the subjective "how" constitute the truth.

But the "how" which is thus subjectively accentuated precisely because the subject is an existing individual, is also subject to a dialectic with respect to time. In the passionate moment of decision, where the road swings away from objective knowledge, it seems as if the infinite decision were thereby realized. But in the same moment the existing individual finds himself in the temporal order, and the subjective "how" is transformed into a striving, a striving which receives indeed its impulse and a repeated renewal from the decisive passion of the infinite, but is nevertheless a striving.

When subjectivity is the truth, the conceptual determination of the truth must include an expression for the antithesis to objectivity, a memento of the fork in the road where the way swings off; this expression will at the same time serve as an indication of the tension of the subjective inwardness. Here is such a definition of truth: *An objective uncertainty held fast in an appropriation-process of the most passionate inwardness is the truth,* the highest truth attainable for an *existing* individual. At the point where the way swings off (and where this is cannot be specified objectively, since it is a matter of subjectivity), there objective knowledge is placed in abeyance. Thus the subject merely has, objectively, the uncertainty; but it is this which precisely increases the tension of that infinite passion which constitutes his inwardness. The truth is precisely the venture which chooses an objective uncertainty with the passion of the infinite. I contemplate the order of nature in the hope of finding God, and I see omnipotence and wisdom; but I also see much else that disturbs my mind and excites anxiety. The sum of all this is an objective uncertainty. But it is for this very reason that the inwardness becomes as intense as it is, for it embraces this objective uncertainty with the entire passion of the infinite. In the case of a mathematical proposition the objectivity is given, but for this reason the truth of such a proposition is also an indifferent truth.

But the above definition of truth is an equivalent expression for faith. Without risk there is no faith. Faith is precisely the contradiction between the infinite passion of the individual's inwardness and the objective uncertainty. If I am capable of grasping God objectively, I do not believe, but precisely because I cannot do this I must believe. If I wish to preserve myself in faith I must constantly be intent upon holding fast the objective uncertainty, so as to remain out upon the deep, over seventy thousand fathoms of water, still preserving my faith. [. . .]

Let us now call the untruth of the individual *Sin*. Viewed eternally he cannot be sin, nor can he be eternally presupposed as having been in sin. By coming into existence therefore (for the beginning was that subjectivity is untruth), he becomes a sinner. He is not born as a sinner in the sense that he is presupposed as being a sinner before he is born, but he is born in sin and as a sinner. This we might call *Original Sin*. But if existence has in this manner acquired a power over him, he is prevented from taking himself back into the eternal by way of recollection. If it was paradoxical to posit the eternal truth in relationship to an existing individual, it is now absolutely paradoxical to posit it in relationship to such an individual as we have here defined. But the more difficult it is made for him to take himself out of existence by way of recollection, the more profound is the inwardness that his existence may have in existence; and when it is made impossible for him, when he is held so fast in existence that the back door of recollection is forever closed to him, then his inwardness will be the most profound possible. But let us never forget that the Socratic merit was to stress the fact that the knower is an existing individual; for the more difficult the matter becomes, the greater the temptation to hasten along the easy road of speculation, away from fearful dangers and crucial decisions, to the winning of renown and honors and property, and so forth. If even Socrates understood the dubiety of taking himself speculatively out of existence back into the eternal, although no other difficulty confronted the existing individual except that he existed, and that existing was his essential task, now it is impossible. Forward he must, backward he cannot go.

Subjectivity is the truth. By virtue of the relationship subsisting between the eternal truth and the existing individual, the paradox came into being. Let us now go further, let us suppose that the eternal essential truth is itself a paradox. How does the paradox come into being? By putting the eternal essential truth into juxtaposition with existence. Hence when we posit such a conjunction within the truth itself, the truth becomes a paradox. The eternal truth has come into being in time: this is the paradox. If in accordance with the determinations just posited, the subject is prevented by sin from taking himself back into the eternal, now he need not trouble himself about this; for now the eternal essential truth is not behind him but in front of him, through its being in existence or having existed, so that if the individual does not existentially and in existence lay hold of the truth, he will never lay hold of it.

Existence can never be more sharply accentuated than by means of these determinations. The evasion by which speculative philosophy attempts to recollect itself out of existence has been made impossible. With reference to this, there is nothing for speculation to do except to arrive at an understanding of this impossibility; every speculative attempt which insists on being speculative shows *eo ipso* that it has not understood it. The individual may thrust all this away from him, and take refuge in speculation; but it is impossible first to accept it, and then to revoke it by means of speculation, since it is definitely calculated to prevent speculation.

When the eternal truth is related to an existing individual it becomes a paradox. The paradox repels in the inwardness of the existing individual, through the objective uncertainty and the corresponding Socratic ignorance. But since the paradox is not in the first instance itself paradoxical (but only in its relationship to the existing individual), it does not repel with a sufficient intensive inwardness. For without risk there is no faith, and the greater the risk the greater the faith; the more objective security the less inwardness (for inwardness is precisely subjectivity), and the less objective security the more profound the possible inwardness. When the paradox is paradoxical in itself, it repels the individual by virtue of its absurdity, and the corresponding passion of inwardness is faith. But subjectivity, inwardness, is the truth; for otherwise we have forgotten what the merit of the Socratic position is. But there can be no stronger expression for inwardness than when the retreat out of existence into the eternal by way of recollection is impossible; and when, with truth confronting the individual as a paradox, gripped in the anguish and pain of sin, facing the tremendous risk of the objective insecurity, the individual believes. But without risk no faith, not even the Socratic form of faith, much less the form of which we here speak.

When Socrates believed that there was a God, he held fast to the objective uncertainty with the whole passion of his inwardness, and it is precisely in this contradiction and in this risk, that faith is rooted. Now it is otherwise. Instead of the objective uncertainty, there is here a certainty, namely, that objectively it is absurd; and this absurdity, held fast in the passion of inwardness, is faith. The Socratic ignorance is as a witty jest in comparison with the earnestness of facing the absurd; and the Socratic existential inwardness is as Greek light-mindedness in comparison with the grave strenuosity of faith.

What now is the absurd? The absurd is—that the eternal truth has come into being in time, that God has come into being, has been born, has grown up, and so forth, precisely like any other individual human being, quite indistinguishable from other individuals. For every assumption of immediate recognizability is pre-Socratic paganism. [. . .]

The immediate relationship to God is paganism, and only after the breach has taken place can there be any question of a true God-relationship. But this breach is precisely the first act of inwardness in the direction of determining the truth as inwardness. Nature is, indeed, the work of God, but only the handiwork is directly present, not God. Is not this to behave, in His relationship to the individual, like an elusive author who nowhere sets down his result in large type, or gives it to the reader beforehand in a preface? And why is God elusive? Precisely because He is the truth, and by being elusive desires to keep men from error. The observer of nature does not have a result immediately set before him, but must by himself be at pains to find it, and thereby the direct relationship is broken. But this breach is precisely the act of self-activity, the irruption of inwardness, the first determination of the truth as inwardness.

Or is not God so unnoticeable, so secretly present in His works, that a man might very well live his entire life, be married, become known and respected as citizen, father, and captain of the hunt, without ever having discovered God in His works, and without ever having received any impression of the infinitude of the ethical, because he helped himself out with what constitutes an analogy to the speculative confusion of the ethical with the historical process, in that he helped himself out by having recourse to the customs and traditions prevailing in the town where he happened to live? As a mother admonishes her child when it sets off for a party: "Now be sure to behave yourself, and do as you see the other well-behaved children do,"—so he might manage to live by conducting himself as he sees others do. He would never do anything first, and he would never have any opinion which he did not first know that others had; for this "others" would be for him the first. Upon extraordinary occasions he would behave as when at a banquet a dish is served, and one does not know how it should be eaten: he would look around until he saw how the others did it, and so forth. Such a man might perhaps know many things, perhaps even know the System by rote; he might be an inhabitant of a Christian country, and bow his head whenever the name of God was mentioned; he would perhaps also see God in nature when in company with others who saw God; he would be a pleasant society man—and yet he would have been deceived by the direct nature of his relationship to the truth, to the ethical, and to God.

If one were to delineate such a man experimentally, he would be a satire upon the human. Essentially it is the God-relationship that makes a man a man, and yet he lacked this. No one would hesitate, however, to regard him as a real man (for the absence of inwardness is not directly apparent); in reality he would constitute a sort of marionette, very deceptively imitating everything human—even to the extent of having children by his wife. At the end of his life, one would have to say that one thing had escaped him: his consciousness had taken no note of God. If God could have permitted a direct relationship, he would doubtless have taken notice. If God, for example, had taken on the figure of a very rare and tremendously large green bird, with a red beak, sitting in a tree on the mound, and perhaps even whistling in an unheard of manner—then the society man would have been able to get his eyes open, and for the first time in his life would be first.

All paganism consists in this, that God is related to man directly, as the obviously extraordinary to the astonished observer. But the spiritual relationship to God in the truth, i.e. in inwardness, is conditioned by a prior irruption of inwardness, which corresponds to the divine elusiveness that God has absolutely nothing obvious about Him, that God is so far from being obvious that He is invisible. It cannot immediately occur to anyone that He exists, although His invisibility is again His omnipresence. An omnipresent person is one that is everywhere to be seen, like a policeman, for example: how deceptive then, that an omnipresent being should be recognizable precisely by being invisible,[4] only and alone recognizable by this trait, since his visibility would annul his omnipresence. The relationship between omnipresence and invisibility is like the relation between mystery and revelation. The mystery is the expression for the fact that the revelation is a revelation in the stricter sense, so that the mystery is the only trait by which it is known; for otherwise a revelation would be something very like a policeman's omnipresence.

FRIEDRICH NIETZSCHE
(1844-1900)

Many of us, when we first read Friedrich Nietzsche, misread him. The idiosyncratic German philosopher lends himself to misinterpretation, as his use by the Nazis bears evidence. At times he sounds like a bitter old man who lashes out at whatever feelings he is incapable of having. But a more attentive reading shows Nietzsche to be a more discerning judge than the cantankerous cynic we may first take him to be. For instance, he does not condemn **everything** about Christianity, just most things. He distinguishes various grades of authenticity in the Christian experience. Christ comes off very well, the apostles less well, the priests poorly, and those in the pews are the butt of his worst scorn. Nietzsche favors leaders rather than followers, as in his respect for Christ despite his scouring criticisms of Christians. He does not regard Christ as the literal son of God, but he does accept the importance of the symbolism of father and son. The father, he says, symbolizes the feeling of "the transfiguration of all things," while the son symbolizes the entry into that feeling.

[4] To point out how deceptive the rhetorical can be, I shall here show how one might rhetorically perhaps produce an effect upon a listener, in spite of the fact that what was said was dialectically a regress. Let a pagan religious speaker say that here on earth, God's temples are really empty, but (and now begins the rhetorical) in heaven, where all is more perfect, where water is air and air is ether, there are also temples and sanctuaries for the gods, but the difference is that the gods really dwell in these temples: then we have here a dialectical regress in the proposition that God really dwells in the temple, for the fact that He does not so dwell in an expression for the spiritual relationship to the invisible. But rhetorically it produces an effect. I have as a matter of fact, had in view a definite passage by a Greek author, whom I do not, however, wish to cite.

Nietzsche experienced the transfiguration of all things, the perfection of the world in its totality despite the wonder and disgust aroused by its parts taken separately. In the fourth part of his famous **Thus Spake Zarathustra** Nietzsche includes what can only be interpreted as the record of a religious or mystic experience, which he could hardly have described so well without first-hand experience. While Nietzsche was really the first to proclaim openly the "death of God," his reason was hardly to argue that the earth was as flat as the mediocrity of enlightenment secularism. He removes "God above" in order to see man above. His world is an "order of rank," a vertical order of sacredness. And Christ is clearly one of the men above.

The wonder is that man could so completely misread the "good news" that he would take a transfigured way of living and turn it into directions for a way of dying. Like Kierkegaard, Nietzsche is amazed at history's obscure ironies. But unlike Kierkegaard he does not see those ironies as God's way of purposely covering his tracks to produce the objective uncertainty that is the condition for faith. Nietzsche sees man's blindness simply as man's blindness. He accounts for the blindness: cowardice, lack of honesty, and a perversion of the will to power. It is, by the way, best to interpret "the will to power" with care. The words do not mean what we usually mean when we say someone is power hungry. Nietzsche offers a psychological analysis of those who lust after power over others as if that power would somehow give them a justification for themselves they otherwise lack. The phrase "will to power" is a coathook on which Nietzsche hangs everything he values. It plays the role of an undefinable first principle in his thought. You must come **to** an understanding of his will to power; do not work **from** your own understanding of "will to power" in order to pass judgment on Nietzsche's use of the phrase, because your initial understanding could not possibly have all the connotations Nietzsche eventually attaches to this centerpole of his thought. Eventually the phrase becomes almost equivalent to a principle of life, or a "will to willing," as Martin Heidegger puts it in his two-volume study of Nietzsche's posthumously published **The Will to Power.**

Try to see in what follows the connotation Nietzsche attaches to the "will to power" through his use of the concept. Consider also the force of Nietzsche's evaluations. He condemns Schopenhauer as a nihilist, as a nay-sayer to life. But many of Nietzsche's judgments are negative. How does the descriptive/evaluative distinction discussed in introducing Schopenhauer work out in relation to Nietzsche? Both these nineteenth-century Germans write in a polemical style and both ask and require an intense vigilance from the reader.

The Antichrist

7

Christianity is called the religion of *pity*. Pity stands opposed to the tonic emotions which heighten our vitality: it has a depressing effect. We are deprived of strength when we feel pity. That loss of strength which suffering as such inflicts on life is still further increased and multiplied by pity. Pity makes suffering contagious. Under certain circumstances, it may engender a total loss of life and vitality out of all proportion to the magnitude of the cause (as in the case of the death of the Nazarene). That is the first consideration, but there is a more important one.

Suppose we measure pity by the value of the reactions it usually produces; then its perilous nature appears in an even brighter light. Quite in general, pity crosses the law of development, which is the law of *selection*. It preserves what is ripe for destruction; it defends those who have been disinherited and condemned by life; and by the abundance of the failures of all kinds which it keeps alive, it gives life itself a gloomy and questionable aspect.

Some have dared to call pity a virtue (in every *noble* ethic it is considered a weakness); and as if this were not enough, it has been made *the* virtue, the basis and source of all virtues. To be sure—and one should always keep this in mind—this was done by a philosophy that was nihilistic and had inscribed the *negation of life* upon its shield. Schopenhauer was consistent enough: pity negates life and renders it *more deserving of negation*.

Pity is the *practice* of nihilism. To repeat: this depressive and contagious instinct crosses those instincts which aim at the preservation of life and at the enhancement of its value. It multiplies misery and conserves all that is miserable, and is thus a prime instrument of the advancement of decadence: pity persuades men to *nothingness!* Of course, one does not say "nothingness" but "beyond" or "God," or *"true* life," or Nirvana, salvation, blessedness.

This innocent rhetoric from the realm of the religious-moral idiosyncrasy appears much less innocent as soon as we realize which tendency it is that here shrouds itself in sublime words: *hostility against life.* Schopenhauer was hostile to life; therefore pity became a virtue for him.

Aristotle, as is well known, considered pity a pathological and dangerous condition, which one would be well advised to attack now and then with a purge: he understood tragedy as a purge. From the standpoint of the instinct of life, a remedy certainly seems necessary for such a pathological and dangerous accumulation of pity as is represented by the case of Scho-

THE ANTICHRIST From *The Portable Nietzsche,* edited and translated by Walter Kaufmann. Copyright 1954 by The Viking Press, Inc. Reprinted by permission of The Viking Press, Inc.

penhauer (and unfortunately by our entire literary and artistic decadence from St. Petersburg to Paris, from Tolstoi to Wagner)—to puncture it and make it *burst.*

In our whole unhealthy modernity there is nothing more unhealthy than Christian pity. To be physicians *here,* to be inexorable *here,* to wield the scalpel *here*—that is *our* part, that is *our* love of man, that is how *we* are philosophers, we *Hyperboreans.*

8

It is necessary to say whom we consider our antithesis: it is the theologians and whatever has theologians' blood in its veins—and that includes our whole philosophy.

Whoever has seen this catastrophe at close range or, better yet, been subjected to it and almost perished of it, will no longer consider it a joking matter (the freethinking of our honorable natural scientists and physiologists is, to my mind, a joke: they lack passion in these matters, they do not suffer them as their passion and martyrdom). This poisoning is much more extensive than is generally supposed: I have found the theologians' instinctive arrogance wherever anyone today considers himself an "idealist" —wherever a right is assumed, on the basis of some higher origin, to look at reality from a superior and foreign vantage point.

The idealist, exactly like the priest, holds all the great concepts in his hand (and not only in his hand!); he plays them out with a benevolent contempt for the "understanding," the "senses," "honors," "good living," and "science"; he considers all that *beneath* him, as so many harmful and seductive forces over which "the spirit" hovers in a state of pure for-itself-ness—as if humility, chastity, poverty, or, in one word, *holiness,* had not harmed life immeasurably more than any horrors or vices. The pure spirit is the pure lie.

As long as the priest is considered a *higher* type of man—this *professional* negator, slanderer, and poisoner of life—there is no answer to the question: what *is* truth? For truth has been stood on its head when the conscious advocate of nothingness and negation is accepted as the representative of "truth."

9

Against this theologians' instinct I wage war: I have found its traces everywhere. Whoever has theologians' blood in his veins, sees all things in a distorted and dishonest perspective to begin with. The pathos which develops out of this condition calls itself *faith:* closing one's eyes to oneself once and for all, lest one suffer the sight of incurable falsehood. This faulty perspective on all things is elevated into a morality, a virtue, a holiness; the good conscience is tied to faulty vision; and no *other* perspective is conceded any further value once one's own has been made sacrosanct with the names of "God," "redemption," and "eternity." I have dug up the theologians' instinct everywhere: it is the most widespread, really *subterranean*, form of falsehood found on earth.

Whatever a theologian feels to be true *must* be false: this is almost a criterion of truth. His most basic instinct of self-preservation forbids him to respect reality at any point or even to let it get a word in. Wherever the theologians' instinct extends, *value judgments* have been stood on their heads and the concepts of "true" and "false" are of necessity reversed: whatever is most harmful to life is called "true"; whatever elevates it, enhances, affirms, justifies it, and makes it triumphant, is called "false." When theologians reach out for *power* through the "conscience" of princes (*or* of peoples), we need never doubt what really happens at bottom: the will to the end, the *nihilistic* will, wants power. [. . .]

15

In Christianity neither morality nor religion has even a single point of contact with reality. Nothing but imaginary *causes* ("God," "soul," "ego," "spirit," "free will"—for that matter, "unfree will"), nothing but imaginary *effects* ("sin," "redemption," "grace," "punishment," "forgiveness of sins"). Intercourse between imaginary *beings* ("God," "spirits," "souls"); an imaginary *natural* science (anthropocentric; no trace of any concept of natural causes); an imaginary *psychology* (nothing but self-misunderstandings, interpretations of agreeable or disagreeable general feelings—for example, of the states of the *nervus sympathicus*—with the aid of the sign language of the religio-moral idiosyncrasy: "repentance," "pangs of conscience," "temptation by the devil," "the presence of God"); an imaginary *teleology* ("the kingdom of God," "the Last Judgment," "eternal life").

This *world of pure fiction* is vastly inferior to the world of dreams insofar as the latter *mirrors* reality, whereas the former falsifies, devalues, and negates reality. Once the concept of "nature" had been invented as the opposite of "God," "natural" had to become a synonym of "reprehensible": this whole world of fiction is rooted in *hatred* of the natural (of reality!); it is the expression of a profound vexation at the sight of reality.

But this explains everything. Who alone has good reason to lie his way out of reality? He who suffers from it. But to suffer from reality is to be a piece of reality that has come to grief. The preponderance of feelings of displeasure over feelings of pleasure is the cause of this fictitious morality and religion; but such a preponderance provides the very formula for decadence.

16

A critique of the *Christian conception of God* forces us to the same conclusion. A people that still believes in itself retains its own god. In him it reveres the conditions which let it prevail, its virtues: it projects its pleasure in itself, its feeling of power, into a being to whom one may offer thanks. Whoever is rich wants to give of his riches; a proud people needs a god: it wants to *sacrifice*. Under such conditions, religion is a form of thankfulness. Being thankful for himself, man needs a god. Such a god must be able to help and to harm, to be friend and enemy —he is admired whether good or destructive. The *anti-natural* castration of a god, to make him a god of the good alone, would here be contrary to everything desirable. The evil god is needed no less than the good god: after all, we do not owe our own existence to tolerance and humanitarianism.

What would be the point of a god who knew nothing of wrath, revenge, envy, scorn, cunning, and violence? who had perhaps never experienced the delightful *ardeurs* of victory and annihilation? No one would understand such a god: why have him then?

To be sure, when a people is perishing, when it feels how its faith in the future and its hope of freedom are waning irrevocably, when submission begins to appear to it as the prime necessity and it becomes aware of the virtues of the subjugated as the conditions of self-preservation, then its god *has to* change too. Now he becomes a sneak, timid and modest; he counsels "peace of soul," hate-no-more, forbearance, even "love" of friend and enemy. He moralizes constantly, he crawls into the cave of every private virtue, he becomes god for everyman, he becomes a private person, a cosmopolitan.

Formerly, he represented a people, the strength of a people, everything aggressive and power-thirsty in the soul of a people; now he is merely the good god.

Indeed, there is no other alternative for gods: *either* they are the will to power, and they remain a people's gods, *or* the incapacity for power, and then they necessarily become *good*. [. . .]

33

In the whole psychology of the "evangel" the concept of guilt and punishment is lacking; also the concept of reward. "Sin"—any distance separating God and man—is abolished: *precisely this is the "glad tidings."* Blessedness is not promised, it is not tied to conditions: it is the only reality—the rest is a sign with which to speak of it.

The consequence of such a state projects itself into a new practice, the genuine evangelical practice. It is not a "faith" that distinguishes the Christian: the Christian *acts,* he is distinguished by acting *differently*: by not resisting, either in words or in his heart, those who treat him ill; by making no distinction between foreigner and native, between Jew and not-Jew ("the neighbor"—really the coreligionist, the Jew); by not growing angry with anybody, by not despising anybody; by not permitting himself to be seen or involved at courts of law ("not swearing"); by not divorcing his wife under any circumstances, not even if his wife has been proved unfaith-ful. All of this, at bottom one principle; all of this, consequences of one instinct.

The life of the Redeemer was nothing other than *this* practice—nor was his death anything else. He no longer required any formulas, any rites for his intercourse with God—not even prayer. He broke with the whole Jewish doctrine of repentance and reconciliation; he knows that it is only in the *practice* of life that one feels "divine," "blessed," "evangelical," at all times a "child of God." Not "repentance," not "prayer for forgiveness," are the ways to God: *only the evangelical practice* leads to God, indeed, it *is* "God"! What was disposed of with the evangel was the Judaism of the con-cepts of "sin," "forgiveness of sin," "faith," "redemption through faith" —the whole Jewish *ecclesiastical* doctrine was negated in the "glad tid-ings."

The deep instinct for how one must *live,* in order to feel oneself "in heaven," to feel "eternal," while in all other behavior one decidedly does *not* feel oneself "in heaven"—this alone is the psychological reality of "re-demption." A new way of life, *not* a new faith.

34

If I understand anything about this great symbolist, it is that he accepted only *inner* realities as realities, as "truths"—that he understood the rest, everything natural, temporal, spatial, historical, only as signs, as occasions for parables. The concept of "the son of man" is not a concrete person who belongs in history, something indi-vidual and unique, but an "eternal" factuality, a psychological symbol re-deemed from the concept of time. The same applies once again, and in the highest sense, to the *God* of this typical symbolist, to the "kingdom of God," to the "kingdom of heaven," to the "filiation of God." Nothing is more unchristian than the *ecclesiastical crudities* of a god as person, of a "kingdom of God" which is to come, of a "kingdom of heaven" beyond, of a "son of God" as the second person in the Trinity. All this is—forgive the expression—like a fist in the eye—oh, in what an eye!—of the evangel—a *world-historical cynicism* in the derision of symbols. But what the signs "father" and "son" refer to is obvious—not to everyone, I admit: the word "son" expresses the *entry* into the over-all feeling of the transfiguration of all things (blessedness); the word "father" expresses *this feeling itself,* the feeling of eternity, the feeling of perfection. I am ashamed to recall what the church has made of this symbolism: Has it not placed an Amphitryon story at the threshold of the Christian "faith"? And a dogma of "immacu-late conception" on top of that? *But with that it has maculated conception.*

The "kingdom of heaven" is a state of the heart—not something that is to come "above the earth" or "after death." The whole concept of natural death is lacking in the evangel: death is no bridge, no transition; it is lack-ing because it belongs to a wholly different, merely apparent world, useful only insofar as it furnishes signs. The "hour of death" is *no* Christian concept—an "hour," time, physical life and its crises do not even exist for the teacher of the "glad tidings." The "kingdom of God" is nothing that one expects; it has no yesterday and no day after tomorrow, it will not come in "a thousand years"—it is an experience of the heart; it is everywhere, it is nowhere.

35

This "bringer of glad tidings" died as he had lived, as he had taught—*not* to "redeem men" but to show how one must live. This practice is his legacy to mankind: his behavior before the judges, before the catchpoles, before the accusers and all kinds of slander and scorn—his behavior on the *cross*. He does not resist, he does not defend his right, he takes no step which might ward off the worst; on the contrary, he *provokes* it. And he begs, he suffers, he loves *with* those, *in* those, who do him evil. *Not* to resist, *not* to be angry, *not* to hold responsible— but to resist not even the evil one—to *love* him.

36

Only we, we spirits who have *become free,* have the presuppositions for understanding something that nineteen centuries have misunderstood: that integrity which, having become instinct and passion, wages war against the "holy lie" even more than against any other lie. Previous readers were immeasurably far removed from our loving and cautious neutrality, from that discipline of the spirit which alone makes possible the unriddling of such foreign, such tender things: with impudent selfishness they always wanted only their own advantage; out of the opposite of the evangel the church was constructed.

If one were to look for signs that an ironical divinity has its fingers in the great play of the world, one would find no small support in the *tremendous question mark* called Christianity. Mankind lies on its knees before the opposite of that which was the origin, the meaning, the *right* of the evangel; in the concept of "church" it has pronounced holy precisely what the "bringer of the glad tidings" felt to be *beneath* and *behind* himself—one would look in vain for a greater example of *world-historical irony*.

Transition:
On
Believing

Whether or not the existence of God is an issue, believing or not believing remains one. Even though the star symbolizing a separate God be struck from the heavens, there remains the question of regarding the world as the flatland of secularism or the transfigured world of sacred and profane. If there is a religiousness that does not derive its meaning from a God, then a problem remains whether or not to believe that reality is indeed sacred in a sense that does not depend on divine grace. What grounds might we have for such a belief? What would be the logic for deciding such an issue? Must it be a completely subjective decision, a totally irrational leap of faith, or does it make sense to weigh the alternatives on some sort of scale?

The following three essays relate to the rightness or wrongness, reasonableness or unreasonableness, of belief in a sacred reality. A common theme in each essay is the role of evidence. Is the question one for which more evidence would be helpful in making a decision? What kind of evidence would be relevant? Or is the question of religious belief based on evidence at all?

Just as Kierkegaard unfolded the objective ambiguity of the religious question, so the following authors acknowledge the unavailability of knock-down-drag-out arguments based on incorrigible evidence. But a common theme of several of the essays is agreement on certain questions that **must** be decided, whether or not one has all the means at one's disposal for making a truly objective or scientific decision. To get a feel for the kind of questions these might be, including the question of religious belief, think again about self-identity. As Sartre and Erikson argued, the self is to some extent a self-creation. The logic of this self-creation is not unlike the logic of religious belief. One faces the same objective ambiguity, the same incompleteness of evidence. If it is true that I become what I do, if it is true that I need not merely play out an essence that remains unchanged from birth to death, if it is true that I do not develop from potentiality to actuality but from one actuality to another actuality to yet other actualities connected by strands of continuity and assimilation, then it is quite impossible at any particular time for me to give a thorough and convincing argument offering fully cogent objective grounds for decisions that will influence my becoming. I cannot appeal to an objectively determinate essence within me as justification for the rightness of following one path or another. In a very real sense I can only know when I get there.

To take a small-scale example, think of the major requirements in the curricula of most colleges and universities. The idea is to give you a taste of many fields of learning in your first years, and then because you cannot study everything, you pick one field to specialize in. Often you are required to choose a major after the sophomore year. Many find this an uncomfortable choice, for it seems to be so important and yet one is so ill equipped to make a choice. How can I know whether I want to major in physics when I haven't yet taken any advanced physics? If I choose physics and take the courses, I will have missed the chance to try out sociology, which happens to be another major interest. And the life of a physicist or engineer is very different from the life of, say, a social worker. The choice seems so critical and there is so little time. The method of totalization sounds like a fine technique to avoid one-sidedness in settling an intellectual question, but in living you simply cannot do everything. You cannot be a butcher, a baker, **and** a candlestick-maker. At some point you must make choices, knowing that those choices influence **who you become,** and also knowing that you lack the means for reaching certainty in making the choice. This frightful exigency, the pressures of time and our finitude, transforms the question of self-identity into an identity **crisis.** And a similar exigency attaches to the question of religious belief, for it is the world one lives in and the life one leads that are at stake in the question of religious belief.

Among approaches to pressing questions we can distinguish possible stances that feel very different on the inside but are sometimes indistinguishable to the external observer. First, there are those who are unaware of the importance of the choice. The river of life flows on and they bob like corks floating along on currents over which they exercise no control. Second, there are those who refuse to choose without adequate grounds for a choice. But that is a choice: to remain upstream. Third are those who choose foolishly. Because objective ambiguity is so painful they hurl themselves thoughtlessly into one current or another and, like the student with no mathematical aptitude who nevertheless majors in physics because labs are fun, end up hurtling over a waterfall into the depths of disaster. (Even if you cannot get **enough** evidence to be certain, you cannot ignore what evidence you have.) Then, fourth, there are those who face a crisis, see its dimensions, struggle with a choice, follow that choice, and looking very much like those in the first stance, go with the flow. Surely more stances could be distinguished but the metaphor is so worn I doubt it will bear further exercise.

Suffice it to say that the high stakes and the objective ambiguity that characterize both identity crises and questions of religious belief render them similar in the logic of exigency. But the questions share more than a common form. Religious belief is part of the content of self-identity. To be a Christian or a Jew or a Muslim or a Buddhist is to maintain or commit oneself to a certain kind of life. Almost all religions speak of the new birth attending faith. The matter of religious belief is indeed the widest circle of self-awareness. When I relate myself (or fail to relate myself) to religious belief, I relate myself (or fail to relate myself) to all that is, was, and ever shall be. I experience (or do not experience) a transfiguration of self and world.

W. K. CLIFFORD
(1845-1879)

W. K. Clifford was a nineteenth-century scientist-philosopher who left little of real distinction in his literary wake. Part of his essay, "The Ethics of Belief," is included here mainly to represent the position James attacks in the essay after. But Clifford is no straw man; the position he represents is formidable and must be understood lest objective ambiguity be confused with an irrational chaos offering equal lack of justification to any and all decisions. Clifford does well to point out, even if slightly melodramatically, the mishaps and tragedies that follow unnecessarily from overzealous credulity.

The Ethics of Belief

The Duty of Inquiry

A shipowner was about to send to sea an emigrant-ship. He knew that she was old, and not over-well built at the first; that she had seen many seas and climes, and often had needed repairs. Doubts had been suggested to him that possibly she was not seaworthy. These doubts preyed upon his mind, and made him unhappy; he thought that perhaps he ought to have her thoroughly overhauled and refitted, even though this should put him to great expense. Before the ship sailed, however, he succeeded in overcoming these melancholy reflections. He said to himself that she had gone safely through so many voyages and weathered so many storms that it was idle to suppose she would not come safely home from this trip also. He would put his trust in Providence, which could hardly fail to protect all these unhappy families that were leaving their fatherland to seek for better times elsewhere. He would dismiss from

THE ETHICS OF BELIEF From W. K. Clifford, *Lectures and Essays by the Late William Kingdon Clifford,* ed. by Leslie Stephen and Frederick Pollock, London, Macmillan and Co., 1879.

his mind all ungenerous suspicions about the honesty of builders and con-tractors. In such ways he acquired a sincere and comfortable conviction that his vessel was thoroughly safe and seaworthy; he watched her depar-ture with a light heart, and benevolent wishes for the success of the exiles in their strange new home that was to be; and he got his insurance-money when she went down in mid-ocean and told no tales.

What shall we say of him? Surely this, that he was verily guilty of the death of those men. It is admitted that he did sincerely believe in the soundness of his ship; but the sincerity of his conviction can in no wise help him, because *he had no right to believe on such evidence as was before him*. He had acquired his belief not by honestly earning it in patient investi-gation, but by stifling his doubts. And although in the end he may have felt so sure about it that he could not think otherwise, yet inasmuch as he had knowingly and willingly worked himself into that frame of mind, he must be held responsible for it.

Let us alter the case a little, and suppose that the ship was not unsound after all; that she made her voyage safely, and many others after it. Will that diminish the guilt of her owner? Not one jot. When an action is once done, it is right or wrong forever; no accidental failure of its good or evil fruits can possibly alter that. The man would not have been innocent, he would only have been not found out. The question of right or wrong has to do with the origin of his belief, not the matter of it; not what it was, but how he got it; not whether it turned out to be true or false, but whether he had a right to believe on such evidence as was before him.

There was once an island in which some of the inhabitants professed a religion teaching neither the doctrine of original sin nor that of eternal pun-ishment. A suspicion got abroad that the professors of this religion had made use of unfair means to get their doctrines taught to children. They were accused of wresting the laws of their country in such a way as to re-move children from the care of their natural and legal guardians; and even of stealing them away and keeping them concealed from their friends and relations. A certain number of men formed themselves into a society for the purpose of agitating the public about this matter. They published grave accusations against individual citizens of the highest position and character, and did all in their power to injure these citizens in the exercise of their professions. So great was the noise they made, that a Commission was ap-pointed to investigate the facts; but after the Commission had carefully in-quired into all the evidence that could be got, it appeared that the accused were innocent. Not only had they been accused on insufficient evidence, but the evidence of their innocence was such as the agitators might easily have obtained, if they had attempted a fair inquiry. After these disclosures the inhabitants of that country looked upon the members of the agitating so-ciety, not only as persons whose judgment was to be distrusted, but also as no longer to be counted honorable men. For although they had sincerely and conscientiously believed in the charges they had made, yet *they had no right to believe on such evidence as was before them*. Their sincere convictions, instead of being honestly earned by patient inquiring, were stolen by listening to the voice of prejudice and passion.

Let us vary this case also, and suppose, other things remaining as before, that a still more accurate investigation proved the accused to have been really guilty. Would this make any difference in the guilt of the accusers? Clearly not; the question is not whether their belief was true or false, but whether they entertained it on wrong grounds. They would no doubt say, 'Now you see that we were right after all; next time perhaps you will believe us.' And they might be believed, but they would not thereby become honorable men. They would not be innocent, they would only be not found out. Every one of them, if he chose to examine himself *in foro conscientiae,* would know that he had acquired and nourished a belief, when he had no right to believe on such evidence as was before him; and therein he would know that he had done a wrong thing.

It may be said, however, that in both of these supposed cases it is not the belief which is judged to be wrong, but the action following upon it. The shipowner might say, 'I am perfectly certain that my ship is sound, but still I feel it my duty to have her examined, before trusting the lives of so many people to her.' And it might be said to the agitator, 'However convinced you were of the justice of your cause and the truth of your convictions, you ought not to have made a public attack upon any man's character until you had examined the evidence on both sides with the utmost patience and care.'

In the first place, let us admit that, so far as it goes, this view of the case is right and necessary; right, because even when a man's belief is so fixed that he cannot think otherwise, he still has a choice in regard to the action suggested by it, and so cannot escape the duty of investigating on the ground of the strength of his convictions; and necessary, because those who are not yet capable of controlling their feelings and thoughts must have a plain rule dealing with overt acts.

But this being premised as necessary, it becomes clear that it is not sufficient, and that our previous judgment is required to supplement it. For it is not possible so to sever the belief from the action it suggests as to condemn the one without condemning the other. No man holding a strong belief on one side of a question, or even wishing to hold a belief on one side, can investigate it with such fairness and completeness as if he were really in doubt and unbiassed; so that the existence of a belief not founded on fair inquiry unfits a man for the performance of this necessary duty.

Nor is that truly a belief at all which has not some influence upon the actions of him who holds it. He who truly believes that which prompts him to an action has looked upon the action to lust after it, he has committed it already in his heart. If a belief is not realized immediately in open deeds, it is stored up for the guidance of the future. It goes to make a part of that aggregate of beliefs which is the link between sensation and action at every moment of all our lives, and which is so organized and compacted together that no part of it can be isolated from the rest, but every new addition modifies the structure of the whole. No real belief, however trifling and fragmentary it may seem, is ever truly insignificant; it prepares us to receive more of its like, confirms those which resembled it before, and weakens others; and so gradually it lays a stealthy train in our inmost thoughts, which may some day explode into overt action, and leave its stamp upon our character forever.

And no one man's belief is in any case a private matter which concerns himself alone. Our lives are guided by that general conception of the course of things which has been created by society for social purposes. Our words, our phrases, our forms and processes and modes of thought, are common property, fashioned and perfected from age to age; an heirloom which every succeeding generation inherits as a precious deposit and a sacred trust to be handed on to the next one, not unchanged but enlarged and purified, with some clear marks of its proper handiwork. Into this, for good or ill, is woven every belief of every man who has speech of his fellows. An awful privilege, and an awful responsibility, that we should help to create the world in which posterity will live.

In the two supposed cases which have been considered, it has been judged wrong to believe on insufficient evidence, or to nournish belief by suppressing doubts and avoiding investigation. The reason of this judgment is not far to seek: it is that in both these cases the belief held by one man was of great importance to other men. But forasmuch as no belief held by one man, however seemingly trivial the belief, and however obscure the believer, is ever actually insignificant or without its effect on the fate of mankind, we have no choice but to extend our judgment to all cases of belief whatever. Belief, that sacred faculty which prompts the decisions of our will, and knits into harmonious working all the compacted energies of our being, is ours not for ourselves, but for humanity. It is rightly used on truths which have been established by long experience and waiting toil, and which have stood in the fierce light of free and fearless questioning. Then it helps to bind men together, and to strengthen and direct their common action. It is desecrated when given to unproved and unquestioned statements, for the solace and private pleasure of the believer; to add a tinsel splendor to the plain straight road of our life and display a bright mirage beyond it; or even to drown the common sorrows of our kind by a self-deception which allows them not only to cast down, but also to degrade us. Whoso would deserve well of his fellows in this matter will guard the purity of his belief with a very fanaticism of jealous care, lest at any time it should rest on an unworthy object, and catch a stain which can never be wiped away.

It is not only the leader of men, statesman, philosopher, or poet, that owes this bounden duty to mankind. Every rustic who delivers in the village alehouse his slow, infrequent sentences, may help to kill or keep alive the fatal superstitions which clog his race. Every hard-worked wife of an artisan may transmit to her children beliefs which shall knit society together, or rend it in pieces. No simplicity of mind, no obscurity of station, can escape the universal duty of questioning all that we believe.

It is true that this duty is a hard one, and the doubt which comes out of it is often a very bitter thing. It leaves us bare and powerless where we thought that we were safe and strong. To know all about anything is to know how to deal with it under all circumstances. We feel much happier and more secure when we think we know precisely what to do, no matter what happens, than when we have lost our way and do not know where to turn. And if we have supposed ourselves to know all about anything, and to be capable of doing what is fit in regard to it, we naturally do not like to find that we are really ignorant and powerless, that we have to begin again at the beginning, and try to learn what the thing is and how it is to be dealt with—if indeed anything can be learnt about it. It is the sense of power attached to a sense of knowledge that makes men desirous of believing, and afraid of doubting.

This sense of power is the highest and best of pleasures when the belief on which it is founded is a true belief, and has been fairly earned by investigation. For then we may justly feel that it is common property, and holds good for others as well as for ourselves. Then we may be glad, not that *I* have learned secrets by which I am safer and stronger, but that *we men* have got mastery over more of the world; and we shall be strong, not for ourselves, but in the name of Man and in his strength. But if the belief has been accepted on insufficient evidence, the pleasure is a stolen one. Not only does it deceive ourselves by giving us a sense of power which we do not really possess, but it is sinful, because it is stolen in defiance of our duty to mankind. That duty is to guard ourselves from such beliefs as from a pestilence, which may shortly master our own body and then spread to the rest of the town. What would be thought of one who, for the sake of a sweet fruit, should deliberately run the risk of bringing a plague upon his family and his neighbors?

And, as in other such cases, it is not the risk only which has to be considered; for a bad action is always bad at the time when it is done, no matter what happens afterward. Every time we let ourselves believe for unworthy reasons, we weaken our powers of self-control, of doubting, of judicially and fairly weighing evidence. We all suffer severely enough from the maintenance and support of false beliefs and the fatally wrong actions which they lead to, and the evil born when one such belief is entertained is great and wide. But a greater and wider evil arises when the credulous character is maintained and supported, when a habit of believing for unworthy reasons is fostered and made permanent. If I steal money from any person, there may be no harm done by the mere transfer of possession; he may not feel the loss, or it may prevent him from using the money badly. But I cannot help doing this great wrong toward Man, that I make myself dishonest. What hurts society is not that it should lose its property, but that it should become a den of thieves; for then it must cease to be society. This is why we ought not to do evil that good may come; for at any rate this great evil has come, that we have done evil and are made wicked thereby. In like manner, if I let myself believe anything on insufficient evidence, there may be no great harm done by the mere belief; it may be true after all, or I may never have occasion to exhibit it in outward acts. But I cannot help doing this great wrong toward Man, that I make myself credulous. The danger to society is not merely that it should believe wrong things, though that is great enough; but that it should become credulous, and lose the habit of testing things and inquiring into them; for then it must sink back into savagery.

The harm which is done by credulity in a man is not confined to the fostering of a credulous character in others, and consequent support of false beliefs. Habitual want of care about what I believe leads to habitual want of care in others about the truth of what is told to me. Men speak the truth to one another when each reveres the truth in his own mind and in the other's mind; but how shall my friend revere the truth in my mind when I myself am careless about it, when I believe things because I want to believe them, and because they are comforting and pleasant? Will he not learn to cry, 'Peace,' to me, when there is no peace? By such a course I shall surround myself with a thick atmosphere of falsehood and fraud, and in that I must live. It may matter little to me, in my cloud-castle of sweet illusions and darling lies; but it matters much to Man that I have made my neighbors ready to deceive. The credulous man is father to the liar and the cheat; he lives in the bosom of this his family, and it is no marvel if he should become even as they are. So closely are our duties knit together, that whoso shall keep the whole law, and yet offend in one point, he is guilty of all.

To sum up: it is wrong always, everywhere and for any one, to believe anything upon insufficient evidence.

WILLIAM JAMES

(1842-1910)

The thesis of James' essay is clearly stated only well into the argument: "Our passional nature not only lawfully may, but must, decide an option between propositions, whenever it is a genuine option that cannot by its nature be decided on intellectual grounds; for to say, under such circumstances, 'Do not decide, but leave the question open,' is itself a decision,—just like deciding yes or no,—and is attended with the same risk of losing the truth." This quotation is not only relevant to the discussion in the last "Transition," but also shows the role played by the phrase, 'genuine option.' In the early part of the essay James takes care to define his terms, and unless one appreciates in advance the importance of his definitions, one is liable to misconstrue the scope of his argument. He is not interested in justifying a Sartrean voluntarism or a Kierkegaardian irrationalism. James is very explicit about the precise conditions under which credulity may be exercised and those under which it may not. Attend to his statements of those conditions.

Beyond its contribution to the question of belief, James' essay also adds to the ongoing debate over the nature of philosophy and its proper method. He makes a powerful case against the Cartesian quest for certainty. James' distinction between the two imperatives: "know the truth," and "avoid error," does indeed characterize two very different kinds of philosophical pursuits. The drive toward ever more technically precise exercises in linguistic analysis follows from the imperative to avoid error. But to the extent that philosophy is driven **only** by a fear of error its products tend to be sterile. Naturally a will to truth wholly unchecked by fear of error may issue in fantasies that are far from sterile, but also far from truth. James' distinction of kinds of philosophy is useful in reviewing other essays that touch on methodology: Descartes, Ryle, Polanyi, Brown, as well as Clifford.

The Will to Believe

1

. . . Let us give the name of *hypothesis* to anything that may be proposed to our belief; and just as the electricians speak of live and dead wires, let us speak of any hypothesis as either *live* or *dead*. A live hypothesis is one which appeals as a real possibility to him to whom it is proposed. If I ask you to believe in the Mahdi, the notion makes no electric connection with your nature,—it refuses to scintillate with any credibility at all. As an hypothesis it is completely dead. To an Arab, however (even if he be not one of the Mahdi's followers), the hypothesis is among the mind's possibilities: it is alive. This shows that deadness and liveness in an hypothesis are not intrinsic properties, but relations to the individual thinker. They are measured by his willingness to act. The maximum of liveness in an hypothesis means willingness to act irrevocably. Practically, that means belief; but there is some believing tendency wherever there is willingness to act at all.

THE WILL TO BELIEVE From William James, *The Will to Believe and Other Essays in Popular Philosophy*, New York, London, and Bombay, Longman's Green and Co., 1897.

Next, let us call the decision between two hypotheses an *option*. Options may be of several kinds. They may be—1, *living* or *dead;* 2, *forced* or *avoidable;* 3, *momentous* or *trivial;* and for our purposes we may call an option a *genuine* option when it is of the forced, living, and momentous kind.

1. A living option is one in which both hypotheses are live ones. If I say to you: "Be a theosophist or be a Mohammedan," it is probably a dead option, because for you neither hypothesis is likely to be alive. But if I say: "Be an agnostic or be a Christian," it is otherwise: trained as you are, each hypothesis makes some appeal, however small, to your belief.

2. Next, if I say to you: "Choose between going out with your umbrella or without it," I do not offer you a genuine option, for it is not forced. You can easily avoid it by not going out at all. Similarly, if I say, "Either love me or hate me," "Either call my theory true or call it false," your option is avoidable. You may remain indifferent to me, neither loving nor hating, and you may decline to offer any judgment as to my theory. But if I say, "Either accept this truth or go without it," I put on you a forced option, for there is no standing place outside of the alternative. Every dilemma based on a complete logical disjunction, with no possibility of not choosing, is an option of this forced kind.

3. Finally, if I were Dr. Nansen and proposed to you to join my North Pole expedition, your option would be momentous; for this would probably be your only similar opportunity, and your choice now would either exclude you from the North Pole sort of immortality altogether or put at least the chance of it into your hands. He who refuses to embrace a unique opportunity loses the prize as surely as if he tried and failed. *Per contra,* the option is trivial when the opportunity is not unique, when the stake is insignificant, or when the decision is reversible if it later prove unwise. Such trivial options abound in the scientific life. A chemist finds an hypothesis live enough to spend a year in its verification: he believes in it to that extent. But if his experiments prove inconclusive either way, he is quit for his loss of time, no vital harm being done.

It will facilitate our discussion if we keep all these distinctions well in mind.

2

The next matter to consider is the actual psychology of human opinion. When we look at certain facts, it seems as if our passional and volitional nature lay at the root of all our convictions. When we look at others, it seems as if they could do nothing when the intellect had once said its say. Let us take the latter facts up first.

Does it not seem preposterous on the very face of it to talk of our opinions being modifiable at will? Can our will either help or hinder our intellect in its perceptions of truth? Can we, by just willing it, believe that Abraham

Lincoln's existence is a myth, and that the portraits of him in McClure's Magazine are all of some one else? Can we, by any effort of our will, or by any strength of wish that it were true, believe ourselves well and about when we are roaring with rheumatism in bed, or feel certain that the sum of the two one-dollar bills in our pocket must be a hundred dollars? We can *say* any of these things, but we are absolutely impotent to believe them; and of just such things is the whole fabric of the truths that we do believe in made up—matters of fact, immediate or remote, as Hume said, and relations between ideas, which are either there or not there for us if we see them so, and which if not there cannot be put there by any action of our own.

In Pascal's Thoughts there is a celebrated passage known in literature as Pascal's wager. In it he tries to force us into Christianity by reasoning as if our concern with truth resembled our concern with the stakes in a game of chance. Translated freely his words are these: You must either believe or not believe that God is—which will you do? Your human reason cannot say. A game is going on between you and the nature of things which at the day of judgment will bring out either heads or tails. Weigh what your gains and your losses would be if you should stake all you have on heads, or God's existence: if you win in such case, you gain eternal beatitude; if you lose, you lose nothing at all. If there were an infinity of chances, and only one for God in this wager, still you ought to stake your all on God; for though you surely risk a finite loss by this procedure, any finite loss is reasonable, even a certain one is reasonable, if there is but the possibility of infinite gain. Go, then, and take holy water, and have masses said; belief will come and stupefy your scruples,—*Cela vous fera croire et vous abêtira.* Why should you not? At bottom, what have you to lose?

You probably feel that when religious faith expresses itself thus, in the language of the gamingtable, it is put to its last trumps. Surely Pascal's own personal belief in masses and holy water had far other springs; and this celebrated page of his is but an argument for others, a last desperate snatch at a weapon against the hardness of the unbelieving heart. We feel that a faith in masses and holy water adopted wilfully after such a mechanical calculation would lack the inner soul of faith's reality; and if we were ourselves in the place of the Deity, we should probably take particular pleasure in cutting off believers of this pattern from their infinite reward. It is evident that unless there be some pre-existing tendency to believe in masses and holy water, the option offered to the will by Pascal is not a living option. Certainly no Turk ever took to masses and holy water on its account; and even to us Protestants these means of salvation seem such foregone impossibilities that Pascal's logic, invoked for them specifically, leaves us unmoved. As well might the Mahdi write to us, saying, "I am the Expected One whom God has created in his effulgence. You shall be infinitely happy if you confess me; otherwise you shall be cut off from the light of the sun. Weigh, then, your infinite gain if I am genuine against your finite sacrifice if I am not!" His logic would be that of Pascal; but he would vainly use it on us, for the hypothesis he offers us is dead. No tendency to act on it exists in us to any degree.

The talk of believing by our volition seems, then, from one point of view, simply silly. From another point of view it is worse than silly, it is vile. When one turns to the magnificent edifice of the physical sciences, and sees how it was reared; what thousands of disinterested moral lives of men lie buried in its mere foundations; what patience and postponement, what choking down of preference, what submission to the icy laws of outer fact are wrought into its very stones and mortar; how absolutely impersonal it stands in its vast augustness,—then how besotted and contemptible seems every little sentimentalist who comes blowing his voluntary smoke-wreaths, and pretending to decide things from out of his private dream! Can we wonder if those bred in the rugged and manly school of science should feel like spewing such subjectivism out of their mouths? The whole system of loyalties which grow up in the schools of science go dead against its toleration; so that it is only natural that those who have caught the scientific fever should pass over to the opposite extreme, and write sometimes as if the incorruptibly truthful intellect ought positively to prefer bitterness and unacceptableness to the heart in its cup.

> It fortifies my soul to know
> That, though I perish, Truth is so—

sings Clough, while Huxley exclaims: "My only consolation lies in the reflection that, however bad our posterity may become, so far as they hold by the plain rule of not pretending to believe what they have no reason to believe, because it may be to their advantage so to pretend [the word 'pretend' is surely here redundant], they will not have reached the lowest depth of immorality." And that delicious *enfant terrible* Clifford writes: "Belief is desecrated when given to unproved and unquestioned statements for the solace and private pleasure of the believer. . . . Whoso would deserve well of his fellows in this matter will guard the purity of his belief with a very fanaticism of jealous care, lest at any time it should rest on an unworthy object, and catch a stain which can never be wiped away. . . . If [a] belief has been accepted on insufficient evidence [even though the belief be true, as Clifford on the same page explains] the pleasure is a stolen one. . . . It is sinful because it is stolen in defiance of our duty to mankind. That duty is to guard ourselves from such beliefs as from a pestilence which may shortly master our own body and then spread to the rest of the town. . . . It is wrong always, everywhere, and for every one, to believe anything upon insufficient evidence."

3

All this strikes one as healthy, even when expressed, as by Clifford, with somewhat too much of robustious pathos in the voice. Free-will and simple wishing do seem, in the matter of our credences, to be only fifth wheels to the coach. Yet if any one should thereupon assume that intellectual insight is what remains after wish and will and sentimental preference have taken wing, or that pure reason is what then settles our opinions, he would fly quite as directly in the teeth of the facts.

It is only our already dead hypotheses that our willing nature is unable to bring to life again. But what has made them dead for us is for the most part a previous action of our willing nature of an antagonistic kind. When I say 'willing nature,' I do not mean only such deliberate volitions as may have set up habits of belief that we cannot now escape from,—I mean all such factors of belief as fear and hope, prejudice and passion, imitation and partisanship, the circumpressure of our caste and set. As a matter of fact we find ourselves believing, we hardly know how or why. Mr. Balfour gives the name of 'authority' to all those influences, born of the intellectual climate, that make hypotheses possible or impossible for us, alive or dead. Here in this room, we all of us believe in molecules and the conservation of energy, in democracy and necessary progress, in Protestant Christianity and the duty of fighting for 'the doctrine of the immortal Monroe,' all for no reasons worthy of the name. We see into these matters with no more inner clearness, and probably with much less, than any disbeliever in them might possess. His unconventionality would probably have some grounds to show for its conclusions; but for us, not insight, but the *prestige* of the opinions, is what makes the spark shoot from them and light up our sleeping magazines of faith. Our reason is quite satisfied, in nine hundred and ninety-nine cases out of every thousand of us, if it can find a few arguments that will do to recite in case our credulity is criticised by some one else. Our faith is faith in some one else's faith, and in the greatest matters this is most the case. Our belief in truth itself, for instance, that there is a truth, and that our minds and it are made for each other,—what is it but a passionate affirmation of desire, in which our social system backs us up? We want to have a truth; we want to believe that our experiments and studies and discussions must put us in a continually better and better position towards it; and on this line we agree to fight out our thinking lives. But if a pyrrhonistic sceptic asks us *how we know* all this, can our logic find a reply? No! certainly it cannot. It is just one volition against another,—we willing to go in for life upon a trust or assumption which he, for his part, does not care to make.[1]

As a rule we disbelieve all facts and theories for which we have no use. Clifford's cosmic emotions find no use for Christian feelings. Huxley belabors the bishops because there is no use for sacerdotalism in his scheme of life. Newman, on the contrary, goes over to Romanism, and finds all sorts of reasons good for staying there, because a priestly system is for him

---

[1] Compare the admirable page 310 in S. H. Hodgson's "Time and Space," London, 1865.

an organic need and delight. Why do so few 'scientists' even look at the evidence for telepathy, so called? Because they think, as a leading biologist, now dead, once said to me, that even if such a thing were true, scientists ought to band together to keep it suppressed and concealed. It would undo the uniformity of Nature and all sorts of other things without which scientists cannot carry on their pursuits. But if this very man had been shown something which as a scientist he might *do* with telepathy, he might not only have examined the evidence, but even have found it good enough. This very law which the logicians would impose upon us—if I may give the name of logicians to those who would rule out our willing nature here—is based on nothing but their own natural wish to exclude all elements for which they, in their professional quality of logicians, can find no use.

Evidently, then, our non-intellectual nature does influence our convictions. There are passional tendencies and volitions which run before and others which come after belief, and it is only the latter that are too late for the fair; and they are not too late when the previous passional work has been already in their own direction. Pascal's argument, instead of being powerless, then seems a regular clincher, and is the last stroke needed to make our faith in masses and holy water complete. The state of things is evidently far from simple; and pure insight and logic, whatever they might do ideally, are not the only things that really do produce our creeds.

4

Our next duty, having recognized this mixed-up state of affairs, is to ask whether it be simply reprehensible and pathological, or whether, on the contrary, we must treat it as a normal element in making up our minds. The thesis I defend is, briefly stated, this: *Our passional nature not only lawfully may, but must, decide an option between propositions, whenever it is a genuine option that cannot by its nature be decided on intellectual grounds; for to say, under such circumstances, "Do not decide, but leave the question open," is itself a passional decision,—just like deciding yes or no,—and is attended with the same risk of losing the truth.* The thesis thus abstractly expressed will, I trust, soon become quite clear. But I must first indulge in a bit more of preliminary work.

5

It will be observed that for the purposes of this discussion we are on 'dogmatic' ground,—ground, I mean, which leaves systematic philosophical scepticism altogether out of account. The postulate that there is truth, and that it is the destiny of our minds to attain it, we are deliberately resolving to make, though the sceptic will not make it. We part company with him, therefore, absolutely, at this point.

But the faith that truth exists, and that our minds can find it, may be held in two ways. We may talk of the *empiricist* way and of the *absolutist* way of believing in truth. The absolutists in this matter say that we not only can attain to knowing truth, but we can *know when* we have attained to knowing it; while the empiricists think that although we may attain it, we cannot infallibly know when. To *know* is one thing, and to know for certain *that* we know is another. One may hold to the first being possible without the second; hence the empiricists and the absolutists, although neither of them is a sceptic in the usual philosophic sense of the term, show very different degrees of dogmatism in their lives.

If we look at the history of opinions, we see that the empiricist tendency has largely prevailed in science, while in philosophy the absolutist tendency has had everything its own way. The characteristic sort of happiness, indeed, which philosophies yield has mainly consisted in the conviction felt by each successive school or system that by it bottom-certitude had been attained. "Other philosophies are collections of opinions, mostly false; *my* philosophy gives standing-ground forever,"—who does not recognize in this the key-note of every system worthy of the name? A system, to be a system at all, must come as a *closed* system, reversible in this or that detail, perchance, but in its essential features never!

Scholastic orthodoxy, to which one must always go when one wishes to find perfectly clear statement, has beautifully elaborated this absolutist conviction in a doctrine which it calls that of 'objective evidence.' [. . .] You believe in objective evidence, and I do. Of some things we feel that we are certain: we know, and we know that we do know. There is something that gives a click inside of us, a bell that strikes twelve, when the hands of our mental clock have swept the dial and meet over the meridian hour. The greatest empiricists among us are only empiricists on reflection: when left to their instincts, they dogmatize like infallible popes. When the Cliffords tell us how sinful it is to be Christians on such 'insufficient evidence,' insufficiency is really the last thing they have in mind. For them the evidence is absolutely sufficient, only it makes the other way. They believe so completely in an anti-christian order of the universe that there is no living option; Christianity is a dead hypothesis from the start.

6

But now, since we are all such absolutists by instinct, what in our quality of students of philosophy ought we to do about the fact? Shall we espouse and indorse it? Or shall we treat it as a weakness of our nature from which we must free ourselves, if we can?

I sincerely believe that the latter course is the only one we can follow as reflective men. Objective evidence and certitude are doubtless very fine ideals to play with, but where on this moonlit and dream-visited planet are they found? I am, therefore, myself a complete empiricist so far as my theory of human knowledge goes. I live, to be sure, by the practical faith that we must go on experiencing and thinking over our experience, for only thus can our opinions grow more true; but to hold any one of them— I absolutely do not care which—as if it never could be reinterpretable or corrigible, I believe to be a tremendously mistaken attitude, and I think that the whole history of philosophy will bear me out. There is but one indefectibly certain truth, and that is the truth that pyrrhonistic scepticism itself leaves standing,—the truth that the present phenomenon of consciousness exists. That, however, is the bare starting-point of knowledge, the mere admission of a stuff to be philosophized about. The various philosophies are but so many attempts at expressing what this stuff really is. And if we repair to our libraries what disagreement do we discover! Where is a certainly true answer found? Apart from abstract propositions of comparison (such as two and two are the same as four), propositions which tell us nothing by themselves about concrete reality, we find no proposition ever regarded by any one as evidently certain that has not either been called a falsehood, or at least had its truth sincerely questioned by some one else. The transcending of the axioms of geometry, not in play but in earnest, by certain of our contemporaries (as Zöllner and Charles H. Hinton), and the rejection of the whole Aristotelian logic by the Hegelians, are striking instances in point. [. . .]

But please observe, now, that when as empiricists we give up the doctrine of objective certitude, we do not thereby give up the quest or hope of truth itself. We still pin our faith on its existence, and still believe that we gain an ever better position towards it by systematically continuing to roll up experiences and think. Our great difference from the scholastic lies in the way we face. The strength of his system lies in the principles, the origin, the *terminus a quo* of his thought; for us the strength is in the outcome, the upshot, the *terminus ad quem*. Not where it comes from but what it leads to is to decide. It matters not to an empiricist from what quarter an hypothesis may come to him: he may have acquired it by fair means or by foul; passion may have whispered or accident suggested it; but if the total drift of thinking continues to confirm it, that is what he means by its being true.

7

One more point, small but important, and our preliminaries are done. There are two ways of looking at our duty in the matter of opinion,—ways entirely different, and yet ways about whose difference the theory of knowledge seems hitherto to have shown very little concern. *We must know the truth;* and *we must avoid error,*— these are our first and great commandments as would-be knowers; but they are not two ways of stating an identical commandment, they are two separable laws. Although it may indeed happen that when we believe the truth *A,* we escape as an incidental consequence from believing the falsehood *B,* it hardly ever happens that by merely disbelieving *B* we necessarily believe *A*. We may in escaping *B* fall into believing other falsehoods, *C* or *D,* just as bad as B; or we may escape B by not believing anything at all, not even A.

Believe truth! Shun error!—these, we see, are two materially different laws; and by choosing between them we may end by coloring differently our whole intellectual life. We may regard the chase for truth as paramount, and the avoidance of error as secondary; or we may, on the other hand, treat the avoidance of error as more imperative, and let truth take its chance. Clifford, in the instructive passage which I have quoted, exhorts us to the latter course. Believe nothing, he tells us, keep your mind in suspense forever, rather than by closing it on insufficient evidence incur the awful risk of believing lies. You, on the other hand, may think that the risk of being in error is a very small matter when compared with the blessings of real knowledge, and be ready to be duped many times in your investigation rather than postpone indefinitely the chance of guessing true. I myself find it impossible to go with Clifford. We must remember that these feelings of our duty about either truth or error are in any case only expressions of our passional life. Biologically considered, our minds are as ready to grind out falsehood as veracity, and he who says, "Better go without belief forever than believe a lie!" merely shows his own preponderant private horror of becoming a dupe. He may be critical of many of his desires and fears, but this fear he slavishly obeys. He cannot imagine any one questioning its binding force. For my own part, I have also a horror of being duped; but I can believe that worse things than being duped may happen to a man in this world: so Clifford's exhortation has to my ears a thoroughly fantastic sound. It is like a general informing his soldiers that it is better to keep out of battle forever than to risk a single wound. Not so are victories either over enemies or over nature gained. Our errors are surely not such awfully solemn things. In a world where we are so certain to incur them in spite of all our caution, a certain lightness of heart seems healthier than this excessive nervousness on their behalf. At any rate, it seems the fittest thing for the empiricist philosopher.

8

And now, after all this introduction, let us go straight at our question. I have said, and now repeat it, that not only as a matter of fact do we find our passional nature influencing us in our opinions, but that there are some options between opinions in which this influence must be regarded both as an inevitable and as a lawful determinant of our choice.

I fear here that some of you my hearers will begin to scent danger, and lend an inhospitable ear. Two first steps of passion you have indeed had to admit as necessary,—we must think so as to avoid dupery, and we must think so as to gain truth; but the surest path to those ideal consummations, you will probably consider, is from now onwards to take no further passional step.

Well, of course, I agree as far as the facts will allow. Wherever the option between losing truth and gaining it is not momentous, we can throw the chance of *gaining truth* away, and at any rate save ourselves from any chance of *believing falsehood,* by not making up our minds at all till objective evidence has come. In scientific questions, this is almost always the case; and even in human affairs in general, the need of acting is seldom so urgent that a false belief to act on is better than no belief at all. Law courts, indeed, have to decide on the best evidence attainable for the moment, because a judge's duty is to make law as well as to ascertain it, and (as a learned judge once said to me) few cases are worth spending much time over: the great thing is to have them decided on *any* acceptable principle, and got out of the way. But in our dealings with objective nature we obviously are recorders, not makers, of the truth; and decisions for the mere sake of deciding promptly and getting on to the next business would be wholly out of place. Throughout the breadth of physical nature facts are what they are quite independently of us, and seldom is there any such hurry about them that the risks of being duped by believing a premature theory need be faced. The questions here are always trivial options, the hypotheses are hardly living (at any rate not living for us spectators), the choice between believing truth or falsehood is seldom forced. The attitude of sceptical balance is therefore the absolutely wise one if we would escape mistakes. What difference, indeed, does it make to most of us whether we have or have not a theory of the Röntgen rays, whether we believe or not in mind-stuff, or have a conviction about the causality of conscious states? It makes no difference. Such options are not forced on us. On every account it is better not to make them, but still keep weighing reasons *pro et contra* with an indifferent hand. [. . .]

The question next arises: Are there not somewhere forced options in our speculative questions, and can we (as men who may be interested at least as much in positively gaining truth as in merely escaping dupery) always wait with impunity till the coercive evidence shall have arrived? It seems *a priori* improbable that the truth should be so nicely adjusted to our needs and powers as that. In the great boarding-house of nature, the cakes and the butter and the syrup seldom come out so even and leave the plates so clean. Indeed, we should view them with scientific suspicion if they did.

9

Moral questions immediately present themselves as questions whose solution cannot wait for sensible proof. A moral question is a question not of what sensibly exists, but of what is good, or would be good if it did exist. Science can tell us what exists; but to compare the *worths,* both of what exists and of what does not exist, we must consult not science, but what Pascal calls our heart. Science herself consults her heart when she lays it down that the infinite ascertainment of fact and correction of false belief are the supreme goods for man. Challenge the statement, and science can only repeat it oracularly, or else prove it by showing that such ascertainment and correction bring man all sorts of other goods which man's heart in turn declares. The question of having moral beliefs at all or not having them is decided by our will. Are our moral preferences true or false, or are they only odd biological phenomena, making things goods or bad for *us,* but in themselves indifferent? How can your pure intellect decide? If your heart does not *want* a world of moral reality, your head will assuredly never make you believe in one. Mephistophelian scepticism, indeed, will satisfy the head's play-instincts much better than any rigorous idealism can. Some men (even at the student age) are so naturally cool-hearted that the moralistic hypothesis never has for them any pungent life, and in their supercilious presence the hot young moralist always feels strangely ill at ease. The appearance of knowingness is on their side, of *naïveté* and gullibility on his. Yet, in the inarticulate heart of him, he clings to it that he is not a dupe, and that there is a realm in which (as Emerson says) all their wit and intellectual superiority is no better than the cunning of a fox. Moral scepticism can no more be refuted or proved by logic than intellectual scepticism can. When we stick to it that there *is* truth (be it of either kind), we do so with our whole nature, and resolve to stand or fall by the results. The sceptic with his whole nature adopts the doubting attitude; but which of us is the wiser, Omniscience only knows.

Turn now from these wide questions of good to a certain class of questions of fact, questions concerning personal relations, states of mind between one man and another. *Do you like me or not?*—for example. Whether you do or not depends, in countless instances, on whether I meet you half-way, am willing to assume that you must like me, and show you trust and expectation. The previous faith on my part in your liking's existence is in such cases what makes your liking come. But if I stand aloof, and refuse to budge an inch until I have objective evidence, until you shall have done something apt, as the absolutists say, *ad extorquendum assensum meum,* ten to one your liking never comes. How many women's hearts are vanquished by the mere sanguine insistence of some man that they *must* love him! he will not consent to the hypothesis that they cannot. The desire for a certain kind of truth here brings about that special truth's existence; and so it is in innumerable cases of other sorts. Who gains promotions, boons, appointments, but the man in whose life they are seen to play the part of live hypotheses, who discounts them, sacrifices other things for their sake before they have come, and takes risks for them in advance? His faith acts on the powers above him as a claim, and creates its own verification.

A social organism of any sort whatever, large or small, is what it is because each member proceeds to his own duty with a trust that the other members will simultaneously do theirs. Wherever a desired result is achieved by the co-operation of many independent persons, its existence as a fact is a pure consequence of the precursive faith in one another of those immediately concerned. A government, an army, a commercial system, a ship, a college, an athletic team, all exist on this condition, without which not only is nothing achieved, but nothing is even attempted. A whole train of passengers (individually brave enough) will be looted by a few highwaymen, simply because the latter can count on one another, while each passenger fears that if he makes a movement of resistance, he will be shot before any one else backs him up. If we believed that the whole car-full would rise at once with us, we should each severally rise, and train-robbing would never even be attempted. There are, then, cases where a fact cannot come at all unless a preliminary faith exists in its coming. *And where faith in a fact can help create the fact,* that would be an insane logic which should say that faith running ahead of scientific evidence is the 'lowest kind of immorality' into which a thinking being can fall. Yet such is the logic by which our scientific absolutists pretend to regulate our lives!

10

In truths dependent on our personal action, then, faith based on desire is certainly a lawful and possibly an indispensable thing.

But now, it will be said, these are all childish human cases, and have nothing to do with great cosmical matters, like the question of religious faith. Let us then pass on to that. Religions differ so much in their accidents that in discussing the religious question we must make it very generic and broad. What then do we now mean by the religious hypothesis? Science says things are; morality says some things are better than other things; and religion says essentially two things.

First, she says that the best things are the more eternal things, the over-lapping things, the things in the universe that throw the last stone, so to speak, and say the final word. "Perfection is eternal,"—this phrase of Charles Secrétan seems a good way of putting this first affirmation of religion, an affirmation which obviously cannot yet be verified scientifically at all.

The second affirmation of religion is that we are better off even now if we believe her first affirmation to be true.

Now, let us consider what the logical elements of this situation are *in case the religious hypothesis in both its branches be really true.* (Of course, we must admit that possibility at the outset. If we are to discuss the question at all, it must involve a living option. If for any of you religion be a hypothesis that cannot, by any living possibility be true, then you need go no farther. I speak to the 'saving remnant' alone.) So proceeding, we see, first that religion offers itself as a *momentous* option. We are supposed to gain, even now, by our belief, and to lose by our nonbelief, a certain vital good. Secondly, religion is a *forced* option, so far as that good goes. We cannot escape the issue by remaining sceptical and waiting for more light, because, although we do avoid error in that way *if religion be untrue,* we lose the good, *if it be true,* just as certainly as if we positively chose to disbelieve. It is as if a man should hesitate indefinitely to ask a certain woman to marry him because he was not perfectly sure that she would prove an angel after he brought her home. Would he not cut himself off from that particular angel-possibility as decisively as if he went and married some one else? Scepticism, then, is not avoidance of option; it is option of a certain particular kind of risk. *Better risk loss of truth than chance of error,*—that is your faith-vetoer's exact position. He is actively playing his stake as much as the believer is; he is backing the field against the religious hypothesis, just as the believer is backing the religious hypothesis against the field. To preach scepticism to us as a duty until 'sufficient evidence' for religion be found, is tantamount therefore to telling us, when in presence of the religious hypothesis, that to yield to our fear of its being error is wiser and better than to yield to our hope that it may be true. It is not intellect against all passions, then; it is only intellect with one passion laying down its law. And by what, forsooth, is the supreme wisdom of this passion warranted? Dupery for dupery, what proof is there that dupery through hope is so much worse than dupery through fear? I, for one, can see no proof; and I simply refuse obedience to the scientist's command to imitate his kind of option, in a case where my own stake is important enough to give me the right to choose my own form of risk. If religion be true and the evidence for it be still insufficient, I do not wish, by putting your extinguisher upon my nature (which feels to me as if it had after all some business in this matter), to forfeit my sole chance in life of getting upon the winning side,—that chance depending, of course, on my willingness to run the risk of acting as if my passional need of taking the world religiously might be prophetic and right.

All this is on the supposition that it really may be prophetic and right, and that, even to us who are discussing the matter, religion is a live hypothesis which may be true. Now, to most of us religion comes in a still further way that makes a veto on our active faith even more illogical. The more perfect and more eternal aspect of the universe is represented in our religions as having personal form. The universe is no longer a mere *It* to us, but a *Thou,* if we are religious; and any relation that may be possible from person to person might be possible here. For instance, although in one sense we are passive portions of the universe, in another we show a curious autonomy, as if we were small active centres on our own account. We feel, too, as if the appeal of religion to us were made to our own active good-will, as if evidence might be forever withheld from us unless we met the hypothesis half-way. To take a trivial illustration: just as a man who in a company of gentlemen made no advances, asked a warrant for every concession, and believed no one's word without proof, would cut himself off by such churlishness from all the social rewards that a more trusting spirit would earn,—so here, one who should shut himself up in snarling logicality and try to make the gods extort his recognition willy-nilly, or not get it at all, might cut himself off forever from his only opportunity of making the gods' acquaintance. This feeling, forced on us we know not whence, that by obstinately believing that there are gods (although not to do so would be so easy both for our logic and our life) we are doing the universe the deepest service we can, seems part of the living essence of the religious hypothesis. If the hypothesis *were* true in all its parts, including this one, then pure intellectualism, with its veto on our making willing advances, would be an absurdity; and some participation of our sympathetic nature would be logically required. I, therefore, for one, cannot see my way to accepting the agnostic rules for truth-seeking, or wilfully agree to keep my willing nature out of the game. I cannot do so for this plain reason, that *a rule of thinking which would absolutely prevent me from acknowledging certain kinds of truth if those kinds of truth were really there, would be an irrational rule*. That for me is the long and short of the formal logic of the situation, no matter what the kinds of truth might materially be.

I confess I do not see how this logic can be escaped. But sad experience makes me fear that some of you may still shrink from radically saying with me, *in abstracto,* that we have the right to believe at our own risk any hypothesis that is live enough to tempt our will. I suspect, however, that if this is so, it is because you have got away from the abstract logical point of view altogether, and are thinking (perhaps without realizing it) of some particular religious hypothesis which for you is dead. The freedom to 'believe what we will' you apply to the case of some patent superstition; and the faith you think of is the faith defined by the schoolboy when he said, "Faith is when you believe something that you know ain't true." I can only repeat that this is misapprehension. *In concreto,* the freedom to believe can only cover living options which the intellect of the individual cannot by itself resolve; and living options never seem absurdities to him who has them to consider. When I look at the religious question as it really puts itself to concrete men, and when I think of all the possibilities which both practically and theoretically it involves, then this command that we shall put a stopper on our heart, instincts, and courage, and *wait*—acting of course meanwhile more or less as if religion were *not* true[2]—till doomsday, or till such time as our intellect and senses working together may have raked in evidence enough,—this command, I say, seems to me the queerest idol ever manufactured in the philosophic cave. Were we scholastic absolutists, there might be more excuse. If we had an infallible intellect with its objective certitudes, we might feel ourselves disloyal to such a perfect organ of knowledge in not trusting to it exclusively, in not waiting for its releas-

[2] Since belief is measured by action, he who forbids us to believe religion to be true, necessarily also forbids us to act as we should if we did believe it to be true. The whole defence of religious faith hinges upon action. If the action required or inspired by the religious hypothesis is in no way different from that dictated by the naturalistic hypothesis, then religious faith is a pure superfluity, better pruned away, and controversy about its legitimacy is a piece of idle trifling, unworthy of serious minds. I myself believe, of course, that the religious hypothesis gives to the world an expression which specifically determines our reactions, and makes them in a large part unlike what they might be on a purely naturalistic scheme of belief.

ing word. But if we are empiricists, if we believe that no bell in us tolls to let us know for certain when truth is in our grasp, then it seems a piece of idle fantasticality to preach so solemnly our duty of waiting for the bell. Indeed we *may* wait if we will,—I hope you do not think that I am denying that,—but if we do so, we do so at our peril as much as if we believed. In either case we *act,* taking our life in our hands. No one of us ought to issue vetoes to the other, nor should we bandy words of abuse. We ought, on the contrary, delicately and profoundly to respect one another's mental freedom: then only shall we bring about the intellectual republic; then only shall we have that spirit of inner tolerance without which all our outer tolerance is soulless, and which is empiricism's glory; then only shall we live and let live, in speculative as well as in practical things.

JOHN WISDOM
(1904-   )

The following essay appears in John Wisdom's book appropriately titled **Philosophy and Psychoanalysis.** In his many essays on many themes Wisdom brings the training of a contemporary British analytic philosopher to questions steadfastly avoided by some of his more cautious peers. To use James' distinction, he knows how to avoid error but he also pursues truth.

Wisdom returns to the theme raised in the introduction "On relating to the Divine." He agrees that the question of the existence of God is less of the "betting sort" than it used to be. In other words, religious belief does not hang on whether there is or is not a God to whom one might appeal in attempting to explain certain features of experience, features that might then be taken as positive evidence for the existence of God. Where James' answer to Clifford argues for the need to make decisions even where the evidence is incomplete, Wisdom tries to show how questions of evidence can be finally irrelevant. He offers cases in which two people with the very same evidence at their disposal come to different conclusions, and then he investigates the reasons for their differences. Finally it comes down to something like a difference in evaluation rather than a difference about facts being described. (See again the introductions to Schopenhauer and Nietzsche.) But the conceptual distinction between evaluative and descriptive dimensions should not be taken to imply that the descriptive dimension is irrelevant to the evaluative dimension. I avoid saying that **facts** are relevant to **values** because the very use of the different nouns 'fact' and 'value' severs the unity of judgment in precisely the way criticized by those who object to the objectivity of so-called facts. If, as Polanyi, Kierkegaard, and James suggest in their various ways, there is no such thing as a domain of purely objective facts, then it is equally true that values are not purely subjective. Just as the subjective and objective were joined in James' "Does Consciousness Exist?" so the factual and the evaluative are no more than distinguishable dimensions of the same judgments. While it makes sense to make the distinction in order to account for the kind of disagreements Wisdom describes, when people agree about the "facts" of a question but disagree about how to answer the question, that sensible distinction should not be taken to imply that either "facts" or "values" can be wholly abstracted from one another. They are at least as loosely wedded as, say, the size and weight of material objects. Size does not determine weight, nor weight size, but knowing one gives you a good hint about the other. And the two are always wedded: without size there is no weight, and while it is possible to **indicate** a shape with a size, that shape cannot be the shape **of** a material object unless that object has weight.[1] One can think of other distinguishables that are not separate from one another in existence, for example, the distinction of velocity into speed and direction. Try to think of other analogies that capture the relationship between the factual and the evaluative in judgment.

The way Wisdom preserves the factual dimension in religious evaluation is significant from the perspective of earlier themes. He speaks of the "Connecting Technique." In describing the Connecting Technique he uses the example of looking at art. Finding beauty in a thing is rather like finding the university among its many buildings or sacredness in the world: it is not a matter of finding another building (or another fact to prove the existence of God); rather, it is like seeing the connections and relations among the buildings one has already seen or the pattern of one's own experience that constitute a transfiguration of the same old figures. It is all there all the time. It is only a question of **how** we see it. (Note the similarity to the existentialist claim that it is not so much **what** one does that counts as **how** one does it. But of course the how and the what are no more rigidly distinct than fact and value.)

Though I balk at multiple metaphors and parenthetical additions, these stylistic atrocities are unavoidable at this stage of our analysis. If you have followed this book in something like the or-

---

[1] Weightlessness in outer space might be a counterexample except that it suggests an extension of the analogy: value-free inquiry, if at all possible, is about as rare and difficult as travel in outer space. Generally and for the most part facts and values are as closely wedded as size and weight.

der in which it was composed you should be able to see many strands crowding together here toward the end. Wisdom's essay is a complement to Erikson's; both suggest ways to read virtually every other essay. Where Erikson stresses the forward-looking, dynamic opening-up to all the issues that must enter into the consolidation of one's historical identity, Wisdom's essay suggests a more retrospective, esthetic assimilation of everything that is already available. The connecting technique reflects the method of totalization, and at the same time it shows why that method is often difficult to employ: even the broadest range of "facts" is open to differing evaluations. Granting that a broader range of facts usually issues in more reasonable evaluations (just as big things are usually heavier), still the possibility remains that differences persist even after totalization. Perhaps these are the differences that finally constitute human freedom precisely because they are the differences beyond all determination of facts.

Gods

1. *The existence of God is not an experimental issue in the way it was.* An atheist or agnostic might say to a theist 'You still think there are spirits in the trees, nymphs in the streams, a God of the world.' He might say this because he noticed the theist in time of drought pray for rain and make a sacrifice and in the morning look for rain. But disagreement about whether there are gods is now less of this experimental or betting sort than it used to be. This is due in part, if not wholly, to our better knowledge of why things happen as they do.

It is true that even in these days it is seldom that one who believes in God has no hopes or fears which an atheist has not. Few believers now expect prayer to still the waves, but some think it makes a difference to people and not merely in ways the atheist would admit. Of course with people, as opposed to waves and machines, one never knows what they won't do next, so that expecting prayer to make a difference to them is not so definite a thing as believing in its mechanical efficacy. Still, just as primitive people pray in a business-like way for rain so some people still pray for others with a real feeling of doing something to help. However, in spite of this persistence of an experimental element in some theistic belief, it remains true that Elijah's method on Mount Carmel of settling the matter of what god or gods exist would be far less appropriate to-day than it was then.

2. *Belief in gods is not merely a matter of expectation of a world to*

GODS From John Wisdom, *Philosophy and Psycho-Analysis.* Published by Basil Blackwell Publishers. Copyright © 1957. Also from "Proceedings of the Aristotelian Society," New Series, Vol. XLV, 1944–45. Published by Harrison and Sons, Ltd. Reprinted by permission.

come. Someone may say 'The fact that a theist no more than an atheist expects prayer to bring down fire from heaven or cure the sick does not mean that there is no difference between them as to the facts, it does not mean that the theist has no expectations different from the atheist's. For very often those who believe in God believe in another world and believe that God is there and that we shall go to that world when we die.'

This is true, but I do not want to consider here expectations as to what one will see and feel after death nor what sort of reasons these logically unique expectations could have. So I want to consider those theists who do not believe in a future life, or rather, I want to consider the differences between atheists and theists in so far as these differences are not a matter of belief in a future life.

3. *What are these differences? And is it that theists are superstitious or that atheists are blind?* A child may wish to sit a while with his father and he may, when he has done what his father dislikes, fear punishment and feel distress at causing vexation, and while his father is alive he may feel sure of help when danger threatens and feel that there is sympathy for him when disaster has come. When his father is dead he will no longer expect punishment or help. Maybe for a moment an old fear will come or a cry for help escape him, but he will at once remember that this is no good now. He may feel that his father is no more until perhaps someone says to him that his father is still alive though he lives now in another world and one so far away that there is no hope of seeing him or hearing his voice again. The child may be told that nevertheless his father can see him and hear all he says. When he has been told this the child will still fear no punishment nor expect any sign of his father, but now, even more than he did when his father was alive, he will feel that his father sees him all the time and will dread distressing him and when he has done something wrong he will feel separated from his father until he has felt sorry for what he has done. Maybe when he himself comes to die he will be like a man who expects to find a friend in the strange country where he is going, but even when this is so, it is by no means all of what makes the difference between a child who believes that his father lives still in another world and one who does not.

Likewise one who believes in God may face death differently from one who does not, but there is another difference between them besides this. This other difference may still be described as belief in another world, only this belief is not a matter of expecting one thing rather than another here or hereafter, it is not a matter of a world to come but of a world that now is, though beyond our senses.

We are at once reminded of those other unseen worlds which some philosophers 'believe in' and others 'deny', while nonphilosophers unconsciously 'accept' them by using them as models with which to 'get the hang of' the patterns in the flux of experience. We recall the timeless entities whose changeless connections we seek to represent in symbols, and the values which stand firm[1] amidst our flickering satisfaction and remorse, and the physical things which, though not beyond the corruption of moth and rust, are yet more permanent than the shadows they throw upon the screen before our minds. We recall, too, our talk of souls and of what lies in their depths and is manifested to us partially and intermittently in our own feelings and the behaviour of others. The hypothesis of mind, of other human minds and of animal minds, is reasonable because it explains for each of us why certain things behave so cunningly all by themselves unlike even the most ingenious machines. Is the hypothesis of minds in flowers and trees reasonable for like reasons? Is the hypothesis of a world mind reasonable for like reasons—someone who adjusts the blossom to the bees, someone whose presence may at times be felt—in a garden in high summer, in the hills when clouds are gathering, but not, perhaps, in a cholera epidemic?

4. *The question 'Is belief in gods reasonable?' has more than one source.* It is clear now that in order to grasp fully the logic of belief in divine minds we need to examine the logic of belief in animal and human minds. But we cannot do that here and so for the purposes of this discussion about divine minds let us acknowledge the reasonableness of our belief in human minds without troubling ourselves about its logic. The question of the reasonableness of belief in divine minds then becomes a matter of whether there are facts in nature which support claims about divine minds in the way facts in nature support our claims about human minds.

In this way we resolve the force behind the problem of the existence of gods into two components, one metaphysical and the same which prompts the question 'Is there *ever any* behaviour which gives reason to believe in *any* sort of mind?' and one which finds expression in 'Are there other mind-patterns in nature beside the human and animal patterns which we can all easily detect, and are these other mind-patterns super-human?'

Such over-determination of a question syndrome is common. Thus, the puzzling questions 'Do dogs think?', 'Do animals feel?' are partly metaphysical puzzles and partly scientific questions. They are not purely metaphysical; for the reports of scientists about the poor performances of cats in cages and old ladies' stories about the remarkable performances of their pets are not irrelevant. But nor are these questions purely scientific; for the stories never settle them and therefore they have other sources. One other source is the metaphysical source we have already noticed, namely, the difficulty about getting behind an animal's behaviour to its mind, whether it is a non-human animal or a human one.

But there's a third component in the force behind these questions, these disputes have a third source, and it is one which is important in the dispute which finds expression in the words 'I believe in God', 'I do not'. This source comes out well if we consider the question 'Do flowers feel?' Like

[1] In another world, Dr. Joad says in the *New Statesman* recently.

the questions about dogs and animals this question about flowers comes partly from the difficulty we sometimes feel over inference from *any* behaviour to thought or feeling and partly from ignorance as to what behaviour is to be found. But these questions, as opposed to a like question about human beings, come also from hesitation as to whether the behaviour in question is *enough* mind-like, that is, is it enough similar to or superior to human behaviour to be called 'mind-proving'? Likewise, even when we are satisfied that human behaviour shows mind and even when we have learned whatever mind-suggesting things there are in nature which are not explained by human and animal minds, we may still ask 'But are these things sufficiently striking to be called a mind-pattern? Can we fairly call them manifestations of a divine being?'

'The question', someone may say, 'has then become merely a matter of the application of a name. And "What's in a name?" '

5. *But the line between a question of fact and a question or decision as to the application of a name is not so simple as this way of putting things suggests.* The question 'What's in a name?' is engaging because we are inclined to answer both 'Nothing' and 'Very much'. And this 'Very much' has more than one source. We might have tried to comfort Heloise by saying 'It isn't that Abelard no longer loves you, for this man isn't Abelard'; we might have said to poor Mr. Tebrick in Mr. Garnet's *Lady into Fox* 'But this is no longer Silvia'. But if Mr. Tebrick replied 'Ah, but it is!' this might come not at all from observing facts about the fox which we have not observed, but from noticing facts about the fox which we had missed, although we had in a sense observed all that Mr. Tebrick had observed. It is possible to have before one's eyes all the items of a pattern and still to miss the pattern. Consider the following conversation:

' "And I think Kay and I are pretty happy. We've always been happy."

'Bill lifted up his glass and put it down without drinking.

' "Would you mind saying that again?" he asked.

' "I don't see what's so queer about it. Taken all in all, Kay and I have really been happy."

' "All right," Bill said gently, "Just tell me how you and Kay have been happy."

'Bill had a way of being amused by things which I could not understand.

' "It's a little hard to explain," I said. "It's like taking a lot of numbers that don't look alike and that don't mean anything until you add them all together."

'I stopped, because I hadn't meant to talk to him about Kay and me.

' "Go ahead," Bill said. "What about the numbers." And he began to smile.

' "I don't know why you think it's so funny," I said. "All the things that two people do together, two people like Kay and me, add up to something. There are the kids and the house and the dog and all the people we have known and all the times we've been out to dinner. Of course, Kay and I do quarrel sometimes but when you add it all together, all of it isn't as bad as the parts of it seem. I mean, maybe that's all there is to anybody's life."

'Bill poured himself another drink. He seemed about to say something and checked himself. He kept looking at me.'[2]

Or again, suppose two people are speaking of two characters in a story which both have read[3] or of two friends which both have known, and one says 'Really she hated him', and the other says 'She didn't, she loved him'. Then the first may have noticed what the other has not although he knows no incident in the lives of the people they are talking about which the other doesn't know too, and the second speaker may say 'She didn't, she loved him' because he hasn't noticed what the first noticed, although he can remember every incident the first can remember. But then again he may say 'She didn't, she loved him' not because he hasn't noticed the patterns in time which the first has noticed but because though he has noticed them he doesn't feel he still needs to emphasize them with 'Really she hated him'. The line between using a name because of how we feel and because of what we have noticed isn't sharp. 'A difference as to the facts', 'a discovery', 'a revelation', these phrases cover many things. Discoveries have been made not only by Christopher Columbus and Pasteur, but also by Tolstoy and Dostoievsky and Freud. Things are revealed to us not only by the scientists with microscopes, but also by the poets, the prophets, and the painters. What is so isn't merely a matter of 'the facts'. For sometimes when there is agreement as to the facts there is still argument as to whether defendant did or did not 'exercise reasonable care', was or was not 'negligent'.

And though we shall need to emphasize how much 'There is a God' evinces an attitude to the familiar[4] we shall find in the end that it also evinces some recognition of patterns in time easily missed and that, therefore, difference as to there being any gods is in part a difference as to what is so and therefore as to the facts, though not in the simple ways which first occurred to us.

6. *Let us now approach these same points by a different road.*

6.1. *How it is that an explanatory hypothesis, such as the existence of God, may start by being experimental and gradually become something quite different can be seen from the following story:*

Two people return to their long neglected garden and find among the weeds a few of the old plants surprisingly vigorous. One says to the other 'It must be that a gardener has been coming and doing something about these plants'. Upon inquiry they find that no neighbour has ever seen anyone at work in their garden. The first man say to the other 'He must have

---

[2] *H. M. Pulham, Esq.,* p. 320, by John P. Marquand.

[3] e.g. Havelock Ellis's autobiography.

[4] 'Persuasive Definitions', *Mind,* July, 1938, by Charles Leslie Stevenson, should be read here. It is very good.

worked while people slept'. The other says 'No, someone would have heard him and besides, anybody who cared about the plants would have kept down these weeds'. The first man says 'Look at the way these are arranged. There is purpose and a feeling for beauty here. I believe that someone comes, someone invisible to mortal eyes. I believe that the more carefully we look the more we shall find confirmation of this.' They examine the garden ever so carefully and sometimes they come on new things suggesting that a gardener comes and sometimes they come on new things suggesting the contrary and even that a malicious person has been at work. Besides examining the garden carefully they also study what happens to gardens left without attention. Each learns all the other learns about this and about the garden. Consequently, when after all this, one says 'I still believe a gardener comes' while the other says 'I don't' their different words now reflect no difference as to what they have found in the garden, no difference as to what they would find in the garden if they looked further and no difference about how fast untended gardens fall into disorder. At this stage, in this context, the gardener hypothesis has ceased to be experimental, the difference between one who accepts and one who rejects it is now not a matter of the one expecting something the other does not expect. What is the difference between them? The one says 'A gardner comes unseen and unheard. He is manifested only in his works with which we are all familiar', the other says 'There is no gardener' and with this difference in what they say about the gardener goes a difference in how they feel towards the garden, in spite of the fact that neither expects anything of it which the other does not expect.

But is this the whole difference between them—that the one calls the garden by one name and feels one way towards it, while the other calls it by another name and feels in another way towards it? And if this is what the difference has become then is it any longer appropriate to ask 'Which is right?' or 'Which is reasonable?'

And yet surely such questions *are* appropriate when one person says to another 'You still think the world's a garden and not a wilderness, and that the gardener has not forsaken it' or 'You still think there are nymphs of the streams, a presence in the hills, a spirit of the world'. Perhaps when a man sings 'God's in His heaven' we need not take this as more than an expression of how he feels. But when Bishop Gore or Dr. Joad write about belief in God and young men read them in order to settle their religious doubts the impression is not simply that of persons choosing exclamations with which to face nature and the 'changes and chances of this mortal life'. The disputants speak as if they are concerned with a matter of scientific fact, or of trans-sensual, trans-scientific and metaphysical fact, but still of fact and still a matter about which reasons for and against may be offered, although no scientific reasons in the sense of field surveys for fossils or experiments on delinquents are to the point.

6.2. *Now can an interjection have a logic?* Can the manifestation of an attitude in the utterance of a word, in the application of a name, have a logic? When all the facts are known how can there still be a question of fact? How can there still be a question? Surely as Hume says '. . . after every circumstance, every relation is known, the understanding has no further room to operate'?[5]

6.3. When the madness of these questions leaves us for a moment *we can all easily recollect disputes which though they cannot be settled by experiment are yet disputes in which one party may be right and the other wrong* and in which both parties may offer reasons and the one better reasons than the other. *This may happen in pure and applied mathematics and logic.* Two accountants or two engineers provided with the same data may reach different results and this difference is resolved not by collecting further data but by going over the calculations again. Such differences indeed share with differences as to what will win a race, the honour of being among the most 'settlable' disputes in the language.

6.4. *But it won't do to describe the theistic issue as one settlable by such calculation,* or as one about what can be deduced in this *vertical* fashion from the facts we know. No doubt dispute about God has sometimes, perhaps especially in mediaeval times, been carried on in this fashion. But nowadays it is not and we must look for some other analogy, some other case in which a dispute is settled but not by experiment.

6.5. *In courts of law* it sometimes happens that opposing counsel are agreed as to the facts and are not trying to settle a question of further fact, are not trying to settle whether the man who admittedly had quarrelled with the deceased did or did not murder him, but are concerned with whether Mr. A who admittedly handed his long-trusted clerk signed blank cheques did or did not exercise reasonable care, whether a ledger is or is not a document,[6] whether a certain body was or was not a public authority.

In such cases we notice that the process of argument is not a *chain* of demonstrative reasoning. It is a presenting and representing of those features of the case which *severally co-operate* in favour of the conclusion, in favour of saying what the reasoner wishes said, in favour of calling the situation by the name by which he wishes to call it. The reasons are like the legs of a chair, not the links of a chain. Consequently although the discussion is *a priori* and the steps are not a matter of experience, the procedure resembles scientific argument in that the reasoning is not *vertically* extensive but *horizontally* extensive—it is a matter of the cumulative effect of several independent premises, not of the repeated transformation of one or

---

[5] Hume, *An Equiry concerning the Principles of Morals.* Appendix I.

[6] *The Times,* March 2nd, 1945. Also in *The Times* of June 13th 1945, contrast the case of Hannah v. Peel with that of the cruiser cut in two by a liner. In the latter case there is not agreement as to the facts. See also the excellent articles by Dr. Glanville L. Williams in the *Law Quarterly Review,* 'Language and the Law', January, and April 1945, and 'The Doctrine of Repugnancy', October, 1943, January, 1944, and April, 1944. The author, having set out how arbitrary are many legal decisions, needs now to set out how far from arbitrary they are—if his readers are ready for the next phase in the dialectic process.

two. And because the premises are severally inconclusive the process of deciding the issue becomes a matter of weighing the cumulative effect of one group of several inconclusive items against the cumulative effect of another group of severally inconclusive items, and thus lends itself to description in terms of conflicting 'probabilities'. This encourages the feeling that the issue is one of fact—that it is a matter of guessing from the premises at a further fact, at what is to come. But this is a muddle. *The dispute does not cease to be* a priori *because it is a matter of the cumulative effect of severally inconclusive premises.* The logic of the dispute is not that of a chain of deductive reasoning as in a mathematic calculation. But nor is it a matter of collecting from several inconclusive items of information an expectation as to something further, as when a doctor from a patient's symptoms guesses at what is wrong, or a detective from many clues guesses the criminal. It has its own sort of logic and its own sort of end—the solution of the question at issue is a decision, a ruling by the judge. But it is not an arbitrary decision though the rational connections are neither quite like those in vertical deductions nor like those in inductions in which from many signs we guess at what is to come; and though the decision manifests itself in the application of a name it is no more merely the application of a name than is the pinning on of a medal merely the pinning on of a bit of metal. Whether a lion with stripes is a tiger or a lion is, if you like, merely a matter of the application of a name. Whether Mr. So-and-So of whose conduct we have so complete a record did or did not exercise reasonable care is not merely a matter of the application of a name or, if we choose to say it is, then we must remember that with this name a game is lost and won and a game with very heavy stakes. With the judges' choice of a name for the facts goes an attitude, and the declaration, the ruling, is an exclamation evincing that attitude. But *it is an exclamation which not only has a purpose but also has a logic,* a logic surprisingly like that of 'futile', 'deplorable', 'graceful', 'grand', 'divine'.

6.6. *Suppose two people are looking at a picture or natural scene.* One says 'Excellent' or 'Beautiful' or 'Divine'; the other says 'I don't see it'. He means he doesn't see the beauty. And this reminds us of how we felt the theist accuse the atheist of blindness and the atheist accuse the theist of seeing what isn't there. And yet surely each sees what the other sees. It isn't that one can see part of the picture which the other can't see. So the difference is in a sense not one as to the facts. And so it cannot be removed by the one disputant discovering to the other what so far he hasn't seen. It isn't that the one sees the picture in a different light and so, as we might say, sees a different picture. Consequently the difference between them cannot be resolved by putting the picture in a different light. And yet surely this is just what can be done in such a case—not by moving the picture but by talk perhaps. To settle a dispute as to whether a piece of music is good or better than another we listen again, with a picture we look again. Someone perhaps points to emphasize certain features and we see it in a different light. Shall we call this 'field work' and 'the last of observation' or shall we call it 'reviewing the premises' and 'the beginning of deduction (horizontal)'?

If in spite of all this we choose to say that a difference as to whether a thing is beautiful is not a factual difference we must be careful to remember that there is a procedure for settling these differences and that this consists not only in reasoning and redescription as in the legal case, but also in a more literal re-setting-before with re-looking or re-listening.

6.7. *And if we say as we did at the beginning that when a difference as to the existence of a God is not one as to future happenings then it is not experimental and therefore not as to the facts, we must not forthwith assume that there is no right and wrong about it,* no rationality or irrationality, no appropriateness or inappropriateness, no procedure which tends to settle it, *nor even that this procedure is in no sense a discovery of new facts.* After all even in science this is not so. Our two gardeners even when they had reached the stage when neither expected any experimental result which the other did not, might yet have continued the dispute, each presenting and representing the features of the garden favouring his hypothesis, that is, fitting his model for describing the accepted fact; each emphasizing the pattern he wishes to emphasize. True, in science, there is seldom or never a pure instance of this sort of dispute, for nearly always with difference of hypothesis goes some difference of expectation as to the facts. But scientists argue about rival hypotheses with a vigour which is not exactly proportioned to difference in expectations of experimental results.

The difference as to whether a God exists involves our feelings more than most scientific disputes and in this respect is more like a difference as to whether there is beauty in a thing.

7. *The Connecting Technique.* Let us consider again the technique used in revealing or proving beauty, in removing a blindness, in inducing an attitude which is lacking, in reducing a reaction that is inappropriate. Besides running over in a special way the features of the picture, tracing the rhythms, making sure that this and that are not only seen but noticed, and their relation to each other—besides all this—there are other things we can do to justify our attitude and alter that of the man who cannot see. For features of the picture may be brought out by setting beside it other pictures; just as the merits of an argument may be brought out, proved, by setting beside it other arguments, in which striking but irrelevant features of the original are changed and relevant features emphasized; just as the merits and demerits of a line of action may be brought out by setting beside it other actions. To use Susan Stebbing's example: Nathan brought out for David certain features of what David had done in the matter of Uriah the Hittite by telling him a story about two sheepowners. This is the kind of thing we very often do when someone is 'inconsistent' or 'unreasonable'. This is what we do in referring to other cases in law. The paths we need to trace from other cases to the case in question are often numerous and difficult to detect and the person with whom we are discussing the matter may well draw attention to connections which, while not incompatible with those we have tried to em-

phasize, are of an opposite inclination. A may have noticed in B subtle and hidden likenesses to an angel and reveal these to C, while C has noticed in B subtle and hidden likenesses to a devil which he reveals to A.

Imagine that a man picks up some flowers that lie half withered on a table and gently puts them in water. Another man says to him 'You believe flowers feel'. He says this although he knows that the man who helps the flowers doesn't expect anything of them which he himself doesn't expect; for he himself expects the flowers to be 'refreshed' and to be easily hurt, injured, I mean, by rough handling, while the man who puts them in water does not expect them to whisper 'Thank you'. The Sceptic says 'You believe flowers feel' because something about the way the other man lifts the flowers and puts them in water suggests an attitude to the flowers which he feels inappropriate although perhaps he would not feel it inappropriate to butterflies. He feels that this attitude to flowers is somewhat crazy *just as it is sometimes felt that a lover's attitude is somewhat crazy even when this is not a matter of his having false hopes about how the person he is in love with will act.* It is often said in such cases that reasoning is useless. But the very person who says this feels that the lover's attitude is crazy, is inappropriate like some dreads and hatreds, such as some horrors of enclosed places. And often one who says 'It is useless to reason' proceeds at once to reason with the lover, nor is this reasoning always quite without effect. We may draw the lover's attention to certain things done by her he is in love with and trace for him a path to these from things done by others at other times[7] which have disgusted and infuriated him. And by this means we may weaken his admiration and confidence, make him feel it unjustified and arouse his suspicion and contempt and make him feel our suspicion and contempt reasonable. It is possible, of course, that he has already noticed the analogies, the connections, we point out and that he accepted them— that is, he has not denied them nor passed them off. He has recognized them and they have altered his attitude, altered his love, but he still loves. We then feel that perhaps it is we who are blind and cannot see what he can see.

8. *Connecting and Disconnecting.* But before we confess ourselves thus inadequate there are other fires his admiration must pass through. For when a man has an attitude which it seems to us he should not have or lacks one which it seems to us he should have then, not only do we suspect that he is not influenced by connections which we feel should influence him and draw his attention to these, but also we suspect he is influenced by connections which should not influence him and draw his attention to these. It may, for a moment, seem strange that we should draw his attention to connections which we feel should not influence him, and which, since they do influence him, he has in a sense already noticed. But we do—such is our confidence in 'the light of reason'.

---

[7] Thus, like the scientist, the critic is concerned to show up the irrelevance of time and space.

Sometimes the power of these connections comes mainly from a man's management of the language he is using. This is what happens in the Monte Carlo fallacy, where by mismanaging the laws of chance a man passes from noticing that a certain colour or number has not turned up for a long while to an improper confidence that now it soon will turn up. In such cases our showing up of the false connections is a process we call 'explaining a fallacy in reasoning'. To remove fallacies in reasoning we urge a man to call a spade a spade, ask him what he means by 'the State' and having pointed out ambiguities and vaguenesses ask him to reconsider the steps in his argument.

9. *Unspoken Connections. Usually, however, wrongheadedness or wrongheartedness in a situation, blindness to what is there or seeing what is not, does not arise merely from mismanagement of language but is more due to connections which are not mishandled in language, for the reason that they are not put into language at all.* And often these misconnections too, weaken in the light of reason, if only we can guess where they lie and turn it on them. In so far as these connections are not presented in language the process of removing their power is not a process of correcting the mismanagement of language. But it is still akin to such a process; for though it is not a process of setting out fairly what has been set out unfairly, it is a process of setting out fairly what has not been set out at all. And we must remember that the line between connections ill-presented or half-presented in language and connections operative but not presented in language, or only hinted at, is not a sharp one.

Whether or not we call the process of showing up these connections 'reasoning to remove bad unconscious reasoning' or not, it is certain that in order to settle in ourselves what weight we shall attach to someone's confidence or attitude we not only ask him for his reasons but also look for unconscious reasons both good and bad; that is, for reasons which he can't put into words, isn't explicitly aware of, is hardly aware of, isn't aware of at all—perhaps it's long experience which he *doesn't* recall which lets him know a squall is coming, perhaps it's old experience which he *can't* recall which makes the cake in the tea mean so much and makes Odette so fascinating.[8]

I am well aware of the distinction between the question 'What reasons are there for the belief that S is P?' and the question 'What are the sources of beliefs that S is P?' There are cases where investigation of the rationality of a claim which certain persons make is done with very little inquiry into why they say what they do, into the causes of their beliefs. This is so when we have very definite ideas about what is really logically relevant to their claim and what is not. Offered a mathematical theorem we ask for the proof; offered the generalization that parental discord causes crime we ask for the correlation co-efficients. But even in this last case, if we fancy that only the figures are reasons we underestimate the complexity of the logic

---

[8] Proust: *Swann's Way,* Vol. I, p. 58, Vol. II. Phoenix Edition.

of our conclusion; and yet it is difficult to describe the other features of the evidence which have weight and there is apt to be disagreement about the weight they should have. In criticizing other conclusions and especially conclusions which are largely the expression of an attitude, we have not only to ascertain what reasons there are for them but also to decide what things are reasons and how much. This latter process of sifting reasons from causes is part of the critical process for every belief, but in some spheres it has been done pretty fully already. In these spheres we don't need to examine the actual processes to belief and distil from them a logic. But in other spheres this remains to be done. Even in science or on the stock exchange or in ordinary life we sometimes hesitate to condemn a belief or a hunch[9] merely because those who believe it cannot offer the sort of reasons we had hoped for. And now suppose Miss Gertrude Stein finds excellent the work of a new artist while we see nothing in it. We nervously recall, perhaps, how pictures by Picasso, which Miss Stein admired and others rejected, later came to be admired by many who gave attention to them, and we wonder whether the case is not a new instance of her perspicacity and our blindness. But if, upon giving all our attention to the work in question, we still do not respond to it, and we notice that the subject matter of the new pictures is perhaps birds in wild places and learn that Miss Stein is a birdwatcher, then we begin to trouble ourselves less about her admiration.

It must not be forgotten that our attempt to show up misconnections in Miss Stein may have an opposite result and reveal to us connections we had missed. Thinking to remove the spell exercised upon his patient by the old stories of the Greeks, the psycho-analyst may himself fall under that spell and find in them what his patient has found and, incidentally, what made the Greeks tell those tales.

10. *Now what happens, what should happen, when we inquire in this way into the reasonableness, the propriety of belief in gods?* The answer is: A double and opposite-phased change. Wordsworth writes:

> . . . And I have felt
> A presence that disturbs me with the joy
> Of elevated thoughts; a sense sublime
> Of something far more deeply interfused,
> Whose dwelling is the light of setting suns,
> And the round ocean and the living air,
> And the blue sky, and in the mind of man:
> A motion and a spirit, that impels
> All thinking things, all objects of all thought,
> And rolls through all things. . .[10]

[9] Here I think of Mr. Stace's interesting reflections in *Mind,* January, 1945, 'The Problems of Unreasoned Beliefs'.

[10] *Tintern Abbey.*

We most of us know this feeling. But is it well placed like the feeling that here is first-rate work, which we sometimes rightly have even before we have fully grasped the picture we are looking at or the book we are reading? Or is it misplaced like the feeling in a house that has long been empty that someone secretly lives there still. Wordsworth's feeling *is* the feeling that the world is haunted, that something watches in the hills and manages the stars. The child feels that the stone tripped him when he stumbled, that the bough struck him when it flew back in his face. He has to learn that the wind isn't buffeting him, that there is not a devil in it, that he was wrong, that his attitude was inappropriate. And as he learns that the wind wasn't hindering him so he also learns it wasn't helping him. But we know how, though he learns, his attitude lingers. It is plain that Wordsworth's feeling is of this family.

Belief in gods, it is true, is often very different from belief that stones are spiteful, the sun kindly. For the gods appear in human form and from the waves and control these things and by so doing reward and punish us. But varied as are the stories of the gods they have a family likeness and we have only to recall them to feel sure of the other main sources which co-operate with animism to produce them.

What are the stories of the gods? What are our feelings when we believe in God? They are feelings of awe before power, dread of the thunderbolts of Zeus, confidence in the everlasting arms, unease beneath the all-seeing eye. They are feelings of guilt and inescapable vengeance, of smothered hate and of a security we can hardly do without. We have only to remind ourselves of these feelings and the stories of the gods and goddesses and heroes in which these feelings find expression, to be reminded of how we felt as children to our parents and the big people of our childhood. Writing of a first telephone call from his grandmother, Proust says: '. . . it was rather that this isolation of the voice was like a symbol, a presentation, a direct consequence of another isolation, that of my grandmother, separated for the first time in my life, from myself. The orders or prohibitions which she addressed to me at every moment in the ordinary course of my life, the tedium of obedience or the fire of rebellion which neutralized the affection that I felt for her were at this moment eliminated. . . . "Granny!" I cried to her . . . but I had beside me only that voice, a phantom, as unpalpable as that which would come to revisit me when my grandmother was dead. "Speak to me!" but then it happened that, left more solitary still, I ceased to catch the sound of her voice. My grandmother could no longer hear me . . . I continued to call her, sounding the empty night, in which I felt that her appeals also must be straying. I was shaken by the same anguish which, in the distant past, I had felt once before, one day when, a little child, in a crowd, I had lost her.'

Giorgio de Chirico, writing of Courbet, says: 'The word yesterday envelops us with its yearning echo, just as, on waking, when the sense of time and the logic of things remain a while confused, the memory of a happy hour we spent the day before may sometimes linger reverberating within us.

At times we think of Courbet and his work as we do of our own father's youth.'

When a man's father fails him by death or weakness how much he needs another father, one in the heavens with whom is 'no variableness nor shadow of turning'.

We understood Mr. Kenneth Graham when he wrote of the Golden Age we feel we have lived in under the Olympians. Freud says: 'The ordinary man cannot imagine this Providence in any other form but that of a greatly exalted father, for only such a one could understand the needs of the sons of men, or be softened by their prayers and be placated by the signs of their remorse. The whole thing is so patently infantile, so incongruous with reality. . . .' 'So incongruous with reality'! It cannot be denied.

But here a new aspect of the matter may strike us.[11] For the very facts which make us feel that now we can recognize systems of superhuman, subhuman, elusive, beings for what they are—the persistent projections of infantile phantasies—include facts which make these systems less fantastic. What are these facts? They are patterns in human reactions which are well described by saying that we are as if there were hidden within us powers, persons, not ourselves and stronger than ourselves. That this is so may perhaps be said to have been common knowledge yielded by ordinary observation of people,[12] but we did not know the degree in which this is so until recent study of extraordinary cases in extraordinary conditions had revealed it. I refer, of course, to the study of multiple personalities and the wider studies of psycho-analysts. Even when the results of this work are reported to us that is not the same as tracing the patterns in the details of the cases on which the results are based; and even that is not the same as taking part in the studies oneself. One thing not sufficiently realized is that some of the things shut within us are not bad but good.

Now the gods, good and evil and mixed, have always been mysterious powers outside us rather than within. But they have also been within. It is not a modern theory but an old saying that in each of us a devil sleeps. Eve said: 'The serpent beguiled me.' Helen says to Menelaus:

> . . . And yet how strange it is!
> I ask not thee; I ask my own sad thought,
> What was there in my heart, that I forgot
> My home and land and all I loved, to fly
> With a strange man? Surely it was not I,
> But Cypris there![13]

[11] I owe to the late Dr. Susan Isaacs the thought of this different aspect of the matter, of this connection between the heavenly Father and 'the good father' spoken of in psychoanalysis.

[12] Consider Tolstoy and Dostoievsky—I do not mean, of course, that their observation was ordinary.

[13] Euripides: *The Trojan Women,* Gilbert Murray's Translation. Roger Hinks in *Myth and Allegory in Ancient Arat* writes (p. 108):

Elijah found that God was not in the wind, nor in the thunder, but in a still small voice. The kingdom of Heaven is within us, Christ insisted, though usually about the size of a grain of mustard seed, and he prayed that we should become one with the Father in Heaven.

New knowledge made it necessary either to give up saying 'The sun is sinking' or to give the words a new meaning. In many contexts we preferred to stick to the old words and give them a new meaning which was not entirely new but, on the contrary, *practically* the same as the old. The Greeks did not speak of the dangers of repressing instincts but they did speak of the dangers of thwarting Dionysos, of neglecting Cypris for Diana, of forgetting Poseidon for Athena. We have eaten of the fruit of a garden we can't forget though we were never there, a garden we still look for though we can never find it. Maybe we look for too simple a likeness to what we dreamed. Maybe we are not as free as we fancy from the old idea that Heaven is a happy hunting ground, or a city with streets of gold. Lately Mr. Aldous Huxley has recommended our seeking not somewhere beyond the sky or late in time but a timeless state not made of the stuff of this world, which he rejects, picking it into worthless pieces. But this sounds to me still too much a looking for another place, not indeed one filled with sweets but instead so empty that some of us would rather remain in the Lamb or the Elephant, where, as we know, they stop whimpering with another bitter and so far from sneering at all things, hang pictures of winners at Kempton and stars of the 'nineties. Something good we have for each other is freed there, and in some degree and for a while the miasma of time is rolled back without obliging us to deny the present.

The artists who do most for us don't tell us only of fairylands. Proust, Manet, Breughel, even Botticelli and Vermeer show us reality. And yet they give us for a moment exhilaration without anxiety, peace without boredom. And those who, like Freud, work in a different way against that which comes over us and forces us into deadness or despair,[14] also deserve critical, patient and courageous attention. For they, too, work to release us from human bondage into human freedom.

Many have tried to find ways of salvation. The reports they bring back are always incomplete and apt to mislead even when they are not in words

---

'Personifications made their appearance very early in Greek poetry. . . . It is out of the question to call these terrible beings "abstractions". . . . They are real daemons to be worshipped and propitiated. . . . These beings we observe correspond to states of mind. The experience of man teaches him that from time to time his composure is invaded and overturned by some power from outside, panic, intoxication, sexual desire.'

What use to shoot off guns at unicorns?
Where one horn's hit another fierce horn grows.
These beasts are fabulous, and none were born
  Of woman who could lay a fable low.—
    The Glass Tower, Nicholas Moore, p. 100.

[14] Matthew Arnold: *Summer Night.*

but in music or paint. But they are by no means useless; and not the worst of them are those which speak of oneness with God. But in so far as we become one with Him He becomes one with us. St. John says he is in us as we love one another.

This love, I suppose, is not benevolence but something that comes of the oneness with one another of which Christ spoke.[15] Sometimes it momentarily gains strength.[16] Hate and the Devil do too. And what is oneness without otherness?

Transition:
Mysticism

Let me lengthen the title of this transition to express a ratio: religion is to mysticism as knowledge is to wisdom and as speech is to silence. Because knowledgeable speech is at issue in understanding this ratio I am naturally at a loss for unambiguous words. To meet the mystics on their own terms I resort to allegory. The following allegory is about words, and the need for allegory will be explained by the allegory.

Imagine a city. It is a city of words. Outside the city lie peaceful pastures and forests of silence. As one approaches the suburbs he finds a few houses, modest edifices of words, mere opinions compared to the larger structures that knowledge has built within the city proper. Now each of us who is a user of language, a knower of truths, or a holder of opinions resides somewhere within the confines of this city or its suburbs. The quest for knowledge leads us deeper into the heart of the city where ever newer buildings are being built. The quest for wisdom— philosophy—takes us in the opposite direction, toward the city limits, beyond which lies the silence of mysticism. This silence is neither absolute quiet nor a refusal to speak. Similarly, mysticism is not the opposite of philosophy, nor wisdom the opposite of knowledge. The silence of mysticism is like nature's silence: nondidactic sounds that are heard only when you listen, a "speech" in rhythms about the fullness of time.

Now I want to draw out the allegory by showing how it helps to answer some perennially baffling questions about the nature of philosophy, such as why philosophy makes no cumulative progress. Other fields of knowledge seem to make advances, but in philosophy we still read the ancient Greeks. What is more, one of those ancients claimed to know nothing, yet we still read about him. What did Socrates mean when he said his wisdom consisted in knowing that he was ignorant?

[15] St. John xvi, 21.

[16] 'The Harvesters' in *The Golden Age,* Kenneth Graham.

What is the relation between philosophy and knowledge? What is the difference between wisdom and knowledge? The picture of the city of words suggests a very simple answer: The quest for knowledge takes one toward the center of the city, the love of wisdom takes one toward the periphery. Philosophy makes no cumulative advances because it builds no buildings. It does not erect any new edifices of words. Yet it uses words in new and different ways because its task is to construct a word map showing the way out of the city of words. Philosophy must acquaint itself with each new project in urban renewal, not in order to add its own new knowledge, but to revise the map leading out of the city. Socrates was well acquainted with the knowledge of his day, but he insisted that he had no special knowledge that others lacked. He could not build any new buildings in the city of words. He could only lead others out of the city.

The picture also helps us understand two other curious phenomena about philosophy: first, Socrates' need to talk to different people in different ways, and second, the proliferation and survival of different and conflicting philosophies. Because different people reside at different places within the city of words, different paths mark the shortest routes to the periphery. Consequently Socrates will lead different people along different paths, and the history of philosophy, unlike the history of science, does not have to shut off one path in order to open another. Urban renewal requires the destruction of one building to make way for another, but philosophy is not about erecting new knowledge that will be the same for all who approach it. One philosophy shows the way out of one part of the city, another philosophy shows the way out of another.

Part of the importance of self-knowledge derives from the need to know one's location in the city. You cannot use a map until you know where you are located on the map. And the lover of wisdom who has the good fortune to make his way out of the city must recognize that his way out will not necessarily serve others who start somewhere else. Here we can see a distinction between the wisdom of the artist who has access to a silence beyond knowledge, and the achievement of the philosopher who knows that it is not enough merely to have left the city. Though he too can describe the peace and beauty of the surrounding pastures, his real task is a return trip to map as many paths as he can so that others may find the beauty described so evocatively by artists —and mystics.

The relationship between philosophy and mysticism can be complementary. Contemporary attitudes often reveal an unnecessary antagonism between those pursuing philosophy and those drawn toward mysticism. Because the philosopher sees the need for words, even in the quest for a silence beyond words, he distrusts the mystic's hasty leap into paradox, irrationalism, and silence. Because the mystic truly does reside outside the city of words he sometimes talks as if words are a hindrance, an unnecessary obstruction to higher states of consciousness. The picture of the city and its surroundings suggests that the philosopher and the mystic are simply preoccupied with different parts of the same journey. The word maps are necessary to lead the lover of wisdom to where it finally makes sense to transcend words, at which point the mystic way is necessary for further progress. But the mystic can speak only to those who have ears to hear, that is, to those who have made it to the outer limits, whether through philosophy or through accidental wanderings (grace, they used to call it). It is a mistake to imagine that one can, while residing at the middle of the city, utter a few mystic incantations and find oneself seated in pastures of eternal bliss. It is also a mistake to imagine that as you approach the edge of the city you can expect another book, another piece of knowledge, another string of words to take you from knowledge to wisdom. But who knows when he stands at the edge? How much further have you to go? The path is so constituted that you can see behind you but you cannot see ahead. The one who can help you most is one who knows where you are because he knows you and has traversed the same path before you. With the exception of Socrates, the western tradition has placed very little emphasis on the role of guru, the spiritual master whose individual insight into the student's place enables him to see where the next step should lead. We have placed our trust instead in a religion that tends to treat everyone equally. Christianity has had its beneficial side effects in promoting a spirit of egalitarianism whose democratic ideals led to a political order that is perhaps more just than the caste system in India. But Christian egalitarianism has been confused with the idea that everyone is in the "same place" so that religion can present itself much like a body of knowledge, a temple standing alongside other buildings in the heart of the city. Western religion tends to ignore the importance of differences among individual locations within the secular city. Though almost in spite of itself the church has housed many mystics and many gurus, the favored form of religious education has remained the preacher who speaks the same words to an entire congregation. Using the term "religion" to refer primarily to western religion, I therefore contrast public religion to the privacy of the mystic way just as I contrast the public, intersubjectivity of knowledge to the privacy or at least the particularity of locations on the way to wisdom. Language is the public, intersubjective medium. Its unambiguous, literal use broadcasts the same message to all. Art and allegory, on the other hand, evoke the silences between their words. Within the interstices of nonliteral speech you may hear, if you listen in your own way, a hint of the mystic silence.

DAISETZ T. SUZUKI
(1870-1966)

Many westerners first learned of Zen Buddhism from Daisetz T. Suzuki. For years he has been writing books on Zen. I have chosen the following little known essay partly because his other works are easily available, partly because this essay includes so many points of close relation to other themes in the present volume.

Suzuki contrasts the "outward way" and the "inward way." The inward way leads through self-knowledge to different forms of consciousness. Suzuki's description of the inward way recalls the picture just painted in the preceding transition, as well as the examination of consciousness called for by Marin, Descartes, James, Snyder, and Laing, among others. Suzuki's descriptions of the obscure and seemingly nonsensical sayings of the Buddhist monks also bear comparison with Breton's description of Surrealist methods. Could Surrealism be a western version of the Zen **mondo**—the nonsensical question and answer?

Finally, consider once again the theme of individualism and/or subjectivism. Throughout the following essays on mysticism you might keep in mind a typically paradoxical possibility within the mystic tradition: The way to transcending possessive individualism lies not in the immediate **denial** of self but rather at the end of a path that leads **through** the self—the inward way.

The Awakening of a New Consciousness in Zen

1

My position in regard to "the awakening of a new consciousness," summarily stated, is as follows:

The phrasing, "the awakening of a new consciousness" as it appears in the title of this paper, is not a happy one, because what is awakened in the

THE AWAKENING OF A NEW CONSCIOUSNESS IN ZEN From Daisetz T. Suzuki, "The Awakening of a New Consciousness in Zen," in *Eranos Jahrbuch,* Vol. XXIII, *Mensch und Wandlung,* edited by Olga Frobe-Kapteyn. Published by Rhein-Verlag. Copyright © 1955. Reprinted by permission of Matsugaoka Bunko (The Pine Hill Library).

Zen experience is not a "new" consciousness, but an "old" one which has been dormant ever since our loss of "innocence," to use the Biblical term. The awakening is really the re-discovery or the excavation of a long-lost treasure.[1]

There is in every one of us, though varied in depth and strength, an eternal longing for "something" which transcends a world of inequalities. This is a somewhat vague statement containing expressions not altogether happy. "To transcend" suggests "going beyond," "being away from," that is, a separation, a dualism. I have, however, no desire to hint that the "something" stands away from the world in which we find ourselves. And then "inequalities" may sound too political. When I chose the term I had in mind the Buddhist word *asama* which contrasts with *sama,* "equal" or "same." We may replace it by such words as "differentiation" or "individualisation" or "conditionality." I just want to point out the fact that as soon as we recognise this world to be subject to constant changes we somehow begin to feel dissatisfied with it and desire for something which is permanent, free, above sorrow, and of eternal value.

This longing is essentially religious and each religion has its own way of designating it according to its tradition. Christians may call it longing for the Kingdom of Heaven or renouncing the world for the sake of divine love or praying to be saved from eternal damnation. Buddhists may call it seeking for emancipation or freedom. Indians may understand it as wishing to discover the real self.

Whatever expressions they may use, they all show a certain feeling of discontent with the situation in which they find themselves. They may not yet know exactly how to formulate this feeling and conceptually represent it either to themselves or to others.

I specified this obscure feeling as a longing for something. In this, it may be said, I have already a preconceived idea by assuming the existence of a something for which there is a longing on our part. Instead of saying this, it might have been better to identify the feeling of dissatisfaction with such modern feelings as fear or anxiety or a sense of insecurity. But the naming is not so important. As long as the mind is upset and cannot enjoy any state

---

[1] Cf. "The Ten Oxherding Pictures," IX, entitled "Returning to the Origin, Back to the Source." In the *Lankāvatara Sūtra,* reference is also made to visiting one's native town where every road is familiar. "A new consciousness" is not at all new. Hakuin (1685–1768) refers to Ganto, an ancient master of the T'ang dynasty, while Kosen (1816–1892) brings out Confucius as a witness to his *satori* experience. In Zen literature we often come across such expressions as "Back at home and quietly sitting," "Like seeing one's family in a strange town," etc.

The term "new" may be permissible from the point of view of psychology. But Zen is mainly metaphysical, and it deals with a total personality and not parts of it. Rinzai talks about "the whole being in action" (*zentai sayu*). This is the reason why in Zen beating, slapping, kicking, and other bodily activities are in evidence. Concrete experiences are valued more than mere conceptualisation. Language becomes secondary. In Zen, consciousness in its ordinary scientific sense, has no use; the whole being must come forward. The whole elephant is needed and not its parts as studied by the blind. This will be clearer later on.

of equilibrium or perfect equanimity, this is a sense of insecurity or discontent. We feel as if we were in the air and trying to find a place for landing.

But we do not know exactly where this place for landing is. The objective is an altogether unknown quantity. It can nowhere be located and the fact adds a great deal to our sense of insecurity. We must somewhere and somehow find the landing.

Two ways are open: outward and inward. The outward one may be called intellectual and objective, but the inward one cannot be called subjective or affective or conative. The "inward" is misleading, though it is difficult to designate it in any other way. For all designations are on the plane of intellection. But as we must name it somehow, let us be content for a while to call it "inward" in contrast to "outward."

Let me give you this caution here: as long as the inward way is to be understood in opposition to the outward way,—though to do otherwise is impossible because of the human inability to go beyond language as the means of communication—the inward way after all turns to be an outward way. The really inward way is when no contrast exists between the inward and the outward. This is a logical contradiction. But the full meaning of it will I hope become clearer when I finish this paper.

The essential characteristic of the outward way consists in its never-ending procession, either forward or backward, but mostly in a circular movement, and always retaining the opposition of two terms, subject and object. There is thus no finality in the outward way, hence the sense of insecurity, though security does not necessarily mean "standing still," "not moving anywhere," or "attached to something."

The inward way is the reverse of the outward way. Instead of going out endlessly and dissipating and exhausting itself, the mind turns inwardly to see what is there behind all this endless procession of things. It does not stop the movement in order to examine what is there. If it does, the movement ceases to be a movement; it turns into something else. This is what the intellect does while the inward way refuses to do so. As soon as there is any kind of bifurcation, the outward way asserts itself and the inward way no longer exists. The inward way consists in taking things as they are, in catching them in their is-ness or suchness. I would not say, "in their one-ness" or "in their wholeness." These are the terms belonging to the outward way. Even to say "is-ness" or "suchness" or "thusness" or in Japanese *"sono-mama"* or in Chinese *"chi-mo,"* is not, strictly speaking, the inward way. "To be" is an abstract term. It is much better to lift a finger and say nothing *about* it. The inward way in its orthodoxy generally avoids appealing to language though it never shuns it.

The inward way occasionally uses the term "one" or "all," but in this case "one" means "one that is never one," and "all" means "all that is never all." The "one" will be "a one ever becoming one" and never a closed-up "one." The "all" will be "an all ever becoming all" and never a closed-up "all." This means that in the inward way the one is an absolute one, that one is all and all is one, and further that when "the ten thousand things" are reduced to an absolute oneness which is an absolute nothingness, we have the inward way perfecting itself.

Buddhism, especially Zen Buddhism as it developed in China, is rich in expressions belonging to the inward way. In fact, it is Zen that has effected, for the first time, a deep excavation into the mine of the inward way. To illustrate my point read the following—I give just one instance:

Suigan at the end of the summer session made this declaration: "I have been talking, east and west, all this summer for my Brotherhood. See if my eye-brows are still growing."[2]

One of his disciples said, "How finely they are growing!"

Another said, "One who commits a theft feels uneasy in his heart."

A third one without saying anything simply uttered "Kwan!"[3]

It goes without saying that all these utterances of the disciples as well as of the master give us a glimpse into the scene revealed only to the inward way. They are all expressions directly bursting out of an abyss of absolute nothingness.

Now we come to the psycho-metaphysical aspect of the inward way. Buddhists call this "abyss of absolute nothingness" *kokoro* in Japanese. *Kokoro* is *hsin* in Chinese and in Sanskrit *citta,* or *sarvasattvacitta* to use the term in Aśvaghosha's *Awakening of Faith. Kokoro* is originally a psychological term, meaning "heart," "soul," "spirit," "mind," "thought"; it later came to denote the kernel or essence of a thing, becoming synonymous metaphysically with "substance" and ethically "sincerity," "verity," "faithfulness," etc. It is thus difficult to give one English equivalent for *kokoro.*

[2] An old Indian tradition states that if a man utters an untruth all his facial hair such as beards and eyebrows will fall off. Suigan has spent his summer talking about things that can never be talked about, hence his allusion to his eyebrows still growing.

[3] Language deals with concepts and therefore what cannot be conceptualised is beyond the reach of language. When language is forced, it gets crooked, which means that it becomes illogical, paradoxical, and unintelligible from the viewpoint of ordinary usage of language or by the conventional way of thinking. For instance, the waters are to flow and the bridge is to stay over them. When this is reversed the world of senses goes topsy-turvy. The flowers bloom on the ground and not on rock. Therefore, when a Zen master declares, "I plant the flowers on rock," this must sound crazy. This crookedness all issues from language being used in the way not meant for it. Zen wants to be direct and to act without a medium of any kind. Hence "Katz!" or "Kwan!" Just an ejaculation with no "sense" attached to it. Nor is it a symbol, it is the thing itself. The person is acting and not appealing to concepts. This is intelligible only from the inward way of seeing reality.

Out of this *kokoro* all things are produced and all things ultimately go back to it. But this must not be understood in relation to time. The *kokoro* and all things are one and yet not one; they are two and yet not two. A monk asked Chao-chou (Joshu in Japanese), "I am told that the ten thousand things all return to the One, but where does the One return to?"

Chao-chou answered, "When I was in Ching-chou, I had a robe made which weighed seven *chin*." This *mondo*[4] demonstrates eloquently the difference between the outward way and the inward way. If this sort of question was asked of the philosopher he will go on writing one book after another. But the Zen master who thoroughly knows the inward way does not stop to think and instantly gives his answer which is final, with no going-on-and-on.

The *kokoro* is not to be confused with the *Ālaya-vijñāna* of the Yogā-cāra, one of the Mahāyāna schools. The *kokoro* reveals itself only when the Ālaya is broken through. The Ālaya may be considered as corresponding to "the Unconscious" or to "the Collective Unconscious," but the Ālaya is more than mere Unconscious as distinguished from the Conscious, for it comprises both. The *kokoro*, however, is not the Ālaya, in which, I would say, there is still something savouring of intellection. The *kokoro* is thoroughly purged of all sorts of intellection, it is an abyss of absolute nothingness.

And yet there is something moving in the midst of the *kokoro*. From the point of view of the outward way, this will be incomprehensible, because how could "absolute nothingness" be made to "move" at all? That such a thing should actually take place is a mystery. Some may call it "the mystery of being." As if from the unfathomable depths of an abyss, the *kokoro* is stirred. The *kokoro* wants to know itself. As long as it remains in itself all is quiet: the mountain remains a mountain towering up to the sky; the river flows as a river singing its way down to the ocean. But as soon as a tiny speck of cloud appears in the blue, it in no time spreads out enveloping the whole universe, even vomiting thunders and lightnings. The *kokoro* is in all this, but human intellectuality loses sight of it and would go on bewildered and annoyed and full of fearful thoughts. The *kokoro* is lost in the maze of perplexities.

In Western terminology, the *kokoro* may be regarded as corresponding to God or Godhead. God also wants to know himself; he did not or could not remain himself eternally absorbed in meditation. Somehow he came out of his is-ness and uttered a *mantram*, "Let there be light!" and lo, the whole world leaped out into existence. From where? Nowhere! Out of nothing! Out of the Godhead! And the world is God and God is the world, and God exclaims, "It is good!"

---

4 "Question and answer."

According to Aśvaghosha, "In the midst of the *kokoro* a *nen* is spontaneously awakened." A *nen* (*nien* in Chinese, *cittakshāna* in Sanskrit) is a moment of consciousness coming to itself; it is, one might say, a consciousness rising from the unconscious, though with a certain reservation. The Sanskrit, *ekacittakshāna,* literally means "one-mind-(or thought) moment." It is "a thought-instant" or "a consciousness-unit" which constitutes consciousness like a second or a minute which is a unit-measure for time. "Spontaneously" (*kotsunen* in Japanese) describes the way a *cittakshāna* rises in the *kokoro.* God uttered his fiat just as spontaneously. When the *kokoro* is said to have raised a thought to know itself, there was no conscious intentionality in it; it just happened so—that is, spontaneously.

But what we must remember in this connection is that when we say "no intentionality" we are apt to understand it in the outward way along the intellectual line and may find it difficult to reconcile it with the idea of human consciousness. It takes a long series of discussions to make this point clear, and as it does not directly concern us here, let it pass with this remark that with God as with the *kokoro* freedom and necessity are one.

When Buddhists make reference to God, God must not be taken in the Biblical sense. When I talk about God's giving an order to light, which is recorded in the Genesis, I allude to it with the desire that our Christian readers may come to a better understanding of the Buddhist idea of the inward way. What follows, therefore, is to be understood in this spirit.

The Biblical God is recorded as having given his Name to Moses at Mount Sinai as "I am that I am." I do not of course know much about Christian or Jewish theology, but this "name," whatever its original Hebrew meaning of the word may be, seems to me of such significance that we must not put it aside as not essential to the interpretation of God-idea in the development of Christian thought. The Biblical God is always intensely personal and concretely intimate, and how did he ever come to declare himself under such a highly metaphysical designation as he did to Moses? "A highly metaphysical designation," however, is from the outward way of looking at things, while from the inward way "I am that I am" is just as "spontaneous" as the fish swimming about in the mountain stream or the fowl of the air flying across the sky. God's is-ness is my is-ness and also the cat's is-ness sleeping on her mistress' lap. This is reflected in Christ's declaration that "I am before Abraham was." In this is-ness which is not to be assumed under the category of metaphysical abstractions, I feel like recognising the fundamental oneness of all the religious experiences.

The spontaneity of is-ness, to go back to the first part of this paper, is what is revealed in the "eternal longing" for something which has vanished from the domain of the outward way of intellectualisation. The *kokoro's* wishing to know itself, or God's demanding to see "light" is, humanly expressed, no other than our longing to transcend this world of particulars. While in the world, we find ourselves too engrossed in the business of "knowing" which started when we left the garden of "innocence." We all now want "to know," "to think," "to choose," "to decide," "To be responsible," etc., with everything that follows from exercising what we call "freedom."

"Freedom" is really the term to be found in the inward way only and not in the outward way. But somehow a confusion has come into our mind and we find ourselves madly running after things which can never be attained in the domain of the outward way. The feeling of insecurity then grows out of this mad pursuit, because we are no more able to be in "the spontaneity of is-ness."

We can now see that "The awakening of a new consciousness" is not quite a happy expression. The longing is for something we have lost and not for an unknown quantity of which we have not the remotest possible idea. In fact, there is no unknown quantity in the world into which we have come to pass our time. The longing of any sort implies our previous knowledge of it, though we may be altogether ignorant of its presence in our consciousness. The longing of the kind to which I have been referring is a shadow of the original *kokoro* cast in the track of the inward way. The real object can never be taken hold of until we come back to the abode which we inadvertently quitted. "The awakening of a new consciousness" is therefore the finding ourselves back in our original abode where we lived even before our birth. This experience of home-coming and therefore of the feeling of perfect security is evinced everywhere in religious literature.

The feeling of perfect security means the security of freedom and the securing of freedom is no other than "the awakening of a new consciousness." Ordinarily, we talk of freedom too readily, mostly in the political sense, and also in the moral sense. But as long as we remain in the outward way of seeing things, we can never understand what freedom is. All forms of freedom we generally talk of are far from being freedom in its deepest sense. Most people are sadly mistaken in this respect.

That the awakening of a new consciousness is in fact being restored to one's original abode goes in Christianity with the idea of God's fatherhood. The father's "mansion" can be no other than my own home where I was born and brought up till I became willful and left it on my own account. But, really, however willful I may be I can never leave my original abode behind and wander away from it. I am always where I was born and I can never be anywhere else. It is only my imagination or illusion that I was led to believe that I was not in it. To become conscious of this fact is to awaken a new consciousness so called. There is nothing "new" in this, it is only the recovery of what I thought I had lost; in the meantime I have been in possession of it; I have been in it; I have been carrying it all the time; no, I am it and it is I.

The Shin Buddhists are quite emphatic in asserting this idea of restoration or rather of identification. They go further and say that Amida is always pursuing us and that even when we wanted to run away from him he would never let us go, for we are held firmly in his arms. The harder we struggle to get away from him the tighter he holds us, just as the mother does to her baby who tries to assert its self-will.[5]

In Zen the idea of restoration or re-cognition may be gleaned from Yeno's reference to "the original (or primal) face" which he wanted his disciples to see. This "face" is what we have even prior to our birth. In other words, this is the face of "innocence" which we have before our eating of the fruit from the tree of knowledge. "The tree of knowledge" is the outward way of intellection. When it begins to operate, "innocence" which is the inward way hides itself and becomes invisible. Most people take the "innocence" in a moral sense, but I would interpret it symbolically. "Innocence" corresponds to Aśvaghosha's "Original (or primal) Enlightenment" in which we were or are. It has never been lost even when "knowledge" is in full operation, because without it our existence has no significance whatever and "knowledge" itself of any kind would be altogether impossible. In this sense, "the inward way" is at once inward and outward. When it is separated and considered in opposition to "the outward way" it ceases to be itself.

Incidentally, Zen is often criticised as not having any direct contact with the world of particulars, but the critics forget the fact that Zen has never gone out of this world and therefore that the question of contact has no sense here.

Aśvaghosha's great work on the Mahāyāna is entitled *The Awakening of Faith,* but Zen generally does not use the term. The reason is that faith implies a division and Zen is emphatic in denying it in any sense. But if it (faith) is used in its absolute sense—which is in accordance with the inward way of seeing things—faith may be regarded as another name for *satori* and is no other than the awakening of "a new consciousness" though, as I have repeatedly said, there is really nothing "new" in Zen. Whatever this may be, "the awakening of a new consciousness" is the awakening of faith in Aśvaghosha's sense, that is, in its absolute sense. Then, faith corresponds to becoming aware of "Original Enlightenment" in which we are all the time. Faith is coming back to ourselves, to our own is-ness, and has nothing to do with the so-called objective existence of God. Christians and other theists seem to be unnecessarily busy in trying to prove God as objec-

---

[5] It may interest you to know that there is no word in European languages, as far as I know, equivalent for the Japanese word *oya. Oya* is neither father nor mother, it means both and applies to either of them. *Oya* is the quality to be found in each and both of them. It has no sex; therefore, its relationship to us is not that of progenitor; it is love pure and simple, it is love personified. Cannot we say that in the Jewish and Christian conception of God as father one feels him somewhat cold, distant and critical; and further that it is for this reason that Maria with Christ-child in her arms is needed to occupy an important niche in the Christian hierarchy? In Shin, Amida as *oya-sama* has nothing to do with the business of forgiving. We simply find ourselves in his grip when a new consciousness is awakened in us. Amida is neither father nor mother, he is *oya,* he is above sex, he is love itself.

tively existing before they believe in him. But from the Zen point of view the objectivity of God is an idle question. I would say that those who are so engrossed in the question of this sort have really no God whatever, that is, subjectively as well as objectively. As soon as they have faith, they have God. Faith is God and God is faith. To wait for an objective proof is the proof—the most decisive one—that they have no God yet. Faith comes first and then God. It is not God who gives us faith, but faith that gives us God. Have faith and it will create God. Faith is God coming to his own knowledge.[6]

When the Zen man has a *satori,* the whole universe comes along with it; or we may reverse this and say that with *satori* the whole universe sinks into nothingness. In one sense, *satori* is leaping out of an abyss of absolute nothingness, and in another sense it is going down into the abyss itself. *Satori* is, therefore, at once a total annihilation and a new creation.

A monk asked a Zen master, "Does 'this' go away with the universe when the latter is totally consumed by fire at the end of the kalpa?" The master answered, "Yes." When the same question was proposed to another master, he said, "No." From the inward way, "Yes" and "No" are one; destruction and construction are one.

The awakening of a new consciousness is the awakening of faith, and the awakening of faith is the creating of a new universe with infinite possibilities.[7] It is a new universe, yes, but in reality an old, old universe, where

[6] Cannot I say that Christians wanted Christ and so they have him? And also that they still wanted his mother Maria and therefore they have her? Being Christ's mother, she could not stay with us on earth, so she was made to go up to Heaven. Where Heaven is, is immaterial. In our religious experience, what we in our logical way think to be the law of causation is reversed, the effect comes first and then the cause. Instead of the cause proceeding to the effect, the effect precedes the cause.

When a Shin Buddhist was asked, "Can Amida really save us?" he answered, "You are not yet saved!" Christians may have the same way of expressing their faith. They would tell us to have faith first and all other things will follow. Is it not a somewhat futile attempt on the part of the Christian theologian to try to prove the historicity of Christ and then to proceed to tell us that for this reason we must believe in him? The same thing can be said of the crucifixion and the resurrection.

One may ask: If it is faith that is needed first, why so many different expressions of it? One faith goes out to Christ, another to Krishna, and still another to Amida, and so on. Why these variations? And why the fighting among them as we actually see in history?

I do not know if my interpretation of the phenomena is sufficient, but a tentative one is that faith, as soon as it goes out to express itself, is liable to be conditioned by all accidental things it finds around it, such as history, individual temperaments, geographical formations, biological peculiarities, etc. As regards the fighting among them, this will grow less and less as we get better acquainted with all these conditional accidents. And this is one of our aims in the study of religion in all its differentiations.

[7] The statement that faith creates God may be misconstrued. What I mean is that faith discovers God and simultaneously God discovers the man. The discovery is mutual and takes place concomitantly. To use Buddhist terms, when Amida is enlightened all beings are enlightened, and when we are enlightened we realize that Amida attained his enlightenment whereby our rebirth into the Pure Land is assured. The objective interpretation betrays that the critic has not deeply delved into the matter.

beings, sentient and non-sentient, have been dreaming their dreams, each in his way, ever since "Let there be light" came to work out its destiny. Here the Biblical time has no meaning. [. . .]

We talk ordinarily so much of self-consciousness as if we knew all about it, but in reality we have never come to a full knowledge of what self-consciousness is. Consciousness has always been conscious of something other than itself. As to "the Self" it has never even attempted to know, because the Self cannot be conscious of itself insofar as it remains dichotomous. The Self is known only when it remains itself and yet goes out of itself. This contradiction can never be understood on the level of the outward way. It is absolutely necessary to rise above this level if the meaning of self-consciousness is to be realised to its full depths.

The awakening of a new consciousness so called, as far as the inward way of seeing into the nature of things is concerned, is no other than consciousness becoming acquainted with itself. Not that a new consciousness rises out of the Unconscious but consciousness itself turns inwardly into itself. This is the home-coming. This is the seeing of one's own "primal face" which one has even before one's birth. This is God's pronouncing his name to Moses. This is the birth of Christ in each one of our souls. This is Christ rising from death. "The Unconscious" which has been lying quietly in consciousness itself now raises its head and announces its presence through consciousness.

We humans have the very bad habit of giving a name to a certain object with a certain number of attributes and think this name exhausts the object thus designated, whereas the object itself has no idea of remaining within the limit prescribed by the name. The object lives, grows, expands, and often changes into something else than the one imprisoned within the name. We who have given the name to it imagine that the object thus named for ever remains the same, because for the practical purposes of life or for the sake of what we call logic it is convenient to retain the name all the time regardless of whatever changes that have taken place and might take place in it. We become a slave to a system of nomenclature we ourselves have invented.

This applies perfectly to our consciousness. We have given the name "consciousness" to a certain group of psychological phenomena and another name "unconscious" to another group. We keep them strictly separated one from the other. A confusion will upset our thought-structure. This means that what is named "conscious" cannot be "unconscious" and vice versa. But in point of fact human psychology is a living fact and refuses to observe an arbitrary system of grouping. The conscious wants to be unconscious and the unconscious conscious. But human thinking cannot allow such a contradiction: the unconscious must remain unconscious and the conscious conscious; no such things as the unconscious conscious or the conscious unconscious must take place, because they cannot take place in the nature of things, logicians would say. If they are to happen, a time-agent must come in and make consciousness rise out of the unconscious.

But Zen's way of viewing or evaluating things differs from the outward way of intellection. Zen would not object to the possibility of an "unconscious conscious" or a "conscious unconscious." Therefore, not the awakening of a new consciousness but consciousness coming to its own unconscious.

Language is used to give a name to everything, and when an object gets a name, we begin to think that the name is the thing and adjust ourselves to a new situation which is our own creation. So much confusion arises from it. If there is one thing Zen does for modern people, it will be to awaken them from this self-imposed thralldom. A Zen master would take up a staff, and, producing it before the audience declare, "I do not call it a staff. What would you call it?" Another master would say, "Here is a staff. It has transformed itself into a dragon, and the dragon has swallowed up the whole universe. Where do you get all these mountains, lakes, and the great earth?" When I got for the first time acquainted with Zen I thought this was a logical quibble, but I now realise that there is something here far more serious, far more real, and far more significant, which can be reached only by following the inward way.

W. T. STACE

(1886-1967)

The next two essays constitute a dialogue between two thinkers with fairly similar backgrounds. Both pursued a good part of their careers in England, both are scholars of Hegel, both have taught philosophy in America—Stace at Princeton and Findlay at Yale—and both have ventured into the philosophy of mysticism. To describe their controversy in Hegelian terms, it expresses a difference in identity. Their dialogue is rich and meaningful because it is built on a shared basis, a sameness in difference.

The key issue in the following debate is the extent to which mysticism has a logic. Stace argues that any attempt to explain or attain the mystic experience through logic is doomed to failure. Findlay argues that there is indeed a "Logic of Mysticism." Part of their difference depends on the breadth each allows to logic, but part depends on their substantively different stances toward mysticism. The debate over the logic of mysticism relates to Kierkegaard's Christianity of paradox. Consider whether Kierkegaard would be more sympathetic to Stace or Findlay.

Mysticism
and Human Reason

Anyone who is acquainted with the mystical literature of the world will know that great mystics invariably express themselves in the language of paradox and contradiction; and it is to this aspect of mysticism that I especially want to draw your attention tonight. But before I do so I would like to make a few introductory remarks about mysticism in general. Mysticism is not a regional or local phenomenon. It is universal. By this I mean that it is found in every country, in every age, in every culture, and in association with every one of the great world-religions. I do not speak here of primitive cultures and primitive religions. No doubt mysticism expresses itself in them in primitive ways. But I am only speaking about advanced cultures and advanced religions. For instance, those ancient inspired documents, the Upanishads, which go back in time from 2,500 to 3,000 years, and which are the fountainheads both of the Hindu religion and of the Vedanta philosophy, are a direct report of mystical experience. Buddhism, too, is a mystical religion throughout. It is founded upon the mystical experience of Gautama Buddha. In the East, in India, the word "mysticism" or any word corresponding to it is not generally used. It is called "enlightenment" or "illumination." But the enlightenment experience of the East is basically the same as what is called the mystical experience in the West. In the Mohammedan religion the Sufis were the great representatives of mysticism. Mysticism appears in China in connection with Taoism. The Tao is a mystical conception. Judaism produced notable mystics. The history of Christianity is rich with the names of great mystics and some of these names are household words: Meister Eckhart, Saint Teresa, St. John of the Cross, and many others. Even outside the boundaries of any institutional religion, in the ancient Greco-Roman pagan world, not attached, perhaps, to any particular religion, Plotinus was one of the supremely great mystics.

Now, of course, as between these mysticisms in the various cultures, there are certain differences. For instance, Hindu mysticism is not quite the same as Christian mysticism. But I believe that the resemblances, the common elements, the elements which are universally found in all these mysticisms, are far more striking than the differences. I should say that the differences are superficial, while the common, basic, universal elements in all mysticism are fundamental. Should you ask me: "What are those common elements which appear in mysticism in all these different cultures and religions?" I can, perhaps, very briefly, summarize them.

In the first place, the absolutely basic, fundamental characteristic of all

MYSTICISM AND HUMAN REASON   From W. T. Stace, "Mysticism and Human Reason," University of Arizona Bulletin Series, Vol. XXVI, No. 3, May 1955. Copyright by University of Arizona Press, 1955: Riecker Memorial Lecture No. 1. Reprinted by permission.

mystical experience is that it is called "the unitary consciousness," or, as it is sometimes called, "the unifying vision." We may contrast the mystical consciousness with our ordinary, everyday, rational consciousness. Our ordinary, everyday consciousness is characterized by multiplicity. I mean that both the senses and the intellect, which constitute our everyday consciousness, are in contact with and are aware of a vast number, a plurality, a multiplicity of different things. In our ordinary consciousness we discriminate between one thing and another. But the mystical consciousness transcends all differences and all multiplicity. In it there is no multiplicity and no division of difference. "Here," says Eckhart "all is one, and one is all." He goes on to say that in that supreme vision there are "no contrasts." "Contrast" is Eckhart's word for the difference between one thing and another, for instance between yellow and green. He even goes so far as to say that in that experience there are no contrasts, i.e. differences, between grass, wood, and stone, but that all these "are one."

Closely connected with, and perhaps as a result of this characteristic of transcending all multiplicity, discrimination, and division are other characteristics common to mystical experience in all religions. It is non-sensuous, non-intellectual, and non-conceptual. And since all words except proper names stand for concepts, this means mystical experience is beyond all words, incapable of being expressed in any language; "ineffable" is the usual word. Another characteristic is that what is experienced is beyond space and beyond time. It is timeless; and timelessness is eternity. And therefore the mystical consciousness, even though it lasts only for a very short while, perhaps only a moment, is nevertheless eternal. For that moment gathers into itself all eternity. It is an eternal moment.

Another universal characteristic is that mystical consciousness is blessedness—it is the peace which passeth all understanding. One might quote at length from the utterances of great mystics in all religions to prove that these are the common characteristics. I have time for only one quotation which I choose because it happens to include most of them in a few sentences. In the Mandukya Upanishad it is written:

It is neither inward experience nor outward experience. It is neither intellectual knowledge nor inferential knowledge. It is beyond the senses, beyond the understanding, beyond all expression. It is the pure unitary consciousness wherein awareness of the world and of multiplicity is completely obliterated. It is ineffable peace. It is the supreme good. It is the One without a second.

One other common element I must mention. The mystic everywhere, except perhaps in Buddhism, which is a rather doubtful case here, invariably feels an absolute certainty that he is in direct touch with, and not only in direct touch with, but has entered into actual union with, the Divine Being. Plotinus expressed this by saying that "the man"—the mystic, that is—"is merged with the Supreme, sunken into it, one with it." And William James in his famous book, *Varieties of Religious Experience,* has an excellent brief chapter on mysticism, and in that he uses these words:

> This overcoming of all barriers between the individual and the Absolute is the great mystic achievement. In mystic states we become one with the Absolute. This is the everlasting and triumphant mystic tradition, hardly altered by differences of climate, culture, or creed. In Hinduism, in Neo-Platonism, in Sufism, in Christian mysticism, we find the same recurring note, so that there is about mystic utterances an eternal unanimity which ought to make the critic stop and think.

Now, of course, this mystical experience, basically the same in all cultures as it is, might nevertheless be nothing but a beautiful dream. It is possible that it is a purely subjective state of the mystic's own mind, and that he is under an illusion when he thinks that he is in contact with some great being objective and outside himself. The only logical argument, the only piece of evidence which can be used to show that it is more than a beautiful dream, that it does actually reveal contact with an objective, divine being is this remarkable agreement, as regards basic features, of the different mysticisms in all the cultures of the world. Of course one may be convinced by faith, or intuition, or feeling. But I am speaking here of logical argument or evidence.

Regarding this I will quote you a few words written by Professor C. D. Broad of Cambridge, England. He says this:

> I am prepared to admit that although the experiences have differed considerably at different times and places, there are probably certain characteristics which are common to all of them, and which suffice to distinguish them from all other kinds of experience. In view of this, I think it more likely than not that in mystical experience men come into contact with some Reality or some aspect of Reality which they do not come into contact with in any other way.[1]

The reason I read this very guarded statement—you see, he doesn't speak of this aspect of Reality as God—the reason I read this is because Broad happens to be a very remarkable kind of witness in such a matter. He says, in the same book which I am quoting, that he has no religious beliefs. He says also that he has never had anything which could be called a mystical or even a religious experience. But he claims that he has absolutely no bias, either for religion or against it. He thus claims to be entirely impartial. His is certainly a critical mind, inclined to be skeptical, certainly not inclined to accept any moonshine. Any of my philosophical colleagues who are acquainted, as they all are, with Broad's writings, will bear out the fact that this is a correct description of Broad. You will see that the evidence

---

[1] *Religion, Philosophy, and Psychical Research,* pp. 172–173.

which he himself quoted for supposing that mystical experience is something more than a beautiful subjective dream is precisely the unanimity, the universal character of certain basic characteristics of it.

I consider that Broad's opinion is a reasonable one, and I shall adopt it, going, however, just one little step—or is it a little step?—further than Broad. For this aspect of reality, or this reality, with which the mystic is in contact, I shall use, as he does not, the name "God." I use this word partly because it is the word that the mystics themselves use, but also because, whatever it is, the experience possesses the kind of qualities or characteristics that we think of as divine qualities: supreme value, blessedness, supreme goodness, love, and so on. But I do not wish to be understood as saying more than I actually am saying. I mean by the word "God" only what I have just said, namely, a reality which is possessed of divine qualities. I do not wish that there should be included in the connotation of the term the many superstitions and anthropomorphic meanings which have often clustered around it.

I turn now to what is the essential subject of my lecture, the paradoxes of mysticism. There are many such paradoxes. Their general character is this: that whatever is affirmed of God must be at the same time and in one and the same breath categorically denied. Whatever is said of the Divine Being, the opposite, the contradictory, must also be said. There are many such paradoxes, but I am going to speak tonight only about one, which is perhaps the most startling of them. This may be expressed by saying that God is both being and non-being. If you like, you can say it means that God both exists and does not exist; or again that God is beyond both existence and non-existence. There is thus both a positive and negative aspect. There is the positive divine and the negative divine. As to the positive divine, it is hardly necessary for me to say much about it because it is well known to everyone. It is the content of popular religion everywhere. We begin, I suppose, by saying that God exists. "Exist" is a positive word. We go on to say that he is a mind, a spirit, a person. These, too, are positive conceptions. Finally, we say that God is love, justice, mercy, power, knowledge, wisdom, and so on. All these are positive terms. And you will recognize that statements of this kind about the Divine Being are the content of ordinary, everyday, popular religious thought. This is true not only of Christianity but, I think, of all the great religions of the world, with the possible exception of Buddhism which is often called an atheistic religion. I don't think that there is really very much disagreement between the great world religions in regard to these basic attributes of God. There may be some difference of emphasis. No doubt it is the case that in Christianity the emphasis is upon God as love. In Hinduism the emphasis is on God as bliss. In Islam perhaps the emphasis is on God as power, and so on.

If we turn now to the negative divine, we pass into a region which is not so well known. This is usually especially associated with mystical religion. It may be expressed by saying that, just as for the positive divine God is being, here God is non-being. Even more striking words than this are used by the great mystics. God is "Nothing." He is "empty." He is "the Void." He is "the bottomless abyss of nothingness." And sometimes metaphors are used. Darkness as the absence of light, and silence as the absence of sound, are negative. Therefore God is spoken of as the great darkness, the great silence.

I am going to document these statements by referring very briefly (I cannot give very much of the evidence in a short lecture) to some of the great mystic utterances in the different religions of the world. I want to show that this is universal.

To begin with Christianity: Meister Eckhart, as you know, was a great Roman Catholic mystic of the 13th century. In one place he says: "God is as void as if he were not." Elsewhere he says: "Thou shalt worship God as he is, a non-God, a non-form, a non-person." One of his followers wrote this of him: "Wise Meister Eckhart speaks to us about Nothingness. He who does not understand this, in him has never shone the divine light." Using the metaphor of darkness, Eckhart says: "The end of all things is the hidden darkness of the eternal Godhead." He also refers on many occasions to God as "the nameless nothing." Another well-known Christian mystic, Tauler, uses the same kind of language. He, too, refers to God as "the nameless nothing." Albertus Magnus writes this: "We first deny of God all bodily and sensible attributes, and then all intelligible attributes, and lastly, that being which would place him among created things." Notice that being, existence, is here said to be the mark of created things.

Turning to Judaism we find that Jewish mystics often referred to Jehovah as "the mystical Nothing." And again, "in the depths of His nothingness" is a common phrase. One of the Hassidic mystics wrote: "There are those who worship God with their human intellects, and others whose gaze is fixed on Nothing. He who is granted this supreme experience loses the reality of his intellect, but when he returns from such contemplation to the intellect, he finds it full of divine and inflowing splendor."

Turning to Buddhism we find a rather difficult case for our exposition because it is often said that Buddhism is an atheistic religion. This is true with some reservations. It is true that you do not find the Western concept of God in Buddhism. And it therefore might be said that it is obvious that Buddhism can have neither a positive nor a negative conception of God. This, however, is really not a justifiable conclusion. I can't go into the matter in any great detail here. On the whole, the concept of Nirvana is what corresponds in Buddhism to the Christian and Jewish concept of God. Nirvana, the experience of Nirvana, is, I think, what we would recognize as the divine experience, the experience of the divine element in the world. It is not important that the word God is not used. If Nirvana corresponds to the concept of the divine, then one can say that the concept of Nirvana has both the positive and negative aspects. Positively, it is bliss unspeakable. Negatively, it is the Void. This conception of the Void which you see that Eckhart also uses, is basic to Buddhism. Ultimate reality is the Void.

I find that in Hinduism this positive-negative paradox is more fully developed, more clear than it is in Christianity, Judaism, or Buddhism. In Hinduism it may be said that this paradox has three aspects. Brahman is the name used in the Upanishads and generally in Hindu thought for the ultimate, supreme God. The first aspect of the paradox is that Brahman both has qualities and yet is without any qualities at all. On the positive side the qualities of Brahman are the usual divine qualities to which I have already referred. On the negative side he is "unqualified." This is often expressed in the Upanishads by using a string of negative terms. For example, it is said that Brahman "is soundless, formless, shapeless, intangible, tasteless, odorless, mindless." Notice this last word, "mindless." This quotation is similar in meaning to the one which I read from Albertus Magnus. First we deny all physical qualities. He is "soundless, formless, shapeless, intangible, odorless, and tasteless." Next we deny all "intelligible," i.e. psychological or spiritual attributes. He is "mindless." But the negative of the paradox, the denial of all qualities, is summed up in a very famous verse in the Upanishads. Brahman is here, as often, referred to as the Self. The verse says: "That Self is to be described as not this, not that." One of the earlier translators worded it thus: "That Self is to be described by 'No! No!'." The force of this "No! No!" is clear. Whatever attribute you suggest, whatever predicate you suggest, whatever quality you suggest, of Brahman, the answer always is "No." Is he matter? No. Is he mind? No. Is he good? No. Is he evil? No. And so throughout every word that you can possibly choose.

The second aspect of the paradox in Hinduism is that Brahman is both personal and impersonal. His personality is carried by the very word "Self." He is the Self. He is personal and as such is wise, just, good, and so on. But he is also wholly impersonal. The word "mindless" contains this implication. For a person must necessarily be a mind. Also he is specifically referred to as "the impersonal Brahman." And sometimes the word "he" and sometimes the word "it" is used of Brahman. "He" conveys the notion of personality, "it" the notion of impersonality.

The third and final aspect of the paradox in Hinduism is that Brahman is both dynamic and static. Dynamic means that he is active, static means that he is actionless. On the positive side God is dynamic. He is the creative energy of the world, the creator. Also he acts in the world, guides and controls the world. On the static side it is specifically stated in the Upanishads that he is wholly actionless.[2] And the entire paradox is summed up in the following verse from the Upanishads:

That One, though never stirring, is swifter than thought; though standing still, it overtakes those who run. It moves and it moves not.

---

[2] Rudolph Otto in his *Mysticism East and West* claims it is as a superiority of the Christian God over the Hindu, that the latter is merely static, the former dynamic. He has missed the paradox and been misled by the frequent statements that Brahman is inactive.

In this phrase, "It moves and it moves not," you have the whole paradox of the dynamic and static character of God summed up in five words.

Perhaps you will say, "Well, this is just poetic language. Everybody knows that poets like pleasant sounding phrases. And they like a balance of clauses. 'It moves and it moves not' sounds very well but it is mere words." I think you are quite mistaken if you take that interpretation. This is a literal statement of the paradox of the dynamic and the static.

Now I am persuaded that this entire paradox, and particularly that of the dynamic and the static character of the divine being, is not peculiar to Hinduism but is a universal characteristic of the religious consciousness everywhere, although in Hinduism it is more explicit, more baldly stated, than in other religions. In other religions it is present but tends to be veiled. Let us look at Christianity, for example. No one will deny that the Christian God is active. He is the creator of the world; he guides and controls it. But where, you will ask me, do you find evidence that the Christian God is static, inactive? It is true that you must look under the surface to find this. It is implied, implicit rather than explicit, in the concept of God as *unchangeable and immutable*. The changelessness, the immutability of God, is not only a Christian idea. It is a universal intuition of the religious consciousness found in all religions. "In him is no shadow of turning," and there is a well-known hymn which begins with the words:

> O strength and stay upholding all creation
> Who ever dost thyself *unmoved abide*.

The last two words convey the idea of the motionless, actionless character of God. We hardly realize when we speak of God as "immutable" and yet as the Creator of the world that we are uttering a paradox. There is, in fact, a contradiction between God as active and God as unchanging, because that which acts necessarily changes—changes from that state in which the action is not done to that state in which the action is done. Therefore, that which is wholly unchanging is also wholly inactive. The same idea also appears in poetry. T. S. Eliot twice to my knowledge in his poems uses the phrase, "The still point of the turning world." The literal meaning of this is obvious. It refers to the planet, the periphery and the outer parts of which are turning, while the axis in the middle is motionless. But the mystical meaning is also clear. It means that this world is a world of flux and change and becoming, but at the center of it, in the heart of things, there is silence, stillness, motionlessness.

So much, then, for the exposition of this paradox. But the human intellect, when it comes to a logical contradiction, necessarily attempts to get rid of it, attempts to explain away the contradiction. It tries to show that although there is an apparent contradiction, there is not really one. To get rid of a contradiction is essential to the very nature of our logical and rationalistic intellect.

Mystics themselves often show this characteristic since they are rational beings. I will give you two examples of attempts by religious thinkers to explain this paradox of the positive and negative divine logically, to make it comprehensible to the logical intellect. One logical way of getting rid of a contradiction is to separate the contradictory predicates and to declare that they apply to two different things. For example, if we speak of a square circle, this is a contradiction. If I say this desk top in front of me is both square and circular, this is a contradiction. But if I say the concept "square" applies to one thing and the concept "circular" to something else, if I say "this thing over here is square, and that thing over there is circular," then of course the contradiction disappears. This method of getting rid of the contradiction of the positive and negative has been used by mystics themselves. The great Hindu philosopher Sankara, who lived in the eighth century A.D. and who wrote a great commentary upon the Upanishads and endeavored to systematize the Vedanta philosophy, was very clearly and well aware of this contradiction about which I have been speaking. He attempted a solution by saying that there are really two Brahmans. One of them, which he called the Higher Brahman, is void, empty, qualityless, impersonal, actionless, negative. The other Brahman, which he calls the Lower Brahman, carries the usual divine attributes—that is, he is the creator of the universe, he is personal, wise, just, and so on. He is, in fact, the God of popular religion. Sankara held, however, that the ultimate ground of the world is the Higher Brahman, and the Lower Brahman merely issues forth from this ultimate ground as its first manifestation. Thus the contradiction is got rid of because the Higher Brahman carries the inactive, the negative character, while the Lower Brahman carries the positive attributes.

One may be quite sure that this is the wrong solution because the religious intuition is peremptory that God is one and not two, and this is especially the case in Hinduism since everywhere Brahman is spoken of as the One, and more emphatically as "the One without a second."

It is extremely instructive and interesting to see that exactly the same solution of this paradox is offered by the Christian mystic, Meister Eckhart, of course in complete independence of Sankara. Eckhart makes a distinction between God and the Godhead. It is the Godhead, according to him, which is void, empty, and negative. God has the usual positive, divine attributes. As before, one must say that this is the wrong solution. But Eckhart, in a sense, withdraws it himself. For he identifies the Godhead with God the Father, and God with God the Son. And in accordance with the doctrine of the Trinity these two are one in spite of their duality. Yet Eckhart, like Sankara, declares that it is the void Godhead which is the ultimate ground of all things.

My own belief is that all attempts to rationalize the paradox, to make it logically acceptable, are futile because the paradoxes of religion and of mysticism are irresoluble by the human intellect. My view is that they never have been, they never can be, and they never will be resolved, or made logical. That is to say, these paradoxes and contradictions are inherent in the mystical experience and cannot be got rid of by any human logic or ingenuity. This, in my opinion, is an aspect of what is sometimes called the mystery of God or the incomprehensibility of God. This mystery of God is not something which we can get rid of, something which we could understand by being a little more clever or a little more learned. It is ultimate, it is an ultimate and irremovable character of the divine. When you say that God is incomprehensible, one thing you mean is just that these contradictions break out in our intellect and cannot be resolved, no matter how clever or how good a logician you may be. And I think that this view is in the end the view of the mystics themselves, including Eckhart, in spite of his apparent attempt to explain the paradox.

In order to show that this is in fact the view of the mystics themselves in all religions, I will read to you from a Christian mystic, a Hindu, and a Buddhist. The Christian example again is Eckhart. Rudolph Otto writes that "Eckhart establishes a polar unity between rest and motion within the Godhead itself. The eternally resting Godhead is also the wheel rolling out of itself." And in Eckhart's own words: "This divine ground is a unified stillness, immovable in itself. Yet from this immobility all things are moved and receive life."

The Hindu from whom I wish to quote is Aurobindo, who died only a few years ago. There is no doubt in my mind that he himself experienced the mystical vision in full measure. He says:

> Those who have thus possessed the calm within can perceive always welling out from its silence the perennial supply of the energies which work in the world.

I wish to comment on this sentence. "Those who have thus possessed the calm within" means those who have possessed mystical vision. "Can perceive always welling out from its silence"—"silence" is the motionlessness, the stillness, the inactivity of the divine. "The perennial supply of the energies which work in the world" refers to the creative activity of the divine. These creative energies are said to "well out from the silence." In other words, they issue out of the empty void. Finally, we see the paradox of the static and the dynamic directly stated as an *experience*. The word "perceive" is used. This is not an intellectual proposition, a theory, an intellectual construction, a philosophical opinion. It is a direct perception or vision of reality.

My last example is Suzuki, the well-known Zen Buddhist mystic, now teaching in New York. He writes:

> It is not the nature of "prajna" to remain in the state of "sunyata," absolutely motionless.

("Prajna" is the word for mystical intuition, while "sunyata" means the void.) So he is saying it is not the nature of mystical consciousness to remain in a state of void, absolutely motionless.

It demands of itself that it differentiate itself unlimitedly and, at the same time, it deserves to remain in itself undifferentiated. This is why "sunyata" is said to be a reservoir of infinite possibility, and not just a state of mere emptiness. Differentiating itself and yet remaining in itself undifferentiated, it goes on eternally in the work of creation. We can say of it that it is creation out of nothing. "Sunyata" is not to be conceived statically but dynamically, or better, as at once static and dynamic.

David Hume asked ironically, "Have you ever seen a world created under your eyes—have you ever observed an act of creation of the world?" The answer is: Yes, there are men who have seen this.

I conclude that these contradictions and paradoxes are impossible of logical adjustment or resolution. What, then, should we think about the matter? Should we say that there is contradiction in the nature of God himself, in the ultimate being? Well, if we were to say that, I think that we shouldn't be saying anything very unusual or very shocking. Many people have said this or at any rate implied it. Does not the Christian doctrine of the Trinity itself imply this? What could be a greater paradox than that? And it is not to be believed that the three-in-one, the three which is one and the one which is three, could be understood or explained by a super-Einstein, or by a higher mathematics than has yet been invented. It is irremovable and an absolute paradox. Also one might quote the words of Jacob Boëhme suggesting that there is contradiction in the heart of things, in the ultimate itself. Schwegler, a distinguished German historian of philosophy, writes this:

> The main thought of Boëhme's philosophizing is this: that self-distinction, inner diremption is the essential characteristic of spirit, and, consequently of God. God is the living spirit only if and insofar as he comprehends within himself difference from himself.

One might also perhaps quote Boëhme's well-known statement that God is both "the Eternal Yea" and "the Eternal Nay," but this perhaps might also be taken simply as a brief expression of the negative-positive paradox.

Although I do not think it would be anything seriously erroneous if we would say that there is contradiction in the Ultimate, yet I would prefer myself to use other language. I should say that the contradiction is in us, in our intellect, and not in God. This means that God is utterly and forever beyond the reach of the logical intellect or of any intellectual comprehension, and that in consequence when we try to comprehend his nature intellectually, contradictions appear in our thinking. Let me use a metaphor to express this. We speak of God as the "Infinite" and of ourselves as "finite" minds. As a matter of fact what the word "infinite" means in this connection is itself a difficult problem in the philosophy of religion. It is certain that the word "infinite," when applied to God, is not used in the same sense as when we speak of infinite time or infinite space or the infinite number series. What it does mean is a problem. I believe that it can be solved, that is to say, it is possible to give a clear meaning to the word "infinite"—different from the infinity of space and time—as the word is applied to God. However, if I am allowed to use this language of finite and infinite, my metaphor is that if you try to pour the infinite into the finite vessels which are human minds, these finite vessels split and crack, and these cracks and splits are the contradictions and paradoxes of which I have been talking. Therefore this amounts to saying that God is utterly incomprehensible, incapable of being intellectually understood. In order to make my final point I will use the word "unknowable." It means that God is, in a sense, unknowable. But we must be very careful of this. If God were absolutely unknowable, and in no sense knowable, then there could be no such thing as religion, because in some sense or other religion is the knowledge of God.

The explanation of this is that he is unknowable to *the logical intellect,* but that he can be known in direct religious or mystical experience. Perhaps this is much the same as saying that he can be known by "faith" but not by "reason." Any attempt to reach God through logic, through the conceptual, logical intellect, is doomed, comes up against an absolute barrier; but this does not mean the death of religion—it does not mean that there is no possibility of that knowledge and communion with God which religion requires. It means that the knowledge of God which is the essence of religion is not of an intellectual kind. It is rather the direct experience of the mystic himself. Or if we are not mystics, then it is whatever it is that you would call religious experience. And this experience of God—in the heart, shall we say, not any intellectual understanding or explanation—this experience of God is the essence of religion.

JOHN FINDLAY

(1903-   )

As noted in the previous introduction to Stace, John Findlay comes to mysticism with a background in Hegel studies. Findlay's approach to Hegel and mysticism is more thoroughly Hegelian than Stace's. As Findlay states in his comments on the role of philosophy, he conceives the task of philosophy as finding connections where none may be obvious. This was Hegel's great talent, and Findlay applies it to the phenomena of mysticism. He argues that the logic of mysticism is basically the logic of a nonatomic, unified world, that our ordinary logic is inadequate to the mystical experience only because our ordinary logic derives from a very partial type of experience of a nonunified world. Findlay opposes this atomic metaphysics of common sense to the monistic metaphysics of mysticism, and he is willing to argue that the latter is in the last analysis more true than the former, though the monistic metaphysics must also account for the experience of pluralism, disparateness, imperfection, and evil.

Although Findlay addresses many of his remarks to Stace's 1960 book, **Mysticism and Philosophy,** Stace's views remain substantially unchanged from what they were in the earlier 1955 address.

The Logic of Mysticism

. . . I am calling my present lecture 'The Logic of Mysticism' because I wish to study what is admittedly a very important and widespread form or set of forms of human experience from a predominantly logical point of view. I intend, that is, to study a whole range of notions and assertions and reasonings that could be called 'mystical', and the peculiar language in which they express themselves, rather than any highly specific, greatly prized experiences which lie behind these notions and assertions. And I wish to see whether there are not peculiar rules and guiding principles governing these mystical notions and assertions, and whether it is not possible to raise questions of the well-formed and the ill-formed, of validity and invalidity, in regard to them, as we can in other fields of discourse, e.g., of discourse on probability or on morals. I am approaching mysticism in this way because there is a widespread persuasion abroad that mysticism, so far from having a peculiar logic that can be studied and evaluated, has no trace of logic in its utterances at all, that it is in fact the very antithesis of the logical, and that the experiences it embraces, and which inspire its peculiar utterances, are not even experiences of which a satisfactory verbal expression is possible. They are intrinsically ineffable experiences, as the mystics themselves often allege, while expressing them so richly and so eloquently as to demonstrate their extraordinary effability. They are also experiences whose expression delights to flout all logical rules rather than to obey them, and which accordingly admit of no logical treatment whatever. The experiences which lie behind mystical assertions are often thought, further, to be experiences of a very peculiar class of persons called mystics, people liable to trances, seizures, illuminations and unmotived convictions: if we value them, we value them as we do clairvoyants or people gifted with extra-sensory per-

THE LOGIC OF MYSTICISM   From John Findlay, "The Logic of Mysticism," in *Religious Studies.* Published by Cambridge University Press. Copyright © 1972. Reprinted by permission.

ception, and if we do not value them, we think of them as physically and psychologically abnormal beings who must certainly not be encouraged. In neither case is there anything of profound philosophical importance in what they say, let alone anything of *logical* significance. Whereas what I want to hold is that mystical utterances reflect a very peculiar and important way of looking at things which is as definite and characteristic as any other, which, while it may override and sublate ordinary ways of looking at things, and so have an appearance of senselessness and inconsistency, none the less has its own characteristic, higher-order consistency, and I wish further to suggest that this mystical way of looking at things, so far from being the special possession of peculiar people called mystics, rather enters into the experience of most men at many times, just as views of the horizon and the open sky enter into most ordinary views of the world. At the horizon things become confused or vastly extended, parallel lines meet and so on; just so, in the mystical sectors of experience, some things behave and appear quite differently from things in the near or middle distances of experience. Some people refuse to cultivate mystical ways of looking at things, and in fact resolutely exclude them. In the same way some people never look beyond the physical situation in which they immediately find themselves. This kind of experiential and logical myopia only shows that there are many myopic people, and that some are deliberately myopic: it shows nothing about the logical or illogical character of mystical utterances and experiences. On the view to which I adhere the so-called great mystics, people like Plotinus, Jalalud'in Rumi, St Teresa and so on, are merely people who carry to the point of genius an absolutely normal, ordinary, indispensable side of human experience and attitude, just as some other people carry to the point of genius the numerical, additive way of looking at things which all men possess in some degree. There are people whose incapacity for mathematics leads them to form an aversion from the whole subject, and there are people whose incapacity for mysticism leads them to form a similar aversion, yet it does not follow that either capacity is not a form of normal human endowment, expressing itself in a peculiar type of utterance and discourse, in fact with such regularity as to merit the title of a 'logic'. Such, at least, will be the assumption on which the present lecture will proceed.

In the lecture I am about to give I have been greatly assisted by W. T. Stace's excellent book *Mysticism and Philosophy,* published in 1961.[1] This book is valuable because it deals with the essential questions which concern mysticism, and deals with them in what I consider a reasonably adequate manner. Stace starts, not by attempting to define mysticism or the mystical, which would *assume* that there was one uniform phenomenon called 'mysticism' in all the experiences and utterances that we cover by this name, but by asking whether there is not what he calls a 'common core' to all the experiences and utterances in question. [. . .] Stace then elaborately shows, by quoting a wealth of material, that there are immense similarities of ap-

---

[1] [W. T. Stace, *Mysticism and Philosophy,* Philadelphia, Lippincott, 1960.]

proach in utterances called 'mystical', which stem from the most varied sources, and have few or no historical links: a Christian saint uses much the same astounding language as a Moslem devotee or a Hindu Yogi, without being aware of the wide community he exemplifies. Profound differences there certainly are between varied styles of mysticism, but the resemblances are much more striking, even oppressively so, and they are not at all like the loose family resemblance embodied in, say, the Hapsburg features or countenance. Stace arrives at the view, after considering all the material, that there is something like a uniform core to the many cases that we unhesitatingly class as instances of 'mysticism', and he further arrives at the view that this core diverges into two main specifications which he calls 'extrovertive' and 'introvertive' mysticism respectively. Of each of these varieties he gives a careful and well-documented characterisation, and he does so without claiming for it either exhaustiveness or definitory exactness, and without rejecting the possibility of isolated cases which deviate from it. Some performances and utterances may have *some* of the marks of the mystical without the others, but the marks cluster together in a great number of cases, and have moreover, a character of mutual 'belongingness' which makes such a clustering seem natural and appropriate.

Having thus pinned mysticism down as a more or less treatable, uniform phenomenon, Stace considers the question of the validity of mystical utterances: he deals with this under the heading of 'The Problem of Objective Reference'. Is mysticism, in other words, a merely personal, subjective way of looking at things, or does it really contribute to our vision of the world? I do not myself at all agree with Stace's interpretation of this question, nor with the answer he gives to it. For he practically identifies objectivity with membership of a law-governed causal system, and, while mysticism as an *attitude* may fit in with such a system, and so be 'objective', the matters it claims to reveal, that it takes a stance towards, certainly lie quite outside any such system. Mysticism does not profess to acquaint us with something like high entropy or the Aurora Borealis, and it is in this obvious sense not objective. But, since it makes no claim to be filling in a particular gap in a law-governed cosmic picture, mysticism is not, in Stace's view, subjective either. What it reveals is not hallucinatory or delusive like, say, ectoplasm or the canals on Mars. Mysticism, says Stace, is neither subjective nor objective, but trans-subjective: it is a community of attitude that many people share. Now I am not in the least satisfied with all this, for mystical moods and persons, are, above all, assertive, and they put something before us as *true,* as *real,* whether anyone thinks so or not. Mysticism is characterised throughout by the noetic quality on which William James laid such stress in his account of religious experience. If mysticism tells us nothing about the world, then it is, in a deep sense, very false indeed, since it certainly professes to tell us something about it. I certainly therefore wish to answer this question as to the validity of mysticism in a manner different from Stace, and I do not wish to assume that whatever validates a mystical utterance is also what validates a scientific utterance. The truth of mysticism may be deeper than the truth of science, and it may only be in the light of mystical truth that scientific truth is fully intelligible. But Stace has proceeded usefully in separating the question of validity from the question of phenomenological description, and in showing the peculiar difficulty of the questions 'Is mysticism true?', 'Are mystical assertions valid?'. [. . .]

I now wish to follow Stace's method by documenting mysticism with quotation. I could quote from the Upanishads or the Buddhist Sutras, or the Tao-teh-King or St Teresa or Ruysbroeck etc., but, since we are all philosophers, and our purpose philosophical, I shall mainly cite from one who is as great a philosopher as he is a mystic, namely Plotinus. He certainly practised mysticism to the limit, since he achieved the uttermost ecstasy or union with the Absolute on at least four occasions, as his biographer Porphyry relates. My first quotation is from *Ennead* V, Treatise viii, paragraphs three and four, *On Intelligible Beauty*; it describes the manner of existence in the true, the intelligible world. 'For all there is heaven: earth is heaven and the sea is heaven, and so are animals and plants and men, all heavenly things in that heaven. . . . And life is easy yonder, and truth is their parent and nurse, their substance and sustenance, and they see all things, not such as are in flux but as have true being, and they see themselves in others: for all things are transparent, and nothing is dark and resistant: everything is inwardly clear to everything and in all respects: light is made manifest to light. And each holds all within itself, and again sees all in each other thing, so that everything is everywhere, and all is all, and each all, and the glory infinite. Each of those things is great, since even the small is great, and the sun yonder is all the stars, and each star the sun, and again all the stars. One thing stands forth in each, though it also displays all. . . . Each there walks, as it were, on no alien earth, but is itself always its own place; its starting-point accompanies it as it hastens aloft, and it is not one thing and its region another.'[2] In this passage we have the mystical doctrine of interpenetration, of seeing the diverse things in the world as in some deep sense one and the same. This doctrine is put forward by Meister Eckhart when he says: 'All that a man has here externally in multiplicity is intrinsically one. Here all blades of grass, wood and stone, all things are one. This is the deepest depth.' And again: 'Say, Lord, when is a man in mere understanding? I say to you, when a man sees one thing separated from another. And when is he above mere understanding? That I can tell you. When he sees all in all, then a man stands above mere understanding.'[3] I could also quote famous utterances from Mahayanist Buddhist sutras in which the same doctrine of mystical interpenetration is put forward.

I return, however, to a second quotation from Plotinus of a somewhat different tenor: it comes from *Ennead* VI, Treatise ix, paras. 5, 6, 11. 'This

---

[2] It is interesting to report that Leo Robertson wrote a poem on this passage.

[3] See Otto, *Mysticism, East and West*, p. 61, quoted by Stace, *loc. cit.* pp. 63–4.

is the point of the rule which governs our mysteries, that they should not be divulged to outsiders: one is forbidden to reveal the divine to one who has not enjoyed the vision of it. Since seer and seen were then not twain, and the seen was united with the seer rather than seen by it, the seer retains an image of the Supreme when he remembers his union with it. He himself was the One, having no difference towards anything in himself, nor towards other things. All then was still with him, no stirring, no desire was with him when he rose to that state, nor any notion nor act of thinking, nor if one may so put it, himself. But as if caught up, rapt, he has passed in quiet to an unshaken state of solitude, completely at rest, and become as it were, rest itself.' (The last phrase 'rest itself' is a typical piece of mystical syntax.) 'He no longer moves among beauties and has outstripped beauty itself, has outstripped the choir of the virtues also, and is like one who, entering an inner sanctuary, leaves behind the statues in the temple that will again be the first to greet him, as secondary spectacles, after the spectacle and the communion within, a communion not with a statue or an image, but with the thing itself. Perhaps, however, there was no spectacle there, but an approach other than sight, an ecstasy, a simplification, a surrender of self, a reaching towards contact, a peace, a contrivance of harmony that brings what is in the sanctuary into view. To look otherwise is to find nothing there.' This extraordinary passage can be paralleled by many passages from St Teresa where she speaks of a beam of light being temporarily lost in a larger light, or of the water in a bucket being temporarily lost in a larger body of water in which it is immersed. Or one can quote from the *Brihadaranyakopanishat*, VI, iii, 21, 23, 32, where it says that 'Now as a man, when embraced by a beloved wife, knows nothing that is without, nothing that is within, thus this person, when embraced by the intelligent self, knows nothing that is without, nothing that is within. . . . And when he does not see, yet he is seeing, though he does not see. For sight is inseparable from the seer, because it cannot perish. But there is then no second, nothing else different from him that he could see.' One is not operating very differently if one turns to Wittgenstein's *Tractatus*: 'The world and life are one' (5.621); 'I am my world' (5.632); 'The subject does not belong to the world, but it is a limit of the world' (5.632); 'The philosophical I is not the man, not the human body or the human soul of which psychology treats, but the metaphysical subject, the limit, not a part of the world' (5.641); 'The contemplation of the world *sub specie aeterni* is its contemplation as a limited whole. The feeling of the world as a limited whole is the mystical feeling' (6.45); 'There is certainly something ineffable: this shows itself, it is the mystical' (6.522); 'My propositions are elucidatory in this way: he who understands me finally recognises them as senseless when he has climbed out through them, on them, over them: he must so to speak throw away the ladder after he has climbed up on it' (6.54). This last proposition is paralleled by an aphorism from the founder of Zen Buddhism about throwing away a raft once it has taken one to the further shore.

I shall now consider the enumeration of the basic traits of mysticism, its 'universal core', which occurs in Stace's book. Stace, as I have said, distinguishes two varieties of mysticism, an extrovertive and an introvertive, and for the extrovertive he enumerates the following. (I rephrase his words a little.)

1. The unifying vision, expressed by the formula 'All is one'. The one is perceived in and through the multiplicity of objects.
2. The more concrete apprehension of One as an inner subjectivity, a life, a consciousness, a living presence in all things, 'Nothing is really dead'.
3. The sense of objectivity or reality: what is apprehended is absolutely real.
4. The feeling of extreme blessedness, joy, happiness, satisfaction, etc.
5. The feeling that what is apprehended is holy or sacred.
6. The feeling that what is apprehended is paradoxical.

And with reservations he adds:

7. The allegation that what is apprehended is 'ineffable'. 'Such phrases as "inexpressible", "unutterable" bespatter the writings of mystics all over the world.'

For introvertive mysticism Stace gives the same list of features, except that its first two members are different. In introvertive mysticism we have, instead of a unifying vision connected with all empirical contents and objects, 'a unifying consciousness from which all the multiplicity of sensuous or conceptual or other empirical content has been excluded, so that there remains only a void and empty unity'. Instead of the One which is All, one has, in short, the One which is Nothing. And instead of (2), the sense of a universal life and consciousness in things, one has the idea of something essentially non-spatial and non-temporal, and otherwise uninvolved. Stace here quotes from a Buddhist sutra: 'There is, monks, an unborn, not become, not made, uncompounded, and were it not, monks, for this unborn, not become, not made, uncompounded, no escape could be shown for what is born, has become, is made, is compounded.'[4]

I think Stace's account of mysticism has deep faults which reflect its method. It is an external, empirical account based on mere examination of single cases, and an attempt to find common traits which occur in them all. Its outcome is a rag-bag of empirical features, having no plain philosophical significance. Some people, it seems, like to speak in terms of an absolute unity present in all things, or utterly separate from them all, they like to say that this unity is objective or real, they feel bliss and awe in its contemplation, they like to say paradoxical things about it, they profess to find it indescribable, etc. Such people, it seems, are also liable to appear all over the

4 *Loc. cit.* p. 126.

world and at any point of time, like mongols or cretins, and the things they say are always remarkably uniform. But all this is a mere fact of human experience and behaviour like, for example, the basic characters and the many mutations of the sexual instinct. I myself am a philosopher who is utterly uninterested in anything which is a mere matter of fact, externally observed, even if it is a fact connected with what people think and say, and I do not regard any mere decanting and classification of empirical fact as genuine philosophical investigation. Philosophy is to me the bringing forth, not the mere registration or discovery, of conceptions which are what I should call intelligible unities, whose various components hang together necessarily, or with some approach to rational necessity, and which alone can illuminate the complex windings of fact. Philosophy I regard as the overcoming of notional contingency, of the kind of loose combination of traits into a concept because such traits often occur together in actual cases, or are combined together in people's actual usage. If mysticism or the mystical is to be a worthwhile theme for philosophical study, it must be a coherent, notional unit, and a coherent notional unit which is necessary for the understanding of man and the world, and so rightly reckoned as fundamental. I am not at all interested in mysticism if it is a mere natural fact, or body of natural facts, about man, or if its concept is a mere natural fact, or body of natural facts, about human language. I think there is such a thing as belongingness or mutual affinity among conceptual features which moves us to combine them into a single concept, and to use a single term more or less to cover them all, and that their analytic discoverability in the meaning or use of that term is a consequence of this affinity. And I think the business of philosophers is to make concepts more of a notional unity, involving a deeper belongingness, than do the concepts which occur in ordinary usage. Philosophical analyses that profess to concern themselves with mere facts of usage in fact do not do so. The usages they select and consider together, always have a notional unity and importance, and the concepts they use to illuminate them, even when geared to what the ordinary man thinks or says, always depart far from the ordinary man's style of thinking. The immense merit of Austin is to have shown how fantastically far ordinary usage is from philosophy, but the concepts he himself elaborates, to *deal* with ordinary usage, the illocutionary, perlocutionary, etc., suggests that philosophers like himself do well to depart far from ordinary usage. The notion of the perlocutionary, for example, is not one that ordinary speakers ever have framed or could frame.

Leaving these methodological issues aside, I proceed to sketch the mystical in what I feel to be a more satisfactory manner, and I am led to say, first of all, that mysticism is essentially a frame of mind connected with an *absolute* of some sort, meaning by an absolute an object of very peculiar type having very peculiar logical properties. By an absolute I mean something which, on the one hand, is irremoveable and necessarily existent and self-existent, which could not meaningfully be supposed absent, nor dependent for its existence on anything else, and on which all contingencies of existence, whether within or without itself, are wholly dependent, and which further has the uniqueness and singleness which goes with its absolute status. I also wish to mean by it something which shows forth absolutely *every* recognised type of excellence or value in a fashion so transcendent that it can perhaps be rather said to *be* all these types of excellence than merely to embody or exemplify them, which *is* them all of necessity and is them all *together,* and which is certainly the sole cause for their presence in any finite case or contingent manifestation. I do not doubt that you will see what I mean by saying that the features of an absolute have logical affinity, that, while it is logically significant to conceive of them apart from each other, and so to build up the notion of a quasi-absolute which has some of these traits and not others—value-free quasi-absolutes are certainly constructed by many—the features in question do belong together and do complete each other, and that what they furnish is an integrated whole, the conception of something superlative, self-explanatory and all-explanatory, which rounds off all our concepts and valuations, and provides the necessary background for all of them. The various features which Stace laboriously discovers all arise because mysticism is oriented towards an absolute: the feature of absolute unity because an absolute is necessarily single and unique, the feature of reality because an absolute can only be thought of as inescapable, necessarily existent, the emotional colouring of bliss and awe, because an absolute is thought of as embodying all values and embodying them necessarily, the features of paradoxicality and ineffability, because an absolute necessarily differs in category, we may say, from any ordinary, finite object, being necessarily self-existent while ordinary objects exist contingently and dependently, and being all excellences whereas an ordinary object cannot have one excellence without inevitably failing to have another, and so on. Many would say that what I have called an absolute is a deeply contradictory or senseless notion, since the notions of necessary existence and unsurpassable excellence are either meaningless or self-contradictory. But whether this is true or not, self-contradictory and empty notions play a vast part in human experience and attitude, and this is certainly true of man's limiting notions of absolutes. Even philosophies which repudiate absolutes in their logic, and have professedly built up radically contingent, value-free systems, generally smuggle in absolutes of some sort, matter, logical space, the totality of atomic states of affairs, etc. etc. The paradoxicality and ineffability of mystical absolutes is simply a logical consequence of their being absolutes at all: every absolute differs *toto caelo* [completely] from any ordinary, empirical existent.

The traits of absolutes we have so far mentioned would, however, be found in purely intellectual approaches of various sorts that are anything but mystical. Much orthodox theology, for instance, is concerned with the unique properties of a transcendent deity, without there being the slightest spice of mysticism in its approaches to this being. It may even be held that strict theism is essentially unmystical, and this is why mysticism is frequently condemned in a theistic period of orthodoxy. Meister Eckhart, perhaps the greatest of Christian mystical philosophers, was condemned as a heretic by John XXII, the worst of the Popes. Mysticism may in fact be said to arise when an absolute is treated witth extreme seriousness, both in theoretical vision and in practice: it is the sort of absolute we get when the logic of absoluteness is pursued to its furthest limit. Above all, what characterises mysticism is a refusal to accept and use the notions of identity and diversity which the ordinary logic applies so confidently, whether in the relation of finite objects to the absolute, or of finite objects to one another. Ordinary logic assumes confidently that we can always pick out a number of separate items, *a, b, c, d, e,* etc., which, however much alike and intimately related, have each their own numerically distinct individuality, and can maintain it for a considerable period, during which they have absolutely no tendency to pass over into other things, or coalesce with them, or lose themselves in them. Whereas, if the uniqueness and omni-responsibility of an absolute is taken seriously, and there is not thought to be anything that is not an extension or expression of itself, then there can be no *a, b, c, d, e,* etc., which are not simply different names and guises of the same absolute, and which do not really differ from each other otherwise than as the morning star differs from the evening star. To take the notion of an absolute quite seriously is in fact to put the ordinary notion of diversity, and with it the ordinary notion of identity, out of action. Both can be only notions of the surface, of the first regard, which can be given an immediate, but not an ultimate, application. Mystics do not believe that the effective use of a notion in ordinary situations is sufficient to establish its ultimate legitimacy. The only sort of identity that can be ultimately admitted is one that can be stretched in varying degrees, which can come nearer and nearer to the limit of sheer diversity, otherness, without ever reaching it. We may say, if we like, that the absolute may be *alienated* from itself in different degrees in different forms or phases, and these in different degrees from one another, without ever reaching the breaking-point of sheer diversity. What we ordinarily wish to say will appear in a new form in a fully developed mystical logic, in which all absurdity will be carefully circumvented. But a mystical logic, like any other logic, takes a long time in construction, and, before it is fully developed, there will be phases in which we shall seem merely to be subverting ordinary forms of expression, without putting anything effective and lucid in their place. We can understand how, plagued by the seeming absurdity of two conflicting schemes of diction, there should be a desire to say of an absolute that it has *none* of the mutually exclusive characters of its forms and phases, that it is, in some quite non-ordinary sense, wholly *other* than them, or beyond them, that it is not to be called a *thing* or an *entity,* and that it is in some very deep sense Nothing at all. Most Japanese teahouses have a symbol for the ultimate Nothingness which blessedly underlies tea-drinking like all finite objects, but it is plain that this Nothingness is only a step removed from the Everythingness and All-pervadingness of more positive mystical characterisations. Even of some of our packed thoughts it is as proper to say that they are very rich in distinct items as that they are wholly void of any distinct items at all, and such seemingly contradictory characterisations, which are certainly only analogical, are *a fortiori* no objection when applied to so remote and difficult an object as a mystical absolute.

To take this notion of an absolute seriously is further to treat the identity of everything, including oneself, with the absolute, as no mere remote intellectual conviction, but as something that ought to be capable of being realised so vividly and compellingly that it becomes a direct personal experience. Mystical experiences are not to be assimilated to queer extrasensory perceptions. They are the understandings of an identity as logically perspicuous as 'If *p* then *p*' or 'If *p.q.* then *q.p.*'. Only, while the theorems of the propositional calculus can be understood without passion, being adjusted to our normal state of alienation, the theorems of mysticism can only be understood with passion; one must oneself live through, consummate the identity which they postulate. All mysticism involves a doctrine and a practice and an experience of ecstasy, and the experiential character of mysticism is simply a consequence of the meaning of the identity it posits, an identity in which the ordinary person is taken out of his alienation, and taken up, or partially taken up, into the ultimate mystical unity.

Some of you will perhaps have been charitable enough to concede that what I have so far said may be quite all right as describing what mystics *think* is the logic of their utterances, but will none the less doubt whether there is any serious logic of this putative sort. The notion of an identity underlying plainly incompatible specifications is, they would say, a purely self-contradictory notion, especially when the absolute is not thought of as broken up into parts, and as admitting incompatible characterisations of its several parts. The notion of an identity underlying separable entities is likewise a wholly empty conception: it points to nothing and tells us nothing about anything. The notion that sheer diversity and complete independence are impossible is likewise inadmissible: they are perfectly possible, and should be recognised as such in any sound logic. And the notion of what exists of necessity is purely meaningless: necessity only connects characterisations of possible existents with one another, and existence always involves the connection of characterisations and descriptions with extralinguistic reality. A necessary existent, were it admissible, would, moreover, be there whatever were the case, like the number Two or the ideal of Chastity, and this would make its so-called existence a wholly empty, abstract case of subsistence. Only what could be absent from the world could also contribute to its content, could exist in an ordinary sense, and could exercise all those saving, illuminative virtues which mystical thinkers have always been ready to attribute to their absolute. There is, finally, no meaning in the notion of perfection, in the joint embodiment of all excellence in an unsurpassable form: it is the nature of valuable qualities to conflict with other valuable qualities, and to be such as to have no maximum, but to permit always of being surpassed.

The answer to these and to many other similar objections is difficult: all that I here have to say is that the difficulties raised are to a large extent question-begging; they rest on a metaphysic or ontology which lies securely ensconced behind the very forms of our common utterances, of our ordinary logic, and which so absolutely commits us to a certain way of regarding the world and anticipating its contents, that it seems to commit us to nothing at all. The forms of our common utterance are by no means vacuous and innocuous: though they may not *say* that the world consists of certain types and ranges of elements and no others, or that it permits of certain sorts of treatment and no others, they may be said to *imply* that this is the case, and what they imply may be open to question, it may not, on reflection, be the only nor the truest way of viewing the facts in the world. The forms of our common utterance imply the existence or the possibility of an independent array of logical subjects, *a, b, c, d, e,* etc., each capable of existing or not existing separately without others, and permitting the attribution of characters, the possession of which by one logical subject tells us nothing as to the possession of the same character by another logical subject. They also imply the presence of relations among subjects which are external and indifferent to their existence and their character. The forms of this type of utterance readily lead to the development of a metaphysical atomism even more drastic than that worked out by Wittgenstein in the *Tractatus Logicophilosophicus,* an atomism of wholly independent existences, quite contingently characterised and related. But there is nothing to prevent us from holding this metaphysic to be merely an abstract or surface way of regarding the world, completely absurd if regarded as setting forth in completeness what a world conceivably could be, unable to make sense of the rational procedures which enable us comprehensively to understand the world and the beings who share it with us, and yet presupposing these procedures in the comprehensive, *soi-disant* [so called] intelligible view it sets forth of what is. Faced by deep reflection on what I may call the unitive aspects of our experience, we may well move towards a Spinozistic logic in which, instead of saying things about separate finite logical subjects, we say them in a somewhat transformed guise of a single logical subject *in so far* as it is expressed in this or that modification. Instead of saying that John is tall, and Paul fat, we may say that the absolute substance is tall in its Johannine aspect, fat in its Pauline one. We may then, taking into account certain deeper strands of experience, progress to Meister Eckhart's statement that this blade of grass is this wood and this stone: properly understood, this is no more illogical and no more destructive of ordinary beliefs suitably expressed, than saying that the morning star is the evening star. If certain philosophers here object that we are merely talking about ordinary facts in an extravagant and unenlightening way, we may question the whole metaphysics of hard facts indifferent to the conventions of our language, and we may say that the whole structure of the world and thinking subjects, and the structure of any world and any thinking subjects, makes certain ways of talking about the world more deeply revelatory of its being, truer to its deep structure, than others. [. . .]

The notion of unsurpassable, all-inclusive excellence or perfection likewise raises considerable difficulties, but these can perhaps best be met by holding, as mystical people in fact frequently hold, that the absolute does not so much *have* all excellences as *is* them all: that is, the absolute is not beautiful but beauty itself, not just but justice itself, etc. etc. In the case of the absolute, in short, the distinction of type and instance falls away: it is not a case of goodness, nor an abstract character of such cases, but it is, if you like, a character which is also a unique case, and a unique case which is also a character. I am not sure that this is not exactly what was present in the mind of Plato when he talked about the causality of the Forms and of the Form of the Good which engendered them all. If there is difficulty in the notion of a subsistent perfection, or set of subsistent perfections, there is certainly no difficulty in a mind which contemplates and desires them all, and which only contingently contemplates or desires particular instances of them, and which is so intrinsically one with what it desires and contemplates as to be rightly said to *be* them all, and to be them all in unity. I do not think it is at all difficult to conceive a profound spiritual simplicity in which all possibilities of being and goodness will be enjoyed together in a single vision, and which is such that any instantiation of such a comprehensive unity will necessarily be one-sided and partial and piecemeal, or in other words creaturely. Nor is it hard to imagine that the relation of finite instantial beings to the all-embracing seminal absolute is neither one of mere otherness nor of simple identity, but a unique variable relation of logical remoteness or alienation. It is not one of mere otherness, since it is arguably of the essence of a mystical absolute that its ideal perfections should be variously forthshadowed in actual instances, and, since each of those instances embodies an aspect, a side of its eternal essence, and can be mystically seen as embodying precisely this, but it is also not one of mere identity, since any realised instance differs categorially from a spiritual simplicity which involves the thought of all realisable instances, and sorts of instances, whatever.

This is not the time nor the place to develop a complete mystical logic and mystical theology, nor do I think that more than the rudiments of it exist in such works as the *Summae* of Thomas Aquinas, or the Commentaries on the *Vedanta Sutras* of Shankaracharya and Ramanujacharya. Suffice it to say that I think that, while mysticism and its logic can be developed in an undisciplined chaotic or poetic way, in which no attempt is made to achieve genuine consistency, and contradictions are even reverenced as stigmata of higher truth, mysticism can also be developed in a manner which has complete logical viability, even if it involves many concepts strange to ordinary thought and reflection. The logic of a mystical absolute is the logic of a limiting case, and we must not expect a limiting case to behave in the same logical manner as a case which does not fall at the limit. If even in mathematics we can regard a straight line as a queer limiting case of an ellipse, we must not steer clear of similar queernesses in the construction of a viable mystical absolute. The outcome of my statements is clear: the forms of utterance that we adopt in our ultimate view of the world should not be arbitrary, but should reflect our profound reflections on what, considered most carefully, is really necessary and possible, and the fact that our ordinary, unconsidered forms of utterances have little or nothing that is mystical about them, does not prove that the forms of utterance which will survive in the deepest and most careful reflection will not be entirely mystical. It is not a question of being inconsistent or illogical, but of deciding what form one's consistency or logicality may take. Ultimately there may prove to be only one such wholly satisfactory pattern of consistency or logicality, and that a mystical one.

It is, however, one thing to remove the main sources of objection to mysticism, and quite another thing to recommend it strongly and positively. And it is here, of course, that a lot of persuasive argument is necessary, for most men at most times, and some men at all times, feel no impulse to pass beyond the sundered, dismembered, sorry world of our common experience, and see nothing but an irrelevant expression of temperament in the utterances of mystics. Even if they at times see the world in a mystical light, as involving 'something far more deeply interfused' and Wordsworthian, they are at other times no more inclined to see anything more deeply revealing in their vision than is seen in the euphoria of drunkenness, the ecstasy of sex or the dead sea dryness of jaundice. Mysticism, they think, is an attitude, deeply and widely human, which paints the world in peculiar, transcendental colours: these colours are an insubstantial pageant which reflects nothing deeply rooted in the nature of things.

To counter this line of attack, I shall first argue that mystical unity at the limit or centre of things alone guarantees that coherence and continuity at the periphery which is involved in all our basic rational enterprises. Unmystical ways of viewing the world would see it as composed of a vast number of wholly independent entities and features, and this, as is well known, raises a whole host of notional quandaries, of ontological and epistemological problems. How can we form a valid conception of the structure of all space and time from the small specimens given to us? How can we extrapolate the character and behaviour of an individual from the small segment known to us? How can we generalise from the character and behaviour of one individual to the character and behaviour of a whole infinite class of individuals, wherever it may be distributed in the infinite reaches of space and time? Why, finally, do we think experienced things will have that affinity with our minds and our concepts that will enable us to plumb their secrets? It is well known that, on a metaphysic of radical independence and atomism, all these questions admit of no satisfactory answer. Whereas, on a mystical basis, the profound fit and mutual accommodation of alienated, peripheral things is precisely what is to be expected: it is the alienated expression of a mystical unity which, however much strained to breaking point, never ceases to be real and effective.

Much the same holds if we turn to that deep understanding of the interior life of others which arguably underlies all our interpretation and prediction of other people's behaviour, all acts of communication and co-operation, and all the ethical experiences and endeavours which arise in our relations with them. It is surely clear that unmystical views have the greatest difficulty in rendering these matters intelligible. They cannot make plain why we should be clear that others feel as we do in similar circumstances, and even how we attach meaning to such a presumption. They are forced to give unsatisfactory, behaviouristic analyses of what we are so sure of, or justify our certainty in strange left-handed ways. Whereas, on a mystical basis, our understanding of others rests on the fact that they are not absolutely others, but only variously alienated forms of the same ultimate, pervasive unity, which expresses itself in the inkling, whether clear or remote, of what may be present in the experience of others. [. . .]

I should, however, be misrepresenting the difficulty of all that I have been saying if I did not indicate further presumptions and tasks which I think the acceptance of a mystical logic would certainly involve. A mystical system must not only explain and justify what I may call the unitive aspects of our experience, but also the patent disunity, confusion, imperfection and badness which the world at its surface exhibits. It must, to be a satisfactory logic, integrate the surface of the world with its centre, show each to be necessary to the other. This it is plain is what many mystical ways of regarding things certainly have not done, and they have accordingly become largely an empty form of words, inflated with an emotional inspiration which meaninglessly babbles of a profound unity, embodying and unifying all value, behind the job-lot which actually confronts us. There are, however, forms of mysticism which make alienation and deep-identity mutually dependent: the absolute must alienate itself in limited, instantial forms so that it may steadily reduce and overcome their alienation, and in so doing truly possess and enjoy and recognise itself. This is more or less the creed of some of the great Christian mystics, mainly Germans, who include Meister Eckhart; it is a view which also runs through the whole philosophy of Hegel, and so may fitly be called the 'Germanic Theology'. Some form of the Germanic Theology is, I think, necessary to giving a viable sense to mystical utterances. And I should go further in thinking that a fully developed working mysticism demands a developed otherworldly cosmology, in which numerous states of being are postulated which mediate between the extreme of alienation characteristic of this world and the extreme of unity characteristic of a mystical ecstasy. There must be levels of experience and being achieved either in or after this life, in which things become steadily more manageable and dreamlike, more fluid and interpenetrating, more general, more marked by personal attitude and communion, more dominated by values than things in this life, until in the end the extreme of mystical unity is reached. Competent mystics like Plotinus, Dante, Swedenborg, the Buddhists, have described such transitional states, and it is my conviction that this world and this experience only makes sense if it is linked, not only to an ultimate mystical unity, but also to the transitional states in question. Mysticism is a logical matter, but a logic is only acceptable if it finds the right sort of empirical material to fit it, and the right sort of material must include worlds and lives stricken with less dispersion and diversity than our present life.

In concluding this lecture on mysticism I shall not apologise for the way in which I have dealt with the subject, that is as a committed partisan, concerned to put on mystical phenomena a very special logical slant of my own. The subject is so vast, difficult and complex that without a strong, simplifying, personal line, one cannot hope to get anywhere among its intricacies. I believe that mysticism enters into almost everyone's attitudes, and that it is as much a universal background to experience as the open sky is to vision: to ignore it is to be drearily myopic, and to take the element of splendour and depth out of everything, and certainly out of philosophy. That element of splendour and depth is certainly present in Plato and Aristotle, in Plotinus, Aquinas, Spinoza, Hegel, and let me finally say in Wittgenstein. And there is no reason why we should let it be squeezed out of philosophy by any form of logic-chopping or minute analysis.

Transition:
The Quest
for Cosmic
Consciousness

During the last decade interest in spiritual matters has increased, as reflected not only in the number of people participating in various religious movements but also in the proliferation of different paths toward salvation or enlightenment. You could argue that all the esoteric cults have always been around, but only in the last decade did their existence become known to so many. Of course it is possible that an entire nation or culture might simply ignore traditions or insights central to another culture. The social reinforcement toward the uniformity that constitutes an identifiable culture inevitably creates a certain provincialism, a certain distrust of the ways of other cultures. But some of that distrust has broken down: during the last decade the interest in spiritual matters has broadened to include virtually every access to the spiritual known to the history of man.

How are we to understand the phenomenon of increased interest in spirituality? Note how this question is different from, How are we to understand our spirituality? The latter question is nonhistorical; it is the religious question dealt with in the previous five essays. The former question is historical, possibly even sociological. It speaks to our specific situation at this point in history and asks, "What difference does it make to the spiritual quest that right now it is being pursued so energetically by so many people in so many different ways?'' Or to put it another way, it is one thing to grow up into the same religious beliefs held by one's entire community, whether fervently or with an enlightenment spirit of conscious agnosticism; it is another thing to adopt a set of religious beliefs foreign to one's cultural heritage. It is remarkable that so many are now able to step outside their cultural heritage, to transcend a strong provincialism operating until only recently. Of course it is easier when one has the support of so many others in a new spiritual movement. But still, the question remains, why do these various movements attract such support now when the seeds have been around for such a long time?

When posing a historical question about religious movements it is difficult to know how to begin to answer because the nature of the historical phenomenon in question presupposes eternal realities that transcend history. The **historical** or **sociological** answer is apt to conflict with the **religious** answer. The historical or sociological answer appeals to contingent historical situations: times are bad and people are looking for an escape; the increase in drug use tunes people in to the spiritual; the decline of western culture is being symptomized by a new planetary consciousness. But the religious response to the historical question tends to reject such answers as not giving credit to the eternal realities forming the content of religious belief. Consequently the historical question poses a paradox to religious belief just as Kierkegaard claimed. How can you ask, ''Why **now?**'' when the answer is supposed to come from an eternal source that transcends all particular nows? With respect to the historical Christ, Kierkegaard asked how the believer's faith in an eternal happiness can depend on an event (the crucifixion) that took place at a historical moment in time. The same question poses itself with a different reference today: How can so many pursue paths toward spiritual enlightenment when that spiritual quest seems to be so obviously based in a particular historical situation? Isn't it strange to be in possession of eternal truths if it is a historical accident that one even has access to those truths? Isn't it peculiar to base one's eternal happiness on the teachings of a Meher Baba or a Krishnamurti or a Baba Ram Dass when it is clear that if one had been born fifty years earlier one would never have heard of these men? Isn't it odd that so many can acknowledge that the consumption of a manmade drug introduced them into a consciousness that seems to transcend the petty affairs of men? These modern analogues to the historical paradox posed by Kierkegaard strike me as very difficult questions.

The mere posing of such questions may seem to suggest a critique of the religious impulse as rooted in nothing but historical-variable human needs. Whether or not we finally accept such a critique of the new mysticism, we need to be aware of its force. Now, as rarely before, the problem of the false prophet presses upon us. When so many offer salvation in so many different ways, how can one help but suspect that someone is being sold a bill of goods? Our credulity is strained. Clifford begins to make more sense when we are faced with the fanaticism of some Jesus-freaks or a band of orange-clad headshaven Hare Krishna converts. We begin to fear the allconsuming fire of a driving irrationalism, and the voice of reason and the testaments of history provoke an uninvited anticipation of new crusades, inquisitions, and religious wars.

As has always been the case with religious movements, part of the phenomenon may cause alarm but part reflects an important coming to terms with the spiritual dimensions of human existence. To ignore that dimension is to be less than fully human; to inflate the spiritual dimensions into fanaticism is to pervert the religious impulse. We cannot use a blanket criticism of the new mysticism to hide us from the difficult task of steering an even course between the two extremes of ignoring and perverting our spiritual life. I find in the next two selections encouraging aspects of the new mysticism that reinforce truths developed in the rest of this volume. Though a perversion of the religious impulse could derail the contemporary spiritual movement at any moment, if we avoid the fanatical spurs and sidings we may be on the right track toward a more whole human existence.

Let us compare point for point the ideas reflected in earlier essays and the beliefs central to the new mysticism. I shall only **begin** this comparison, and a lot remains to be done by the reader.

1. **The Critique of What Is Otherworldly**

Nietzsche's attack on the life-denying flight into otherworldliness and a life beyond seems to me—and to Nietzsche elsewhere in his writings—less applicable to Buddhism than Christianity. True, many Christians stress the thisworldly aspects of their religion, and there are traces of escapism in the Buddhist will to nothingness and the transcending of all desires, nevertheless, Jung's generalization is as correct as any can be: "The Christian principle which unites opposites is the **worship of God,** in Buddhism it is the **worship of the self —self development"** (**Psychological Types,** Paragraph 375).

2. **The Self**

The importance of beginning with the self, which has informed the entire structure of this volume, is reflected in the "inward way" of the new mysticism. Though there are false prophets who ask for subservience to the most varied doctrines, much of the new mysticism stresses the importance of finding whatever one can find within oneself.

3. **Individualism**

Yet the inward way leads to transcending ego rather than reinforcing it. An emphasis upon the self does not entail the selfishness of possessive individualism or the atomism of the individualist meta-physics of the self. The inward way simply takes seriously the importance of identifying the situatedness of one's perspective. Subjectivism is inescapable, certainly as long as one has not uncovered the unconscious influences of one's private provincialism. But the inward way is like Kant's transcendental deduction: once we uncover the sources of our consciousness we are better able to distinguish the anatomy of appearances. We are in a better position to distinguish merely subjective bias from trans-subjective or objective truth. Consequently we are closer to joining a transpersonal, nonindividualistic spiritual community.

4.   The Body

One of the sources of our consciousness is the incarnateness of consciousness. While this is clearly the message of the incarnation of Christ and the resurrection of the whole body, the perversion of this truth by the historical Church led to a denial of body-consciousness in the Christian tradition. This loss is being restored in the new mysticism with its stress on the importance of certain kinds of food and physical training in yoga, and its regard for the healthy body as both a symptom and a symbol of organic wholeness in human existence.

5.   Rationalism and Expanded Awareness

Without in the least denigrating the importance of reason, Laing, Goffman, Polanyi, Brown, Leonard, Dewey, and many others agree that we have tended to define reason too narrowly in the western tradition. We have taken conscious logical processes like mathematics as the paradigm, and we have ignored the many subtleties of affective and symbolic consciousness in our attempts to define what is reasonable. We have developed what Marcuse calls an irrational rationality, which promotes the cult of efficiency at the heart of technology. The new mysticism might counter the onesidedness of rationalism without an attack on reason in general.

6.   Authoritarianism

Having seen that paternalism in many of its forms has come under attack (Brown, Greer, Locke, Laing, Reich, and Fanon) we should take note of the different dynamics of authority in eastern cultures. While relations of authority are hardly absent—the spiritual guru is more blatantly authoritarian than most Protestant ministers (read servants) would ever dare be—the eastern religious teachings seem to point more toward the transcendence of authority relationships than to their preservation. Rather than replacing the father with a God, the worship of the self is aimed at the realization that "there is no one over you," as Marin puts it.

7.   Transfiguration

Seventh, and finally, we come full circle to another aspect of the thisworldliness of the new mysticism. Despite the esoteric talk of astral planes and hidden realms, a dominant theme of the new mysticism seems to reflect a transfiguration of this world rather than a flight into some other. What is at stake is an accurate picture of what this world of human experience really does contain. Is it the flatland of secularism (with or without a transcendent God above), or can we experience this world as transfigured into a sacred existence? Each of the previous six comparisons enters into a doctrine of the possibility and actuality of transfiguration: (1) an emphasis on the finality of this world; (2) the sacredness of the self; that is, (3) community of the self with the cosmos rather than its isolation in individualism; the potential richness of experience that comes with a recognition of (4) incarnate consciousness; and (5) expanded modes of awareness that transcend a onesided rationalism; and finally (6) the realization that the resources lie within and do not depend on the dispensation of some father above. This is not to say that the individual can stand up to the cosmos with a pride unbecoming so small a part of the cosmos; transcending authority does not justify a return to a rationalism in which the individual fancies his mind sufficient to master the world. All six features taken together generate a transfiguration in the seventh circle of self-awareness. The wholeness of human existence adds a sacredness to every part traversed separately. When the pattern is complete, when the method of totalization has included every appearance in its partiality, the parts together take on new meaning. Some people call it being high, others call it being enlightened, and still others call it wisdom.

ALAN WATTS

(1915-   )

Following Suzuki, his elder contemporary, Alan Watts ranks among the major influences in the deprovincialization of the young American consciousness. Throughout the 1950's and 1960's Watts helped introduce eastern religious thought through his writings, lectures, and radio shows. That the new mysticism is strongest in California probably has something to do with Watts' direct influence there, though other elements certainly render California the richest soil for the seedlings he would transplant from the East.

In the following essay Watts relates responsible drug use to the mystical experience. I am inclined to agree with him that the proper attitude to take toward the question of drug use cannot be authoritarian imperatives against any and all use. Elders cannot hide their heads like ostriches at the approach of danger. To imagine that negative imperatives will work is to bury one's head in the sand of ignorance. Drugs are so easy to get and their reputation so enchanting that the likelihood of their use by many must be regarded as a fact we cannot hide from. So the responsible reaction to the question of drug use is to attempt intelligent distinctions between their use and abuse. To offer such intelligence no more counts as advocacy of indiscriminate drug use than offering birth-control information is advocacy of promiscuity.

But the question of responsible drug use is not simple. The thought of charting out a set of rules is absurd. Because drugs are **mind** drugs, discussions of their use amount to discussions of the mind; to abuse drugs is to abuse the mind. Education against the abuse of drugs is nothing less than education as a whole. The best educators can do about drugs is educate well, with wisdom and honesty. Watts' attempt to orient the question of drugs in the context of our dominant social values is a step in the right direction. We need further steps in the right direction because most drug use today is drug abuse, a careless, thoughtless, and very dangerous flirtation with human tragedy.

Psychedelics and Religious Experience

The experiences resulting from the use of psychedelic drugs are often described in religious terms. They are therefore of interest to those like myself who, in the tradition of William James, are concerned with the psychology of religion.[1] For more than thirty years I have been studying the causes, the consequences, and the conditions of those peculiar states of consciousness in which the individual discovers himself to be one continuous process with God, with the Universe, with the Ground of Being, or with whatever name he may use by cultural conditioning or personal preference for the ultimate and eternal reality. We have no

PSYCHEDELICS AND RELIGIOUS EXPERIENCE   From Alan W. Watts, "Psychedelics and Religious Experience," in *California Law Review*, Vol. 56, No. 100. Copyright © 1968, California Law Review, Inc. Reprinted by permission.

[1] James, William: *The Varieties of Religious Experience: A Study of Human Nature* (Longmans, Green & Co., New York, New York), 1911.

satisfactory and definitive name for experiences of this kind. The terms "religious experience," "mystical experience," and "cosmic consciousness" are all too vague and comprehensive to denote that specific mode of consciousness which, to those who have known it, is as real and overwhelming as falling in love. This article describes such states of consciousness as and when induced by psychedelic drugs, although they are virtually indistinguishable from genuine mystical experiences. It then discusses objections to the use of psychedelic drugs which arise mainly from the opposition between mystical values and the traditional religious and secular values of western society.

The Psychedelic Experience

The idea of mystical experiences resulting from drug use is not readily accepted in western societies. Western culture has, historically, a particular fascination with the value and virtue of man as an individual, self-determining, responsible ego, controlling himself and his world by the power of conscious effort and will. Nothing, then, could be more repugnant to this cultural tradition than the notion of spiritual or psychological growth through the use of drugs. A "drugged" person is by definition dimmed in consciousness, fogged in judgment, and deprived of will. But not all psychotropic (consciousness-changing) chemicals are narcotic and soporific, as are alcohol, opiates, and barbiturates. The effects of what are now called psychedelic (mind-manifesting) chemicals differ from those of alcohol as laughter differs from rage or delight from depression. There is really no analogy between being "high" on LSD and "drunk" on bourbon. True, no one in either state should drive a car, but neither should one drive while reading a book, playing a violin, or making love. Certain creative activities and states of mind demand a concentration and devotion which are simply incompatible with piloting a death-dealing engine along a highway.

I myself have experimented with five of the principal psychedelics: LSD-25, mescaline, psilocybin, dimethyl-tryptamine (DMT), and cannabis. I have done so, as William James tried nitrous oxide, to see if they could help me in identifying what might be called the "essential" or "active" ingredients of the mystical experience. For almost all the classical literature on mysticism is vague, not only in describing the experience, but also in showing rational connections between the experience itself and the various traditional methods recommended to induce it—fasting, concentration, breathing exercises, prayers, incantations, and dances. A traditional master of Zen or Yoga, when asked why such-and-such practices lead or predispose one to the mystical experience, always responds, "This is the way my teacher gave it to me. This is the way I found out. If you're seriously interested, try it for yourself." This answer hardly satisfies an impertinent, scientifically minded, and intellectually curious westerner. It reminds him of archaic medical prescriptions compounding five salamanders, powdered gallowsrope, three boiled bats, a scruple of phosphorus, three pinches of henbane, and a dollop of dragon dung dropped when the moon was in Pisces. Maybe it worked, but what was the essential ingredient?

It struck me, therefore, that if any of the psychedelic chemicals would in fact predispose my consciousness to the mystical experience, I could use them as instruments for studying and describing that experience as one uses a microscope for bacteriology, even though the microscope is an "artificial" and "unnatural" contrivance which might be said to "distort" the vision of the naked eye. However, when I was first invited to test the mystical qualities of LSD-25 by Dr. Keith Ditman of the Neuropsychiatric Clinic at the UCLA Medical School, I was unwilling to believe that any mere chemical could induce a genuine mystical experience. At most it might bring about a state of spiritual insight analogous to swimming with water wings. Indeed, my first experiment with LSD-25 was not mystical. It was an intensely interesting aesthetic and intellectual experience which challenged my powers of analysis and careful description to the utmost.

Some months later, in 1959, I tried LSD-25 again with Dr. Sterling Bunnell and Dr. Michael Agron, who were then associated with the Langley-Porter Clinic in San Francisco. In the course of two experiments I was amazed and somewhat embarrassed to find myself going through states of consciousness which corresponded precisely with every description of major mystical experiences that I had ever read.[2] Furthermore, they exceeded both in depth and in a peculiar quality of unexpectedness the three "natural and spontaneous" experiences of this kind which had happened to me in previous years.

Through subsequent experimentation with LSD-25 and the other chemicals named above (with the exception of DMT, which I find amusing but relatively uninteresting) I found I could move with ease into the state of "cosmic consciousness," and in due course became less and less dependent on the chemicals themselves for "tuning-in" to this particular wave length of experience. Of the five psychedelics tried, I found that LSD-25 and cannabis suited my purposes best. Of these two, the latter, which I had to use abroad in countries where it is not outlawed, proved to be the better. It does not induce bizarre alterations of sensory perception, and medical studies indicate that it may not, save in great excess, have the dangerous side effects of LSD, namely chromosomal damage and possible psychotic episodes.

For the purposes of this study, in describing my experiences with psychedelic drugs, I avoid the occasional and incidental bizarre alterations of sense perception which psychedelic chemicals may induce. I am concerned, rather, with the fundamental alterations of the normal, socially induced consciousness of one's own existence and relation to the external world. I am trying to delineate the basic principles of psychedelic awareness. But

---

[2] Johnson, Raynor Carey: *Watcher on the Hills* (Hodder & Stoughton, Ltd, London, England) 1959. An excellent anthology of mystical experiences.

I must add that I can speak only for myself. The quality of these experiences depends considerably upon one's prior orientation and attitude to life, although the now voluminous descriptive literature of these experiences accords quite remarkably with my own.

Almost invariably, my experiments with psychedelics have had four dominant characteristics. I shall try to explain them—in the expectation that the reader will say, at least of the second and third, "Why, that's obvious! No one needs a drug to see that." Quite so, but every insight has degrees of intensity. There can be obvious$_1$ and obvious$_2$—and the latter comes on with shattering clarity, manifesting its implications in every sphere and dimension of our existence.

The first characteristic is a slowing down of time, a *concentration in the present*. One's normally compulsive concern for the future decreases, and one becomes aware of the enormous importance and interest of what is happening at the moment. Other people, going about their business on the streets, seem to be slightly crazy, failing to realize that the whole point of life is to be fully aware of it as it happens. One therefore relaxes, almost luxuriously, into studying the colors in a glass of water, or in listening to the now highly articulate vibration of every note played on an oboe or sung by voice.

From the pragmatic standpoint of our culture, such an attitude is very bad for business. It might lead to improvidence, lack of foresight, diminished sales of insurance policies, and abandoned savings accounts. Yet this is just the corrective that our culture needs. No one is more fatuously impractical than the "successful" executive who spends his whole life absorbed in frantic paperwork with the objective of retiring in comfort at sixty-five, when it will all be too late. Only those who have cultivated the art of living completely in the present have any use for making plans for the future, for when the plans mature they will be able to enjoy the results. "Tomorrow never comes." I have never yet heard a preacher urging his congregation to practice that section of the Sermon on the Mount which begins, "Be not anxious for the morrow. . . ." The truth is that people who live for the future are, as we say of the insane, "not quite all there"— or here; by overeagerness they are perpetually missing the point. Foresight is bought at the price of anxiety, and, when overused it destroys all its own advantages.

The second characteristic I will call *awareness of polarity*. This is the vivid realization that states, things, and events which we ordinarily call opposite are interdependent, like back and front or the poles of a magnet. By polar awareness one sees that things which are explicitly different are implicitly one: self and other, subject and object, left and right, male and female—and then, a little more surprisingly, solid and space, figure and background, pulse and interval, saints and sinners, police and criminals, and in-groups and out-groups. Each is definable only in terms of the other, and they go together transactionally, like buying and selling, for there is no sale without a purchase, and no purchase without a sale. As this awareness becomes increasingly intense, you feel that you yourself are polarized with the external universe in such a way that you imply each other. Your push is its pull, and its push is your pull, as when you move the steering wheel of a car. Are you pushing it or pulling it?

At first, this is a very odd sensation, not unlike hearing your own voice played back to you on an electronic system immediately after you have spoken. You become confused, and wait for it to go on! Similarly, you feel that you are something being done by the universe, yet that the universe is equally something being done by you, which is true, at least in the neurological sense that the peculiar structure of our brains translates the sun into light and air vibrations into sound. Our normal sensation of relationship to the outside world is that sometimes I push it, and sometimes it pushes me. But if the two are actually one, where does action begin and responsibility rest? If the universe is doing me, how can I be sure that, two seconds hence, I will still remember the English language? If I am doing it, how can I be sure that, two seconds hence, my brain will know how to turn the sun into light? From such unfamiliar sensations as these the psychedelic experience can generate confusion, paranoia, and terror, even though the individual is feeling his relationship to the world exactly as it would be described by a biologist, ecologist, or physicist, for he is feeling himself as the unified field of organism and environment.

The third characteristic, arising from the second, is *awareness of relativity*. I see that I am a link in an infinite hierarchy of processes and beings, ranging from molecules through bacteria and insects to human beings, and, maybe, to angels and gods—a hierarchy in which every level is in effect the same situation. For example, the poor man worries about money while the rich man worries about his health; the worry is the same, but the difference is in its substance or dimension. I realize that fruit flies must think of themselves as people, because, like ourselves, they find themselves in the middle of their own world, with immeasurably greater things above and smaller things below. To us, they all look alike and seem to have no personality— as do the Chinese when we have not lived among them. Yet fruit flies must see just as many subtle distinctions among themselves as we among ourselves.

From this it is but a short step to the realization that all forms of life and being are simply variations on a single theme; we are all in fact one being doing the same thing in as many different ways as possible. As the French proverb goes, *plus ça change, plus c'est la même chose*—"the more it varies, the more it is one." I see, further, that feeling threatened by the inevitability of death is really the same experience as feeling alive, and that as all beings are feeling this everywhere, they are all just as much "I" as myself. Yet the "I" feeling, to be felt at all, must always be a sensation relative to the "other"—to something beyond its control and experience. To be at all, it must begin and end. But the intellectual jump which mystical and psychedelic experience makes here is in enabling you to see that all these myriad I-centers are yourself—not, indeed, your personal and superficially conscious ego, but what Hindus call the *paramatman,* the Self of all selves.

> [Thus Hinduism regards the universe, not as an artifact, but as an immense drama in which the One Actor (the *paramatman* or *brahman*) plays all the parts, which are his (or "its") masks or *personae.* The sensation of being only this one particular self, John Doe, is due to the Actor's total absorption in playing this and every other part. For fuller exposition, see 6; 10:355–463; 8.—A. W.]

As the retina enables us to see countless pulses of energy as a single light, so the mystical experience shows us innumerable individuals as a single Self.

The fourth characteristic is *awareness of eternal energy,* often in the form of intense white light, which seems to be both the current in your nerves and that mysterious *e* which equals mc^2. This may sound like megalomania or delusion of grandeur, but one sees quite clearly that all existence is a single energy, and that this energy is one's own being. Of course there is death as well as life, because energy is a pulsation, and just as waves must have both crests and troughs the experience of existing must go on and off. Basically, therefore, there is simply nothing to worry about, because you yourself are the eternal energy of the universe playing hide-and-seek (off-and-on) with itself. At root, you are the Godhead, for God is all that there is. Quoting Isaiah just a little out of context: "I am the Lord, and there is none else. I form the light and create the darkness: I make peace, and create evil. I, the Lord, do all these things."[3] This is the sense of the fundamental tenet of Hinduism: *Tat tvam asi*—"THAT (i.e., "that subtle Being of which this whole universe is composed") art thou."[4] A classical case of this experience from the west is in Tennyson's *Memoirs:*

> A kind of waking trance I have frequently had, quite up from boyhood, when I have been all alone. This has generally come upon me thro' repeating my own name two or three times to myself silently, till all at once, as it were out of the intensity of the consciousness of individuality, the individuality itself seemed to dissolve and fade away into boundless being, and this not a confused state, but the clearest of the clearest, the surest of the surest, the weirdest of the weirdest, utterly beyond words, where death was an almost laughable impossibility, the loss of personality (if so it were) seeming no extinction but the only true life [7:320].

Obviously, these characteristics of the psychedelic experience, as I have known it, are aspects of a single state of consciousness, for I have been describing the same thing from different angles. The descriptions attempt to

[3] Isaiah 45:6, 7.

[4] *Chandogya Upanishad* 6.15.3.

convey the reality of the experience, but in doing so they also suggest some of the inconsistencies between such experience and the current values of society.

Opposition to Psychedelic Drugs

Resistance to allowing use of psychedelic drugs originates in both religious and secular values. The difficulty in describing psychedelic experiences in traditional religious terms suggests one ground of opposition. The westerner must borrow such words as *samadhi* or *moksha* from the Hindus, or *satori* or *kensho* from the Japanese, to describe the experience of oneness with the universe. We have no appropriate word because our own Jewish and Christian theologies will not accept the idea that man's inmost self can be identical with the Godhead, even though Christians may insist that this was true in the unique instance of Jesus Christ. Jews and Christians think of God in political and monarchical terms, as the supreme governor of the universe, the ultimate boss. Obviously, it is both socially unacceptable and logically preposterous for a particular individual to claim that he, in person, is the omnipotent and omniscient ruler of the world, to be accorded suitable recognition and honor.

Such an imperial and kingly concept of the ultimate reality, however, is neither necessary nor universal. The Hindus and the Chinese have no difficulty in conceiving of an identity of the self and the Godhead. For most Asians, other than Muslims, the Godhead moves and manifests the world in much the same way that a centipede manipulates a hundred legs— spontaneously, without deliberation or calculation. In other words, they conceive the universe by analogy with an organism as distinct from a mechanism. They do not see it as an artifact or construct under the conscious direction of some supreme technician, engineer, or architect.

If, however, in the context of Christian or Jewish tradition an individual declares himself to be one with God, he must be dubbed blasphemous (subversive) or insane. Such a mystical experience is a clear threat to traditional religious concepts. The Judaeo-Christian tradition has a monarchical image of God, and monarchs, who rule by force, fear nothing more than insubordination. The church has therefore always been highly suspicious of mystics because they seem to be insubordinate and to claim equality or, worse, identity with God. For this reason John Scotus Erigena and Meister Eckhart were condemned as heretics. This was also why the Quakers faced opposition for their doctrine of the Inward Light, and for their refusal to remove hats in church and in court. A few occasional mystics may be all right so long as they watch their language, like St. Teresa of Avila and St. John of the Cross, who maintained, shall we say, a meta-physical distance of respect between themselves and their heavenly King. Nothing, however, could be more alarming to the ecclesiastical hierarchy than a popular outbreak of mysticism, for this might well amount to setting up a democracy in the kingdom of heaven—and such alarm would be shared equally by Catholics, Jews, and fundamentalist Protestants.

The monarchical image of God with its implicit distaste for religious insubordination has a more pervasive impact than many Christians might admit. The thrones of kings have walls immediately behind them, and all who present themselves at court must prostrate themselves or kneel because this is an awkward position from which to make a sudden attack. It has perhaps never occurred to Christians that when they design a church on the model of a royal court (basilica) and prescribe church ritual, they are implying that God, like a human monarch, is afraid. This is also implied by flattery in prayers:

> O Lord our heavenly Father, high and mighty, King of kings, Lord of lords, the only Ruler of princes, who dost from thy throne behold all the dwellers upon earth: most heartily we beseech thee with thy favor to behold . . .[5]

The western man who claims consciousness of oneness with God or the universe thus clashes with his society's concept of religion. In most Asian cultures, however, such a man will be congratulated as having penetrated the true secret of life. He has arrived, by chance, or by some such discipline as Yoga or Zen meditation, at a state of consciousness in which he experiences directly and vividly what our own scientists know to be true in theory. For the ecologist, the biologist, and the physicist know (but seldom feel) that every organism constitutes a single field of behavior, or process, with its environment. There is no way of separating what any given organism is doing from what its environment is doing, for which reason ecologists speak not of organisms in environments but of organism-environments. Thus the words "I" or "self" should properly mean what the whole universe is doing at this particular "here-and-now" called John Doe.

The kingly concept of God makes identity of self and God or self and universe inconceivable in western religious terms. The difference between Eastern and Western concepts of man and his universe, however, extends beyond strictly religious concepts. The western scientist may rationally perceive the idea of organism-environment, but he does not ordinarily *feel* this to be true. By cultural and social conditioning, he has been hypnotized into experiencing himself as an ego—as an isolated center of consciousness and will inside a bag of skin, confronting an external and alien world. We say, "I came into this world." But we did nothing of the kind. We came *out* of it in just the same way that fruit comes out of trees. Our galaxy, our cosmos, "peoples" in the same way that an apple tree "apples."

Such a vision of the universe clashes with the idea of a monarchical God, with the concept of the separate ego, and even with the secular, atheist-

---

[5] *Book of Common Prayer,* Order for Morning Prayer, A Prayer for the King's Majesty (Church of England) 1904.

agnostic mentality, which derives its common sense from the mythology of nineteenth century scientism. According to this view, the universe is a mindless mechanism and man a sort of accidental micro-organism infesting a minute globular rock which revolves about an unimportant star on the outer fringe of one of the minor galaxies. This "put-down" theory of man is extremely common among such quasi-scientists as sociologists, psychologists, and psychiatrists, most of whom are still thinking of the world in terms of Newtonian mechanics, and have never really caught up with the ideas of Einstein and Bohr, Oppenheimer and Schrödinger. Thus to the ordinary institutional-type psychiatrist, any patient who gives the least hint of mystical or religious experience is automatically diagnosed as deranged. From the standpoint of the mechanistic religion he is a heretic and is given electroshock therapy as an up-to-date form of the thumbscrew and rack. And, incidentally, it is just this kind of quasi-scientist who, as a consultant to government and law enforcement agencies, dictates official policies on the use of psychedelic chemicals.

Inability to accept the mystical experience is more than an intellectual handicap. Lack of awareness of the basic unity of organism and environment is a serious and dangerous hallucination. For in a civilization equipped with immense technological power, the sense of alienation between man and nature leads to the use of technology in a hostile spirit—to the "conquest" of nature instead of intelligent cooperation with nature. The result is that we are eroding and destroying our environment, spreading Los Angelization instead of civilization. This is the major threat overhanging western, technological culture, and no amount of reasoning or doom-preaching seems to help. We simply do not respond to the prophetic and moralizing techniques of conversion upon which Jews and Christians have always relied. But people have an obscure sense of what is good for them —call it "unconscious self-healing," "survival instinct," "positive growth potential," or what you will. Among the educated young there is therefore a startling and unprecedented interest in the transformation of human consciousness. All over the western world publishers are selling millions of books dealing with Yoga, Vedanta, Zen Buddhism, and the chemical mysticism of psychedelic drugs, and I have come to believe that the whole "hip" subculture, however misguided in some of its manifestations, is the earnest and responsible effort of young people to correct the self-destroying course of industrial civilization.

The content of the mystical experience is thus inconsistent with both the religious and secular concepts of traditional western thought. Moreover, mystical experiences often result in attitudes which threaten the authority not only of established churches, but also of secular society. Unafraid of death and deficient in worldly ambition, those who have undergone mystical experiences are impervious to threats and promises. In addition, their sense of the relativity of good and evil arouses the suspicion that they lack both conscience and respect for law. Use of psychedelics in the United States by a literate bourgeoisie means that an important segment of the population is indifferent to society's traditional rewards and sanctions.

In theory, the existence within our secular society of a group which does not accept conventional values is consistent with our political vision. But one of the great problems of the United States, legally and politically, is that we have never quite had the courage of our convictions. The Republic is founded on the marvelously sane principle that a human community can exist and prosper only on a basis of mutual trust. Metaphysically, the American Revolution was a rejection of the dogma of original sin, which is the notion that because you cannot trust yourself or other people, there must be some superior authority to keep us all in order. The dogma was rejected because if it is true that we cannot trust ourselves and others, it follows that we cannot trust the superior authority which we ourselves conceive and obey and that the very idea of our own untrustworthiness is unreliable!

Citizens of the United States believe, or are supposed to believe, that a republic is the best form of government. Yet vast confusion arises from trying to be republican in politics and monarchist in religion. How can a republic be the best form of government if the universe, heaven, and hell are a monarchy?

[Thus, until quite recently, belief in a Supreme Being was a legal test of valid conscientious objection to military service. The implication was that the individual objector found himself bound to obey a higher echelon of command than the President and Congress. The analogy is military and monarchical, and therefore objectors who, as Buddhists or naturalists, held an organic theory of the universe often had difficulty in obtaining recognition.—A. W.]

Thus, despite the theory of government by consent, based upon mutual trust, the peoples of the United States retain, from the authoritarian backgrounds of their religions or national origins, an utterly naive faith in law as some sort of supernatural and paternalistic power. "There ought to be a law against it!" Our law enforcement officers are therefore confused, hindered, and bewildered—not to mention corrupted—by being asked to enforce sumptuary laws, often of ecclesiastical origin, which vast numbers of people have no intention of obeying and which, in any case, are immensely difficult or simply impossible to enforce—for example, the barring of anything so undetectable as LSD-25 from international and interstate commerce.

Finally, there are two specific objections to the use of psychedelic drugs. First, this use may be dangerous. However, every worthwhile exploration is dangerous—climbing mountains, testing aircraft, rocketing into outer space, skin-diving, or collecting botanical specimens in jungles. But if you value knowledge and the actual delight of exploration more than mere duration of uneventful life, you are willing to take the risks. It is not really healthy for monks to practice fasting, and it was hardly hygienic for Jesus to get himself crucified, but these are risks taken in the course of spiritual adventures. Today the adventurous young are taking risks in exploring the psyche, testing their mettle at the task just as, in times past, they have tested it—more violently—in hunting, dueling, hot-rod racing, and playing football. What they need is not prohibitions and policemen but the most intelligent encouragement and advice that can be found.

Second, drug use may be criticized as an escape from reality. However this criticism assumes unjustly that the mystical experiences themselves are escapist or unreal. LSD, in particular, is by no means a soft and cushy escape from reality. It can very easily be an experience in which you have to test your soul against all the devils in hell. For me, it has been at times an experience in which I was at once completely lost in the corridors of the mind and yet relating that very lostness to the exact order of logic and language, simultaneously very mad and very sane. But beyond these occasional lost and insane episodes, there are the experiences of the world as a system of total harmony and glory, and the discipline of relating these to the order of logic and language must somehow explain how what William Blake called that "energy which is eternal delight" can consist with the misery and suffering of everyday life.[6]

The undoubted mystical and religious intent of most users of the psychedelic drugs, even if some of these substances should be proved injurious to physical health, requires that their free and responsible use be exempt from legal restraint in any republic which maintains a constitutional separation of church and state.

["Responsible" in the sense that such substances be taken by or administered to consenting adults only. The user of cannabis, in particular, is apt to have peculiar difficulties in establishing his "undoubted mystical and religious intent" in court. Having committed so loathsome and serious a felony, his chances of clemency are better if he assumes a repentant demeanor, which is quite inconsistent with the sincere belief that his use of cannabis was religious. On the other hand, if he insists unrepentantly that he looks upon such use as a religious sacrament, many judges will declare that they "dislike his attitude," finding it truculent and lacking in appreciation of the gravity of the crime, and the sentence will be that much harsher. The accused is therefore put in a "double-bind" situation in which he is "damned if he does, and damned if he doesn't." Furthermore, religious integrity—as in conscientious objection—is generally tested and established by membership in some church or religious organization with a substantial following. But the felonious status of cannabis is such that grave suspicion would be cast upon all individuals forming such an organization, and the test cannot therefore be fulfilled. It is generally for-

[6] Watts, Alan: *The Joyous Cosmology: Adventures in the Chemistry of Consciousness* (Pantheon Books, New York, New York) 1962.

gotten that our guarantees of religious freedom were designed to protect precisely those who were *not* members of established denominations, but rather such screwball and (then) subversive individuals as Quakers, Shakers, Levellers, and Anabaptists. There is little question that those who use cannabis, or other psychedelics, with religious intent are now members of a persecuted religion which appears to the rest of society as a grave menace to "mental health," as distinct from the old-fashioned "immortal soul." But it's the same old story.—A. W.]

To the extent that mystical experience conforms with the tradition of genuine religious involvement, and to the extent that psychedelics induce that experience, users are entitled to some constitutional protection. Also, to the extent that research in the psychology of religion can utilize such drugs, students of the human mind must be free to use them. Under the present laws, I, as an experienced student of the psychology of religion, can no longer pursue research in the field. This is a barbarous restriction of spiritual and intellectual freedom, suggesting that the legal system of the United States is, after all, in tacit alliance with the monarchical theory of the universe, and will, therefore, prohibit and persecute religious ideas and practices based on an organic and unitary vision of the universe.

[Amerindians belonging to the Native American Church, who employ the psychedelic peyote cactus in their rituals, are firmly opposed to any government control of this plant, even if they should be guaranteed the right to its use. They feel that peyote is a natural gift of God to mankind, and especially to natives of the land where it grows, and that no government has a right to interfere with its use. The same argument might be made on behalf of cannabis, or the mushroom *psilocybe mexicana Heim.* All these things are natural plants, not processed or synthesized drugs, and by what authority can individuals be prevented from eating them? There is no law against eating or growing the mushroom *amanita pantherina,* even though it is fatally poisonous and only experts can distinguish it from a common edible mushroom. This case can be made even from the standpoint of believers in the monarchical universe of Judaism and Christianity, for it is a basic principle of both religions, derived from Genesis, that all natural substances created by God are inherently good, and that evil can arise only in their misuse. Thus laws against mere possession, or even cultivation, of these plants are in basic conflict with Biblical principles. Criminal conviction of those who employ these plants should be based on proven misuse. "And God said, 'Behold, I have given you *every* herb bearing seed, which is upon the face of all the earth, and every tree, in the which is the fruit of a tree yielding seed; to you it shall be for meat.' . . . And God saw every thing that he had made, and, behold, it was very good" [Genesis 1:29, 31].—A. W.]

J. KRISHNAMURTI
(1895-   )

Precisely because he does not proselytize with exciting tales of breakthroughs to ecstasy, J. Krishnamurti is one of the best eastern thinkers for western readers. In reading eastern philosophy we run a constant danger of misreading; if we attach a romantic vision to the exotic quest for mystical enlightenment we shall be most assured of failure. Krishnamurti is aware of this danger, as the form of his writings shows: each of his dialogues is preceded by a short description of an utterly mundane scene, his vision of the here and now. These short descriptions are important; they carry as much of his message as the words of his dialogues. Do not skim the introductions to get to the meat of his thought. Read them carefully and try to relate them to the following dialogues.

The next two selections, which appear in sequence in their original form, reflect more than others in his **Commentaries on Living** the major themes of previous writers in this volume—the quest for self-awareness, the relation of self to society, and finally, the transcendence of rigid ego boundaries at the end of the "inward way."

ON TRANSCENDING SELF AND SOCIETY

To Change Society,
You Must Break Away from It

The sea was very calm that morning, more so than usual, for the wind from the south had ceased blowing, and before the north-easterly winds began, the sea was taking a rest. The sands were bleached by the sun and salt water, and there was a strong smell of ozone, mixed with that of seaweed. There wasn't anyone yet on the beach, and one had the sea to oneself. Large crabs, with one claw much bigger than the other, moved slowly about, watching, with the large claw waving in the air. There were also smaller crabs, the usual kind, that raced to the lapping water, or darted into round holes in the wet sand. Hundreds of seagulls stood about, resting and preening themselves. The rim of the sun was

ON TRANSCENDING SELF AND SOCIETY   From J. Krishnamurti, *Commentaries on Living,* Third Series, edited by D. Rajagopal. Published by The Theosophical Publishing House. Copyright © 1960 and reprinted by permission of Krishnamurti Writings, Inc., Ojai, Calif.

just coming out of the sea, and it made a golden path on the still waters. Everything seemed to be waiting for this moment—and how quickly it would pass! The sun continued to climb out of the sea, which was as quiet as a sheltered lake in some deep woods. No woods could contain these waters, they were too restless, too strong and vast; but that morning they were mild, friendly and inviting.

Under a tree above the sands and the blue water, there was going on a life independent of the crabs, the salt water and the sea-gulls. Large, black ants darted about, not making up their minds where to go. They would go up the tree, then suddenly scurry down for no apparent reason. Two or three would impatiently stop, move their heads about, and then, with a fierce burst of energy, go all over a piece of wood which they must have examined hundreds of times before; they would investigate it again with eager curiosity, and lose interest in it a second later. It was very quiet under the tree, though everything about one was very much alive. There was not a breath of air stirring among the leaves, but every leaf was abundant with the beauty and light of the morning. There was an intensity about the tree —not the terrible intensity of reaching, of succeeding, but the intensity of being complete, simple, alone and yet part of the earth. The colours of the leaves, of the few flowers, of the dark trunk, were intensified a thousand-fold, and the branches seemed to sustain the heavens. It was incredibly clear, bright and alive in the shade of that single tree.

Meditation is an intensification of the mind which is in the fullness of silence. The mind is not still like some tamed, frightened or disciplined animal; it is still as the waters are still many fathoms down. The stillness there is not like that on the surface when the winds die. This stillness has a life and a movement of its own which is related to the outer flow of life, but is untouched by it. Its intensity is not that of some powerful machine which has been put together by cunning, capable hands; it is as simple and natural as love, as lightning, as a full-flowing river.

He said he had been in politics up to his ears. He had done the usual things to climb the ladder of success—cultivated the right people, got on familiar terms with the leaders who had themselves climbed the very same ladder—and his climb had been rapid. He had been sent abroad on many of the important committees, and was regarded with respect by those who count; for he was sincere and incorruptible, albeit as ambitious as the rest of them. Added to all this, he was well-read, and words came easily to him. But now, by some fortunate chance, he was tired of this game of helping the country by boosting himself and becoming a very important person. He was tired of it, not because he couldn't climb any higher, but because, through a natural process of intelligence, he had come to see that man's deep betterment does not lie entirely in planning, in efficiency, in the scramble for power. So he had thrown it all overboard, and was beginning to consider anew the whole of life.

What do you mean by the whole of life?

"I have spent many years on a branch of the river, as it were, and I want to spend the remaining years of my life on the river itself. Although I enjoyed every minute of the political struggle, I am not leaving politics regretfully; and now I wish to contribute to the betterment of society from my heart and not from the ever-calculating mind. What I take from society must be returned to it at least tenfold."

If one may ask, why are you thinking in terms of giving and taking?

"I have taken so much from society; and all that it has given me I must give back to it many times."

What do you owe to society?

"Everything I have: my bank account, my education, my name—Oh, so many things!"

In actuality, you have not taken anything from society, because you are part of it. If you were a separate entity, unconnected with society, then you could give back what you have taken. But you are part of society, part of the culture which has put you together. You can return borrowed money; but what can you give back to society as long as you are part of society?

"Because of society I have money, food, clothing, shelter, and I must do something in return. I have profited by my gathering within the framework of society, and it would be ungrateful of me to turn my back on it. I must do some good work for society—good work in the large sense, and not as a 'do-gooder'."

I understand what you mean; but even if you returned all you have gathered, would that absolve you from your debt? What society has yielded through your efforts is comparatively easy to return; you can give it to the poor, or to the State. And then what? You still have your 'duty' to society, for you are still part of it; you are one of its citizens. As long as you belong to society, identify yourself with it, you are both the giver and the taker. You maintain it; you support its structure, do you not?

"I do. I am, as you say, an integral part of society; without it, I am not. Since I am both the good and the bad of society, I must remove the bad and uphold the good."

In any given culture or society, the 'good' is the accepted, the respectable. You want to maintain that which is noble within the structure of society; is that it?

"What I want to do is to change the social pattern in which man is caught. I mean this most earnestly."

The social pattern is set up by man; it is not independent of man, though it has a life of its own, and man is not independent of it; they are interrelated. Change within the pattern is no change at all; it is mere modification, reformation. Only by breaking away from the social pattern without building another can you 'help' society. As long as you belong to society, you are only helping it to deteriorate. All societies, including the most marvellously utopian, have within them the seeds of their own corruption. To change society, you must break away from it. You must cease to be what society is: acquisitive, ambitious, envious, power-seeking, and so on.

"Do you mean I must become a monk, a *sannyasi?*"

Certainly not. The *sannyasi* has merely renounced the outer show of the world, of society, but inwardly he is still a part of it; he is still burning with the desire to achieve, to gain, to become.

"Yes, I see that."

Surely, since you have burnt yourself in politics, your problem is not only to break away from society, but to come totally to life again, to love and be simple. Without love, do what you may, you will not know the total action which alone can save man.

"That is true, sir: we don't love, we aren't really simple."

Why? Because you are so concerned with reforms, with duties, with respectability, with becoming something, with breaking through to the other side. In the name of another, you are concerned with yourself, you are caught in your own cockle-shell. You think you are the centre of this beautiful earth. You never pause to look at a tree, at a flower, at the flowing river; and if by some chance you do look, your eyes are filled with the things of the mind, and not with beauty and love.

"Again, that is true; but what is one to do?"

Look and be simple.

Where the Self Is, Love Is Not

The rose-bushes just inside the gate were covered with bright red roses, heavy with perfume, and butterflies were hovering about them. There were also marigolds and sweet peas in bloom. The garden overlooked the river, and that evening it was full of the golden light of the setting sun. Fishing boats, shaped somewhat like gondolas, were dark on the still surface of the river. The village among the trees on the opposite side was over a mile away, and yet voices came clearly across the water. From the gate there was a path leading down to the river. It joined a rough road which was used by the villagers on their way to and from the town. This road ended abruptly at the bank of a stream that flowed into the big river. It was not a sandy bank, but heavy with damp clay, and the feet sank into it. Across the stream at this point they would presently build a bamboo bridge; but now there was a clumsy barge laden with the quiet villagers, who were returning from their day of trading in the town. Two men punted us across, while the villagers sat huddled in the evening cold. There was a small brazier to be lit when it got a little darker, but the moon would give them light. A little girl was carrying a basket of firewood; she had put it down while crossing the stream, and was now having difficulty in lifting it again. It was quite heavy for a little girl, but with some help she got it carefully placed on her small head, and her smile seemed to fill the universe. We all climbed the steep bank with careful steps, and soon the villagers went chattering off down the road.

Here it was open country, and the soil was very rich with the silt of many centuries. The flat, well-cultivated land, dotted with marvelous old trees, stretched out to the horizon. There were fields of sweet-smelling peas, white with blossom, as well as winter wheat and other grain. On one side flowed the river, wide and curving, and overlooking the river there was a village, noisy with activity. The path here was very ancient; the Enlightened One was said to have walked on it, and the pilgrims had been using it for many centuries. It was a holy path, and there were small temples here and there along that sacred way. The mango and tamarind trees were also very old, and some were dying, having seen so much. Against the golden evening sky they were stately, their limbs dark and open. A little further along there was a grove of bamboos, yellowing with age, and in a small orchard a goat tied to a fruit tree was bleating for its kid, which was jumping and skipping all over the place. The path led on through another grove of mangoes, and beside a tranquil pond. There was a breathless stillness, and everything knew the blessed hour. The earth and everything upon it became holy. It was not that the mind was aware of this peace as something outside of itself, something to be remembered and communicated, but there was a total absence of any movement of the mind. There was only the immeasurable.

He was a youngish man, in his early forties he said; and though he had faced audiences and spoken with great confidence, he was still rather shy. Like so many others of his generation, he had played with politics, with religion, and with social reform. He was given to writing poetry, and could put colour on canvas. Several of the prominent leaders were his friends, and he could have gone far in politics; but he had chosen otherwise, and was content to keep his light covered in a distant mountain town.

"I have been wanting to see you for many years. You may not remember it, but I was once on the same boat with you going to Europe before the second world war. My father was very interested in your teachings, but I drifted away into politics and other things. My desire to talk to you again finally became so persistent that it could not be put off any longer. I want to expose my heart—something I have never done to anyone else, for it isn't easy to discuss oneself with others. For some time I have been attending your talks and discussions in different places, but recently I have had a strong urge to see you privately, because I have come to an impasse."

Of what kind?

"I don't seem to be able to 'break through'. I have done some meditation, not the kind that mesmerizes you, but trying to be aware of my own thinking, and so on. In this process I invariably fall asleep. I suppose it is because I am lazy, easy-going. I have fasted, and I have tried various diets, but this lethargy persists."

Is it due to laziness, or to something else? Is there a deep, inward frustration? Has your mind been made dull, insensitive, by the events of your life? If one may ask, is it that love is not there?

"I don't know, sir; I have vaguely thought about these matters, but have never been able to pin anything down. Perhaps I have been smothered by too many good and evil things. In a way, life has been too easy for me, with family, money, certain capacities, and so on. Nothing has been very difficult, and that may be the trouble. This general feeling of being at ease and having the capacity to find my way out of almost any situation may have made me soft."

Is that it? Is that not just a description of superficial happenings? If those things had affected you deeply, you would have led a different kind of life, you would have followed the easy course. But you have not, so there must be a different process at work that is making your mind sluggish and inept.

"Then what is it? I am not bothered by sex; I have indulged in it, but it has never been a passion with me to the extent that I became a slave to it. It began with love and ended in disappointment, but not in frustration. Of that I am pretty sure. I neither condemn nor pursue sex. It's not a problem to me, anyway."

Has this indifference destroyed sensitivity? After all, love is vulnerable, and a mind that has built defences against life ceases to love.

"I don't think I have built a defence against sex; but love is not necessarily sex, and I really do not know if I love at all."

You see, our minds are so carefully cultivated that we fill the heart with the things of the mind. We give most of our time and energy to the earning of a livelihood, to the gathering of knowledge, to the fire of belief, to patriotism and the worship of the State, to the activities of social reform, to the pursuit of ideals and virtues, and to the many other things with which the mind keeps itself occupied; so the heart is made empty, and the mind becomes rich in its cunningness. This does make for insensitivity, doesn't it?

"It is true that we over-cultivate the mind. We worship knowledge, and the man of intellect is honoured, but few of us love in the sense you are talking about. Speaking for myself, I honestly do not know if I have any love at all. I don't kill to eat. I like nature. I like to go into the woods and feel their silence and beauty; I like to sleep under the open skies. But does all this indicate that I love?"

Sensitivity to nature is part of love; but it isn't love, is it? To be gentle and kind, to do good works, asking nothing in return, is part of love; but it isn't love, is it?

"Then what *is* love?"

Love is all these parts, but much more. The totality of love is not within the measure of the mind; and to know that totality, the mind must be empty of its occupations, however noble or self-centred. To ask how to empty the mind, or how not to be self-centred, is to pursue a method; and the pursuit of a method is another occupation of the mind.

"But is it possible to empty the mind without some kind of effort?"

All effort, the 'right' as well as the 'wrong', sustains the centre, the core of achievement, the self. Where the self is, love is not. But we were talking of the lethargy of the mind, of its insensitivity. Have you not read a great deal? And may not knowledge be part of this process of insensitivity?

"I am not a scholar, but I read a lot, and I like to browse in libraries. I respect knowledge, and I don't quite see why you think that knowledge necessarily makes for insensitivity."

What do we mean by knowledge? Our life is largely a repetition of what we have been taught, is it not? We may add to our learning, but the repetitive process continues and strengthens the habit of accumulating. What do you know except what you have read or been told, or what you have experienced? That which you experience now is shaped by what you have experienced before. Further experience is what has been experienced already, only enlarged or modified, and so the repetitive process is maintained. Repetition of the good or the bad, of the noble or the trivial, obviously makes for insensitivity, because the mind is moving only within the field of the known. May not this be why your mind is dull?

"But I can't put away all that I know, all that I have accumulated as knowledge."

You are this knowledge, you are the things that you have accumulated; you are the gramophone record that is ever repeating what is impressed on it. You are the song, the noise, the chatter of society, of your culture. Is there an uncorrupted 'you', apart from all this chatter? This self-centre is now anxious to free itself from the things it has gathered; but the effort it makes to be free is still part of the accumulative process. You have a new record to play, with new words, but your mind is still dull, insensitive.

"I see that perfectly; you have described very well my state of mind. I have learnt, in my time, the jargons of various ideologies, both religious and political; but, as you point out, my mind has in essence remained the same. I am now very clearly aware of this; and I am also aware that this whole process makes the mind superficially alert, clever and outwardly pliable, while below the surface it is still that same old self-centre which is the 'me'."

Are you aware of all this as a fact, or do you know it only through another's description? If it is not your own discovery, something that you have found out for yourself, then it is still only the word and not the fact that is important.

"I don't quite follow this. Please go slowly, sir, and explain it again."

Do you know anything, or do you only recognize? Recognition is a process of association, memory, which is knowledge. That is true, isn't it?

"I think I see what you mean. I know that bird is a parrot only because I have been told so. Through association, memory, which is knowledge, there is recognition, and then I say: 'It is a parrot'."

The word 'parrot' has blocked you from looking at the bird, the thing that flies. We almost never look at the fact, but at the word or the symbol that stands for the fact. The fact recedes, and the word, the symbol, becomes all-important. Now, can you look at the fact, whatever it may be, dissociated from the word, the symbol?

"It seems to me that perception of the fact, and awareness of the word representing the fact, occur in the mind at the same time."

Can the mind separate the fact from the word?

"I don't think it can."

Perhaps we are making this more difficult than it is. That object is called a tree; the word and the object are two separate things, are they not?

"Actually it is so; but, as you say, we always look at the object through the word."

Can you separate the object from the word? The word 'love' is not the feeling, the fact of love.

"But, in a way, the word is a fact too, isn't it?"

In a way, yes. Words exist to communicate, and also to remember, to fix in the mind a fleeting experience, a thought, a feeling; so the mind itself is the word, the experience, it is the memory of the fact in terms of pleasure and pain, good and bad. This whole process takes place within the field of time, the field of the known; and any revolution within that field is no revolution at all, but only a modification of what has been.

"If I understand you correctly, you are saying that I have made my mind dull, lethargic, insensitive, through traditional or repetitive thinking, of which self-discipline is a part. To bring the repetitive process to an end, the gramophone record, which is the self, must be broken; and it can be broken only by seeing the fact, and not through effort. Effort, you say, only keeps the recording machine wound up, so in that there is no hope. Then what?"

See the fact, the what *is,* and let that fact operate; don't you operate on the fact—the 'you' being the repetitive mechanism, with its opinions, judgments, knowledge.

"I will try," he said earnestly.

To try is to oil the repetitive mechanism, not to put an end to it.

"Sir, you are taking everything away from one, and nothing is left. But that may be the new thing."

It is.

A   3
B   4
C   5
D   6
E   7
F   8
G   9
H   0
I   1
J   2